A SHORT HISTORY OF
BRITISH EXPANSION

A SHORT HISTORY OF
BRITISH EXPANSION

*

THE OLD COLONIAL EMPIRE

BY

JAMES A. WILLIAMSON

AUTHOR OF 'MARITIME ENTERPRISE, 1485-1558,' ETC.

THIRD EDITION

LONDON
MACMILLAN & CO LTD
NEW YORK · ST MARTIN'S PRESS
1961

MACMILLAN AND COMPANY LIMITED
London Bombay Calcutta Madras Melbourne

THE MACMILLAN COMPANY OF CANADA LIMITED
Toronto

ST MARTIN'S PRESS INC
New York

PREFACE TO THE FIRST EDITION, 1922

THIS book is an attempt to relate briefly the history of the British people in what, for want of a better term, may be called its external aspects. These include not merely colonization and the administration of tropical dependencies but also movements which antedated, ran parallel to, and influenced both—foreign trade, the rise and decline of economic theories, religious and secular incentives to emigration, and broad changes in national character and outlook. The purely continental phases of British relations with the peoples of Europe are omitted, as falling more naturally within the scope of political history. The events of one period form the clue to the comprehension of the next, and it is therefore necessary to begin the study of the subject with a glance at the commercial organizations of the Middle Ages, when Englishmen first began to acquire external interests of a non-political order.

To write the history of so many centuries from a study of the original sources would be an endless task. It is rendered avoidable by the fact that a multitude of students have published the results of their original research in almost every branch of the subject. Particularly in the past twenty-five years material has been examined which collectively involves a restatement or even a rediscovery of certain chapters of our external history. The present work is accordingly based, as far as possible, upon information obtained from these sources. Its writer wishes to acknowledge his indebtedness not only to the authorities cited in the footnotes but also to others mentioned in the bibliographical sections at the end of each part ; and at the same time he must assume full responsibility for the use made of facts and opinions combined from so many independent quarters.

The division of the narrative into five periods arises naturally from the well-marked central characteristics of each. Foreign trade confined to the seas of Europe is that of the first, preparing the way for oceanic trade and a variety of cognate adventures in the second, the dividing line being the discovery of America and India at the close of the fifteenth century. In the third period, corresponding with the rule of the Stuart kings in England, colonization begins in earnest, and a colonial empire on a mercantile basis takes shape. The fourth period, covering nearly a century from the Revolution of 1688, is that of the material growth of the mercantile empire, its collision with the parallel

organization set up by France, and its violent disruption by the revolt
of the American colonies. In all these four periods the dominant
motive is economic. The fifth period, in which we ourselves live, is
altogether different. It is a recommencement on new lines, having
no precedent in the history of modern nations. In its essence it is
the record of an overflow of population much more voluminous and
much less under the guidance of a national policy than ever before,
and its principal interest is not economic but social and political. Also
it is not, like the other periods, a finished tale. It breaks off in the midst
of a chapter, and the outcome is for the future to reveal.

Such is the scope of the subject. To unfold it entails working sometimes from the centre, to obtain a proportioned view and to deal with
ideas and policy, and sometimes in compartments, to trace the history
of various undertakings. The method involves some repetition, but
its advantages appear to counterbalance its defects.

Footnote references to authorities are inserted where the facts stated
are disputable or of recent discovery, and also to acknowledge the
source of quotations, and sometimes to indicate generally the authority
followed. The lists of works at the end of each part are not exhaustive.
They aim rather at suggesting courses of reading and indicating the
particular uses of the books mentioned. They omit many older works
whose authority is good, but whose substance is included in more
recent writings.

PREFACE TO THE SECOND EDITION, 1930

THE re-writing and enlargement of that part of the book which deals
with British expansion after 1783 has necessitated the issue of the
second edition in the form of two volumes. The present volume
therefore contains Parts I-IV and treats of the history of the Old
Colonial Empire. Certain corrections, particularly in the account of
the West Indian colonies in the seventeenth century, have been made
in accordance with the results of recent research. These corrections
were first introduced in the reprint of the first edition in 1927.

PREFACE TO THE THIRD EDITION, 1945

EXTENSIVE corrections have been made throughout the volume. In
particular, the work of recent years having very greatly modified conceptions of the maritime history of the Tudor period, Chapters III and
IX of Part II have been partly, and Chapter VI entirely, re-written.
Elsewhere many re-statements have been made in accordance with the
findings of research.

CONTENTS

PART I

OVERSEAS COMMERCE IN THE MIDDLE AGES

CONTENTS

PART III

THE FOUNDATION OF THE MERCANTILE EMPIRE

PART IV

THE ZENITH AND FALL OF THE MERCANTILE EMPIRE

CONTENTS

LIST OF MAPS

PART I

OVERSEAS COMMERCE IN THE MIDDLE AGES

CHAPTER I

FROM THE NORMAN CONQUEST TO EDWARD I

IT is a well-worn saying that the British Empire is based upon sea-power. The Great Wars have provided ample proof that the principle is still a vital one, as vital as it was amid the Dutch wars of the seventeenth century, the French wars of the eighteenth, and the world-wide expansion of the nineteenth. But in the general teaching of the history of our empire it has been somewhat customary to overlook the fact that this sea-power came into existence some centuries before we dreamt of sending settlers across the ocean to found the first rudiments of an offshoot from the mother country. Such, however, is the truth. English sea-power was born and grew silently amid daunting perils in the Middle Ages, the possession and the achievement of a class set somewhat apart from the main stream of national life, until in the days of the Tudors it secured full recognition and took a lasting hold upon the imagination of the people. It follows, therefore, that a general survey of our expansion must take into account the beginnings of sea-power, and the causes, geographical, political, and economic, which affected its growth.

During the generations which followed the Conquest of 1066, whilst Norman and Saxon elements were gradually blending to produce the English nation, we must picture the population of this country as living almost exclusively by labour upon the land, organized in little manorial communities, each producing on its own soil well-nigh all the commodities necessary to its life. Such a society, with its members firmly attached, by the complicated feudal services which took the place of money payments, to the locality in which each was born, had evidently little need of commerce and shipping for the maintenance of its economic life ; and it was not until industries began to employ an appreciable number of hands, and agriculture began to produce certain commodities in excess of the local demands, that the elements of an extensive sea-borne commerce came into being. At the time of the Conquest there was undoubtedly some small traffic with the continent ; but it was limited to the casual export of scanty supplies of lead and tin from the English mines and the corresponding import of French wines and fine apparel for the wealthy the whole upon so petty a scale that it could be dealt with in the undecked, clinker-built boats with which the Bayeux tapestry has made us familiar. It is scarcely permissible to dignify such vessels with the title of a mercantile marine.

The towns, which were in later days to be the centres of manufacture and intercourse, were in Norman times little better than hamlets, their population dependent upon the lord of the neighbouring manor, and engaged, like his other villains, upon the tilling of the soil. But to this there were some few exceptions. London, as the centre of what little continental trade there was, had passed beyond this stage in the Saxon period. York, as the Domesday survey tells us, had 1600 households—perhaps 10,000 people. Bristol and Chester had some local traffic with Ireland, and were visited by Scandinavian traders from the north. Other towns, by reason of their position upon river-ford, harbour or estuary, were ripe for emergence from the village state so soon as settled government should permit the development of industry.

Settled government, indeed, was the undoubted boon conferred by the Norman supremacy. The Conqueror himself had a passion for discipline and order, rough and ready as were the methods by which he enforced it : " A man might go through his realm with his bosom full of gold unhurt." William Rufus may have plundered the Church and the magnates, but at least he permitted no lesser man to misbehave. Groan as they might at the licentious oppression of his entourage, the people had to admit that private wars and raids of pirate bands from over the seas were now things of the past. In Henry I. Norman kingship reached the height of its excellence ; and his reign of five-and-thirty years was a period of almost unbroken peace and firm, consistent government. With the miserable Stephen-Matilda contest which broke out upon the death of Henry in 1135 the prospect changed suddenly and violently for the worse, and the terrible forces of anarchy which underlay the surface of feudalism burst forth with unrestrained exuberance. Civil war conducted with decency soon gave place to partisan strife. Private warfare for avowedly private interests speedily followed, and thence it was but a step to pure brigandage which laid the whole industry and life of the country at the mercy of innumerable bands of ruffians. But, fortunately, this interlude of evil was a short one. After nineteen years of anarchy (1135-54) a new king of strength and public spirit took the reins of government in the person of Henry II. So enduring was his work, and set on such firm foundations, that it survived the perils caused by the absence of his successor Richard I., who spent less than one year of his ten years' reign in England, the violent eccentricities of John, and the long minority and weak character of Henry III. From Henry II. indeed to Edward I. we may truly say that the prosperity and the social improvement of England never halted in their progress.

The essence of the health of a community is change, provided that change is peaceful and orderly, evolutionary not revolutionary. And so it came about that the self-sufficing feudal state bore within itself the seeds of a new growth which was destined ultimately to alter its whole aspect. Under Henry I., or even earlier, the production of wool gave rise to the manufacture of cloth in certain districts, and this industry in its turn favoured the growth of the towns both in population and political power. Conclusive evidence is lacking, but it is probable that Flemish immigrants were responsible for the new handicraft. The English cloth manufacture was not a mushroom growth ; for several centuries its produce was coarse and inferior, not to be compared in quality with that which came from the great cities of Flanders and Italy. At first also its sale was limited to the home markets, then it was carried to the remote Scandinavian north, and only after long experience could it compete with its continental exemplars. But if Flemings and Italians remained contemptuous of English cloth, they early grew eager to buy the wool with which it was made ; and raw wool became the first considerable article of export.

For two principal reasons this early commercial intercourse remained the virtual monopoly of foreign merchants. The first was geographical : England lay at the terminus, or more properly beyond the terminus, of the mediaeval trade routes, whereas the cities of the Rhine delta and basin, and those of Italy, were astride of those routes, trading not only with their own products but also dipping their fingers in the trade of others, which had necessarily to pass through them. Out of this arose the second reason : that the merchants of the regions named had much greater capital resources, and were fully trained and organized whilst the English were yet in the stage of apprenticeship. The trade routes indeed are the key to a correct understanding of mediaeval English expansion. But it will be convenient to defer a full considera-tion of them to the next chapter, and for the present to turn to an examination of the various foreign organizations which dominated our early commerce.

The word Hanse or Hansa serves to designate those merchant bodies which were of Teutonic birth ; and three distinct Hansas are to be recognized in traffic with our island. The Hansa of Cologne, or " men of the Emperor," had a factory in London in 1157, at the beginning of the reign of Henry II. The king's parentage—he was the son of the Empress Matilda, whose first husband had been the Emperor Henry V.—probably accounts for the favour shown to them. They controlled the Rhine waterway through which came the wares of the south after transit across the mountain passes from Italy. They obtained extensive privileges from Henry II. and Richard I., but after an early period of success their trade dwindled under the stress of Burgundian wars and Italian sea-borne competition using the longer route by the Straits of Gibraltar.

Contemporary with them was the Flemish society known as the Hanse of London. It included the merchants of all the cities of Flanders and north-eastern France, possibly also of Paris itself. These places produced woollen cloth of fine quality, arms and armour, and all kinds of manufactured metal goods. Although the name of Hansa dropped out of use as applied to this association, the Flemish cities remained in vigorous participation of English trade throughout the Middle Ages. Their business being based principally upon the disposal of their own manufactures, they were not so liable as the men of Cologne to suffer by a deflection of the trade routes.

The third and ultimately the most active and aggressive of the Hansas was of somewhat later development. It arose from the coalition of the seaports of the North Sea and Baltic coasts from Bremen to Riga. The merchants of these ports were mainly of German nationality—in England they were known as the Easterlings—and it was their consistent aim to dominate the trade and fisheries of the North Sea, balancing the wares drawn from Flanders, England and Norway with those they obtained from eastern Europe through Poland and the great mart of Novgorod in northern Russia. Rising to prominence in the thirteenth century, they succeeded to the English privileges of the Cologne traders whom, in their declining days, they admitted to the great confederacy. In this way they were able to establish houses in London, Ipswich, Yarmouth, Lynn, Boston and Hull, and to arrogate to themselves the exclusive use of the title of the Hanseatic League. Their chief characteristic was their uncompromising insistence upon absolute supremacy, and it was against them that the nascent English sea-power had to fight its hardest battles.

The Norwegians and Danes had in pre-Conquest days had much maritime intercourse with England. The military side of it is that which has left the deepest impress upon historical records, but there is no doubt that trade followed in the wake of the conquering Vikings and became especially active during the temporary union of this country with the northern kingdoms under Canute. From Norway the principal import was the salted fish which served as the staple food in the early part of the year, when religious observance and the scarcity of flesh combined to produce a large demand. The Norse mariners, following the route by the Shetlands, Orkneys and Hebrides, traded with the western ports of England and Wales, and with the Irish ports of Norse foundation—Dublin, Wexford and Waterford. In the twelfth century, as William of Malmesbury relates, "Bristol was a commodious and safe receptacle for all ships directing their course for the same from Ireland, Norway and other outlandish and foreign countries." As the English shipping industry made progress Englishmen began to take this trade into their own hands, sailing to the Norwegian staple town of Bergen to buy fish, and to the coasts of Iceland to catch it.

The Normans, bringing their continental tastes into English life, introduced the habit of wine drinking. Soon after the Conquest the merchants of Rouen carried French wines into this country, and the accession of Henry II., controlling his wife's possessions in Aquitaine, stimulated a similar trade from Bordeaux and Bayonne. Here again the foreign merchants, ranking equally with the English as subjects of the crown, long held a virtual monopoly of the traffic. But under the Plantagenet kings the English towns grew rich, and their citizens began more and more to seek their own markets across the seas, chartering first the ships of strangers, then building ships of their own. The Crown, for several reasons, continued its patronage of the aliens long after it might have recognized that its duty was to foster English sea-power. Consequently that power had to make its way in face of opposition abroad and neglect at home, and the days of its apprentice-ship were unduly prolonged ere it became firmly established.

A consideration of two other classes of foreigners in England will complete the survey of its early mercantile condition. The Jews, more as financiers than as merchants, obtained a firm grip on mediaeval society. The law of the Church forbade Christians to lend money at interest, and here the Jew found his opportunity. The object of universal hatred, he would have had little chance of recovering his wealth from powerful debtors had it not been for the royal protection. Successive kings countenanced the Jews in this manner, and repaid themselves by seizing their debts in times of stress and proving them-selves harsher creditors than the original lenders had power to be. When Edward I. expelled the Jews from the realm in 1290 public opinion held that by so doing he had promoted the interests of the nation at the expense of his own purse. But already another breed of financiers were prepared to fill the position thus left vacant. In the great Italian cities the craft of banking developed with the growth of trade ; and the Florentines succeeded in London to the traffic of the Jews. Successive royal defalcations ruined the great Florentine firms, and their ascendancy passed next to the Genoese and the Venetians. These latter, combining the wool trade with banking, based their position upon firmer foundations. But the development of their commerce with England scarcely falls within the period covered by the present chapter, and is therefore left to later con-sideration.

The impression derived from the facts above examined is that during the hundred and fifty years at least which succeeded the Conquest Englishmen had a minor share in English sea-borne trade. In that time, however, they developed a considerable internal trade in the produce which aliens imported ; for the latter suffered considerable restrictions of their activities within the country, the most important being that they might only sell by wholesale. About the beginning of the thirteenth century more of the overseas traffic began to fall into English hands. In later days the great English companies of the Staplers and the Merchants Adventurers each claimed to have originated at this period. It is possible that the Staplers may have done so ; but all that is certain is that there were some societies of Englishmen, of whom precise knowledge has not survived, who were carrying goods abroad as early as the reign of King John. An ordinance of the first year of his reign says : " It is our will that foreign merchants be vouchsafed the same favour in England which is granted unto English merchants in those places from whence they come."

An examination of the record of English shipping provides further evidence to the same effect. At the time of the Conquest the organization of the Cinque Ports was already in existence. Harold indeed had mobilized a fleet from the Ports to withstand the expected invasion, but had been unable to keep it together long enough for it to be of use. The records of various Saxon kings show that numerous ships were owned in England in very early times, but it must be remembered that these so-called ships were only large open boats. Their usual employment was probably fishing and the petty traffic with France and Flanders already described.

William I. and his successors issued charters defining the duties and privileges of the Cinque Ports (Hastings, Romney, Hythe, Dover and Sandwich, with which were associated almost from the beginning " the two ancient towns " of Winchelsea and Rye). From these charters it appears that the Ports had between them to find fifty-seven ships for fifteen days in each year without payment ; but the small size of the ships is apparent from the fact that each crew was to consist of twenty-one men and a boy. The Cinque Ports fleet so constituted was evidently intended to be the counterpart of the feudal land forces whose primary object was defence against invasion. It had also the further duty of " the honourable transportation and safe conduct of the King's own person or his army over the Narrow Seas." Such offices could easily be performed in the fifteen days of gratuitous service, and to them the early conception of the uses of a naval force was limited. There was no provision for the protection of commerce against pirates. The owners of merchantmen were for the most part aliens, and might be left to defend themselves. The mariners of the Ports, in fact, became notorious for piracy themselves, especially during the thirteenth century under the loose rule of Henry III. ; and their negotiation of a formal treaty with the shipmen of France for the regulation of plunder, prisoners, and ransoms, shows that they had begun to regard themselves almost in the light of a sovereign power.

The cheapness of the service obtained from the privileged Ports rendered the Crown slow to set about the establishment of a royal fleet under the direct command of the King. From the time of Richard I., however, onwards to that of Henry V., we may trace the continuous existence of a royal navy of greater or less dimensions. Richard I. led a considerable naval force to the Third Crusade, but it is uncertain that any large part of it was English built and manned. John possessed several royal ships, and the office of Clerk or Keeper of the King's Ships—the germ of the Navy Board—dates from his reign. Besides contriving amid the general disaffection to retain the loyalty of the Cinque Ports he made use of Portsmouth as a dockyard establishment and built some fortifications for its protection. Henry III. continued his father's policy, and Edward I. in his turn developed it with his usual energy, spending what were for that time considerable sums on the acquisition of new vessels.

The first signal illustration of the advantage of a fleet to the national defence occurred a year after John's death. Louis, the son of the French king, was in England at the invitation originally of the rebellious barons. They had asked him to come in order that they might confer upon him the crown which they were determined to take from John. But the death of the tyrant in 1216 had led to a revulsion of feeling in favour of his son Henry, and the French prince found his English supporters deserting him. In these circumstances the sailing of a reinforcement from France was of vital importance. Led by a notorious freebooter of the time, known as Eustace the Monk, it crossed the straits and seemed to be making for the Thames estuary. Hubert de Burgh, who had held Dover stedfastly both for John and his son, hastened to mobilize the Cinque Ports fleet. Off Sandwich the English mariners, although in inferior strength, intercepted the invaders, and by a skilful manoeuvre attacked them at a disadvantage. The single-masted, square-sailed ships of the time were hopelessly slow in beating to windward, and the Portsmen, gaining the weathergage before closing, were able to overwhelm the nearer Frenchmen before their fellows could come to their support. The casting of bags of quicklime into the French decks added to their confusion, and the victory was speedily complete. By the " custom of the sea " the vanquished could expect little mercy. In each captured ship two or three only were spared, the remainder slaughtered. Eustace the Monk surrendered, offering large ransom for his life ; " but there was one there named Stephen of Winchelsea, who recalled to him the hardships which he had caused them both upon land and sea, and who gave him the choice of having his head cut off either upon the hatch or upon the rail of the ship. Then he beheaded him." [1]

The details of the Battle of Sandwich may serve to typify many a forgotten Channel fight of the period. The Cinque Ports increased greatly in power during the thirteenth century, and there is indirect evidence that the ships had become, if not larger, at least better found. In 1277 when Edward I. launched a great campaign against the Welsh his army had the support of a fleet from the Ports, which supplied the troops with provisions from the sea. This service marks a considerable advance upon that contemplated by the framers of the early charters. In 1293 again the Ports fleet, in alliance with the Gascon wine carriers, inflicted a great overthrow upon the seamen of Normandy, fighting in a quarrel of their own private origination at a time when the kings of the two countries were at peace.

A fighting sea-force nearly always implies the existence of a mercantile marine, and more especially was this true in the Middle Ages.

---

[1] *English Historical Review*, xxvii. 649-670.

when the warship of one day was the merchantman of the next. We may, therefore, draw the conclusion that the thirteenth century saw the development of English sea-borne commerce to a point much in advance of the fishing and passenger-carrying across the Straits of Dover which had been its status at the Norman Conquest. The native traffic of other ports than those of the south-east coast must also have been silently coming into being; for in the middle of the next century—in 1346—we find Edward III. concentrating before Calais a huge fleet of 700 English ships drawn from eighty-three several havens in England and Wales. The average number of men per ship in the Calais roll works out curiously enough at (within a fraction) the twenty-one of the Cinque Ports charters.

The reign of Edward I. (1272-1307) marks a turning-point in the early stage of English expansion. The general legislation of his reign extended the sense of social security, favouring the growth of a middle class both in town and country, and creating a healthy public opinion which began consciously to express itself upon matters pertaining to the public welfare. At the fit moment also he provided, by the summoning of representative parliaments, a medium through which the public voice might make itself heard. Parliament, developing as it did into a regular institution of the realm at the conclusion of a century in which the towns had increased vastly in wealth and independence, gave exactly the opportunity which was needed for the conversion of local into national privileges, of local aspirations into a truly national policy.

In the twelfth century the towns had begun to obtain freedom from obligations to the territorial magnates, and by so doing to draw apart from the feudal organization which had hitherto embraced the whole population in purely agricultural interests. In the thirteenth the majority of them secured rights of self-government more or less complete; and these changes coincided with the rise and progress of the cloth manufacture. Here, then, was favourable ground for the birth of a mercantile middle class, " a busy, hard, prosperous, pugnacious middle class," which was destined ultimately to obtain a preponderating voice in the direction of national affairs.

The mercantile legislation of Edward I. affected principally the foreign traders, who were still, in the eyes of the Crown, of greater importance than those of English nationality. He substituted fixed money payments for the old royal rights to take toll of cargoes in kind. This revenue, called the Ancient or Great Custom, was defined in 1275 and again in the Confirmation of the Charters in 1297 ; and no later sovereign until James I. made any attempt to increase the rates in so far as they applied to Englishmen. But in 1303 the King, being hard pressed for money, concluded an agreement known as the *Carta Mercatoria* with the foreign corporations which conducted the greater part of our trade. In consideration of royal promises of full security for their persons and goods, speedy justice by the international code of

" law merchant," and trial of disputes by juries of which half the members were to be foreigners, they consented to pay an additional duty on all articles of common trade, known as the New or Petty Custom.   This agreement illustrates the uniform policy with regard to commerce which was to prevail for some time to come.   The Crown preferred to deal with foreigners because it could obtain from them taxes which its own subjects would strongly have objected to paying. The foreigners made no such objection because, having a virtual monopoly, they could pass on the tax to the general body of consumers in the shape of higher prices.   Only when native commerce had increased did the protective function of these duties become apparent.

We may sum up the work of the king by a quotation from a high authority on these matters : [1] " Edward I. laid the foundations of a system of national regulation of industry and commerce, and this gradually outgrew the municipal institutions ; he rendered it possible for his successors to survey the commercial condition of the country as a whole, and to form a definite policy for the development of national resources and for establishing satisfactory relations with foreign powers."

During the whole period from the Conquest to the death of Edward I. the country steadily progressed both in material wealth, in population, and in the art of government.   The population is reckoned to have been about two millions in 1066, to have increased to four millions by 1222, and possibly to five millions by the middle of the fourteenth century.   The Black Death and the French wars then caused a heavy decrease until the total stood at about two-and-a-half millions in 1377. There was no correspondingly rapid recovery, and there were probably not many more than three million Englishmen at the time of the accession of Henry VIII.   The above figures are only approximations based on no conclusive evidence, and some authorities doubt that the population ever exceeded two-and-a-half millions during the Middle Ages.

But however faulty may be our knowledge of statistics, we are at least justified in regarding the commencement of the fourteenth century as the period in which feudal England had reached its prime. Thenceforward the conception of a self-contained state based upon the cultivation of the land tended to degenerate, and out of its decay began growth in new directions.   Peasants became craftsmen, gentry became merchants ; and the next two centuries witnessed an increasing consciousness of the need for sea-power and a demand for a national policy for its encouragement.

---

[1] Ven. Archdeacon W. Cunningham : *The Growth of English Industry and Commerce during the Early and Middle Ages*, 5th ed. Cambridge, 1910, p. 265.

CHAPTER II

THE LATER PLANTAGENETS, 1307–1399

WE have already seen that the rise of England as a maritime power was to depend upon the grasp which she might be able to obtain of the sea-borne commerce of the Middle Ages. It is time now to turn to a consideration of the mediaeval trade routes in order to understand the nature of this system into which the English adventurers sought to force an entry.

A map of the trade routes of modern Europe would be an exceedingly complex affair, traversed in all directions by intersecting tracks on land and sea, out of which would emerge no simple arrangement of principal routes. Modern commerce, in fact, is widely diffused and decentralized, like the system of veins in the human body. Mediaeval commerce, on the other hand, resembled the arteries, its currents flowing strongly and in bulk along a comparatively few main channels, and leaving large areas untouched and but indirectly conscious of its existence. It is not difficult, therefore, to present a general plan of the circulation of commodities in the Middle Ages.

Taking first the trade connections of Christendom with lands outside its boundaries, we find that in the fourteenth century, although Portugal was beginning to awaken to the importance of Africa, the regions of the Near and Middle East were the only ones with which any large traffic was maintained. This traffic from Asia followed two great main routes : one by the river system of Russia to the mart town of Novgorod and thence to Riga, or across Poland to the more southerly Baltic ports ; the other by caravans to the Black Sea coasts or the Syrian cities such as Damascus and Aleppo, or by Arab shipping into the Red Sea, followed by the short land journey to Alexandria, all coming equally within the range of the Christian traders of the Mediterranean. These two great lines of commerce we may call the Northern and the Mediterranean routes respectively. The former had been worked originally by the Northmen of Scandinavia, but by the twelfth century they had given place to the Hanseatic League, whose energy developed the trade to an unprecedented extent. The chief share in exploiting the Mediterranean route was long contested between Genoa and Venice, with the balance of success inclining ultimately to the latter.

Turning now to the internal commerce of Europe itself, we find that its main streams passed between the depots or distributing centres of the two great routes from Asia (the Hanseatic and Italian cities respectively) and certain well-defined producing areas which possessed valuable commodities in excess of the needs of their own inhabitants. These producing areas were : first, the populous cities of Flanders and the Rhine delta, turning out cloth, hardware and munitions of war ; next England, with its ever-increasing quantities of wool and hides, its half-manufactured cloth, and its small supplies of lead and tin ; then the coasts of Norway and Iceland with their valuable fisheries providing a fair percentage of the food supply of northern Europe ; the wine-growing districts of south-western France and the middle Rhine ; and lastly Italy itself, which, from being primarily a distributing centre for the Mediterranean trade, became increasingly a producing area for many kinds of finely manufactured goods.

Taking these regions in the order given above, we find that in the north the Hanseatic League had practically complete control of the traffic between its own distributing cities and the producing areas of Iceland and Norway, England, Flanders and Aquitaine. In the middle of the fourteenth century the League included eighty-six cities and towns, under common commercial control although subject to diverse political allegiance. Its easterly outpost was at Novgorod in Russia, and its principal European factories were at London, Bruges and Bergen. The North Sea was therefore a Hanseatic lake, and if ever its alternative title of the German Ocean was justified it was during the period when the great League was in its prime.

But although the Easterlings—as the Hanse merchants were early called in England—monopolized the trade between their own cities and the areas named, they never obtained the same exclusive grip upon the cross-traffic between the areas themselves. We find therefore certain trade routes not subject to the League's control linking England with other lands. The most important of these was the short sea passage to Flanders, monopolized originally by the Flemish Hanse. Along this route passed English raw wool in one direction and Flemish manufactured goods in the other. In the fourteenth century, as we shall see, the English traders began to obtain a larger share of this traffic than they had possessed in the earlier part of the Middle Ages. With Iceland and Norway also the trade in salt fish became a field for English enterprise from Bristol and the east coast ports. The wine trade from the Rhine was largely in the hands of the Easterlings from the time when they admitted Cologne to their fellowship. That from Aquitaine remained in possession of the Gascon seamen until in the fourteenth century Englishmen began to take a share in it also. Chaucer's typical shipman, it may be remembered, was the master of a Dartmouth barge which brought cargoes of wine from Bordeaux.

England, then, in the early Middle Ages was commercially a dependency of the Northern or Hanseatic trading system. With the Mediterranean system she had no such intimate connection until the early years of the fourteenth century. Previously to that time the small trade between England and Italy had passed mainly by the overland route, up the Rhine and along the Alpine roads. The Italians first rose to prominence in England as financiers and collectors of papal taxation, the proceeds of which they frequently transmitted in the shape of raw wools. As manufactures flourished in the Italian cities the demand for wool increased, and both Venetians and Genoese began to send merchantmen to England by the long passage through the Straits of Gibraltar. In 1317 the government of Venice went a step further by inaugurating the state trading fleets or Flanders galleys. These fleets consisted of three, four, or five vessels of the largest size, owned by the state but laden with the goods of private merchants, who bought their share of cargo space at a public auction. They sailed annually in close company as far as the English Channel, where the fleet divided, some of the ships entering English ports, the remainder going on to Flanders. The operations of the state fleets did not involve the cessation of the voyages of privately-owned Italian merchantmen to England or the abandonment of the Rhine route ; but their inauguration may serve to mark the entry of England into the same close contact with the Mediterranean trading system as it already possessed with that of the North. It is to be remarked that the Italians long maintained a monopoly of the trade ; at no time during the fourteenth century is there any record of English ships penetrating to the Levant.

While it would be an overstatement to assert that there was ever a time when the trade of this country was exclusively in foreign hands, it is nevertheless true that for the two hundred years following the Conquest it was predominantly so. We have now, therefore, to trace the early stages of its transference from alien to native control. The whole process occupied fully three centuries (mid-thirteenth to mid-sixteenth), and considerable obscurity enshrouds its origination. It is certain, however, that the export of raw materials was the first branch of trade to fall mainly into English hands. At some time in the reign of Henry III. the merchants dealing in wools, hides, tin and lead formed themselves into an association afterwards known as the Merchants of the Staple. They carried their goods to the markets of Flanders, their nearest and best customer. The exact conditions under which the early Staplers traded are unknown, but it is improbable that they enjoyed a monopoly of the traffic. Soon, however, the importance of the wool export became apparent to the government. England produced more wool than she needed for her own crude cloth manufacture ; and English wool had peculiar properties which made it indispensable for the weaving of the best kinds of cloth in other lands. To exploit this natural advantage the Crown imposed heavy duties upon the export of the Staple commodities, and foreign manufacturers found thenselves obliged to pay the resultant enhanced prices.

Edward II. in 1313 fixed definite marts at which alone the wool might be sold. Edward III. abolished them, but re-established them in Flanders in 1343. At this time the Crown was chronically in straits for money to carry on the French wars, and the advantages arising from collective bargaining with the merchants led to a strict incorporation of the Company and a definite grant of monopoly rights. No aliens of the north of Europe were permitted to buy the staple articles save from merchants of the Staple. Only the Italians exporting direct to their own cities were still allowed freedom of trade. It is not clear that the Company as reorganized by Edward III. was identical with that which had traded in earlier days. There is ground for believing that the later Staplers arose from a combination of the packers, weighers, customers and other state officials who had amassed wealth from the performance of their duties.

Edward III. himself had no idea of developing shipping by thus concentrating the sale of wool in English hands. A mercantile marine, it is evident, was looked upon, not as an national asset, but as a liability which was troublesome by reason of the protection it demanded from pirates and the king's enemies. This view, in fact, appears in a petition of the merchants themselves, wherein they desired the removal of the Staple to England in order that losses upon the seas might fall upon aliens. In 1353, therefore, on the occasion of a quarrel with the authorities of Bruges, Edward took the questionable step of removing the marts to this country, appointing ten towns at which wool might be sold, and forbidding any Englishman to carry it abroad. Aliens were henceforth to come in their own ships and employ their own mariners to conduct the chief export of the country. At this time the annual amount of wool shipped out of England is stated to have been 30,000 sacks, or nearly 5000 tons. The evils of this policy no doubt became apparent even to Edward III., and before many years elapsed he transferred the Staple to his recent conquest of Calais. Here, after certain further changes, it became permanently settled until England lost the town in the middle of the sixteenth century.

The Merchants of the Staple, thus finally organized, became an exceedingly close corporation, jealously guarding their privileges against interlopers, and restricting the enterprise of their own members within narrow limits. Whenever the government issued licences to non-Staplers to export wool the monopolists were loud in their complaints. The money accruing from the export dues on their wares formed an appreciable fraction of the royal revenue, and the Staplers were charged moreover with maintaining the fortifications of Calais, a duty which they neglected with disastrous results in 1558.

No sooner had the wool trade been concentrated in the hands of an English company than English merchants began also to seek a share in the kindred export of cloth. English cloth in the Middle

Ages, as we have already noticed, was a coarse product, and it would seem that much of it went overseas in a semi-manufactured condition, without having undergone all the finishing processes of dyeing, rowing, barbing, fulling and shearing which were necessary before its appearance upon the retail market.   It was for this reason that the cloth-making cities of Flanders were among the best customers of the English cloth merchants, although certain classes of Flemish craftsmen must have viewed the import of the alien material with jealousy from the outset. Hence the history of the English cloth trade with Flanders is one of perpetual disputes with the Flemings, resulting often in commercial warfare and breaches of intercourse.

Not content with obtaining a grip upon this traffic, the English cloth merchants began during the same century to carry their wares to Spain, Portugal, and the Baltic.   About the year 1380 Bristol shipped some 750 pieces of cloth annually to Portugal.   In 1390 the number had risen to 2158.   At first, as in all other trades, the majority of the bottoms employed were of foreign ownership ;   then by slow degrees the English began to use their own shipping.

In carrying their trade into the Baltic the English were making a daring attack upon a monopoly which the Hanseatic League had always regarded as its own.   In view of the privileges the Hansa enjoyed in England it could not decently issue a formal prohibition of its rival's enterprise.   It sought instead to extinguish it by permitting all kinds of piracy and lawlessness to flourish unrestrained.   We may cite one case which is typical of many : " About the feast of Easter in the year of our Lord 1394 Henry van Pomeren, Godekin Michael, Clays Sheld, Hans Howfoote, Peter Hawfoote, Clays Boniface, Rainbek, and many others with them, of Wismar and Rostock, being of the society of the Hansa, took by main force a ship of Newcastle-upon-Tyne called the Godezere sailing upon the sea towards Prussia, being of the burthen of two hundred tons and belonging unto Roger de Thorneton, Robert Gabiford, John Paulin and Thomas de Chester : which ship together with the furniture thereof amounteth unto the value of four hundred pounds ;   also the woollen cloth, the red wine, the gold and the sums of money contained in the said ship amounted unto the value of 200 marks English money :   moreover they unjustly slew John Patanson and John Russell in the surprising of the ship and goods aforesaid, and there they imprisoned the said parties taken and, to their utter undoing, detained them in prison for the space of three whole years."   From many similar records of complaints it is evident that the English merchants were doing a considerable trade to the Baltic in the last twenty years of the century, in spite of the misdeeds of a gang of Hanse pirates who infested the North Sea.

In face of difficulties also the English fishermen made their annual voyages to the coasts of Iceland.   The Norwegian-Danish kings, the owners of that island, sought to prohibit them altogether.   They preferred that their own subjects should do the fishing and sell their

takings in the Staple of Bergen, where it was easier to collect the royal
dues. But even here the jealous hatred of the Easterlings made itself
felt. The men of Lynn alone had twenty houses in Bergen, and all
these, they complained, were burnt in 1394 by the pirates of Wismar
and Rostock.

Although complete statistics are lacking, it is evident that these
various branches of English enterprise developed considerably during
the fourteenth century. They did so, as we shall see, with little or no
encouragement from the government. Consequently we find that the
pioneers had no recognized incorporation as had the Merchants of the
Staple. But regulation and mutual support were the necessities of
life to the mediaeval trader. Amid swarms of bitter enemies the
isolated individual could not hope to make an honest living ; he
tended inevitably to degenerate into piracy. In default of government
action, then, the more responsible merchants began to band together
into informal corporations for common defence and the fixing of prices.
In London the principal members of the Mercers' and Drapers'
Companies took the lead in regulating the overseas trade in cloth.
Under Richard II. the Bristol men formed a fellowship of merchant
venturers, and similar bodies were early inaugurated at Lynn, York
and Newcastle. From this it was but a step to the amalgamation of
the local bodies into a national corporation ; but that step was not
taken until the beginning of the fifteenth century.

Throughout the greater part of the fourteenth century the policy of
the government towards commerce showed little appreciation of the
fact that a powerful overseas merchant class and shipping industry
might be beneficial to the general interests of the country. The
dominant motives, as they appear to-day, seem to have been first the
easy raising of revenue from customs dues, and second, the promotion
of the interests of the consumer in preference to those of the producer.
In Bacon's well-known phraseology, the Crown placed considerations
of plenty before considerations of power. The first-named of these
motives indeed led Edward III. to adopt a more definite and comprehensive commercial policy than any of his predecessors had done.
Intermingled with his schemes of conquest in France were plans for a
confederation of the three producing areas of England, Flanders and
Gascony. The wool of England was to supply the looms of Flanders ;
the wine of Bordeaux was to minister to the tastes of Englishmen and
Flemings and to be paid for in cloth from either country ; the woad of
Toulouse, extensively used in dyeing, would add to the self-sufficiency
of the union. From the whole interplay of trade revenues would
pour into the coffers of the King. But the King himself was not
merely King of England. He was also the tenant-in-chief of Aquitaine,
and hoped to be the suzerain of Flanders. To secure the allegiance of
the Flemings is even said to have been his principal motive in claiming
the crown of France. Since, therefore, he regarded the Flemings and
the Gascons as his subjects equally with the English, he showed the

latter no favour in his shipping policy. Their loyalty at least was secure, and they had to content themselves with the advantages of a cheap and plentiful supply of foreign goods. The men of Flanders and Gascony were in possession of the chief share of the trade of those provinces with England, and Edward saw every inducement to maintain and strengthen their position.[1] It is this policy which has caused some to accord to Edward III. the title of " the Father of English Commerce." But the title is a misleading one : English commerce, in so far as it progressed at all in his reign, did so by reason of the energy and enterprise of private Englishmen, and in despite of the efforts of the King.

The naval history of the reign shows, as one might expect, a decline of English sea-power in comparison with that of other nations. The great fight in the harbour of Sluys in 1340 gave the victory to the English fleet over that of the Normans in the service of Philip of Valois. The command of the sea thus secured made possible the blockade and reduction of Calais in 1346-7, and the destruction in the battle off Winchelsea in 1350 of a fleet of armed Spanish merchantmen passing down the Channel from Flanders. But twenty years later the fatal results of the policy of cheapness were apparent. In 1372 the Earl of Pembroke sailed with an army for Aquitaine. A Spanish fleet encountered him in the Bay of Biscay, inflicting upon him a decisive defeat wherein he himself was captured and his armament destroyed. That this was no mere unlucky accident, but a real loss of the command of the sea, subsequent transactions were to prove. In the following year the only means of getting reinforcements to the south-west of France was by sending them to march the whole length of the country from Calais. To a mediaeval army such a march through an enemy country spelt rapid deterioration. Only a remnant of the force reached Bordeaux in fighting order, and the loss of sea-power resulted in the loss of all but the coastal fringe of Aquitaine. The Commons in Parliament spoke truly when they laid a share of the blame upon the policy of the government.

With the accession of Richard II., a boy of nine years of age, the delegation of the royal powers to a committee afforded an opportunity to the mercantile interests to express their views in an authoritative manner. Among the men who obtained a share in the administration in the early part of the reign we find the names of Michael de la Pole, Earl of Suffolk, the son of a wealthy merchant of Hull ; and of Nicholas Bramber, William Walworth and John Philipot, three prominent merchants of London. The Parliaments of the time had also a strong infusion of the new element. It is not surprising, therefore, that a series of statutes was enacted, some of which embodied an entirely new view of commercial policy. In 1381 an Act prohibited the carrying of gold and silver out of England, the current theory being that the

[1] A statute of 1353, for regulating the price of wine, had the effect of restricting the shipments of Englishmen from Bordeaux whilst leaving free those of the Gascons.

practice tended to "the destruction of the realm." The idea itself was not a new one, but it is from this time onwards that we find the principle continually insisted upon. In the following year Parliament passed a Navigation Act, the first of a notable series of such measures, which were destined to exercise an immense influence upon the course of English expansion—intermittently until 1651, continuously from that date until within a century of the present day. The Act of Richard II., undoubtedly inspired by the naval disasters in the later years of Edward III., laid down that no English merchants were to import or export goods save in English ships, the idea being not to limit English trade but to inforce an increase of English shipping and the employment of English mariners. The underlying motive was the strengthening of military power at sea, and the promoters of the measure showed an entire appreciation of the fact that fighting and mercantile sea-power are in essence one and the same thing. In 1391 the Crown gave leave to the merchants doing business in the Baltic to elect a governor and officials. Two other Acts further illustrate the trend of the new policy. That of 1392 prohibited aliens from selling by retail in England, a privilege which Edward III. had allowed them ; and that of 1394 permitted the hitherto forbidden export of corn.

Here, then, we have the outline of a new theory of the use of commerce, undreamt of even by such a statesman as Edward I. Commerce in future was to subserve the increase of national power, not merely to act as a means of filling an empty treasury at periods when the people were unwilling to pay direct taxes. The interests of the producer were to rank before those of the consumer ; the new policy might increase the cost of living to individuals, but the reward would be an increase of security for the whole nation. " The encouragement of natives and discouragement of foreigners, the development of shipping, and the amassing of treasure—these were the three main points of the mercantile programme, and they were all deliberately adopted by the Parliament of Richard II., who deliberately rejected the opposite policy which had been pursued in each of these particulars by Edward III." [1]

Such was the programme on paper. But its translation into actual performance must not be taken too seriously. The key-measure of the whole, the Navigation Act, remained effective for only a few months. It was too sudden and sweeping, and consequently impracticable of enforcement, for it was obviously premature to enjoin the exclusive use of English ships when such ships did not exist in anything like the requisite numbers. The Navigation Act, then, became a dead-letter, and when a century later Henry VII. drafted a new one, he did so, as we shall see, in a much more cautious and practical spirit, and his moderation was rewarded by success. The remaining parts of the system of Richard II. were dependent upon consistent administration for their usefulness. But, unfortunately, the history of English

---

[1] Cunningham, *op. cit.* p. 470.

administration from his time to the Battle of Bosworth in 1485 resembles a perilous passage across a quaking morass with but one or two spots of firm ground occurring in its course. During all that century of faction and revolt, governments fighting for their lives had little taste for a dispassionate study and manipulation of commerce.

The real interest of the mercantile legislation of the end of the fourteenth century lies in this : that it expressed in public enactments the aspirations of the trading and seafaring sections of the community ; and once expressed, those aspirations, being vital to the national ambition for expansion, remained always in men's minds as an ideal to be worked towards even if impossible of present realization. Patriotic men of the fifteenth century struggled hopefully through adverse conditions until, with a sigh of relief, they reached the haven of sound government under Henry VII.

The question of the actual strength of English shipping in the fourteenth century is not one upon which it is easy to speak clearly. The fleet which won the Battle of Sluys was a formidable one, although it would appear that the fighting was of the type familiar in the land battles of the period, a heavy discharge of arrows followed by an attack with hand-to-hand weapons in which boarding decided the victory. Sluys, then, was a soldiers' victory which affords no conclusive proof of the superiority of the English ships and seamen. The Calais Roll, again, containing the list of the fleet which held the Narrow Seas during the siege, indicates the presence of a large number of vessels drawn from all ports of England and Wales. Altogether there were 700, with 14,151 men, or an average of just over twenty in each crew. The majority must, therefore, have been fishing boats or coasters, whilst a few were of larger size and capable of carrying large cargoes on the longer voyages to the Baltic, Iceland and Spain. From other sources we know that at least one English ship of 300 tons existed in this reign, and several of 200.

However distributed, the fact that fourteen thousand seamen were available for a campaign out of a total population not exceeding five millions implies that English sea-power had already become considerable. Indeed, from the Battle of Sandwich down to the middle of the fourteenth century the English had no difficulty in securing the command of the Channel whenever they desired it. But in twenty years the prospect completely altered. Not only did the English fleets lose the command of the sea in 1372, but for several years following they were unable to regain it. In 1377 the south coasts were swept from end to end by French and Spanish raiders, who landed with impunity and penetrated far inland. To what must this decline be attributed ? Largely, no doubt, to Edward III.'s commercial policy, although this does not provide a complete answer to the question, since English shipping had never previously had any protection from government, and yet had contrived to grow formidable. The Black Death of 1350 which, with succeeding epidemics, caused the population to decline from five to two-and-a-half millions in the space of twenty-five years, would easily explain the matter had it been confined to England. But all western Europe suffered equally heavily. The pestilence may, however, have struck the maritime population with exceptional severity.

Whatever may have been the reason for the relative decay of our sea-power, the middle classes, as we have seen, were determined upon an alteration of the policy laid down by Edward III. That monarch, although he was present at two naval battles, never showed any appreciation of the value of sea-power. His revival of the title " Lord of the Seas " seems superficially to indicate the contrary. But his words were not supported by deeds, and piracy, which he hoped to suppress by the dread of his name, increased to an unprecedented extent throughout the century.

An examination of the Calais Roll throws an interesting light upon the distribution of English shipping in 1346. The Roll does not state the tonnage of the vessels, but it gives the numbers of ships and mariners found by each port. After making allowance for the fact that many of the men must have been fishermen, and for the probability that not every seaport contributed the same proportion of its strength, we obtain a little light on the relative shares held by Englishmen in the different branches of foreign trade. Yarmouth stands easily at the head of the list with 1057 mariners. Next come Fowey and Dartmouth with 770 and 757 respectively ; then London, Bristol and Plymouth with between 600 and 700 each ; Winchelsea, Southampton and Sandwich, 500 to 600 ; Hull, 466 ; and Lynn, Boston, Dover, Shoreham, Looe and Newcastle, each with 300 to 400 men. Thus of the first sixteen seaports of the country we find on the North Sea coasts only six, or seven if we include Sandwich, whose trade, however, went mostly down Channel. But it is certain from all other evidence that the North Sea trades, to Flanders, Germany, the Baltic and the North, preponderated greatly over those with France and the Peninsula. We must, therefore, conclude that, imperfect as was the hold of Englishmen upon the southern trade routes, it was nevertheless much more considerable than their share of the more important traffic with the east, the centre and the north of Europe. The principal competitors in shipping were, and long were to remain, the Easterlings and the Flemings.

CHAPTER III

LANCASTER AND YORK, 1399–1485

THE revolution which deposed Richard II. and gave the crown to Henry IV. was favourable to the development of the commercial policy. The new king was alive to the importance to the realm of an overseas trade in native hands, and set himself to further the wishes of the mercantile element which made its first attempt at self-assertion under Richard II. Henry himself had spent the period of his exile previous to 1399 in the Baltic lands, as the guest of the Grand Master of the Teutonic Knights. He had seen the conditions under which Englishmen were attempting to trade in Danzig and other Prussian towns of the Hanseatic League, and when as king he began a negotiation to improve those conditions he had the advantage of being personally known to the potentates with whom he was in correspondence.

The keynote of his policy was the suppression of piracy and the inauguration of a " well ordered trade " under government supervision. Of piracy both Englishmen and Easterlings had been guilty, although the latter as a body had less excuse, since the discipline of their league was strict, and the conduct of individuals was, therefore, a reflection of the opinions of their rulers. To settle old scores and prevent a renewal of disorders Henry sent Sir William Esturmy and John Kington as his ambassadors to frame a treaty with the Baltic cities ; and at the same time he took steps to reduce the loose individualism of the English traders to the more controllable form of a regulated company.[1] On June 6, 1404, he issued to the merchants trading in Prussia and the Hanse towns a charter authorizing them to meet at any place convenient and choose governors from among their number. The governors so chosen, and their deputies, were empowered to rule all English merchants dwelling in the countries named, to make ordinances for the conduct of the trade, to settle disputes, to ensure the good behaviour of the English towards foreigners, and to demand reparation for wrongs sustained by any Englishman at their hands. A later grant of 1408 created a similar jurisdiction for Denmark,

---

[1] It would appear that the organization for those merchants suggested by Richard II. had, like the remainder of his commercial legislation, been allowed to lapse.

Norway and Sweden.   In this manner arose the company which undertook the difficult task of planting English outposts in the Baltic in face
of Hanse opposition.   When, in the sixteenth century, it was revived
and reconstituted, it took the name of the Eastland Company, and it
will be convenient to apply that designation to it from the outset.

The Eastland Company, like all others of mediaeval formation, was
of the " regulated " type, its constitution developing out of those of
the guilds which had long supervised the internal industry of the towns.
There was no joint capital with profits distributed to the members in
the shape of interest on shares, as in a modern trading company.
Each merchant traded on his own separate capital, making his own
profit or loss.   Membership of the company meant that he enjoyed
his share of the common privileges obtained from foreign governments,
stored his wares in the common " house " in the foreign port, bought
and sold at prices fixed by the officers of the company, and generally
obeyed all other rules for the good conduct of the trade.   In return
for thus surrendering a part of his liberty of action he received the
immense benefit of the protection of a corporation which might
negotiate with governments almost in the character of a sovereign
power.   Since the governor and his assistants were responsible for the
conduct of all their fellow-countrymen in the foreign country, it
followed of necessity that no Englishman could be permitted to trade
unless he were a member of the company.   Thus quite naturally arose
the monopolies of the companies in the several branches of foreign
trade.

We have already noticed the rise of local societies of merchant
adventurers during the latter part of the fourteenth century.   The
opening years of Henry IV. saw also the linking-up of all such bodies
as were interested in the cloth trade with Flanders.   In imitation, no
doubt, of the Baltic merchants, they petitioned the king for a regular
incorporation.   In 1407 he issued to them a charter constituting them
a regulated company with the same machinery of governor and
assistants as in the case of the Eastland Company.   In after years the
Merchants Adventurers, as this association came to be called, claimed
a much earlier date of origin than 1407.   Sir Thomas Gresham speaks
of a copy of privileges granted to them in 1296.   But, although they
undoubtedly existed as a trading body in the fourteenth century and
possibly earlier, the best informed opinion holds that the charter of
Henry IV. was their first official recognition : " the Adventurers now
proposed to enter the decent ranks of recognized associations, and
exchange their roving wars for the more formal aggressions of a
chartered company." [1]

The London Merchants Adventurers, to whom those of other ports
became affiliated, were an offshoot of the Mercers' Company.   Their
London headquarters until the time of Charles II. were in the Mercers'

---

[1] Mrs. A. S. Green, *Town Life in the Fifteenth Century*, London, 1894 (repr. 1908),
L p. 95.

Hall, and down to 1526 the transactions of both companies' meetings were entered in the same minute-book. But on several occasions the members from the other east-coast ports made stout resistance to the dominance of the Londoners in the company. It was, perhaps, on account of the unwillingness of the several ports to acknowledge any one of their number as head that the governor, secretary and other officials of the company resided normally in the Netherlands, first at Bruges, and then at Antwerp. The English house overseas thus became a little oasis of English rule in a foreign land.

In chartering and supporting these companies Henry IV. probably gave more effective aid to the English shipping industry than would have resulted from a strict enforcement of the Navigation Act. In spite of fair words the Hansa was not slow to show by deeds its disapproval of the recognition of its rivals. A fresh catalogue of crimes upon the sea formed the subject of a new negotiation in 1409 ; and no sooner had the slate been wiped clean than the score began again to accumulate. It may seem surprising that, in despair of securing better treatment for their subjects, Henry IV. and his successors did not retaliate by abrogating the substantial privileges the Germans enjoyed in England. But for many years to come no English king dared to consider such a step. The Hansa was a mighty naval power. If it had sided with France the English shores would have been ravaged from end to end. In that age of sudden rebellions, banishments and fugitive claimants, there was ever the possibility that an invading force might land any day upon the east coast with Hanse assistance, and in a few weeks subvert the throne. So Henry IV. himself had come in 1399 ; and so Edward IV. was to appear in 1471. English governments might as yet think only of propitiating the Hansa ; they were in no position to defy it.

Under Henry V. (1413-22) commerce flourished. There is a significant cessation of complaints of Hanse piracy. The trade with the Peninsula increased so that English ships went frequently to Lisbon and even to Morocco. Henry, in fact, secured respect because he maintained a large navy for the purposes of his French war, and was doubtless able to spare some of his ships for the duty of keeping order generally upon the seas. For protection against rovers it became the custom for the merchants in each branch of the foreign trade to despatch their ships in company, and when the navy was strong it provided vessels to " waft " or convoy the merchant fleets. Thus each year saw the departure from English shores of several wool fleets for Calais, of three or four cloth fleets for Bruges or Antwerp, another for the Baltic, a wine fleet for Bordeaux, a fishing fleet for Iceland, and a convoy of varying size for Spain and Portugal. The wool was shipped principally from Southampton, London and Boston, and the cloth for Flanders and the Baltic from all the east coast ports. From them also and from Bristol went the Iceland fleet, departing in the spring and returning in the autumn. The wine-ships timed their arrival at

Bordeaux between November and February, when the new vintage was ready for export. In the latter part of the fifteenth century it was stated that there were as many as 8000 Englishmen in the town at one time during the winter season. In Spain the English traded principally at Seville and San Lucar in the south, obtaining at the latter place privileges from the Duke of Medina Sidonia. The Bordeaux and Peninsula trades were conducted chiefly by the merchants of the southern and western ports of England.

So far the fifteenth century had promised well for English maritime expansion. But scarcely two decades of it had passed when Henry V. died in France, leaving his throne to a child not twelve months old. Civil dissension added to the burden of foreign war fatally weakened the authority of the government, and England speedily lost that discipline by which alone the young commerce of the native merchants could make headway against foreign competition. The navy of Henry V. had numbered fourteen large ships of 300 to 1000 tons, ten of medium size, and fourteen small craft—a greater force than any previous king had wielded. Within a few years of his death it had ceased to exist, the Council having sold the ships to private owners to avoid the expense of their upkeep. The fate of the navy was ominous of that in store for merchant shipping. In all directions a period of decline set in which was destined to last for many years.

One important result of Henry V.'s diplomacy had been his alliance with the young Duke Philip of Burgundy, whose father, John the Fearless, had been callously murdered by the Dauphin at the Bridge of Montereau in 1419. The Dukes of Burgundy had large interests in the Low Countries, the whole of which fell gradually under their control. The political alliance, therefore, improved the position of the Merchants Adventurers at Bruges. Their shipments of cloth grew ever larger, until they began seriously to compete with the labour of the Flemish craftsmen. But their position was dependent upon politics, and politics failed them. In 1434 the Duke of Burgundy began to think of abandoning his military alliance with England in the French war ; at the same time he entirely prohibited the importation of English cloth into the Netherlands. Here was the opportunity for a strong government to interfere on behalf of its merchants. But no government support was forthcoming, and it was not until twelve years later (1446) that the English obtained a charter of privileges from the duke by which their position was restored, their mart being now transferred to Antwerp.

From government weakness the Eastland merchants were naturally greater sufferers than the Merchants Adventurers, for their industry had always been more precarious. Henry VI. renewed their charters in 1428. In 1432 they made complaint that the subjects of the King of Denmark had robbed the merchants of York and Hull of £5000 in one year, and the other merchants of England of £20,000. Four years later Englishmen found themselves entirely excluded from trade at

c

the Staple at Bergen.   They attributed this to the machinations of the
Hansa, and demanded the revocation of the latter's privileges in
England ; but, for reasons already explained, their petition was
unavailing.   In 1440 Henry VI. bestirred himself so far as to send a
remonstrance to the Grand Master of the Teutonic Knights on the
subject of the ill-treatment of Englishmen in the Baltic.   Danzig and
Lubeck seem to have been the prime evil-doers at this period.   But
both Danes and Germans had taken the measure of Henry VI.   They
paid no heed to his nerveless diplomacy, and in the course of the next
thirty years made war so effectively upon the Eastland Company that
they fairly wiped its commerce off the seas.   When at the end of
the century we find a few English traders carrying on a precarious
traffic with the Baltic, they are doing so as free-lances, the well-devised
organization of Henry IV.'s charters having lapsed into oblivion.

   Until the middle of the fifteenth century the English frequented the
coasts of Iceland and other northern regions for the purpose of trading
and fishing.   The Kings of Denmark, the over-lords of Iceland, had
disapproved of this traffic, but had been unable to stop it.   The
situation, in fact, with its triangle of interests, resembles that produced
in the Spanish colonies when Hawkins began selling negroes in the
following century.   The English went direct to the fishing grounds
because there they obtained the largest and cheapest supplies of fish ;
the Icelanders welcomed them because of the cloth and other indispensable commodities which they brought ; and the Danish king
sought to prohibit direct intercourse and force all exchange through
the bottle-neck of his Staple at Bergen, because there alone he could
collect effectively such dues as seemed right to him.   The royal
argument at this early date is identical with that of the Spanish
sovereigns of the sixteenth century, and indeed with that of our own
rulers in the eighteenth : What is the use of having acquired colonies
unless we make something out of them by converting them into
monopolies for our own enjoyment ?   Owing to Danish pressure
applied for this reason the government of Henry VI. forbade by a law
of 1430 any trade by its subjects otherwise than at Bergen ; and in
1450 the two kingdoms concluded a treaty to the same effect.   The
result of this diplomatic harshness upon the mariners of an undisciplined age was what might have been expected : trade did not flow
smoothly through the channel appointed, but degenerated instead into
a wild orgy of piracy which made the northern seas a battle-ground for
Englishmen, Scots, Easterlings and Scandinavians until the last decade
of the century.

   Turning to the southern and western trade routes we find a course
of development distinct from that of the North Sea.   The trades with
Gascony, Spain and Portugal, and late in the century the beginnings
of the Levant trade, were never during the Middle Ages incorporated,
even in so mild a form as that of a regulated company.   It is interesting
to seek out the reasons for this difference in policy.   In the first place,

until the loss of Aquitaine in 1453, Englishmen trading at Bordeaux and Bayonne were as safe from unwarranted interference as they would have been at Dover or Newcastle, for the Gascon ports were the possessions of the English crown ; and even after the expulsion of the English garrisons local feeling still remained favourable to those who had been for centuries the best customers of the province. Then again, in exchanging English cloth for the wines of Bordeaux, or the wines, oil, leather and fruits of Spain and Portugal, the merchants on either side were but bartering the surplus commodities of their respective countries. The Gascons, Spaniards and Portuguese of this period profited by trade, but their national existence did not depend exclusively upon it as did that of the Hanseatic League and the Flemish cities. There was thus an absence of incentive to that desperate, merciless competition which made the North Sea so hard a school of commerce. But perhaps the principal reason for the absence of incorporation in these trades lies in the mentality of the men bred in our southern and western seaports. These men of Southampton, Plymouth, Fowey and Bristol, and all the ports between, were instinctively individualists, hating any form of regulation and control. There was more essential difference of outlook between them and the Londoners and east-coast men than there is between Englishmen and Americans to-day. Well-governed, collective effort made no appeal to them. Therefore, there was no serious attempt to " regulate " the Spanish trade until 1530 ; and in the other trades, so far as we know, no attempt at all. Of all the south-western towns but one, Exeter, is recorded as taking any part in the national association of Merchants Adventurers incorporated by Henry IV.

As regards the fortunes of these trades during the period ending in 1485, we find that the Bordeaux wine-carrying slipped largely out of English hands. The Gascons themselves brought much of their wine to England, and the Easterlings developed a considerable carrying trade between London and Flanders and the south, so that when Henry VII. came to the throne he made it his first business to remedy the complaints of " decay " in this traffic. The commerce with Portugal, after continuing to flourish during the first part of the fifteenth century, fell into disorder amid the anarchy which followed ; and for the first time the amity between the two nations was shaken by outbreaks of piracy and reprisal on the seas. The galleys of Venice and the carracks of Genoa continued to monopolize the rich trade between England and the Mediterranean. The goods they brought were of high value in comparison with their bulk, and complaints were consequently frequent that the Italians besides lading their fleets with wool and cloth drained the country of money in order to redress the balance of value. This, in the eyes of mediaeval economists, was a crime against the nation, and the Italians were highly unpopular in consequence. In addition to this, a petition in Parliament in 1439 charged them with acting as carriers between Spain, Portugal, France and England, and so contributing to the decay of English shipping. The first recorded venture of an Englishman to the Levant—on a trading voyage, that is to say, and in an English ship—took place in 1458. The merchant in question, Robert Sturmy of Bristol, reached the East in safety but was captured and robbed by the Genoese on his return. They attacked him, it is said, because it was rumoured that he was bringing green pepper and other spices to plant in England and so render the country independent of the Italian trade.

With the death of Henry V., then, there began a prolonged depression in the various branches of English overseas enterprise. How great the decline was we have no means of estimating, the necessary statistics not having been preserved ; but that it existed there is no doubt, since it is avouched both by the men of the evil time and by those of the next age, when a stronger government had effected an improvement. When all allowance has been made for exaggeration, a residue of truth must remain in the contemporary evidence.

One of the most interesting documents of mediaeval English history is the product of this unhappy period. *The Libel of English Policy* was written, as internal evidence shows, in 1436-7. The author was a man of classical reading, a wide knowledge of commercial matters, and modern-sounding theories on the uses of sea-power. His identity is not certainly known, but he is generally thought to have been Adam de Moleyns, Bishop of Chichester, who was murdered by some mutinous seamen in 1450. Although he intended his work to be a serious essay on policy he wrote it in verse ; but he was appealing to the men of his own generation, and he knew that the rough rhymes in which he clothed his doctrines gave them the greatest chance of a wide circulation. And in fact their circulation was a wide one, so that they bore fruit long after the hand that had written them was dead.

" The true process of English policy," he begins, " is this . . . Cherish merchandise, keep the Admiralty, that we be masters of the Narrow Sea." With a naval force in the Channel, he says, we are able to bring all our foes to terms by pressure upon their commerce ; then, bethinking him of the sad state to which incompetence had reduced the once powerful fleet of Henry V., he exclaims, " Where be our ships, where be our swords become ? Our enemies bid for the ship [on the noble] set a sheep." After this prologue the author proceeds to examine in turn each branch of foreign trade, and also the trade routes of other nations which pass through the English Channel. He mentions all commodities in detail, and is ever ready for securing political results by the manipulation of trade :

> " . . . for the wool of England
> Sustaineth the Commons Flemings I understand.
> Then if England would her wool restrain
> From Flanders, this followeth in certain,
> Flanders of need must with us have peace,
> Or else she is destroyed . . ."

> " Therefore if we would manly take in hand,
> To keep this sea from Flanders and from Spain,
> And from Scotland, like as from petty Britain [Brittany]
> We should right soon have peace for all their boasts,
> For they must needs pass by our English coasts."

The Easterlings also carry on much trade with Flanders and the
Bay of Biscay, and may be brought to reason in the same manner :

> " Thus if they would not our friends be,
> We might lightly stop them in the sea :
> They should not pass our streams [coasts] withouten leave
> It would not be, but if we should them grieve."

The Italian trade, he considers, is altogether injurious, since it brings
mere luxuries into the country, but carries out staple goods such as
wool and tin :

> " The great galleys of Venice and Florence
> Be well laden with things of complacence,
> All spicery and of grocers' ware :
> With sweet wines all manner of chaffare
> Apes and japes and marmosets tailed
> Nifles and trifles that little have availed :
> And things with which they featly blear our eye
>
> .   .   .   .
>
> Thus these galleys, for this licking ware
> And eating ware, bear hence our best chaffare,
> Cloth, wool and tin . . . ."

In a strong navy and a strong mercantile marine he sees the salvation
of England :

> " And if I should conclude all by the King
> Henry the Fifth, what was his purposing,
> When at Hampton he made the great dromons,
> Which passed other ships of all the commons ;
> The Trinity, the Grace de Dieu, the Holy Ghost,
> And others more, which as now be lost.
> What hope ye was the king's great intent
> Of those ships, and what in mind he meant ?
> It was not else but that he cast to be
> Lord round about environ of the sea.
>
> .   .   .   .
>
> For if merchants were cherished to their speed,
> We were not likely to fail in any need.
> If they be rich, then in prosperity
> Shall be our land, lords and commonalty."

It is impossible in a few short extracts to do justice to a composition
of some twelve hundred lines. But enough has been quoted to show
that the mercantile policy outlined in the time of Richard II. still lived
in the minds of men in the feeble reign of Henry VI. Patriots like this
unknown author saw a way out of the nation's difficulties even though
they might despair of ever getting that way adopted.

The last twenty years of the French war, from the death of the Duke of Bedford to the end in 1455, witnessed unbroken disasters to the English arms.   First Paris and the regions of the Isle of France were lost, then Normandy, and finally Bordeaux and the last remnants of Aquitaine.   The Burgundian alliance which Henry V. had concluded was broken off, nor was it renewed while the House of Lancaster remained upon the throne.   Under Henry V. England had undertaken an impossible task, the conquest and permanent subjection of a nation as strong as itself.   The surpassing military genius of the king had for a time made the attempt seem feasible ; after his death the momentum of victory had carried his followers forward for a few more years, until with the campaigns of Jeanne Darc the tide inexorably turned and the folly of the undertaking became apparent.   But the English people themselves were the last to realize that this was the case.   They blamed their king, their commanders overseas, and the lukewarm party in the Council, whom they regarded as traitors ; and their stubborn pride insisted upon prolonging the struggle long after it was virtually decided.   As a result Calais alone of all the overseas possessions remained in English hands, and the government of Henry VI., contemned and browbeaten by its own subjects, fell into such a state of decay that it was ripe for overthrow by a feudal revolution.

A faction of the nobles headed by Richard, Duke of York, and the Earl of Warwick raised the standard of revolt.   In the struggle known as the Wars of the Roses Richard of York lost his life, but his son Edward, with Warwick's aid, gained the throne by the decisive victory of Towton in 1461.   Within four years Henry VI. of Lancaster was a prisoner in the Tower whilst Edward IV. of York wore the crown in his stead.

During this period no one in authority gave heed to the external interests of the country.   The middle classes in the towns, hopeless of aid from either party, remained for the most part aloof and indifferent. The Londoners, indeed, intervened with effect when at a critical moment they closed their gates to the Lancastrians and opened them to the Yorkists.   But they did so only because they feared the plundering proclivities of the northern troops who formed the bulk of Henry VI.'s army.   The shipping interest turned more and more from trade to piracy.   In the Channel cross-raids upon the towns of either coast were frequent ; the east-coast mariners fought Danes and Easterlings and Flemings ; the Merchants Adventurers lost ground in Flanders to the Hansa, by reason of their own indiscipline and the unpopularity of the Lancastrian government with the Duke of Burgundy.   Anarchy, in fact, had reached its height.

Edward IV., when he had secured the throne, took up the cause of the Merchants Adventurers.   Unlike the Lancastrian leaders he was on friendly terms with Philip of Burgundy, whose son Charles afterwards married Edward's sister Margaret.   Accordingly, in 1462, the Merchants Adventurers received a confirmation of their charter, allowing them to elect a governor and twelve assistants for their better government. The King, in fact, appointed the first governor of the new series, William Obray, who had held that office before the outbreak of the disorders which necessitated the new grant. For the maintenance of better discipline the new governor's powers were made so extensive as to give him the complete control of the trade in all its stages. There was a cessation of intercourse with the Low Countries in 1464, probably owing to the jealousy of the Flemings at the revival of the English trade ; but the dispute did not long endure. William Caxton, before introducing the craft of printing in England, served for a period as Governor of the Merchants Adventurers at Bruges.

With the Hansa Edward IV. was not at first on good terms. Their intolerance of English traffic across the North Sea led to a period of sharp reprisals and almost open warfare. In 1463 Edward actually went so far as to abrogate the Hanse privileges, although he soon restored them again, moved presumably by the bribes or threats of the League. Warwick the King-maker, his principal supporter, had always been an enemy of the Easterlings, having preyed upon their ships at sea when he filled the post of Captain of Calais. But in 1470 Warwick turned against his master, declared for the imprisoned Henry VI., and drove Edward from the country. Edward retired to Flanders, patched up his quarrel with the Hanseatic merchants, and with their aid and that of the Burgundians reappeared in 1471 upon the east coast of England. Regaining the throne by the two victories of Barnet and Tewkesbury, he found himself obliged to pay the price of his new friends' assistance. The Duke of Burgundy's reward was of a political nature ; the Hansa demanded a confirmation and extension of its old privileges in England. The treaty, signed at Utrecht in 1474, opens with the provision, " all hostilities to cease," and proceeds to the definition of the concessions. The effect of the latter was that the Germans obtained rights of self-government in their fortified house of the Steelyard in London, and an adjustment of customs duties which placed them in a more favourable position than any other foreigners, and even than the English merchants themselves. The circumstances of the king's restoration explain why these privileged and unpopular foreigners were able to maintain their position in England. It was not until the Royal Navy became a formidable force in the sixteenth century that any English king could dare to offend them with impunity. Although the Treaty of 1474 contained clauses for the safeguard of the English merchants in the Hanse towns, it would seem that they were to a large extent inoperative. The pirate wars with Denmark still continued and, even had the Hansa been genuinely friendly, would have sufficed to throttle English trade with the Baltic. The organization which Henry IV. had granted to the Eastland merchants failed to survive, and their commerce seems to have practically disappeared. Well might the ambassadors of Danzig, returning from signing the

Treaty of Utrecht, make boast : " We have made an end of the English." [1]

We have seen therefore that the Yorkist kings—for Richard III. had little opportunity to vary his brother's arrangements—whilst recognizing the importance of the country's external trade, were unable to adopt a consistent mercantile policy.   Their principal merit in the eyes of their merchants was that they maintained the Burgundian alliance, so important to the interests of the cloth trade.   For this reason they enjoyed the support of the middle classes who, now that the old nobility had well-nigh perished in the civil wars, were of much greater consequence in the country than they had ever been before.

In dealing with English affairs in the fifteenth century there is perhaps a temptation to be too emphatic on the decline of English shipping.   The statements of contemporaries are always prone to exaggerate the evils of their own time in comparison with that which has gone before.   The truth seems to be as follows : the early years of the century were undoubtedly a time of great progress ; in the later ones, although there may have actually been an increase of overseas traffic, that increase did not maintain the earlier rate of expansion, nor did it compare with the advance of the other maritime nations of Europe.   The Easterlings, the Italians and the Portuguese were reaping golden harvests from the development of maritime enterprise in its various forms ; Englishmen were conscious of being left behind in the race, and they knew that with wiser leadership they could do better.   Internal industry was growing also by leaps and bounds. The cloth manufacture absorbed ever increasing quantities of wool, insomuch that the Staplers' exports sensibly declined.   A long list of other industries—iron works in Sussex and the Forest of Dean, copper working, shipbuilding, gunmaking and bell-founding, brickmaking, the weaving of carpets and tapestries, and the making of silk, lace and ribbons—all inaugurated or greatly extended during the fifteenth century, testify to the advance of material civilization, and explain the unrest arising from the insufficiency of the outlet through the medium of English shipping.   There is of course another side to the picture. Agriculture undoubtedly declined.   Through lack of security manuring was neglected and the soil became exhausted ; and for the first time England had need to look to the safeguard of the food supply.   But this led again to the same conclusion—that a strong native marine must be built up in the interest of the national security.   The disappearance of mediaeval kingship at Bosworth in 1485 left to a new dynasty and a changed system of government the task of providing a solution of the problem.

The four centuries with whose history we have hitherto concerned ourselves witnessed an immense advance in the design and construction of shipping and in the art of navigation.   Mediaeval vessels were broadly divided into two main types, long ships and round ships.   The former relied upon oars as the chief means of propulsion, with sails as an auxiliary ; the latter were primarily sailing craft. In addition, a number of bastard types, frequently evolved and discarded, attempted to combine the advantages of both systems.

The Norsemen carried out their raids and invasions in long ships rowed by the warriors who alone composed the crews, open for the greater part of their length, and decked only at the stern. The Norse type long persisted in England under various names such as balyngers, barges and spynes. It was swift and therefore suitable for war, but the absence of a deck and the large number of men required to work it rendered it unfitted for the carriage of merchandise in the rough northern seas. In the Mediterranean the long ship or galley, as the southerners called it, had a much longer life. The use of forced labour at the oars partially solved the economic difficulty. But here again its function was chiefly military, and the merchant used the sailing ship for the general purposes of his trade. In England the long ship had a special use for the service of the Channel passage. The *White Ship* in which Henry I.'s son perished seems to have been a large vessel of this type. Edward I. built several galleys for his navy, two of which pulled sixty oars a side. Much controversy has arisen concerning the design of the classical galley of antiquity with its superposed banks of oars. That of the Middle Ages presents no such difficulty for explanation. It had never more than one bank, but each oar was pulled by two or more rowers.

The round ship (variously called in England a nef, cog, dromond or carrack) differed principally from the galley in having a much greater proportion of beam to length and in discarding the oar as a means of propulsion. We see this type in its early stages in the pictorial epic of the Bayeux Tapestry. As commerce increased it grew rapidly in size, and the provision of a deck rendered it more seaworthy than the Norse oared ship. At first it had only one mast with a great square sail. In the thirteenth and fourteenth centuries two masts became common ; in the fifteenth there were often three, whilst at the opening of the sixteenth century the greatest ships carried four masts with topmasts and topsails and a complicated system of rigging. In the fourteenth century also the primitive steering-oar of the Norsemen gave place to the rudder.

The exigencies of warfare introduced a modification of the hull. In the earlier campaigns merchantmen were hastily adapted for fighting by the erection of high temporary platforms at bow and stern for the accommodation of archers and stone-throwing machines. As piracy developed and insecurity became chronic in the northern seas these erections became a permanent part of the design under the names of forecastle and poop or " summercastle." The introduction of artillery and the mounting of large numbers of little pieces of ordnance increased the size of these castles until they grew to the dimensions shown in pictures of the *Great Harry* and other ships of the Tudor period.

A few figures relating to the size of English ships are available. In the reigns of Edward III. and Richard II. we find mention of vessels of 200 and 300 tons. The navy of Henry V. included the *Jesus*, 1000 tons ; the *Holy Ghost*, 760 ; the *George of the Tower* and the *Christopher of Spayne*, 600 ; and the *Trinity Royal, Marie of Hampton* and *Marie of Sandwich*, between 500 and 600. In 1439 a list of ships shows that at least 36 English merchantmen existed of 100–400 tons ; whilst a similar list of 1451 shows 50 such vessels. John Taverner of Hull possessed in the same period what is described as a great carrack (the term was usually applied to Italian vessels) ; and William Canynges of Bristol owned a ship of 900 tons and several others of large size.

The principal types of foreign merchantmen were the hulks of the Easterlings, large sailing ships ; the great carracks of Genoa ; the caravels of Spain and Portugal, light sailing craft rigged with triangular lateen sails ; and the galleasses of Venice, commonly known as the Flanders galleys. These latter were, in their proportions, a compromise between the long galley and the short round ship. They were driven normally by sails, but used oars as an auxiliary means of propulsion. They were of huge size (reaching 1200 tons) and strongly armed and manned.

Prominent among the improvements in navigation during the Middle Ages was the invention of the mariner's compass in the thirteenth century, the needle being floated in water by means of a cork or rush. This was followed by the introduction of the astrolabe, and later of the cross-staff and the quadrant, for taking latitudes. Their use however was not always practicable at sea, and the *portolani* or pilot's charts of the fifteenth century indicate direction by lines of bearing radiating from fixed points instead of by the modern parallels and meridians.

AUTHORITIES FOR PART I., CHAPTERS I.-III.

Among general histories of the Middle Ages in England the following will be found to give the results of modern research in greater or less detail according to their size : *The Political History of England*, ed. W. Hunt and R. Lane Poole, vols. 1, 2, 3, 4, London, 1905, etc. ; *The Angevin Empire*, London, 1903 ; *The Dawn of the Constitution*, London, 1908 ; *The Genesis of Lancaster*, Oxford, 1913, and *Lancaster and York*, Oxford, 1892, all by Sir J. H. Ramsay ; *England and the British Empire*, by A. D. Innes, vol. 1, London, 1913. The latter covers the whole period in one volume, and includes valuable sections on industry and commerce.

For the general economic history of the time the standard modern authority is *The Growth of English Industry and Commerce during the Early and Middle Ages*, by the Ven. Archdeacon W. Cunningham, 5th ed., Cambridge, 1910. *The Economic History of England*, vol. 1, by E. Lipson, London, 1915, covers the same ground and includes the results of more recent research. *England's Industrial Development*, by A. D. Innes, London, 1912, is of smaller scope and presents the whole subject from early to modern times in one volume.

Of works dealing exclusively with foreign commerce the most indispensable is written in German, and has never been published in our own language—

Englische Handelspolitik gegen Ende des Mittelalters, by G. Schanz, 2 vols., Leipsig, 1881. It contains an accurate and comprehensive survey of all branches of our overseas trade during the period covered by the title, and of the commercial relations of England with foreign powers. *English Merchant*, by H. R. Fox Bourne, London, 1886, is an excellent account of the great mercantile families, and contains much information omitted from more recent works. *The Records of the Merchant Adventurers of Newcastle*, edited for the Surtees Society by Dr. F. W. Dendy, 1894, are preceded by an introduction showing the relationship of the provincial society to the national company of Merchants Adventurers. *The Beginnings of English Overseas Enterprise*, by Sir C. P. Lucas, Oxford, 1917, is a much needed account of the origin of the Staplers, the Merchants Adventurers and the Eastland Company. *The Commercial Relations of England and Portugal*, by Miss V. M. Shillington and Miss A. B. W. Chapman, London, 1907, and *The Outline History of the Hanseatic League*, by C. Walford, in *Transactions of the Royal Historical Society*, orig. ser. ix. pp. 82-136, are titles which explain the contents they cover. *The Libel of English Policy*, quoted in Chapter III., is printed in *Hakluyt's Principal Navigations*, MacLehose edn., Glasgow, 1903, and has since been edited by Sir G. Warner, Oxford, 1926.

For special subjects, *Social England*, ed. H. D. Traill and J. S. Mann, 6 vols., London, 1902, will be found a mine of information, the collection of contemporary illustrations reprinted being especially valuable. Mrs. J. R. Green in *Town Life in the Fifteenth Century*, 2 vols., London, 1894 (repr. 1908), and the Rev. W. Denton in *England in the Fifteenth Century*, London, 1888, devote themselves principally to industrial and agricultural matters respectively, and come to very opposite conclusions as to the conditions of life during the period. The two books should be read side by side. *Social England in the Fifteenth Century*, by Miss A. Abram, London, 1909, contains more recent light upon the same subject. Other useful monographs are : Prof. W. J. Ashley, *Early History of the Woollen Industry in England*, in *Trans. of the American Economic Association*, 1887 ; Prof. G. Unwin, *Finance and Trade under Edward III.*, Manchester, 1918 ; I. D. Colvin, *The Germans in England*, 1066-1598, London, 1915 ; Prof. M. Burrows, *The Cinque Ports*, London, 1888 ; K. Engel, *Organisation of the Hanseatic Merchants in England*, in *English Historical Review*, xxix. 605 ; A. E. Bland, *Establishment of Home Staples in England*, ibid. xxix. 94 ; L. V. D. Owen, *England and Burgundy in the First Half of the Fifteenth Century*, Oxford, 1909 ; and Eileen Power, *The Wool Trade in English Medieval History*, Oxford, 1941.

For the Navy, 1066-1485, the following are useful authorities : Sir W. Laird Clowes, *History of the Royal Navy*, 7 vols., London, 1897-1903 ; D. Hannay, *Short History of the Royal Navy*, 2 vols., London, 1898 ; M. Oppenheim, *History of the Administration of the Royal Navy and Merchant Shipping*, vol. 1, London, 1896. The latter is a work of the deepest research, containing much information not previously brought to light. An incident narrated in Chapter I. is drawn from an article by H. L. Cannon, *The Battle of Sandwich and Eustace the Monk*, 1217, in *English Historical Review*, xxvii. 649-670. The evolution of mediaeval shipping is brilliantly summarized in the 56-page introduction to Sir J. S. Corbett's *Drake and the Tudor Navy*, 2 vols., London, 1898.

PART II

THE TUDOR PERIOD—EXPERIMENTS IN
OCEANIC ENTERPRISE

CHAPTER I

THE REGULATED COMPANIES, 1485–1603

(i) *Characteristics of the Tudor Period*

WITH the commencement of the Tudor period, England enters upon a new stage of national expansion. Its history no longer confines itself to the single topic of the companies trading with European countries. Before the fifteenth century drew to its close Christendom had begun to open up new lands in the east and in the west. With the earliest steps in this development our own country concerned herself only to a limited extent. But she could not remain for ever indifferent to the conquests of the Spaniards and the Portuguese ; and in the latter half of the sixteenth century English enterprise, content no longer with the seas of Europe, extended itself in a determined manner to the oceans of the world. Accordingly we shall have now to consider associations for trade with Africa and Spanish America, for the discovery of a north-eastern or north-western passage to the Far East, and for the planting of colonies in North America ; and finally, before the close of the period, the inception of the East India Company with its destiny of establishing Great Britain as an Asiatic power. We shall see also the development of the navy from a mere police force of the Narrow Seas into an ocean-going service able to blockade a distant coast and strike hard blows on the other side of the Atlantic.

But, although the sixteenth century witnessed the beginning of oceanic undertakings, and is thus sharply distinguished from the mediaeval period which preceded it, the undertakings themselves were all in the nature of experiments ; some were but temporarily successful, others failed, only a few produced solid and lasting results. The failures of course were not all loss. They provided indispensable experience. But they were sufficiently numerous to prevent the new undertakings as a whole from adding immediately to the wealth and prosperity of the country. That prosperity, throughout the century, depended mainly upon the old-established European trades carried on by the old regulated companies whose origin we have already traced, and by two or three new ones formed in imitation of their mediaeval prototypes. In the present chapter therefore we shall trace the history of the commercial undertakings doing business in European seas.

Henry VII., on taking up the reins of government, immediately interested himself in the country's overseas commerce. He found the transference of its control from alien to native hands still incomplete, and he set himself to hasten the process by all the means in his power. To him belongs the credit of putting continuously into practice the doctrines of commercial policy first enunciated in the time of Richard II. and vainly advocated by the trading interests under the Lancastrian and Yorkist dynasties. These doctrines are conveniently grouped under the designation of the mercantile system. The mercantile policy, as understood in Tudor times, meant that the Government applied itself deliberately and consciously to the fostering of sea-power, to the favouring of the interests of its own subjects by depressing those of foreigners, to the accumulation of the precious metals, and to the encouragement, by artificial means if necessary, of industries conducive to the national wealth. Henry pursued this policy consistently ; his successors with occasional lapses due to political considerations ; and the mercantile system as a whole flourished with full vigour until the closing years of the eighteenth century.

In modern England these principles fell into discredit. It was no longer believed that state interference was the ideal means of promoting commercial and colonial expansion. But that need not blind us to the fact that under far different conditions statecraft was wise to apply itself to such tasks, and that unless it had done so we should not stand where we do to-day. We must not regard the mercantile system as always a fallacious one merely because it was unsuited to the circumstances of the nineteenth century. The *laissez-faire* which supplanted it proved unsuitable in its turn to the needs of the twentieth century ; and mercantilism has come back in modern forms. And, returning to the Tudor period, we must notice that practically all the great advances of the time originated in private enterprise, which first took the risks of the pioneer and then looked to the administration for support.

(ii) *Henry VII. and the Promotion of Commerce by Diplomacy,*
1485-1509

From the day of his accession Henry VII. received complaints that the seaports were decayed and shipping was diminishing. His first care was to provide an immediate palliative by granting bounties for the construction of new ships and by drafting a Navigation Act of a moderate and limited application. By this Act (passed in the Parliament of 1485, and amended in 1489) it was ordered that aliens should cease to import into England the wines of Bordeaux and the woad of Toulouse, a commodity much used in dyeing cloth. In future this traffic was only to be carried by English ships employing English crews. This was a much more feasible measure than the abortive Act of Richard II. ; but even so, strict enforcement was not always maintained, and foreign merchants often received (on payment) licences to infringe it.

The affairs of the Merchants Adventurers and of their rivals the Hanseatic League also claimed the king's early attention. In 1493 there arose a prolonged quarrel with the Flemish authorities owing to the fact that Margaret, Duchess of Burgundy (sister of Edward IV. and Richard III.), gave open support to Perkin Warbeck and others who challenged the king's title to the throne. Henry, his very existence thus vitally threatened by a sea power, found himself obliged to make use of commerce as a weapon with which to secure the expulsion of this nest of traitors from the Low Countries. He ordered the cessation of all intercourse and the removal of the Adventurers' headquarters from Antwerp to Calais. The English merchants were hard hit, for at Calais they might sell only to French and other non-Flemish buyers. But they rallied loyally to the king's support, and their wealthier members continued to buy stocks of cloth as usual in order to mitigate the unemployment of the weavers. Much of this cloth, as Bacon tells us, " lay dead on their hands for want of vent." The cloth, however, was to the Flemings a necessary raw material, since they supplied the labour for the finishing processes. At length they gave way. By the *Intercursus Magnus* of 1496, and later treaties of 1497 and 1499, Henry secured the political objects he desired, clearing up at the same time many disputes as to tariffs and restrictions. The Merchants Adventurers returned in triumph to Antwerp.

In the year following the signing of the *Intercursus Magnus* Parliament had to intervene to settle a dispute among the Adventurers themselves. The merchants of the smaller seaports complained that the London members, having gained control of the government of the fellowship, were exacting excessive fees for admission to its privileges. It had never been the intention of the sovereigns who framed the Company's charters to limit membership to a small band of monopolists ; and obviously Henry VII., whose aim was the aggrandisement of national commerce, could not countenance such a policy. An Act was accordingly passed to limit the entrance fee to 10 marks (£6 13s. 4d.), on payment of which sum any Englishman might trade provided that he had served a satisfactory apprenticeship. A few years later a dispute arose between the Merchants Adventurers and the Merchants of the Staple, the latter apparently claiming the right to deal in cloth without paying fees to the former. After a prolonged argument a decision was given to the effect that all exporters of cloth to Flanders must belong to the Merchants Adventurers and all dealers in wools to the Staplers, although there was nothing to prevent the same individual from being free of both Companies.

An accident provided Henry with the opportunity for a stroke of policy characteristic of the man and the time. In 1506 the Archduke Philip, then ruler of the Low Countries, was voyaging to Spain when heavy weather compelled him to land on the English coast. The king had him escorted to London, ostensibly as a guest, in reality as a prisoner, and as the price of his liberty the archduke agreed to a treaty which revised the customs dues substantially in favour of the Merchants Adventurers. This treaty the Flemings named the *Intercursus Malus*, and for the next twenty-five years a diplomatic debate was maintained on the question of its validity, the archduke having died prior to its formal ratification.

The discipline of the Adventurers had become unsatisfactory at this period, as the dispute between the Londoners and provincials had testified. In 1505, therefore, the king issued a new charter defining the legal powers of the governor and his assistants as in former grants, and making it plain that the Company was to include not only London men but also the affiliated societies of the other east-coast ports. But complaints of the wilfulness of " disordered persons " recurred throughout the sixteenth century, and it is evident that the enforcement of discipline in a foreign land was no easy matter. Practically all the great companies for overseas trade suffered from the same disadvantage.

With the Hanseatic League Henry had to proceed warily, for he well knew how dangerous its sea-power might be to a king whose tenure was by no means secure. He confirmed its privileges on his accession, doubtless much against his will. But his hand fell heavily upon the Easterlings whenever their conduct gave him an excuse for harshness. The customers and port officials, their enemies to a man, strained the letter of the law in dealing with their cargoes. During the restraint of trade with the Low Countries in 1495 they were accused of secretly conveying thither the cloth which the native merchants loyally abstained from handling ; and the king exacted from them a bond for £20,000 as a guarantee of their integrity. At the same time the fury of the London mob broke forth in an armed attack upon their London factory of the Steelyard. The Easterlings made a stout defence, and the Lord Mayor dispersed the rioters after, one may suspect, allowing them a reasonable chance of sacking the place. The king's partiality appeared in the fact that although eighty delinquents were arrested they were all dismissed after a few days' detention in the Tower.

By two diplomatic measures Henry further aimed at the Hanse supremacy. In 1490 he made a treaty with the King of Denmark by which the long maritime war dating from the middle of the century was brought to an end. Englishmen were now free to resume their ancient voyage to the Iceland fishery, and the way was made safe for English merchants to revive the Eastland route into the Baltic, provided they could find some foothold in the Hanse towns upon its shores. To effect this Henry entered into a negotiation with the port of Riga in order to detach it from the League's general policy and secure from it a grant of trading privileges. In this he was ultimately unsuccessful, and the Eastland trade had to wait long for better times. In the latter part of his reign Henry suffered much uneasiness from the flight to Germany of the Earl of Suffolk, who had some pretensions to the crown. The old threat of a sudden invasion across the North Sea made it imperative for the king to propitiate the Hansa, and he therefore modified much of the harshness of his early attitude towards it. The whole story of his dealings with the League, and of the claims and counter-claims brought forward in three several diets for the settlement of differences in 1491, 1497 and 1499, provides a good illustration of the working of the mercantile policy as practised at the close of the fifteenth century.

The trade between England and Spain continued on the old lines during the reign of Henry VII., the effects of the West Indian discoveries not making themselves felt until a later period. Here again Henry sought by diplomacy to improve the position of his subjects. A commercial treaty in 1489 regulated the duties and secured the personal liberty of the merchants. Both governments also agreed to revoke all letters of reprisals for injuries on the sea, and so to reduce the extent to which piracy had grown during the middle years of the fifteenth century. The direct traffic between England and Portugal failed to recover from the set-back it experienced during the same period of anarchy. The Portuguese began to export their surplus commodities principally to Antwerp, and that place, after the opening of the sea passage to India, became their staple for trade with northern Europe. But Portuguese merchants and mariners remained influential in Bristol, and at the beginning of the sixteenth century took a prominent part in organizing voyages of discovery from that port.

The Italian merchants had hitherto almost monopolized the trade between England and the Mediterranean. During the reign of Henry VII. the improvement in English shipbuilding and the vigorous diplomacy of the king combined to force an entry for Englishmen into the Italian seaports and the remote waters of the Levant. In addition to the spices brought by the Asiatic caravans to Aleppo, Damascus and Alexandria, the fine fabrics, jewellery, armour and glassware of Italy, and the muscatel and malmsey wines of Candia and Chios provided rich ladings for enterprising traders. The exports of England found a ready market in the south, and early in the reign Englishmen were bringing wines from Candia in quantities sufficient to alarm the Venetian government at the prospect of their competition. The Venetians increased their customs dues. Henry retaliated in the same manner, and sought for allies in the other Italian states. He found the Florentines agreeable to his policy, and concluded with them a treaty by which he undertook to establish at Pisa a wool-staple similar to that of Calais. The plan was to make Pisa the sole

distributing centre for English wool in the Mediterranean. This would
have been a serious blow to Venice, since the Venetians had hitherto
been exempt from the staple system, and had laded their Flanders
galleys at Sandwich or Southampton without being obliged to buy
from the Staplers' Company. The Pisa depot flourished for a time,
and then fell into disuse. Henry probably never intended it as more
than a threat, in which character it was entirely successful. Venice
abandoned her hostile attitude, and English trade became firmly
established.

The regulated type of company laboured under serious disadvantages
in the operation of a distant trade in unsettled regions. The average
duration of a voyage to Chios was at least twelve months out and
home, the risks from Mohammedan pirates were high, and the
merchants were obliged to combine into private syndicates for the
employment of large and well-armed ships. The best means of
conducting such a traffic was afterwards found to be that of the joint-
stock company. But this method of doing business was then un-
developed in England, and consequently we hear of no incorporation
of the Mediterranean traders until the latter years of the sixteenth
century.

(iii) *Commerce and Politics*, 1509-1558

For half a century after the death of Henry VII. the commercial
policy of England sought to follow the lines which he had laid down.
His encouragement of shipping by Navigation Acts, his alliance with
Spain and as a consequence with the Low Countries, and his underlying hostility towards the Hansa—all these features of his system
persisted until the accession of Elizabeth, with this modification,
that whereas Henry VII. had made the encouragement of commerce
his principal object after the securing of his throne, his successors
made it subsidiary, first to an ambitious foreign policy, and afterwards
to the conduct of the religious disputes arising from the Reformation.
The mercantile system remained, therefore, the guiding principle of
English policy, although somewhat blunted in its operation by preference accorded to the interests above mentioned.

The Navigation Acts of Henry VII. remained in force, although
complaints arose of slackness in their administration in the early
years of his son's reign. In order to raise money Henry VIII. became
too lavish in the grant of licences to aliens to import French wines ;
but on realizing that his subjects regarded this as a serious grievance
he promised a stricter enforcement of the law. In 1539 a great though
temporary change took place in the fiscal system inherited from the
past. The adjustment of the duties payable at the ports had hitherto
given Englishmen preference over all foreigners except the Easterlings.
At the date named Henry VIII. was in serious difficulties, threatened
by disaffection at home and by a joint invasion by the King of France
and the Emperor Charles V. acting in the interests of the Catholic

religion. To buy off the emperor's hostility Henry proclaimed that for the ensuing seven years foreign merchants might trade with England in all commodities, wools excepted, on payment of the duties formerly exacted from English traders only. Thus at a stroke England abandoned the fiscal protection of her commerce, the mainstay of the mercantile system. But no sooner had the political danger passed away than the king and his minister, Thomas Cromwell, sought to undo the effects of the enforced concession. By a new Navigation Act in 1540, they provided that foreigners wishing to avail themselves of the reduction in duties must ship their goods in English bottoms. By this means the loss to the native traders became commensurate with the gain to the shipping interest. Both the free-trade concession and the Act of 1540 expired at the end of the allotted seven years, and England returned to the ancient protective system. The above changes had not affected the validity of Henry VII.'s Navigation Acts. They continued in operation until 1552, when a modification was introduced enabling foreigners to import wines and woad at the less busy seasons of the year.

The Merchants Adventurers continued their traffic at Antwerp under the constitution provided for them by the charter of 1505 and under the protection of the treaties which Henry VII. had negotiated. The stability of their position represented the most satisfactory and permanent portion of Henry's work, and for the first thirty years of the sixteenth century they prospered in their trade and contributed substantially to the wealth of the kingdom. Then political difficulties for which they were not responsible ushered in a troublous period. The Emperor Charles V. was by inheritance the ruler of the Burgundian territories and also King of Spain. The divorce of his aunt, Katharine of Aragon, by Henry VIII. alienated his friendship with England and presaged the ultimate rupture of the Burgundian alliance. Religious differences added to the discomfort of the English merchants. Arrests of English goods and shipping became frequent. The threatened invasion of 1538-9 was followed by a prolonged dispute over the Navigation Act of 1540. In 1544 the situation brightened for a time when Henry VIII. and the emperor allied themselves against France. But ere the year had passed Charles broke his engagement, leaving England to carry on the war alone. The high-handed proceedings of the English privateers converted him from a neutral into an almost open enemy, and a prolonged arrest of English trade in the Low Countries still further disorganized the Adventurers. They themselves added to their misfortunes by continual bitter feuds on the limitation of membership and other ancient controversies.

During this time the Hanseatic League took advantage of their rivals' weakness to engross much of the export of cloth to Antwerp. The Flemings themselves could not indulge in this traffic on account of the high duties they had to pay. The Easterlings, not similarly handicapped, made rapid strides, until the Merchants Adventurers

clamoured loudly that they were on the verge of ruin. Henry VIII.,
sympathising with his own merchants, could do little to help them.
Like his father, he dared not quarrel with the Hansa. He needed
a powerful navy to save the country from invasion, the threat of which
hovered over him from the day on which he severed his allegiance to
the papacy ; and the great warships of his day could only keep the
sea by enormous expenditure of pitch, cables, cordage, spars and
canvas, all of which came almost exclusively from the Baltic lands.
Henry, therefore, during his later years maintained fast friendship
with the League, which repaid him with the naval stores above
mentioned, and also sold him several large warships when a great
French armament threatened England with disaster in 1545. The
Jesus of Lubeck, afterwards so famous in our naval annals, was one of
the vessels acquired in this manner.

The prosperity of the London factory of the Hansa had probably
never stood higher than at the date of Henry's death (1547). Five
years later it fell suddenly and, as the event proved, permanently,
from its proud position. The blow which the strongest English kings
had hitherto shrunk from dealing fell from the hand of the Duke of
Northumberland, the virtual ruler of the country during the later
years of Edward VI. ; and it was the weakness rather than the strength
of the duke's position which brought him to his decision. The French
and Scottish wars had compelled the government to run deeply into
debt. The Merchants Adventurers, amongst other groups of capitalists, had lent it large sums. Their leading spirit, Thomas Gresham,
afterwards the founder of the Royal Exchange, was a supporter of
Northumberland's ; and they demanded the revocation of the Hanse
privileges based on the treaty of 1474. They had a long list of accusa-
tions in readiness. The League, they said, had admitted many new
towns to its membership since the grant of its privileges, and yet
persistently evaded a definition of its own extent ; by exporting cloth
to Antwerp it had infringed the legal monopoly of the English society ;
the Easterlings, by the Latin wording of the treaties, were limited
to the import of *suae merces,* the produce of their own cities, and nevertheless the greatest part of their trade was in *exoticae merces,* the wares
of other lands ; and finally the Adventurers produced evidence that
the Germans habitually " coloured " the merchandise of Flemings and
other strangers, fraudulently passing such goods through the customs
at their own reduced rates. The trial proceeded rapidly, the evidence
was held to be conclusive, and on February 24, 1552, the Privy Council
promulgated " The Decree against the Steelyard " by which all the
privileges were annulled and the Easterlings reduced to the status of
other alien merchants.[1]

So matters remained until the accession of Mary in 1553. She,
as an enemy of Northumberland and all his works, restored the Hansa
to its old position. But financial necessity forced her to bow to the

[1] J. A. Williamson, *Maritime Enterprise,* 1485-1558, Oxford, 1913, pp. 164-7.

renewed demands of the Merchants Adventurers. Gresham, whom she had dismissed from his office of Royal Factor at Antwerp, was found to be indispensable. She reinstated him, and after much negotiation revoked the Hanse privileges for the second time. The Hansa, still hoping to regain what it had lost, stopped short of a formal declaration of war, although it arrested all English ships in its ports, proclaimed a cessation of intercourse, and circulated ominous rumours of a maritime coalition of Denmark, France and its own naval resources against England. But the League itself was past the time of its greatest strength. Its misfortunes in England coincided with losses in other directions, and the effects of its hostility were not so serious as many had anticipated. To what extent its stoppage of supplies contributed to the undoubted deterioration of the English fleet in Mary's reign, and thus to the loss of Calais in 1558, is uncertain. The question is one which our naval historians have not fully elucidated.

The Tudor period witnessed the steady decline and virtual extinction of the Merchants of the Staple, at one time the most powerful corporation trading overseas. The principal cause of this decay was a natural one, and not disadvantageous to the general interests of the country : it was simply that the growth of the English cloth manufacture diminished the surplus of raw wool available for export. Although sheep-farming greatly increased during the period from the Black Death to the middle of the sixteenth century, the home demand for wools would alone have sufficed in time to kill the staple export. But other factors hastened the change. The Mediterranean trade, both by Italians and Englishmen, drew off an increasing share of the wool, and this traffic was independent of the Staplers' monopoly. Spain also became a wool-exporting country. The quality of its product was inferior, but its prices were lower than those of England on account of the heavy export duties levied by the English crown. Finally, the loss of Calais in 1558 dealt a blow to the already dying organization from which no recovery was possible. The Staplers attempted, with the aid of a new charter from Elizabeth, to establish depots in the Low Countries. Their shipments were never very regular, and the Spanish war put an end to them. Then James I. sought to revive the early system of Edward III. by appointing staple towns in England. But by this time, for the purposes of foreign trade, little more than the name of the Company survived. An Act of 1660, prohibiting all export of wool, may serve to mark its practical decease. Yet, like its origin, its end is obscure. It was never formally dissolved and may even, in a legal sense, be said to exist to-day.[1]

Henry VIII. confirmed his father's commercial agreements with Spain, and the English traffic with that country increased rapidly during the early years of his reign. The English merchants voyaged principally to Cadiz, San Lucar and Seville. At these Andalusian ports they obtained not only the wines, fruits and oil of Spain itself,

---

[1] Sir C. P. Lucas, *Beginnings of English Overseas Enterprise*, Oxford, 1917, p. 22.

but also by transhipment the merchandise of Italy and the Levant, and the hides and sugar arriving from the new Spanish colonies in the West Indies. Bristol had a preponderant share in this trade, but London and the south-coast ports also engaged in it. We have records showing that the Bristol firms maintained English factors in the Canary Islands, and even that a Bristol man, Thomas Tison, was doing business in the West Indies in 1526. In 1517 the Duke of Medina Sidonia, the feudal lord of San Lucar, granted the English special privileges in his port. They accordingly concentrated their business there and for a time flourished exceedingly. Then the Reformation and the divorce of Katharine of Aragon put an end to the ancient friendship between the two nations. The attitude of the Spaniards became hostile, and the English, hitherto unincorporated, were compelled to draw together for mutual defence. In 1530 they obtained from Henry VIII. a charter granting them the status of a regulated company, and allowing them to set up a machinery of government on the same general lines as that of the Merchants Adventurers.

The English merchants had obviously resorted to this step in anticipation of difficult times to come. Events proved that their fears were well grounded. The enmity between Henry VIII. and Charles V., and the fanatical loyalty of Spain to the papacy, provided occasions for the persecution of the English company. The Spanish buyers complained that the English were selling cloth of poor material and fraudulent workmanship. The officials revived ancient and long dormant statutes as excuses for hindering them in the enjoyment of their privileges. General arrests became frequent and of increasingly long duration. The Inquisition stepped in and claimed jurisdiction over heretics who held that Henry VIII. was the supreme head of the English church. " English subjects," says a report of 1537, " are much molested at the instigation of slanderous preachers suborned thereto by the Bishop of Rome's adherents." In 1539 an unconfirmed, though widely credited, story asserted that three Englishmen had been burnt alive in Seville ; and undoubtedly some suffered torture and imprisonment. " We . . . do live in great peril and fear of our persons and goods," the merchants protested in an official document, " for fear of the extreme punishment and cruel entreating of the fathers of the Inquisition and their deputies, which be in all places where our trade doth lie." [1]

The national quarrel between England and Spain, commonly considered as the product of Elizabeth's reign, may thus be seen to have originated a generation earlier. The Reformation was its cause, and one of its early effects was an outbreak of piracy and privateering which first drew the attention of English rovers to the immense wealth which was crossing the Atlantic in Spanish ships. In 1545 a Southampton adventurer took a ship bound from Hispaniola with a lading worth 30,000 ducats. In spite of such provocation on both sides

[1] Williamson, op. cit. p. 223.

war at the time was avoided, and the English company continued
in the Spanish trade for another forty years. In 1585, three years
before the despatch of the Armada, the end came with a sudden
attempt on the part of the Spanish officials to seize all English ships
in their ports. Thenceforward direct intercourse ceased until the
accession of James I.

The English merchants who pushed their way into the Mediterranean
in the reign of Henry VII. did so at a time when the trading conditions
in that sea were about to undergo great changes. In the Middle
Ages the Venetians and Genoese had possessed numerous colonies and
trading stations in Greece, Syria, Asia Minor, the Black Sea, and the
islands of the Levant. Through these they had controlled the most
important trade route by which eastern goods passed into Europe.
The discovery of the sea passage to India by the Portuguese in 1498
had the effect within a few years of diverting the far-eastern traffic
—the spices which Arab seamen had carried across the Indian Ocean
to the Red Sea and the Persian Gulf—from the Mediterranean to the
Atlantic route. At the same time the rapid advance of Turkish
power began to submerge the Italian outposts of commerce, and to
render precarious the remaining traffic in the products of the Levant
itself and of Persia and Central Asia. After the fall of Constantinople
in 1453 Venice, by the payment of tribute to the Sultan, had contrived to retain for a time her trading privileges in his territories.
Then, with the reign of Selim I. (1512-20), the Ottoman conquests
recommenced with fresh energy. Syria, Egypt, the smaller islands
of the Greek archipelago, and the Venetian possessions on the coast
of Greece all fell to this Sultan ; whilst his successor Solyman the
Magnificent (1520-66) took Rhodes and extended his sway over the
northern coast of Africa.

Into this medley of warfare and piracy came the English traders
of Henry VII. and his son ; and during the first half of the sixteenth
century " divers tall ships of London . . . with certain other ships of
Southampton and Bristol had an ordinary and usual trade to Sicily,
Candia, Chios and somewhiles to Cyprus, as also to Tripoli and Beyrout
in Syria." The commerce of Venice was dying under the stress of
Turkish pressure. The sailings of the Flanders galleys became in-
frequent, ceasing altogether after 1532 ; and the Englishmen succeeded
to their employment. For a time the trade was a rich one, making
the fortunes of some of the commercial families. But in the middle
of the century the Turks became more truculent, and even the Sultan's
safe-conduct became powerless to protect Christian merchants. The
last recorded voyage of this series took place in 1553. Thenceforward
the trade was abandoned for five-and-twenty years. These early
Levant traders, as we have seen, had no incorporation. Each syndicate
fought for its own hand, and only the richest capitalists could bear
the expense of setting forth the heavily armed ships necessary for the
voyage. Warships were especially suitable for the purpose, and the

first three Tudor sovereigns all at various times sent the best ships
of the navy on trading ventures to " Levant's end."

From the foregoing we have seen that during the period 1509-1558
the mediaeval trading system of England reached its highest development, and then speedily began to show signs of decay.   By the date
of Mary's death nearly all the departments of trade, which in Plantagenet days had been in the hands of alien corporations, had fallen to
English companies or individuals.   Only in the Baltic were Englishmen
still in a subordinate position ; but the crushing of the London branch
of the Hansa and its exclusion from competition with the Merchants
Adventurers in the Netherlands gave promise of better conditions in
the Eastland regions.   We may set the completion of this transference
of control to the credit of the mercantile system as operated by the
Tudor sovereigns.   The general decline of the old trades which began
to be apparent in the middle of the century arose from such wider
causes as the progress of world-discovery, the advance of Islam, and
the influence of religion upon European politics.   When the same
ruler, in the person of the Emperor Charles V., presided over Germany
and effectively governed the Low Countries, Spain, the New World
and the greater part of Italy, the old Burgundian alliance concluded
by Henry V. became immensely extended in its scope.   The commercial advantages of that alliance had been strong enough to
overcome the personal enmity of the Duchess of Burgundy towards
Henry VII. ; they were not strong enough to neutralize the religious
passions aroused by the Reformation.   Spain and the Low Countries
became increasingly hostile towards England in the later years of
Henry VIII.   With the marriage of Mary to Philip, the emperor's
heir, the quarrel was patched up for a time.   But Philip used England
merely as a tool in his struggle with France, and the loss of Calais
aroused a storm of indignation which entailed the end of the ancient
alliance.   With the advance of the Turk in the Mediterranean added
to this, it is evident that the whole political system upon which
our mediaeval trade had flourished was rapidly going to pieces.   From
this time forward Englishmen began seriously to devote themselves
to oceanic enterprise in order to compensate for the threatened position
of the older commerce.

(iv) *The Old Trades under Elizabeth*, 1558-1603

At the accession of Elizabeth the political and commercial position
of England was unsatisfactory.   To many contemporary observers
it seemed that the Tudor dynasty and all that it stood for were on the
verge of ruin.   But fortunately the emergency found the man in
readiness to cope with it.   Sir William Cecil, afterwards Lord Burghley,
had been a member of the Privy Council under Edward VI.   In 1558
the new queen made him her Secretary of State, and he remained her
most faithful and trusted adviser until his death forty years later.

Besides directing the political energies of the country during this long period he exercised also an immense influence upon its economic policy, and in his hands the mercantile system received some modifications and a more consistent application than had been possible in the previous generation.[1]

Cecil was eminently a man who took account of realities rather than of labels. The national accumulation of treasure seemed to him a desirable object not so much for its own sake as for that of the warlike commodities treasure would buy. He did not therefore limit his efforts to the hoarding of gold in the coffers of the state, as the rulers of Spain were doing ; he sought also to establish in England the industries conducive to national power—the mining of metals for gun-founding, the growth of raw materials for the manufacture of cordage and canvas. In the shipping interest also he came to the conclusion that much of the existing navigation policy was mistaken, since the benefits accruing were not commensurate with the damage arising from the hostility of other countries. In the parliament of 1559 he accordingly promoted a new Navigation Act which "for the avoidance of disputes with foreign princes" expressly repealed those of Richard II. and Henry VII. In his Act the policy was whittled down to this, that Englishmen who in normal circumstances shipped their goods in foreign bottoms were to pay duties at aliens' rates. But since exceptions were made in favour of the Merchants Adventurers, the Merchants of the Staple, and the merchants of Bristol, the new Act amounted to a considerable abandonment of the old navigation policy. That part of it which remained, as may be seen, concerned the operations of Englishmen rather than of foreigners.

Cecil's distaste for the high hand in external relations appears again in his classification of maritime enterprise under three heads : trading, fishing, and piracy, "whereof the third is detestable and cannot last." Although he miscalculated the outcome of the west-country adventurers' proceedings, predicting from them nothing but national calamity, he approved of all legitimate and inoffensive means of increasing the national sea-power. He did what he could to improve the quality of the Royal Navy and the supply of munitions. He introduced detailed legislation for promoting the consumption of fish, holding that the fisheries were the best breeding-grounds for seamen. He supported all projects for extra-European trading and discovery and asserted the doctrine of effective occupation against the prescriptive claims of Spain and Portugal. He was, in fact, a great minister whom circumstances forced into war against his inclination. But he was emphatically not what in our day is called a pacifist, blindly refusing to make ready for a contingency which he disliked. The success of England in the Spanish struggle was largely due to his wise control during the years of preparation.

[1] For a full treatment of Cecil's mercantile policy see W. Cunningham, D.D., *The Growth of English Industry and Commerce in Modern Times*, Cambridge, 1903, chap. 3.

When Cecil commenced his administration the dispute with the Hanseatic League was still unsettled. Its privileges in England remained in abeyance, and its ports were closed to English shipping. In 1560 he concluded a treaty by which the Easterlings returned to London on terms which decided the matter substantially in accordance with English contentions. For the future the merchants of the Hansa were to export no English cloth to the Low Countries or Italy. On that which they carried to German towns they were to pay the same duties as did the English merchants (not lower ones as had previously been the case). On imports into England they were to pay higher duties than the English, although slightly lower ones than those paid by other aliens. They were also to guarantee reciprocal treatment for Englishmen in the Baltic. This agreement destroyed the ancient preponderance of the Germans in the North Sea and Netherlands trade. Two further steps abolished the last vestiges of their power in England. In 1579, on the occasion of a fresh dispute, the government reduced them to an absolute equality with other aliens in the payment of duties ; and in 1598 it expelled them altogether from the country, their great block of buildings in the Steelyard reverting to the possession of the Crown.

The Merchants Adventurers continued their traffic at Antwerp under increasingly adverse conditions during the early years of Elizabeth. They moved their depot to Emden for a time in 1563, but afterwards returned to Antwerp. In 1568 the Duke of Alva, Philip II.'s commander in the Netherlands, seized all Englishmen and their goods under his jurisdiction in revenge for the detention by Elizabeth of a consignment of treasure intended for the payment of his troops. The Merchants Adventurers then transferred their headquarters to Hamburg, and traded there for several years, afterwards moving to Emden again, and then to Stade on the Elbe. The final rupture with the Hansa deprived them of the use of this place, but by that time the Seven United Provinces comprising the northern part of the Netherlands had made good their independence against Philip II. To them accordingly the English company betook itself, selling its cloth successively at Middelburg, Delft, Rotterdam and Dordrecht. In the seventeenth century the Adventurers re-established their mart at Hamburg without resigning that in the United Provinces. In these two regions they long continued a successful trade. The mart at Dordrecht came to an end in 1751 ; that at Hamburg endured until 1808, when the Company was finally dissolved as a result of Napoleon's conquest of Germany.[1]

The extinction in the fifteenth century of Henry IV.'s organization of the Eastland Company had left the Baltic trade free and unincorporated. From 1485 onwards Englishmen had undoubtedly sailed to this region in increasing numbers, although the subject is an obscure one, and the actual extent of the traffic is difficult to estimate. By

[1] Lucas, *op. cit.* p. 117.

1579 the Hansa had been sufficiently weakened to permit of the revival of the chartered company. In that year, therefore, Elizabeth issued a new charter authorizing the merchants to elect a governor and twenty-four assistants, and granting a monopoly of English trade within the Baltic. For the first fifty years of its existence the new Eastland Company had a more prosperous history than the old. Then it began to suffer from Dutch competition, and from the increasing clamour against commercial monopolies. In 1673 an Act which made every Englishman free of its privileges on payment of forty shillings practically threw the trade open. In the eighteenth century its organization became extinct. Like the Merchants Adventurers, it outlived the period of its usefulness, but in its prime it was of material assistance to the cause of English maritime expansion.

In 1578 Sir Edward Osborne and Richard Staper, merchants of London, sought to revive the Levant trade. They sent William Harborne overland to Constantinople, and through him obtained a grant of safe-conduct and trading privileges from the Sultan. As a consequence the queen issued a charter in 1581 constituting Osborne, Staper and others a recognized corporation with monopoly rights, under the name of the Turkey Company. This company, we should note, was not a regulated one, but was of the new joint-stock type. Circumstances, however, caused its reorganization within a few years as a regulated company, so it will be convenient to consider it in this chapter. Owing to political delays the full operation of the privileges was not achieved until 1584. Thenceforward the Turkey Company conducted a lucrative trade, employing nineteen fair-sized ships and successfully forcing its way through the Straits of Gibraltar in face of armed Spanish opposition.

Meanwhile, owing to a dispute between the English buyers and certain capitalists who sought to force up prices in the currant trade, the queen granted to an English syndicate the sole right to import currants, sweet wines and oils from Venice (1583). The Venice Company was also of the joint-stock type, and prospered almost as much as the Turkey Company. It employed fourteen ships of an average burden of about 180 tons.[1]

The charters of both companies had been granted for short terms, the object being to allow the founders of the trade a chance of recouping their outlay under a monopoly, and then to reconsider the whole matter. Accordingly, in 1592, the charters having expired, the two companies were amalgamated under the name of the Levant Company. The voyage having now become, by the improvement of shipping, both shorter and safer, and conditions in the Turkish dominions having become more settled, it was thought feasible to make the new organization a regulated company. Its first governor was Sir Edward Osborne, and its chief mart Aleppo. It carried on an active career for over two centuries.

[1] For these companies see A. C. Wood, *History of the Levant Company*, Oxford, 1935.

CHAPTER II

THE AGE OF DISCOVERY—PORTUGUESE AND SPANISH

THE great voyages of the age of discovery—those which extended the interests of Christendom to a world many times greater than that which had filled the minds of Europeans in the Middle Ages—were for the most part the work of Portuguese, Italian and Spanish navigators. Yet their grandest results, all achieved in the lifetime of a single generation, are the heritage of mankind at large, and no history of the subsequent maritime expansion of the English, French or Dutch nations can be complete or even intelligible unless it takes them into account. They are the foundation upon which has arisen the whole structure of world civilization as we see it to-day.

But the peoples of the Mediterranean were not the earliest pioneers in ocean discovery. That distinction belongs to the Northmen of Scandinavia, the brilliant, restless race which blazed, meteor-like, through Europe during a brief three centuries, and then subsided into insignificance, having left its mark in every land from Dublin to Jerusalem and from Novgorod to Sicily. In the latter half of the ninth century the Norse rovers began to traverse the northern seas in search of more novel fields for conquest than those afforded by Saxon England and Carolingian France. In 860 they discovered Iceland, and within fifteen years they had established a permanent colony upon its shores. Then, in 877-8, they pushed on to Greenland, whose aspect did not invite a similar immediate settlement; and there for a century their western progress stopped.

After that interval Norse expansion recommenced under the leadership of successive members of one energetic family. In 986 Eric the Red, an Icelander, led a band of settlers to Greenland, he himself choosing that name for the country because, as he said, a good name was useful in attracting pioneers. Three years later a reinforcement following him from Iceland miscalculated their course, passed south of Greenland, and sighted a coast which they named Helluland or Stony Land, probably Labrador. In the last year of the century Leif, the son of Eric the Red, determined to explore this land. Sailing thither, he coasted southwards and discovered successively Markland (Wooded Land) and Vineland, which some have identified with the neighbourhood of Cape Cod. Thorwald, another son of Eric, made further discoveries in Vineland, and fell in battle with the Eskimos (or Indians) who resisted his landing. Finally, in 1006-8, Thorfinn Karlsefne made a serious effort to colonize Vineland, but the numerical strength of the natives forced him to abandon the undertaking.

Thorfinn's attempt marks the culminating point of Norse expansion in the west. Thenceforward sporadic visits to America continued until 1347 without any permanent impression being made. The Greenland settlement existed until the late fifteenth century, when it died out, and Iceland remained as the farthest north-western outpost of Christendom. Climatic changes are thought to have contributed to the shrinkage of the Norse settlements ; for it seems evident from the old sagas that Greenland and Labrador were milder and less forbidding regions than they are to-day. To what extent the records of these Norse explorations persisted in the sea-lore of the fifteenth century is doubtful. Some have conjectured that Columbus and Cabot drew much of their inspiration from this source, but of positive evidence there is no trace.

The Norse school of exploration may have perished without influencing the Latin pioneers whose deeds we have now to consider, but the possibility remains that the Bristol men heard of the western discovery in the course of their trade with Iceland. Another connecting link, the story of the voyages of two Italians, Nicolo and Antonio Zeno, at the end of the fourteenth century, is of such doubtful authenticity that it can only rank among the numerous " not proven " tales of the later Middle Ages. Briefly, it amounts to this, that the two brothers between the years 1380 and 1395 visited Greenland and other northern countries not now identifiable. These are described with much detail except as regards their geographical position, which remains hopelessly vague. The suspicious circumstance is that the account remained buried in a solitary manuscript until it was printed in 1558 by the Italian historian Ramusio, whose critical faculties were not of a high order. The life-history of the manuscript is not convincing, and it is probable that the whole story is a forgery of the sixteenth century.

The undoubted explorations which preluded the great age of discovery rest on surer evidence. They took two opposite directions ; eastward by land into Asia, and westward by sea to the island groups of the Atlantic. The Asiatic travellers were merchants and missionary churchmen who followed in the wake of the Crusaders. Of these the most memorable were the Venetian brothers Nicolo and Maffeo Polo who, with Marco Polo the son of Nicolo, penetrated the entire length of Asia, in a journey occupying the space of twenty-four years (1271-1295), of which they spent seventeen at the court or in the employment of Kublai, the Grand Khan of Cathay. They reached the far east by land, and returned by sea in Chinese junks through the Indian Ocean to the Persian Gulf, and thence overland to Europe. On their return Marco Polo wrote a full account of all they had seen, an account whose substantial accuracy has been confirmed by modern experience of the East. Christendom obtained in this manner a glowing and detailed picture of the vast region it was destined to dominate ; but, supreme as Marco Polo's work stands out in its delineation of social, political and mercantile conditions, it makes little attempt to provide the accurate geographical data of latitudes and distances which were so important in solving the problem of the sea passage to Cathay. Widely known throughout Europe in numerous manuscript copies, it was nevertheless only slowly that it fulfilled its destiny of exciting a determination to bring poverty-stricken Christendom into effective contact with the splendours it depicts. But by the year 1477, when it was first printed, it had accomplished this task, and the men were then living who were to complete the work of the three Venetian wanderers of the thirteenth century.

Whilst the Polos and their less well-known successors were enduring the hardships of land exploration, the seamen of Italy and Portugal were displaying a fortitude of another order by pushing forth into the unknown Atlantic. The material dangers of the sea were real enough to men who undertook long voyages with scarcely any scientific equipment. But the imaginary terrors were greater still in the desolate wastes which no keel had broken since the making of the world. "Most mariners had heard it said that any Christian who passed Bojador would infallibly be changed into a black, and would carry to his end this mark of God's vengeance on his insolent prying. . . . And it was beyond the Cape which bounded their knowledge that the Saracen geographers had fringed the coast of Africa with sea-monsters and serpent rocks and water unicorns instead of place-names, and had drawn the horrible giant hand of Satan raised above the waves to seize the first of his human prey that should venture into his den." [1] Every unknown island was spirit-haunted, tenanted by devilish magicians with flat, reptile heads and long-fanged mouths, or by headless monstrosities whose eyes peered forth from between their shoulders. Beneath the open seas lurked the *kraken* which could devour ship and crew in its enormous jaws. Above the storm-cloud towered the gigantic form of the Bishop of the Seas driving mariners on to their unknown doom. These horrors were as real to the mediaeval seamen as their belief in the saints to whom they prayed for succour ; and yet men of transcendent courage came forward to offer their lives and, as many thought, their souls, in the cause of human progress.

Westward of the Straits of Gibraltar the classical geographers had placed the Fortunate Islands which, however, had not come under the sway of the Roman Empire. They remained undiscovered until 1270, when a Genoese expedition reached the group now known as the Canaries. The find was forgotten until 1341, when Portuguese and Italians rediscovered the islands which they found tenanted by "a naked but not quite savage people" who cultivated the ground and

[1] C. R. Beazley, *Prince Henry the Navigator*, London, 1895, p. 171.

kept flocks of goats. In 1402 Jean de Béthencourt, a gentleman of Normandy, led a party of his compatriots to the conquest and colonization of some of the group. In 1351 also, the Azores were first discovered, and subsequently forgotten until in 1431-2 Gonzalo Cabral rediscovered and occupied them for Portugal. An English adventure of very doubtful authenticity may be quoted for what it is worth. About the year 1370 Robert Macham or Machin of Bristol induced an heiress named Anne d'Arfet to elope across the seas with him. Their ship, making for Spain, was driven southwards by tempests until they came to an island where the pair landed with certain of their crew. A renewal of the storm drove the vessel from her anchorage, and she was never heard of again. Superstitious terror seized the landing party. The woman died " for thought," and Macham himself did not long survive her. The sailors, preferring any fate to the horrors of enchantment, put to sea in the ship's boat and reached the coast of Africa, where they ended their lives in slavery to the Moors. A fellow captive who had learned their story escaped to Portugal in 1416, and as a consequence a Portuguese expedition sought for and found the island, which they named Madeira.

Under the direction of Prince Henry the Navigator the Portuguese began the systematic exploration of the west African coast. Born in 1394, the Prince took a prominent part with his father and his brothers in the capture of Ceuta from the Moors in 1415. After this campaign he settled at Sagres on the promontory of Cape St. Vincent, and devoted himself to the study of navigation and geography and the setting forth of voyages to the southwards. His motives were partly religious and partly political. By reaching the populous districts of Guinea he hoped to convert millions to the Christian religion. By rounding the extremity of the African continent,—then believed to stretch not much further south than the Equator—he designed to open communication with the Christian empire of Prester John, vaguely supposed to exist somewhere in eastern Africa or the Middle East, and so to form a great coalition for the extermination of the Turk, whose growing power in the Levant was threatening the ruin of Christendom. The object of the later voyagers, the finding of a rich trade route to India and Cathay, seems not to have occupied much place in Prince Henry's plans. His spirit was that of the crusader rather than of the merchant ; his " India " was the Christian country which was to aid in overthrowing the infidel. He pursued his aims with all the single-mindedness and cruelty of genius. When cargoes of miserable negroes were landed in Portugal, and their families torn asunder amid loud lamentations at the slave auction, he contemplated the spectacle " with unspeakable pleasure, as to the saving of their souls, which but for him would have been for ever lost."

The first objective, then, was Guinea, already known by repute through the Moslem caravan traders who journeyed thither across the Sahara. In 1434 Gil Eannes, one of the Prince's captains, passed Cape Bojador.

the previous boundary of the unknown. The next year's expedition reached the Rio de Oro. In 1441 Cape Blanco was discovered, and in 1444 the Bay of Arguin. Here the country was populous and the slave trade began in earnest. A great slaving expedition in 1445 brought home 235 captives. In the same year Diniz Diaz discovered Cape Verde. Ten years later, in 1455-6, Ca da Mosto, an Italian captain in the Prince's service, reached Sierra Leone, and passed along the nearer portion of the Guinea Coast, whilst Diego Gomez in 1458-60 explored the Cape Verde Islands. When the Prince died, in 1460, the arduous preliminary work was accomplished, and the gates to rich discoveries stood open to his successors.

There for some ten years the matter rested, until a captain named Fernam Gomez made a contract with King John II. by which he was to conduct the Guinea trade for a fixed period, on condition that he discovered a certain extent of new coastline every year. Under this agreement (1470-5) the ships of Gomez rounded Cape Palmas and traversed the Ivory and Gold Coasts. By 1481 the whole Gulf of Guinea had been explored, and the Portuguese had sailed 2° south of the equator. In the latter year also they founded the fortified post of S. Jorge da Mina on the Gold Coast, as the nucleus of their rich traffic in that region.

Three more memorable voyages completed the discovery of the western coast of Africa. In 1482-4 Diego Cam reached the mouth of the Congo, and in 1485-7 the same navigator attained the southern latitude of 21° 50′ at Cape Cross. In the year of Cam's return from this expedition Bartholomew Diaz sailed for Cape Cross and thence pushed boldly southwards, determined to find the southern extremity of the continent. On his outward voyage he was driven far out into the ocean by stormy weather, and so missed seeing the Cape of Good Hope. But steering eastwards and northwards to regain the coast he found the sea open before him until he came to land again in the neighbourhood of Mossel Bay. Continuing in the same direction he visited Algoa Bay and the mouth of the Great Fish River (the nomenclature is that of a later period). Here the trend of the coast left no room for further doubt. The end of Africa had been turned, and the first European keel was sailing the Indian Ocean. Diaz, his task accomplished, retraced his course, sighting on his homeward passage the point which he named Cabo Tormentoso, but which his king rechristened Cabo de Bona Speranza. He arrived in Portugal in 1488.

Already, before this result had been achieved, the character of Portuguese exploration had been changing, as the rapid progress of the past seven years had proved. The ideals of Henry the Navigator were receding to a secondary position, and the new mercantile projects of the late fifteenth century were taking shape. The motive of these plans was the desire to divert from its ancient course the trade in the wares of the Far East, which had hitherto reached Europe by the Hanseatic and Mediterranean trade routes. The wealth

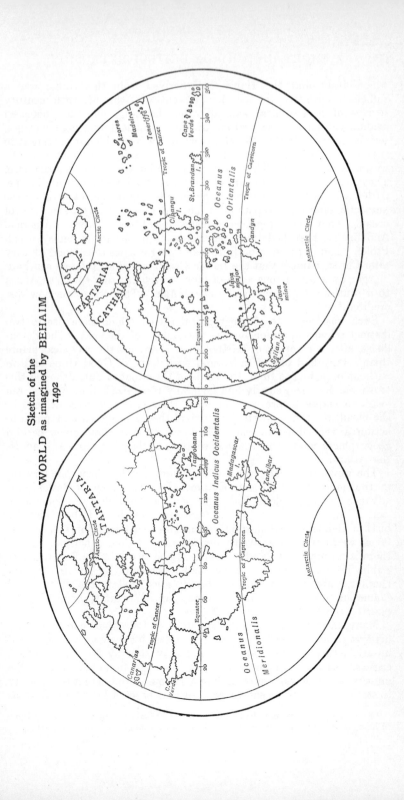

Sketch of the
WORLD as imagined by BEHAIM
1492

which Italy and the Hansa had derived from this traffic was a sufficient incentive to the new adventure ; the fifteenth century revival of geographical and all other learning, and the increased confidence of ocean navigators arising from the Portuguese voyages, seemed to indicate that the means were now available for putting it to the test.   The geographers of the time recognized the fact that the world is a sphere.   They somewhat underestimated its true size. They held that upon its surface were the three continents of Europe, Africa and Asia, together with a possible fourth in the shape of a great antarctic land-mass separated from the known lands by a belt of ocean.   They were altogether unsuspecting of the existence of America. And finally, they had freed themselves from the great heresy which Ptolemy had imposed upon European thought since the second century after Christ, namely that the Indian Ocean was shut in on its southern margin by a continuous strip of land stretching from southern Africa to a southward projection of eastern Asia.   This error was now discredited.[1]

Such was the state of geographical theory which gave rise to two distinct schools of action for the attainment of the goal.   The Portuguese, after the voyage of Bartholomew Diaz, saw the way clear before them : they had but to sail round their Cape of Good Hope and on without impediment to all the lands of the orient.   But, although this truth was by them clearly and generally recognized, they allowed ten years to elapse before sending forth their crowning expedition.   In the meantime the supporters of a rival theory proposed and put into action a very different plan.   This theory was that, given certain geographical conditions, the best route to Cathay lay westwards across the Atlantic.

The westward theory was not a new one ; it had been put forward in the days of the Roman Empire.   But two men of action now advanced definite plans for realizing it without delay.   These men were Christopher Columbus, a Genoese, and John Cabot, also by birth a Genoese, but since 1474 a naturalized citizen of Venice.   So far as we know they arrived independently at their conclusions ; and there is no means of deciding which of the two was the first to make public his ideas.   Of Cabot we shall have more to say in the next chapter.   For the present the story must follow the fortunes of Columbus, who was the first to obtain an opportunity of putting his plan to the test.

Many, in fact nearly all, of the details of Columbus' career prior to his first great voyage have furnished matter for dispute, so vague and unsatisfactory is the evidence ; and only step by step has modern criticism succeeded in distinguishing the true from the false in the multitude of traditions surrounding his name.   And here it is necessary to state that during recent years the whole basis of his title to fame as

[1] Erotosthenes, c. 200 B.C., had made a much more correct guess at the disposition of land and sea, but the authority of Ptolemy had for long superseded his teaching.

a scientific explorer has been challenged by an investigator of deep learning in the subject. This new version of his achievement has not secured general acceptance, and we shall therefore give first the commonly received account, and afterwards a brief summary of the revolutionary conclusions of his latest biographer.

Christopher Columbus was born at Genoa, probably in 1446. His father was a weaver of that city, and he himself followed the same craft for a time, afterwards going to sea in various Genoese ships. In 1476 the vessel in which he was serving formed part of a mercantile squadron which was voyaging to England. Off Cape St. Vincent a fleet of privateers assailed it, Columbus' ship took fire, and he himself seized an oar and swam to land, afterwards making his appearance in Lisbon. For the next few years he remained in Portuguese employment, making and selling charts and voyaging to Madeira and the Guinea coast. During this period he entered into a correspondence with Paolo Toscanelli, a well-known astronomer and mathematician of Florence. Toscanelli (copies of whose letters exist) furnished him with a map of the world as he conceived it, and with scientific evidence of the feasibility of the western route to Cathay. Armed with this testimony, which gave point to the plans he had already revolved in his own less learned mind, Columbus applied to the King of Portugal for the necessary ships and equipment. The king openly refused to consider the scheme, but secretly sent out to the west a caravel which failed to find land in the direction indicated. Columbus then left Portugal, which was on the point of reaching the East by the African route, and therefore disposed to be hostile to any rival project. Passing over into Spain he made similar proposals to the Spanish sovereigns, Ferdinand and Isabella, and at the same time sent his brother Bartholomew to England to lay his case before Henry VII. His terms were high, and some years more elapsed before the Spanish court conceded them. Henry VII. is said also to have yielded, but to have been too slow to make up his mind, so that his acceptance reached Spain only after the explorer had set sail in that country's service.

Be that as it may, Columbus departed from Palos with three ships on August 3, 1492, and steered first for the Canary Islands. His plan, as explained in the correspondence with Toscanelli, depended upon an underestimate of the total circumference of the globe, and an immense overestimate of the breadth of Asia from west to east. Thus, in his expectation, the coasts of Cipango (Japan) and Cathay (China) would be found even nearer to Europe than, as we now know, the American seaboard is actually situated. Had he known accurately the size of Asia and of the earth he could never have set forth on the expedition, since neither the navigation nor the shipping of the period were considered equal to such a voyage.

Armed with letters of recommendation from the Spanish sovereigns to the Grand Khan, he quitted the Canaries on September 6, determined to push steadfastly westward until he reached the goal. On October 12, 1492, he landed upon an island of the Bahama group. Following the directions of the natives he discovered the larger islands of Cuba and Hispaniola (Hayti), and returned in the spring of 1493 with the news that he had found the archipelago long known to exist off the south-east coast of Asia.

Such, in brief outline, is the orthodox account of the inception of the great discovery. But a recent historian of Columbus denies much of its truth.[1] According to his reading of the evidence, the explorer had, prior to the voyage of 1492-3, no expectation of making his way to the coast of Asia, neither had he promised the Spanish sovereigns that he would do so. His intentions, on the contrary, were based upon the secret knowledge imparted to him by an unknown shipmaster or " pilot." This man had been overtaken by a tempest whilst making a trading voyage near the coasts of Europe ; had been blown far across the Atlantic, and had landed on an unknown shore upon the other side ; had returned after losing most of his crew by privation ; and finally had died penniless in Columbus' house after revealing his secret to his benefactor. The latter had thereupon determined to rediscover the land for himself, not for a moment supposing it to be Cathay, and had sailed in 1492 with that purpose. Columbus, this version proceeds, shaped his course to the locality (half way across the Atlantic) where he confidently expected to discover the land, and not finding it, went on in some bewilderment until he discovered the West Indies. Here, struck by some fancied resemblance to Marco Polo's descriptions, he announced to his companions that they had reached the islands of Asia. Several years afterwards some person, probably Bartholomew Columbus, forged the Toscanelli map and correspondence in order to give the lie to the story—then widely current—of the unknown pilot and the accidental character of the discovery.

If the above be the true history of the enterprise, it is evident that Columbus sinks to the position of a somewhat dishonest trafficker in the fruits of another man's labours, and forfeits all claim to the reputation of a great scientific explorer. But there are difficulties in the way of accepting this account, and the majority of the present-day students of the subject remain unconvinced of its validity.[2]

Whatever may be the truth about the motives of Columbus, the effect of his discovery is not in doubt. On his return in March, 1493, he claimed definitely to have reached the outskirts of Cathay. The Portuguese had only the last stage to traverse of their voyage to India. A whole world was but waiting to be seized by European enterprise. In 1493 (May and September) Pope Alexander VI. issued bulls assigning spheres of exploration to the nations of the Peninsula.

---

[1] Henry Vignaud, *Toscanelli and Columbus*, London, 1902 ; and *Histoire Critique de Christophe Colomb*, 3 vols. Paris, 1911.

[2] The above is left as in the second edition (1930). It may be said that at the present date (1944), the Vignaud theory has not gained any further ground.

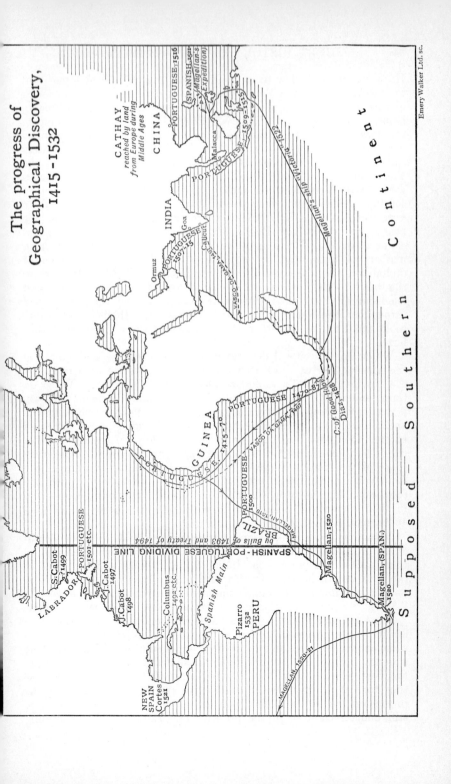

The progress of
Geographical Discovery,
1415–1532

CATHAY
reached by land
from Europe during
Middle Ages

CHINA

PORTUGUESE, 1516

(SPANISH 1521
Magellan's
Expedition)

INDIA

PORTUGUESE 1509–15

Malacca

PORTUGUESE 1509–15

Goa

Calicut

Ormuz

VASCO DA GAMA 1497

Magellan's ship

Magellan's ship Victoria 1522

PORTUGUESE 1479–87

PORTUGUESE 1415–70

PORTUGUESE GUINEA

VASCO DA GAMA 1497

C. of Good Hope
Diaz 1488

Southern   Continent

S. Cabot
1499

LABRADOR

PORTUGUESE
1501 etc.

J. Cabot
1497

J. Cabot
1498

Columbus
1492 etc.

Spanish Main

NEW
SPAIN
Cortes
1521

Pizarro
1532
PERU

SPANISH–PORTUGUESE DIVIDING LINE

by Bulls of 1493 and Treaty of 1494

PORTUGUESE
1500

BRAZIL

MAGELLAN, 1519

Magellan, 1520

Magellan, (SPAN.)
1520

MAGELLAN, 1520–21

Supposed–Southern

Emery Walker Ltd. sc.

In vague language they fixed one hundred leagues west of some point in the Azores or Cape Verde Islands as a dividing meridian. West of this line the Spaniards might take possession of all non-Christian lands, east of it the Portuguese. Probably through defect of geographical learning the exact meaning of the papal award remained disputable. The diplomatists of the interested nations immediately set to work, and in June, 1494, Spain and Portugal concluded the Treaty of Tordesillas, by which they agreed upon a line 370 leagues west of Cape Verde as the boundary. Even this was not a satisfactory solution, since at that date and for long afterwards there existed no means of measuring longitude with even approximate exactness. We hear of no protest from England or France at the preposterous papal claim to dispose of the unknown lands. Orthodox as they were in matters of faith, and absorbed in a purely European system of diplomacy, the statesmen of either country paid no great heed to the matter ; but when the occasion arose both Frenchmen and Englishmen consistently disregarded the bulls and the treaty, and throughout the Reformation period French and English Protestants took the lead in violating the monopolies those documents conferred.

Whilst Spain occupied the next few years in exploring and colonizing the Antilles, Portugal bestirred herself to complete the work of Henry the Navigator and Bartholomew Diaz. On July 8, 1497, Vasco da Gama sailed from the Tagus with four ships and 170 men. Making a westward sweep through the South Atlantic to avoid the currents and calms prevailing near the African coast, he rounded the Cape and entered the Indian Ocean. From the latitude of Madagascar northwards he found himself in a well-peopled maritime world. On every shore of the western Indian Ocean were the trading stations of the Arab seamen and merchants. For centuries they had formed the connecting link between Christendom and the Far East, conducting in their dhows the richest carrying trade in the world ; and now appeared the advanced guard of a power which was to ruin all.

Obtaining pilots from among this seafaring population, the Portuguese proceeded on their way to India. They still expected to find there a Christian power—the India of Prester John and the India of fabulous wealth in one. On May 21, 1498, they dropped anchor at Calicut, an important commercial depot on the Malabar coast. A " Moor " who spoke Portuguese asked them what they sought. " Christians and spices," they replied, and remained under the same illusion throughout their sojourn at the place. The supposed Christians came aboard the ships and did reverence to a painting of Christ and the apostles, mistaking it for a representation of their own deities ; whilst the Portuguese in their turn entered a temple where they saw what they took to be an image of the Virgin, and Europeans and Hindus prostrated themselves in simultaneous worship. The newcomers were still undeceived even in the presence of " saints " with protruding

tusks and four arms apiece.[1] The spices, however, proved to be more
genuine than the Christianity, and after a three months' stay Vasco da
Gama sailed for Portugal with satisfactory ladings. He reached home
in September, 1499, after losing two-thirds of his crews by sickness
and other casualties. But the great task was accomplished. The
spice trade was diverted from the Mediterranean to the Atlantic,
and an era of intense prosperity for Portugal set in.

The conquest of the eastern trading system proceeded rapidly.
Vasco da Gama made a second voyage in 1502. Three years later the
spread of Portuguese acquisitions warranted the appointment of a
viceroy, and in 1509 the great Affonso de Albuquerque succeeded the
first holder of that post. In six years (1509-15) Albuquerque captured
Goa, Malacca and Ormuz, and riveted the grip of Portugal upon all the
intervening trade routes. In 1516 the Portuguese reached China, and
in 1542 Japan. The local native shipping poured into their depots
the commodities which their huge carracks transported to Europe.
Side by side with commercial success the earlier crusading zeal still
manifested itself in the labours of the Jesuit missionaries who, led by
Francis Xavier, strove without much result to convert this vast new
world.

In the west the Spaniards were for a time disappointed with the
outcome of their discoveries. Under the leadership of Columbus and
others they examined the West Indian islands and the neighbouring
coast of South America. Gradually it became evident to them that
they were not in Asia but in some hitherto unknown continent, and
their disillusionment on this point was not at first compensated by
any extraordinary signs of wealth in their new possessions. A small
supply of gold and a few pearls compared very poorly with the
profits made by the Portuguese.

But some thirty years after the original discovery America began to
reveal itself in a new light. In 1518 an expedition from Cuba ranged
along the coast of Mexico, heard tales of a civilized native state under a
great king in the interior, and came upon traces of a large store of gold
in the hands of the Indians. Hernan Cortes, a settler in Cuba, determined to find and conquer this rich land. Taking with him all the
armed forces he could gather, he landed in 1521 and pushed into the
heart of the country. The ruling tribe of Aztecs were savage oppressors
of other subject nations. The latter assisted the Spaniards, and after
desperate fighting in which the whole expedition was face to face with
annihilation Cortes subdued Mexico. An immense hoard of treasure
fell into his hands, and ere long Europe became seriously perturbed by
the influx of the precious metals into Spain.

Hardly had astonishment at this conquest begun to subside when
news came of a similar and even greater achievement. Spanish
pioneers crossing the Isthmus of Panama heard accounts of an empire
to the south, filled like Mexico with gold and silver. In 1532 Francisco

[1] K. G. *Jayne, Vasco da Gama and his Successors,* London, 1910, pp. 52-5.

Pizarro, with less than two hundred followers, sailed down the coast and invaded Peru. He succeeded in gaining control of his prey more easily than Cortes had done, for the Peruvians were a milder and less warlike race than the Mexicans. The original *conquistadores* disgraced themselves by orgies of greed and cruelty and by rebellion against the authority of the Spanish government. But after order had been restored Peru yielded to Spain more treasure than any of her other conquests. Persistent rumours recurred throughout the sixteenth century of yet another treasure-state of fabulous wealth in the interior of South America. But in this case they proved to be illusory, although many adventurers spent their lives in the quest. Sir Walter Raleigh thought he was on the track of this *Eldorado* when he ascended the Orinoco in 1595.

One other exploit remains to be told to complete the bare outline of the great discoveries. In 1519 Ferdinand Magellan, a Portuguese navigator, having left the service of his own country, sailed out of San Lucar in that of Spain. His object was to reveal that western route to the Far East which Columbus and Cabot had projected years before. Skirting the coast of South America, he examined the estuary of the River Plate without success. Farther to the southwards he found what he sought, a passage leading through the land into the Pacific. Called by him the Strait of All Saints and by posterity the Strait of Magellan, it presented to mariners the most dangerous piece of navigation in the world. Jagged rocks, strong currents, furious squalls, and numerous blind turnings combined to threaten disaster to any who essayed to steer a sailing-ship through its intricacies. Magellan nevertheless succeeded. Then he crossed the Pacific and directed his course to the Moluccas, the Spice Islands, which long remained in dispute between Spain and Portugal. He himself fell in a quarrel with natives, but his flagship the *Victoria* returned by the Indian Ocean and the Cape of Good Hope after encompassing the world in a three years' voyage. Such an achievement, unthinkable fifty years before, shows what heights of audacity and endurance distinguished the seamen of the great age. With practically no improvement in ships or instruments they accomplished in bold self-confidence ten times as much as their fathers had contemplated with superstitious dread. Nothing better illustrates the wide yet rapid transition from mediaeval to modern manhood.

CHAPTER III

THE ENGLISH DISCOVERIES, 1485–1547. THE NAVY, 1485–1558

(i) *The Voyages of John and Sebastian Cabot and other Explorations under Henry VII*

WHILST Columbus had been spending many weary years in seeking aid for his discovery of Cathay by a western voyage, a similar idea had developed in the mind of a fellow-countryman of his, John Cabot (variously rendered as John or Zuam Kabotto, Caboto or Cabota). Cabot, like Columbus, was a Genoese by birth, but in 1476 he became a naturalized citizen of Venice, and so figures generally in history as a Venetian. He had traded as a merchant on the old spice route through the Levant. He had travelled to the shores of the Red Sea and had conversed with Arab seamen who told him that their wares came by many hands from the farthest regions of the east. There is little doubt that he had read also the book of Marco Polo, the germ of so many great achievements, and had in his mind a clear impression of the wealthy cities of China and the more fabulous riches of Cipango or Japan, therein so glowingly set forth.

If the truth about Columbus is difficult to unravel, still more is that concerning John Cabot. For centuries his very name was forgotten. A memoir of 1832, which long remained a standard authority, ascribed the whole of his discoveries to his son Sebastian ; and it is only in more recent times that some part of the history of his honourable career has been dragged into the light amid the conflicting arguments of numerous investigators. The principal reasons for this obscurity are that four hundred years ago the English writers of memoirs and chronicles concerned themselves only with the lives of kings and nobles, regarding the struggles of low-born genius as unworthy of record ; [1] and that Sebastian Cabot, the explorer's son, who furnished information to Spanish and Italian historians, remained strangely silent on the subject of his father's voyages, and contrived, wilfully or not, to give the impression that he alone had discovered North

[1] Very little is known concerning the private lives of the majority of the middle-class worthies of the Tudor period. The paucity of surviving detail regarding the life of Shakespeare, so often given a sinister interpretation, is another illustration of the same general rule.

America for Henry VII. The researches of the past eighty years have corrected this error, and the archives of London, Madrid, Venice and Milan have yielded definite proof of the true facts.

The motives which brought John Cabot to England, and the length of his residence in our country, are unknown. He and his family were at Bristol in 1496. He may have travelled thither on hearing of Bartholomew Columbus' mission to Henry VII. and the failure of the negotiation for Christopher Columbus to sail westwards in the English service. A contemporary letter states that Cabot had been in Spain and Portugal seeking aid for his projects. He may also have tried his fortune in France, for the Spanish sovereigns wrote to their ambassador that the western adventure had been suggested to Henry VII. by the French king in order to divert his energies from continental affairs. He came to Bristol more probably as an explorer than as a merchant, for the western seaport was a favourable starting-point. The Bristol men frequented the Iceland fishery, where they may have heard tales of the old Norse discoveries. It was said that for many years they had been sending out ships to explore the Atlantic without result. The evidence on this point is vague, but it is certain that they showed a more enterprising spirit in these matters than did the merchants and mariners of the capital.

Columbus, if indeed he hoped to find Cathay on his first expedition, had based his plans on a great exaggeration of the size of Asia, bringing the eastern shore of that continent within easy sailing distance of Europe. He had accordingly crossed the Atlantic on the latitude of the Canary Islands, somewhat less than 30° north of the equator. Cabot's plan depended less on this geographical error. As we shall see, his idea was to cross the ocean much farther to the north, not far short of 60°, where the lessening circumference of the globe would have the same effect of reducing the distance to be traversed. There is no evidence, therefore, that he was a mere imitator of Columbus. The westward theory had been suggested before either of them was born ; the practical means whereby each sought to realize it were the products of two different geographical conceptions, of which Cabot's was much sounder than that of Columbus. They had this in common, that they both believed that the passage of the Atlantic would bring them to Asia, and neither had any suspicion that an immense unknown continent barred the way.

Henry VII. visited Bristol in 1495-6, and in March of the latter year John Cabot received letters patent authorizing him and his sons Ludovicus, Sebastian and Sanctus to take five ships at their own charges, to navigate any seas to the east, north, or west, and to occupy and possess any new found lands hitherto unvisited by Christians. In the event of success they were to trade only from the port of Bristol, to be exempt from payment of customs, and to enjoy a monopoly as against all other subjects of the king. In return for these privileges they were to pay one-fifth of all profits to the king. Here it is necessary to state that Ludovicus and Sanctus Cabot are mere names to us, appearing on this occasion only upon the page of history. Of the extent of their participation in the voyages and of their subsequent careers nothing is known. Of Sebastian, on the other hand, there will be more to relate.

In the late spring of 1497 John Cabot sailed out of Bristol, not with the five ships permitted by his charter, but in a single tiny vessel named the *Matthew* with a crew of eighteen men. He himself was a poor man, and Bristol, comparatively enterprising as it was, would do no more for him than this. His undertaking, viewed from the starting-point, was thus much more hazardous than that of Columbus with his three caravels and 120 men. After passing to the south of Ireland he steered northwards for a time, then westwards across the Atlantic, and apparently south-westwards again before reaching the other side. On June 24, according to a statement made nearly fifty years later, he sighted land in the neighbourhood of Cape Breton. The landfall, however, is a disputed point, some authorities concluding that it must have been on the coast of Labrador or Newfoundland. John Cabot planted the flags of England and Venice, and coasted for some distance to examine the nature of the country. He found it " a very good and temperate country " and, although he saw no inhabitants, he noticed unmistakable signs of the presence of man—felled trees, snares for game, and the like. His provisions then began to fail and he turned homewards, arriving at Bristol at the beginning of August.

He rode at once to London, taking with him his charts and a globe with which to demonstrate his discoveries to the king. Of the nature of his discovery neither he nor any of his friends had any doubt. Lorenzo Pasqualigo, a merchant residing in London, wrote on August 23, 1497, to his brothers in Venice : " The Venetian, our countryman, who went with a ship from Bristol in quest of new islands, is returned, and says that 700 leagues hence he discovered land, the territory of the Grand Cham." A few months later, on December 18, the Milanese envoy reported to his master : " Perhaps among Your Excellency's many occupations it may not displease you to learn how his Majesty here has won a part of Asia without a stroke of the sword." Then, after describing the voyage and the valuable fishery found on the new coast, he continues : " But Master John Caboto has set his mind on something greater ; for he expects to go further on towards the Levant from that place already occupied, constantly hugging the shore until he shall be over against an island, by him called Cipango, situated in the equinoctial region, where he thinks all the spices in the world, and also all the precious stones, originate . . . by means of which they hope to establish in London a greater storehouse of spices than there is in Alexandria."

Cabot, then, confidently reported that he had found the outlying coasts of Cathay. The greatest enthusiasm prevailed in London and Bristol. The navigator took the title of Admiral, dressed in silk, and was feasted at court. Henry bestowed on him a gratuity of £10 and an annual pension of £20. The merchants of London, with the king's aid, equipped and laded a large ship for the next year's voyage, whilst those of Bristol prepared four smaller ones to accompany her. Cabot promised to lead them from the neighbourhood of his first landfall to the wealthy cities of China and Japan, where they would exchange their English cloth for untold riches of silks, spices and jewels. The Spanish ambassador protested, jealously claiming that the new land was the possession of his own sovereigns. The latter had already written that such enterprises " cannot be executed without prejudice to us and to the King of Portugal." The Bull of Alexander VI. was evidently no empty ceremonial, but a reality with which Englishmen would have to reckon if they were to push their way in the new world which was coming so suddenly above the horizon.

With golden anticipations John Cabot sailed again from Bristol in 1498. A London chronicler, entering up his record towards the close of the year, wrote : " they departed from the west country in the beginning of summer, but to this present month (Oct.-Nov.) came never knowledge of their exploit." The Spanish ambassador reported the fact of their sailing, and also that they met with a storm off the Irish coast which caused one ship to turn back. A manuscript found in the Vatican Library and made public in 1939 declares that John Cabot was lost with his own ship on this voyage, although the statement does not cover the other vessels. The evidence may be incorrect, for Cabot's pension continued to be paid until Michaelmas, 1499, which shows that he was not certainly known to be dead. The payments may have gone on longer : we do not know, for after that date the record fails. There is no direct testimony to the discoveries made in the voyage of 1498. Yet there is indirect and circumstantial evidence that Cabot's expedition (with or without him) reached the other side of the Atlantic again and coasted southward in search of trade ; and further, that it made the unwelcome discovery that it was not upon the coast of Asia, but on that of a savage land whose scanty population had nothing of value with which to lade the ships.

The evidence for this belief is as follows. In 1500 Juan de la Cosa, a Spanish pilot and cartographer, drew a map of the world which is still preserved in Madrid. This map shows that the English had explored a considerable part of the North American coastline. The place-names are written in Spanish and their identification is not a certain matter owing to the crudeness of the drawing, but the extent of English discovery indicated seems too great to have been accomplished in the three months' voyage of 1497. This points to the probability that the Spaniard had learned particulars of the voyage of 1498 before drawing his map. In 1501 a Portuguese expedition visiting Newfoundland found a native in possession of a European sword and a pair of earrings. He could only have obtained them from Cabot's

second expedition, for on the first no natives had been seen. **Then**
again, in 1501 the Spanish sovereigns issued a patent to Alonso de
Hojeda with instructions for pushing westwards along the north coast
of South America " because it goes towards the region where it has
been learned that the English were making discoveries " ; and Hojeda
was ordered to stop the explorations of the English. This shows that
the English had already come far down the North American coast ;
and Cabot's second expedition is the only one we know of which could
have done so by that date. Finally, the next voyages which we shall
have to consider were made to the north-west, which suggests that

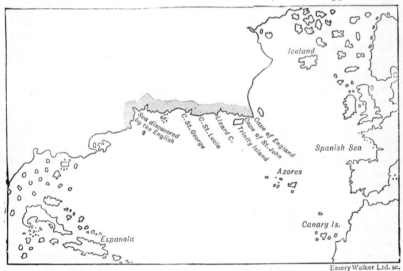

Emery Walker Ltd. sc,

THE NORTH ATLANTIC AS SHOWN IN THE WORLD-MAP OF THE SPANISH
PILOT, JUAN DE LA COSA, DATED 1500.

The shaded portion of the American coast is marked in the original with flags indicating English discovery. The map therefore in all probability illustrates the discoveries of the Cabots.
In the above reproduction the names, all in Spanish in the original, are translated into English,
and many details are omitted for the sake of simplicity.

their promoters realized that the new land was not Asia and were trying to find a way round it. If this was so, it is probable that they drew
their information from the voyage of 1498.

Altogether there is a strong probability, not amounting to certainty,
that Cabot's people made an extensive American coasting in 1498, and
discovered that the New Found Land was not Cathay. They could
have found no opening for profitable trade. The money invested in
the venture was lost, and the London merchants had received a check
to their short-lived enthusiasm for exploration. According to the new
evidence John Cabot lost his life on the voyage, and there is no further
record of him except the pension payment in 1499.

Whether or not it was now understood that the western land was not
Asia, there is no doubt of another result of John Cabot's voyages, the

discovery of the Newfoundland fishery. The fishery had been reported
in 1497, and described as more valuable than that of Iceland. The
mariners of Bristol and the other west-country ports soon abandoned
the Iceland voyage and went instead to Newfoundland, where they
competed with Portuguese, Spaniards, Normans and Bretons in
gathering the harvest of the new fishing grounds.

The Portuguese were particularly active in Newfoundland and the
north-west. In 1499 Vasco da Gama returned from the first sea
voyage to India. It had taken two years, and a shorter route would
have been worth looking for. If Asia had lain across the Atlantic the
western voyage would have provided the shorter route. But it would
seem that the Portuguese, together with the English, had concluded
that the western land was an obstacle on the path to Asia ; for their
efforts took them to the coasts of Greenland and Labrador, which suggests that they were looking for the North-West Passage. As for
Newfoundland, its fishery made it worth claiming, and the impos-
sibility of accurately fixing the longitude gave the Portuguese an
excuse for including it in their hemisphere as laid down by the papal
bulls and the Treaty of Tordesillas. The brothers Gaspar and Miguel
Corte-Real made voyages to Greenland and North America, and
perished in the north-west in 1501 and 1502 respectively ; and the
map which records their discoveries shows Newfoundland under the
name of " Terra del Rey de Portuguall." The claim, however, was not
accompanied by any attempt at effective occupation, and the way
was left clear for English enterprise.

The men of Bristol again took the lead. On March 19, 1501, Richard
Ward, Thomas Ashehurst and John Thomas, merchants of that city,
together with João Fernandes, Francisco Fernandes and João Gon-
salves, Portuguese colonists of the Azores, obtained a patent from
Henry VII. empowering them to find and occupy any new countries
not already known to Christians. The precise achievements of this
syndicate cannot be determined. The patent contains numerous
clauses on the formation of settlements, the monopoly of trade and the
expulsion of intruders, but it does not follow that the patentees attempted to exercise all these powers. It is certain that they had
reasonable hopes of a profitable trade, for neither the government nor
the merchants of England were prepared to spend money merely on the
acquisition of geographical knowledge. Voyages to the north-west
were made in 1501 and 1502. The results must have been encouraging,
for the king rewarded the explorers as he had rewarded John Cabot in
1497. An entry in the Privy Purse accounts of January 7, 1502, runs :
" To men of Bristol that found the Isle, £5 " ; another of September
30, 1502, says : " To the merchants of Bristol that have been in the
Newfound Land, £20 " ; while at the same time two of the Portuguese
adventurers received pensions of £10 a year each " in consideration of
the true service which they have done unto us to our singular pleasure
as captains unto the New Found Land." Some clue to the destination

of the voyages is afforded by a London chronicler who says that in
1502 the adventurers captured three " eaters of raw flesh," evidently
Eskimos, and exhibited them at the king's court at Westminster.

At the end of 1502 the king issued a new patent which omitted three
of the original names from the syndicate, but added a new one, that of
Hugh Elyot, a prominent merchant of Bristol. Documents show that
other men took part besides those named in the patent, and the whole
combination was known as The Company Adventurers to the New
Found Land. It was the first company for overseas expansion in our
history. Its new patent empowered it to establish itself in lands dis-

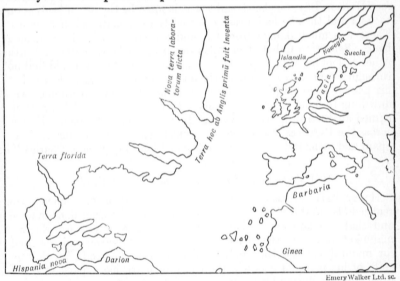

THE NORTH ATLANTIC AS SHOWN IN THE MAP OF ROBERT THORNE, 1527.

Thorne's father was one of the Bristol adventurers of 1501-5, and the inscriptions on the
North-American region of the map may have some reference to their operations.

covered by others if not effectively occupied by them, and the clauses
about colonization and government were very elaborate. We have
scanty records showing that voyages took place every year to 1505
and possibly later, but we know nothing of the location and nature of
the Company's efforts. It may or may not have founded settlements
and trading posts for collecting fish and furs. Its ultimate motive was
very probably that of discovering the North-West Passage to Asia, in
which, as we know, it must have failed.

Several writers of the sixteenth century give details of a voyage
made by Sebastian Cabot, and most of them leave its date vague or
unstated. It was formerly supposed that this voyage was in fact one
of those made by John Cabot, of which Sebastian was unjustifiably
claiming the leadership. There is evidence, however, that Sebastian's
voyage was a separate undertaking, and that it took place in 1509. It

is therefore treated under that date in this account, with a warning to the reader that the whole question of the Cabot voyages contains many uncertainties and that investigators are not in agreement about them. Under the patronage of Henry VII., Sebastian Cabot sailed with two ships for the purpose of discovering the North-West Passage to Asia. The accounts are clear on this point, and it follows that by this date, if not earlier, it was realized that the land across the Atlantic was a new continent distinct from Asia. Cabot pushed into the north-west and found an opening which may be identified with the present Hudson Strait. He passed through and found a broad sea beyond. It was in fact Hudson Bay, but he thought that it must be the ocean leading on to Asia and that he had already passed the northern end of America. There was much danger from ice, and the crews insisted on turning back. Sebastian Cabot then sailed down the Atlantic coast of North America looking for an opening in a warmer climate, but could find no through channel to the west. He returned to England to learn that his patron Henry VII. was dead, and that the new government was unwilling to follow up his discovery. In 1512 Sebastian Cabot accompanied an English army to Spain. It was intended to attack France across the Pyrenees, but came home unsuccessful. Cabot remained in Spain and ultimately rose to the office of Pilot-Major under Charles V.

(ii) *Voyages of Discovery under Henry VIII.*

Henry VIII. was a lover of the sea and a patron of seamen. He realized also that difficult times were in prospect for English commerce and that the necessity existed for seeking new outlets for English manufactures. But the menace of the religious quarrel and the need for maintaining the Burgundian alliance tied his hands, so that in spite of his personal goodwill the cause of maritime expansion made little advance during his reign.

In 1517 John Rastell, brother-in-law of Sir Thomas More, attempted a voyage to North America, but his men mutinied and set him ashore in Ireland. There is no confirmation of a later assertion that Sebastian Cabot was concerned in this venture. Rastell wrote the first English account of America in his *New Interlude* (1519). Some years later, in 1521, a new project took shape. The king and Cardinal Wolsey proposed that the Livery Companies of London should finance an expedition for the opening-up of trade, presumably with Asia, by the north-western route. The London merchants, remembering the failure of John Cabot's Cathay voyage, remained sceptical of success and refused to subscribe sufficient money. Those of Bristol showed more willingness, and promised to equip two ships ; but it does not appear that the scheme was brought to the stage of action. Again, in 1525, an Italian seaman, Paolo Centurioni, was in communication with the king on the subject of the northern voyage. Centurioni came to London, but died there before anything further could be done.

Two years later Henry VIII. got an expedition to sea. It consisted
of two ships, one of them belonging to the Navy, commanded by John
Rut with the assistance of an Italian navigator. Their orders were to
sail into the north-west and seek a passage to eastern Asia.[1] John
Rut in the *Mary of Gilford* possibly reached the mouth of Hudson
Strait, but he had parted company with his consort the *Samson* and
went back to seek her at St. John's, Newfoundland, an agreed rendez-
vous. They never rejoined, and Rut is reported to have reached
England in the autumn of 1527. At the same time an English ship,
presumably the *Samson*, arrived in the Spanish West Indies. Her
captain, whose name is not recorded, told the Spaniards that he had
been far up into the northern ice seeking for a passage to Cathay at
the command of the king of England. He had then coasted North
America and was seeking supplies in the West Indies for his voyage
home. He attempted to trade at Santo Domingo, but was fired on,
and departed with threats to come again with a large force and take
revenge. He was never heard of again, and the Spaniards supposed
that the ship was lost on the way home. This may well have been true,
for there is no further mention of the *Samson* in English records, and
the contemporary English chroniclers of the voyage knew nothing
about the West Indian transactions.

One of the British merchants who had sailed westward in the time
of John Cabot, perhaps in the pioneer voyage of 1497, had been named
Robert Thorne, for whom it was claimed that he and Hugh Elyot had
" discovered the New Found Land." He died in 1519, leaving a son
also named Robert. This Robert Thorne the younger (born in 1492)
was a merchant doing business in Seville, hearing of the tropical lands
revealed by Spain and Portugal, and dreaming of an empire for England
to rival theirs. In 1522 Magellan's ship *Victoria* came home to Spain,
having crossed the Pacific, traded in the Spice Islands and circumnavigated the globe. At once a dispute broke out between Spain and
Portugal on the location of the Spice Islands, either power claiming
them as in its own hemisphere as delimited by the Treaty of Tordesillas.
The emperor Charles V. at one moment thought of selling his claim,
and threw out a hint to Henry VIII. as a possible purchaser. Henry
instructed Edward Lee, his ambassador in Spain, to report on the
value of the spice trade, and Lee consulted the Seville merchant Robert
Thorne. Thorne replied in a celebrated *Letter to Doctor Lee*, which
showed that the writer had long been meditating an English enterprise
in the Pacific. This was in 1527. In the previous year Thorne had
procured places for two English friends of his in a Spanish expedition
intended for that ocean and led by Sebastian Cabot. In fact Cabot did
not reach the Pacific, but spent nearly four years in exploring the course
and tributaries of the River Plate. By 1530 Roger Barlow, one of the

---

[1] Spanish documents published by the Hakluyt Society in 1929 have amplified the
knowledge previously available on this voyage. See *Spanish Documents on English
Voyages to the Caribbean*, ed. I. A. Wright.

Englishmen with him, had come home, and he and Thorne composed an address to Henry VIII., setting forth their project. This writing was entitled *A Declaration of the Indies*. It covered the same ground as the letter to Lee, but did so in a far more concise and polished style, which gives rise to the supposition that although the idea was Thorne's, the final wording may have been Barlow's.[1] The "Indies" that Thorne had chiefly in mind were the great lands, as yet undiscovered, that he expected to find in the tropical latitudes of the vast Pacific Ocean between America and Asia. These, he thought, were the appointed sphere of English expansion, the continent and islands which, before the end of the century, men were calling *Terra Australis Incognita*. He proposed to reach them by sailing due north from England across the pole and then down the opposite meridian to mid-Pacific. Measured on the globe it was a very much shorter route than those by the Cape of Good Hope or the Straits of Magellan. Thorne held that since the tropics had not proved too hot for human endurance the pole would not be found too cold : " there is no land unhabit-able," he said, " and no sea unnavigable." He and Barlow returned to England and bought a ship for the venture. But in 1532 Robert Thorne died in London at the age of forty. His wealth had made the project feasible, and Barlow, a poorer man, could not go on with it alone. At various later dates he put the proposal before the English government, but nothing was done. The only enduring result was thus the *Declaration of the Indies*, which the Elizabethans found worth reading and which has remained worth reading, a gem of early modern prose, to this day.

In 1536 the study of " cosmography " had evidently begun to make headway in England, for we find in that year an expedition of a novel type setting forth for the north-west. Although it had the king's approval it originated neither with him nor with the merchants. Its promoter was a certain Richard Hore of London, a man of good position and fortune, who with a party of friends, for the most part lawyers, was determined to see the wonders of the world for himself. Accordingly they subscribed funds, equipped two ships, and embarked at Gravesend to the number of thirty gentlemen and ninety mariners. In two months they crossed the Atlantic, and began to explore the coasts of Cape Breton and Newfoundland. The natives fled at their approach, and their stock of victuals failed. Many died of hunger, some killed and ate one another, and all would have perished but for the appearance of a French ship upon the coast. They attacked the Frenchman, revictualled themselves at his expense, and returned home. Afterwards, when the aggrieved parties complained to the king, " he was so moved with pity that he punished not his subjects, but of his own purse made full and royal recompense unto the French."

Thus far we have had to chronicle the heroic failures of Englishmen

[1] See Introduction to Barlow's *Brief Summe of Geographie*, edited for the Hakluyt Society by Prof. E. G. R. Taylor, 1932.

in the vain quest for the North-West Passage. In another direction the adventurers of Henry VIII. did succeed in opening up a profitable trade across the ocean.   In 1530 William Hawkins of Plymouth, one of the most prominent merchant-mariners of the west country and a man " for his wisdom, valour, experience and skill in sea causes, much esteemed and beloved of King Henry," set sail in a ship named the *Paul* for Brazil.   This country lay within the sphere of discovery of the Portuguese.   They had visited it in the opening years of the century, although it was only in 1530 that they began to make serious efforts to colonize it.   Hawkins, according to the meagre accounts we have of him, seems to have avoided coming into collision with them.   He traded directly with the natives, making friends with them to such good effect that a chief voluntarily accompanied him to England and was presented to the king.   Hawkins made in person at least three voyages to Brazil and also touched at the Guinea coast on his outward passage, obtaining ivory from the negroes.   Afterwards he continued to send out ships under other captains and evidently conducted a lucrative trade.   The merchants of Southampton and London followed his example, making the voyage so regularly that they found it worth while in 1542 to build a fortified station on the Brazilian coast.   One ship, named the *Barbara* of London, of whose voyage we have details,[1] came home by way of the West Indies, and took a Spanish merchantman off Santo Domingo. Hakluyt describes this trade as " a commodious and gainful voyage " ; but for some unexplained reason it ceased to be frequented towards the end of Henry's reign.   Probably the outbreak of the French war in 1544 led to the retention of all ocean-going ships for the naval service.   Hawkins in his later years found profitable employment for his capital in maintaining a fleet of privateers in the Narrow Seas. Some of his proceedings smacked so strongly of piracy that the Privy Council committed him to prison.   However, his services to the country were valuable, and he was soon at large again.   He represented Plymouth in three several parliaments, and died in 1554. Only the bare outlines of his career have been preserved ; its full story would certainly make exciting reading.

Superficially, the first fifty years of English oceanic history are a record of failure and disappointment, of chimerical projects and promising openings not followed up.   In reality they provided a necessary apprenticeship for the more solid undertakings of the next generation.   The English were unlearned in scientific navigation and the new world-geography to which the great discoveries had given birth.   They had to buy their experience, as the Portuguese had done during the fifteenth century.   Their achievements under the early Tudors would probably appear to us in a more impressive light if they had given rise to a literature recording their heroisms.   But the English chroniclers took no interest in barren discoveries, and

---

[1] See article by R. G. Marsden in *English Hist. Review*, xxiv. p. 96.

successful men of action like William Hawkins had often good reason
for remaining silent on transactions whose strict legality was questionable.   When Richard Eden, our first historian of discovery, began
to write in the reign of Mary, the details of the early expeditions were
already lost ;   and when the industrious Richard Hakluyt at the end
of the century made his great collection of English voyages he could
find nothing but fragments of the record of the first Tudor soveerigns.
He could only lament " the great negligence of the writers of those
times, who should have used more care in preserving of the memories
of the worthy acts of our nation." [1]

(iii) *The Navy*, 1485-1558

With the Tudors begins the history of the modern navy of England.
The powerful fleet of Henry V. had disappeared under his son, whose
ministers thought to save expense by relying upon hired merchantmen
for their naval undertakings.   The Yorkist kings set about the re-
creation of a royal fleet in so far as their limited means would allow ;
and Henry VII. acquired with the throne six small vessels which
represented the navy of his predecessor.   Henry's own additions
to the fleet were not numerous, although they marked a great advance
in quality and specialization for warlike purposes.   He built two
first-class fighting ships named the *Regent* and the *Sovereign*, the
former carrying 225 small guns, and the latter 141.   At his death
these ships and five smaller ones passed to his son.

Henry VIII. from the first years of his reign adopted a vigorous
naval policy.   Not content with building and buying ships on a
lavish scale, he was a keen personal student of naval tactics and
architecture and of the improvement of artillery.   In his reign the
design of war vessels improved enormously, and, profiting by the
experience gained in his French wars, he laid the foundations of a
system of naval administration capable of dealing with a powerful and
permanent national fleet.   By the end of 1512, three and a half years
after the opening of his reign, seventeen new vessels had been added
by purchase or construction to the seven he inherited from his father.

The French war of 1512-14 provided ample work for the new force.
In the former year Sir Edward Howard put to sea as commander-in-
chief, and convoyed the Marquis of Dorset's army to San Sebastian.
The French made no opposition, but later in the year they concentrated
some twenty-two sail at Brest.   Howard sailed to meet them and fought
a general action off that port.   The intensity of the English fire
caused the enemy to lose heart, and their fleet retired hastily into
Brest with the exception of two ships, one of which fought gallantly
for seven hours before giving up the contest.   The other, the *Cordelière*,
grappled by the *Regent* and two other Englishmen, was overwhelmed.

[1] For a fuller treatment of this period of discovery see the present writer's *Voyages
of the Cabots, etc.,* London, 1929.

Her crew fought desperately, and at last the gunner, seeing that escape was impossible, fired the magazine. The explosion set fire to the *Regent* also, and the two finest ships in the respective fleets perished side by side. The battle secured the command of the sea to the English, who were able to sweep the Channel for merchantmen and ravage the French coasts with impunity.

In 1513 Howard was again at sea, and instituted a blockade of Brest, where the French kept close in expectation of the arrival of a reinforcement of galleys from a neighbouring port. The galleys at length made their appearance and forced the blockade, sinking an English ship in the process. Their commander moored them in shallow water close to the shore of Blanc Sablons Bay where the larger English warships could not follow. Howard made a gallant boat attack upon them, in which he met his death. By some mischance he was left almost alone on the deck of the galley he had boarded, and before aid could come the Frenchmen's pikes had thrust him overboard. The other English captains had no better fortune, and the attack was repulsed. After this the shortage of supplies and the fighting prestige of the galleys caused the English to raise the blockade of Brest, but they still held the effective command of the sea and sent armies to the continent at their pleasure. The war ended in 1514 without further sea fighting other than the raiding of the Channel coasts. In the spring the French galleys burned Brighton, in revenge for which Sir John Wallop ravaged the shores of Normandy, destroying twenty-one towns and villages and much shipping.

After the war the enlargement of the navy continued. The *Henry Grace à Dieu* or *Great Harry*, of 1500 tons, was completed in 1514. She was the largest ship yet seen in northern Europe, and carried a number of heavy guns in addition to the light serpentines hitherto considered sufficient. The war of 1522-5 produced no naval incidents of importance because the French refrained from sending a battle fleet to sea. The third war, that of 1544-6, was very different. Francis I. had seen the error of allowing his enemies to land unmolested on the continent, and had strained every nerve to build up a mighty fleet. Henry also had been unremitting in his preparations. In the twelve years following 1530 he had remodelled and extended the navy, applying to the purpose much of the wealth of which he had despoiled the Church. Many of the older ships, the *Great Harry* amongst them, were broken up and more modern ones built to bear the same names. The new *Great Harry*, completed in 1539, was of 1000 tons and very heavily armed. The king also constructed low-built craft of a new type, relying upon gun-power rather than upon hand-to-hand fighting, and evidently designed, by their finer lines and general handiness, to avoid being grappled and boarded by the great " high charged " battleships which remained the ideal type in the minds of the more conservative tacticians. These ships were the prototypes of the nimble English galleons of Drake's day, and had the war produced a great pitched battle they might have surprised the men of that generation as effectively as did their successors in the Armada campaign of 1588.

Although both sides had made great preparations, the outcome was not spectacular. In 1544 England, reinforced by the Emperor's Spanish and Flemish naval power, held the seas without difficulty. Then without warning Charles V. made a separate peace, and England was thrown upon the defensive. In 1545 a great French fleet approached Portsmouth where Lord Lisle, the English admiral, remained in the port covered by land batteries and awaiting the arrival of reinforcements. The privateers of the west country, called in from their profitable employment of ranging the Channel and the Bay of Biscay, increased Lisle's fleet by some sixty sail of small but useful warships. The French, in spite of their initial preponderance, acted feebly. A cannonade took place at the entrance to Portsmouth harbour, but the French would not engage seriously under the fire of the batteries, and Lisle would not advance beyond that protection. The French ships were crowded with troops for the capture of Portsmouth, and a terrible epidemic of typhus broke out amongst them. After vainly attempting to occupy the Isle of Wight they drew off, returned to their own coast, and landed their soldiers. Lisle, with his numbers now increased, followed. Off Shoreham the two fleets met in open water. The French galleys attacked and suffered some loss before the night ended the action. Lisle expected that the great ships would fairly join battle on the following day, and anchored to make preparations. But when morning dawned his opponents were gone. They had tamely declined the contest and retired to their own ports. Although this campaign produced no fighting which can be described as a great battle, it justified Henry's expenditure on the navy, for the mere existence of that force had saved England from the most carefully planned invasion since the Norman conquest.

At the time of Henry's death there were in the navy fifty-three vessels great and small, the total tonnage amounting to 11,268. Six of the ships were of 500 tons and over, and nineteen between 200 and 500 tons. At war strength they carried between them 7780 men and 2087 guns. During the eleven years which intervened between that date and the death of Mary (1558), the numbers, and still more the efficiency, declined. In 1588 there were twenty-six royal ships with a combined tonnage of 7110. The shortage of stores and the decay of organization were such that the sudden emergency of the siege of Calais found not a single great ship of the fleet in a condition to put to sea. It is true that Henry had been accustomed to lay up most of his larger vessels during the winter, but he had always kept a sufficient force afloat to maintain communications with Calais. Mary's naval advisers, in spite of warnings, neglected to do this, and lost Calais as a consequence of their default.

CHAPTER IV

THE WIDENING FIELD OF COMMERCE, 1547–1558

(i) *Changing Conditions*

THE period succeeding the death of Henry VIII. was, as we have seen, one of depression in the old trades with European countries and in the more recently established intercourse with the disturbed regions of the Levant. At the same time manufactures were developing, and a town-dwelling, artisan population was increasing in numbers even if there was no corresponding growth of the agricultural portion of the community. Capital also was accumulating, partly owing to the influx of the precious metals from America, to an extent previously unknown. A Venetian observer, making a report upon England in the middle of the sixteenth century, stated that there were many members of the Merchants Adventurers and Staplers' Companies worth from £50,000 to £60,000 each.[1] All these causes combined to produce an imperative demand for new outlets for English trade. The curtailment of the old markets spelt unemployment and hunger, capable of merely illusory relief by the increase of luxury and extravagant living among the wealthy ; and the national instinct, combining with the deliberate policy of far-seeing men, sent adventurers over the seas in ever increasing numbers to seek a share of the world-commerce hitherto monopolized by the Spaniards and the Portuguese.

In this new commercial movement London bore a preponderating part. Since the beginning of the Tudor period she had been steadily growing at the expense of the other seaports. The customs returns for the fifty years following 1485 show that the trade of Bristol, Exeter, Plymouth and the smaller western ports remained practically stationary ; that of Hull, Ipswich, Newcastle and Boston slightly declined ; that of Southampton fell off by forty per cent. ; whilst that of London, exclusive of the wool export, considerably more than doubled itself. The increase in the size of ships, rendering many of the shallower harbours useless for anything but coasting and fishing craft, undoubtedly contributed to this concentration of commercial energy in the capital.

[1] The figures are possibly exaggerated, but mercantile wealth was certainly on the increase.

The merchants of London, therefore, in close touch with the govern‑
ment, wielding large capital resources, and having at their doors the
labour and the purchasing power of a relatively dense population,
became the promoters of novel enterprises in various directions. As
a class they were large-minded and generous in taking risks where
important ends were in view ; nor did they specialize too narrowly
in particular lines of business. On the contrary, in most of the
speculative undertakings of the time we find the same set of names
constantly recurring. Sir Thomas Gresham, Sir John Yorke, Sir
William Garrard, Sir George Barnes, Sir Andrew Judde, Anthony
Hickman, Edward Castlyn and Miles Mordeyne, to mention only
some of the most prominent, invested their money in adventures to
Barbary, Guinea, the Levant, the Canary Islands and Russia, and
in schemes for finding Cathay by the north-east or the north-west,
besides being members of one or more of the older companies like the
Merchants Adventurers or the Staplers. And these men, engaging
in such widespread activities at a time when the government was
unstable and inclined to be corrupt, had a far greater influence upon
the policy and the future destiny of their country than is commonly
recognized. Their virtues and their failings, the former on the whole
outweighing the latter, determined the moral tone of the nation quite
as effectively as those of the statesmen and courtiers who fill a larger
space in the general history of the time.

(ii) *The African Trade*

The earliest records now extant show that a regular trade with
Africa began in 1551. In that year a partnership of London merchants
sent out a ship named the *Lion* of 150 tons under the command of
Thomas Wyndham. Wyndham had served in the navy against the
French and the Scots, rising to the rank of vice-admiral in the Duke of
Somerset's campaign of 1547. The treaty which surrendered Boulogne
to the French in 1550 put an end to the wars for the time, and
Wyndham spent the remainder of his life in the African expeditions
now to be described. In 1551 he sailed from Portsmouth to a harbour
on the Atlantic coast of Morocco, where he traded successfully and
obtained a cargo of sugar, dates, almonds and molasses. He repeated
the venture with three ships in the following year, making an equally
prosperous voyage and touching at the Canary Islands on his way
home. London merchants had long maintained agents in these
islands, although it would seem that they carried on their trade in
Spanish and Portuguese ships.

The success of the Morocco voyages emboldened the adventurers
to a new departure of a more daring nature. They determined to
send Wyndham to seek a trade in the rich ivory and gold-bearing
regions of Guinea, on that part of the African coast which runs from
west to east into the Bight of Benin. William Hawkins had touched

at the nearer Guinea coast, now Liberia, on his voyages to Brazil ; and it is probable, although evidence is lacking, that the other Brazil adventurers under Henry VIII. had done the same. Be that as it may, it is clear that the trade, if it had ever been frequented, had been discontinued for at least ten years. The climate of the Guinea coast was unhealthy, the navigation difficult and full of pitfalls for the inexperienced, and the position of the Portuguese stations and the condition of the negro tribes but vaguely known in England. These circumstances combined to render the venture extremely hazardous. The interested parties had, however, access to inside information which encouraged them to make the attempt. They got into touch with a Portuguese fugitive named Antonio Pinteado who had served for many years as a pilot on voyages from Lisbon to Guinea and Brazil. This man was now an outcast from his own country, and he undertook to guide an English fleet to the richest and most secret preserves of the Portuguese crown.

The exact status of the persons who found the capital for this and similar voyages is a matter of some uncertainty. A recent historian of such undertakings classifies them as a company, but they would perhaps be more properly described as a syndicate or partnership. They subscribed the necessary money privately, and certainly made no public issue of stock as did the Muscovy Company at the same period. They had no incorporation, monopoly grant or official recognition of any kind. The names of Sir George Barnes, Sir Andrew Judde and several others already mentioned in this chapter appear from time to time among the promoters ; but it is highly unlikely that there was a permanent company at all. Each voyage seems to have been a separate undertaking, completely wound up at its close. The adventurers, if they felt disposed to continue, reinvested their money in the next, and the composition of the syndicate varied as time went on. It is by no means certain indeed that the various voyages were all set forth by one syndicate ; quite possibly two or more rival associations took up the trade when once the initial success had been secured. The merchants who sent out Wyndham and Pinteado in 1553 were evidently in favour with members of the Privy Council, since two of the ships belonged to the navy. But the claim of Portugal to exclusive rights upon the African coast rendered the whole undertaking of doubtful legality, and it was carried on from the outset in a furtive and clandestine manner.

The Guinea coast was divided into regions each named from the most valuable merchandise it produced. The westerly portion, the modern Liberia, was known as the Grain Coast on account of the grains or "hot fruit" obtained there. Next came the Ivory Coast, now in the possession of France, and then the Gold Coast, which still bears its ancient name. Eastward of all these lay the coast of Benin and the delta of the Niger, then principally known as a pepper-growing district. At suitable places along all this expanse of 1400 miles the Portuguese had established trading stations, but between them there were wide unoccupied stretches. The negro chiefs acknowledged a loose vassalage to the Portuguese crown, but retained a large measure of independence. The Portuguese themselves conducted the trade, not by means of a chartered company, but under a system of licences purchased from the government, the whole undertaking being considered as a royal monopoly.

Wyndham and his Portuguese associate set sail in August, 1553, with the *Lion*, Wyndham's old ship, the *Primrose*, and a pinnace named the *Moon*. Near Madeira they met with a large Portuguese warship, sent out, as they thought, expressly to stop them; but they continued on their way without fighting, and arrived without mishap at the Grain Coast. They made no stay there or at the Ivory Coast, but pushed straight on to the Gold Coast where they traded on either side of the fortress of S. Jorge de la Mina, the chief Portuguese stronghold in Guinea. After they had obtained some 150 lb. of gold the supply began to run short. Already the financial success of the venture was assured, and Pinteado was for beginning the homeward voyage at once on account of the lateness of the season. But Wyndham disagreed, demanding that the Portuguese should lead them eastward to Benin to lade pepper, according to his promise. A violent debate ensued, Wyndham "reviling the said Pinteado, calling him Jew, with other opprobrious words, saying : This whoreson Jew hath promised to bring us to such places as are not, or as he cannot bring us unto : but if he do not, I will cut off his ears and nail them to the mast." Pinteado, knowing the dangers into which the expedition was running, submitted against his better judgment, and they ran on to the eastward until they came to an anchor in the mouth of a great river. Pinteado and the merchants went up the river in the pinnace to bargain with a native king for pepper. Meanwhile a terrible epidemic broke out amongst the crews waiting inactive upon the coast. The men died at the rate of four and five a day, and the survivors in a panic demanded to be taken home forthwith. Pinteado, hearing this news, came down the river to plead for a little delay in view of the rich cargo he was collecting. But Wyndham himself was dead before the Portuguese arrived. The men refused to wait, even to send for the English merchants who still remained in the interior. Reduced now to half their original numbers, they sank the *Lion* and set sail in the *Primrose*, taking Pinteado with them. Pinteado sickened also, and died before the voyage was a week old ; and when the *Primrose* at length crept into Plymouth there were but forty men alive of the 140 who had set forth.

In spite of the casualties sustained by the expedition the commercial prospects of the trade had proved encouraging. One hundred and fifty pounds of pure gold represented a large sum, especially when compared with the debased condition of the coinage at the time ; and we do not know that this was the only return of the voyage. The syndicate therefore despatched a larger squadron in the autumn of 1554. It was commanded by John Lok, and consisted of two ships of 140 tons, one of 90, and two pinnaces. Arriving at Guinea before the end of the year, Lok traded successfully on the Grain, Ivory and Gold Coasts. He obtained 36 butts of grains, 400 lb. of gold, and 250 tusks. He arrived in England in the summer of 1555, having lost only twenty-four men by sickness. This was the most profitable of all the Guinea voyages of which we have records. A rough estimate of the value of the cargoes suggests that the gains may have represented as much as 1000 per cent. on the capital invested.[1]

This great success encouraged others to follow in the same track. In the years 1555-8 William Towerson, a London merchant, made three voyages in person to the Guinea coast, all of them more or less successful. Towerson appears to have traded on his own private account, or at least to have represented a different syndicate from that which had sent out Wyndham and Lok. We need not suppose, however, that the latter body ceased its activities, although we have no records of its further voyages until 1561. The survival of such records has been purely a matter of accident and, as we shall see, the parties concerned had often a strong interest in suppressing them. Towerson, who tells his own story, makes reference to other English ships upon the Guinea coast, and from other sources it is evident that for some years the trade tempted numerous adventurers. Then, for two reasons, it declined : the supply of gold was not unlimited, and the negroes, seeing it eagerly competed for, raised their prices ; and the Portuguese increased their armed forces on the coast with a full determination to put down what they regarded as illegal competition. The later history of the Guinea trade will be referred to in a subsequent chapter.

The voyages above described raised an international question of immense importance to the future destiny of England. Before the return of John Lok in 1555 the Portuguese ambassador lodged with the English government a strong protest against the infringement of his master's rights. England at this time was under the rule of Queen Mary, whose marriage to Philip, the heir of Charles V., had but recently taken place. Philip used all his authority with his wife to secure her acquiescence with the Portuguese demands. As prospective King of Spain he saw that he must back to the utmost the validity of the Bulls of Alexander VI., for if the English were permitted to trade with Guinea they would next claim the same privilege in the West Indies. Mary somewhat reluctantly assented to her husband's views, and orders were given to the port authorities to stop all vessels fitting out for the Guinea voyage pending a thrashing-out of the whole matter in the Privy Council. That body, afraid to defy Philip openly, endorsed the prohibition. But although the Council repeatedly

---

[1] W. R. Scott, *Joint Stock Companies to 1720*, vol. ii. Cambridge, 1910, p. 4. Some of the tusks were of 90 lbs. weight.

admonished the merchants, and occasionally took security for their
obedience, it either was unable, or did not honestly desire, to put
an end to the traffic. The latter explanation is more probably the
correct one. There is good reason for believing, from analogy with
better-known transactions, that many of the Privy Councillors were
themselves financially interested in the voyages. The trade therefore
continued in spite of all prohibitions, and England thus effected its
first great breach in the world-monopoly of the Peninsular powers.
That this had happened under a Catholic and conservative regime
rendered it a more remarkable testimony to the existence of an uncontrollable national instinct for expansion ; and Philip, to judge from the
interest he showed in the matter, was quick to realize its importance
to himself.

The English were not the only infringers of the great monopoly.
Numerous French adventurers traded side by side with them both in
Brazil in the time of Henry VIII. and in Guinea at the period now
under discussion ; and French pirates and privateers were harrying
the Spaniards in the West Indies for many years before the English
rovers found their way thither. Francis I. had encouraged these
adventures originally in order to annoy his enemy Charles V. In
later years oceanic enterprises became a special occupation of the
Huguenots.

(iii) *The North-Eastern Discovery and the Muscovy Company.*

The idea of reaching Cathay by a northern voyage had lain dormant
since the middle part of the reign of Henry VIII. The earlier attempts
in this direction had been the work of a few enthusiasts at Bristol, or
of adventurers supported by royal patronage. They had all striven
to open up a passage by pushing northwards along the coast of
Labrador in the hope of finding a westward turning before the ice
became an insuperable obstacle. In the meantime the Portuguese
had successfully worked the South East Passage by the Cape of Good
Hope, and the Spaniards, led by Magellan, had traversed the South
West Passage or Straits of Magellan which, however, they had found
too dangerous for regular use. The north-east seemed therefore the
only quarter which yet remained to be explored if England was to
find a route of her own to the coveted traffic of the orient ; and the
need for some such expansion became increasingly apparent in the
years of stress which followed the death of Henry VIII.

Knowledge of the methods of discovery was still at a low ebb in
England, and in their perplexity the promoters of the new schemes
turned to a man who had once sailed under the English flag, and who
had since applied himself to the building up of a great reputation as
a scientific navigator and cosmographer. Sebastian Cabot, it will
be remembered, had entered the service of Spain in 1512. He had risen
to the office of Pilot-Major of that country, and in 1526 he had com-

manded an expedition intended to pass through the Straits of Magellan and cross the Pacific to the Spice Islands. To the disgust of the investors, but possibly with the secret connivance of Charles V., he did not enter the Pacific but devoted four years to exploring the basin of the River Plate. It was a possible way of approach to Peru, whose wealth was rumoured but had not at that date been reached by the Spaniards. Cabot was officially censured on his return, but retained the Emperor's confidence. Although he had gained no treasure he had indeed done arduous work in the Argentine, and his credit as an explorer and geographer was unimpaired. In 1548 he appeared to the adventurers of the English Privy Council as the master mind of Europe in maritime affairs, and the possessor of secrets which would provide an easy path to wealth for those to whom he would disclose them. They accordingly made him a tempting offer which induced him to depart secretly out of Spain and place his talents at their disposal.

Whether the north-eastern project was already evolved at the time of Sebastian Cabot's flight we do not know. Some years elapsed before it took effect, and in the meanwhile a scheme was discussed for a raid in conjunction with the French upon the Spanish riches in Peru—a plan foreshadowing that of Drake a generation later. Cabot himself betrayed this intention to Charles V.[1]—a fact which casts a revealing light upon his character—and it was never put into effect. But in 1552-3 the Cathay voyage by the north-east was taken seriously in hand, and a company came into existence under government patronage for the purpose of setting it forward.

This company was the first of a public character to be worked by means of a joint stock. The promoters, including the Marquis of Winchester, the Earls of Arundel, Bedford and Pembroke, and Sir William Cecil, together with Sir George Barnes, Thomas Gresham and most of the leading merchants of London, raised a capital of £6000 in £25 shares. The purchaser of a single share became a member of the Company, entitled, not to take a personal part in the trade, but to receive his proportion of the profits arising from expeditions sent out by the Company as a whole. This, the normal modern method of investment, was a novel one in sixteenth-century England. In the regulated companies, hitherto the universal type, every member had had to provide his own stock-in-trade and in most cases his own shipping, and to appoint his own factor to sell his goods overseas if it was not convenient for him to do so in person. In the new undertaking the great length of the prospective voyage and the very uncertain chances of success were probably the reasons which led to the adoption of the joint-stock organization. The Company began its career under the title of " The Merchants Adventurers of England for the discovery of lands, territories, isles, dominions and seignories unknown." Edward VI. undoubtedly granted it a charter of incorporation with a machinery

---

[1] His letter to the emperor is printed in Navarette, *Colección de Documentos inéditos para la Historia de la España*, vol. iii. p. 512.

of governor, consuls and assistants, but this document does not now exist.[1] The first governor was Sebastian Cabot.

Early in May, 1553, the Company's first expedition sailed out of the Thames. It consisted of the *Bona Esperanza*, 120 tons, the *Edward Bonaventure*, 160 tons, and the *Bona Confidentia*, 90 tons ; and each of the ships had a pinnace and a large boat to facilitate trading in shallow waters. Sir Hugh Willoughby, who had won his knighthood on the field during Somerset's invasion of Scotland, sailed in the *Esperanza* as Captain-General. Richard Chancellor, as Chief Pilot, went in the *Edward Bonaventure* and acted as second-in-command of the squadron. Sebastian Cabot, who was too old to go in person, drew up a set of ordinances for the voyage embodying much of the experience in discovery accumulated by the Peninsular nations. In particular he warned the crews against " conspiracies, partakings, factions, false tales and untrue reports," exhorting them to behave always as loyal and honourable men, " toward the common wealth of this noble realm and the advancement of you the travailers in this voyage, your wives and children."

The three ships sailed to the coast of Norway in company. Here a sudden storm separated Chancellor in the *Edward Bonaventure* from Willoughby with the other two ships. Willoughby pushed on, rounding the North Cape and sailing eastwards with a full determination to discover the passage to Cathay. On August 14, 1552, he sighted an unknown coast running north and south in the latitude of 72°. " Early in the morning we descried land," says his journal, " which land we bare withal, hoising out our boat to discover what land it might be : but the boat could not come to land, the water was so shoal, where was very much ice also, but there was no similitude of habitation." This was the coast of Novaia Zemlia, the great double island stretching northwards from the Siberian coast. But Willoughby, supposing it to be a promontory of the continent itself, attempted to round its northern extremity and push on to Cathay. Contrary winds retarded his progress, the *Confidentia* developed a serious leak, and the weather showed signs of an early approach of winter. Willoughby therefore decided to seek a haven where his two ships might lie securely. He had plenty of food and was still in good hopes of accomplishing the discovery in the following year. After examining the desolate northern shores for another month in search of a convenient resting place, he came to an anchor on September 18 in the mouth of the River Arzina on the Murman coast. Here, during the long winter of 1553-4, Sir Hugh Willoughby was frozen to death with every man of his crew. In the following summer Russian fishermen found the ships with the bodies in them, and also Sir Hugh's journal, from which we derive our account of the voyage.

Richard Chancellor, who never saw his chief again after the storm off the Norwegian coast, had better fortune. His ship, the *Edward*

---

[1] Williamson, *Maritime Enterprise*, 1485-1558, p. 312.

Bonaventure, was the largest and most strongly manned of the squadron. Failing to hear news of Willoughby at Vardo, the Norwegian fishing port which marked the extreme boundary of European knowledge, he determined to pursue the discovery alone. Some Scotsmen whom he met at Vardo attempted to dissuade him, repeating to him what they had learnt of the terrors of the Arctic winter ; but " persuading himself that a man of valour could not commit a more dishonourable part than, for fear of danger, to avoid and shun great attempts, he was nothing at all changed or discouraged with the speeches and words of the Scots, remaining stedfast and immutable in his first resolution : determining either to bring that to pass which was first intended, or else to die the death."

" That which was first intended " was the opening up in some new country of a profitable trade for his employers ; and, to the extent of accomplishing so much, Chancellor was successful. Keeping closer to the coast than Willoughby had done on his eastward passage, he discovered the entrance to the White Sea at about the same time that his chief was examining the shores of Novaia Zemlia. The geography of these regions was entirely unknown to Europeans, as the fantastic maps of the preceding period testify ; and Chancellor may well have supposed that here was the mouth of a passage which might lead him to his goal in the Far East. He therefore sailed south-wards into the White Sea, and at its southern extremity sighted an open boat full of barbarians who, never having seen such a ship as the *Edward Bonaventure,* fled in terror before it. Chancellor pursued and overtook them, finding them " in great fear, as men half dead." Reassured by his gentle treatment they conducted him to their village of Nenoksa, some thirty miles from Archangel. Here the English were well received, and learned, to their surprise, that the ruler of these regions was Ivan the Terrible, the Tsar of the vaguely known empire of Muscovy.

Muscovy or Russia had at that time no outlet either on the Baltic or the Black Sea. It had been visited by the Easterlings, who used the land route through Poland ; but no one had hitherto thought of approaching it by the Arctic north-east. Chancellor, however, lost no time in realizing the importance of his discovery. The winter was now setting in, rendering further voyaging impossible for that season, and he employed the time of inactivity in travelling southwards by sledge to Moscow. There he was received by Ivan in the midst of a magnificent court, and presented to him the letters of recommendation with which Edward VI. had furnished the expedition. The Tsar, accustomed to the cringing servility of his own subjects, was pleased with the fearless demeanour of the Englishman, who behaved in all respects as the ambassador of a sovereign power. He wrote a reply to Edward VI., extending a cordial invitation to Englishmen to trade in his dominions. With this Chancellor returned to his ship, and sailed for England as soon as the weather permitted.

Chancellor's arrival with his news in 1554 marks a very definite forward stride in the history of our maritime expansion. For the first time an English expedition had accomplished a new discovery bringing with it the immediate acquisition of commercial advantages. Edward VI. had died shortly after the departure of the first expedition. Chancellor returned too late in 1554 for a new voyage to be set forward in that year. It was in 1555 therefore that the Company despatched its second expedition, but before this it applied for a new charter of privileges from Queen Mary, who had just wedded Philip of Spain. Philip, as we have seen, strongly discountenanced the Guinea voyages which were going on at this period. But towards the White Sea trade he adopted a different attitude. It was evident that it conflicted with none of the existing interests of Spain or Portugal, and many of its promoters were influential men who were already feeling sore at the prohibition of their African adventures. Philip therefore determined to conciliate the mercantile interest by giving his hearty approval to the new trade. In February, 1555, the Company secured a new charter in the names of Philip and Mary wherein its monopoly of northern enterprise was clearly confirmed. The discovery of the North-East Passage now became a secondary object with the adventurers, although it still seemed possible that Willoughby, of whose fate nothing was yet known, might return with news of this achievement also.

During the next three years the Company, henceforward commonly known as the Muscovy or Russia Company, consolidated its position in the newly discovered regions. Chancellor sailed again for the White Sea in 1555. He took with him factors who were to reside in the country and collect Russian goods for transport to England. He established trading stations at Moscow, at Colmogro near the mouth of the Dwina, and at Vologda, about half way between the White Sea and Moscow. He learned also of the finding of the bodies of Willoughby and his men, and recovered some of the goods from their ships. The Tsar made a grant of privileges to the Company's servants, promising freedom from paying customs, freedom from arrest, and full jurisdiction for the chief agent over all Englishmen in Russia. Chancellor remained in Russia for the winter of 1555-6 in order to complete these arrangements.

In 1556 three ships sailed for Russia. One of them, a pinnace named the *Serchthrift*, pushed eastwards along the coast of Siberia in order to continue the search for the passage. Her commander, Stephen Borough, reached the island of Vaigats before turning back at the approach of winter. Thenceforward no more discoveries took place in this direction until the voyage of Arthur Pet and Charles Jackman in 1580. Richard Chancellor sailed for England once more in 1556 in the *Edward Bonaventure*, having in his company the *Philip and Mary* and Willoughby's two ships the *Bona Esperanza* and the *Bona Confidentia*. The voyage was disastrous. The *Esperanza* and the *Confidentia* were lost with all hands in a great gale off the Norwegian coast. The *Edward*, after struggling against adverse weather for four months, was wrecked on the Scottish coast in November. Chancellor and many of the crew were drowned, but a Russian ambassador whom he was bringing to England got safely to shore and travelled by land to London. The *Philip and Mary*, the only ship of the squadron which survived, did not reach the Thames until the spring of 1557.

In spite of these losses the Muscovy Company prospered during its first years, obtaining in exchange for English cloth such valuable commodities as wax, train-oil, tallow, furs, cordage and timber for masts and spars. The last two items were especially important to the national well-being at a time when the quarrel with the Hansa threatened a stoppage of supplies from the Baltic. But the period of unassailable monopoly was a short one. In 1558 Ivan the Terrible captured the port of Narva on the Baltic, and Russia obtained an outlet to civilization much more accessible than that provided by the ice-bound White Sea. The competition of English interlopers using the Baltic route, coupled with the machinations of the Easterlings and the misconduct of some of its own servants, caused the Company to fall upon bad times during the latter half of the sixteenth century. Its extension of English trade to Persia under the leadership of Anthony Jenkinson will be dealt with in a later chapter.

CHAPTER V

GENERAL SURVEY OF ENGLISH EXPANSION UNDER ELIZABETH, 1558-1603

WITH the accession of Elizabeth the task of presenting a justly proportioned picture of English expansion becomes a difficult one—more difficult perhaps than in any other period of our history. The national energy sought its outlets in many different directions at the same moment. Some of these experiments were mutually destructive, yet all were closely interwoven with the fortunes of the others. The daring minds which shaped the destinies of the time chose as their sphere the whole world of practical affairs ; they refused to specialize, to concentrate their efforts in a single narrow groove. That alone is sufficient to differentiate them sharply from the leaders of our own day, in which versatility is commonly mistrusted as a sign of weakness. The Elizabethans scorned such a doctrine. Variety to them was the salt of life. Anthony Jenkinson served his apprenticeship to adventure among the corsairs of the Levant, and occupied his prime in diplomatic work at Moscow, in traversing the plains of Russia and outwitting the bandits of Central Asia ; Frobisher bartered beads for gold dust on the Guinea coast, then sought a passage to Asia through the northern ice, converted that undertaking without a thought of inconsistency into the exploitation of a gold mine, sailed next with Drake to raid the Spanish colonies, commanded a squadron against the Armada, and received his death-wound as an officer of the queen in a land battle on the coast of Brittany ; John Davis reached a record latitude in the Arctic, lost four-fifths of his crew in an attempt to pass the Straits of Magellan, and ended his life in fight with Japanese pirates in the eastern sea. So it was with them all. Not one of the great names of the time is to be identified with one exclusive line of action. It was their strength and their weakness that they made the English name ring through the world as it had never done before, and yet left of definite, finished, lasting work but the merest fragment. But the moral has ever balanced the material in the scales of history, and the brilliant Elizabethans were an indispensable prelude to the sober toilers of the seventeenth century who garnered the fruits of their achievements.

Even to classify the lines of action of the time is not an easy matter. We may arrange them under more than half-a-dozen different heads and still find adventures outstanding, such as Ralegh's expedition to Guiana, which refuse to take their place in the scheme. But some provisional system is essential if we are to view the era as a whole ; without it we lose ourselves in a maze of glittering detail and emerge with no formed conception of its meaning.

Beginning therefore with the first decade of the queen's reign, we find that with the government committed to Protestantism armed trading in the tropics takes a fresh lease of life. The merchants who had sailed illicitly to the Gold Coast under Philip and Mary continued their undertaking with the approval of the queen. But they found that as the years passed they had ever to do more fighting and less trading, and the early series of Guinea voyages came to an end with George Fenner's expedition of 1566-7, which was a continuous conflict with the negroes and Portuguese, culminating in a desperate battle off the Azores on the homeward passage. In the same period John Hawkins found a new use for Guinea as a slave-producing area. He collected his living merchandise by guile and by force and employed the like means to sell it in the West Indies in defiance of the Spanish authorities. Twice he did this with great success. His third expedition ended in the disaster of San Juan de Ulua in 1568. Thus within a year of each other the two experiments in trading sword in hand came to a conclusion.

There followed a period of general reprisals for Spanish and Portuguese exclusiveness. This unofficial warfare was waged partially in home waters by privateers of all nations patronized although disavowed by the English authorities, and more particularly by English adventurers beyond the Atlantic. Drake in 1570-1 and 1572-3 took Spanish ships in the West Indies, landed on Panama and captured a treasure-train, and came successfully home with his spoils. Oxenham imitated his example in 1576, and was captured and hanged as a pirate. Andrew Barker of Bristol, having been robbed whilst trading legitimately, sought his remedy in the same course a year later, and also lost his life. Then Drake in 1577-80 passed the Straits of Magellan, swept up enormous booty on the Peruvian coast, and returned triumphantly by the Indian Ocean and the Cape of Good Hope. The unofficial war by private individuals continued even after the regular conflict between Elizabeth and Philip had been begun. Thomas Cavendish in 1586-8 repeated Drake's exploit of circumnavigation, returning with much captured treasure a month after the dispersal of the Armada. These are but the outstanding names amongst a horde of adventurers of all classes from the noble to the frankly criminal, who, before and after the declaration of war, infested the routes by which Spanish and Portuguese commerce traversed the ocean.

In the meantime men of less flamboyant tastes were seeking by exploration to find a route to the wealth of the East which they could legitimately call their own, and which they could pursue without coming into collision with the original discoverers. Sir Humphrey Gilbert and Michael Lok began to preach anew the doctrine of the North West Passage, ransacking all knowledge theological, geographical and historical for proofs of what they so ardently desired to believe. Lok and his friend Martin Frobisher were first in the field, the latter sailing in 1576 and returning with news of a channel leading westwards to the north of Labrador. But the prospect of discovering gold in this region diverted the energy of the adventurers, and the Company which Michael Lok had formed fell into bankruptcy when the gold mine proved to be illusory. The London merchants financed two more attempts to find a northern passage to Cathay. In 1580 the Muscovy Company despatched two ships to the north-east along the Siberian coast ; and in 1585-7 a private syndicate sent John Davis on three successive voyages which resulted in the exploration of Davis Strait and the correct delineation of Greenland upon the map.

The lure of the East drew men also to penetrate Asia by land explorations. In 1558 Anthony Jenkinson, succeeding Richard Chancellor as chief pioneer of the Muscovy Company, journeyed from Moscow to the Caspian Sea and thence to Bokhara, returning with much commercial intelligence. In 1561 he penetrated farther along the same route and opened up a trade for his employers in Persia, acting as an English ambassador in the same way as Chancellor had done at Moscow. Other servants of the Company followed in his steps until 1580, and the Persian trade, although always hazardous, promised for a time to be lucrative, until wars between the Turks and the Persians extinguished it. Baffled but not yet defeated, the English made one more attempt to traffic with the East by a land route. In 1583 Ralph Fitch and John Newbery penetrated through Syria to Ormuz and thence to Goa, the Portuguese headquarters in India. Here they suffered imprisonment, but escaped to continue their eastward wanderings. At Futtehpore they parted company, Newbery never to be heard of again and Fitch going on to Burma and Siam. He reached London again in 1591.

The history of English colonization begins also under Elizabeth. The grants of Henry VII. to the Bristol syndicates had contained vague language suggesting the foundation of settlements overseas. But these were probably for commercial purposes only, nor do we know that the suggestions were ever carried into effect. Sir Humphrey Gilbert contemplated the planting of a colony in the neighbourhood of Newfoundland, presumably as a base for the discovery of the North-West Passage. In his voyage of 1583 he lost his largest ship and all his stores before deciding upon a site, and he himself was drowned on the homeward passage. Then Ralegh his half-brother took up the task, financing and directing two serious attempts to plant a self-supporting colony in Virginia. The expressed purpose of the promoters was to provide homes for the surplus population who could find no employment in England.   The first batch of colonists deserted the undertaking after a year's experience ; the second moved into the interior of the continent and were heard of no more.   The Spanish war precluded any further prosecution of the design until the reign of James I.

The war itself came as the climax of all the disorders upon the seas since the decay of the ancient Burgundian alliance.   It had other causes in addition—the revolt of the Netherlands, countenanced by Elizabeth, and the determination of the Catholic leaders of Europe to reclaim England to the old religion.   It began with a sudden embargo upon all English vessels in Spanish ports, followed, by way of reprisal, by Drake's great West Indian raid of 1585-6.   Philip II. then prepared to invade England, and Drake smote his unready armaments in Cadiz in 1587, postponing the great undertaking to the following year.   In 1588 the Armada sailed, focussing in the nine days' fight in the Channel all the issues which had so long disturbed the world. It fled, beaten and disgraced, without landing a man of Parma's army, but the war continued for another fifteen years.   The English failed to strike home upon the heels of their great success.   The Spaniards, realizing at length the incredibly defenceless condition of their scattered empire, bestirred themselves to provide armaments suitable to its needs.   So on the English side we have a series of isolated expeditions without continuity of plan, and on the Spanish a slow emergence from the depths, a persistent evolution of a policy of national defence, which might have led to a decision reversing that of 1588 had not the burden proved too crushing to be borne.   The disappearance of all the original actors from the scene left the way open for the signing of a purely negative peace in 1604.

Out of the war and its revelation of Spanish impotence by sea sprang the one permanent material achievement of Elizabethan expansion— the push to the East by the normal route round the Cape of Good Hope. Tentative expeditions preceded the formation of the East India Company.   In 1582 Edward Fenton led a squadron intended to trade with China, but sailed no further than the coast of Brazil.   Next, in 1591, Sir James Lancaster doubled the Cape and traversed the Indian Ocean.   He and a few survivors struggled home after terrible sufferings ; but he had proved the voyage to be a possibility.   Benjamin Wood again sailed for China in 1596, but his three ships were lost on the voyage.   Finally, in 1599-1600, the merchants of London, seeing the success of the Dutch in a similar venture, formed a joint-stock company and obtained a charter of monopoly from the queen.   In 1601 Lancaster sailed in command of the first expedition of the East India Company.

Such are the principal categories into which we may divide the deeds of the Elizabethan adventurers.   The categories themselves are distinct yet interdependent, some arising from the operation of others, some hampered and checked by the same.   Can we find any common factor running through them all, with reference to which we may combine them into a united picture of national development ? Religion has been suggested as such a common factor. Religion had undoubtedly a great influence, but it fails to answer the test as a touchstone of Elizabethan history. Protestantism in the latter half of the sixteenth century was on the defensive, and the Elizabethans were aggressive in every fibre of their being. Had their religion been the mainspring of their actions they would have preached it with missionary zeal ; but of this we find little trace. Again, the thirst for commerce suggests itself as the guiding motive. It was certainly long and deeply implanted in the English character, as our previous history had shown. It carries us a little further than religion ; but yet it will not serve to account for every department of Elizabethan enterprise. There was no profit to be drawn from the Virginian colony, neither had the merchants as a class any sympathy with the earlier proceedings of Drake and the western school of privateers.

Nevertheless there is a common motive power running through every phase of the Elizabethan story, although it is not an easy one to define. The English of the later Middle Age had been superficially an intelligent race, intensely active, interesting themselves keenly in all their material pursuits, yet evincing little taste for pure learning or the speculative employments of the mind. Upon them came the Reformation and then the full force of the Renaissance, shattering all the preconceived system in which they had lived, and which they had taken for granted without any deep examination of its validity. Their world, religious, social, commercial, geographical, was all to make anew, and in setting about the task they displayed the vast stores of mental and moral energy which had slumbered during the centuries of stagnation ; it was this energy which, once the dams were broken, burst forth in an uncontrollable flood, and produced the astonishing phenomena of the Elizabethan age. It was fortunate that in England the Reformation became a settled question before the touch of the Renaissance revealed its power. So was a long civil war averted and the way left clear for national energy to turn to national expansion, the resettlement of agriculture and industry, and the literary exuberance which gave England for the time the pride of place among the cultivated nations of the world. In the sphere of action the accumulated force spent itself prodigally in many experiments until the men of the seventeenth century found means to control and direct it along lines of permanent progress.

One point of view we should beware of, and that is the one which emphasizes the romance of the Elizabethan adventurers. Nothing tends so much to give a false impression of the men themselves, the work they did, and its lesson for us their descendants. The majority of them were soundly practical men, trying with all their faculties to comprehend and make their profit of a world in which many things were obscure. The attempt to give a romantic colouring to their achievements involves the necessity of selecting certain facts and rejecting or minimising others of equal importance, and so of rendering the whole picture untrue. Those few who may justly be treated as romantic characters certainly had not a preponderating influence upon the fortunes of their time. In this respect the Elizabethan period differs in no way from other periods of our history.

CHAPTER VI

ARMED TRADE AND REPRISALS[1]

(i) The Gold Coast Trade and Anglo-Portuguese Hostilities

QUEEN MARY had prohibited voyages to Guinea, and they had never-theless taken place. Queen Elizabeth refused to prohibit them, and the volume of trade expanded. In the first two years after her accession the African expeditions increased in numbers. " They keep sending more ships from here round Cape Verde," reported the Spanish ambassador ; and in 1561 the Portuguese government sent an envoy to protest. He was followed by others in 1562 and 1564. Since they all said much the same thing and received the same answer, the three negotiations may be summarized as follows. The ambassadors claimed that the entire Guinea coast was subject to the Portuguese crown, which had explored and conquered it with the expenditure of blood and treasure, and maintained occupation by means of garrisons in some places and of trade and ecclesiastical activity in others. They declared that the King of Portugal did not allow unrestricted trade even to his own subjects, none of whom might sail to Guinea without special licence ; and that he could not permit any intrusion by foreigners, who would disturb the negroes and ruin the whole system. The English answer, made by the Queen and Sir William Cecil, was that they would respect these claims in places effectively ruled by the Portuguese, but that such places did not by any means constitute the whole coast of Guinea. If the negroes were " under the obedience " of the King of Portugal, he had only to forbid them to trade with the English and so settle the matter ; meanwhile the Queen would not prohibit her merchants from visiting any places where the people were willing to trade with them. In practice this amounted to a prohibition of El Mina, the Portuguese stronghold on the Gold Coast, and licence to trade everywhere else, for it was only under Portuguese guns that the negroes would not do business with the English. Cecil, the inspirer of this policy, was exploiting the doctrine of effective occupation in an

---

[1] This chapter has been re-written for the 3rd edition in accordance with the new evidence on many transactions that has come to light in recent years. For an indication of the new sources of information see " Authorities for Part II.," pp. 147-50.

extreme form. It should be noted that the Portuguese chose to defend their position on the same ground, by arguing that the occupation was effective. They did not appeal to prior discovery or the papal donation.

Meanwhile the English expeditions continued, and the Portuguese send out armed ships to guard the Guinea Coast. Although war between the two countries was not officially declared, a state of war on the sea nevertheless existed, not only in African but in European waters. The products of the East and of Africa were distributed to southern Europe from Lisbon, but to northern Europe from Antwerp. The vessels conveying them had to pass through the English Channel, where they formed rich prizes for English merchants making reprisal for ships lost to the Portuguese in Guinea. Some particulars chosen from many transactions of the 1560's may serve to illustrate what went on.

The old Guinea syndicate which had sent out Wyndham and John Lok in the reign of Mary continued to operate. In 1561 Lok again commanded/ their expedition, which consisted of two ships and two pinnaces from the Navy. In spite of the vessels being twice scattered and driven back by gales before clearing the English coast, they carried out the voyage and returned with profitable cargoes. The Queen, in her public capacity, was an investor in this and subsequent voyages, receiving a share of the profits proportionate to the value of the naval ships taking part. This profit was not paid to the Queen as an individual, but to the Treasurer of the Navy, and was used for the upkeep of the fleet. Next year, 1562-3, the syndicate sent out two ships belonging to the Navy. They had some hard fighting with the galleys and other armed vessels which Portugal was now stationing on the coast, but succeeded in collecting cargoes nevertheless. In 1564 the same adventurers despatched three ships, of which one was destroyed by an accidental explosion of her magazine and another was captured by the Portuguese. In spite of these losses, the third ship, the famous *Minion*, returned with a lading of gold and ivory that more than paid for all, although only a remnant of her crew survived to bring it home. Other adventurers were also at work. The brothers William and George Winter, members of the Navy Board, were among them. In 1565 a ship of theirs named the *Mary Fortune* was sunk by a Portuguese force on the Liberian coast, or Grain Coast, as it was then called. They retaliated by extending the war to home waters and capturing Portuguese shipping in the Channel. Another English ship was captured while watering at the Azores on her homeward voyage in 1566. At the end of the same year George Fenner sailed from Portsmouth with the *Castle of Comfort* and two smaller ships. He had continuous fighting at the Cape Verde Islands and on the adjacent mainland coast, and seems to have thought it unwise to push on to the Gold Coast. Portugal indeed was now taking the matter very seriously and sending out numerous ships-of-war to make good her monopoly. Fenner retired to the Azores, probably to lie in wait for homeward-bound Portuguese merchantmen, and while there fought a celebrated action with seven Portuguese armed ships, which he defeated and drove off in disgrace. Fenner came home with credit, but apparently without profit, and it was evident that the palmy days of the Gold Coast trade were over. But in the meanwhile a new enterprise was being developed on the nearer part of the Guinea Coast.

(ii) *The Enterprise of Sir John Hawkins*

John Hawkins (knighted in 1588), the son of Henry VIII.'s William Hawkins who had made voyages to Guinea and Brazil, carried on a trade with the Spanish colony of the Canary Islands. This trade was quite legitimate, since the Canaries had been in Spanish possession at the time of the Treaty of Medina del Campo in 1489, whereby England and Spain each opened the whole of its dominions to the trade of the other's subjects. The Canaries had a specially close connection with England. In 1479 the islands, then for the most part uncolonized, were made over by Portugal to Spain. In the next seventeen years the conquest of the aboriginal Guanches and the settlement of European colonists was carried out ; and it is on record that many English adventurers took part in this process and remained as landowners in the new colony. The Hawkins family had long been engaged in the Canaries trade, and John Hawkins was on friendly terms with some of the principal people of the islands. From them he learned particulars of the trade and condition of the Spanish colonies in the West.

The trade was concentrated into two great annual convoys, the *flota*, which carried goods to Mexico and brought away that country's produce, chiefly silver ; and the *galeones*, which went to Cartagena on the Spanish Main and then on to Nombre de Dios on the Isthmus of Panama, whither gold and silver were forwarded from Chile and Peru. These two fleets connected with a great quantity of local shipping which concentrated the produce of the West Indian islands, the Spanish Main and Central America at the focal points in direct communication with Europe. All kinds of manufactured goods were taken out from Spain, their cost to the colonists being greatly increased by the slowness of the convoys, the expenses of the armed escort and the multitude of high officers employed, the charges for insurance, and the general atmosphere of regulation, monopoly and bribery that overhung the whole business. The shipping of slaves to the colonial plantations was a separate trade. It was done by means of licences for fixed numbers of negroes granted from time to time to contractors, who obtained their cargoes from the Portuguese in Guinea and delivered them to specified ports in Spanish colonies. The contractors were sometimes, but not always, Spanish merchants ; sometimes the licences were granted to Portuguese or Genoese. But it was illegal to ship slaves without a licence, and the monopoly thus created again enhanced the price of the

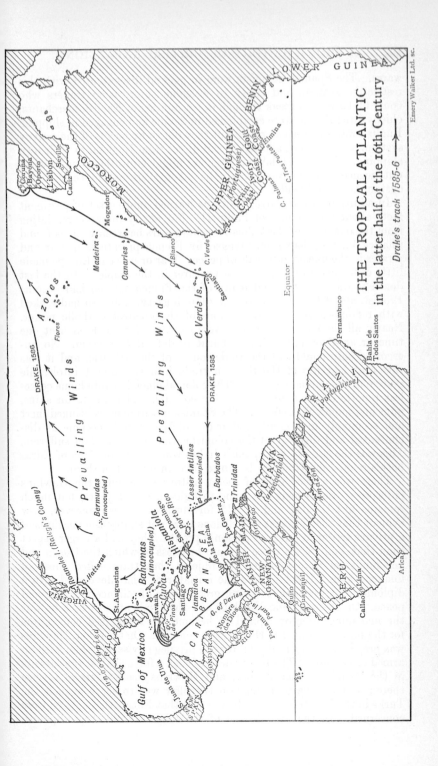

THE TROPICAL ATLANTIC
in the latter half of the 16th. Century

Drake's track 1585-6 ⟶

Emery Walker Ltd. sc.

LOWER GUINEA

UPPER GUINEA
(Portuguese)

Grain | Ivory | Gold
Coast | Coast | Coast

BENIN

C. Palmas

C. Tres Puntas

C. Elmina

MOROCCO

Coruña
Bayona
Oporto
Lisbon
Seville
Cadiz

Mogador

Madeira

Canaries

C. Blanco

C. Verde

Arguin

C. Verde Is.

Santiago

Equator

Azores

Flores

Prevailing Winds

DRAKE, 1586

Prevailing Winds

DRAKE, 1585

Bermudas
(unoccupied)

Roanoke I. (Ralegh's Colony)

C. Hatteras

VIRGINIA

St. Augustine

FLORIDA
(unoccupied)

Gulf of Mexico

S. Juan de Ulua

NEW
SPAIN

HONDURAS

COSTA RICA

Bahamas
(unoccupied)

Havana

Cuba

I. de Pinos

Santiago

Jamaica

Hispaniola

San Domingo

Porto Rico

Lesser Antilles
(unoccupied)

Barbados

Trinidad

C A R I B B E A N   S E A

G. of Darien

Nombre de Dios

Panama

Pearl Is.

Rio de la Hacha

Cartagena

La Guaira

SPANISH MAIN

Orinoco

NEW
GRANADA

GUIANA
(unoccupied)

Amazon

Quito

Guayaquil

PERU

Callao

Lima

Arica

B R A Z I L
(Portuguese)

Pernambuco

Bahia de
Todos Santos

wares. The Spanish colonists were in general discontented with this restrictive system, and ready to welcome enterprising traders who could find a way to break through it. A number of English merchants, chiefly Bristol men, were established in Seville and engaged in shipping English wares to the colonies ; but they did so by means of the convoy system, and were not allowed to sail direct from England in their own shipping. By Spanish law no foreigner might go to the colonies without licence, and no goods might be taken there except through the custom-house of Seville.

In addition to the above, Hawkins learned another set of pertinent facts about the colonies of Philip II. For nearly forty years, dating from the outbreak of the Valois-Hapsburg wars between Francis I. and Charles V., they had been ravaged by French privateers in war and pirates in the uneasy intervals of peace. War or peace in Europe made little difference to the French adventurer in the tropics. In the last dozen years of that period many of the French seamen had become Protestants of the uncompromising Calvinist type, and so had sacked with redoubled zest the possessions of the greatest Catholic power. Nearly all the colonial seaports were captured by the French at one time or another, pillaged, and burnt in default of ransom. No unescorted ship could sail the trade-routes of the Atlantic, and it was this that had forced the Spanish trade into the almost intolerable system of the annual convoys. The colonial officials wrote home ceaseless reports of the enormities of the corsairs, and requests for ships, guns and money for defence. The Spanish government continued inert and seemingly indifferent, and many of the officials became as discontented and disloyal as the colonists who were the chief sufferers. This was the state of the Spanish Indies when at the opening of Elizabeth's reign John Hawkins began to take an interest in them.

There was a good deal of secret history underlying the Hawkins enterprise. Some of it has come to light in recent years, but much remains unfathomed and a field for surmise. It is, however, now evident that the Hawkins expeditions were not simply the ventures of a private trader in quest of personal profit. They had a larger aspect than that, and were a piece of state business in which the Queen and her ministers were involved for objects that transcended those of financial gain. Hawkins was the initiator of what developed into a diplomatic experiment involving great issues of alliance and war and peace. On the one hand Hawkins and the syndicate of which he was the managing director aspired to become the recognized contractors for the supply of slaves to the Spanish colonies. On the other, Hawkins was prepared to pay Philip II. for the privilege by serving him with an armed naval force. The King's need of such a force against the corsairs in the Caribbean was obvious, and Hawkins made offers of service there ; but on one occasion also the offer was to serve against the Turks in the Mediterranean. It was here that Elizabeth and Cecil were concerned. In the first decade of the reign the old Anglo-Spanish alliance still subsisted, yielding solid advantages to both countries. The success of Hawkins's scheme would have confirmed the alliance against the forces which were threatening to dissolve it, besides increasing the sea-power and economic wealth of England in a time of need. In the early years of Elizabeth, it should be remembered, the country's independence seemed threatened not by Spain but by Mary Stuart and the Valois monarchy of France.

In 1559 John Hawkins married Katherine, the daughter of Benjamin Gonson, Treasurer of the Navy, and three years later was able to set out on his first western venture. His backers included not only Gonson, the senior officer of the Navy Board, but also another of its members, Sir William Winter, and the merchants Sir Lionel Ducket and Sir Thomas Lodge, who were already engaging in the Gold Coast trade. Hawkins sailed with four ships in October, 1562, going first to the Canaries, where he had conference with his ally, the merchant Pedro de Ponte at Teneriffe. This man sent word to certain places in the West Indies that Hawkins might be expected with slaves and English goods for sale in the following year. Hawkins meanwhile went on to Cape Verde and thence to Sierra Leone. Between these points he acquired Guinea pepper and ivory and some 400 slaves. The Portuguese government said that he captured his cargoes by methods of piracy, but Hawkins's own men declared that he bought and paid for everything he had. It appears that he took some of his negroes by force of arms and purchased others from the Portuguese slavers. He sent home one ship with the non-human produce and crossed the Atlantic with the other three and a Portuguese vessel picked up on the African coast. Again he was accused of piratical seizure of this ship, but his own evidence was that he lawfully chartered her. She was sailed by her own crew throughout the voyage, which hardly suggests that they were the victims of piracy.

With guidance from a Spanish pilot provided by Pedro de Ponte, Hawkins reached Hispaniola and there traded at Isabella and Monte Christi on its northern coast. The Spanish authorities made a show of disapproval, but were in reality quite willing to allow the trade. Hawkins sold his negroes and his English manufactures, laded his three ships with sugar and hides, and also carried away pearls and gold. He put some of the surplus goods into the Portuguese vessel and some into a Spaniard chartered in Hispaniola. The one ship sailed to Lisbon and the other to Seville, and at either place the authorities confiscated Hawkins's cargo. But the loss was not serious compared with the gains brought home by Hawkins in his three English ships. The voyage left him and his syndicate well satisfied and hopeful of greater things.

Hawkins had acted without permission from Philip II., although he hoped to obtain it. No doubt he reasoned that the best way to qualify for the King's serious consideration was to show that he really could carry on the trade proposed. Philip's reaction was unfavourable. He had so far shown no ability to defend his colonies against the French corsairs, but he could not admit the English. Pride forbade it, and the fear of Protestant heresy, and the instinct for monopoly which was the governing motive in all the old colonial empires. He sent out positive orders to all colonial governors that they were not to allow the English to trade.

Although the Queen's Navy officials had been partners in the first voyage, there is no evidence that she was directly concerned in it. She undoubtedly was in the second. The list of investors who fitted out Hawkins in 1564 includes not only the Navy men and some London merchants, but four of the Queen's privy councillors (Sir William Cecil, the Lord Admiral, and the Earls of Pembroke and Leicester) and the Queen herself. The merchants were again those who were conducting the Gold Coast trade. The old idea that they were hostile to Hawkins because slaving upset the negroes and spoiled the gold trade is no longer tenable. In fact Hawkins never went south of Sierra Leone for his slaves, and that place is hundreds of miles short of the nearest point on the Gold Coast.

Hawkins sailed again in October, 1564, having on this occasion a large vessel from the Navy, the *Jesus of Lubeck*, in addition to his private ships. The *Jesus*, valued at £2000, represented the government's, or, as contemporaries put it, the Queen's investment in the enterprise. Hawkins had an interview with the Queen before sailing, and officially described himself in the course of the voyage as her officer in command of her squadron. He went first to Teneriffe for a meeting with Pedro de Ponte, who would notify prospective customers in the West. Thence he sailed to Africa to collect slaves on the Cape Verde-Sierra Leone coastline. There he had business dealings with the Portuguese slavers, one of whom testified that he heard an Englishman declare that the slave-contract now belonged to "the realm of England" and John Hawkins. We know that the Spanish government gave no such concession, but it is clear that Hawkins's people were confident of obtaining it ; and it would seem that the Queen and her ministers shared the belief that something more than an illicit trade would proceed from the venture. In the West, Hawkins went this time to the Spanish Main, the coast of what is now Venezuela and Colombia. There he sold his negroes at Borburata, Curaçoa, Cabo de la Vela and Rio de la Hacha. The general course of events was that the Spanish officials made a token resistance to Hawkins's demand for trade, putting up in some cases a sham fight in which no one was hurt, and then submitting to what they described as his overwhelming force. In reality the officials were as eager as the planters to buy negroes and English manufactures. Hawkins passed up the North American coast after quitting the Caribbean, visited a struggling French colony in Florida, and reached England in 1565 after a very profitable voyage.

Philip II. was highly incensed at the conduct of his officers in the West, and at least one colonial governor was sent home for trial. Meanwhile Hawkins was carrying on conversations with Guzman de Silva,

the Spanish ambassador in London, seeking to open up a new path to
recognition by the Spanish government. In 1566 there was much talk
between them of Hawkins serving Spain with an armed squadron in
the Mediterranean, and Hawkins, in anticipation of the reward for such
service, was quietly fitting out another expedition for Africa and the
Indies. It was on a smaller scale, and Hawkins did not lead it in person.
In his place went Captain John Lovell, accompanied by Francis Drake,
who here made his first appearance in events of national importance.
Lovell made the usual round voyage in 1566-7, but with less success
than Hawkins. He fought the Portuguese on the African coast, where
Hawkins seems to have bluffed them amicably into selling slaves, and at
Rio de la Hacha he was defrauded of payment for ninety negroes whom
he delivered to the planters. At other places he may have done better,
but there is no record. Hawkins did not employ him again.

The negotiations with Guzman de Silva broke down, and Philip
decided finally against having anything to do with Hawkins. Nevertheless Hawkins prepared a greater expedition than ever in 1567, to
which the Queen contributed two ships, the *Jesus* and the *Minion*.
De Silva protested to the Queen against any new intrusion in the
Indies, but was assured that Hawkins was only going to Africa. In
fact there were two Portuguese renegades in England with a tale of a
rich African gold mine. Hawkins conveniently based his preparations
on this story, which all concerned professed to believe. Then, when the
ships were ready to sail, the Portuguese decamped to France, and the
Queen gave Hawkins permission to carry out the usual slaving expedition, which had perhaps been intended from the outset.

On this voyage (1567-9) Hawkins started with six ships, and was
joined by two French crews on the African coast. Since he had last
been there, war with the Portuguese had become undisguised, and he
attacked them wherever he met them. At Sierra Leone he completed
his cargoes by assisting a native king to defeat another and taking some
of the prisoners in payment. He crossed the Atlantic and again passed
along the Spanish Main. One or two of the officials made an effort to
enforce the King's orders, and at Rio de la Hacha Hawkins had to
storm the town before he could do business. But in general the
colonists were glad to see him and, notably at Santa Marta, the resistance was farcical and staged solely with a view to making a plausible
report to the Spanish government. At Cartagena, however, the
governor's refusal was genuine, and the place was too strong to be captured. Hawkins therefore sailed for home, having sold most of his
lading. Off the western end of Cuba a storm damaged the *Jesus of
Lubeck* so seriously that she could not cross the Atlantic without
repair. More bad weather drove the fleet deep into the Gulf of Mexico,
and in default of any other refuge Hawkins unwillingly entered San
Juan de Ulua, the port from which all the treasure of Mexico was
shipped to Spain. At that moment a *flota* was expected, to carry away
the year's output of silver.

Hawkins was in a difficult position. He needed victuals, and he was obliged to carry out repairs. If the *flota* arrived while the *Jesus* was dismantled, he would be at the Spaniards' mercy, for he would be greatly outnumbered both in ships and men. He occupied the batteries on the low island which covered the anchorage, and assured the town's officials that they had nothing to fear. Next day the *flota* appeared, thirteen ships, having on board Don Martin Enriquez, the new Viceroy of Mexico. With the batteries in his possession, Hawkins could have kept the Spaniards out, but it would have been an act of war contrary to the Queen's policy and his own. He therefore admitted them on a solemn pledge to abstain from hostilities and to permit him to complete his repairs and victualling. The Viceroy, the personal representative of the King of Spain, and the guardian of his honour, was a party to the agreement. He entered the port, and two days later he made a sudden and unprovoked attack on the English ships. The *Jesus* was unrigged and impossible to move. Hawkins escaped in the *Minion* after burning and sinking the two best Spanish ships. Drake got away in a small vessel, and the others were lost. This was the fight of San Juan de Ulua, which, more than any other single event, made the English seamen enemies of Spain. Hawkins found the *Minion* devoid of victuals and crowded with over two hundred survivors. Half of them elected to take their chance in Mexico and were landed, to become, with a few exceptions, prisoners of the Spaniards. The other half sailed for England with Hawkins, and the great majority died of hunger on the voyage ; in fact, the Spanish ambassador stated that there were only fifteen alive when the *Minion* reached Plymouth in January, 1569.

(iii) *The War of Reprisals*

In treacherously attacking a fleet containing two of the Queen of England's ships and sailing under her royal standard, the Viceroy of Mexico had given serious offence, as his master Philip II. was soon to find. When Hawkins came home in 1569, a new period was opening in European politics. In France the Valois monarchy was visibly weakening, and the Wars of Religion could not be stayed. The Huguenots were making La Rochelle their capital, and from that port were sending out swarms of privateers to prey upon all Catholic shipping. In the Netherlands Philip's representative the Duke of Alva had provoked a revolt by his severities. He had for the moment put it down in a successful opening campaign, but the situation was uneasy and he was short of money for the upkeep of his army. In England Mary Stuart was a prisoner, having ridden over the border to escape from her Scottish subjects who would otherwise have put her to death, while Scotland was precariously controlled by a clique of Protestant nobles who looked to Elizabeth for support. The former English need of Spanish friendship against a strong France allied with a strong Scotland was therefore inoperative. The Spanish need of English friendship in order to keep the Channel safe for communication with the Netherlands was stronger than ever. But Spain took no trouble to repair and maintain the eighty years-old alliance. The revolt of the Netherlands became increasingly a religious war in which England sympathized with the rebels ; and slowly Philip came to the conclusion that Elizabethan England was the stronghold of heresy and that the Catholic world would never have peace until it was overthrown.

Such being the makings of a new departure in diplomacy, Hawkins's tale of wrong did not represent a matter to be glossed over. A few weeks before Hawkins returned, Philip had borrowed from Genoese financiers a large sum of money for the support of Alva's Netherland forces. The money was sent up Channel, and the Huguenot rovers chased the ships that carried it. Some entered Plymouth for refuge, and others Southampton. Negotiations were proceeding for its safe transmission when the tragedy and treachery of San Juan de Ulua were revealed. On Cecil's advice the Queen then retained the money, for which she made herself responsible to the Genoese bankers, whom she afterwards repaid in full. To pay his troops Alva had to impose crushing taxes, thus stimulating a new Netherland revolt that was destined to shatter Spain's hold on the Dutch provinces. Philip could not risk formal war with England, but embargoed shipping and arrested merchants and their goods. England did the like, and for four years a state of non-belligerent hostility existed between the two countries, the background of the events in the Caribbean that have now to be considered.

John Hawkins was naturally eager to right his wrongs by making reprisals on Spanish shipping. He applied for leave to do so on the grand scale by attacking a returning plate-fleet with a dozen armed ships. But he was now England's most eminent sea-commander, and the government refused to let him go so far from home during this risky period when war might at any time break out. He was obliged to content himself with sending out illicit traders and privateers to the Caribbean under captains in his employ. It is known that he did this on a considerable scale, although the details of nearly all the voyages have been lost. Others among the Queen's officers, notably Sir William Winter, Surveyor of the Navy, and Sir Edward Horsey, Captain of the Isle of Wight, were doing the same ; and there is no doubt that these expeditions took place with the consent and approval of the Queen, who was determined to make Spain understand that she would not be a passive victim of aggression.

Drake was one of the privateer captains sent out after San Juan de Ulua, and in 1570 and 1571 he made two voyages of which little record has survived. In the first he may have taken slaves from Guinea to Hispaniola, and in the second he captured some booty on the coast of the Isthmus of Panama, but there is some confusion between a number of English and French captains operating in this region, and Drake's proceedings are by no means clear.

In 1572-3 Drake carried out the undertaking which first made him
famous, the raid on the treasure-stream flowing from Peru to Spain.
He sailed in May, 1572, with two small vessels and seventy-three men,
and made for a secluded harbour on the Darien coast which he had
found in the previous year.   There he fitted together three pinnaces
which he had brought out in sections.   His purpose was to use them
for a secret advance along the coast to Nombre de Dios and a surprise
attack upon that place.   Nombre de Dios was the port from which the
treasure was shipped to Spain after coming north from Peru by way
of Panama ;   and the English expected to find it full of valuable
plunder.   Drake duly surprised Nombre de Dios and captured it by a
bold night attack.   But he was disabled by a wound received in the
action, and his men broke off the attempt and retreated to their shipping without gaining any treasure.   He next made alliance with the
Cimaroons, escaped negro slaves who lived at perpetual war with their
former Spanish masters.   Nombre de Dios could not be surprised a
second time, and the best chance now was to waylay a mule-train
bearing treasure across the isthmus.   With the guidance of the Cimaroons Drake made the attempt not far from Panama.   Again success
eluded him ;   the captured mules bore victuals and luggage, but no
treasure.   For the third time, in alliance with the crew of a French
corsair, he tried near Nombre de Dios.   This time the prize was good.
The triumphant adventurers made off with as much gold as they could
carry, leaving quantities of silver behind.   Recently discovered documents show that the English share of the booty was 50,000 gold *pesos*,
equivalent to about £20,000, a great prize at that time for so small an
expedition.   Drake arrived in England with this booty at an inopportune moment, when a reconciliation was being patched up with
Spain after the four years' quarrel over the Genoese treasure.   Damages
were being settled and trade resumed, and so Drake retired into
obscurity with his winnings to avoid having them cast into the general
balance.

Many other captains, English and French, were cruising against
Spanish commerce, and the Spanish official documents made public in
recent years give the impression that at times the Caribbean was
swarming with corsairs.   Not all of them were successful.   John Noble
in 1574 was captured with his crew of twenty-eight, and all except two
boys were put to death.   In the same year Gilbert Horseley sailed from
Plymouth with twenty-five men in an 18-ton vessel.   Along the Main
and the Central American coast he captured a number of Spanish
ships, from which he obtained a moderate amount of treasure.   He
came home with two-thirds of his men from what must have been
accounted a very prosperous little venture.   Some of these captains
carried on a trade with the Cimaroons, who purchased English linens
and weapons with the gold taken from Spanish treasure-trains attacked
while crossing the Isthmus.

Andrew Barker of Bristol led two ships to the Caribbean in 1576.

He was a merchant who had sent a ship and cargo to the Canaries on the faith of the Anglo-Spanish reconciliation of 1573. By the treaty of 1489 the Canaries were a legitimate field of English trade, but Barker's ship and goods were seized by the Inquisition on the ground that their absent owner was a heretic. He took legal action, but had no means of enforcing judgment for redress, and so sailed on a voyage of reprisal. He captured a number of prizes in the western Caribbean, but was ruined by a mutiny. His own men set him ashore near Truxillo, where the Spaniards found and killed him. The mutineers suffered various misfortunes, and only a handful got back to England in 1578.

At the same time John Oxenham, one of Drake's men, was engaged in an expedition of a novel kind, which might have produced momentous consequences. Although its mystery and tragedy had long given it a romantic interest, very little about this adventure was truly known until the publication of previously undiscovered Spanish documents in 1932, and even its date had been incorrectly recorded. Oxenham sailed from Plymouth with fifty-seven men in the spring of 1576. In pursuance of a plan which he had discussed with Drake, he meant to cross the Isthmus of Panama and attack the shipping proceeding to Panama from the treasure ports of Peru. He intended to strike the treasure-stream, in fact, one stage earlier in its flow than Drake had done when he lay in wait for the mule-trains crossing from Panama to Nombre de Dios. There are good indications also that Oxenham had in mind a further purpose, namely, to form an alliance with the Cimaroons and occupy the Isthmus in permanence, creating a strategic protectorate of the kind that Ralegh afterwards proposed in Guiana. This project, if realized, would have paralysed the Spanish treasure traffic, and the Spanish authorities were so gravely concerned that they made an altogether exceptional effort to overcome Oxenham. The authorities at Panama sent out all the men they could raise to march through the Isthmus in mobile columns. At the same time they asked for reinforcements from Peru, and these were sent up the coast to Panama. The result was that after a preliminary success Oxenham was overwhelmed. Having concealed his shipping on the north coast of the Isthmus he struck inland to join the Cimaroons. On one of their rivers he launched a pinnace and rowed down to the South Sea. There he captured a quantity of treasure from the unarmed vessels that conveyed it from Peru to Panama. By that time the Spaniards were gathering, and soon they were out in force against him. They surprised and scattered his little party and severely punished the Cimaroons for aiding them. Oxenham and most of the survivors were captured. About a dozen made good their escape. They built a boat on the north coast, captured a Spanish ship, and in her sailed for England ; but there is no record that they ever arrived. Oxenham and the other prisoners were hanged by the Spaniards. All this had taken a considerable time, and Oxenham was not captured until October, 1577, some fifteen months after his landing on the Isthmus.

In the meantime a project of a very different kind had been taking shape. Geographers had long been convinced that the equatorial zone of the Pacific was full of valuable islands and that the South Pacific was bordered by a vast continent whose coast stretched from the Straits of Magellan to the region now known to be occupied by northern Australia. The continent was generally called Terra Australis Incognita, and most of it was imaginary. The two ends of its long coastline rested on realities, the actual Australia and the land seen by Magellan to the south of his straits, but the thousands of miles between were pure assumption. Yet they were firmly believed in by all European geographers from the time when the idea was popularized by Mercator and Ortelius towards 1570 until it was proved erroneous by Captain James Cook two centuries later. In 1570 Abraham Ortelius, a Flemish cartographer, published an atlas which gave prominence to the Southern Continent, and it was then that the idea was taken up in England as a basis for empire-building. Already in 1567 a Spaniard, Mendaña, sailing from Peru, had discovered some large islands near the equator which he believed to be identical with the Ophir from which King Solomon's expeditions had brought back great wealth. These Solomon Islands were considered to lie in the same relationship to the Southern Continent as the West Indies did to South America. In 1574 an English syndicate headed by Sir Richard Grenville and backed by the magnates of Devon petitioned the Queen for a patent to occupy any hitherto unknown lands in the southern hemisphere. They proposed to reach these lands by a voyage through the Straits of Magellan, and expected to find them full of rich commodities which would increase the trade, wealth and shipping of England. The Queen at first consented, and a patent was drawn up. But afterwards she withdrew her consent for fear lest the adventurers should use their position as a base from which to attack the Spaniards in Peru. That would not have suited the national policy, which in 1574 was still directed to reconciliation with Spain. Grenville therefore had his preparations forbidden and abandoned the enterprise.

Three years later it was revived by Drake and a different set of backers, a government group consisting of the Queen's ministers and the Navy officials who had stood behind John Hawkins in times past ; and the Queen gave her consent and encouragement. Relations with Spain had once more deteriorated, and it was thought good to proceed with an enterprise which would cause Spain uneasiness. In the summer of 1577 some preliminary instructions were made out for Captain Francis Drake. He was to pass through the Straits of Magellan and examine the unknown continent beyond, making friends with the people and reporting on their commodities and the opportunities for English trade. He might spend five months on the new coast and was then to return by the same way. It is evident that before Drake sailed this idea of a mere reconnaissance of the new continent had been superseded by a plan for fuller development of the discovery, for the

actual expedition was stronger in men and ships than the original
intention would have required. But indeed there was a plan within
the plan, and what Drake really meant to do was different from what
the majority of his backers expected.

There was, it seems, an inner syndicate consisting of the Queen, Sir
Francis Walsingham and Drake himself. Their intention was to attack
the treasure route on its first stage from Chile and Peru to Panama.
To ensure surprise the utmost secrecy was to be preserved, and the
syndicate at large together with the officers of the expedition were to
be left in the belief that the object was discovery and trade in the
Pacific. Even that was not made public, and it was given out that
the ships were bound for Alexandria, and the crews were engaged for
that destination. The Queen enjoined Drake to discretion and warned
him that Lord Burghley (Sir William Cecil) must be kept in the dark.
Burghley was a supporter of legitimate projects for the expansion of
enterprise in all continents and oceans, but he strongly disapproved
of treasure-raiding as productive of international disorder and diplomatic difficulties. Drake had a friend named Thomas Doughty, who
was to accompany the expedition. By some means Doughty wormed
himself into the secret, which he betrayed to Burghley. The minister
must have been annoyed at what was going on, and it is just possible
that Doughty's subsequent conduct was due to his instructions, but
of that there is no evidence. Finally, it should be noted that when
Drake sailed Oxenham was known to have set out on his Panama
expedition, but it was not yet known that Oxenham had failed and had
been taken prisoner. There was thus the possibility that Drake arriving on the West Coast with armed shipping might find the Isthmus
of Panama already under English control. So much we are entitled to
say, but whether Drake suggested to the Queen such a combined
stranglehold on the treasure route we do not know. The details of
their understanding are not revealed ; but what Drake did is not
necessarily what he set out to do.

He sailed in December, 1577, with three armed ships, the *Pelican*,
Elizabeth and *Marigold*, and two auxiliary vessels. During the passage
southward through the Atlantic Doughty gave trouble by his seditious
talk and his claims to an authority equal to Drake's. He was trying
to arouse discontent, and in a large measure he succeeded. At Port St.
Julian Drake brought him to trial and beheaded him for inciting to
mutiny. Whether Doughty was acting on Burghley's orders or only
on what he supposed was Burghley's policy has never been determined.
It was, however, now clearly known that Drake intended a raid on the
treasure-route, and this caused some dissatisfaction among those who
had believed themselves to be engaged in a voyage of discovery. He
faced them boldly and asserted his mastery, and passed successfully
through the Straits of Magellan. A month of gales from the west and
north-west then smote the expedition. The *Marigold* was lost, and the
Elizabeth driven back into the Straits. Her commander, John Winter,

was long accused of deserting Drake, but recently discovered evidence shows that this is untrue : Winter did his best to persuade an unwilling crew to continue, but they insisted on going home ; and it was one of these fainthearts who afterwards originated the accusation against his captain.   Drake in the *Pelican*, which he renamed the *Golden Hind*, at length conquered the weather and made headway up the Chilean coast.

At this point the raid began, in December, 1578.   The West Coast was entirely unprepared and unsuspecting, without an armed ship on the sea and with very few armed men on land.   From Valparaiso northwards Drake took prizes and treasure from men who had no inkling of his approach.   At Callao he heard that a ship laden with riches had left for Panama.   He pursued and captured her, with hardly a blow struck, in a sea where no flag but that of Spain had ever flown before.   The *Golden Hind* had now all the treasure she could carry, and Drake did not attempt Panama ; he must have learned from his prisoners that Oxenham's expedition had been destroyed.

Drake passed on to the North Pacific and searched for the North-West Passage, which was thought to debouch from the Atlantic in the latitude of 40°.   He went higher than this and found no opening.   Then he sailed back to the neighbourhood of the present San Francisco and stayed a month to refit in a country which he called New Albion.   It is probably an exaggeration to suggest that Drake thought of planting a colony here, but he seems to have thought that a refreshing station for other Englishmen making Pacific voyages would be useful, particularly if the North-West Passage should be opened.   Leaving the Californian coast in July, 1579, the *Golden Hind* crossed the Pacific.   In the Moluccas or Spice Islands Drake made friends with the Sultan of Ternate, who promised that the English should have liberty to buy spices in his kingdom.   This so-called treaty was welcomed in England as a serious step towards an opening of the long-desired trade with the Far East.   The eastern archipelago was full of perils, and the ship narrowly escaped destruction on a reef upon which she stuck fast for twenty hours.   The passage through the Indian Ocean and round the Cape occupied six months.   On September 26, 1580, Drake completed the first English circumnavigation by entering Plymouth Sound with the richest lading that any ship had yet brought into an English port.

Others followed in his track.   Thomas Cavendish made a successful circumnavigation in 1586-8, returning with much treasure taken in the Pacific.   He tried again in 1591, but failed to pass the Straits and died on the way home.   John Chidley sailed in 1589, but failed to get through the Straits and died in the attempt.   Richard Hawkins, son of Sir John Hawkins, reached the West Coast in 1593-4, but was captured after a desperate fight by the superior forces that Spain had now learnt to employ on the treasure-route.   This was the last Elizabethan venture into the Pacific.

CHAPTER VII

THE PUSH TO THE EAST

(i) *The Approach to Asia by Land*

WHILE Drake and his associates were following their warlike courses, other men were making plans for expansion by discovery alone without intrusion upon the regions exploited by Spain and Portugal. The difference between the two groups was of method rather than ultimate aim. Both sought national security, but they differed in estimating its conditions. Drake and his disciples looked forth upon a world wherein the two favoured nations of the Church of Rome claimed a joint monopoly of all the harvest of discovery. The material claim was the embodiment of the religious ; the counter-reformation had issued its challenge and was maturing its plans for the subjection of Christendom. To the more ardent spirits this state of affairs was an intolerable wrong which must be fought immediately and at all costs. By force of arms alone, as it seemed to them, could the world be made a fit place for free men to dwell in ; and upon England alone fell the task of heading the crusade for liberty. Cooler and more conservative minds viewed the matter differently. Looking back upon their country's history, they saw that she had never yet waged a successful offensive war. They denied that an inevitable defensive war was immediately to be thrust upon them ; with tact and statecraft it might be postponed until the country should be more fit to meet the peril. In the meantime, they argued, let England grow rich by all peaceful methods of expansion. Let her leave the tropic seas to their first discoverers and seek a route of her own to the riches of the east. More and more she was becoming the producer of the staple goods of world-commerce. Once let her find an unassailable avenue for her shipping to exploit her productions and she might live in solid state, the equal and more of her southern rivals, rich and strong to resist all attacks. Granted only the existence of an alternative route to Asia, this contention of the peace party was a sound one ; and upon the discovery of that route their capitalists and their pioneers expended as much effort as did the armed traders and the privateers whose exploits we have just considered.

The Muscovy Company, never forgetting that its original object had been the discovery of Cathay, was the first to take up the task. In the person of Anthony Jenkinson, a merchant who had travelled widely in the Levant and secured favours from the Sultan, it found a worthy successor to Richard Chancellor both as explorer and ambassador. Jenkinson sailed for Russia in 1557, and immediately obtained the confidence of the Tsar. Ivan IV. was at that moment at the turning-point of his career, about to enter upon the downward path which earned him the surname of the Terrible. Hitherto he had been an enlightened despot, leading his people to the conquest of their encircling enemies and to the adoption of ideas from the more civilized west. Henceforward his nature degenerated until he ended his life in 1584 as an insane tyrant, drenching his country in unnecessary bloodshed and losing one by one the fruits of his earlier successes. During this gloomy time the English would certainly have lost their commercial footing in Russia had it not been for the diplomatic genius of Anthony Jenkinson. The latter's first exploits, however, were in the field of exploration.

In the spring of 1558 Jenkinson and two other Englishmen departed from Moscow with Ivan's safe-conduct to reconnoitre the approach to Cathay through the region which our modern maps name Turkestan. It was the road by which Marco Polo and other mediaeval travellers had reached their goal from the Levant, and the English hoped that by striking it at right angles from the north they might divert to their White Sea terminus some of the diminished stream of commerce which still flowed westwards to Aleppo and Beyrout. Following the waterways from Moscow Jenkinson and his companions came to Kazan, and then journeyed by the Volga southwards through a Tartar country to its outflow into the Caspian Sea. Here stood the city of Astrakhan, recently conquered by the Tsar and now the outpost of his possessions. At Astrakhan they obtained a vessel fit for navigation in the Caspian. In her they skirted the northern shores of the sea and after a month's voyage landed in Koshak Bay. They were now in wild lands inhabited only by predatory peoples without settled government. Joining a caravan of native merchants they set forward through a desolate country and came, after many adventures, to Urgendj. They found the people much impoverished by continual wars, and little trade to be done. Another journey through a desert country, in which they beat off robber bands and endured much hunger and thirst, brought them to Bokhara. Here Jenkinson abode three months, learning much concerning the mercantile conditions of the East. He found that owing to the anarchy which was now chronic in Central Asia it was impossible to push on to India or China. He therefore returned by the way he had come, arriving at Moscow in 1559 and sailing for England in the following year.

The knowledge gained in Jenkinson's first expedition pointed to Persia as the most promising terminus for the Company's overland

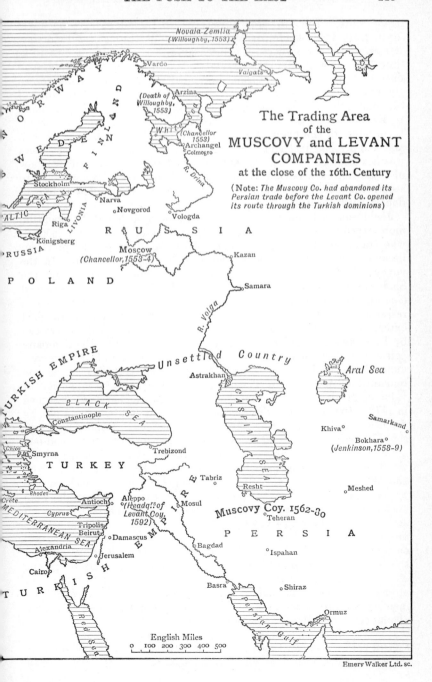

The Trading Area
of the
MUSCOVY and LEVANT
COMPANIES
at the close of the 16th. Century

(Note: *The Muscovy Co. had abandoned its Persian trade before the Levant Co. opened its route through the Turkish dominions*)

Novaia Zemlia
(Willoughby, 1553)

Vardo

Valgats

Arzina

(Death of Willoughby, 1553)

White

(Chancellor 1553)

Archangel
Colmogro

NORWAY

SWEDEN

FINLAND

R. Dwina

Stockholm

BALTIC SEA

LIVONIA

Narva

Novgorod

Vologda

Riga

Königsberg

PRUSSIA

R U S S I A

Moscow
(Chancellor, 1553-4)

Kazan

POLAND

Samara

R. Volga

Unsettled Country

Astrakhan

Aral Sea

TURKISH EMPIRE

B L A C K   SEA

Constantinople

CASPIAN SEA

Samarkand

Khiva

Bokhara
(Jenkinson, 1558-9)

Chios

Smyrna

Trebizond

T U R K E Y

Tabriz

Resht

Meshed

Rhodes

Crete

Antioch

Aleppo
(Headq.s of Levant Coy. 1592)

Mosul

Muscovy Coy. 1562-80

Cyprus

MEDITERRANEAN SEA

Tripolis

Beirut

Damascus

Teheran

P E R S I A

Alexandria

Jerusalem

Bagdad

Ispahan

Cairo

Basra

Shiraz

T U R K I S H

Red Sea

Ormuz

Persian Gulf

English Miles
0 100 200 300 400 500

Emery Walker Ltd. sc.

trade-route. The Tsar was quite alive to the advantages he might draw from a rich trade passing in this manner through his dominions. He approved the project, appointed an ambassador of his own to go into Persia with Jenkinson, and set him forward from Moscow once more in 1562. Jenkinson descended the Volga and sailed down the western shore of the Caspian Sea, landing at the Persian town of Shabran. He was well received by a vassal prince, and journeyed inland to Kazbin where the Shah then dwelt. The time, however, was unfavourable for the realization of his scheme. A peace between Persia and Turkey had just ended a long period of hostilities, and the Shah was not disposed to offend his new ally the Sultan by diverting the flow of trade from the Levant to the north. Jenkinson therefore failed to secure the concessions he sought, although the Shah allowed him to depart with a considerable quantity of merchandise.

Jenkinson still clung to the Persian project, although he made no more expeditions in person. In 1564 he despatched three Englishmen who traded in the outlying regions of Persia. The people, however, became hostile, and murdered the leader of the expedition. In the voyage of 1565 Arthur Edwards reached Kazbin and found that the Shah was now better disposed towards the English. Edwards obtained a substantial grant of privileges, although they were seldom in practice respected. In the fourth voyage (1568-9) Lawrence Chapman travelled extensively in Persia but reported that the trade was firmly engrossed by Turks and Armenians from the Levant. Nevertheless the Company persevered, despatching in 1569 twelve Englishmen and forty Russians under Thomas Bannister and Geoffrey Ducket. This expedition remained some years in Persia, accumulating a large quantity of valuable goods. Ducket, the senior merchant who survived, returned in 1573. In the Caspian Sea he was captured by pirates after a plucky defence in which all the Englishmen were wounded. Robbed of everything he arrived at Astrakhan, whose governor made haste to send out a force against the pirates. They were defeated and some £5000 worth of goods recovered of a lading which had been worth from £30,000 to £40,000. A further loss occurred by shipwreck in the Volga ; but the attractive possibilities of the Persian trade were evidenced by the fact that after all these misfortunes there was no actual loss on the whole voyage. The last Persian expedition set out in 1579. On arrival in the regions where the English had been accustomed to trade it found all in confusion. A Turkish army occupied the frontier provinces, and communication with the interior was cut off. In these circumstances there was nothing for it but to retire, and after doing some small trade by permission of the Turkish leaders the merchants returned to Russia. The Muscovy Company now definitely abandoned its overland traffic with Asia.

It was at this time that the London merchants were seeking to revive the sea traffic between England and the Levant, and it is evident that there were some ambitious spirits who hoped to make the new Turkey

Company (incorporated in 1581) the basis of a direct English trade with India through Syria and the Persian Gulf. The eight years' wandering of Ralph Fitch in Southern Asia (1583-91) resulted in the acquisition of much detailed information concerning all the lands between Palestine and Siam, but his reports proved fairly conclusively that the obstacles to an overland route were insuperable.

(ii) *The North-West Passage*

Since the voyage of John Rut in 1527 no English expedition had made a definite attempt to discover a passage to Asia by the north-west. The records of the early expeditions to this region had perished. Richard Hakluyt, the great historian of our maritime enterprise in the latter part of Elizabeth's reign, could find only accounts at second or third hand of Sebastian Cabot's achievements, wherein he stated that he had discovered the Passage and had been prevented from following it by a mutiny of his crew. Hakluyt knew nothing of the Anglo-Portuguese voyages from Bristol in 1501-5, and had only a verbal tradition of Rut's expedition, which did not even preserve the name of the explorer. Since that time Jacques Cartier of St. Malo had explored and charted the Gulf of St. Lawrence, and New-foundland had been proved to be an island, but the maps still gave fanciful representations of the coasts further to the north. Green-land was not known to be a separate country from North America, and purely imaginary lands such as Frisland and Estotiland were set down under the influence of the apocryphal adventures of the Zeni, first published in 1558.

As the need for an English route to Asia became more pressing men began to look to this unknown north-west as the quarter which would provide a solution of their difficulty. Sir Humphrey Gilbert, in an interval between military service in France and Ireland, meditated deeply on the matter. His conclusions, however, were only published ten years after he wrote them,[1] appearing from the press in 1576 as the *Discourse* in which he sought to prove the existence of the Passage : (1) By authority, *i.e.* by quotations from classical, mediaeval and renaissance philosophers and geographers. (2) By reason, appealing to various considerations such as the fauna of America and the accepted theory of the tides and ocean currents. (3) By experience, based upon the stories of Sebastian Cabot and other explorers. (4) By circumstance, *i.e.* by the citation of historical accounts of " Indians " having at divers times been driven upon the coasts of Germany, the which Indians could only have arrived by the North West Passage. Much of Gilbert's reasoning and his estimation of the value of his authorities were puerile in the extreme. That part of it which was sound tended only to prove that America was an island, a circumstance which he took for granted as implying the existence of a navigable channel between

[1] W. G. Gosling, *Life of Sir Humphrey Gilbert*, London, 1911, p. 59

it and eastern Asia.   Like Robert Thorne forty years earlier he had little conception of the realities of Arctic navigation.   The *Discourse* was Gilbert's only contribution to the solution of the north-west problem, for the famous voyage in which he lost his life in 1583 was undertaken as a colonizing venture.   The fact that he is commonly regarded as one of our north-western pioneers is an instance of the power of attraction so often possessed by a celebrated name.

A more practical worker in the same field existed at this time in the person of Michael Lok, a man whose efforts to serve his country have never secured the recognition they deserve.   The son of a knight and alderman of London, he served his apprenticeship as a Merchant Adventurer at Antwerp.   Then he spent many years in wandering about Europe and the Levant, and at the beginning of Elizabeth's reign returned to London and obtained employment as an agent of the Muscovy Company.   In the course of his travels he had spent much money on the acquisition of books and charts, and had accumulated "a ream of notes" by which, like Gilbert, he persuaded himself of the existence of the Passage.   For many years he found no opportunity of furthering the design.   Then in 1574 he fell in with Martin Frobisher, a sea-captain whom he had known in his youth.   Frobisher also, he found, was an enthusiast for the north-western discovery, and the two decided to join forces in the quest.

By the terms of their widely drawn charters the Muscovy Company were the monopolists of all trade with Asia by the north.   Although they had never made an expedition to the north-west they at first declined to grant permission to Frobisher to do so.   Frobisher, however, made interest at court and put his case before the Privy Council. That body, under Lord Burghley's direction wrote a strong letter to the Company which then abated its claims and gave Frobisher a free hand.   At the same time Lok quitted the Company's service in order to devote all his energies to the new project.   With great difficulty the two partners raised sufficient money at court and in the city to equip two small vessels for a voyage in 1576, Lok advancing nearly half the cost from his own purse.   With these ships, the *Gabriel* and the *Michael* of 25 tons each, Frobisher set sail, arriving at what is now called Baffin Land with the *Gabriel* only.   Here he entered a deep gulf which still bears his name.   In reality it was a *cul de sac*, but he was convinced from various indications that it was a passage between America and Asia.   He had now only thirteen men left, five having been captured by the Eskimos, and without pursuing the discovery further he came home to announce that the North West Passage was found.

The news created a great sensation, and the mercantile party in London hastened to support the project in full confidence that a valuable trade would result.   Subscriptions of capital came in more freely, and the pacific nature of the undertaking obtained for it the support of Lord Burghley.   Before the end of 1576 the queen granted a charter of incorporation constituting the original adventurers the Company of Cathay with full monopoly rights in the new trade. Michael Lok became governor and Frobisher admiral, each with a grant of one per cent. of all merchandise to be imported by way of their Passage. Preparations were put in hand for a trading expedition to Cathay in the following year. Before it could set sail a new circumstance arose which altered the intentions of the promoters. A piece of ore brought home by one of the seamen in the first voyage showed traces of gold on being assayed. The explorers declared that large quantities of this mineral were lying close to the shores of their strait. Remembering what the Spaniards had found in Mexico and Peru, the shareholders jumped to the conclusion that they were the owners of a rich gold mine. They instructed Frobisher to lade his largest ship with the ore and to prospect for further deposits. Only if these failed was he to proceed with the discovery of Cathay.

With these orders Frobisher sailed again in 1577 having under his command the *Aid* of 200 tons, belonging to the queen, together with the two small craft of the previous voyage. The fact that the queen was now an investor showed the favourable opinion held upon the prospects of the undertaking. The expedition returned to the supposed strait found in the previous year, sighting on the way the shores of Greenland, which the explorers took to be the legendary Frisland. They took in some two hundred tons of mineral, not, however, at the same spot as that which produced the original sample, and without attempting further discoveries sailed for England at the end of the Arctic summer. The arrival of this quantity of ore raised excitement to fever-pitch. London provided no facilities for wholesale smelting, and pending the construction of furnaces the goldsmiths continued to assay samples and to vie with one another in their declarations of the wealth of the discovery. It was perhaps the first of the great speculating manias in our history, and although the amount of floating capital in the country was in those days infinitesimally small the stock of the Company had swollen to £20,000 by the spring of 1578.

In May of that year, although the precise value of the ore was still undetermined, Frobisher sailed for the third time with fifteen ships, the largest English squadron which had ever sailed beyond the coasts of Europe. He took with him Captain Edward Fenton whom he was instructed to leave with a hundred men as a permanent garrison to repel intruders from the mines. The expedition encountered much stormy weather, and the mariners, eager to be away from a dangerous coast, collected under the name of gold-ore any rubbish that came to their hands. The only discovery effected was the accidental one of Hudson's Strait, which the fleet entered whilst searching for the original Frobisher's Sound.

Frobisher led his ships home at the end of the year only to find that the enterprise had come to a sudden and disastrous end. Further experiments with the ore had cast doubts upon its value, and although even now no considerable amount of it had been tested a panic set in which was quite as violent and unreasonable as the first enthusiasm. Lok, as governor and treasurer of the Company, made calls upon the adventurers for further sums with which to carry on the work. They refused to part with any more money. Twelve hundred tons of the ore remained derelict at Dartford, where the furnaces were to have been set up; the shipowners and mariners were unpaid; and the Company of Cathay was hopelessly bankrupt two years after its inauguration. Frobisher accused Lok of incompetence and malversation. Lok returned the charge of dishonesty, and with some justice, for the admiral on returning from the second voyage had not disclosed the fact that his cargoes had not been collected at the place where the original sample had been found. Everyone, however, combined to lay the blame on Michael Lok, who lost all his fortune and was thrown into prison for the Company's debts. So ended the first Elizabethan attempt on the problem of the north-west.

After the lapse of some years the project was revived by Captain John Davis, whose career earned him the reputation of being at once a great practical seaman and the chief scientific navigator of the period. He obtained the support of William Sanderson, a wealthy merchant who found most of the necessary funds, Doctor Dee the philosopher, Sir Walter Ralegh, and many of the leading shipowners of London, Exeter and Dartmouth. In his first voyage in 1585 he examined the western shore of Greenland and then stretched westwards to Baffin's Land (Meta Incognita as it had been named since Frobisher's voyages). Here he entered Cumberland Sound, which he thought to be the mouth of the Passage. On his return he told Sir Francis Walsingham that "the North West Passage is a matter nothing doubtful." Sailing again in 1586 he explored the same coasts more fully, and rediscovered Hudson's Strait, but lost some of his faith in Cumberland Sound on a closer examination of its shores. This voyage confirmed the impression that "the north parts of America are all islands." His principal achievement was the fruit of his third expedition (1587). The west-country merchants had now exhausted their enthusiasm, and it was with Sanderson's support alone that Davis could obtain the use of three ships. Two of them he was obliged to send fishing in order to pay some of the expenses of the voyage. In the third, a small and leaky pinnace, he pushed northwards up the great strait between Greenland and America. At a point which he named "Sanderson his hope" he reached the latitude of 72° 12′ N. and saw the sea open to the north and west. A gale drove him back, after which he rediscovered Frobisher's Sound and noted "the furious overfall of the tide" at the entrance to Hudson's Strait, a fact which seemed significant to him of the existence of a large sea to the westward.

The Spanish war precluded further attempts to follow up this clue, but Davis had done the best work yet accomplished in this region. He charted accurately all the coasts which he visited, cleared up the

confusion hitherto existing between Greenland, " Frisland," Labrador
and Baffin Land,[1] and found four distinct openings, any of which, he
claimed, might be the sought-for passage. Modern discovery has
proved that two of them are actually channels leading clear round the
north of America, although so choked with ice as not to be available
for navigation.

(iii) *The true Road to Asia*

The final push to the east by the only practicable route, the Cape
of Good Hope and the Indian Ocean, grew out of the Spanish war, with
its revelation of a state of affairs incredible to the landsmen but long
recognized by the forward school of seamen, the impotence of Spain
and Portugal to make good their world-monopoly. With the conclusion of Davis' explorations the party of peaceful expansion had to
admit that their northern passage, however much they might believe
in its existence, had yet eluded their search. At the same time the
course of events had settled over their heads the question of peace or
war. For good or ill England was at war with the world-powers, and
so the merchants who still thirsted for an Asiatic trade despatched their
expeditions to the south and east, and we hear no more of the North
West Passage for fifteen years to come.

As early as 1541 the English government had asked permission for
its merchants to accompany the Portuguese to Calicut to buy spices
for English consumption, and had submitted to the inevitable refusal.
The English connection with the Guinea coast, had it been permanently
established, would have furthered the larger project. The chief natural
difficulty was the length of the voyage, necessitating an equipment for
which English resources were judged inadequate. The Portuguese
met this by carrying their trade in huge carracks of three or four times
the tonnage of the largest English merchantmen. Then came Drake's
voyage of circumnavigation with its proof that a light, swift-sailing
English galleon could safely traverse the seas in which the great
carracks commonly lost half their crews by the diseases of the long
tropic passage. Drake also brought information of the hostility of
some of the native powers in the Moluccas towards the Portuguese.
These circumstances resulted in the despatch of the only expedition
intended for a trading voyage to the east before the declaration of
war.

In effect this voyage was something of a compromise between the
aims of the two great parties in the national policy. Its backers

---

[1] This confusion, arising from the lack of any accurate method of determining
longitude, renders it extremely difficult to arrive at a clear impression of northern
discovery in the sixteenth century. Coasts already visited and vaguely charted
were rediscovered as something new and assigned different positions by subsequent
navigators. The same name was applied to different lands by successive geographers.
" Greenland " had two and possibly three distinct significations. When Davis began
his explorations he was evidently under the impression that Frobisher's discovery had
been on the east coast of the true Greenland. See Sir C. R. Markham, *Life of John
Davis*, London, 1889.

included some who had financed Frobisher and others who had supported Drake. Its commander was Edward Fenton, one of Frobisher's
men, but amongst the officers were some who had gone round the
world with Drake. The instructions given to Fenton were very
explicit. He was to sail by the Cape of Good Hope to the Moluccas,
and not to pass through the Straits of Magellan either going or returning
" except upon great occasion incident." On his homeward voyage he
might attempt the North West Passage from the Pacific side provided
he did not pass northward of 40°. He was not on any account to
plunder the property of the queen's friends or allies, a designation which
at the time of sailing included Spain and Portugual, and he was to
trade in strict honesty and courtesy with the nations of the east.

With these orders Fenton sailed from Southampton in May, 1582,
having under his command the galleon *Leicester* of 400 tons and three
other vessels. He touched first at the coast of Guinea and then stood
over to Brazil. Here he stayed some time trading with the Portuguese
colonists and seeking information about the Straits of Magellan, through
which, in spite of his instructions, it was his intention to pass. While
he was still hesitating to continue the voyage three Spanish ships,
part of an expedition despatched to fortify and garrison the Straits,
fell upon him in a Brazilian harbour. In the action which ensued one
Spaniard was sunk, the English receiving little damage. Dissensions
now broke out between Fenton and his officers. Two of his ships
parted company, and the voyage was abandoned without any attempt
to round the Cape of Good Hope.

Nine years elapsed before the project was renewed. Then the war
provided two incentives to a revived interest in Asiatic trade. In
1587 the English captured off the Azores a homeward-bound carrack
named the *San Felipe*. Besides a cargo worth £108,000 in the money
of the time she was found to contain documents and charts giving
fuller information about the trade than any of the English merchants
had yet obtained. In the following year Thomas Cavendish came home
from his circumnavigation, and published a detailed report upon
China and other eastern countries.

Again the London merchants set forward an East Indies voyage.
In 1591 George Raymond and James Lancaster sailed with three well
found ships. In the passage to the Cape the crews suffered so much
from scurvy that the commanders sent home one ship with the weaker
men. Proceeding with the other two, they had barely doubled the
Cape when Raymond's vessel went down with all on board in a storm.
Lancaster continued alone, sailing up the east coast of Africa and
thence across to Cape Comorin. Losing many men by sickness he
reached the Eastern Archipelago, where he took two Portuguese ships.
He made his way back to Ceylon, and would have lingered there in the
hope of a richer prize but his crew insisted on sailing for England.
On the long voyage round the Cape more men died. The lack of victuals
made it hopeless to attempt to reach England by a direct passage.

Lancaster therefore made for the West Indies to obtain supplies. Hardship had rendered the survivors mutinous, and whilst he was ashore they carried off the ship. He himself with a few companions obtained a passage home in a French privateer, arriving in England in 1594. The disasters of this voyage did not deter him from being willing to repeat the attempt. He considered that all might have been well if he had been able to sail from England at the fit season of the year.

The London adventurers were of the same opinion. The capture of another carrack in 1592 with a cargo worth £150,000 stimulated their determination to share in the richest trade in the world. In 1596 they despatched Captain Benjamin Wood with three ships, Sir Robert Dudley taking a principal share in the outlay. Wood was the bearer of letters from the queen to the emperor of China. He rounded the Cape and crossed the Indian Ocean to Ceylon and the Straits of Malacca. He captured Portuguese shipping, but sickness steadily diminished his crews. With his last remaining ship he was wrecked on the coast of Burma. Wood's fate is unknown, for nothing more was heard of him. A handful of the men in a native boat crossed the Indian Ocean to Mauritius, at that time an uninhabited island. There one sole survivor was rescued in 1601 by a Dutch ship making the eastern voyage.[1]

The sufferings and losses of these voyages might well have given all concerned a horror of the undertaking. Nevertheless men were found to persevere in it. The Dutch also were beginning to interest themselves. Their first eastern venture sailed in 1595, and between that date and 1601 no less than fifteen Dutch expeditions were set forth. In 1602 the amalgamation of several minor concerns produced the Dutch East India Company, a national institution with a capital of over £500,000. The publication in 1595-6 of a great work upon India by Jan Huyghen van Linschoten, a Hollander who had lived six years at Goa, revealed to the world how insecure was the Portuguese grip upon the east. Linschoten's book was speedily translated into English, Latin, German and French. Its effect in England was complementary to that of Ralph Fitch's narrative, published after his return in 1591.

Once more London took up the task. In 1599 the sum of £30,000 was subscribed for the Indian voyage. Some of the promoters, such as Thomas Smith and Richard Staper, were members of the Levant Company, which had tried and failed to establish an overland trade with India. For diplomatic reasons, the government stayed the project. Peace with Spain was in prospect, and it was not until the negotiations failed that the queen would give her consent. During the delay the views of the adventurers broadened. They doubled their capital and petitioned for a regular grant of incorporation. On

---

[1] The above version of the facts of this obscure voyage is based on the account given by Sir W. Foster in *England's Quest of Eastern Trade*, pp. 138-41.

December 31, 1600, they received their charter, and the **East India**
Company, the greatest trading and empire-building corporation in
our history, entered on its long career.   The directors immediately
set about the purchase of shipping, and early in 1601 Sir James Lancaster sailed with four vessels ranging from 600 to 240 tons.   Before
he returned from a brilliantly successful voyage Elizabeth **was** dead,
and a new era in English expansion had begun.

CHAPTER VIII

ELIZABETHAN ATTEMPTS AT COLONIZATION

ALTHOUGH under Henry VII. there had been in England an interest in discovery, and the adventurers had obtained charters which contemplated the establishment of permanent settlements in new lands, it is not until the reign of Elizabeth that we find the germs of colonial expansion of the kind with which the later history of the empire has made us familiar. The explanation is that until well on in the sixteenth century social and industrial conditions were developing in a slow and orderly manner upon lines already laid down, and that in consequence there was no marked excess of population for which provision was lacking in the mother country. The colonies contemplated by the early discoverers had therefore been trading posts on the route to Cathay, to be held by temporary residents rather than by true colonial communities with a life of their own detached from that of the country which gave them birth. And, as we have seen, it is doubtful whether any of these so-called colonies were actually planted, and certain that in any case they survived only for a few years at most. By the time of Elizabeth's accession, on the other hand, the old social conditions had been rudely disturbed by the confiscations of church property, the innovations of the new class of landowners, the dislocation of European trade, and the great rise of prices following on the influx of gold and silver from America. Beggars, tramps and masterless men became a social menace during the last years of Henry VIII.; and at the same time, in spite of, or perhaps because of, the break-up of static conditions population began to increase after remaining nearly stationary for two centuries.

The reorganization of agriculture and industry silently carried out by Elizabeth and her ministers finally mastered the worst symptoms of the trouble ; but the distress, before it subsided, gave rise among men of original mind to an ambition to found " plantations " [1]—true and living offshoots of the English race—in the fair and vacant lands across the Atlantic. By so doing, they contended, they would turn

---

[1] " To plant," in the sense of " to form a settlement " was an expression in common use in the sixteenth century. " Plantation," meaning a colony, was first used in 1610, after which it soon became the customary term.

criminals into honest men and provide a relief for the population of
England which, as it seemed to them, was becoming excessive. " We
might inhabit some part of those countries," wrote Sir Humphrey
Gilbert, " and settle there such needy people of our country, which now
trouble the commonwealth, and through want here at home are enforced
to commit outrageous offences, whereby they are daily consumed with
the gallows." Hakluyt recognized in Virginia the heaven-provided
home for the unfortunates whom he saw in England " go idle up and
down in swarms for lack of honest entertainment." Ralegh, Sir
George Peckham and Christopher Carleill all wrote to the same effect,
the last-mentioned being particularly concerned at the "mighty
increase " of the home population.

This altruistic motive was undoubtedly uppermost in the minds
of the chief promoters of the movement ; but it was necessary also
to attract investors, and they therefore enlarged upon commercial
advantages in addition. Carleill, seeking to induce the Muscovy
merchants to subscribe funds, wrote : " But when this of America
shall have been haunted and practised thirty years to an end, as the
other [i.e. the Russian trade] hath been, I doubt not by God's grace,
that for the ten ships that are now commonly employed once the
year into Muscovia, there shall in this voyage twice ten be employed
well, twice the year at the least " ; and again, " by the good prospering
of this action there must of necessity fall out a very liberal utterance
of our English cloths into a main country, described to be bigger than
all Europe. . . . The like will be also of many other things, over many
to be reckoned, which are made here by our artificers and labouring
people, and of necessity must be provided from hence." And behind
all this, hovering in the background to appeal to the large-minded
capitalist, there was ever the vision of the Asiatic passage, which
might even yet be found in one of the deep inlets of an uncharted
coastline. The hope of stumbling upon it influenced the actions
of all the early colonial projectors, and furnished one more instance
of that doubleness of motive which characterized the Elizabethan
undertakings.

Sir Humphrey Gilbert, as we have seen, began his connection with
oceanic undertakings as an advocate of the north-western search.
At the time of the first drafting of his *Discourse* (about 1565) he brought
to the queen's notice his plan for the discovery of the Passage coupled
with the colonization of the intermediate lands. The Muscovy Company, as later in the case of Martin Frobisher, raised an objection
based upon the terms of their own charter. A conference followed
between Gilbert and Anthony Jenkinson, and it was agreed that
Gilbert should carry out his plan as a member of the Company.[1]
Nothing, however, came of the proposal, and Gilbert spent the next
few years (1566-70) as a soldier in Ireland where he interested himself
in a scheme for the plantation of Ulster. During the years which

[1] Gosling, *Life of Gilbert*, pp. 69-73.

followed his mind seems to have inclined more and more towards the colonizing aspect of his first idea; his *Discourse* was published in 1576, in all probability without his consent; he took no more than a shareholder's interest in the undertaking of Frobisher and Lok; and when the Cathay Company was on the verge of collapse he came forward with a purely colonial plan for which he obtained a patent from the queen in June, 1578.

Gilbert's patent has often been spoken of as the title-deed of our colonial empire, as if it had been the first document of its kind. In reality it differs little in essentials from the original charter granted to Cabot by Henry VII. in 1496 and from those subsequently obtained by the Bristol syndicates in 1501-2. We know that the ideas inspiring it were new ones, but the actual wording is so vague as to give it little claim to be considered as a document of fundamental importance. It conferred upon Gilbert full powers to inhabit and fortify any barbarous lands not actually in the possession of a Christian sovereign, without geographical limitation. These rights were to extend over a radius of 200 leagues from any spot at which he should make a settlement within the six years ensuing from the date of the grant. He was to hold his conquests by homage from the crown of England and to govern them as far as possible in accordance with English common law. One-fifth of all precious metals discovered were to be reserved to the crown. No hostile acts against friendly powers were to be committed by the patentee on pain of forfeiture of the grant. This clause represented a piece of calculated duplicity, for Gilbert had already suggested to the Queen that he should cruise against Spanish shipping under cover of a patent expressly forbidding such a proceeding. She would thus be able to disavow him if necessary. It seems, however, that while the government was ready to connive at anti-Spanish action in distant seas, it set its face against anything savouring of piracy in home waters.

Gilbert lost no time in preparing to carry his grant into effect. In the autumn of 1578 he collected an imposing squadron of ten or eleven ships and over 500 men. After delays caused by bad weather he finally got clear of the English coast on November 19. What he did next remains a mystery, for no definite information concerning the voyage was ever allowed to leak out. All that is known is that some of his ships deserted and that he had returned by April, 1579, having suffered losses, but whether by storm or battle is uncertain. The Spaniards charged him with piracy, but he seems to have made good his personal innocence in the matter and thus to have avoided the forfeiture of his patent. Whatever may have actually happened, it is certain that he failed to plant his colony and so crippled his fortune that for some years to come he could make no further attempt.

The patent, however, had to be acted upon within six years of its issue. In 1582, therefore, we find Gilbert in negotiation with two Catholics, Sir George Peckham and Sir Thomas Gerrard. They were

representatives of that loyal majority of the old faith who were resolved
to be good Englishmen whilst preserving their opinions, and were
disgusted with the attempts of Cardinal Allen and his English Jesuits
to make them the tools of a foreign conspiracy. They took up the
idea of an American colony as a refuge for those members of their
religion who could not reconcile themselves to life in Protestant England, and they were willing to make their attempt under the licence
of Gilbert. The proposal was a perfectly open one, approved by the
English government, and in particular by Sir Francis Walsingham,
the most ardent Protestant among the queen's ministers.[1] In the
end nothing came of it as a separate undertaking, the promoters throwing in their lot with a combined expedition under Gilbert ; but it is
interesting as foreshadowing the conception of colonies as a refuge
for oppressed religionists, a conception which bore such remarkable
fruit in the following century. The French Huguenots had already
made two experiments in the same direction, one in Florida and the
other in Brazil.

With the assistance of Ralegh, Walsingham and Peckham, Gilbert
had once more the prospect of carrying out his scheme. He was unable,
however, to raise sufficient money in London. He therefore came to an
arrangement with the merchants of Southampton, promising in return
for their help to use the port exclusively for the trade of his colony.
A private joint-stock company was formed under the title of " The
Merchants Adventurers with Sir Humphrey Gilbert." [2] On June 11,
1583, the squadron set sail from Cawsand Bay. It consisted of the
Delight, 120 tons, in which sailed Gilbert himself, the *Bark Ralegh*,
200 tons, the property of Ralegh, the *Golden Hind*, 40 tons (not Drake's
old flagship), the *Swallow*, 40 tons, and the *Squirrel*, 10 tons, usually
referred to as the " frigate." Two days out the *Bark Ralegh* deserted,
her captain alleging an outbreak of sickness. Edward Hayes, the
captain of the *Golden Hind* and author of the best account of the
voyage, says : " The reason I could never understand. Sure I am
no cost was spared by their owner, Master Ralegh, in setting them
forth : therefore I leave it unto God." The incident was mysterious,
and ominous of the indiscipline which helped to ruin the expedition,
but on the facts as we have them there is no ground for supposing, as
some have done, that Ralegh himself played false. On the voyage
across the Atlantic the *Swallow* parted company. She rejoined Gilbert
on the Newfoundland coast, her captain reporting that his men had,
against his will, robbed a French fishing boat and treated her crew
with great brutality. The *Swallow's* men were in fact pirates, having
been caught red-handed in the Channel and transferred to Gilbert's
expedition as an alternative to the gallows.

In the harbour of St. John's were thirty-six sail of fishing craft of
all nations. At first the fishermen were doubtful of the intentions
of the newcomers, but when Gilbert displayed his commission they

[1] Gosling, *op. cit.* pp. 185-200.   [2] *Ibid.* p. 206.

received him with all courtesy and promised to supply his wants. On August 5 he had a tent set up ashore, and in the presence of all, " as well Englishmen as Spaniards, Portugals and other nations," he read his patent and solemnly took possession of Newfoundland for the crown of England, signifying to the cosmopolitan assembly that they were henceforth to be governed by English law as administered by himself. The foreigners, according to the English accounts, made no objection : possibly they took their new governor less seriously than he did himself. After further ceremonies, including the setting up of the royal arms and the granting of parcels of land in fee-simple to various applicants, he reorganized his fleet preparatory to proceeding with the voyage ; for it was his intention to plant his settlement on the mainland. Gilbert had little of the tact and mastery by which Drake had led his crews to success. Many of the men and of the officers also had become fainthearted. Some deserted in Newfoundland, stole a vessel from the fishing fleet and took their departure. For the others who were unwilling to proceed the Admiral detached the *Swallow*, and in her they returned to England. With the three remaining ships he sailed from Newfoundland on August 20, going southwestwards to examine the shores of Nova Scotia and choose a site for a colony.

Events now marched rapidly to their tragic climax. Fogs and storms prevented a proper exploration of the coasts, and a week after the departure from Newfoundland the *Delight*, through the negligence of her officers as Hayes asserted, went aground and was beaten to pieces by the force of the waves. All her crew perished except sixteen who made their way in the ship's boat to Newfoundland ; and all the stores for the prospective settlement were lost. Gilbert himself had sailed in the *Squirrel* during this part of the voyage, and so had escaped the disaster. But with the winter approaching and the stores lost there was nothing for it but to turn homewards. He put a good face upon the matter, saying, " Be content, we have seen enough, and take no care of expense past : I will set you forth royally the next Spring, if God send us safe home " ; and being asked how he would raise the necessary money, he replied, " Leave that to me ; I will ask a penny of no man." From which, and from other circumstances, Hayes believed that he had privately discovered a rich mine in Newfoundland. Perhaps he had some such illusion ; but he was not, like Frobisher, fated to degrade his noble project into a gold-hunt. On September 9, when the *Golden Hind* and the *Squirrel* were north of the Azores, a great tempest overtook them. In the afternoon Hayes saw the *Squirrel* nearly overwhelmed, but she recovered ; and as the two ships came within hailing distance Gilbert cried out, " We are as near to heaven by sea as by land." About midnight the watch saw the *Squirrel's* light suddenly disappear, and reported that she had foundered. It was true, although Hayes still clung to a hope that they had only parted company in the storm. But as the weeks passed after the *Golden Hind's* return and no news came of the missing ship it became evident that England had lost one of the noblest if not the most successful of her leaders.

In Gilbert's mind there had been a plan for founding another colony in addition to the one which he actually attempted. This was to have been in a more southerly position on the American seaboard. His half-brother, Walter Ralegh, now took up this part of the project and for the next five years worked hard to bring it to success. During the whole of that time Ralegh was prevented by circumstances beyond his own control from crossing the Atlantic in person. It is quite possible that this was no disadvantage to the venture, for in after years he showed himself little more competent as a leader than Gilbert himself. Both were personally brave, but while Gilbert failed by reason of his neglect of detail and easy-going optimism, Ralegh was handicapped by his unpopularity with his equals and the persistent suspicion of double-dealing with which, justly or not, they regarded him. In his colonial schemes he was served by men whose capability on the whole was high, and the chief cause of their failure lay in sheer bad luck and the outbreak of the Spanish war at the critical period of the undertaking.

In March, 1584, Ralegh obtained a patent very similar in its terms to that of Gilbert, and a month later he despatched two small vessels under Philip Amadas and Arthur Barlow to reconnoitre the southern part of the American coastline. Taking a course by way of the Canaries and the West Indies, they came after little more than a two months' voyage to the coast of what is now North Carolina. Here they found a chain of long narrow islands lying parallel with the mainland and separated from it by broad sounds with inlets penetrating far into the continent. The climate and the vegetation appeared delightful, as also did the character of the Indians who came fearlessly to meet them. " We found the people," said Barlow, " most gentle, loving and faithful, void of all guile and treason, and such as live after the manner of the golden age." This country, in which they reported the presence of pearls, copper, great red cedars, corn which ripened within two months of sowing, and abundant game, seemed exactly what they had come to seek, and after taking formal possession they returned to describe what they had seen. Ralegh received his knighthood after their arrival, and the new land was christened Virginia [1] in honour of the queen.

Ralegh hastened to follow up the discovery. Forbidden by the queen to leave England, he appointed Sir Richard Grenville to plant the first settlement. In spite of the fact that Grenville's name is a

---

[1] For the first thirty years after its invention the name Virginia was applied to the whole coastline from Cape Breton southwards. The English in the time of the Cabots had called it the New Land ; the French after the voyage of Verrazzano in their service in 1524 had named it New France ; and subsequently the Spaniards had christened it Florida. All these names thus stood for the same coast in the sixteenth century, and it was not until long afterwards that Virginia and Florida became localized to the particular regions which bear them to-day.

household word in English mouths, very little is known of his career except in connection with the Virginia venture [1] and the fight in which he met his death in 1591 ; and conflicting estimates of his character have been formed. In 1585 he undertook to command the fleet on its voyage across the Atlantic and see the colonists safely installed. Another officer, a soldier of fortune named Ralph Lane, was to remain as the permanent governor. Sailing in April with seven ships and about a hundred colonists in addition to the crews Grenville landed at Hispaniola and was courteously entertained by the Spanish governor, whose civility the English somewhat ungenerously attributed to fear. Then he stood over to the peninsula of Florida and coasted northwards until he came to the island of Wokokon. Here Grenville, Lane and forty others went over to the mainland to explore, leaving the bulk of the expedition to proceed northwards to Roanoke Island and found the settlement on the scene of Barlow's exploration. On the mainland Grenville quarrelled with the Indians on account of a theft, and burnt a village in retaliation. The bad effect of this on the subsequent fortunes of the colony has probably been exaggerated, for the Roanoke Indians had themselves been at war with those of the mainland. On August 25 Grenville sailed for England, promising to return with supplies in the following year. His departure was not lamented by the settlers, who complained that his conduct had been harsh and tyrannical. It is fairly evident that in his determination to avoid the weakness which had ruined Gilbert he had gone too far to the other extreme.

Left to themselves the colonists made their camp on the north-east corner of the island of Roanoke, where the outlines of their entrenchment may still be traced.[2] They seem to have shirked the hard work which was essential to success, the minds of many being obsessed with the idea that in any strange land gold was certain to be had for the gathering. In spite of the fertility of the soil they became short of food, and the Indians grew increasingly unwilling to supply them. Lane devoted most of his time to exploration, intent upon discovering mines and pearl fisheries, and led away by delusive indications of a passage to the Pacific. In April, 1586, the Indians gathered force and planned to surprise and massacre the intruders. Lane heard of their design and took the offensive himself, routing the savages and killing many of them. As the summer advanced and Grenville failed to appear all grew apprehensive that they were to be abandoned by those at home. At length, on June 8, a great fleet was seen approaching the coast. It was Drake's expedition homeward bound from its triumphant raid through the West Indies. Drake offered the colonists

---

[1] This is no longer true since the publication in 1937 of Mr. A. L. Rowse's *Sir Richard Grenville*, in which the whole career is traced with the aid of new research. [Note to 3rd edn.]

[2] J. A. Doyle, *The English in America*, London, 1882, p. 83.

such supplies as he could spare, and particularly a vessel named the *Francis* of 70 tons, in which they might make their escape if the position became untenable. Scarcely had this been agreed upon when a storm drove the *Francis* out to sea. She did not return, and Lane refused the offer of a larger ship on account of the insecurity of the anchorage. The sight of the English fleet proved a temptation too strong to resist. The settlers determined to abandon the colony, and all took passage with Drake to England. A fortnight later Grenville reached the site with three relief-ships, equipped principally at Ralegh's expense. Finding the enterprise abandoned he made some further explorations and departed to cruise for Spanish prizes. He left behind fifteen volunteers with supplies for two years. These men were never seen again, but it was learnt afterwards that some were killed by the Indians and that the survivors disappeared into the interior.

Ralegh still found means to persevere with his plan. In 1587 he despatched another expedition with John White as governor and a council of twelve assistants. On July 2 they reached the island only to find that Grenville's fifteen men were gone. They reoccupied the fort at Roanoke and determined to effect a permanent settlement. Of the 150 colonists seventeen were women, one of whom, the daughter of White and wife of Ananias Dare, gave birth to a daughter, Virginia Dare, the first English child born in America. It was agreed that some person of weight who had been on the spot should go to England to represent the interests of the colony, and at the general request John White undertook this duty. Before his departure (August 27, 1587) the question of removing to the mainland had been considered, and the colonists promised that if they quitted Roanoke they would leave some indication of their whereabouts.

White arrived in England in November, and shortly afterwards Ralegh equipped another fleet to be commanded by Sir Richard Grenville. Owing to the Spanish preparations to invade the country this fleet was retained for service with the navy. Anxious to maintain touch with the colony, White obtained permission to sail with two small vessels in April, 1588. He was, however, unable to fulfil his purpose. The ships parted company, and the crews converted the voyage into a privateering adventure, neither reaching Virginia. In the following year, 1589, Ralegh transferred his rights to a syndicate consisting of Sir Thomas Smith, John White, and others. By his own account he had expended £40,000 on the colony. But even if he had borne the entire burden, which is doubtful, the amount seems exaggerated : a contemporary estimate placed the expense of planting a hundred settlers at £4000. The transference of the proprietorship and the need of shipping for the great expedition to Portugal in 1589 precluded the sending of relief in that year. When at length White was able to sail to Virginia in 1590 he found the colony again abandoned, neither was he able to obtain any news of the colonists.

The mystery of their fate is one which has never been certainly solved. White himself found no signs of a massacre. The word " Croatan " carved upon the trunk of a tree near the deserted fort he took to be an indication of the locality on the mainland to which they had migrated ; and the absence of a prearranged mark of distress (a cross) above the name convinced him that they had gone of their own free will. The crews of his ships refused to wait for further investigations, and many years elapsed before another English vessel visited the place. The colonists of later times gleaned two contradictory accounts from tales current among the Indians. One was to the effect that a band of white captives had been kept for years in slavery and finally massacred.[1] The other was that they had joined forces with a friendly tribe and intermarried with them, and that their descendants in North Carolina were still to be distinguished by certain European characteristics as late as the nineteenth century.[2] But either of these stories might quite well refer to the survivors of a shipwrecked crew having no connection with the colony. In 1602 Ralegh sent a small ship to Virginia to glean some information, but it returned without even reaching the neighbourhood of Roanoke.

This, with the exception of an abortive voyage to a more northerly region set forth in the same year by the Earl of Southampton, was the last Elizabethan attempt to found an American colony. Before Ralegh's death in the next reign the task in which, by no fault of his own, he had failed, was accomplished by other hands. He himself seems to have lost interest in it, for when a period of disgrace at court afforded him the opportunity of crossing the ocean in 1595 it was not to Virginia but to Guiana that he betook himself. There he ascended the Orinoco in search of the fabled Eldorado, the lost city of the Incas. He found no trace of the city but, like many other adventurers of the time, he convinced himself of the existence of huge gold deposits in the basin of the river. On his return he published an elaborate account of his discoveries, but his enemies openly disbelieved them, and the country as a whole showed little interest.

[1] Doyle, *op. cit.* p. 97.

[2] See Hamilton McMillan, *Sir Walter Ralegh's Lost Colony*, Ralegh, N.C., 1907, in which all the evidence on the subject is set forth.

CHAPTER IX

THE SPANISH WAR, 1585-1603

In May, 1585, Philip II., having by promises of protection induced a number of English merchantmen to enter Spanish ports with cargoes of corn, suddenly arrested them all and cast their crews into prison. One, the *Primrose* of London, made good her escape, bringing with her to England the Corregidor of Bilbao who had come aboard in person to seize the ship in the guise of a friendly merchant. This act is generally taken to mark the beginning of the Spanish war, although neither side issued a formal declaration. The causes were numerous —the depredations of Drake and his imitators, the machinations of the Catholic Church involving plots against Elizabeth's throne and life, the countenance given by the queen to the revolt of the Nether-lands, the forcible annexation of Portugal and its colonies by Philip in 1580-1. The cumulative effect of these had been a slow and steady march to an inevitable war, the more certain to involve the whole strength of the conflicting nations because long delayed by the pacific efforts of leaders on both sides who would fain have avoided the issue.

Throughout the struggle England had never any prospect of a military conquest of Spain itself ; her most aggressive captains aspired to nothing more than the occupation of strategic points from which they might dominate the trade-routes. Spain, on the other hand, had from the outset a clear intention of invading and conquering England with an overwhelming army. To clear the way for this army to cross the sea, and at the same time to protect the commerce which was to provide the sinews of war, was therefore the first task she had to perform ; and since she never accomplished it the war was always a naval one to the end, and England relied for her defence upon her maritime resources.

We have seen that when Elizabeth came to the throne the navy of Henry VIII. had decreased in numbers and efficiency. Some new ships were added just after the queen's accession, and thenceforward the total was not greatly altered for twenty years. During that time, although the nominal head of the Navy Board was the Treasurer, Benjamin Gonson, the fleet was substantially under the administration of Sir William Winter, the surveyor of the ships, a seaman of experience *in* the mid-century wars. Meanwhile a new influence was growing powerful. After the cessation of his western voyages in 1569, John Hawkins was regarded, until the rise of Drake, as the country's leading sea commander, and was consulted on questions of naval policy. Winter's vision was limited to campaigns against France and Scotland in home waters, and the navy was designed to that end. Hawkins foresaw that Spain was the future enemy, and that she must be struck on the ocean and in the distant American seas. For that purpose he desired to modernize the fleet, cutting down the high upper works which had been thought necessary to constitute floating castles impregnable to boarding, and making the ships low-built, fast and sea-worthy, relying for victory on their guns rather than a multitude of men. The new ships were called galleons, and under Hawkins's guidance England adopted the galleon type many years before Spain followed the example. Apart from these technical reforms, Hawkins knew that corruption was rampant under Winter's control, and that much of the queen's naval expenditure was going into private pockets. In 1577 Hawkins succeeded his father-in-law Gonson as Treasurer of the Navy, defeated the reactionary influence of Winter, and was able to rebuild and enlarge the fleet before war broke out in 1585. In spite of much calumny from those whose peculations he had checked, he stuck to his task and was able to declare that the fleet was more efficient while costing less. The accounts prove the second claim, and the war was to support the first.

At the beginning of the war there was no ocean-going Spanish navy. Philip had under his control a large force of oared galleys generally recognized as unserviceable outside the Mediterranean ; a few well-armed ships paid for by tolls levied on the West Indian merchants, and allocated to the duty of convoying their cargoes ; and about a dozen Portuguese galleons which he acquired on his annexation of that country. For his early undertakings he supplemented these forces by arming his own large merchantmen and hiring others from the Hanseatic League and the Italians. Experience, however, soon revealed the defects of this heterogeneous fleet, and before the war had been many years in progress Spain began to undertake in earnest the construction of a national navy after the English model.

At the time of the arrest of the English merchantmen Drake had been negotiating with the queen for the conduct of a new raid upon the Spanish colonies. The arrest provided an excellent excuse for reprisals, and in September, 1585, after much hesitation on the queen's part, he put to sea at the head of a fleet of twenty-one ships and eight pinnaces. Of these vessels only two belonged to the navy, the remainder being privateers and armed merchantmen from London and the south-western ports. The expenses were paid by a joint-stock company, and the object of the expedition was twofold, to obtain sufficient plunder to yield a profit. and to strike a real blow at Philip's colonial system by dislocating the transport of the treasure upon which he was basing his preparations for the invasion of England. Martin Frobisher sailed as vice-admiral of the squadron, and Christopher Carleill, Walsingham's son-in-law, as general of a body of soldiers provided for land operations.

Drake sailed first to Vigo Bay, where he took some booty and defied the Spaniards on their own soil to interfere with him. Thence he went southwards to the Canaries and the Cape Verde Islands, where he burned the city of Santiago. Crossing the Atlantic in eighteen days, he came to the Windward Islands and prepared at once to attack San Domingo in Hispaniola, the capital city of the West Indies. On the first day of 1586 he landed Carleill's troops without the knowledge of the Spaniards, and Carleill appearing from the land side whilst Drake attacked from the sea, the city was taken with very small loss. The yield of plunder was disappointing, and after burning a large part of the place Drake accepted £6000 as ransom for the remainder and sailed to repeat the exploit at Cartagena, the capital of the Spanish Main. Here the Spaniards had received warning and were prepared for a stout defence. But Drake's eye seized the weak point in fortifications which they believed impregnable. Again he landed Carleill and his soldiers with orders to take an entrenchment upon a narrow isthmus covering the approach to the city. The English force, wading along the tide-beach up to their knees in the sea, were able to avoid the fire which would have stopped them had they used the high-road. After a stiff fight in which Carleill slew the Spanish standard-bearer with his own hand, attackers and defenders crowded through the gates together, and Cartagena was taken. Drake remained six weeks in the hope of extorting a ransom of £100,000. In the end he accepted a quarter of that sum for the bare walls of the place, having gutted it of all portable property. He had considered the question of leaving a garrison to hold it permanently, but sickness and fighting had reduced his force, and he abandoned the idea. Very possibly the queen, as yet not resolute for regular warfare, would have reversed a decision to hold it. The programme of the voyage had included the sack of Panama, the third greatest town of Philip's colonies. This also had to be given up owing to the ravages of the epidemics which smote impartially every expedition, English and Spanish, in this war. The fleet sailed home by way of Florida and Virginia, missing by twelve hours the capture of a squadron of treasure ships on the way. As a privateering venture the voyage had failed, the adventurers receiving back only fifteen shillings in the pound of their investment. As a warlike stroke against the resources of Spain it had been a brilliant success. Instead of drawing money from his colonies Philip had now for some time to spend large sums on their defence. Two hundred and forty guns of all sizes were but one item in the military captures; and the private mariners, who had spent their lives so freely, were known to have obtained large plunder in the sack of the two great cities. The Spanish king found his credit broken, and was thought by good judges to be on the verge of bankruptcy.

So matters stood in the summer of 1586. Again a period of insincere negotiation followed, Elizabeth hoping that Philip, having felt the weight of her hand, would even now come to an accommodation, Philip desirous to lull the English preparations whilst he made headway with his own and extorted financial support from the pope. Next came the discovery of the Babington conspiracy to murder the queen, a plain indication of the real aims of the country's enemies. At the end of the year Mary Stuart was brought to trial and convicted of complicity. Her execution in February, 1587, cleared from Philip's path one of his principal difficulties, for he could now conquer England for his own benefit and not for that of the Scottish queen with her leanings towards his rivals in France. He gave orders to his admiral, the Marquis of Santa Cruz, to hasten his preparations. At Lisbon, Cadiz, and within the Mediterranean, the great Armada was collecting, its units waiting only for their guns and stores to concentrate and sail for the Channel that very summer. Elizabeth was shaken for the moment from her dreamland of a diplomatic settlement, and realized the imminence of her peril. In a mood of resolution she gave the word to Drake, waiting in readiness at Plymouth, to sail at once " to impeach the joining together of the King of Spain's fleets." Drake hastened away before the cold fit should follow the hot, and scarcely had he gone when a further order arrived forbidding him to enter any Spanish port or commit any act of war otherwise than on the open sea —in a word, to do what his mind was set upon. He had trusty friends at Plymouth and the order never reached him, the bark which pursued him with it being blown back by a convenient gale.

Drake with twenty-one sail, royal and mercantile, made for Cadiz. His vice-admiral was William Borough, a veteran who had seen service with the Muscovy Company in the White Sea and the Baltic. Arrived at Cadiz, Drake gave orders for an immediate entrance into the port in disregard of the fire of the land defences. Borough protested vainly, alleging that such a proceeding was contrary to all the rules of war. Drake went in and the fleet followed. In Cadiz were many ships destined for the Armada, in various stages of unreadiness, together with a number of galleys which were supposed to be especially formidable in a land-locked water. The English gunnery routed the galleys, and Drake remained for thirty-six hours in the harbour, burning or carrying off everything he could reach within it. The Spaniards themselves admitted the loss of twenty-four sail ; the English claimed thirty-six, amounting together to 13,000 tons. Leaving Cadiz, Drake went next to Lisbon, capturing much shipping on the way. At Lisbon he found Santa Cruz unready to put to sea, but the strength of the fortifications prevented him from repeating the Cadiz exploit. He then took up his station by Cape St. Vincent, and by so doing paralysed the concentration of the scattered Spanish fleet. To secure safe riding at St. Vincent he had to land a force to capture Sagres Castle and other works, and tumble their guns into the sea. Borough again protested and was placed under arrest for his pains. Having effectively postponed the sailing of the Armada for the summer the English departed to the Azores where they waylaid and captured a homeward bound carrack, the *San Felipe*. She was Philip's own ship, containing an enormously rich cargo. During this part of the voyage the ship in which Borough was a prisoner deserted and sailed for home. Drake accused Borough of being the instigator of the mutiny, assembled a court-martial, and condemned his luckless vice-admiral to death in his absence. The sentence was afterwards remitted. Having shown how it was possible to prevent "the Enterprise of England" from ever getting under way, Drake returned to receive, not honours and rewards, but a reprimand from his inconstant mistress for hitting the enemy too hard. "Her Majesty is greatly offended at him," wrote Burghley to the Hollanders on the morrow of the admiral's return.

To the very last Elizabeth clung to the idea of negotiating a peace before the invasion should be launched. Fortunately she was served by men who placed their country's interests before the risk of her displeasure, although there were others at her ear who were actually in the pay of Spain. Santa Cruz died, worn out with the fruitless toil of 1587. His successor, the far less competent Duke of Medina Sidonia, found the disorganization and rottenness of his command at their height. In vain in the early months of 1588 Drake clamoured to be let loose to finish his work. A fresh negotiation had begun, and the queen was obdurate, believing in her heart that left to itself the Armada would never sail. Nevertheless, as the spring drew on, the information became more and more certain that it would sail. Philip, hidden in his room in the Escurial, never visiting his troops or seeing one of his ships, was bent, by sheer force of his will-power, on forcing it to sea in face of every difficulty. Every protest, every objection of lack of this or insufficiency of that, he met with the same answer, that the thing must be done, that those who hung back were cowards and fools. His sneers killed the honest and capable Santa Cruz; they drove the shiftless Sidonia helpless to disaster.

At length the great armament sailed from Lisbon in the third week of May. A fortnight later adverse winds drove it into Coruna, already short of provisions and suffering from epidemics. For a month it lay there, repairing damages and weeding out the sick. Meanwhile Lord Howard of Effingham, the Lord Admiral, had joined Drake at Plymouth, and the whole English fleet was ready to strike. The admirals wished to sail southwards and attack at once, but the queen vacillated between yea and nay, and when she was favourable the winds, as luck would have it, were adverse. At the beginning of July Howard and Drake got to sea; when they were almost in sight of the Spanish coast a southerly gale drove them back, and as they entered Plymouth Medina Sidonia sailed finally out of Coruna.

As it drew near to the mouth of the Channel the Armada numbered 120 ships and 24,000 men.[1] Half the ships were transports or victuallers not available for fighting. The combatant vessels were of larger average size than those of the English, but their gun-power was weaker and their ammunition insufficient. Soldiers outnumbered the seamen in the crews by more than two to one ; and the whole fleet, in spite of the warnings of Spanish officers who knew better, was organized on the assumption that the fighting would be decided by boarding and a hand-to-hand struggle across the decks. The Battle of Lepanto, the great sea victory which the Spaniards had won against the Turks in 1571, had been fought on these lines, and was quoted in support of the fatal policy of Philip and his advisers. Another weakness lay in the fact that the officers and men were not of one race and speech, being drawn from Portugal, Italy and the several diverse provincial strains which had hardly yet been welded into the single nationality of Spain. Medina Sidonia's instructions were to sail up the Channel, seize Margate or some other landing-place in the Thames estuary, and convoy across from the Low Countries the veteran army of the Duke of Parma, adding to it a proportion of the soldiers from his own ships. He had no definite orders, and apparently no clear plan, for dealing with the English navy. It seems to have been taken for granted that Drake only with a small force would be found at Plymouth, and that Howard with the main fleet would be in the Narrow Seas. For the event as it actually fell out the Spaniards were unprepared.

The approach of the Spaniards was unexpected by Howard and Drake, who thought they were still lying at Coruna. Nevertheless they made haste to get their fleet out of Plymouth, and during the first evening succeeded by skilful seamanship in working to the westward of the Armada and so obtaining the advantage of the weathergage. Under Howard's orders were some fifty fighting ships and forty pinnaces, and in the course of the next few days he was joined by many more vessels of secondary rank until his total numbers of all kinds reached 197 sail,[2] with 16,000 men. Three of the queen's first-class ships, with an attendant following of privateers and merchantmen, remained off Dunkirk under Lord Henry Seymour to prevent Parma's army from putting to sea in its barges and transports. With Howard were most of the prominent English leaders of the time—John Hawkins, his son Richard, Frobisher, Fenner, Fenton, Raymond, Lord Sheffield, Lord Thomas Howard, and Sir Robert Southwell. Drake acted as vice-admiral and Hawkins as rear-admiral. Ralegh and

---

[1] The above figures are given by Sir J. K. Laughton, *State Papers relating to the Defeat of the Armada*, Navy Records Society, vol. i. p. xl. Other modern authorities are in substantial agreement.

[2] Laughton, *op. cit.* p. xli. But Sir J. S. Corbett points out that there were never more than 140 ships together at one time. The actual fighting was done by about fifty vessels on either side.

Grenville were not at sea. They were employed in organizing the land forces of the south-west, as part of the general levy of which Leicester was commander-in-chief.

On the morning of July 21 the Armada was drawing abreast of Plymouth Sound, with the bulk of the English fleet lying to the westward of it. Howard attacked, and in the fighting which followed neither side secured a decisive advantage. The Spaniards were alarmed by the ease with which the English fired into their exposed vessels and drew off without themselves receiving any damage. The English on their side were impressed by the solidity of the Armada and its cunning organization in disciplined squadrons by which any vessel in difficulties was immediately supported and rescued.[1] The result of the morning's fighting was that the Armada was driven past Plymouth, thus losing the chance of entering and taking it, and that neither fleet had yet lost a ship, although the Spaniards had two badly damaged. To Howard and his officers it now seemed probable that Medina Sidonia would attempt to seize the Isle of Wight as a convenient base for the operations of Parma's army ; and in the Spanish councils the plan was considered, although it was contrary to Philip's orders. Howard therefore determined to pursue closely. In the night the two damaged Spaniards failed to keep up the pace and were abandoned to the English. Drake incurred much criticism by quitting his station at the head of the fleet in order to take possession of one of these prizes ; for, since every captain was ordered to follow his light, the whole fleet was thrown into confusion by his change of course. He himself explained his action as the fruit of a misapprehension, but some of his contemporaries charged him with preferring plunder to the queen's service.

The next action occurred off Portland on July 23. Here again, in a whole day of confused fighting, there was no decisive result. The Spaniards lost a number of men by the English fire, but no ships, and they inflicted little damage in return. Frobisher distinguished himself by a great defence when surrounded by superior forces, and shortage of ammunition caused the English to break off the action. Howard now reorganized his fleet into four squadrons commanded respectively by himself, Drake, Hawkins and Frobisher. On July 25 the two fleets, having been delayed by calms, were south of the Isle of Wight. This was now regarded as the decisive position, for there was no harbour anywhere to the eastward in which Sidonia might shelter his fleet whilst opening communications with Parma. Howard therefore attacked with all his strength, and by hard fighting and skilful manoeuvring forced the Spaniards to abandon all thought of

[1] Modern research has disproved the oft-repeated story of the crescent formation of the Armada. Its fighting ships sailed in two great divisions, the one following the other and subdivided into smaller squadrons. Between the two were the victuallers and transports. The Spaniards sailed in lines abreast ; the English, apparently, in lines ahead. Corbett, *Drake and the Tudor Navy*, ii. 210-221.

making use of the landlocked waters about the Isle. Sidonia continued his course eastwards to the roadstead of Calais, sending orders
to Parma to join him there at all costs. Parma was unable to do any
such thing. He was closely watched by a combined English and
Dutch squadron, and he naturally expected the Spanish fleet to drive
off these blockaders before he would think of embarking his army.

At Calais Sidonia was allowed no time to make new arrangements
in place of those which had broken down. The English, following as
closely as his shadow, had come to anchor a cannon-shot to the westward of him. His men were becoming demoralized by the deadliness
of the English gunnery and the inefficacy of their own. His officers
now realized the folly of the plan to which they were committed, the
attempt to carry out an invasion without securing the command of
the sea. On the evening of the arrival at Calais Seymour joined
Howard with five large ships and seven smaller ones. The anchorage
outside the little port was open and unprotected. A sense of failure
and a dread of what was to come pervaded the whole Armada. At
this fateful moment Howard and Drake delivered a blow which an
unshaken enemy might successfully have turned aside. They sent
eight fireships blazing into the ranks of the crowded fleet. Upon
men waiting, as one of them confessed, " with a great presentiment of
evil from that devilish people and their arts," the effect was what the
English had calculated. Making no attempt to deal with the fireships
the Spanish captains cut their cables and drifted away eastwards
on wind and tide. The stratagem had accomplished what a week's
fighting had failed to do. It had broken the orderly formation of the
Armada, which was now a struggling mass of ships without shape,
cohesion or rallying-point. One of the four galleasses, the greatest
ships of the fleet, was left rudderless and aground under the guns of
Calais. She fell ultimately into the hands of the French. All the
remainder got away, although many received damage by collisions.
But the fireships had justified their expenditure.

When morning dawned the Armada was scattered for miles along
the coast. Medina Sidonia did his best to rally it and reform his
battle order. Before he could do so Drake, Hawkins and most of the
English were upon him. Howard alone turned aside, as Drake had
done near Plymouth, to attack the disabled Spaniard which had been
left behind. This day's battle is known as that of Gravelines. It
decided the fate of the campaign by driving the Spaniards away from
the Flemish coast and depriving them of all hope of returning to join
hands with Parma. Medina Sidonia, collecting his best ships, tried in
vain to stand his ground. Throughout the day, in a steadily rising
wind, the English squadrons circled about him, pouring in the most
terrible fire that had ever been known in a sea battle. The Spanish
captains and their crews died gloriously, refusing to surrender even
when all hope was gone. One or two great ships went down with
nearly all their hands, and three drifted ashore on the Flemish sands

to be taken by the light Dutch craft which awaited them. The remainder, with their rigging shot to pieces and their sides full of shot holes, seemed doomed to the like fate when a sudden shift of the wind delivered them. But they had no thought of returning to carry out the invasion. Drawing together as well as they could they fled northwards into waters unknown to all, seeking to reach Spain once more by the north of Scotland and the west of Ireland.

The English, their powder and victuals exhausted, saw them past the Firth of Forth, and then returned to the Thames estuary. They had lost little more than a hundred men in all the actions, but after they regained port a terrible outbreak of typhus carried off more than ten times that number, and was only stayed by the disbandment of the infected crews. The Spaniards had lost eleven good ships and 8000 men in the fighting, but the full effects of the battle of Gravelines only showed themselves on the homeward voyage. In the two months following reports came in of wholesale shipwrecks on the northern and western coasts. On the shores of Connaught the death-roll was particularly heavy; and of the thousands who struggled to land scarcely a few score escaped massacre at the hands of the Irish peasantry whom they had boasted they were coming to deliver from English tyranny. " God," reported an English officer in Ireland, " hath suffered this nation to blood their hands upon them, whereby, it may be hoped, is drawn perpetual diffidence between the Spaniards and them as long as this memory endureth." Not half the ships, and much less than half the men, of the Armada returned to Spain to reveal the full extent of the disaster. The unfortunate Duke of Medina Sidonia was one of the survivors. He had known from the first that he was incompetent for the command, and had told his master so in vain ; yet whenever he saw his duty clear before him he had played the man to the utmost of his powers. Philip doubtless recognized his own error, for he added no word of reproach to the storm of execration which burst from all sides upon the unhappy commander's head.

Drake was now in the ascendant in the English councils, and he demanded an immediate counterstroke to drive home the success. Don Antonio, the exiled claimant to the Portuguese throne, had been vainly soliciting English aid for years. He declared that all Portugal would rise in his favour if he could land with an English force at his back. Drake, with the idea of establishing a second Netherlands at Philip's own doors, proposed the capture of Lisbon as the best means of accomplishing the design. Early in 1589 he set about organizing a fleet for the purpose, and Sir John Norreys, a distinguished Low Countries soldier, raised an army. In April the two put to sea with some 15,000 men conveyed in 130 ships, of which only eight belonged to the navy. The expenses were defrayed by a joint-stock company of which the queen was the largest shareholder. Drake was not allowed to proceed straight to Lisbon ; his instructions enjoined the previous attack of the northern Spanish ports. Accordingly he besieged Coruna, captured the lower town, and withdrew after doing much military damage and losing many men. The inevitable epidemic now broke out, and it was with reduced forces that Norreys landed at Peniche and began his march to Lisbon. He reached the outskirts of the city, only to find it strongly held by the Archduke Albert, who had by now received ample warning. Of the Portuguese rising there was no sign. Norreys therefore retreated to the coast and re-embarked. Drake was on the point of entering the Tagus with the fleet when he heard of the retreat. He was severely blamed for not supporting Norreys more promptly, and passed the next five years in disgrace and without employment of importance. The expedition, in comparison with what was expected of it, was reckoned a failure, but it had not failed so utterly as the Armada in the previous year.

Sir John Hawkins had already proposed an alternative plan. Philip II.'s armed forces, serving not only in Portugal but in Italy, France and the Netherlands, could be maintained only by means of the treasure received from the West. The king's European revenues did not nearly defray the costs of government and armaments. The American possessions of Spain and the East Indian monopoly of the crown of Portugal (now Philip's) alone yielded the surplus for carrying on the war. If naval action could prevent the king from receiving this revenue, he would be unable to continue. Hawkins contended that naval action could do so. For reasons of navigation the homecoming fleets from East and West had to pass the Azores, and generally to call there. Hawkins proposed to hold the Azores station permanently by sending six fighting galleons and a proportion of auxiliaries to cruise there. Such a squadron would stay out for four months and would then be relieved by another, and by this means the treasure-route would be blocked the whole year round. The plan was half-heartedly accepted and never put into operation. In 1589 Drake's Lisbon expedition diverted energies. In 1590 Hawkins and Frobisher were at sea for six months, but the Azores were unwatched for the other six, and in both years the treasure got through. With this money Philip was able to begin his naval rearmament, as was unpleasantly demonstrated in 1591. Lord Thomas Howard and Sir Richard Grenville were at the Azores awaiting a great Spanish convoy due from the West. Philip was able to send out from Spain to escort it some twenty fighting ships against Howard's six, and in the ensuing action off Flores the English had to retreat, while Grenville and the famous *Revenge* were lost. This was the fight of " the one and the fifty-three," the higher number being obtained by counting in the Spanish auxiliary vessels. The *Revenge* actually did engage fifteen Spaniards in successive groups, and sank four of them.

After this few of the queen's ships were employed, and commerce-raiding at the Azores became a business for the privateers. In 1592 they captured an East Indian carrack and destroyed another, but there was never any success against the western treasure. During all these years the English privateers multiplied in numbers and audacity. Spanish merchantmen could only cross the Atlantic in great convoys, and even so all stragglers were set upon and captured ; in some years trade was almost at a standstill. In spite of all losses Philip worked patiently to remedy the errors which the Armada disaster had revealed. From the day of its return he set himself to construct a real navy, and the great fleet which destroyed Grenville in 1591 provided a serious shock for Elizabeth's government, which now saw that it had a more formidable enemy to face than in 1588. The invasion of England remained the principal object of Philip's plans. To open the way he entered into alliance with the Guise party in France with the object of obtaining Brest as a base for his next attempt. A Spanish force landed on the Breton coast and fortified itself at Crozon, near Brest. Frobisher and Sir Henry Norreys attacked it in November, 1594, and although they were successful in storming the defences Frobisher was killed.

In the years after 1588 the chances of ending the war had been allowed to slip. The Queen was conscious that things were going badly and alarmed at the reviving power of Spain, for all reports showed that Philip had at last a regular navy of far better quality than the Armada. The basis of its strength was the western treasure, which summer cruises to the Azores had failed to intercept. The continuous blockade advised by Hawkins had never been tried, and would now require greater forces than when he first proposed it. The remaining remedy seemed to be a stroke at the sources of Spanish wealth, in the manner of Drake's great raid of 1585-6.

Before the close of 1594 Drake and Hawkins were making preparations for the new western expedition. For reasons that were not explained they were made joint commanders with equal authority, an arrangement obviously likely to create dissension. Each engaged his own men and provided his own victuals, and their methods were so different that the fortune of the expedition was prejudiced. The original plan was to seize Panama with a view to capturing the treasure coming up from Peru ; but this was not the purpose with which the commanders finally sailed. In July, 1595, they were ready to start, but the Queen hesitated. Intelligence from Spain pointed to a new attempt at invading England next year, and she was unwilling to let Drake and Hawkins go off on a long expedition. Then came a piece of news which altered the position. A Spanish treasure-ship had put into San Juan de Porto Rico in distress with two million ducats on board. The ship was a wreck, and the money was there until transport should be sent from Spain. The Queen therefore allowed Drake and Hawkins to sail for the capture of the Porto Rico treasure on their promise to be home within six months.

Speed and surprise were essential, for it was known that a force was being sent from Spain. But no sooner was the fleet at sea than Drake demanded a divergence from the plan. He was short of victuals and proposed to attack the Canary Islands and extort a ransom of food-stuffs. Hawkins was incensed, for the delay would imperil the object of the voyage. After some heated argument he yielded, but he regarded the voyage as overthrown from that moment, as indeed it was. The attack on the Canaries failed and yielded no victuals, after which the expedition crossed the Atlantic on its original supplies. But some Englishmen were made prisoners at Grand Canary and revealed the destination ; and the governor sent a warning to Porto Rico which outstripped the English. Five well-armed ships also reached the place from Spain before the English appeared, and an alert and powerful garrison stood ready to resist attack. Hawkins died in his cabin as the fleet reached Porto Rico, and Drake organized the assault. He was beaten off with loss, and then stood south to the Spanish Main and passed along it to Nombre de Dios. He landed his troops to attack Panama, but they were repulsed and retreated to the ships. After this disease smote the expedition, and nothing more was attempted. Drake died off Porto Bello on January 27, 1596. Sir Thomas Baskerville, the military commander, brought the fleet home after beating off an attack by the Spanish fleet on the way.

The old commanders who had made England an oceanic power were dropping out one by one, giving place to new men who, for the most part, had served their apprenticeship at court rather than on the seas. Of the younger generation Sir Walter Ralegh and Robert Devereux, Earl of Essex, were the most prominent ; and the latter, in spite of the defects of his character, had perhaps a larger share than any man of the qualities which had made Drake great. With their advent the war revived. Elizabeth's eyes were now fully opened to the opportunities she had wasted, and the year 1596 saw the first regular attack on the new Spanish navy which Philip had been silently organizing since the defeat of 1588.

Whilst the news of Drake's failure and death was yet unknown a great armament was in preparation to drive home his expected victories by a blow at the ports and shipping of Spain itself. The scale of the expedition was such that the Lord Admiral came forth to lead it in person with his son Lord Thomas Howard as vice-admiral, Ralegh as rear-admiral, and Essex as general of the land forces. Delays arose from the bad news from the West Indies and the capture of Calais by the Spanish army in the Netherlands. These produced the customary vacillations in the queen's intentions. Finally her doubts were overcome, and on June 3, 1596, the fleet set sail. It consisted of forty-seven men-of-war and over sixty transports conveying an army of 8000 men. With great speed and secrecy it made straight for Cadiz, its chief point of attack, and the surprise was so far successful that the Spaniards had less than two days' warning of its approach. After its arrival the Lord Admiral, old and cautious, wasted time in councils of war and the deliberation of formal plans of attack. In the end Lord Thomas Howard, Ralegh and Essex took things very much into their own hands. The two former attacked the shipping whilst Essex landed the army and stormed the city. The Spanish warships fought hard, but were unable to stop the English fleet. All except a few galleys perished, destroyed by the English or burned by their own crews, together with a number of laden merchantmen. In all nearly fifty ships, worth twelve million ducats, were thus lost to Spain. The action ceased only when the English were masters of the city and the harbour a mass of blackened wrecks. Essex was in favour of permanently holding Cadiz, as the best bridle upon Spanish naval power. But he was overruled, and after giving the place to the flames the expedition sailed homewards, committing further depredations by the way.

Essex had vainly pleaded for sufficient delay to permit of an attempt on the homeward-bound treasure-fleet and the East Indian carracks. In this also he had been overruled. His wisdom was recognized when it became known that these rich convoys had come safely into port soon after the departure of the English ; and Ralegh, who had been most eager to return home, fell into discredit. Although more might have been done the success was yet brilliant. Philip, stung to loss of self-control by the disgrace and disappointment, swore to be revenged. Working feverishly all through the summer he collected a fleet of a hundred sail in the ocean ports of Spain and Portugal. In spite of all advice he drove it to sea in the last week of October, bent upon invading England at a season when precautions might be relaxed. Again fortune failed him. A storm shattered this Armada also, destroying thirty-two large ships and two thousand men ; and not a single Spanish sail came in sight of the English coast.

So for seven more years the see-saw continued, each side attacking in turn and neither being able to deal a mortal blow. In 1597 Essex and Ralegh made great preparations for one more stroke at Spain with fleet and army. The weather dispersed their force as it had done Philip's, although English seamanship prevented the terrible casualties of the previous autumn. Landing their soldiers, they set forward again on a purely naval adventure intended for the interception of the treasure-fleet at the Azores. This, the well-known " Islands Voyage," was a melancholy series of misfortunes and mistakes. Ralegh's behaviour offended the fiery temper of Essex ; the treasure-fleet blundered unsuspecting into the midst of the archipelago whilst the English were there, and was missed by a bare three hours ; and a carrack of 2000 tons was almost in their grasp when, being prematurely fired upon, she was beached and burnt by her own crew. The commanders came home in bitter enmity whilst Philip was preparing his last Armada. As in the previous year, it sailed in the late autumn, only to be scattered and driven back by the Biscay storms. In 1598 Philip II. died, to the relief of many of his subjects who had come to believe that fortune would never smile upon his flag. But the new king, Philip III., although eager to maintain the contest, effected little. The chief point of interest lay now in Ireland, where continual rebellions seemed to offer the Spaniards their best opportunity. In 1601 Don Juan de Aguila landed at Kinsale, and for a time the English forces were in a serious position. But the intrepidity of the Deputy, Lord Mountjoy, turned the scale, and Aguila surrendered after the defeat of the Irish levies which had marched to join him. In the West Indies the outstanding event of these years was the capture of Porto Rico by the Earl of Cumberland with a privateer force in 1598.

The long tragedy came to an end with the death of Elizabeth in 1603. James I., her successor, made haste to proclaim that he did not consider himself at war with Spain, and commissioners from either side concluded the peace of 1604. By this treaty the causes of the war were ignored. Not a word was said of the position of England as an oceanic power, or of her rights to trade and colonize in the west. Philip II., dying in despair, had warned his son that he must in the end concede trade in the Indies to his foes. The situation had not altered since that date, but James demanded less than Spain had steeled herself to give. The real result of the war, however, is not to be looked for in the treaty. It lay plain for all the world to see in the contrast between the power and prestige of England in 1558 and 1603. At the former date she had seemed barely fitted to survive as a European kingdom, destined rather, in the opinion of many, to become an appanage of France or Spain. At the latter, she stood forth tried and proved in conflict with the greatest world-power, and ready now to become a world-power herself.

AUTHORITIES FOR PART II.

GENERAL.

The results of modern research in the general history of England during the Tudor period will be found in *The Political History of England*, vols. 5 and 6 ; the relevant chapters in vols. 1, 2 and 3 of the *Cambridge Modern History* ; and in two volumes of the *Oxford History of England*, by J. D. Mackie and J. B. Black respectively. Although of older date and subject to correction in certain matters, James Anthony Froude's *History of England* (from the Fall of Wolsey to the Defeat of the Armada), 12 vols., London, 1856-70, is still the most brilliant and broadly conceived exposition of the time.

Among accounts of particular reigns are *England under the Tudors*, by W. Busch (unfinished, Henry VII. only), London, 1895 ; *Henry VII.*, by J. Gairdner, London, 1889 ; *Henry VIII.*, by A. F. Pollard, London, 1905 ; *England under Protector Somerset*, by A. F. Pollard, London, 1900 ; *Queen Elizabeth*, by J. E. Neale London, 1934.

Cunningham's *Growth of English Industry and Commerce during Early and Middle Ages* extends to the middle of the sixteenth century. The subject is continued by the same author in *The Growth of English Industry and Commerce during Modern Times*, 2 vols., Cambridge, 1903. Other works on social and economic matters for the period are Innes' *England's Industrial Development*, and Traill and Mann's *Social England* (see Auth. Pt. I.) ; and *Shakespeare's England*, by various contributors, 2 vols., Oxford, 1916.

Works on maritime affairs are dealt with under the headings of particular chapters. *English Seamen in the Sixteenth Century*, by J. A. Froude, London, 1895, is of general application, providing as it does accounts of many of the better-known voyages. The great original collection of overseas undertakings of the time is Richard Hakluyt's *Principal Navigations of the English Nation*, 1st ed., 1 vol., 1589 ; 2nd ed. 3 vols., 1599-1600 ; best modern edition, 12 vols., printed for the Hakluyt Society, 1903 ; cheap modern edition (with omissions), 8 vols., in Messrs. Dent's Everyman Library. Clues to many of the projects of the period are obtainable from the ideas examined in E. G. R. Taylor's *Tudor Geography*, London, 1930.

CHAPTER I. THE REGULATED COMPANIES, 1485-1603.

The European trades in relation to general economic history are dealt with in the works of Cunningham and Innes already mentioned. Schanz's *Englische Handelspolitik* (see Auth. Pt. I.) ends at the year 1547. *Foreign Commerce under the Tudors*, by J. B. Williamson, Oxford, 1883, is a still useful sketch covering the whole period. The history of the Staplers, the Merchants Adventurers and the Eastland Company is followed through the period in *Beginnings of English Overseas Enterprise*, by Sir C. P. Lucas, Oxford, 1917. *The Early Chartered Companies*, by G. Cawston and A. H. Keane, London, 1896, provides a sound outline of the subject. The circumstances accompanying the fall of the Hansa in England are set forth in *The Germans in England*, 1066-1598, by I. D. Colvin, London, 1915. Useful monographs are *The Internal Organisation of the Merchants Adventurers*, by W. E. Lingelbach, *Trans. of Royal Historical Society*, vol. xvi. (1902) ; *History of the Levant Company*, by A. C. Wood, Oxford, 1935 ; and *Acts and Ordinances of the Eastland Company* (Introduction), by Miss M. Sellers, Camden Society, 1906.

CHAPTER. II. THE AGE OF DISCOVERY—PORTUGUESE AND SPANISH.

Cambridge Modern History, vol. i. ch. i. and ii., forms an introduction that is now growing somewhat out of date. More recent conclusions are in *The Great Age of Discovery*, London, 1932, ed. A. P. Newton. Some of the Portuguese discoveries are to be found in *Prince Henry the Navigator*, by C. R. Beazley, London, 1894, and others in *Vasco da Gama and his Successors*, 1460-1580, by K. G. Jayne, London, 1910. The only comprehensive treatment in English of the Portuguese achievements is *The Portuguese Pioneers*, by Edgar Prestage, London, 1933. The life of Columbus contains disputable passages, and the late Henry Vignaud set forth an unorthodox view supported by great learning and research in *Toscanelli and Columbus*, London, 1902, and *Histoire critique de Christophe Colomb*, 3 vols., Paris, 1911. Some worthless biographies of Columbus have been written by persons lacking the necessary knowledge and judgement. A thoroughly sound and well-written work embodying the more conservative interpretations of the evidence is S. E. Morison's *Christopher Columbus*, Oxford, 1942. Among other works on the discoveries are those on *Magellan*, by F. H. H. Guillemard, London, 1890 ; *Martin Behaim*, by E. G. Ravenstein, London, 1908 ; *The Spanish Conquistadores*, by F. A. Kirkpatrick, London, 1934 ; and (in part) *The Exploration of the Pacific*, by J. C. Beaglehole, London, 1934. Those who desire to read English translations of the contemporary accounts of discoveries will find almost all of them in the volumes published by the Hakluyt Society in the past hundred years. The editors' introductions to these volumes provide useful historical accounts of the various subjects.

CHAPTER III. THE AGE OF DISCOVERY, ENGLISH; AND THE NAVY, 1485-1558.

The discoveries of the Cabots have given rise to more controversial writing than has any other historical problem of this period. The *Cabot Bibliography*, by G. P. Winship, London, 1900, contains the names of no less than 579 books in all languages bearing upon the subject. Of the more modern works in English the following present the matter in all its bearings : *Voyages of the Cabots*, by S. E. Dawson, in *Trans. of the Royal Society of Canada*, 1894 ; *John and Sebastian Cabot*, by H. Harrisse, London, 1896 ; *John and Sebastian Cabot*, by C. R. Beazley, London, 1898 ; *Voyages of the Cabots and Corte Reals*, by H. P. Biggar, Paris, 1903 ; and *Voyages of the Cabots*, by J. A. Williamson, London, 1929. The account given in the present chapter follows the conclusions arrived at in the last-mentioned work ; but in such a complicated matter the most satisfactory course is for the student to examine the evidence (small in bulk and fully set forth in most of the above) and form his own opinion.

The subsequent English discoveries are treated in the above-mentioned books of Harrisse, Beazley and Williamson. *The Discovery of North America*, by H. Harrisse, London, 1892, treats the subject from the geographical point of view, and includes reproductions of many of the ancient maps which survive. *The Voyage of the Barbara of London*, by R. G. Marsden, *English Historical Review*, vol. xxiv., throws new light on the Brazil trade in the time of Henry VIII.

For the navy, 1485-1558, see the works of Sir W. Laird Clowes, D. Hannay, M. Oppenheim and Sir J. S. Corbett, mentioned in the Authorities for Part I.

CHAPTER IV. THE NEW COMMERCE.

The Guinea enterprises of Mary's reign have not, generally speaking, received as much attention from historians as their importance in international relations warrants. The voyages and the Anglo-Portuguese negotiations to which they gave rise are described in J. W. Blake's *European Beginnings in West Africa*, London, 1937. Their business organization and financial arrangements receive attention in *Joint Stock Companies to 1720*, by W. R. Scott, 3 vols., Cambridge, 1910, etc. The same authority treats also of the establishment and early operations of the Muscovy Company. The original narratives of the Russian expeditions are collected in *Early Voyages to Russia and Persia*, ed. E. Delmar Morgan, 2 vols., Hakluyt Society, 1886.

CHAPTER VI. ARMED TRADE AND REPRISALS.

The story of the Guinea trade under Elizabeth may be read in Blake's *European Beginnings in West Africa* and in J. A. Williamson's *Sir John Hawkins*, Oxford, 1927. The latter book also gives an account of the slave-trading voyages of 1562-9. Spanish accounts of the slaving enterprises and of the fight at San Juan de Ulua are printed in *Spanish Documents concerning English Voyages to the Caribbean, 1527-1568*, ed. I. A. Wright, Hakluyt Society, 1929. A second volume edited by Miss Wright, *Documents concerning English Voyages to the Spanish Main, 1569-1580*, Hakluyt Society, 1932, covers most of the reprisal period in the West Indies, adding considerably to our knowledge of Drake and Andrew Barker, and revealing the true story of John Oxenham for the first time. The standard life of Drake is still that of Sir J. S. Corbett, *Drake and the Tudor Navy*, London, 1898. For the voyage of circumnavigation it is supplemented by Spanish documents in *New Light on Drake*, ed. Z. Nuttall, Hakluyt Society, 1914. Later considerations on the same voyage are expressed in H. R. Wagner's *Sir Francis Drake's Voyage around the World*, San Francisco, 1926 ; but shortly afterwards revolutionary new evidence came to light in documents printed by Prof. E. G. R. Taylor in *Geographical Journal*, Jan., 1930, and *Mariner's Mirror*, Apr., 1929, and Apr., 1930. The new conclusions are sketched in the present writer's *Age of Drake*, London, 1938 ; but a full-dress life of Drake, based on the above discoveries and other research still to be performed, is now needed.

CHAPTER VII. THE PUSH TO THE EAST.

For the Persian trade see Morgan's *Early Voyages to Russia and Persia* (under Ch. IV.). Frobisher's attempts on the North-West are fully elucidated, with all the original narratives reprinted, in *The Three Voyages of Martin Frobisher*, by Vilhjalmur Stefansson, London, 1938. The Rev. F. Jones's *Life of Sir Martin Frobisher*, London, 1878, has not yet been superseded by any better general biography, although additional facts have since come to light. Similarly Sir C. R. Markham's *Life of John Davis*, London, 1889, is still the only general account of its subject. A well-written history of the early East Indian expeditions occurs in Sir W. W. Hunter's *History of British India*, vol. 1, London, 1899 ; but a fuller and more accurate account is now available in *England's Quest of Eastern Trade*, by Sir W. Foster, London, 1933.

CHAPTER VIII. ELIZABETHAN ATTEMPTS AT COLONIZATION.

Richard Hakluyt and the English Voyages, by G. B. Parks, New York, 1930, the only full-scale life of Hakluyt, laid the foundations of the recent investigation of the Elizabethan colonial activities. Two other works of research published by the Hakluyt Society have notably advanced the same study : *The Original Writings and Correspondence of the Two Richard Hakluyts*, ed. E. G. R. Taylor, 2 vols., 1935 ; and *The Voyages and Colonising Enterprises of Sir Humphrey Gilbert*, ed. D. B. Quinn, 2 vols., 1940. The former of these contains the best available text of Hakluyt's *Discourse of the Western Planting*. W. G. Gosling's *Life of Sir H. Gilbert*, London, 1911, is a good general authority now rendered somewhat out of date. For the Virginian enterprise the standard histories of the United States (see below, p. 318) should be consulted, and also the various lives of Ralegh, of which that by E. Edwards, although published in 1868, is still useful for its thoroughness and accuracy. The most recent *Life*, by E. Thompson, London, 1935, is more valuable for Ralegh's later rather than his earlier career. A penetrating appreciation of Ralegh with much new light on his South American project is to be found in *The Discovery of Guiana*, ed. V. T. Harlow, London, 1928.

CHAPTER IX. THE SPANISH WAR.

Corbett's *Drake and the Tudor Navy*, and its continuation, *The Successors of Drake*, London, 1900, give the most detailed modern history of the war. See also the naval histories of Laird Clowes, Hannay and Oppenheim. The original documents are collected in *State Papers relating to the Defeat of the Armada*, ed. Sir J. K. Laughton, 1894 ; and *Papers relating to the Navy in the Spanish War*, ed. Sir J. S. Corbett, 1898, both published by the Navy Records Society. The editors' introductions provide a careful analysis of the evidence on disputed points. A useful summary of the war occurs in *The Cambridge Modern History*, III. ch. ix. (Laughton). For the Spanish version see the work of Fernandez Duro already mentioned. The present writer's *Sir John Hawkins* includes the administration of the Navy and Hawkins's part in the fighting. A. L. Rowse's *Sir Richard Grenville*, London, 1937, one of the outstanding biographies of recent years, gives the story of Grenville's last fight authenticated by newly-discovered evidence, and is also valuable for the Virginian enterprise.

PART III

THE FOUNDATION OF THE MERCANTILE EMPIRE

CHAPTER I

GENERAL SURVEY OF ENGLISH EXPANSION UNDER JAMES I. AND CHARLES I., 1603-1649

WITH the accession of the Stuarts we enter a new age in English history. In the sphere of politics it differs markedly from that which preceded it. In the external activities with which this book is concerned there is, on the other hand, no sudden breach with the past, but rather an intensification of effort along the old lines, and an increasing embodiment of the fruits of experience in overseas undertakings. We have therefore to consider modifications, not a revolution, in methods, accompanied by much more solid achievements. It is in achievement indeed that the Tudor age differs from the Stuart. The one groped uncertainly towards an oceanic empire; the other founded and developed it.

Turning to the names of those with whom the story now concerns itself, we find much evidence of continuity. The greatest Elizabethans, indeed, were gone, but the younger generation had still their parts to play. Foremost among the merchants stood Sir Thomas Smith, grandson of Sir Andrew Judde and, like him, interested in nearly every trading venture of his time. Smith was governor of the East India Company from its inception until 1621, governor of the Muscovy and Somers' Islands Companies, treasurer of the Virginia Company, and a prominent member of the Levant Company. He mixed in politics to the extent of being implicated in Essex's treason. For this he passed some months in the Tower, to be released and knighted in 1603. Next year he went on an embassy to Russia, and later in life became a commissioner for the navy and member of Parliament. Amid all these interests he found leisure to be a patron of Arctic exploration. Next to Smith in importance came Lord Rich, the owner of many privateers, continuing to drive the old trade under foreign flags even after James I. had forbidden it to his subjects. Other Elizabethans surviving in full vigour included John Davis, Sir George Somers, Sir James Lancaster and Christopher Newport, among the seamen; Sir Thomas Dale and Sir Thomas Gates, soldiers of the

Netherlands; Ralegh and Southampton; and Richard Hakluyt, still active in the cause of colonization, and training a successor to his labours in the person of Samuel Purchas. We have cited only those who were to bear a part in promoting overseas expansion. Were the list to include leaders in other branches of thought and action it might be extended indefinitely: Shakespeare himself, it is well to remember, did not attain the fulness of his powers until the great queen was dead. It is only after the lapse of several years that we find men typical of a new era coming to the front—the younger Lord Rich, afterwards Earl of Warwick, his kinsman Sir Nathaniel Rich, Sir George Calvert, Sir Edwin Sandys, John Pym, William Bradford and John Winthrop, all tinged with religious dissent and becoming leaders of English expansion largely on that account.

There was, then, no sudden change in the trend of national thought in 1603. The Spanish period in our development continued although, as we can now see, Spain was not nearly so important as in the imagination of the time she seemed to be. Contemporaries looked at the treaty of 1604, and saw that on paper it decided none of the questions on which the long war had been waged. Thus it was natural for them to expect a renewal of the contest in the near future, and to frame their conduct accordingly. This misunderstanding of the real result of the struggle persisted for fifty years, and produced two more wars with Spain before the true facts became apparent. Elizabethan tradition in fact had a great influence upon the foreign policy of Cromwell.

Meanwhile a new rival, unregarded at first, was taking the place of worn-out Spain. The United Provinces, even before their independence was secure, were sending great merchant fleets to sea. In 1603 their East India Company, with its capital of half-a-million pounds, was an accomplished fact. In 1609 Spain consented to a twelve years' truce, the complement of the English peace of 1604. And here again the significance lay rather in the facts than in the words. Spain was exhausted, the Dutch triumphant and growing stronger year by year. The whole Dutch nation set itself to monopolize the carrying trade of the world. For this purpose it had three assets: its skill in shipbuilding and seamanship, its geographical position, and its freedom from the shackles of mediaeval organization. The first permitted its shipowners to charge freights less by one-third than Englishmen could profitably work for; the second gave access to the North Sea, the Baltic, the Arctic and the Atlantic as easy as that of London, whilst its command of the internal communications of Europe was far superior; the third permitted the state to frame a mercantile policy with sole reference to the needs of the time, unhampered by fixed ideas and vested interests of ancient hold upon the community. Thus equipped, the Dutch set out to carve for themselves a grip upon the commerce of the world comparable to that which the Hansa had enjoyed of old upon the northern seas of Europe. The menace aimed principally at the future prosperity of England. It showed itself equally and simultaneously in the Spice Islands of the east, in trade and colonization in the west, in the markets of the Levant, in the vital Baltic producing-area of naval stores, in the herring-fishery of the North Sea and in the whale-fishery of the Arctic. Everywhere the Hollander, by intrigue, by force of arms, by sheer business ability, set himself to oust the Englishman. Yet for many a year neither English kings nor the English nation realized the existence of the challenge. The Elizabethan legend still blinded them. The Dutch were Protestants, the Spaniards were Catholics; they had helped the former to win their freedom, they had fought the latter so long that war with Spain seemed part of the established order of life. Thus the Dutch period in the English struggle for expansion, whilst in reality dating from 1595 when Cornelis Houtman first rounded the Cape of Good Hope, begins in contemporary estimation at least thirty years afterwards. We may date it, in fact, from the last year of James's life, when news came to hand of the Amboyna massacre.

Such were the facts of the new age, and so slow were they to make their impression upon the minds of Englishmen. Nevertheless, as the years passed, the Elizabethan picture of adventurous progress with sword in hand became less and less distinct, and in the interim before the Dutch menace was grappled, a new conception took place, of steady expansion by means of the arts of peace. The Elizabethan ambitions of colonization, discovery and oceanic trade all gained a stronger hold upon the people, with this modification, that men now realized that in patient toil rather than military enterprise lay the key to success. So we find the Tudor undertakings pursued with a changed attitude of mind, born of experience. We are still in an age of experiments, but each experiment is pursued with a greater concentration of purpose rendered possible by the cessation of foreign war; and the result is a far higher percentage of permanent successes.

In colonization this development is very marked. The English emigration of the early seventeenth century took place in two distinct waves, having very different underlying motives. The first produced the permanent American colonies of Virginia and Maryland, together with establishments in the West Indies and South America, some successful, others transient; the second resulted in the foundation of the Puritan states of New England.

The first colonizing impulse began immediately upon the conclusion of the Spanish war. Voyages of exploration along the American coastline resulted in the formation of two companies to plant respectively upon the northern and southern sections of the continent. The northern company did nothing effective. The southern one developed into the Virginia Company, founding, after a gallant struggle against apparently hopeless conditions, the colony from which it took its name (1606-24). The Virginia colony occupied only the southern half of the attractive shores of Chesapeake Bay. Sir George Calvert, first Lord Baltimore, obtained from the Crown in 1632 a concession to plant in the northern part of the Bay. The project, carried through by his son, resulted in the establishment of Maryland (1634). At the same time Sir Robert Heath had in view the plantation of Carolina, to the south of Virginia, the scene of Ralegh's original experiments. He obtained a grant for that purpose but circumstances prevented him from acting upon it. In the meanwhile the decay of Spanish power threw open the West Indies and South America as a possible field of expansion. The occupation of the Bermudas (1609-10) grew naturally out of the Virginia enterprise, since they lay in the track of ships voyaging to that colony. Deeper in the Spanish sphere were Barbados and St. Christopher, taken in hand in 1624-5, and Nevis, Antigua and Montserrat (1627-32). On the mainland of the south Guiana became the scene of persistent though unsuccessful attempts. Immediately after the peace a few adventurers sought to found a settlement there in pursuit of Ralegh's plans announced on his return from the Orinoco in 1595. Robert Harcourt repeated the attempt in 1609, and secured by patent a large grant of territory in 1613. Next followed Ralegh's final tragic adventure of 1617-8. In spite of his disaster Englishmen still saw possibilities in this region. Roger North planted a small and evanescent colony on the Amazon in 1619, and eight years later founded an incorporated Guiana Company which long survived without durable result. Then for a time the English abandoned the mainland of South America.

The above survey, covering a period of some thirty years, represents an outburst of colonizing energy which renders the Elizabethan achievements insignificant in comparison. We have now to consider more fully the motives which produced so powerful and widespread a movement.

The most important of these motives was undoubtedly the economic belief that colonies, suitably chosen and managed, would strengthen the whole nation. Three important classes of commodities, regarded as essential to English well-being, were only obtainable from foreign countries, and their supply was dependent upon the favour and friendship of foreigners. These commodities were : (1) gold and silver, upon the possession of which the mercantile theory laid great emphasis, holding it to be the essence of a nation's strength ; (2) naval stores—timber, cordage, canvas, pitch—then obtained only from the White Sea and the Baltic ; (3) the spices of the far east, precariously obtained hitherto by the Levant Company and the newly established East India Company, fighting its way against Portuguese and Dutch competition in the Indian Ocean. Reports of numerous explorers gave rise to hopes that the precious metals would be found both in North America and in Guiana ; and, even when these hopes proved groundless, the more advanced mercantilists still looked for an indirect advantage from colonization by the sale to foreigners of wares exclusively produced in English plantations. With regard to naval stores, again, the discoverers' accounts had been unanimous in raising expectations that North America would provide a new area of supply. Orders from home constantly enjoined upon the early Virginia settlers the necessity for collecting cargoes of shipbuilding material, and ultimately a shipbuilding industry did arise in the New England colonies. Finally, the connection of western colonization with the spice trade was also very apparent to the projectors of the time. The quest of the North West Passage was not a dead ideal ; it was still active in contemporary thought, and there was a universal hope that the American colonists would find a short way to Asia in the course of their explorations. In addition to these purely mercantile considerations a social change provided another argument for territorial expansion. In spite of increasing prosperity and a higher standard of living, unemployment in England seemed to be on the increase. The real reason was that a more complicated industrial system produced local dislocations with accompanying distress, but contemporaries drew the conclusion that England was grossly overpopulated, and that provision must therefore be made for the surplus in plantations overseas. It should be noted that this alleged overpopulation provided only a fleeting argument for colonization ; it was soon found difficult to recruit settlers for Virginia ; and before the end of the century the cry became that colonies depopulated the mother country and, in themselves, were only a source of weakness.   But the important inferences drawn from this change of opinion will fall to be considered at a later stage.

Economic advantage undoubtedly stands foremost among the motives of the first emigration ; but its promoters also put forward other arguments based upon military and religious grounds. With regard to the former, it was claimed that Virginia would form an excellent base of operations against the West Indies in the event of a future war with Spain. In contemporary phrase, it would be " a bit in the ancient enemy's mouth." In the days of Drake England, with nothing but her own shores to defend, had been at war with a colonial and ocean-trading power. The situation had been at first sight an attractive one, but the later events of the war had cast doubts upon its real soundness. The Spanish authorities, once they had grasped the elements of the problem, had been able to take successful measures in defence of their colonies, and the treasure fleets had throughout reached home with fair regularity. The English fleets could not strike effectively at fortified colonies because there were no English bases in the west ; and naval opinion ended by regretting as a capital error the abandonment of Cartagena in 1586. The conclusion now reached by the thinkers of the early seventeenth century was that American and West Indian colonies, although involving added responsibilities, would be worth acquiring on military grounds alone. The religious motive already referred to was that of converting the heathen to Christianity. It appears in most of the discussions of colonization, but since in actual fact it appealed to but a limited number of minds no great stress need be laid upon it. The English were not yet a missionary nation, nor, until the nineteenth century, did they become one. A final argument for colonization, that of its advantage to the mercantile marine, is best expressed in the words of a writer of 1609 : " We shall rear again such merchants' ships both tall and stout, as no foreign sail that swims shall make them vail or stoop, whereby to make this little northern corner of the world the richest storehouse and staple for merchandise in all Europe."

The reader of the above will be struck at once by the Elizabethan and " Spanish " aspect of the first wave of colonization. All the arguments in its support might as fitly have been advanced by Gilbert and Ralegh before the Armada as by the inheritors of their labours under James I. Both the ideas and their promoters were in fact distinctively Elizabethan ; in national expansion as in literature the age outlived the queen herself by fully twenty years, and when we are tempted to accuse the Elizabethans of instability and infirmity of purpose we should remember that they did indeed fulfil many of their promises in that long afterglow which followed the setting of the Tudor sun.

Already before the first outward impulse had spent itself another had set in, the work of a younger generation, typical of the seventeenth century, and wholly dissimilar to that which had peopled the shores of Chesapeake Bay. Puritans, in fact if not in name, had existed in England since the days of Mary Tudor and Cardinal Pole. Until the accession of James I. they had lived for the most part within the allegiance of the Anglican church, occupying many of its livings, securing a tacit acquiescence in some of their practices, and yielding the same to many things of which they did not approve. The mass of them, indeed, regarded themselves not as dissenting from but as constituting the Church of England. They had not yet faced the necessity of defining themselves, and it has been justly said that at this period " Puritanism was an attitude of mind rather than a system of theology." The change of dynasty and the transition from war to peace disturbed this state of quasi-toleration. Under James I. and still more under his son the Church of England fell under the control of bishops who abhorred the Puritan outlook, and who, enjoying greater political power than Elizabeth had ever allowed them, set about the enforcement of their views in sternly practical fashion. Intolerance begat intolerance, and although among the majority the progress of the schism was very gradual, certain small congregations broke into open revolt in the first years of James I. Having done so, they had to choose between remaining at home in face of persecution or seeking an asylum across the seas. They decided upon the latter alternative, and from 1608 onwards they emigrated to the Dutch Netherlands in increasing numbers.

From these men sprang the effective colonization of New England. They had good reasons for curtailing their sojourn in the Dutch provinces. The isolation and emptiness of America attracted them, as they had attracted the Huguenots of France some seventy years before ; and in 1620 a small party whom the world has known as the Pilgrim Fathers crossed the Atlantic in the *Mayflower* and founded the settlement of Plymouth within the northward curve of Cape Cod. Their experiment, after much loss of life, proved successful, and the growing Arminianism of the English Church drove many hitherto conforming Calvinists to think of imitating their example. The leaders of these later malcontents, men of greater wealth and social influence than the Pilgrims, formed the Massachusetts Bay Company, and obtained a regular charter from Charles I. In 1628-9 they planted their colony, which quickly became the most populous of all the American settlements. Charles I.'s absolute government, coinciding with Laud's religious tyranny, drove across the Atlantic thousands of Englishmen who would never else have dreamed of quitting their homes. Massachusetts rapidly produced offshoots in Rhode Island, Connecticut and New Haven, and extended its jurisdiction northwards along the shores of Maine. Nor did Puritan emigration stop at these limits. The leaders of the party at home formed an association to exploit the West Indies. In 1631 they planted the Island of Providence near the Mosquito Coast of Honduras. But this venture, after some years' prosperity, failed to take permanent root. The Spaniards captured the island in 1640, and the experiment came to an end.

Such was the Puritan emigration of the seventeenth century. It began feebly in 1620, swelled in volume in 1629, when parliamentary government seemed finished for ever in England, continued unabated until 1640, and ceased abruptly in that year, when the Long Parliament took up the task of abasing the pride of bishops and the arbitrary power of kings. It was an unnatural phenomenon in the national life, arising not from a healthy instinct for expansion, but from a schism in the church and the state so deep and so embittered that the passions to which it gave rise never wholly subsided in the Puritan colonies. In effect the English nation had split itself into two hostile communities, of which the smaller never forgave the larger for the wrongs it had inflicted. This circumstance, as we shall see, is the key to all the subsequent history of New England, and ultimately of America at large ; and it differentiates the New England colonies very sharply from those farther to the south whose foundation we have already considered.

In the mechanism of their establishment the early colonies followed no settled model. In Virginia a chartered company, appealing to investors on patriotic and financial grounds, undertook the pioneer work. For the first three years it acted under the strict supervision of a government committee ; from 1609 to 1624 it exercised almost entire control over the colony ; and in the latter year it was suppressed. Thenceforward the crown appointed the governor and the council with powers modified by an assembly elected by the settlers themselves.

Maryland was a proprietary colony, the crown delegating the powers it exercised in Virginia to a proprietor who financed the early work of settlement and recouped his expenditure by disposing of estates. The proprietor thus appointed the governor and the council, and influenced the framing of the laws, but, as in the older colony, a popular assembly engrossed a large share of political power. The Pilgrim Fathers' colony of Plymouth was, so far as internal affairs were concerned, an independent community. Its members made haste to discharge their debt to the English financiers who provided the funds for their establishment, and thenceforward governed themselves, electing their own officials without reference to the home authorities. Only in such external relations as those of trade and defence did they share in the rights and duties of the English nation as a whole, and in them to an extent which was greater in theory than in practice. The same applies to the larger colonies of New England. Massachusetts began under the aegis of a chartered company. But the members, investing for religious and political rather than commercial reasons, took a course of action differing greatly from that of the Virginia Company. The stockholders, the council and the governor removed in a body to America. The Company thus became identical with the colony, which remained virtually an independent state throughout the seventeenth century. Rhode Island, Connecticut and New Haven, as offshoots from Massachusetts, enjoyed the same political conditions. Of the West Indian settlements, Providence Island was founded and ruled by a chartered company resembling that of Virginia. In the ten years of its existence its constitution underwent no change. The remaining island colonies were proprietary in type, the proprietors usually exercising greater powers than in Maryland. Amid all this diversity one type of colonial experiment was yet lacking. There was no crown colony founded and controlled by government enterprise from the outset. This was the more remarkable in an age when the crown was seeking to arrogate to itself powers of initiative which it had not possessed before. It exemplifies the permanence of the stamp which the Tudor policy had impressed upon English methods of expansion.

Although independent and private enterprise accomplished the whole work of founding the early colonies, their increase in numbers and diversity of circumstance necessitated ere long the formation of a national policy to regulate their relations with the mother country. A policy involved also the creation of a government department for its supervision. Hence we find in this period the rudiments of what is called the old colonial system together with tentative experiments in central administration. Of the former it will be more convenient to speak after reviewing the development of oceanic trade. Of the latter the principal stages were as follows. In the reign of James I. the short-lived Royal Council for Virginia (1606-9) might have grown into a colonial department had not the incorporation of the Virginia

Company put an end to its existence;[1] thenceforward the king, advised by the Privy Council, dealt directly with the colonies. In 1623, when the House of Commons attempted to discuss his treatment of the Virginia Company, he told them plainly that such matters concerned himself and the Privy Council alone, and they accepted the rebuff. Under Charles I. a Commission of Trade was appointed in 1625 to consider colonial as well as commercial matters. It was, however, of a temporary nature, expiring in 1626.[2] In 1630 the duty of supervising external activities was divided, the Privy Council Committee of Trade and various temporary Plantation Commissions working side by side. The latter, however, were only appointed for special exigencies. Next, in 1634, Charles called into existence a more permanent Commission for Plantations with Archbishop Laud at its head. In theory it had power to make laws, impose penalties, remove governors, appoint judges, hear complaints and review charters.[3] In practice it was powerless to deal effectively with the Puritan colonies to restrict whose independence it had been created ; and it found no occasion to interfere with Virginia and Maryland. Laud's commission disappeared in 1641 amid the rising tide of parliamentary encroachment on the powers assumed by the crown. The Privy Council again became the controlling body until the outbreak of the Civil War, when the Parliament appointed a new Commission for Plantations, consisting of eighteen members with the Earl of Warwick as president. This body ended with the king's life in 1649. From the above we may see that, as in so many other matters with which we have had to deal, a period of experiment preceded the definite creation of a new institution.

Colonization was but one branch of English expansion in the seventeenth century ; complementary to it was the steady growth of oceanic trade. We have already seen the rise and swift decline of a semi-illicit traffic with Africa and the West Indies prior to the Spanish war. In the later years of that war, as the returns from privateering decreased, English shipowners revived a precarious intercourse with certain places on the Spanish Main and the adjacent islands—in the year 1602-3 over two hundred vessels, English and Dutch, visited the coast of Venezuela to sell European produce and lade salt in return.[4] With the conclusion of peace this trade became illegal, but was not altogether extinguished. In the meantime the East India Company had entered upon its career, and ere long there followed persistent attempts to revive the African trade. The Levant Company, although confining its voyages to the seas of Europe, was in reality attempting

[1] See ch. ii. pp. 173-4.

[2] A Commission of Trade formed in 1622-3 had dealt with the cloth trade only. On these matters see C. M. Andrews, *British Committees, Commissions and Councils of Trade and Plantations*, 1622-75, Baltimore, 1908.

[3] Andrews, *op. cit.* pp. 16-17.

[4] A. P. Newton, *Colonising Activities of the English Puritans*, New Haven, 1914, p. 14.

to conduct an Asiatic trade through Syria and Mesopotamia ; and the Muscovy Company was still active in a somewhat conservative and unenterprising manner. For the first time this world trade became comparable in its bulk and importance to the ancient European trading system inherited from the Middle Ages.

The East India Company began its operations at an auspicious moment. The Portuguese, its already established enemies in the east, were losing prestige and efficiency by reason of their subjection to Philip III. of Spain ; the Dutch, the most stubborn rivals of the coming time, were yet feeling their way as newcomers, and dared not show their true colours whilst their independence was still at stake in Europe. For the first few years, then, the English traded in the Eastern Archipelago with fair success. Dutch opposition, evident to some extent from the outset, hardened perceptibly after the truce of 1609. The Dutch Company employed four times as many ships and men in the east as its English rival, and the trial of strength could have but one ending. By 1623 the English flag had almost disappeared from the islands of Asia, the richest mine of commercial produce in the world. Foiled in the Archipelago the English Company turned towards India, then reckoned as a secondary field of enterprise. There they showed themselves as superior to the Portuguese as they had been inferior to the Hollanders ; and whereas they had succumbed in the islands to superior force, on the continent they made headway against it. The decade 1612-22 witnessed the final humiliation of Portugal in the Indian Ocean. In the former year a paltry pair of English ships under Captain Best drove a large Portuguese squadron from the mouth of the Tapti, and by so doing secured the concession of a factory at Surat ; in the latter an English armament cleared the Persian Gulf and captured the island fortress of Ormuz. Circumstances thus modified the original intentions of the Company and decided that India rather than the Archipelago was to be the scene of its greatest operations. Thenceforward it extended its sway by the successive acquisition of factories in all parts of the Indian peninsula.

The success of the East India Company stimulated a revival of interest in the western coast of Africa. In 1618 Sir William St. John, after preliminary voyages of a private character, secured a charter for his Company of Adventurers of London trading to Guinea and Benin. The Company established a factory on the Gambia River. It was consistently unfortunate and soon degenerated into a privateering concern without having made one successful trading voyage. For ten years the Guinea trade was practically open to any who cared to engage in it. But the local conditions, although they favoured slave-hunting by freelances, demanded an organization of forts and factories for any sustained legitimate trade. Accordingly the year 1630 saw the grant of a new charter to the Company of Merchants trading to Guinea (or Sir Nicholas Crisp's Company). Until 1636 this body achieved no success. Then, when it was virtually bankrupt, a single ship belonging to it brought home gold to the value of £30,000. This lucky stroke gave it a fresh lease of life. It was reconstituted in 1651, and six years later, when it was once more in trouble, the East India Company took over its forts and factories. The further history of the African trade belongs to the period following the Restoration.[1]

The Muscovy Company, the oldest of the joint-stock corporations, enjoyed an uneventful career until 1636. Ten years of adverse fortune followed, culminating with the expulsion of all Englishmen from Russia in 1646. The Tsar was moved to this step by Dutch allegations that the Company made unfair profits, and also by monarchical sympathy with the misfortunes of Charles I. Cromwell subsequently obtained a partial restoration of the Company's position, but the Dutch were now firmly established in the trade, and the old prosperity never returned. After the Restoration the joint-stock was wound up, and the merchants continued to do business as a regulated company. A by-industry arising from the Muscovy Company's Arctic voyages was the Greenland whale fishery. The adventurers interested soon formed themselves into a separate body, and sought to create a monopoly. But the conditions of a sea-fishery rendered this virtually impossible, and even had English competitors been disposed of, the Dutch remained sufficiently formidable.

The universal tendency to monopoly in all these new undertakings has already been remarked. It was justified by the extreme risks of oceanic voyages, the advantage of corporate negotiation with savage or semi-civilized potentates, and the necessity for supervising the conduct of English pioneers in lands where the national reputation for honest dealing was yet to make. But the early Stuart period witnessed at home an embittered agitation against monopolies in internal trade and industry. Most of these latter were manifestly unjust, and the external monopolies suffered much unfair attack by the confusion in the public mind arising from the misuse of a popular catchword. The crown was not always to be relied upon for the maintenance of the East India Company's chartered rights. James I. licensed at least one English and one Scotch courtier to make independent voyages of their own ; and the behaviour of the English interloper in the eastern seas was so atrocious that he imperilled the whole credit of his countrymen in the eyes of Asiatics. Charles, in constant need of money, instigated the formation of a rival association, that of Sir William Courteen, and the East India Company fell into a state of disorganization from which it was only rescued by Cromwell in 1657. Both James and his son displayed lamentable weakness in the conduct of negotiations with the Dutch on the disputes between the rival companies of the two nations. Another and, to the beliefs of the time, a more plausible, line of attack upon the East India Company, lay in the allegation that its traffic drained the country of wealth. It paid

---

[1] For these African ventures see W. R. Scott, *Joint Stock Companies to 1720*, 3 vols. Cambridge, 1910, vol. ii. pp. 10-16.

for its spices partly by the export of manufactured goods, but more largely by carrying silver coin to the east.   To the older bullionists this was an economic crime ; the newer mercantilists were content with a less simple theory of trade, and as it became evident that the returns from the sale of eastern produce in the long run greatly exceeded the outlay, this form of agitation gradually lost its force.   From the confusion caused by the changing conditions of the time there emerged ultimately the theory of the balance of trade, by which it was reckoned that so long as exports exceeded imports in total value, the commerce of the country was in a healthy condition, since the difference must imply an accumulation of treasure.

This mercantile theory, coupled with the ideal of national self-sufficiency, whereby the mother-country and its dependencies should between them produce all the necessaries of national life, determined the line of policy pursued towards the colonies.   In the period 1603-49 this policy, commonly called the old colonial system, was only in process of evolution.   It did not receive its permanent form until the passage of the Navigation Acts in the latter half of the century.   Nevertheless its rudiments are traceable in the reigns of the early Stuarts. The Virginians were continually enjoined to produce, not tobacco, to them the most profitable crop but to the mother country a pernicious luxury, but naval stores, wine and silk, necessary articles not obtainable in England.   The West Indian Islands were little valued until they found in sugar (introduced c. 1640) a staple commodity which satisfied the canons of the mercantile system.   From 1621 onwards the American settlers received constant commands to ship their goods exclusively to England.   Charles I. went still further, attempting to restrict the colonial trade to English shipping.   The weakness of his administration, however, deprived his policy of much of its effect ; and the Dutch maintained their hold upon the carrying trade throughout his reign.   To the conception of a self-sufficing empire, a mother-country surrounded by a ring of outposts each contributing its quotum of necessary produce, the New England colonies remained a hindrance rather than a help.   For, resembling the parent state both in climate and agricultural tendency, they competed with it in their demands and their productions, and developed a cross-traffic with the other colonies which aroused grave disapproval among the mercantilists at home. In commerce, as in politics and religion, New England seemed marked from its origin as the rebellious child in the family of English communities.

The record of the navy under James I. and Charles I. is not a matter for pride.   Already in the last years of Elizabeth there had been signs of deterioration.   The Earl of Essex gave promise of maintaining the great work of Drake and Hawkins, but he withdrew from the sea service after the Islands Voyage and died on the scaffold in 1601. Thenceforward Lord Howard (now Earl of Nottingham), the conqueror of Philip's Armada, remained in nominal control, retaining the office of Lord Admiral until 1618. Although personally honest, his great age and his partiality for his own kinsmen rendered him blind to the advancing wave of corruption which engulfed his once splendid fleet. Of the shameful period which synchronized with the accession of James I. the presiding genius was Sir Robert Mansell, treasurer of the navy from 1604 to 1618.   Mansell embezzled the public funds in the most barefaced manner. Besides taking toll of every item of current expenditure he charged for the upkeep of establishments and travelling expenses for himself and his friends at exorbitant rates, he kept ships on his books for years after they had ceased to exist, he carried out shoddy repairs and represented them as new construction, and he created sinecures to such an extent that at times there were as many admirals on full pay as ships in commission. His audacity in swindling passes belief ; and when James had the truth clearly and indubitably laid before him he contented himself with an exhortation to better conduct in the future.[1]

Such an administration brought honest officers to a loathing of the king's service. In addition, the treatment of the sailors became steadily worse. Elizabeth's government had been fairly heartless in this respect, but at least her admirals had been seamen, understanding the conditions of their trade, sharing the life of their men, and never hesitating to speak their minds when moved thereto by patent abuses. Under Mansell it became a common practice for admirals to remain ashore throughout their commission, and to perform their duties by deputy. Barbarous customs and punishments had been inherited from the remote past but never before legalised.   " They were now part of ordinary discipline, and mark the downward progress of the sailor in self-respect and social estimation.   They were easier and cheaper to apply than good government, but they bore their Nemesis in the next reign." [2]

The scandal came to a climax in 1618, and the Duke of Buckingham, prompted by ambition and a genuine enthusiasm for the service, undertook the task of reform. Mansell and the Earl of Nottingham were dismissed, the former unpunished, to go down to posterity as a pattern of successful villainy; and Buckingham became admiral, assisted by a Board of Commissioners, whose leading member was a public-spirited merchant named Sir Lionel Cranfield. The new administration checked corruption and strengthened the material side of the navy by a regular programme of new construction, but it failed to restore fighting efficiency to a generation which had forgotten the Elizabethan tradition. Lord Wimbledon's expedition to Cadiz in 1625, and Buckingham's to the relief of Rochelle in 1627, failed disgracefully ; and in a war which pressed by no means heavily on the national resources the sufferings of the seamen from

---

[1] For details of Mansell's administration see Oppenheim, pp. 189-196.

[2] Oppenheim, p. 188.

sheer lack of good management surpassed any records which former times could show. Every folly and defect which had brought into contempt the Spanish Armada of 1588 was repeated in the English expedition of 1625.

Apart from these wars the principal duty of the navy during the period should have been the safeguarding of the trade-routes against the depredations of the Barbary corsairs. These Mohammedan rovers had hitherto confined themselves to the Mediterranean, to which sea their galley type of shipbuilding and seamanship had alone been suitable. In the early years of the seventeenth century, taught sailing tactics by a renegade English privateer,[1] they extended their activities to the Atlantic, and from Algiers, Tunis, and the new port of Sallee in western Morocco, they roved in swarms against the commerce of Europe. In 1612 they inflicted damage amounting to £40,000 upon the Newfoundland fishing fleet alone. In 1616 thirty of their craft were reported to be cruising in the Atlantic, and one was captured in the mouth of the Thames. The south-coast towns had to construct fortifications against them, and they even reversed the ordinary process of the slave trade by carrying off peasants from the English fields. During one period of seven years they took English merchantmen at the rate of nearly seventy a year.[2] Such details are an eloquent witness to the decay of the navy. Charles I. at length bestirred himself to vindicate the national honour. A detachment of his ship-money fleet in 1637 did useful work at Sallee in cleansing the seas of these pests, a fact which is worth remembering to his credit, and as some set-off to the tyrannical means by which he equipped his force. But the pirates were not effectively curbed until England, by the occupations of Tangier and Gibraltar in a later age, became definitely a Mediterranean power.

With his one outburst of vigorous action Charles I.'s naval record comes to an end. When the Civil War broke out in 1642 the seamen showed that they had lost all loyalty to the Stuart crown. The navy sided with the Parliament from the outset, and by so doing contributed perhaps the decisive factor to the downfall of the royal cause.

In all the developments dealt with in this chapter the personal influence of the early Stuart kings had an evident effect. The policy of James I. is self-contradictory and puzzling ; for whereas, viewed from the European standpoint, his subservience to Spain renders him contemptible, it is precisely in relation to Spain that his colonial proceedings stand out in a favourable light. He chartered the Virginia Company two years after signing the treaty of 1604. He maintained the colony in the face of Spanish protests, and when he destroyed the Company he did so only to take its achievement under his own patronage. He gave his royal sanction to West Indian and South

---

[1] For the full story see Sir J. S. Corbett, *England in the Mediterranean*, i. pp. 10-13.
[2] Oppenheim, pp. 198-9.

American projects, from which he looked backward only when he ordered Ralegh to the block in 1618. It is more than probable that, had it not been for his firm attitude, the early struggles of Virginia would have been ended by a military blow from Spain similar to that which destroyed the Huguenots in Florida in 1565. Turning to the East, and bearing in mind that Portugal and its empire remained under Spanish domination from 1580 to 1640, we find a like definiteness of policy. The actual wording of the treaty gave the East India Company little excuse for its intrusion. But James held in true Elizabethan fashion that European treaties did not run beyond the Cape of Good Hope, and he never countenanced the contention that English trade was illegitimate in the Indian Ocean. Thus far English expansion may be seen to have owed more to James I. than many historians, prejudiced by the record of home affairs, have cared to acknowledge. But, as regards the Dutch, the story is different. The conflict in the Spice Islands came at an unlucky juncture. The Spanish marriage project had just failed, the Thirty Years' War was beginning, and political reasons urged an alliance with the nation which had behaved with barbarous injustice in the distant east. A stronger king might have carried his point in both matters; James sacrificed imperial interests to the game of European statecraft.

One continued element of English policy emerges from the history of his reign. England did not pretend to recognize the papal award of 1493. In time of peace she was prepared to respect Spanish and Portuguese rights based upon effective occupation, but, in default of the latter, she claimed that all non-Christian lands were open to any who were prepared to step in and exploit them. By the close of the seventeenth century the peninsular nations had each given a formal assent to this view.

Charles I., like his father, began his reign with a genuine kindliness towards commerce and colonization. Virginia had little cause for complaint in his treatment of her interests. Nor was he intolerant towards the religious element in expansion. His grant to the Catholic proprietor of Maryland was a model of liberality. He winked also at the obvious intention of the Massachusetts projectors to establish a nonconformist state across the seas : " His Majesty," wrote Winthrop, " did not intend to impose the ceremonies of the Church of England upon us ; for it was considered that it was the freedom from such things that made people come over to us." In trade also he was anxious to promote the common welfare, and his ordinances showed him to be abreast of the advanced economic thought of the time. Then, with the fatal resolution to be absolute in Church and state, a deterioration appeared in his attitude towards national ambitions. Laud demanded universal submission to the Laudian religion, and Charles placed him at the head of the Commission of Plantations which would assuredly have goaded New England into revolt had not the Civil War broken out at home. Commerce suffered also from the eleven years' tyranny. By 1640 the government was bankrupt, after long resorting to shifts which could not be reconciled with economic doctrines. Towards Portugal and the United Provinces Charles's policy is parallel to that of his father. He truckled to the Dutch, relying upon a diplomacy which both parties knew would not be backed by force ; and one of his last diplomatic acts before the catastrophe was the conclusion of a treaty with Portugal (1642) by which English claims in the east were substantially recognized. For the colonial policy of the last seven years of his life he is not, of course, responsible : the Parliament, controlling the navy, controlled the maritime interests of the country.

CHAPTER II

VIRGINIA, 1603–1624

ALTHOUGH there is an apparent break of several years between the abandonment of Ralegh's efforts to colonize Virginia and the resumption of the task under James I., the subject in reality had never faded from the thoughts of English adventurers. As the contest with Spain declined in intensity the interested parties began again to send ships to reconnoitre the American coastline. We have already mentioned the expeditions of 1602. In the following year Richard Hakluyt and others sent out Martin Pring from Bristol with two ships. Their purpose was exploration and trade, rather than actual settlement. Pring examined the Virginian coast and returned with a favourable report. Still more notable was the voyage of George Waymouth in 1605, under the patronage of the Earl of Southampton. Waymouth gave a very glowing account of the prospects of successful colonization. In the meanwhile the treaty with Spain had been signed in 1604. Negative in all important respects, it omitted any express recognition by England of Spanish rights in North America. The Spaniards had pressed for such a recognition,[1] but the influence of the English colonizing interest had been strong enough to secure the rejection of the clause, in spite of the undignified haste of James I. to conclude the peace. The way was thus open for the government to renew its patronage of the Virginia venture. In other respects also the time was favourable. The king's determination to put an end to privateering set free for colonization the services of many adventurers and the capital of the owners of private warships. Some of these energies were diverted to the East Indies ; the remainder looked for their outlet in North, Central and South America, and more especially in Virginia.

Waymouth's report precipitated these floating aspirations. In April, 1606, not two years after the signing of the Spanish treaty, James issued a patent constituting a Royal Council for Virginia with the duty of supervising colonization on the American coast between the latitudes of 34° and 45° N. The adventurers willing to participate grouped themselves naturally into two divisions, those belonging to

[1] Prof. E. Channing, *History of the United States,* New York, 1905, i. p. 159.

London, and those hailing from Plymouth and the west country. It was therefore determined that, in accordance with the project originally conceived by Sir Humphrey Gilbert, two colonies should be founded, one by the Plymouth Company in the northern part of the assigned area, the other by the London Company in its southern sector. The companies themselves were to enjoy commercial advantages and to furnish the needed capital, but the administration of the settlements was to remain in the hands of the crown acting through the medium of the Royal Council already mentioned. The arrangement was further complicated by the assignment of overlapping boundaries to the London and Plymouth Companies, the former having the right to plant between 34° and 41°, and the latter between 38° and 45° N. This division, which might have been a fruitful cause of future disputes, is possibly traceable to the devious mental processes of James I., whose talent for devising such subtleties earned him the title of " the wisest fool in Christendom."

As the event fell out no trouble actually arose from this source, the London Company alone proving to possess any vitality ; and we may here conveniently dispose of the Plymouth Company before proceeding with the main course of events. In 1607 its directors despatched an expedition under George Popham and Ralegh Gilbert, who planted a settlement which they named St. George in the estuary of the Kennebec River (44° N). The settlers held out during a winter of great suffering and privation, and the survivors abandoned the enterprise in 1608. Thenceforward the Plymouth Company continued in practical abeyance until 1620, when Gilbert, Sir Ferdinando Gorges, and others belonging to it secured a reconstitution of its powers under the name of the Council for New England. Their subsequent proceedings will be dealt with later.

The London Company, which thus remained for practical purposes the sole Virginia Company, acted with greater perseverance. It was fortunate in securing the patronage of Sir Robert Cecil, and its influential members included Hakluyt, Sir Thomas Smith, Robert Rich, afterwards Earl of Warwick, Sir George Somers and Sir Thomas Gates. The original Royal Council for Virginia was evidently intended to be a government department for the regulation of colonial affairs in general.[1] Later in 1606, the king appointed a special council to deal with the Virginia colony. It consisted ultimately of twenty-five members, and, itself remaining in England, was to nominate a resident council in the colony, who were to govern in accordance with instructions from home and to elect a president from among their own number. It is thus evident that the home authorities intended to keep a very tight control upon the doings of the actual colonists. It was further provided that the Company was to pay to the crown one-fifth of all precious metals that might be obtained. It might also, for a period

[1] H. E. Egerton, *Short History of British Colonial Policy*, 3rd edit., London, 1910, p. 28.

of twenty-one years, levy a duty of 2½ per cent. on Englishmen and 5 per cent. on foreigners trading with the colony. Under this fina arrangement the Company set to work, and had its first expedition ready to sail in December, 1606.

The broad motives of English colonization at this period have already been considered. The particular designs of the London Company are revealed in the instructions to Captain Christopher Newport and his associates in the command of the first voyage. They were to find a navigable river and select a spot for the settlement as far inland as a 50-ton ship could penetrate, paying special attention to the defensibility and healthiness of the site chosen. On arrival they were to open sealed orders which they carried from England, in which they would find the names of the resident councillors appointed by the home council. Two-thirds of the colonists were to be employed in building and fortifying the settlement and in tilling the soil ; the remaining third were to accompany Newport on an exploration of the interior, wherein he was to seek especially for deposits of precious metals and a passage to the South Sea. At the settlement itself all trade was to be for the public account, under the supervision of a " cape " or head merchant ; the Church of England worship was to be maintained ; conversion of the Indians was to be attempted, and they were to be treated with justice and kindness. Newport was to return two months after the establishment of the colony.

Captain Newport, the same who had brought the captured *Madre de Dios* to England in 1591, sailed from the Downs on January 1, 1607, with two ships and a pinnace carrying 120 emigrants [1] in addition to the crews. He took the southerly route used by Ralegh's expeditions, by way of the Canaries and the West Indies, and entered Chesapeake Bay on April 16. Chesapeake Bay forms an inland sea making a breach nearly two hundred miles deep westwards and northwards into the American seaboard. The estuaries of many rivers disembogue into it, dividing the coastal region of Virginia [2] into long peninsulas, themselves notched and jagged by smaller creeks and inlets. Of the larger estuaries two, those of the James and York Rivers, lead into the bay at its southern extremity, opposite the opening to the Atlantic ; and between these two rivers lies the peninsula upon which the pioneers of 1607 laid the foundation of Jamestown, the first permanent English colony beyond the seas. It was at Yorktown not twenty miles away upon this same tongue of land that Lord Cornwallis surrendered to Washington one hundred and seventy-four years later, and by so doing signalized the end of British power in the old colonies on the very soil which had been the scene of its earliest sufferings and triumphs. The site of Jamestown (called James Fort in the earlier despatches) was chosen on May 13. It was low-lying,

---

[1] Channing, i. p. 165 ; J. A. Doyle, *The English in America*, London, 1882, says 143 (p. 152). Only 104 actually landed.

[2] The name " Virginia " is henceforward used in its more limited, modern significance

malarious, bordered by swamp and covered with trees, and deficient
of fresh-water springs.[1] To compensate for these drawbacks, which
the settlers regarded lightly until bitter experience revealed their
significance, it was secure against attacks from the sea, and the water
was sufficiently deep for the ships to be moored close under the bank
of the stream.

Newport opened the sealed document and revealed the names of
the seven councillors. They included that of Captain John Smith,
without doubt the most striking personality in the little band. His
energy and resource were alone to avert the failure of the enterprise.
But these very qualities rendered him a man who could not
suffer fools gladly, and his service in the colony was one continual
succession of quarrels with his less gifted colleagues. He arrived, in
fact, in irons, as a result of disputes which had broken out during the
five months' voyage, and was only released when his name was found
in the list of councillors. His *History*, written some years later, is the
authority for many of the early transactions of the settlement. Its
truth has been called in question, but even when all possible deductions
have been made from his achievements he still stands forth as the
undoubted saviour of the undertaking. The councillors chose Edward
Maria Wingfield as their first president.

Newport, after seeing a triangular fort marked out and armed with
a few guns from the ships, pushed into the interior and made friends
with Powhatan, the head chief of a confederation of thirty-four small
tribes of the neighbourhood.   He failed in his objects of finding gold and
the South Sea passage, and returned to learn that some of the Indians
had attacked the fort in his absence. In spite of his tactful handling
of Powhatan the settlement suffered for some years from sporadic
Indian attacks. Newport departed for England at the end of June.

Left to themselves the colonists failed to settle down to steady work.
Smith saw what was needed, but his bad relations with the remainder
of the council prevented him from taking control. The prime necessity
was that of corn, and he devoted himself to the task of securing supplies
from the Indians. On one of his excursions he was ambushed and
taken prisoner, two of his companions being killed. His own story,
which has been most strongly criticized, asserted that he himself was
on the point of being tortured to death when he was saved by the
intercession of Pocahontas, the daughter of Powhatan. The old
king, moved by his daughter's entreaties, renewed the alliance from
which he had wavered, and remained the friend of the English for the
remainder of his life.[2] The dissensions among the leaders continued,
and when Newport arrived with reinforcements in January, 1608, he

---

[1] L. G. Tyler, *England in America*, 1580-1652, New York, 1904, p. 50.

[2] The objections to belief in this story rest on inconsistencies in Smith's own accounts
and on the fact that Pocahontas was only twelve years old at the time. Doyle and
Channing are sceptical. Tyler, however, accepts the tale, quoting arguments in its
support and a parallel case from Spanish experiences in Florida (p. 47).

found that of the original councillors, Bartholomew Gosnold, the most able character after Smith, was dead of sickness ; another had been hanged for mutiny ; and Smith and Wingfield were in prison, the former under sentence of death. The rank and file had also suffered severely, more than half of them having succumbed to fever and privation.

Apart from Newport's fresh supplies of men and victual, and his opportune arrival in time to save Smith's life, his presence was rather a hindrance than a blessing. The Company was already looking for commercial returns, principally it would seem, in the shape of the " naval stores " which bulk so largely in the mercantile strategy of the time, and the energies of the settlers were diverted to the provision of cargoes for his ships. Wingfield went home with him, and Smith became the president of the colony. A second small reinforcement appeared later in 1608, but in spite of this the numbers of the colonists were rapidly diminishing as disease and starvation took their ever increasing toll, and a spirit of despair settled upon the hearts of the survivors. The hope of treasure, the heritage of the sixteenth century, was already dead ; the settlers had as yet found no staple industry, no commodity, needed by the mother-country, which they could supply in abundance ; most of them had come out in a spirit of adventure, prepared for combat and movement, and the prospect of dreary, purposeless toil appalled them. They had not even the incentive of working for their own individual advantage ; for all the products of industry went to the common stock, in which the idle shared equally with the industrious. They were in fact a besieged garrison, slowly giving ground to intangible enemies, without hope of permanent relief, and without a definable ideal to spur them to self-sacrifice. Smith alone held them to their task, and even he seems to have seen little prospect of success for the colony as it was then organized, for he devoted himself principally to exploring the shores of Chesapeake Bay with a view to wider schemes in the future.

It was thus evident that the undertaking must receive stronger backing or perish ; and the critical decisions must be looked for in England rather than in Virginia. As the true state of affairs began to be known at home in 1609 an unexpected wave of enthusiasm for the colony swept over the surface of public opinion. Pamphleteers and preachers joined hands with the original promoters in declaring that the country must bestir itself. For the first time the idea of true colonization as opposed to treasure-hunting and the discovery of trade-routes took possession of the English people, and the national energy, dispersed in many directions in the Elizabethan period, now centred itself upon the preservation of Virginia.

Whilst offers of capital and personal service were flowing in, the government placed the undertaking on firmer foundations by the issue of a new charter (May 23, 1609). By this charter the Virginia Company, now definitely so-called, was placed in control of the colony it was creating.   A council and treasurer at home, all chosen from among the members of the Company, were to appoint a governor and officials in the colony to act in accordance with their instructions. The capital was to be reckoned in shares of £12 10s. each (the estimated cost of planting one settler), and personal emigration [1] was to count as the subscription of one share.   All labour was to be for the common benefit for the first seven years, after which time the land was to be divided among the settlers and the home investors in proportion to the number of shares held by each.   Until that time should arrive the Company was to feed, clothe and supply the settlers with all necessaries. Under this arrangement the adventurers at home gained confidence from the fact that the Company and not the crown was to administer the colony ; whilst the emigrants received the incentive of an ultimate reward for their labour in the possession of a landed estate.   This was all to the good, although, as we shall see, it was not sufficient in itself to make the temporary communal society a success.

Thus endowed with fresh life, the Company was able to set forth a great expedition in 1609.   On June 1, 500 new settlers sailed in nine ships under the command of Sir George Somers, Sir Thomas Gates and Christopher Newport.   Lord Delaware had been appointed governor under the new constitution, but remained in England until the following year.   Somers [2] and the other leaders sailed all in the same ship, the *Sea Adventure*.   On the passage out a hurricane struck the fleet.   One vessel foundered, seven reached Virginia, and the *Sea Adventure*, isolated from the rest, was run ashore upon the uninhabited Bermuda Islands in order to save her from sinking.   Somers and all hands were saved, but they found themselves effectually marooned until they could contrive to construct new vessels from the timbers of the wreck, a task which occupied ten months.

In the meantime the bulk of the 1609 emigrants landed in the colony, which was now, by the death or departure of all the other councillors, under the sole government of John Smith.   They brought insufficient supplies with them, and they found the existing colonists already starving.   Smith, in fact, had divided the latter into three bodies, one to live on the charity of the Indians, one to fish at Cape Comfort, and the third to support life on the oyster banks twenty miles below Jamestown—a diet which caused their skins to " peel off from head to foot as if they had been flayed."   The newcomers, unseasoned to the climate and appalled by the contrast between their glowing anticipations and the stern reality, began to sicken and die like flies.   Smith was injured by an explosion of gunpowder and had to go home with the ships, leaving the settlement without a leader of outstanding character. The winter of 1609-10 lived in Virginian annals as " the starving time."

[1] An emigrant family received a share for each of its members over ten years old. Doctors, clergymen and others received double or treble shares.

[2] Somers was notable as the captain who, in conjunction with Sir Amyas Preston, had commanded in a successful raid on the Spanish Main in 1595.

The famishing wretches ate the bodies of the dead, and even killed the living for food. One man at least was executed for murdering and eating his wife. Another cast his Bible into the fire and raved in the market-place that there was no God in heaven. In the summer of 1609 there had been 500 inhabitants in Jamestown. By the spring of 1610 sixty alone were left.

Somers and Gates, subsisting through the same winter at Bermuda upon the hogs which some Portuguese navigator of past time had turned loose to breed upon the island, had busied their men in building two pinnaces. In these they sailed up the James in May, 1610. The sixty half-dead survivors met them. Together they had but a fortnight's provisions remaining. To stay, in default of help from England, was to perish. They decided to embark all hands, make for Newfoundland, and try there to obtain food for the voyage home. So irrevocable the decision seemed that someone proposed to burn the houses before departure, but Somers forbade it. On June 7, they dropped down the river, leaving Jamestown a deserted ruin, the walls broken down, the gates rotting from their hinges, the houses gutted of their woodwork. To the despairing band the Virginia enterprise seemed at an end, with all its misery and waste of life of no avail. But at the river's mouth they met a pinnace bringing news that English ships were coming in from the sea. It was Lord Delaware arriving to take up his command, with new men, food, and new hope. All returned to Jamestown, and the darkest hour of the colony was past. The words of a survivor best epitomize it : " a miserie, a ruine, a death, a hell."

Delaware took active measures to restore the undertaking. He appointed a new council, censured the idle and the fainthearted, and made a beginning of the strict discipline essential to success. He despatched Sir George Somers and Captain Samuel Argall to Bermuda for a supply of the wild hogs of the island. Argall missed his way, but Somers reached the scene of his shipwreck, to die there at the close of 1610. In spite of Delaware's activity famine and fever again smote the settlement, and many more deaths occurred before better conditions were fully established. His representations led the Company to adopt the rule of sending out a year's supplies with every new batch of colonists. In 1611 failing health forced him to return to England. No sooner had he gone than discipline again became slack, work was neglected, and the shiftless inhabitants of Jamestown spent their days in loafing and playing bowls in the street, whilst their houses and crops decayed for lack of attention.

But retribution was at hand. Later in the year there arrived as deputy-governor Sir Thomas Dale, an old soldier, strong of will and merciless of nature. He saw at once that military discipline alone could secure the performance of necessary labour ; and he proceeded to establish military discipline as he had learned it in the Netherland wars. To a code of laws already sent out by Sir Thomas Smith, and used by Delaware, he made additions of his own. Under his administration flogging and death became the penalties for the slightest insubordination of attitude, even when evidenced in such trivial matters as speaking ill of the Company or neglecting to attend divine service. His severity was more than certain natures could endure. Some men fled to live among the savages rather than remain under his rule ; others conspired to overthrow it, and were hanged for their pains. But, terrible though his system may appear, there is little doubt that it was necessary : where he slew men by dozens their own slothfulness had slain them by hundreds, and his justification lies in the material prosperity which steadily increased from 1611 onwards. The whole story of Virginia up to this time illustrates the inherent weakness of a communal state of society in which good and bad share alike in the fruits of common industry. Such a society inevitably sinks into decay unless governed by a despotism.

Dale remained in the colony until 1616. During part of this period Sir Thomas Gates, another old soldier of the same kidney, was governor, Dale serving as high marshal or chief officer of justice. The two worked amicably together, and devoted themselves to something more than the maintenance of a reign of terror. Realizing that half the early disasters were traceable to the unhealthy situation of Jamestown, they broke fresh ground higher up the river, founding Henrico and other new settlements and removing the bulk of the colonists to them. After the departure of Gates in 1614 Dale effected a pacification with the Indians which lasted for several years. He did this by utilizing the love for the English already evinced by Pocahontas, the old king's daughter. Pocahontas married John Rolfe, a prominent settler, and the two races subsided into a peace which bade fair to be permanent. To the Dale-Gates régime also belongs the inauguration of tobacco-planting as the staple industry. Rolfe experimented with tobacco in 1612, and in the following year despatched the first cargo to England. Once established, tobacco culture spread rapidly, much to the disgust of James I. and the mercantilists at home, who would have preferred to see their colony produce naval stores or corn, and so add to the self-sufficiency of the nation. The current objection to tobacco sprang partly from this reason, partly from an idea that its consumption would prove to be but a passing fashion, and largely from a genuine belief that its sale was harmful and immoral. The conservative opinion of the time regarded it much as we regard the opium traffic now, and was proportionately ashamed of this firstfruit of successful colonization.[1]

In the last year of Dale's rule the seven years of common ownership prescribed by the 1609 charter expired, and the governor began the allotment of individual plantations to the surviving pioneers. This was undoubtedly a step which was urgently needed as a preliminary to the relaxation of rule by martial law. Dale also pressed upon the

[1] G. L. Beer, *Origins of the British Colonial System*, 1578-1660, New York, 1908, ch. iv.

Company another improvement, that of the class of emigrant which they were sending out. He protested against the idea that Virginia was a fit receptacle for the failures of England, and contended that it was a land worthy to receive better inhabitants. His own words are worth quoting : " I have seen the best countries of Europe ; I protest unto you, before the living God—put them all together, this country will be equivalent unto them, it being inhabited with good people." [1]

The next governor was George Yeardley, who gave place after a short interval to Samuel Argall (1617-19). Argall's rule marks a step backward. His appointment was due less to his merits than to the intrigue of a faction in the Company. He used his office solely as a means of filling his own purse, arresting the grants of land to the planters,[2] and treating them practically as a slave-gang for his own service. Such at least is the tenor of the colonists' complaints against him ; and as he was never brought to trial, he found no public opportunity of disproving the charges. When reports of his proceedings began to arrive in England the Company decided to send out Lord Delaware with instructions to establish representative government by means of a popular assembly. Delaware died on the voyage, and after some delay Yeardley received the appointment in his stead. Argall decamped without awaiting his successor's arrival. He never returned to Virginia, but evidently gained the favour of James I., for he was subsequently knighted and employed in positions of trust.[3]

Yeardley arrived to take up his second term of office in the spring of 1619. His instructions were to put into operation the privileges accorded to the colonists by the Company's resolutions of the previous year—privileges to which some have accorded the title of the Magna Charta of Virginia. He lost no time therefore in summoning a representative assembly of two burgesses from each of the eleven settlements which now composed the colony. With the aid of this assembly, which in imitation of the English Commons appointed a speaker and a sergeant-at-arms, he enacted a new code of laws for the future regulation of the colony's life. In general they resembled the current statutes of the mother-country with special modifications to suit local conditions. Their significance is that, in conjunction with an extended allotment of estates, they mark the end of military communism and the inauguration of the social order normal to Englishmen

---

[1] Historians' estimates of Dale naturally vary. Channing considers him " the best of the early governors of Virginia." Doyle condemns his "atrocious code," and Bancroft says that it " added new sorrows to the wretchedness of the people, who pined and perished under despotic rule." Taken by itself this latter statement would almost imply that they had done otherwise than pine and perish when left to their own unruly devices.

[2] H. L. Osgood, *The American Colonies in the Seventeenth Century*, New York, 1904, l. p. 77.

[3] It should be noted that Dale, Gates, Yeardley (first period) and Argall were, strictly speaking, deputy-governors for Lord Delaware, who retained the title of governor from 1609 to his death in 1618.

living under settled conditions. Some of the enactments sought to modify the colony's exclusive dependence upon tobacco by enjoining the production of foodstuffs, silk, flax, and wine. But in spite of a progressive fall in its value tobacco remained the only remunerative crop, and all attempts failed to establish other branches of industry.

The extension of the tobacco estates and the prolonged peace with the Indians tempted the planters to quit the shelter of their fortified settlements and live in more scattered habitations. They had apparently good ground for their confidence, for the savages had shown themselves increasingly docile for some time, listening to the teaching of missionaries, and sending their children to school. But appearances were deceptive. The old king Powhatan died. His successor was Opecancanough, long erroneously described as his brother, but in reality a stranger of another race, who had in his youth been driven out by the Spaniards from territory far to the southward.[1] This man harboured an implacable hatred of all white men, and possessed the strength of purpose, rare among the savages, to conceal his designs until the time was ripe. In 1622 he struck hard and suddenly, and before resistance could be organized massacred the outlying planters to the number of over three hundred. The result was a guerilla warfare lasting several years, the cessation of attempts to civilize the red men, and a temporary contraction of the cultivated area. The colonial leaders sought to exterminate the Indians by a systematic destruction of their crops. After many years they gave up the attempt and the war gradually died down. Opecancanough lived to carry out another massacre twenty-two years afterwards.

During this period the history of the Company's fortunes in England is full of interest. In 1612 it obtained a third charter amplifying the powers of control conferred upon it in 1609. The 1612 charter provided for quarterly meetings of the shareholders to elect members of the council, and also added the recently discovered Bermudas or Somers' Islands to its territories. The three most prominent members of the directorate were Sir Thomas Smith, Robert Rich, Earl of Warwick, and Sir Edwin Sandys, with the last of whom the Earl of Southampton, Shakespeare's patron, was generally found in association. Each of these leaders had a following among the stockholders, and their mutual disagreements, springing originally from mere matters of business but expanding into broad divergences of principle, ultimately ruined the whole corporation. Until 1619 Smith filled the office of treasurer. He looked undoubtedly for some return upon the money invested, and viewed the undertaking in the same light as the Muscovy and East India Companies, with which he was closely connected. A disagreement with Warwick led the latter to intrigue for the appointment of his protégé Samuel Argall as governor in 1617. But when Argall fell into manifest discredit Warwick and Smith made up their quarrel and united to oppose the new ideals personified by Sandys and Southampton.

[1] T. J. Wertenbaker. *Virginia under the Stuarts*, Princeton, 1914, p. 89.

These ideals were broadly that the social welfare of the settlers and the expansion of the colony in the national interest must henceforward be the Company's chief care. Instead of looking for immediate profits, this party sought to promote " the honour and safety of the Kingdom, the strength of our Navy, the visible hope of a great and rich trade." [1]

The theory that these factions in the Company represented the Court and Puritan parties in general politics was long held, and is now discredited. Sandys, it is true, was an advanced liberal in political and religious matters, but so also was the Earl of Warwick, who opposed him. The parallel therefore breaks down.[2] Whatever may have been the origin of the cleavage, the tension became acute in 1618-9. In the former year Sandys secured the grant of political privileges to the settlers and the successive appointments of Delaware and Yeardley to carry it out. Smith, who had approved the martial administration of Dale and Gates, resigned the treasurership in 1619. Sandys became treasurer in his stead. An examination of Smith's accounts revealed negligence on his part, and in his disgust he became a bitter enemy of the Company and its new managers. Sandys now commenced another campaign to popularise emigration. In his enthusiasm he painted colonial life in too rosy colours. He secured thousands of new emigrants, and these, unseasoned to the climate, fell victims to a great outbreak of fever which raged in Virginia from 1620 to 1624. The news of the Indian massacre was another blow, and hard upon it came the publication of *The Unmasking of Virginia*, by Nathaniel Butler, specially commissioned by the Smith-Warwick faction to reveal as many damaging facts about the colony as possible.

So matters stood in 1623, when it was evident that the Virginia Company was in difficult waters. It had never been profitable and was now insolvent. The king distrusted Sandys and his friends. He also disapproved strongly of the tobacco trade, although he entered into a tobacco contract with the Company in 1622 on terms very favourable to himself. Count Gondomar, the Spanish ambassador, is also said to have been in league with the enemies of Sandys, yet it is not clear that Spain could expect much advantage from the taking over of Virginia by the Crown ; for James always made it plain that although the Company might be offensive to him he was a staunch supporter of the colony itself. Gondomar's influence is not proven, but the other considerations sufficed to bring the king to a decision. In 1623 he opened proceedings for the confiscation of the Virginia Company's charter. The friends of Sandys sought to debate the matter

---

[1] This represents the Sandys faction's own account of itself. But in justice to Smith it should be noted that, whilst the Company's records for his term of office are missing, those for 1619-24 are still extant. We have thus a proper presentation of the case for one party only.

[2] A. P. Newton, *op. cit.* p. 25. C. M. Andrews, in *Our Earliest Colonial Settlements*, New York, 1933, pp. 47-52, endorses the revised view and shows that the Sandys party ruined the Company, not by their liberalism, but by mismanagement.

in parliament and were silenced by the royal command. In 1624 the
case was concluded, and the Company ceased to exist. Historians are
fairly unanimous in their judgments upon the step : morally and
politically the abrogation may have been unjustifiable ; in its practical
effects it was a benefit to all concerned.[1]

[1] Doyle, p. 242 ; Channing, i. p. 225 ; Egerton, pp. 35-7. The same conclusion may
be inferred from *Camb. Hist. of Br. Empire*, i. pp. 150-2.

CHAPTER III

VIRGINIA AND MARYLAND, 1624–1649

WHEN James I. dissolved the Company Virginia had a population of about 1200 settlers. The general plan of its future development was already sketched out, dictated principally by the climatic and geographical characteristics of the country. The most important of these was the river system, by which ocean-going ships could penetrate at many points far inland from the coast. There was thus no concentration of external trade at one great depot, as happened in certain later colonies. Port facilities being widely diffused, the business population remained equally scattered, and there was no development of large towns. To this decentralization the growth of the tobacco industry and the failure of attempts to establish manufactures also contributed. In spite of extensive emigration the population had hitherto remained small, owing to the deadly nature of the climate in the coastal areas. Two factors now combined to remove this check. The punishment inflicted upon the Indians after the massacre of 1622 gradually lightened their pressure upon the older settlements ; and the distribution of individual estates attracted in place of the older military adventurers two new types of settler, the man with capital able to open up new districts, and the agricultural labourer willing to work as an indentured servant for a term of years with the prospect of himself attaining to proprietorship in the course of time. A movement thus set in, by which population quitted the malarious creeks and swamps of which Jamestown had formed such a fatal example, and sought the healthier undulating country of the interior, which, with its alternating patches of woodland and meadow, more nearly resembled the English landscape of the period. The crown, entering into possession of the late Company's territorial rights, adopted a fairly liberal land policy. Men with money and energy found no hindrance from lack of space, and the foundations were laid of that enduring social order based upon the exploitation of large estates which for over two centuries was to render Virginia the type of a plantation colony. The subsequent introduction of negro slaves in place of white labour tended to stabilise these conditions. In

1624, however, the negroes were only present in insignificant numbers.[1]

Such were the prospects of Virginia when the crown assumed control. It was perhaps fortunate for the colony that the death of James I. shortly followed, for his capricious nature and tortuous modes of thought rendered it unsafe to prophesy upon his future conduct of the undertaking. Nevertheless it is but fair to say that his attitude towards Virginian affairs represents the most pleasing aspect of his otherwise feeble record. When we consider his truckling to Spain in other transactions, it is a matter for congratulation that Virginia received steadfast support from home throughout its early tribulations. Charles I., before he became entangled in the courses which led to his ruin, displayed a statesmanlike moderation and breadth of view in American policy which are also at variance with his general conduct. He issued a new charter in 1625, by which the appointment of the governor and council of Virginia was vested in the crown. The elected assembly received no formal recognition, but in practice Charles made no attempt to curtail its powers, and his appointments were usually on sound principles, without the jobbery and corruption which disgraced the later period of the Restoration.

During the years from 1625 to 1640 Virginia steadily improved in population, wealth and security of life and property. By 1635 the inhabitants numbered 5000, and the importation of negroes was on the increase. At the same time there were more than twenty different settlements returning representatives to the assembly ; the occupation of the peninsula between the York and James Rivers was fairly complete, extending seventy miles inland from its extremity ; and there were also about 1000 settlers on the Northampton peninsula, the northern arm of Chesapeake Bay. The tobacco output showed a proportionate advance, increasing from 20,000 lb. in 1617 to 500,000 lb. in 1627, when the period of prosperity was only at its beginning. But the West Indian islands of both England and Spain were also producing tobacco, and the European markets became glutted. The consequent fall in price led the assembly to pass enactments forbidding newcomers to grow tobacco, and restricting the number of plants to be cultivated by the older planters. Such legislation was typical of the time, and we are not obliged to believe that it was fully enforced. A more hopeful remedy lay in the appointment of inspectors to condemn tobacco of poor quality and thus to stimulate a healthy competition with the Spanish product, hitherto acknowledged the best. Secondary effects of the over-production were a period of strained relations between the planters and the merchants, and a revival of corn cultivation by which the colony became more self-supporting.

As the years elapsed and the developments outlined above displayed their effects, we find a remarkable change of tone in the descriptions of colonial life. Letters from Virginia are no longer a dreadful

[1] The first small consignment arrived in 1619.

catalogue of famine, pestilence, and death. Instead, they descant
upon the delights of a community in which the rich man lived in
dignified ease, untroubled by the political oppression which weighed
upon his brother at home, and the poor man enjoyed better food,
lighter toil and more prospect of advancement than could be looked
for by the agricultural labourer of England. We hear much of the
hospitality of plantation life, whereby a stranger might travel in
comfort through a land in which inns were unknown ; and a writer
of the middle of the century goes so far as to say that few who had
once lived in Virginia ever wished to leave. The picture, like that of
the earlier days of martial law, may be over-coloured ; but at least it
indicates a change for the better.

We come now to the foundation of Maryland, the second English
colony upon Chesapeake Bay. In point of time the New England states
preceded it by a few years ; but since in locality, social conditions, and
the events of its early history, Maryland is closely linked to Virginia,
it will be convenient to trace their development side by side.

One of the original members of the Virginia Company had been
George Calvert who, after entering upon a political career under the
patronage of Sir Robert Cecil, had become successively a knight, a
secretary of state, and an advocate of the Spanish marriage of Prince
Charles. On the failure of that project he became a convert to Roman
Catholicism and retired from public life in England. James I. rewarded
him with a grant of Irish lands and the Irish title of Lord Baltimore.
He now interested himself in colonization and secured a proprietary
grant of territory in Newfoundland. His settlement in the Avalon
peninsula, founded in 1623, was at first prosperous. Then French
attacks and Puritan complaints of the toleration he accorded to his
co-religionists rendered the position difficult, and the severity of the
northern winters seems finally to have decided him to abandon the
scene of his first efforts and seek a milder climate for his colonists in
the south. He therefore sailed for Virginia in 1629, intending to settle
in that country. But the Virginians disliked his religious views as
strongly as the Puritans had done. They required him to take the
oath of supremacy or leave the colony. He chose the latter alternative
and returned to England before the close of the year. At home large
schemes of colonial development were in the air ; the Massachusetts
Bay Company had entered upon its career, and Sir Robert Heath had
just received a vaguely defined grant of Carolina, in the south. Baltimore himself seems to have obtained a promise of lands between
Virginia and Carolina, but the jealousy of the Virginians frustrated
its fulfilment. They despatched William Claybourne to England to
keep an eye upon Baltimore's designs, and the issue of the latter's
patent was deferred until 1632. As finally framed, it conferred the
right to plant in an area whose boundary to the south-west was the
Potomac River and to the north the fortieth parallel of latitude.
This territory, at the king's suggestion, received the name of Maryland.

The terms of the charter are of interest since it led to the founding of the first permanent proprietary colony. The proprietor, although remaining an English subject, became a monarch in miniature. He enjoyed the right to make laws for his settlers, subject to the advice and consent of the free men among them. The colony was to be exempt from taxation by the crown. The religious establishment was to be that of the Church of England, and there was no expressed toleration of Catholicism. Such a definite pronouncement was hardly to be expected from an English king in the then state of public opinion, but that toleration was implied can hardly be doubted when we consider the subsequent proceedings of the Calverts and the fact that they remained in favour with Charles I. This proprietary grant, one of several issued at the same period, marks a reversion from the policy of colonization by chartered companies to the original Tudor method illustrated by the patents of Ralegh, Gilbert, and the adventurers of Henry VII.

The first Lord Baltimore died immediately after the receipt of his grant. Cecilius Calvert, the second Lord Baltimore, then took control. Although he never visited his colony he remained in active control of it for many years. His personal character has been variously interpreted. He was undoubtedly a keen man of business, but while some have ascribed his religious policy to a genuine love of freedom, others can see in it only the result of complete cynicism.[1] However, the effect rather than the motive of his career is of practical importance, and the effect was that Maryland became from the outset a singularly prosperous and enlightened colony.

Before the end of 1633 the first expedition set sail from the Thames under the command of Leonard Calvert, the proprietor's brother. Its two ships, the *Ark* and the *Dove,* carried 300 settlers of a type superior to those who had first gone to Virginia. It was Baltimore's aim that they should be " not a chance assemblage of individuals, but a formed and articulate body transplanted complete." [2] Most of the leading men were Catholics, and it would seem that the humbler settlers were also predominantly but not exclusively of that faith. Before clearing the English coast they took on board two Jesuit priests. Arriving in Chesapeake Bay in February, 1634, they received a friendly welcome from Sir John Harvey, the governor of Virginia, and then proceeded northwards up the Bay. Calvert chose a site on a tributary flowing into the Potomac from the north, and named the first settlement St. Mary's. The priests, contrary to the cautious instructions of the proprietor, marked the foundation by a public celebration of mass. Baltimore had enjoined the private exercise of the Catholic faith.[3]

A wise innovation in colonial practice combined with favourable local conditions to render the first settlement a success. There was

[1] Doyle, p. 373 ; Tyler, p. 125.   [2] Doyle, p. 399.

[3] The proprietor continued to insist on impartial toleration, and had some consequent disagreement with the Jesuits. The original Catholic majority in the population gradually disappeared.—*Cam. Hist. of Brit. Empire,* i. pp. 170-1.

no preliminary period of communal working; the gentlemen and servants having come out in due proportions and with proper equipment, it was possible to allot individual plantations from the outset. The pioneer work also was facilitated rather than hindered by the Indians of St. Mary's, who welcomed the white men as protectors against more powerful tribes dwelling in the interior. With these warlike savages the colonists ultimately came into conflict, but for the first few years they were able to devote themselves, unhampered by military considerations, to the establishment of the settlement on sound economic lines. The cultivation of corn was immediately successful, the output even exceeding the needs of the colony. Tobacco was then taken in hand, and became the staple article of trade. The conditions upon which the proprietor distributed the land tended to the formation of large estates worked by indentured labour; and although the surviving records of early Maryland are scanty, they convey a general impression of social justice and fair play which is perhaps traceable to the influence of religious toleration.

The most unsparing enemies of the Maryland pioneers were men of their own race. We have already seen that the Virginians were suspicious of the whole project from its origination. Through the medium of Claybourne they had protested in London against the grant of Baltimore's charter. On the arrival of Leonard Calvert in America Governor Harvey had been alone in offering him a civil welcome; and ere a year had elapsed from the founding of St. Mary's a fierce boundary dispute had broken out. Harshly and illiberally as the Virginians behaved, they had yet a genuine grievance. As early as 1625, years before the Maryland grant had been thought of, they had established a trading post upon the Isle of Kent, deep in the northern recesses of Chesapeake Bay. William Claybourne was the person chiefly interested in this enterprise, intended for traffic with the unsubdued Indians of that region, and this accounts for his energy in opposing the designs of the Calvert family. The government, in fixing the boundaries of Maryland, ignored his rights, and Leonard Calvert insisted from the beginning upon the claim of Maryland to include the disputed island. This was not the only example of carelessness on the part of Charles I.'s colonial advisers. Practically the whole frontier of Maryland, although definitely described upon paper, proved difficult to delimit on the spot, owing to uncertainty in determination of latitude and longitude and in the application of geographical names. The quarrel with Claybourne was probably exasperated by personal feeling. He had been one of the prime movers in the expulsion of the first Lord Baltimore from Virginia in 1629. He was now prepared to continue his trade at Kent Island as a private citizen, but Leonard Calvert speedily found opportunity for charging him with treason and ordering his arrest. The pretext for this was that a scandalmonger had accused him of inciting the Indians to attack St. Mary's. The charge appears to have been groundless. Feeling ran so high that a conflict took place in 1635 between the rival partisans, and five men were killed in a boat action in the Chesapeake. The home government, on appeal being made to it, decided in favour of the Maryland contention. The Virginians gave up Kent Island, and Claybourne had to swallow his defeat until a change in the political situation gave him his chance of revenge.

Meanwhile the development of Maryland continued somewhat more slowly than the initial success had given warrant to expect. Lord Baltimore, having sunk much of his fortune in the venture, was obliged to exact higher terms for his land than did the crown in Virginia. Capitalists therefore preferred the latter colony, and the exploitation of Maryland fell increasingly to the smaller freeholders. Socially, no doubt, this was desirable, but in the local circumstances it was not of economic advantage. In religious matters the enthusiasm of the enfranchised Catholics outran the cautious ideas of the proprietor. He became alarmed for the security of his patent as reports began to arrive of increasing disregard of the English religious code. In 1641, when affairs at home began to take a serious turn, he asserted his authority to curb the Jesuits, whom he accused of working for his ruin under the mask of religion. Thenceforward their activities continued on a more moderate scale. Baltimore's intervention had been necessary, for it must be remembered that the population of Maryland had never been exclusively Catholic, and that the Protestant element increased as time went on. Any attempt to secure more than a limited toleration would have imperilled the whole Catholic position.

The political evolution of the colony presents special features. Originally the governor summoned all the free men—a term which he interpreted to mean freeholders—to deliberate in one body with himself and his council. The proprietor intended to limit the powers of this assembly to mere assent or dissent to his own legislative proposals. The colonists, however, speedily made it plain that they meant to initiate legislation of their own, and they carried their point. As the settlements were extended personal attendance at the assembly became inconvenient, and a custom sprang up of entrusting one man with the proxies of his neighbours. Further growth necessitated the election of representatives as in Virginia, but the system remained long uncrystallised in a formal constitution. One man at least, having voted for a defeated candidate, claimed to sit in person since otherwise he would not have been represented ; and his claim was allowed.[1] The final step in the establishment of the normal English mode of government was taken in 1647 when the assembly began to sit as a separate chamber from the council. In its machinery of government Maryland was now on a level with Virginia ; in practice it was more independent of home control, for its proprietor, who appointed governor and council, could not hope to enjoy the prestige of the crown, which filled the corresponding offices in the older colony.

[1] Doyle, p. 385.

After the settlement of the Kent Island dispute the history of Virginia drifted apart from that of Maryland until events arising from the outbreak of the Civil War in England again linked the two colonies together. The favour shown by the English government to Maryland produced much irritation in Virginia, and led to the first contest between the colonists and the crown. In 1635 the leading Virginians picked a quarrel with their governor, Sir John Harvey, placed him under constraint, and shipped him to England. His offence had been that, acting under orders from home, he had not supported Claybourne and his party. The insurgents sent deputies to England to explain their case. The deputies suffered some months' imprisonment, and Harvey returned in triumph with powers to indemnify himself at their expense. The soreness arising from this incident had no permanent effect upon the loyalty of the Virginians. In 1641 the king appointed Sir William Berkeley as governor. He was a staunch royalist, and, being personally frank and popular in his earlier years, he was able to confirm the royalist and Anglican tone of the colony. During the Civil War many exiled cavaliers made their homes in Virginia.

The Claybourne party seems now to have become a minority. But it was watching its opportunity. The outbreak of hostilities in England in 1642 provided an excuse for privateering on the seas. In 1643 Leonard Calvert obtained letters of marque from the king. A little later Richard Ingle, a Puritan captain, cruised in Chesapeake Bay with a similar authority from the Parliament. Claybourne joined forces with Ingle, and in 1645 they fell upon St. Mary's, capturing it and driving Calvert to take refuge in Virginia. In spite of their grievances against Calvert the Virginians supported him as a fellow royalist. He returned to St. Mary's in the following year, dying there in 1647. Lord Baltimore in England, more in touch with the realities of the Civil War than were the colonists in America, felt himself obliged to conciliate the now triumphant parliamentary party. He appointed a Virginian Protestant, William Stone, to succeed his brother as governor. His conduct excited the resentment of the royalists, and the fugitive Charles II. proclaimed him a traitor in 1649. Before Stone could take over his charge the conservative elements in Maryland repudiated the authority of Parliament and asserted their allegiance to the king. In Virginia also the royalists, under Berkeley's leadership, professed adherence to Charles I., and when the news of his execution arrived in 1649 they recognized his son and prepared for resistance against the Commonwealth. The reign of Charles I. thus closes with the two southern colonies in revolt, not against the mother-country as such, but against the political party dominant in it for the time being.

CHAPTER IV

THE PURITAN EMIGRATION TO NEW ENGLAND, 1620–1649

(i) *The Pilgrim Fathers*

IN 1608 a congregation of Puritan dissenters, driven from their homes by persecution, emigrated from Scrooby and the neighbouring villages and made their way in poverty and distress to Amsterdam in the Protestant Netherlands; in August, 1609, Henry Hudson, in the Dutch ship *Half Moon*, discovered the Hudson River and so drew the attention of his employers to the project of establishing Dutch trade and colonies in North America; five years later Captain John Smith, the Virginia pioneer, examined and charted the coasts of Maine, New Hampshire and Massachusetts, and christened them New England; and in 1620 Sir Ferdinando Gorges and others of the influential colonizing projectors of the time secured a reconstitution of the moribund Plymouth Company of Virginia under the name of the Council for New England. These were the leading events in a series which preceded the emigration of the discontented English Puritans to America, and determined which part of the continent should be the scene of their labours.

The Scrooby exiles were a band small in numbers and drawn for the most part from the poorer section of the middle class—farmers and tradesmen of a group of villages upon the great highroad from London to the north. Their leading spirits at the time of their flight were William Brewster, postmaster of Scrooby and a former dependent of the secretary Davison whom Elizabeth had made the scapegoat for the execution of the Queen of Scots; Richard Clifton and John Robinson, two clergymen dispossessed of their livings for nonconformity; and William Bradford who, although but a youth—he was born in 1590—was already evincing qualities of mind and character which were to place him at the head of the movement. By existing statutes it was illegal for this congregation to leave the country, and their first plan of evasion in 1607 was foiled by the treachery, it was said, of the shipmaster who was to transport them. Their second attempt, in 1608, barely succeeded. Before the embarkation was complete, a cry arose that the magistrates were upon them. The ship's crew made sail, leaving on the quay of Boston the personal belongings and some of the wives of the passengers ; and those who were on board arrived penniless in Amsterdam after a stormy passage which occupied a fortnight.[1] From Amsterdam they soon removed to Leyden, where they joined hands with other religious exiles from various parts of England. In the cities of the Netherlands they led a hard life. Most of them had abandoned their worldly goods in England, and they had to gain a living by manual labour in unaccustomed trades, with the added handicap of being aliens in a competitive industrial population. Their children, forced to take part in the struggle for bread, grew up weakly and regretful of their fathers' austere choice. Some of the fainthearted gave up the contest and returned to England ; some of the younger men married in the country or enlisted in the Dutch armies. There was no guarantee even of a continuance of existing conditions, for religious factions were rife in Holland and there was ever the menace of a reconquest by Catholic Spain. As the years went by it became clear that to remain at Leyden meant at best a loss of their English nationality. For these reasons they began to look more and more to the empty lands across the Atlantic, where spiritually they might be at peace and where material circumstances could scarcely be harsher than in Europe.

They had originally no intention of settling in New England. The locality first proposed was Guiana, which had received so much attention already from English pioneers under James I. We can understand now that Guiana was hopelessly unsuitable for the type of settlement the Leyden congregation had in mind, and the fact that it should have been seriously considered throws an interesting sidelight on the general information concerning America current at the time. After abandoning the idea of Guiana the exiles next approached the Dutch authorities on the question of a settlement near the Hudson, and finally obtained a patent from the Virginia Company conferring leave to occupy the extreme northern limits of that corporation's territory. Sir Edwin Sandys was at this period (1619-20) in control of the Virginia Company's policy, and it was probably to his Puritan leanings that the intending emigrants were indebted for the concession. Sandys indeed may have had personal acquaintance with William Brewster, who had been a tenant of his brother at Scrooby.

The next difficulty was the lack of funds. The estimated cost of planting each member of the colony was £10, and that sum accordingly became the share unit of a company privately formed to carry out the enterprise. The required sum could not be raised among those who sympathized for religious reasons. The emissaries of the Leyden congregation therefore entered into an agreement with a syndicate of London financiers headed by Thomas Weston. Weston and his friends viewed the project purely as a commercial investment,

[1] There was already at Amsterdam a separatist congregation which had emigrated before the death of Elizabeth.

and drove a somewhat hard bargain as the price of their support. All land was to be worked in common for the first seven years ; personal emigration, as in Virginia, was to rank as equivalent to the subscription of one share ; and trading rights were to be reserved to the syndicate. Communal working was thus forced upon the settlers from without, and not undertaken, as some have supposed, from any design of imitating early Christian methods. The emigrants, indeed, pleaded for individual ownership of small plots of land from the outset, but this was refused by the syndicate.

These arrangements having been concluded, the advance party left Leyden in July, 1620, and sailed from Delft to Southampton in the ship *Speedwell*. Additional emigrants from England joined them, and a larger ship, the *Mayflower*, was chartered to accompany the original vessel across the Atlantic. The two left Southampton in company on August 5, but ere long the *Speedwell* developed a leak, and they put into Plymouth. Here some of the passengers abandoned the voyage, and the *Speedwell* was left behind, the *Mayflower* finally sailing alone with one hundred colonists on September 6. Taking the northerly route across the ocean the *Mayflower* made a landfall at Cape Cod in New England on November 11, 1620. The intended destination had been the shore of Delaware Bay, just within the northern limit of the Virginia Company's claims, and some 400 miles to the southward of the actual point of arrival. The Pilgrim Fathers now abandoned their original intention and decided to pitch their camp upon the shores of New England instead. Two possible intrigues have been suggested as the cause of this radical change of plan. One is that the Dutch had bribed the *Mayflower's* captain to deposit his passengers in a region remote from the New Netherlands ; this story is first traceable some forty years later, and receives no support from the writings of the Pilgrims themselves. The other is that Thomas Weston, the chief of the London syndicate, was a secret agent of Sir Ferdinando Gorges and the Council for New England, and likewise bribed the shipmaster to cut short the voyage at Cape Cod. For this supposition also there is no real evidence, although it squares very well with the known facts of the situation. The New England Council were not disposed to invest money in planting their concession ; nevertheless it was to their interest to attract settlers, since they hoped to make their profit from the development of trade and fisheries. Actually they showed no displeasure when they heard that the Pilgrims had invaded their territory, and made no difficulty in according them a formal recognition. Yet the simple explanation is probably the true one. There were grave disadvantages in a prolonged coasting voyage at the advanced season of the year ; and the Pilgrim Fathers were undoubtedly pleased with the aspect of the bay enclosed by Cape Cod. After a month's exploration they decided to settle at the harbour of Plymouth [1] on the western shore of the bay.

[1] So named by John Smith in 1614.

Soon after the first landing the Pilgrims executed a mutual agreement acknowledging their allegiance to the king of England and promising to abide by such laws and ordinances as might be enacted for the common good. This document, known as the Mayflower Compact, remained the basis of the colony's future government, since there was no royal charter to define the constitution as in Virginia and in the later cases of Massachusetts and Maryland. The small number of the settlers rendered electoral machinery unnecessary for many years to come, and the whole body met in primary assembly to choose their officers and pass such measures as they thought fit.

The first governor was John Carver, and on his death early in 1621 William Bradford was elected to the office. Bradford remained governor until 1657, the year of his death, with the exception of short intervals amounting to five years when, at his own desire, another was appointed. To the mind of a scholar he united the character of a man of action and a statesman, and he displayed a large-hearted toleration and complete absence of self-seeking which were the more remarkable when contrasted with the narrowness of his upbringing and the bitter struggles of his early years. Every community takes much of its tone and corporate character from its head, and the colony of Plymouth undoubtedly owed to William Bradford much of the purity and simplicity which distinguished it throughout its independent career. William Brewster and Edward Winslow, who survived for many years at Plymouth, were likewise leaders of character and learning. One professional soldier, Miles Standish, also threw in his lot with the Pilgrim band, although not belonging to their church, and played on a smaller scale a part comparable to that of John Smith in Virginia.

Of the courage and determination of these men the immediate future had an ample test in store. No sooner had they chosen the site of their settlement than winter set in in bitter earnest and sickness began to take toll of their scanty numbers. In five months fifty of the hundred were dead ; of the eighteen wives who accompanied their husbands, only four outlived the first winter. To lack of shelter was added shortage of food, although the New England woods teemed with game and the seas with fish. On this point an American historian has the following explanation. " In those days," he says, " middle-class Englishmen knew little of sport. In England and in Holland, not one of them probably had ever gone in pursuit of a wild animal, and few, if any, had ever caught a fish." [1] This, of English farmers and villagers, is strange reading. But the circumstances of the case account for the famine. Much of the fishing tackle of the expedition had, by an oversight, been left behind in the *Speedwell* ; hunting in the depth of winter was not always practicable, and if the young and active members of the party had been permitted to scatter and rove there would have been a speedy end to the hard work needed for planting the settlement. Later, when the summer set in, Bradford

[1] Channing, i. p. 310.

kept all hands strictly to the task of raising crops, and there is no doubt that he was wise to do so, for to the man of northern Europe bread is a more necessary food even than meat.

The victory over the first winter, gained at such terrible cost, determined the success of the experiment. Thenceforward progress was slow but steady. In 1622 a reinforcement arrived, although the London partners failed to send with it a sufficiency of supplies. Even with men of high moral character the system of communal working proved a failure. Bradford became convinced of the fallacy of the idea " that the taking away of property and bringing in community into a commonwealth would make them happy and flourishing as if they were wiser than God." Sir Thomas Dale had shown the one method of making the arrangement workable. But the Pilgrims had not fled from one despotism to set up another, and in 1623 they divided the corn lands into individual lots as the only means of coping with the chronic scarcity. The result justified their decision, for in two years they had so much corn that they were able to barter some to the Indians. But the step was a breach of the agreement with the financiers. The Pilgrims reserved to the latter the proceeds of the fur trade with the natives, and set themselves to clear off their remaining indebtedness. In 1627 they paid Weston and his partners £1800 for their entire interest in the colony, and thus dissolved the bond which restricted their independence.

At this period Plymouth consisted of log houses built in two streets, with a governor's house and a combined church and granary. Cannon were mounted at the crossroads and on the church, and the whole was surrounded by a palisade. With the Indians the Pilgrims' relations were fortunate. Shortly before their arrival a pestilence had swept away most of the red men of the vicinity, leaving cornfields already cleared for the newcomers to cultivate. With other tribes along the coast a fur trade sprang up, and the honest dealings of the English secured an amity which was seldom broken. When two savages were killed in a chance scuffle it was regarded as a matter for extreme regret and even for grave condolences in letters sent across the Atlantic. The Dutch at the mouth of the Hudson also showed no hostility towards the colony, evidently not foreseeing in it the germ of a movement which was to oust their flag from the continent.

As we have seen, it was not the policy of the New England Council to adventure its own members' money in colonies. It granted licences freely to intending settlers and fought hard to retain its trading and fishing monopoly against would-be interlopers from home. In this manner a number of small settlements sprang up along the New England coast during the decade following the voyage of the *Mayflower*. One of these was despatched by Thomas Weston to the site of the present Boston in 1622. Its members speedily fell into necessity and quarrelled with the Indians. A despairing appeal for aid reached Plymouth, and Miles Standish led a party to the rescue. He drove off the Indians and brought away the starving white men, the majority of whom returned to England. Another venture was that of Thomas Morton, who set up, also in the Boston neighbourhood, as a fur-trader and drink-seller to the Indians. He and his reprobate followers called their station Merrymount and caused great scandal to the Pilgrims, who complained that they frisked round a maypole and drank pounds worth of liquor in a morning. When they added to these offences that of selling muskets to the red men the nuisance became intolerable. Standish went to Merrymount and arrested its proprietor. The Plymouth elders banished him from the country, but he soon returned to his old trade, to be dealt with ultimately by some new neighbours of sterner mould who began to make their appearance in 1629. By the latter date there were eight small trading posts on the New England coast, some of them of a more respectable type than Merrymount.

Plymouth itself grew slowly in population, and began to throw off new townships. In 1624 there were 180 settlers ; in 1630, 300 ; and in 1642, 3000. By the latter date the number of townships had risen to ten. This extension necessitated the formation of an elective assembly, which came into being in 1636-8. A fishing station was established at Cape Ann, but salt works at the same place failed to prosper. An export trade in corn and cattle began to thrive, and, coupled with the fur trade, ensured solid prosperity. This steady but unbrilliant progress became the keynote of the colony in material affairs, as a certain broadness of outlook, unusual in Puritan communities, was that of its religious history. In Plymouth, in fact, seventeenth-century Puritanism was seen at its best. Its more vigorous, if in some ways less pleasing, aspect appears in the undertaking we have next to consider.

(ii) *Massachusetts*

The ten years following the voyage of the *Mayflower* witnessed a large transformation and development of English Puritanism. The great body of opinion which had vainly sought reforms at the Hampton Court Conference, but had not been prepared to follow the emigrating separatists of 1608, began to appear as a political power in the later parliaments of James I. and the early parliaments of his son. Its leaders were men of greater wealth and standing than the Pilgrim Fathers. Its strength lay among the merchants of London and the squires of the eastern counties ; in the person of Sir Edwin Sandys it controlled the later fortunes of the Virginia Company ; and its adherents in the ranks of the peerage included the Earls of Warwick and Lincoln and Lords Saye and Brooke. Although tinged throughout with the prevailing religious dissent, much of the force of the movement was political : the advanced Englishman of the seventeenth century would no longer consent to be governed by the arbitrary power of sovereigns who by their own actions had forfeited much of his respect.

The establishment of Plymouth and other small settlements to the north of Cape Cod, in the sphere allotted to the New England Council, diverted the attention of many influential men from the discouraging politics of England to the possibilities of America.   In March, 1628, six partners obtained from the New England patentees a grant of the land between the Merrimac and Charles Rivers, a tract which subsequently became the colony of Massachusetts.

Of the original six partners, one only, John Endicott, crossed the Atlantic in person and became prominent in the development of the venture.   He was an ardent Puritan, ripe to throw off his nominal allegiance to the Anglican Church, and his early proceedings in Massachusetts indicated the advent of a militant force and the opening of a new chapter in the history of America.   Arriving at Salem with sixty followers in September, 1628, he found the place occupied by a small party of secular colonists having no connection with the Plymouth Pilgrims.   He came to an arrangement which safeguarded the interests of these existing settlers, and then proceeded to impress his vigorous personality on the whole district.   He deported to England two members of his own party who claimed the right to use the Anglican prayer-book, telling them that " New England was no place for them."   He hewed down the Merrymount maypole, and rechristened the site Mount Dagon, with a stern admonition to the occupants " to look well that there be better walking."   Whatever may have been the intentions of his partners in England it is evident that he regarded himself as the pioneer of a strictly Puritan community.

In the meantime preparations were going on at home for the exploitation of the Massachusetts grant on a large scale.   The original holders of the concession from the New England Council threw open the project to investors and formed the Massachusetts Bay Company, which received its charter from Charles I. on March 4, 1629.   The company was at first ostensibly secular in its objects, but the majority of its members were Puritans, some holding very pronounced views, and these leading spirits probably entertained from the outset purposes which they did not think fit to make public until a later stage had been reached.   Evidence pointing in this direction lies in the fact that whilst the charter was being drafted its promoters obtained the ruling out of a clause which would have enforced the residence of the governing body in England.   This was a customary provision in such documents, and its omission is significant in view of what followed.   The terms of the grant followed in general the precedent of the Virginia Company, but there was to be no preliminary period of communal ownership, and the allotment of estates was to begin at once.

In the summer of 1629 the underlying motives in the scheme became apparent.   Three hundred recruits went out to join Endicott's advanced party, but the great expedition was postponed to the following year, and at a meeting of the shareholders Matthew Cradock, the

governor, announced that he had received a suggestion for the entire
body to transfer itself to Massachusetts, and desired those concerned
to think over the matter.   Several gentlemen of the eastern counties
declared their willingness to emigrate with their dependents, and
before the end of the year the decision was taken.   Ten of the wealthier
members bought up the stock of those who preferred to remain at home.
Matthew Cradock resigned the governorship and John Winthrop
with a new body of assistants took his place.[1]   The members of the
reconstituted company dispersed to their homes to wind up their
affairs and prepare to cross the ocean in the following spring.   It was
the year which had witnessed the dissolution of Charles' third tumultu-
ous parliament after the Puritan commons had held their Speaker in his
chair whilst they concluded their business, with the king's guards
hammering at the door.   Sir John Elyot and other leaders in that
defiant act were now prisoners in the Tower, and the king had entered
upon the reckless course of tyranny which was to bring him in twenty
years to the scaffold.   His allowance of the proceedings of the Massachusetts Bay Company has not been satisfactorily explained.   The
Puritans were still influential in high places, and bribery may have
aided their purposes.

John Winthrop, who now became the leader of the emigrants,
was a Suffolk squire born in the Armada year.   He was a man of
legal training, cool temperament and a large capacity for administration.   But for his religious convictions he might have looked forward
to a distinguished career at home.   But the trend of affairs made it
increasingly evident that the England of Charles I. had no promise
for such men as he ; at that date the most imaginative among them
could not have forecasted the Puritan ascendancy which the future
had in store.   For Winthrop there was no question of a conflict between
his practical ambitions and his religious belief.   He made the one
subserve the other ; and when, in 1629, his opinions lost him his
office of attorney of the Court of Wards, he threw himself heartily into
the Massachusetts project.   His guiding motive, and that of his
fellow colonists, is well expressed in a letter written by him in the
summer of 1629 : " My dear wife, I am verily persuaded God will
bring some heavy affliction upon this land, and that speedily ; but if
the Lord seeth it will be good for us, he will provide a shelter and a
hiding place for us and others, as a Zoar for Lot, a Sarephthah for his
prophet."   Again in the same year he wrote : " Evil times are coming,
when the church must fly to the wilderness."   This conception of themselves as men fleeing from the wrath to come accounts for much of the
indifference of the New England Puritans to the subsequent struggle in
the mother-country.   Their brethren left at home had not girded themselves and fled ; they might therefore fight out their battle unaided, for
they had ceased to be of any concern to the elect in Massachusetts.

[1] The stages in the development of the scheme are discussed in C. M. Andrews,
Our Earliest Colonial Settlements, New York, 1933, pp. 59-79.

Winthrop duly set sail in the spring of 1630, and arrived at Salem on June 12 with eleven ships and 900 settlers. This was the greatest number of colonists which had yet crossed the Atlantic in one party and, in keeping with its inauguration, the development of the colony continued on a larger and more rapid scale than had previously been seen. The new arrivals found that Endicott's pioneers had suffered much from sickness and privation, and they themselves had a hard time in the winter of 1630-1. Some two hundred died and as many returned to England before the problem of the food supply had been effectively taken in hand. The leaders, however, acted with energy. They incorporated with their own community the scattered settlements already existing upon their land, and by the end of the first winter Massachusetts had eight recognized townships. Winthrop chose Boston as the seat of government. One of his first acts on seeing the local conditions had been to send for fresh stocks of food. A ship arrived with supplies from England in February, and these, with another cargo from Virginia, relieved the most pressing necessity and gave the colonists a chance to await the ripening of their own harvest in 1631. Thenceforward the material success of the community was never in doubt. A moderate number of recruits arrived in 1631 and 1632. In the following year the stream swelled in volume, and by May, 1634, Winthrop estimated the population at 4000. In 1642, when the Civil War interrupted the westward flow, it amounted to 16,000, to convey which nearly two hundred ships had crossed the Atlantic.

Winthrop's expedition, like that of the Pilgrim Fathers, had been the transference of an already organized community. Its leaders arrived with their intentions clear-cut in their own minds, and since they bore with them their charter and their whole machinery of government, they were able to put their ideas into practice without delay and without interference from home. The identity of the colony with the Company secured by the personal emigration of all the stockholders paved the way for the rapid development and the practical independence of Massachusetts as compared with the older plantation of Virginia.

By the terms of the charter the election of the governor and the officials lay with the stockholders or free men of the Company. These, after the readjustment of 1629, were only twelve in number. The remaining settlers had thus at the outset no political rights. To withhold such rights from influential men who had brought their families and dependents from England by reason of political oppression was manifestly impossible. Accordingly the ruling circle decided in 1631 to throw open the freedom of the colony to members of churches already established therein or afterwards to be established with the approval of the existing churches. By this means, although the franchise was extended, the original founders perpetuated their power. Religious conformity became the basis of the colony's political life, and the penalty of dissent was to be the loss of civic rights. No man might be a church member unless his opinions satisfied the scrutiny of a very narrow circle of the leading spirits, who had in their own hands the power of admitting new members to their body and of expelling any who might show signs of independent thought. Nor were these powers less in practice than in theory. They were acted upon to the full. The early political history of Massachusetts is that of a close and intolerant oligarchy utterly untouched by the democratic ideals which have often been loosely ascribed to it. Winthrop and his friends would have scouted the suggestion that they were founding a democratic state in the modern sense of the word. Their political standpoint was that of the ordinary country gentleman of their time, with a natural assumption of authority stiffened by the Puritan conviction that they, the chosen servants of God, must be right and all others wrong; and they had not, like the poor separatists of Leyden, learned the beauty of toleration in the hard school of adversity. They hated William Laud and all his opinions, but to his methods they paid the practical compliment of adopting them themselves.

The magistrates of Boston soon found occasion to exercise their authority. Thomas Morton, the Merrymount gun-trader, returned to his old haunts from his banishment in England. Winthrop's men seized him and deported him once more, after ceremoniously burning his house as an example to evil-doers. He revenged himself by giving information to Archbishop Laud of their religious practices, and by writing a book satirising "the New English Canaan." But it would seem that America had for him an irresistible attraction, for he returned once more in his old age, suffered further rough treatment, and died in the country. An undesirable of similar character was a self-styled knight named Sir Christopher Gardiner. He was accused of loose living and banished, to give valuable information in his turn to the enemies of the colony. In 1631 also "one Ratcliffe" was flogged, lost his ears, and was banished for defaming the government; and other cases of the kind are likewise recorded.

The above proceedings were but typical of the current English practice in dealing with disorderly characters, and might be justified by a consideration of the special dangers besetting a new community. On a very different footing was the case of Roger Williams, a young Welsh preacher who landed in the colony in 1631. Although of kindly nature and of high moral character he was opinionated and pugnacious, and speedily discovered that he was at variance with the generality on a fundamental matter. He objected to a state church, the mainspring of Massachusetts life. Passing on to Plymouth in the hope of finding more congenial society, he soon fell out with Governor Bradford and returned of his own free will to Massachusetts. Here he secured a following at Salem and for three years engaged in disputes with Winthrop and the officials on a variety of subjects. They were

loath to proceed against him, for Winthrop himself had designated him
" a godly minister." But at length the supremacy of the religious
oligarchy was felt to be in danger, and they decided that he must
go. He eluded the pursuit of those who sought to ship him to England
and made off southwards to lay the foundation of the independent
colony of Rhode Island. Another religious dissentient was Mistress
Anne Hutchinson, probably the most masterful character, after
Winthrop, in New England. She criticized first the doctrines and then
the conduct of the ministers. She developed a theological system
which is unintelligible to any but an expert in such matters ; and,
proving steadfastly recalcitrant, she also was banished, to form a new
settlement of her own near that of the exiled Williams. Dr. Robert
Child, another Puritan divine, was fined for objecting to church membership as a test of citizenship. He sailed for England of his own motion
and so probably forestalled the usual sentence upon malcontents.
Whilst the leaders of these several movements suffered in the manner
above described, their adherents were fined, disfranchised and admonished with varying degrees of severity.

In secular matters the government of Massachusetts acted usually
with wisdom and foresight. It was careful to secure a title to its
lands by purchase from the Indians ; it forbade the sale of drink to
them, and it encouraged missionaries to begin the work of civilization.
In consequence it had no Indian war to fight on its own account for a
generation. For economic as much as for ethical reasons it prohibited
the cultivation of tobacco, in which the colony could scarcely have
expected to compete with the warmer regions to the southward.
Corn-growing, fur-trading, fishing and shipbuilding became ultimately
the staple industries, and a vigorous intercourse sprang up with the
West Indies in despite of the mercantile policy which the mother-
country was building up.

The principal dangers to the colony arose from the jealousy of the
New England Council and the growing influence of Archbishop Laud
in the English world. The New England Council, although it had
been anxious to forward the settlement of its lands, could only view
with alarm the vitality and independence of the community which
now occupied the choicest part of them. Its disregard of geography
in the making of its various grants provided material for an abundant
crop of disputes. In 1635 it was dissolved, its members dividing its
claims to unallotted territory amongst themselves. Sir Ferdinando
Gorges obtained the principal share, and in 1639 received a royal
grant for the proprietorship of Maine. Prior to that date he had made
active complaints about the trend of events in Massachusetts, and had
suggested the formation of one united crown colony of New England
with himself as governor. There is little doubt that he would have
given serious trouble had not the outbreak of the Civil War occupied
all the king's energies at home. Before this it had become plain that
Charles I. regretted his complaisance to the Puritan projects. In

1634 he placed Laud at the head of a Commission for Plantations with very extensive powers. Laud, his animosity already whetted against "King Winthrop," determined to be master of the New England Puritans equally with those at home. He began proceedings against the Massachusetts rulers for exceeding the privileges embodied in their charter. Of this Winthrop had undoubtedly been guilty, trusting that his remoteness from the source of authority would permit him to carry matters with a high hand. He now played a waiting game, returning soft answers although resolute not to make any material submission. His prudence was justified by the course of events, for the Civil War saved him from Laud as it did from Gorges. But had Charles successfully maintained his role of absolute monarch there is little doubt that Massachusetts would have fought for its independence rather than give way.[1] The principal restraining influence seems to have been not the sentiment of loyalty but the practical consideration that the New Englanders, by remaining English subjects, preserved their right to inherit property at home.

Winthrop long maintained his ascendancy in the colony he had made, although his tenure of the governorship was not unbroken. In 1634 Thomas Dudley filled that office; in 1635 John Haynes; and in 1636 the younger Sir Henry Vane, lately arrived from England. Vane, however, was not sufficiently firm with religious dissentients to satisfy the dominant party, and Winthrop returned to power in the following year. He was governor from that date until 1640, again from 1642 to 1644, and from 1645 until his death in 1649.

(iii) *Rhode Island, Connecticut and New Haven*

Roger Williams, on his expulsion from Massachusetts, travelled southwards with a few adherents, and made friends with the Indians of Narragansett Bay. In 1636 he purchased, according to his own account, a tract of land from these allies, and established a settlement which he named Providence near the northern end of the bay. He allowed his neighbours complete religious liberty—in fact, he could not consistently do otherwise, for his own opinions were constantly changing—and in political matters the settlement lived with the minimum of organized control. Other emigrants from Massachusetts joined him, and in two years Providence had sixty settlers.

In 1638 Anne Hutchinson and her fellow exiles passed through Providence on their way to seek a new habitation. Her husband, a peace-loving man of colourless character, accompanied her, but her principal lieutenant was William Coddington, who became the magistrate of the little community when it formally declared itself a body politic. The party finally chose a site at Portsmouth on the Island of Aquidneck in Narragansett Bay. They altered the name to Rhode

---

[1] Beer, *Origins of the British Colonial System*, pp. 325-30.

Island, and this became ultimately the title of the whole group of settlements now under discussion. A year later Coddington founded Newport on the southern side of the island. After these townships had been established the restless Mrs. Hutchinson made yet another removal. Taking with her her children and grandchildren, sixteen persons in all, she went westwards to Long Island, and there the entire party were massacred by Indians in 1643. " God's hand is apparently seen therein," was Winthrop's comment when he heard the news.

The fourth constituent portion of Rhode Island was the township of Shawomet, afterwards Warwick, founded in 1638 by Samuel Gorton. This man, like the neighbouring pioneers, was a religious exile from Massachusetts. He had lived there little more than a year when he had to leave by reason of his unorthodox and blasphemous opinions. Plymouth and Portsmouth in their turn cast him out, and he acquired from the Indians the estate of Shawomet, a few miles south of Providence. Massachusetts adopted generally a policy of ignoring the subsequent proceedings of those whom she had deemed unworthy of her own citizenship, but Gorton was suspected of fomenting unrest among the red men, and he certainly continued to write abusive letters to Winthrop and his friends. They therefore sent an expedition which seized him and brought him prisoner to Boston. He sailed for England and laid his case before the Earl of Warwick, now president of the Parliamentary Commission for Plantations. Backed by Warwick's support, he returned to Shawomet, renamed it in honour of his patron, and ended his life there without further disturbing incident.[1]

Hitherto the Rhode Island communities had been independent of one another. Their position, however, was insecure since they had no legal title to the possession of their lands. Massachusetts had a royal charter, and Plymouth a formal grant from the New England Council. Rhode Island now determined to seek a similar recognition. In 1643 Roger Williams took ship for England and approached the Parliamentary Commission. In doing so he took a serious risk, for the Civil War was at this date by no means decided, and the king's displeasure might have fallen heavily on those who treated his enemies as the sovereign power. However, Williams obtained a parliamentary charter organizing Providence, Portsmouth and Newport as one colony, with power to admit Warwick and other townships which might arise in the district. From his return in 1644 dates the history of Rhode Island as a corporate colony. The grant was not acted upon until 1647, when the leading men of the four settlements met at Portsmouth and framed the rudiments of a democratic constitution. In general it may be said that all householders were enfranchised, but the arrangements fluctuated until the period of the Restoration, when it became necessary to seek a royal charter for the colony. As might be expected from the circumstances of its foundation, there was no attempt to set

[1] Channing, i. 390-3.

up a religious test for citizenship as in the case of Massachusetts.
"Rhode Island," it has been said,[1] "was to New England what New
England as a whole was to the mother-country"—that is, a schismatic
and suspect community.

Some ninety miles west of Massachusetts Bay runs the fertile valley
of the Connecticut River which, rising near the present Canadian
boundary, flows nearly due south for the greater part of its course, and
turns south-eastward for the last thirty miles before finding its exit
to the sea at the mouth of Long Island Sound.   This valley became the
scene of another development of New England expansion which took
place contemporaneously with the foundation of the Rhode Island
settlements.   Already, before 1633, English and Dutch pioneers had
visited the Connecticut.   In that year the Dutch established a fort
on its lower reaches.   Immediately on hearing of this, the men of
Plymouth, foreseeing that the Indian trade of the region might be
valuable, planted a rival settlement fifteen miles higher up the stream.
But it was not from Plymouth that the principal influx of Englishmen
was to proceed.   In 1635 there began from Massachusetts Bay an
overland emigration which resulted in the establishment of townships
at Wethersfield, Hartford, Windsor and Springfield, all on the banks
of the Connecticut River.   The leaders of this movement were not
political exiles like Williams and Mrs. Hutchinson, but respected
citizens of Massachusetts, John Haynes, an ex-governor, Roger'
Ludlow, and Thomas Hooker, a preacher.   Their migration was partly
due to dissatisfaction with the trend of events in the parent colony,
but was also inspired by a desire for elbow-room and the superior
quality of the Connecticut soil ; at least there was no serious quarrel,
and they remained on terms of amity with their former comrades.
By the end of 1636 there were 800 inhabitants in the new settlements.
Springfield, the most northerly of the group, was afterwards found
to be within the limits of Massachusetts, and remained under its
jurisdiction.

At the same period the leaders of English Puritanism, then at the
nadir of their fortunes at home, had marked the Connecticut region
as the scene of a possible refuge for themselves should the king's
measures drive them to emigrate.   The Earl of Warwick, president
of the New England Council, granted in 1632 a patent for plantation
to Lords Saye and Brooke, John Pym, John Hampden and others.[2]
In 1635-6, these associates sent out an advanced party under John
Winthrop the younger and Lyon Gardiner to survey the coast near
the mouth of the river and prepare the ground for their own arrival.
The English expedition founded the settlement of Saybrook, but with
that the efforts of the English Puritans came to an end.[3]   The ship-

[1] Doyle, *The Puritan Colonies*, London, 1887, vol. i. p. 240.
[2] A. P. Newton, *Colonizing Activities of the English Puritans*, pp. 83-4.
[3] Newton, pp. 176-185.

money contest, the Scottish rising, and the assembly of the parliaments of 1640 riveted their attention upon home affairs, and they abandoned their purpose of emigrating to America. The Saybrook pioneers lived on friendly terms with the Massachusetts emigrants high up the river, assisted them to repel Dutch intruders from New Amsterdam, and finally in 1644 coalesced with them to form the united colony of Connecticut.

The next stage in the development of Connecticut was an Indian war on an extensive scale, the first of importance in the history of New England. The Pequods were a strong tribe inhabiting the country between the Connecticut and Rhode Island. They committed hostile acts against the new settlements, which thereupon organized a punitive expedition. Under John Mason and John Underhill the force sailed along the coast to Narragansett Bay, landed there, and advanced westwards upon the Pequod stronghold. The latter was stormed, large numbers of its defenders killed, and the Pequods as a nation practically wiped out (1638).

In the following January, 1639,[1] the Connecticut townships felt themselves sufficiently established to devise a political constitution. They declared themselves a commonwealth with a governor, six assistants and a number of deputies increasing with the growth of the colony. Church membership was required ostensibly of the governor alone, but it was probably an unwritten condition of the enjoyment of political rights in general, as in Massachusetts. The latter state made no objection to this separation of its offspring from itself, neither did the men of Connecticut think it necessary to obtain the authority of the English government for the step they had taken. They remained without legal title to their land and without official recognition of their constitution until after the Restoration.

Although the Earl of Warwick, Pym, Hampden, and the other Puritan leaders of the first rank had contemplated for a moment only the abandonment of their struggle against absolutism, there was yet one more group of lesser importance which sailed in a body across the Atlantic ere the great Puritan exodus came to an end. In 1637 John Davenport and Theophilus Eaton arrived at Boston with their followers. The party was small in numbers, but comprised several men of considerable wealth. The two leaders had been friends from boyhood, and were at one in holding the most advanced views on the relationship of church and state. For them the scriptures were a complete and exclusive guide to the conduct of civil affairs, and they designed the setting up of a Bible commonwealth exemplifying the rule of the saints uncontaminated by any mundane allegiance ; at the same time they remained practical business men, with a keen eye to the material prosperity which would accrue from the occupation of a strategic position upon the lines of American trade. The rulers of Massachusetts

---

[1] Doyle, *Puritan Colonies,* i. p. 213, gives the date as 1638 ; Channing, i. p. 404, says January, 1638-9, *i.e.* by modern usage, 1639.

welcomed them as men after their own hearts, and invited them to
settle their church within the colony's territories. But Davenport
and Eaton preferred to retain their independence. They remained in
Massachusetts only for a few months, employing the winter of 1637-8
in studying New England conditions and collecting information upon
which to base their choice of a site for their experiment.

In the spring of 1638 they moved along the southern coast to a
position about thirty miles west of the estuary of the Connecticut.
The Indian name of the place was Quinnipiac, which the new settlers
altered to New Haven. Like the men of Connecticut and Providence
they had no authority from the crown for their undertaking, but this
did not deter them from acting as an independently constituted community. In 1639, when the successful accomplishment of the pioneer
work gave them leisure to turn to political matters, a meeting of the
freemen drew up the constitution of the colony. Government was to
be in the hands of the church members, whose reading of the scriptures
was to be the basis of authority. Church membership, in this sense,
was at first limited to seven of the leading men, with power to admit
others. The arrangement contemplated the existence of but one
township and one church, but as the years passed other settlements
sprang up along the coast westwards towards the Dutch posts at the
mouth of the Hudson. As they developed, these later churches
became affiliated to that of New Haven, and the whole northern shore
of Long Island Sound became a colony which pushed the ideals of
Massachusetts to their extreme conclusion and formed a complete
antithesis to the liberal Puritanism of Rhode Island.

The commercial ambitions of New Haven suffered disappointment
from the proximity of the Dutch settlements and a series of accidental
misfortunes. These are typified in the oft-repeated story of a final
commercial venture in which the New Haven capitalists combined to
set forth their remaining wealth in a large new ship. The vessel sailed
for Europe and was never heard of again ; but according to the
evidence of contemporary witnesses her ghostly form was seen one day
to re-enter the harbour, drop anchor and then vanish from the sight
of the watchers on the quay. The story is narrated by so grave an
authority as John Winthrop in his *History of New England*.

(iv) *The New England Confederation and the Civil War*

In 1643 the four colonies of Massachusetts, Plymouth, Connecticut
and New Haven entered into a pact known as the New England
Confederation. Their expressed reasons for so doing were the promotion of their religious ideals and the necessity for common measures
of defence against the French, the Dutch and the Indians. But since
there was at the time no immediate prospect of attack from any of
these three sources, it is likely that the true, although unexpressed,

motive lay in the English Civil War,[1] and the desirability of a uniform attitude towards whichever party might prove victorious in that struggle.   Whatever may be the truth on this point, the four colonies determined to entrust their external relations to a committee composed of two delegates from each, at the same time preserving their internal jurisdictions unimpaired.   They excluded Rhode Island from the alliance on account of its unsatisfactory religious policy, and they omitted likewise the scattered settlements planted in Maine under the patronage of Sir Ferdinando Gorges.   These settlements were secular in their objects and trivial in wealth and corporate importance, and therefore of no weight in the Puritan councils.

The significance of the New England Confederation in its early years lies not so much in its proceedings as in the mere fact of its existence ; for it shows that the conception had even then been vaguely formed of America as a united commonwealth prepared to act in independence of, perhaps in opposition to, the wishes of the parent country.   There was no formulation of the idea in written words ; that was rendered unnecessary by the course of events for many years to come.   Charles I., contrary to expectation, returned to Whitehall to die under the axe.   Had he returned as a conqueror the Confederation would doubtless have appeared in history in a very different role to that which it actually filled ; and so much, we may believe, lay in the minds of the far-seeing men who founded it.

The attitude of the New Englanders towards the Civil War was therefore one of watchful aloofness.   They hoped for the victory of the Parliament, but at the same time remained on their guard lest that victory should lead to a closer union with the mother-country, a union which the latter's relative weight must inevitably render one-sided.   New England desired no such close union, even with a Puritan Old England.   Massachusetts returned cordial thanks for an ordinance of Parliament which freed the trans-Atlantic trade from customs duties, and it declined with civility an offer of favourable legislation at Westminster, lest a precedent should thereby be founded to bear harmful fruit under a royalist reaction.   Individuals returned to fight under Cromwell's standard in the Civil War, but New England took no corporate measures in support of its friends at home.   The Earl of Warwick's Parliamentary Commission of Plantations dealt principally with the recalcitrant cavaliers in Virginia and the West Indies, and left the Puritan colonies alone.   The general outcome of the Puritan victory in England was thus to afford to the northern American commonwealths the opportunity of clinching that independence which had been their aim through all the years since the *Mayflower* had sailed from Southampton.

[1] Hostilities began in England in 1642, and for the first two years there seemed every probability that the king would gain the upper hand.

CHAPTER V

NEWFOUNDLAND, GUIANA AND THE WEST INDIES

(i) *Newfoundland and Nova Scotia*

AFTER Sir Humphrey Gilbert's departure in 1583 there was no officially recognized attempt to take possession of the soil of Newfoundland until 1610. Gilbert had proclaimed the sovereignty of the English crown over the whole island, but in practice the French had rights based upon occupation which were equal to those of England. This occupation consisted in the seasonal operations of thousands of fishermen, who landed to repair their nets and cure their fish during the summer months. It is quite possible that a few persons connected with the industry remained throughout the year. For these purposes the English used principally the eastern coast and the south-eastern Peninsula of Avalon, and the French the south-western and western coasts looking towards Cape Breton and the Gulf of St. Lawrence. The fishery had been continuously frequented since its discovery by John Cabot. At first the French, Spaniards and Portuguese had predominated over the English. Towards the end of the sixteenth century the Spaniards and Portuguese declined in numbers, those who remained working principally in the French sphere of operations. The English fishermen hailed almost exclusively from Bristol and the seaports of Cornwall, Devon, Dorset and Hampshire.

In 1610 a company of adventurers of London and Bristol received a patent for the colonization of Newfoundland. Its leading promoter was John Guy, a Bristol merchant; the Earl of Northampton and Sir Francis Bacon were members, and some of the money seems to have been advanced by the crown.[1] Guy, who acted as governor from 1610 to 1615, took out a party of about forty colonists in the former year and founded a settlement at Cuper's or Cupid's Cove, in the Avalon Peninsula. Almost immediately hostilities broke out with the west-country fishermen, whose claims to the use of the coast proved irreconcilable with those of the settlers. For this reason the colony remained the scene of disorders throughout its career, the large floating population of visitors proving uncontrollable by the small

---

[1] D. N. Prowse, *History of Newfoundland*, 2nd edit. London, 1896, p. 94.

body of permanent colonists. Guy was succeeded as governor by John Mason, 1615-21, and by Robert Hayman, 1621-7. By the latter date the settlement was decayed and the vitality of the Company exhausted. It had lived principally on fishing and fur-trading, and on the hope of finding iron and silver mines. After 1628 it is heard of no more.

In the meantime other projectors had founded settlements on the Newfoundland coast. Of Sir George Calvert's proceedings we have already spoken.[1] Contemporary with him were Lord Falkland, father of the royalist hero of the Civil War, who formed a colonizing syndicate in Dublin ; Sir William Alexander, a Scotsman ; and others. Between them they planted settlers in six distinct localities, the most important of which was Calvert's establishment of Ferryland. By 1637 all these grants were declared forfeited by neglect and desertion, and Laud's Commission for Plantations regranted the whole colonizing rights in the island to the Duke of Hamilton and Sir David Kirke. Whether the forfeiture was merited is an open question. The settlements were certainly in a struggling and precarious condition, but it appears that the vested rights of such planters as remained were swept away in a very arbitrary fashion for the benefit of persons who had hitherto done nothing for the colony.[2] Sir David Kirke went out as governor of the new colony in 1638. He remained, with one interval, until 1651, when he was recalled by the Commonwealth to answer a charge of rendering assistance to Prince Rupert. He died in England in 1653.

The prime importance of Newfoundland in the early days of English expansion lies undoubtedly in the fishery. As a training ground for seamen it outweighed the East Indian trade, and the men were more easily available in times of emergency. In 1615 it employed 5000 men and 250 ships of an average burden of 60 tons. In the period 1630-40 these figures were doubled, the men numbering 10,680, and the total tonnage 26,700.[3] At a time when the navy depended almost entirely upon the mercantile marine for its personnel, these figures are very significant, and go far to explain the sudden strength of the Commonwealth fleets in the Dutch war of 1652-4. Charles I., always in theory a supporter of maritime interests, usually favoured the claims of the fishermen against those of the colonists. He recognized the ancient custom whereby the first fishing skipper to enter a Newfoundland port at the opening of the season became admiral for the year with a comprehensive jurisdiction on sea and land. He also went so far on one occasion as to order all settlers to withdraw to a distance of six miles from the coast in order to leave the fishermen's activities unhampered. In the development of the mercantile policy the fishery was an

[1] *Ante*, ch. iii. p. 183.

[2] Prowse, *op. cit.* pp. 140-1 ; see also *Historical Geography of the British Colonies,* vol. v. pt. iv. by J. D. Rogers, Oxford, 1911, p. 69.

[3] Beer, *op. cit.* pp. 292-3.

important element.   A large proportion of the fish went to Spain and
the Mediterranean countries where it was exchanged for wine, salt
and sugar.   " From the purely economic standpoint . . . Newfoundland
conformed most closely to the canons of the mercantile system, and
was the most valuable of the English dominions beyond the seas." [1]

Nova Scotia or Acadia was the scene of feeble attempts at settlement
by the British and French in the early Stuart period.   In 1604 some
French adventurers founded a settlement at Port Royal (Annapolis)
in the Bay of Fundy.   Jesuit priests continued the enterprise, but
their undertaking was destroyed by Samuel Argall of Virginia in 1613.
Eight years later James I. granted a patent for colonization to Sir
William Alexander and a Scottish syndicate, who gave to the region
the name it now bears.   Their settlements were still in the embryonic
stage when war with France broke out in 1627.   English privateers
cut off the food supplies of the French posts in the St. Lawrence.
The inhabitants of Quebec, the principal settlement, were perishing
from hunger, and surrendered to the English in 1629.   If the conquest
had been retained the whole subsequent history of America would
have been very different.   But Charles I. had no prophetic intuition
of its value.   By the Treaty of St. Germain-en-Laye in 1632 he returned
it to France, and also resigned the British claim to Nova Scotia.
Alexander's enterprise thus came to an untimely end.

(ii) *The English in Guiana*

Ralegh's expedition of 1595, with its commander's glowing accounts
of wealth, had drawn attention to the interior of Guiana, the unoccupied
territory lying between the settlements of the Spanish Main and the
Portuguese coasts of Brazil.   A little later the west-country merchants,
finding privateering somewhat overdone, had begun to traffic upon
the Main itself in salt and tobacco.   The peace of 1604 ostensibly
put an end to this trade, but the seamen of the outlying ports continued
to make clandestine voyages to Trinidad and Venezuela in spite of
the royal prohibition. [2]   Their route carried them close to the mysterious
Guiana coast, and this helped to keep alive the English interest in the
region.   The Dutch at the same time were penetrating Guiana and
driving a brisk trade with the natives, besides forming tobacco
plantations.

Early in 1604 Charles Leigh made the first attempt at settlement by
leading a band of colonists to the River Wiapoco, the present boundary
between French Guiana and Brazil.   He himself and a number of his
men died of fever, a reinforcement failed to reach the river, and the
survivors abandoned the undertaking in 1606.   Robert Harcourt tried
at the same place in 1609.   He planted thirty men on the Wiapoco
and returned to organize further operations.   Financial misfortunes

[1] Beer, p. 294.

[2] A. P. Newton, *Colonizing Activities of the English Puritans*, Yale, 1914, pp. 25-6.

prevented him from doing so, but in 1613 he obtained a proprietary grant of Guiana from James I. and tried to form a company to exploit it. Subscribers, however, would not come forward, and the enterprise collapsed. Harcourt's men had remained in Guiana until 1612, when most of them had come home. Meanwhile, a new projector, Sir Thomas Roe, made a thorough exploration of the region. In 1610-11 he entered the Amazon and penetrated 300 miles inland. Thence he passed along the Guiana coast to Trinidad. He thought well of the Amazon and left a party of colonists near its mouth. Two subsequent expeditions went out to maintain touch with them, but the enterprise was on too small a scale and expired at some date which is not certainly known.

Sir Walter Ralegh now reappeared in the business. He obtained the king's consent to an expedition to exploit the gold mine he claimed to have found on the Orinoco in 1595. James gave permission only on the understanding that there should be no fighting with the Spaniards and no trespass on their territory. It was an impossible condition, for Spain claimed the whole Orinoco basin and had established a settlement at San Thome in the neighbourhood of the supposed mine. Ralegh probably knew as much, but he was rendered desperate by long imprisonment and trusted to force the king's hand by a brilliant success. In June, 1617, he sailed for the Orinoco with fourteen ships and 900 men. Remaining at the mouth of the river, he sent his son with Captain Keymis to ascend the stream and find the mine. They found that they had to pass San Thome before they could reach their destination, and they therefore took the town by assault, although they were unable to drive the Spaniards from the neighbourhood. Young Ralegh had been killed in the action, and Keymis soon found it impossible either to push farther into the interior or to remain at San Thome. He returned to the coast, told his news to Sir Walter, and stabbed himself in despair. The expedition had indeed failed, and its leader might expect no mercy. The king's only thought was now to exculpate himself by sacrificing Ralegh, a course for which he had already prepared by the instructions given at the outset. No trial was necessary, for Ralegh was already under sentence of death for his alleged treason in 1604. The sentence was executed in 1618, and the anger of Spain was appeased. The whole undertaking had been based upon a web of falsehood for which Ralegh, although not blameless, had some excuse ; but James cut a sorry figure.

Soon afterwards another project came to birth. Its promoter was Captain Roger North, an officer of Ralegh's expedition and a kinsman of the Earl of Warwick. North was a believer in the Amazon as the most promising region for an English effort, and in 1619 he secured a patent from the king and formed the Amazon Company to finance the undertaking. Early in 1620 he was ready to sail with the intention of forming a plantation in the Amazon delta. Once more the king wavered and listened to the protests of the Spaniard Gondomar, who asserted that the delta was already occupied by his sovereign's vassals the Portuguese. North could not get permission to sail and finally went without it, risking his head as Ralegh had done. He planted a settlement in the delta, attracted to it some English and Irish free-lances already in the vicinity—probably survivors of Roe's colony—and returned in person at the close of the year. James had by this time swung back to the side of Spain. He sent North to the Tower, dissolved the Amazon Company, and forbade any further expedition. Once again an English colony was bereft of aid from home. Its members supported themselves by planting tobacco and trading with the Dutch, who had also some settlements in the delta. In 1623 the end came in consequence of an attack from the Portuguese fort at Pará. Many of the planters were killed, and the remainder abandoned the undertaking.

When Charles I. went to war with Spain, North revived his Amazon scheme, and Harcourt joined forces with him. Together they launched the Guiana Company, which received its patent in 1627. Next year this body sent out an expedition which re-established the Amazon colony and built a strong fort on the island of Tocujos in the delta. In 1629 the Portuguese attacked this place and took it, and the work was all to begin again. Meanwhile Harcourt had led a party to the Wiapoco, a site more to his liking. He successfully established a colony, but died there in 1631. The fate of his men is unknown ; they were perhaps massacred by the Indians. North disapproved of Har-court's proceeding and determined to concentrate the Company's efforts upon the Amazon. He sent out further expeditions, all with the same result—a promising start followed by capture and massacre at the hands of the Portuguese. By 1635 the Guiana Company was bankrupt, and after that date it is heard of no more. An independent adventurer, the Earl of Berkshire, tried his hand with the like result, and so the whole movement died out.[1] The causes of failure may be stated as insufficiency of capital and lack of government support. The Portuguese, from their base at Pará, struck down all the plantations in turn ; but a regular expedition might well have captured Pará and with it the whole Amazon delta.

The Guiana attempts form a series of colonial undertakings from which much was hoped at the time of their inception, although they have since passed almost completely out of memory. In the early years of James I. Guiana appeared more promising than Virginia, and even as late as 1619 we have seen the Pilgrim Fathers considering a plan to settle in Guiana in preference to North America; they abandoned the idea only because they feared it would involve hostilities with Spain and Portugal. Had they persisted in it, the whole current of Puritan emigration might have followed them to South America, with important results upon the course of subsequent world-history.

[1] See in general, J. A. Williamson, *English Colonies in Guiana and on the Amazon*, 1604-1668, Oxford, 1923.

(iii) *The Bermudas and the West Indies*

The English occupation of the Bermudas arose, as we have seen, from the shipwreck of Sir George Somers upon them in 1609. The Virginia Company claimed the Islands, and used them at first as a source of food supply for Jamestown. The Virginia charter of 1612 included the Somers Islands, as they were now called, in the Company's jurisdiction. The pioneers early recognized that the new acquisition possessed advantages of its own as a tobacco plantation. A group of investors, most of them members of the Virginia Company, bought out that corporation's rights, and formed an independent Somers Islands Company, which obtained a royal charter in 1615. The ubiquitous Sir Thomas Smith presided over this undertaking. The struggle between the Sandys and the Smith-Warwick factions which ruined the parent company was reflected in its offspring; but the latter preserved its charter until nearly the end of the Stuart period. In 1620 the Company allowed the planters representative government. Tobacco, cultivated by indentured and servile labour, became the principal product, and the population increased to some 15,000 persons. The planters alleged that the Company frequently oppressed them and also restricted their freedom of trade with the mother-country. Owing to its small size the colony early reached the limit of its development. From the national standpoint its chief importance lay in its strategic position, which made it useful as a naval station. In 1684 the Company was dissolved, and the Bermudas became a crown colony.

In the West Indies proper the English found colonization more difficult. Soon after the original discovery Spain had occupied the four great islands of Cuba, Hispaniola, Porto Rico and Jamaica. Then, with the opening up of the Spanish Main, Mexico and Peru, the focus of interest and energy had passed on westwards and southwards, leaving the West Indies in a somewhat stagnant condition. In the Greater Antilles the Spanish settlements contracted, until the northern shores of Hispaniola were left unoccupied, and Jamaica was held only by scattered bands of hunters; in the Bahamas and the Windward and Leeward groups the Spaniards never colonized at all, leaving them in the possession of the ferocious Caribs, whose man-eating reputation made them a terror to seamen. But, while Spain left the islands untouched, she still claimed the sole right to navigate the Caribbean Sea. The long Elizabethan war reduced her naval power to a shadow; but a generation after its close we find a distinct revival and a return to the old aggressive methods throughout the Indies. It was at this period that the English made their first attempts at planting the islands.

In 1624 Thomas Warner, one of the colonists abandoned in Guiana, made his way with some followers to St. Christopher (frequently shortened to St. Kitts), an island lying within the outer ring which shuts in the Caribbean Sea on the east and north. He succeeded in establishing himself, although much troubled by Carib attacks. When, shortly afterwards, a French rover, the Sieur d'Esnambuc, put in to repair his ship, Warner welcomed him amicably, and offered to share the island. The two nationalities accordingly settled side by side. In 1629 disaster overtook them. A Spanish force captured St. Kitts and dispersed the colonists. Ultimately they returned, and the joint occupation of the island continued undisturbed until the outbreak of the Anglo-French war of 1666.

In spite of its troubled career the early colony of St. Kitts acted as a parent to other English settlements in the neighbourhood, some of which outlived it. In 1628 Englishmen from St. Kitts occupied Nevis, the next island to the southward. From thence they pushed on to Montserrat and Antigua in 1632.

In 1627 Charles I. granted to the Earl of Carlisle a proprietary patent for the colonization of all the Caribbees. The earl died in 1636, and in 1647 his son leased the grant to Lord Willoughby of Parham, whose proceedings we shall have to notice later.

In the meantime Barbados, the wealthiest of the early West Indian colonies, had been taken in hand. It has often been said that some of the Guiana adventurers landed in Barbados in 1605 and proclaimed its annexation; but this story rests upon a misprint in an old book, and is untrue. Favourable reports on the island then reached the ears of Sir William Courteen, a wealthy London merchant of Flemish extraction, whom we shall meet again in connection with the East Indian trade. Courteen's continental kinsmen, a merchant family of Middleburg, were at the time making a fortune in the Dutch Guiana enterprises, in which he himself seems to have had some interest. In 1625 he sent a small expedition to claim Barbados, acting under the patronage of the Earl of Pembroke, who procured a grant for that purpose. This patent, which overlapped that granted to Carlisle, caused a great deal of wrangling and litigation, but ultimately the Earl of Carlisle made good his claims above all other competitors. Courteen's colonists, forty in number, arrived in 1627. They founded the settlement of Jamestown, and sent to their Dutch friends in Guiana for tobacco and other plants wherewith to establish their industries. In its early years Barbados produced tobacco, cotton, indigo and fustic wood. Its population increased to a remarkable extent, reaching, according to one account, the number of 18,000 at the time of the introduction of sugar planting, about 1640. Such a weight of numbers rendered the colony immune from any attacks the Spaniards were in a position to organize. Sugar-growing increased the wealth but decreased the population of the island, which tended thenceforward to fall into the hands of large proprietors. Lord Willoughby of Parham and many other royalists took refuge in Barbados on the decline of the king's cause. Their influence caused the colony to repudiate the authority of the Commonwealth when the news arrived of the tragedy of 1649.

Both English and French made attempts to occupy the larger islands of the eastern Antilles—Dominica, Guadeloupe, St. Lucia, and Tobago. All such attempts were immediate failures or only precariously maintained for a few years, by reason of the power of the Caribs. These savages, secure in the hilly fastnesses of the larger islands, could not be dislodged by the small numbers of European colonists who attempted the task, and it was well on in the eighteenth century before the cannibals of Dominica and St. Lucia were subdued. Defoe, with his talent for setting, has given in his description of Crusoe's Island a vivid picture of savage life in the West Indies and of the ruffianly European types who did the pioneer work in the seventeenth century.[1]

Whilst the outer islands were being successively attempted, a Puritan organization similar in character to the Massachusetts Company was venturing boldly into the heart of the Spanish waters. The Earl of Warwick was perhaps the strongest hater of Spain who survived into the reign of Charles I. He was also a Puritan leader who, like John Winthrop, saw the necessity for colonies as a refuge for the oppressed. In 1629 Massachusetts was only in embryo, and its success was by no means assured. Warwick therefore conceived the idea of planting a Puritan colony on the island of Santa Catalina, lying off the Mosquito Coast of Nicaragua, and about equidistant from Jamaica and Cartagena, the capital of the Main. The island was healthy and defensible, and lay close to the track of Spanish ships homeward bound from Cartagena. To Warwick, with his eye to privateering, the latter was its principal recommendation. He formed a company among his friends and obtained in 1630 a royal charter for the plantation of Providence Island, as the adventurers renamed their possession.

The Providence Island Company began its career by sending out settlers, some from Bermuda, in which Warwick had an interest, and some from England. They took possession of the island, and began the planting of corn and tobacco. The seafaring members of the Company also used it as a centre for roving expeditions. Some of the French and English colonists of St. Kitts and Nevis, expelled by the Spaniards in 1629, had taken refuge at the island of Tortuga at the north-western corner of Hispaniola. They found food plentiful and the prospects of preying upon Spanish commerce encouraging. In 1631 they sought and obtained admission to the Providence Island Company, which bestowed upon Tortuga the new name of Association.

---

[1] It is perhaps still necessary to state that Crusoe's island was not Juan Fernandez. Defoe describes Crusoe as on a voyage in the Atlantic, driven along the Guiana coast and wrecked on an island near Trinidad. The island most nearly answering to the description is Tobago, but Crusoe's island was in fact imaginary, although vivified with the local colour of the contemporary West Indies which Defoe had so assiduously collected. The Alexander Selkirk of fact had almost nothing in common with the Robinson Crusoe of fiction, and Selkirk's Juan Fernandez was in the South Pacific.

The Association settlers included few Puritans and were frankly piratical almost from the outset. Those of Providence became increasingly lawless as time went on. In 1635 Spanish expeditions attacked both islands. They captured Association and were beaten off from Providence. Association was afterwards reoccupied by the French, and became the base from which they spread over the western end of Hispaniola. The turn of Providence came in 1641. Don Francisco Diaz de Pimienta collected at Cartagena a force of twelve ships and two thousand men. After fierce fighting he captured the island and expelled the settlers. The Puritan members of the Company at home, absorbed in the struggle with the king, abandoned the idea of retaking it, and the enterprise came to an end.[1]

In two more localities in the West Indies English settlers gained a footing before the death of Charles I. On the mainland of Honduras corsairs and wood-cutters frequented the inlets of the coast, the name Belize being a Spanish corruption of Willis, a buccaneer who flourished towards 1640. In the uninhabited Bahamas, to the north of Cuba, pioneers from Bermuda established a salt-making station on the island of Eleuthera in 1646. Next year they began to plant cotton and tobacco in another island of the group to which they gave the name of New Providence. In general, we may regard the period above considered as one of beginnings and experiments in the West Indies. The great days of the English islands, when sugar cultivated by negro labour was the staple product, belong to the latter half of the seventeenth and the whole of the eighteenth centuries.

---

[1] The transactions of the Providence Island Company are narrated at length in A. P. Newton's work already cited.

CHAPTER VI

THE EAST INDIA COMPANY, 1600–1657

(i) *The origin and development of the Company's constitution*

In its early constitution the East India Company combined some of
the distinctive features of both the regulated and joint-stock types
of chartered corporation. The charter of 1600 enumerated a list of
members, who alone were free to take part in the trade. This body
elected a governor and a committee of twenty-four assistants. But
the freemen were not, in theory, compelled to share in every venture
of the Company. To the expenses of any given voyage they might or
might not subscribe, at their discretion ; and, having done so, they
were liable to additional calls for unforeseen outlay upon that voyage
alone without regard to the other undertakings of the Company.
Regulated company principles thus governed the subscription of
capital for each venture ; but the capital once collected was administered on purely joint-stock lines. The governor and a sub-committee
for the voyage hired or purchased the shipping, appointed the captains
and factors, provided the lading, and framed the instructions and
general policy to be followed. All trading was for the joint account,
no private member of the Company being allowed to venture an
individual stock of merchandise ; and on the return of the expedition
the cargoes were sold and the profits distributed on a percentage ratio
to the principal invested. At this point the methods of the past
again came into play : for each expedition was to be completely
wound up at its conclusion and the capital returned to those who had
invested it, precisely as if their connection with the trade were being
permanently severed. The early East India Company was thus a
regulated body conducting its separate voyages on joint-stock methods.
It was not a joint-stock company of the normal modern type, since it
had no permanent capital to be used for continuous operations over
an unlimited period of time.

Such was the theory of the Company's constitution. In many
particulars that theory was destined to be practically modified almost
from the outset by the operation of circumstances unforeseen by its
framers. Elizabeth's charter granted to the original freemen and such

others as they might admit to the fellowship a monopoly of the trade for fifteen years with this reservation, that the crown might at any time give two years' notice and recall the grant if its operation were judged to be prejudicial to the national interests. The queen, in sanctioning the trade at all, had fettered her hands in the impending negotiations for the conclusion of the Spanish war. In return for this disability she expected the Company to conduct its trade on a larger and more vigorous scale than it seemed at first prepared to do. She looked in fact for a steady influx of wealth into London as the result of the despatch of annual trading squadrons to the East. The regular arrival of the treasure-fleets at Cadiz was the pattern of oceanic enterprise present in her mind ; for nothing less had she consented to raise such an obstacle to the negotiation of peace. The merchants viewed the matter differently. They had invested large sums in a hazardous business. They desired to go slowly, to see how unascertained factors would affect the venture, to feel their way cautiously from the known to the unknown, and above all, to realize the profits of one voyage before adventuring in the next. A voyage to and from eastern Asia occupied two or three years, hundreds of tons of spices could not be sold to advantage in a week or two, and thus there was inevitable delay before the prudent merchant could determine whether or no it was worth his while to continue. As a consequence, long before any news of the first expedition had reached home the queen was clamouring for the despatch of a second, for which the capital was not forthcoming. Her death in 1603, and the change of dynasty, added to the uncertainties of the directors. But if nothing were done they knew the charter would be forfeited. They brought strong pressure to bear upon the members, and secured a grudging subscription for a second voyage, which set sail three years after the departure of the first. They obtained this result only by agreeing to pool the expenses and profits of the two ventures, in breach of the principle of separate voyage trading.

Other factors contributed to the same end. It was necessary to maintain resident servants in the Asiatic ports, and it became difficult to apportion the expense to the various subscriptions of capital. The voyages began to overlap, and the overseas officials had to keep separate books for each. The interests of one set of investors were not identical with those of another, and contradictory orders began to arrive at the outlying factories. After twelve years the confusion and wastage were seen to be intolerable, and much of the regulated element in the Company's methods had to be discarded.

The principle, however, died hard. Its influence was seen in the expedient which succeeded it. This was to raise a terminable joint-stock for a stated period of years. The directorate were to operate on this capital as vigorously as possible without limit to the number of voyages they might set forth. But at the end of the period the stock was to be wound up and the capital returned to the investors.

The overlapping was reduced, but it still remained to a certain extent. This system had a longer life than that of the separate voyages. It endured until 1657. Only then was a permanent and continuous joint-stock adopted, in which the investors could never demand the return of their capital, but had instead to withdraw from the enterprise by the sale of their shares for what they would fetch on the stock-market. Not until 1657, therefore, did the East India Company become a purely joint-stock concern in the modern sense.

(ii) *The period of Separate Voyages*, 1600–12

The Company's first expedition sailed from the Thames in the spring of 1601, and finally cleared from Torbay on April 22. It consisted of the *Red Dragon* of 600 tons, a private warship purchased from the Earl of Cumberland ; the *Hector*, 300 ; the *Ascension*, 260 ; and the *Susan*, 240. The united crews numbered 480 men. The lading comprised English manufactured goods to the value of £6860 and coined silver worth £28,742. The whole was under the command of Sir James Lancaster, the surviving captain of the voyage of 1591. The squadron reached Achin in Sumatra in June, 1602. Lancaster presented the queen's letters to the native sovereign of that place, and entered into friendly relations. He found, however, that the local pepper crop had failed, and went on to Bantam in Java, capturing a Portuguese carrack with a rich lading by the way. He obtained pepper and spices at Bantam and the neighbouring islands, left factors to collect future cargoes, and sailed for England. The *Ascension*, the first of his ships to reach home, arrived in June, 1603, and the rest of the fleet came into port in September.

Lancaster's return was opportune, for the Company's affairs were at a low ebb. James I. had confirmed the late queen's charter, and was showing favour to Sir Thomas Smith, the governor, mainly on account of the latter's implication in Essex's treason of 1601. But James, like his predecessor, expected something more than the despatch of one voyage in three years. The cessation of hostilities with Spain had thrown many adventurers out of employment, and the eastern trade tempted them to bid for the king's countenance in opposition to the chartered Company. Unless, therefore, the Company acted with energy it was likely to lose its privileges. But its troubles were by no means ended by Lancaster's arrival. He brought with him 1,000,000 lb. of pepper. To flood the market hurriedly with this quantity would entail a disastrous fall in prices. The plague, also, was raging in London, and business was at a standstill. Many years in fact elapsed before the first voyage could be wound up, and even then some of the proceeds had to be distributed in kind instead of in cash. Ultimately the profit, in conjunction with that of the second voyage, worked out at 95 per cent., but the delay, with the money, worth normally 10 per cent. per annum, locked up for eight years, reduced the actual net gain to about 20 per cent.—by no means a great return for such a risk.

The second expedition, its financial fortunes pooled with the first, consisted of the same ships under the command of Sir Henry Middleton. So difficult had the raising of subscriptions proved that it carried a freight worth only £12,300, mostly in specie. Middleton found a cargo of pepper awaiting him at Bantam, and pushed on to Amboyna in the midst of the Moluccas for the more valuable spices. After a successful voyage he returned in 1606.

Already jealousy and the king's infirmity of purpose had dealt the Company a heavy blow. Sir Edward Michelborne, a courtier, had been one of its original members, but had been expelled for non-payment of his venture in the first expedition. In 1604 he obtained from James a licence to make an independent voyage in violation of the royal charter. For two years he cruised in the eastern archipelago, doing very little trade but robbing any ships which came in his way. His victims included Dutch and Chinese merchants, and he thoroughly compromised the position of his fellow-countrymen in the islands. He returned in 1606, and died not long afterwards, the Company never obtaining any redress for the damage he had done to their interests. His injuries to the Dutch were particularly unfortunate, for they afforded that nationality the grievance which they were seeking as an excuse for hostility against their English rivals. John Davis, the Arctic explorer, accompanied Michelborne as his chief navigator, and was killed in action with a Japanese ship.

Of the subsequent voyages of the early period, the third (1607), financed jointly with the fifth (1609), a single ship venture, returned the huge profit of 234 per cent., discounted of course by the usual delay in the winding-up. One ship of this expedition landed Captain William Hawkins [1] on the mainland of India to proceed on a mission to the Great Mogul at Agra. Hawkins obtained in 1607 a grant of permission to establish a factory at Surat in the Gulf of Cambay. Portuguese machinations, however, prevented this from becoming fully operative until some years afterwards. The fourth voyage, set forth in 1608, was unlucky. Of its two ships one, the *Ascension*, ran aground near Surat, and was lost with all her cargo, although the crew escaped. The other, the *Union*, traded prosperously in the islands, and was driven by a storm on the coast of Brittany when almost in sight of home. The Company asserted that the Breton fishermen deliberately wrecked her for the sake of plunder. It took action in the French courts to secure restitution of some of the goods, but never obtained any satisfaction.

In 1609, when the profits of the third and fifth voyages had yet to be divided, the Company was again in difficulties, and had to make a strong appeal for public support. It was the year which witnessed

[1] He was possibly the same William Hawkins, nephew of Sir John Hawkins, who had sailed with Fenton in 1581, but the identity is not proved.

the great revival of interest in the Virginia colony, and the East India
Company, like that of Virginia, obtained a new and more favourable
charter and an accession of influential members. The coincidence
was probably due to the fact that Sir Thomas Smith presided over the
fortunes of both Companies. By the charter of 1609 James promised
a perpetual monopoly, in place of the original term of fifteen years,
and the period of notice for resumption by the Crown was extended
from two years to three. The grant also included a strong clause
against the intrusion of interlopers.

Thus fortified, the Company set forth its sixth voyage in 1610 with
a capital of £82,000. It built for the trade a great ship of 1100 tons,
the largest constructed in England since the monster warship *Great
Harry* had been completed a century before. James in person attended
the launch, and named the new ship the *Trade's Increase*. His royal
favour brought no good fortune, for she was maliciously fired and
destroyed whilst careening at Bantam on her first voyage. In spite
of this disaster the sixth voyage returned a profit, as did the seventh
and eighth, of 1611 and 1612, which were also on a large scale.

A summary of the results of the separate voyages, which now came
to an end, shows that from 1601 to 1612 twenty-six large ships sailed
for the east, representing a total investment of £466,179, of which
£138,127 was exported in money and £62,413 in goods, the remainder
being consumed by working expenses. The average profit for the
period, allowing for losses by delay in winding up, was about 20 per
cent. per annum.[1] The above figures, when compared with those of
the Elizabethan ventures, even with such an inflated undertaking as
Michael Lok's Cathay Company, indicate the enormous increase in
national wealth which had taken place during half a century. The
impression is strengthened when we remember that the East India
Company was only one among many concerns which were exploiting
the capital and manufactures of the country.

(iii) *The struggle with the Dutch*, 1609–23

Hitherto we have regarded the operations of the Company from the
point of view of the adventurers at home. We have now to trace
the fortunes of their servants abroad and the events of the bitter
struggle which was destined to divert the energies of the English in
Asia into channels never contemplated by those who inaugurated the
movement thither. The East India Company, in brief, was formed to
carry on a trade in spices with the archipelago lying off the south-east
coasts of Asia ; within twenty-five years of its foundation it had been
completely expelled from that trade and had taken up, as an alternative, the exploitation of India proper, a continental country with a
vast population, whose productions seemed to offer less favourable

[1] Hunter, *British India*, i. p. 293 and table on p. 291. The author does not vouch
for the 20 per cent. average, but quotes it as " an unofficial estimate."

opportunities to a chartered company than did the pepper, cloves and nutmegs of the islands. The cause of this enforced change of plan lay in the strength and hostility of the Dutch.

The Dutch were our precursors by some six years in the island trade, and to this fact they owed some of their predominance. They began, as we did, with a series of separate undertakings (1595–1601) conducted by independent companies competing with one another, which was in fact the position of the several groups of investors operating the separate voyages of the English company. They realized, as the English ultimately did, the disadvantages of this system, and they had a stronger incentive than their rivals to tackle the problem and place their trade upon a sounder basis. The United Provinces were still waging their war of independence against Spain, and they came to the conclusion that the surest means to success lay in building up a maritime supremacy, and with it a wealthy state, by developing to its utmost the East Indian trade. For the Dutch then, this trade spelt the very existence of their country ; for the English it was merely a means whereby a limited class in the community might enrich themselves. Hence the Dutch government made the furtherance of eastern commerce the prime motive of its policy, whilst the Stuart kings used it as a subordinate counter in a diplomatic game played with widely different objects in view.

In 1602 the Dutch authorities took the first step towards supremacy by abolishing competition within their own house. They enforced the amalgamation of their various undertakings into a United East India Company with a joint-stock of over half a million pounds. This Company became practically a department of the state, and consequently had nothing to suffer from the intrigues and official encouragement of interlopers which frequently menaced its London competitor. With its huge capital, subscribed in perpetuity, it sent strong fleets to the east, and wrested one by one the strategic points in the Archipelago from Portuguese (i.e. Spanish) control. In 1602 a Dutch fleet defeated the Portuguese near Bantam and forced its way through the straits of Sunda into the island-strewn waters beyond. In 1605 the Hollanders established a virtual protectorate over Amboyna in the region of the rarest spices. Two years later a treaty with the King of Ternate gave them a footing in the heart of the Moluccas, and in 1609 they secured the entrance to the Archipelago by a similar treaty with the ruler of Bantam. Everywhere they appeared in the guise of deliverers of the native chiefs from Portuguese tyranny ; it was not until their position was unassailable that they turned tyrants themselves.

During these years the English, inferior in numbers and organization, were also trading in the islands. The Dutch resented the intrusion, considering that their own achievements entitled them to a monopoly. But the time for active hostilities had not arrived. The war of independence dragged on at home, Spain was visibly exhausted yet not convinced that all was lost, and the Dutch government counted on the good offices of England to bring about a triumphant peace. James I. failed to act up to their expectations. The Dutch considered that his tenderness for Spain cheated them of a full recognition of their victory, and gave them instead the mere truce for twelve years with which the struggle ceased in 1609. Their resentment wiped out their gratitude for past obligations to England, and the respite at home gave them leisure to adopt an aggressive policy in the east. In 1609 they claimed the exclusive sovereignty of the Spice Islands, and appointed Pieter Both as the first governor-general of their Asiatic dependencies. With his arrival at Bantam in 1611 begins the acute period of the contest for the island trade.

Both began vigorously to consolidate what his countrymen had won and to extend their influence by a new series of treaties with the native chiefs. The English factors found themselves everywhere flouted or forestalled. In 1613-14 the Dutch opened veiled hostilities under cover of the native powers. A year later the English complained that they could not trade in peace at Bantam, their earliest port of call. In 1617 forty Englishmen were reported to be imprisoned with great severity at Amboyna, and at the same time their enemies adopted the ingenious device of maltreating the natives whilst sailing under the English flag. The London company sent out a strong fleet to support its servants, but the Dutch had more ships in addition to fortifications on land. Sir Thomas Dale, the ex-governor of Virginia, commanded the English squadron. He fought pitched battles in 1619, in one of which more than 3000 rounds of great shot were fired. With native assistance he burned the Dutch settlement of Jaccatra in Java, but had ultimately to evacuate the island and retire to India, where he died.

Concurrently with the war in the east negotiations went on in Europe. The English company appealed to the king for assistance, and a tortuous haggling was protracted for several years, first in London, then at the Hague, then again in London. The English company offered the Dutch free trade at Surat in return for the like in the islands. The Dutch demanded as their price what amounted to a political alliance—joint territorial conquest in Asia and joint hostilities against Spain and Portugal. The former the English merchants considered unnecessary, the latter King James would not allow. Finally he compelled his subjects to agree in 1619 to a treaty which assigned to them one-third of the island trade on their under-taking to share the expenses of fortifications and warships. The flaw in the arrangement was that the fortifications in question remained under Dutch control and the English residents in them under Dutch jurisdiction.

The inevitable consequence followed. The treaty arrived in the east in 1620, and Jan Coen, Both's successor as governor-general, determined to take full advantage of its one-sided terms. He had just founded a new capital for his empire at Batavia, and had decided that the time was ripe for the assertion of Dutch sovereignty throughout the Archipelago. By straining the law his officers of justice rendered life a torment to the English factors. The word of a native, they complained, was always preferred to theirs. Their letters home were full of requests to be recalled from an intolerable position. In 1621-2 Coen expelled the English by force from Lantor and Pulo Run in the Banda group in spite of a plucky defence in which the chief agent, Nathaniel Courthope, lost his life. In 1623, after Coen's departure for Europe, one of the blackest deeds in history terminated the career of the English company in the Spice Islands.

At Amboyna, north-west of the Bandas, an English agency consisting of eighteen merchants under Gabriel Towerson was maintaining a precarious position. At the same station were 200 Dutchmen with some hundreds of native troops and eight warships under their command. Herman van Speult, the governor, had been reproved by Coen for over-scrupulousness. He was evidently determined to prove that such an aspersion was an injustice to his character. In February, 1623, he seized a Japanese soldier of the garrison and charged him with conspiring with the English to gain possession of the fort. By the use of torture he obtained the man's confession, and that of other Asiatics to the same effect. He next arrested the eighteen Englishmen —who were living scattered in five different places, and not all in the same island—and taxed them with the plot. One and all denied stoutly that they had ever thought of such a thing. One after another they were tortured with water and fire until their eyes protruded and their burnt flesh putrified. The process extended over several days, and from every one, except perhaps Towerson himself, some kind of confession was obtained. Nearly all, however, denied their confessions as soon as the torment was relaxed, and some found opportunity to write their denials in their prayer books and other belongings which ultimately came home to England. Whilst the trial was in progress a letter arrived for Towerson, recalling him and his subordinates from the island. Van Speult read it, and continued on his course. When his evidence was complete he proceeded to consummate the tragedy. On February 27, ten English merchants and nine Japanese soldiers were executed in the presence of the native population, assembled to witness the triumph of the Dutch. This ghastly affair, of which the details rest upon unshakable evidence,[1] rivals the most exaggerated horrors of the Inquisition. The Inquisitors, indeed, had the excuse of believing that they saved the soul by killing the body. Van Speult and his fellows committed their crime for the sake of commercial advantage.

When the news reached England in 1624 it aroused extreme horror and indignation. King James wept as the tale was recited to him, and the country at large woke suddenly from its Elizabethan dream of Spain as the national enemy, and realized for the first time that it

---

[1] It may be read at length in Hunter's *British India*, i. pp. 383-434.

had to deal with a foe harder and more ruthless than either of the Catholic powers, a fit successor to the grasping Easterlings of the past. The Dutch nation as a whole shared in the guilt, for no leading man in it expressed regret or made a genuine move to bring the criminals to justice. The popular fury in England continued unabated for some time. Dutchmen were insulted if they appeared in the streets ; and when an artist commissioned by the East India Company painted a picture of the scene in the torture chamber of Amboyna, the government had to prohibit its public exhibition lest it should lead to a massacre in London. In the end, little was done. James soon dried his tears and continued his game of European statecraft, in which the co-operation of the Dutch Republic was essential to him. Charles I., who succeeded him a few months later, made a show of demanding reparation. On meeting with a refusal he arrested some Dutch ships in the Channel, and quietly released them again without having carried his point. But, although their sovereigns had betrayed them, the Company and the nation never forgot the Amboyna massacre. When Cromwell, thirty years afterwards, came to a reckoning with the Dutch, he extorted compensation to the surviving relatives of the victims. The blood feud between the two chief Protestant nations endured longer still. As late as the beginning of the eighteenth century we find such bitter sneers as Swift's account of the interview of Gulliver with the Emperor of Japan, in which the latter is made to say " that he began to doubt whether I [Gulliver] was a real Hollander, or no ; but rather suspected I must be a Christian."

In the east the crime brought success to its perpetrators. From 1623 English trade ceased in the Spice Islands. Two years later the English factors even in Java began to despair, and themselves urged the Company to turn its chief attention towards continental India. A factory established at Firando in Japan by William Adams and Richard Cocks failed at the same time,[1] and the Company had perforce to act on its servants' advice, and abandon all connection with the farthest east. Fortunately, it had, during the previous decade, made progress in India commensurate with its losses elsewhere.

(iv) The Establishment of the English in India

Whilst the Dutch were grasping the monopoly of the Spice Islands the English Company was taking steps to establish its trade in India. Here it found the Portuguese already in occupation, with strongly fortified stations at Ormuz in the Persian Gulf, at Goa in western

[1] Adams arrived in Japan in a Dutch ship in 1600. He obtained favour with the authorities and was granted an estate, dying in the country in 1620. When he heard of the existence of the English company he furthered its interests. But Iyeyasu, the great Shogun, who had favoured the English, died in 1616 ; and ultimately, to prevent the spread of Christianity, all Europeans except the Dutch were excluded from Japan until 1850.

India, and at several places on the Malabar Coast in the south.   Portugal held also the island of Ceylon, and by means of this chain of possessions sought to dominate the whole trade of India both with Europe and the farther east.   But Portugal had already passed the zenith of its power.   In its best days the nation had not produced enough men to maintain its world-wide possessions against a determined assault, and its subjection to Spain since 1580 had destroyed the energy of its administration.   In the east the Portuguese were everywhere hated by the native populations on account of the savage cruelty which they had consistently used to mask their deficiency in real force.   That cruelty had been employed for religious as well as political ends.   The Portuguese never forgot that their move to the east had been in its origin a crusade ; and the Inquisition at Goa had probably a longer roll of executions to its credit than any other branch of that tribunal.

In 1607 William Hawkins travelled to the court of the Mogul Emperor Jehangir.   His business was to negotiate a treaty by which the Company might trade in the Mogul dominions.   He was kindly treated by the Emperor, but his status was not that of an ambassador, and the Portuguese and some native interests were against him.   He obtained permission to trade at Surat, but the Portuguese were able to intrigue with the local governor and prevent the grant from coming into operation.   In 1609, however, there were some English factors in the place.   Two years later Sir Henry Middleton led thither some of the ships of the sixth voyage.   A Portuguese fleet prevented him from landing, and he passed on to the islands after some precarious bartering with native boats at sea.

Next year, 1612, Captain Thomas Best arrived with two ships, the *Red Dragon* and the *Hosiander*.   The Tapti river was not navigable as high as Surat, and the Englishman sought to anchor and land his goods at Swally Roads, an anchorage protected by sandbanks at the river's mouth.   Four Portuguese warships with a number of oared craft were ready to resist his entrance.   He waged a prolonged battle with them, the fighting extending, with intervals, over a full month.   At length the superior seamanship and gunnery of the English gained the victory, and the Portuguese retired from the neighbourhood.   The Mogul governor then gave permission for the English to establish their factory at Surat, with branches in three other towns of the vicinity; and the grant was confirmed by the emperor at Agra.   Thomas Aldworth, who had come out with Best, became the organizer of the first permanent English trading post in the Mogul's dominions.

Best's two ships had formed part of the last separate expedition of the Company.   The first terminable joint stock was formed in the following year with a capital of £429,000 subscribed for four years.   Early in 1614 the shareholders despatched four ships to Surat under the command of Nicholas Downton, a captain already experienced in eastern voyages.   Downton arrived at the mouth of the Tapti in October, and found the Mogul governor at war with the Portuguese.

The natives pressed for Downton's assistance, but he declined to be the aggressor, being limited by the king's injunctions to fighting in self-defence. Nevertheless the Portuguese were themselves determined to force an issue, for they realized the significance of the Surat factory. The Viceroy of Goa collected all his available forces and advanced to overwhelm the English at the head of nine sailing ships and sixty frigates, or row-barges, as they were called by the English seamen. The odds were enormous, 234 guns and 2600 Portuguese together with 6000 natives against Downton's 80 guns and 400 men, weak from a long voyage. The campaign lasted from January 20 to February 13, 1615. In that period Downton, by hard fighting and skilful manœuvring, completely defeated the great armament of his enemies, who retired to Goa, leaving the future of the Surat factory secure. The English leader did not survive to receive the rewards which were his due, and which even King James, with his talent for promoting the wrong men, could hardly have refused him. His only son had been killed in the fighting, and he himself died later in the same year.

Downton's victory had been the triumph of modern over mediaeval methods. The collapse of the Portuguese empire rapidly followed. In 1616 they lost a great carrack with a rich lading, wrecked by its own captain to avoid surrender to the English. Two years afterwards the latter took another with half a million in money aboard. The Spanish government showed complete indifference to the ruin of its subject-empire. During three years not a single official letter from home reached the authorities at Goa. In 1620 the English appeared in the Persian Gulf. After preliminary hostilities they combined with the Shah's forces to capture the island fortress of Ormuz (1622). The Shah retained the conquest, but granted his allies a factory at Gombroon (Bender Abbas). The English now concluded that it was impolitic to press their vanquished rivals further. The Dutch, however, were less lenient. They continued the attack in their own sphere, capturing Malacca in 1641 and Ceylon in successive stages from 1638 to 1658. In their exhaustion the Portuguese conceded liberty for English trade in all Indian ports by a local agreement in 1635, confirmed by treaties in London in 1642 and 1654. The 1635 agreement should be noted for, as will be shown later, it turned greatly to the English Company's disadvantage.

In the meanwhile the Company improved its position in the Mogul empire. From 1615 to 1618 Sir Thomas Roe resided at Agra with the full rank of an ambassador from the king. He was not completely successful in his negotiations, for the Moguls looked upon all Europeans as inferiors, and Jehangir's personal character was similar in some respects to that of the English king. Roe desired to embody the Company's privileges in a definite treaty. To this the emperor listened favourably, but always eluded committing himself by a formal ratification. Presents to the sovereign and bribes to his ministers entailed a heavy expense, and Roe departed with his object unachieved.

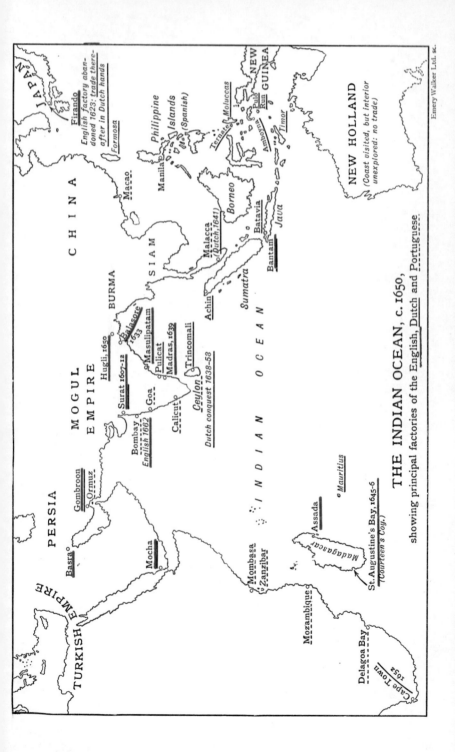

THE INDIAN OCEAN, c. 1650,
showing principal factories of the English, Dutch and Portuguese.

Emery Walker Ltd. sc.

TURKISH EMPIRE

PERSIA

Basra°

Gombroon
Ormuz

Mocha

MOGUL EMPIRE

Surat 1607-12
Bombay
English 1662
Goa
Calicut
Hugli 1650

BURMA

Balasore
1633

Masulipatam
Pulicat
Madras, 1632
Trincomali

Ceylon
Dutch conquest 1638-58

SIAM

CHINA

JAPAN

Firando
English factory aban-
doned 1623: trade there-
after in Dutch hands
Formosa

Macao

Manila

Philippine
Islands
(Spanish)

Borneo

Achin

Sumatra

Malacca
(Dutch 1641)

Ternate
Moluccas
Amboyna
Pulo
Run

NEW GUINEA

Batavia
Java
Bantam

Timor

NEW HOLLAND
(Coast visited, but interior
unexplored: no trade)

INDIAN OCEAN

Mombasa
Zanzibar

Mauritius

Assada

Madagascar

St. Augustine's Bay, 1645-6
(Courteen's Coy.)

Mozambique

Delagoa Bay

Cape Town
1652

But he had carried himself with dignity in a difficult situation, and could at least claim that he had increased rather than diminished the prestige of his countrymen.

The Surat factory, under Aldworth's presidency, long enjoyed a prosperous career. It became a depot for the cotton, muslins, saltpetre, indigo and dyestuffs from all parts of the interior. Before long the Dutch appeared to claim trading facilities. The immanence of the Mogul power precluded the English from expelling them with a high hand, as they themselves had been driven from the islands ; but the Dutch merchants failed to prosper in their dealings with the Indian rulers, and their competition never became dangerous. They committed piracies, however, upon the native craft conveying pilgrims to Mecca, and, the blame being laid upon the English factors at Surat, all were imprisoned in 1623. The English afterwards gained favour with the emperor by policing the pilgrim route. In 1630 a terrible famine in Gujarat depressed the trade, which failed to recover for several years. Six years later the English merchants were again placed under arrest on account of the piracies of their own countrymen whom Charles I. allowed to visit the east in defiance of the Company's charter. Nevertheless Surat remained on the whole the most satisfactory of the English trading stations until nearly the end of the seventeenth century. It continued to be the senior factory until 1687, when political changes caused the transference of the headquarters to Bombay.

On the eastern side of India, where the Mogul power was less firmly established, Dutch competition was more formidable. In 1609 the Dutch opened a factory at Pulicat on the Coromandel Coast. The English tried their fortune at Pettapoli, an unhealthy place at the mouth of the Kistna. They held on until 1621, when the heavy mortality forced them to abandon the station. It was reoccupied later, but never became a great trading centre. Masulipatam, a little farther north, seemed to promise better. A factory was established there in 1611, and was precariously maintained in face of Dutch aggression throughout the century. Madras, which ultimately became the chief English port on the Coromandel Coast, was founded by Francis Day of Masulipatam in 1639. Day secured for the Company the sovereignty of a strip of land upon which he erected Fort St. George, the first fortified factory possessed by his countrymen in India. The directors at home blamed him severely for involving them in what they considered an unnecessary expense, but the outcome proved his wisdom, and Madras became in 1658 the head factory of the eastern coast.

Extending northwards into the Bay of Bengal, the Company's servants established themselves in 1633 at Balasor in Orissa, midway between the mouths of the Mahanadi and the Ganges. Here again the unhealthy climate nearly proved fatal to the enterprise, but Francis Day reinforced it when it was on the point of being abandoned. In the Ganges delta itself an outpost for the Balasor depot was founded at Hughli in 1650.[1] But the principal English development in this region did not arise until the end of the century.

During the last five-and-twenty years of the period ending in 1657 the Company's servants in India were extending its hold upon the country's trade with very little support from home. In England their masters' affairs were in confusion, and the complete break-up of the corporation seemed more than once at hand. But the Indian establishments displayed a wonderful vitality of their own which fully justified the saying that " if the Company succeeded, or if it failed, it went on."

(v) *The Company's fortunes at home*

For the first century of its existence the East India Company's chief troubles at home arose from the fact that its charter was of royal and not parliamentary origin. This laid it open to attacks of two kinds : liberal politicians were tempted to declare its monopoly unjust by analogy with the clearly oppressive monopolies granted by the crown in internal trade ; and the crown itself, regarding the Company as its own creature dependent on its pleasure, violated its charter without compunction, and made inroads upon its funds when in need of money.

Within a very few years of its inauguration attacks developed on both these lines. We have already mentioned James I.'s license to Sir Edward Michelborne in 1604, and the damage wrought by that adventurer to the Company's interests. In 1617 again the king granted a charter to Sir James Cunningham for the formation of a Scottish company to trade with the East Indies. The London company raised loud protests, but could only secure the cancellation of the grant by paying compensation to Cunningham and his associates. In 1624 the crown claimed £20,000, one-fifth of the spoils of Ormuz, although the place had been taken entirely by the Company's forces. The political opponents of the monopoly armed themselves with economic arguments. As early as 1601 Gerard de Malynes in *A Treatise of the Canker of England's Commonwealth* denounced the export of silver for the purchase of spices, alleging that his countrymen were as simple as West Indian savages in exchanging precious metals for luxuries and trifles. Other writers took up the cry, notably " J. R." in *The Trade's Increase*, 1615, the very title of which was a gibe at the Company, being that of their lost leviathan. Puerile arguments were pressed into the service, such as the assertions that the Company's construction of shipping had raised the price of timber and that its voyages were prejudicial to the national defence by denuding the realm of seamen.[2] Political theorists, in fact, and would-be inter-

---

[1] Sir W. W. Hunter considers that the tradition of a factory at Pipli in 1633-4 is not supported by clear evidence : *British India*, ii. p. 91 note.

[2] J. R., however, brought forward the serious statement that of 3000 seamen who had sailed to the east 2000 had never returned.

lopers deliberately used fallacious reasoning in order to appeal to popular prejudice, and their efforts were so far successful that for half a century the harassed shareholders and directors were commonly regarded as a clique of unpatriotic self-seekers.

For the Company Sir Dudley Digges replied in *The Defence of Trade*, 1615, and Thomas Mun in *A Discourse of Trade from England into the East Indies*, 1621. Mun also wrote (*c.* 1630) *England's Treasure by Forraign Trade*, but the work was not printed until 1664. These brochures prove that more reasonable economic principles were already being formed, but popular tradition was against them, and they required clearer thinking for their appreciation than could be expected from the prejudiced public to which they were addressed. The most serious charge against the Company was that of exporting the national wealth. Mun aptly replied to this by comparing it to the action of the farmer who sows grain in order to obtain a harvest. And statistics, so far as the Company disclosed them, bore him out, for about three-quarters of the spices brought home from the east were re-exported for payment in cash or goods of much more than their original cost. As knowledge of the Indian trading conditions improved, also, the proportion of specie exported decreased. The 1601 expedition carried eastwards £29,000 in money and £7000 in goods, but the second joint-stock in 1617-20 sent out nearly £300,000 in English manufactures and only £152,000 in coin. The Company had thus a sound contention in favour of its public utility. An undoubted ground of suspicion, even to impartial observers, lay in the fact that, whilst the profits of the Indian trade were obviously large enough to be worth fighting for, the Company was for ever bewailing its losses and crying out for help. The explanation was probably to be found in the delay in winding up the various ventures. Whilst one set of investors were quietly pocketing their gains, the stage was already occupied by another set still in the throes of uncertainty as to the outcome.

As originally formed in 1600 the Company had consisted almost exclusively of merchants, the only member of rank being the Earl of Cumberland, whose connections in the city were extensive. For a man to avail himself of the privileges of an ordinary regulated company it was indeed necessary for him to have had a commercial training. But it was soon realized that such training was not essential to a speculator in the East Indian voyages, because all the details of the trade were in the hands of the Company's officials. When, therefore, the king renewed and strengthened the charter in 1609, a host of courtiers and persons of rank sought admission, headed by the Earls of Salisbury, Nottingham, Southampton, and Worcester; and some years later James himself offered to become a freeman, a dangerous compliment which the governing body skilfully declined. The period of greatest prosperity in the early history of the corporation followed. The first terminable joint-stock, 1613-16, amounted to £429,000, sent out twenty-nine ships in four voyages, and made a total profit of 87½ per cent. The second joint-stock, 1617-32, raised a capital of £1,629,000, despatched twenty-five ships in three voyages, and at first promised a satisfactory return.[1] The loss of the islands trade was then severely felt, and a period of financial decline set in. Separate voyages had again to be resorted to in 1628-30 and a third joint-stock could not be raised until 1632.

Charles I. was ever a broken reed for the Company to rely upon. His father had alternated between support and desertion of its interests ; he himself consistently betrayed them. His feeble conduct of the Amboyna question caused the directors to appeal in despair to Parliament in 1628. Their case was ably presented by Thomas Mun, but the Commons, absorbed in the constitutional struggle, looked coldly upon a body enjoying a monopoly of royal creation, and rendered no efficient aid. Charles then demanded a passage to the east for the Earl of Denbigh, whose object was most probably to reconnoitre the prospects for an independent trade of his own. Denbigh returned from India in 1633, and apparently abandoned his projects.

The next move was more serious. In 1635 Sir William Courteen, a financier of Flemish extraction, and Sir Paul Pindar, a merchant of great wealth, approached the king through the good offices of Endymion Porter,[2] a groom of the bedchamber. The Company had just concluded its agreement for trade in the Portuguese possessions. Captain John Weddell had been instrumental in this negotiation. He now deserted the Company and took service with Courteen and Pindar. Charles issued, in December 1635, a license to these associates to trade in the east, stilling his own conscience and endeavouring to soothe the indignation of the Company by an assurance that the new body should not intrude into places where the Company was already established. The ostensible design, in fact, was to take advantage of the late treaty and trade in the Portuguese stations. The king was already under financial obligations to Courteen and Pindar, and hoped to draw large sums from the new concession. At a later date he avowed that Endymion Porter's name was merely inserted as a screen for his own.

In 1636 Weddell and other captains sailed under the flag of their new employers. They appeared at Goa and even at Surat, where they caused considerable perplexity to the resident factors, as yet ignorant of the details of the intrigue. Weddell himself led an expedition to China, but was lost on the homeward voyage. But their principal occupation was sheer piracy, which they pursued everywhere from the Red Sea to Canton. It was on account of their misdeeds that the Mogul government imprisoned the unfortunate Surat merchants. The next project was the establishment of a colony in Madagascar, to

---

[1] For full financial details and an analysis of the various ventures see W. R. Scott's *Joint Stock Companies*, ii. pp. 91-128.

[2] Porter had already sent two privateers to the Indian Ocean in the early part of 1635, before the Portuguese agreement was known in England.

act as an entrepot between the east and the west. Prince Rupert, his military career not yet begun, was flattered into accepting the command, but ultimately his relatives decided against it and despatched him to the continental wars instead. The Madagascar settlement remained in the air until 1645, when 140 colonists went out to plant in St. Augustine Bay. The experiment was a terrible failure, lasting little more than a year. At the end of that time twenty-three survivors abandoned the place, and less than a dozen saw their native land again. In 1639 Charles, by a fresh change of front, revoked his grant to Courteen's association ; but it continued nevertheless to carry on trade and piracy and the export of base coin throughout the period of the Civil War.

The king's new regard for the East India Company brought it no good fortune. In 1640, in desperate need of money, he took possession of pepper to the value of £60,000 in its London warehouses. He promised repayment, and perhaps honestly believed he could keep his word, but circumstances were too strong for him. The Company recovered about half the amount by withholding payment of customs.

During the Civil War the Company suffered by an inevitable splitting of its members into royalist and parliamentarian factions. The former were in a minority, and after they had been purged out the main body again appealed to Parliament for the extinction of the Courteen association. In 1646 the Commons agreed to this, but the Lords rejected their decision, and nothing was done. So hopeless did the position seem that the directors in 1646-7 and again in 1649 resolved to abandon their factories, recall their servants and wind up all their affairs. For some years no money could be raised and no ships sailed to the east except those of private speculators with or without license. But the final act of abandonment was not carried out, and the Company continued to exist as an official body, although doing no business. The overseas factors really kept it alive, maintaining themselves principally by private trade. At the end of 1649 the original body coalesced with the Courteen association, also in a moribund condition, without effecting any immediate improvement.

At the conclusion of the Dutch war (1654) all concerned looked to Cromwell's strong statesmanship to reorganize the East Indian trade. He approached the question with an eye solely to the national convenience, having no personal connection with the interests involved. He found three conflicting bodies of opinion : that of the unattached merchants of London and Bristol, who professed to desire an entirely open trade ; that of the old East India Company, wishing to continue on a joint-stock basis ; and finally, that of a schismatic party in the Company itself, who were eager to refound it as a purely regulated body allowing its members to make individual voyages. These traders called themselves the New Adventurers, and were already sending out their ships in anticipation of the decision. In 1656 Cromwell completed his investigation, and in the following year issued his charter, which put an end to the long period of anarchy.   He decided in favour of a joint-stock trade and a complete monopoly, on the lines laid down by James I.   So far as can be ascertained, there was nothing very new in the document itself.[1]   But it was accompanied by changes which amounted to a revolution.   A new machinery of election brought the governor and officials into closer touch with the shareholders. Admission to the privileges of the Company could be obtained on payment of £5.   And, above all, the new joint-stock became permanent and indissoluble, with a consequent extinction of the old vicious system of overlapping interests.

[1] It does not now exist.   For a reconstruction of its terms see Hunter, ii. pp. 132-3.

CHAPTER VII

MARITIME DISCOVERY IN THE FIRST HALF OF THE SEVENTEENTH CENTURY

(i) *Australia and the South Seas*

UNTIL nearly the end of the sixteenth century the world-maps compiled by the great geographers are unanimous in showing the southern portion of the earth as covered by a great land-mass, whose coastline runs in an irregular circle round the globe in latitudes varying from 20° to 60° S. This great southern continent—the *Terra Australis nondum cognita*—was thought to form the southern shore of the Straits of Magellan, and the maps show a northward projection of it in the region since found to be occupied by Australia, with New Guinea drawn as a separate island off the main coast. This indication of land on the actual site of Australia was either a lucky guess on the part of the map-makers or the fruit of a real discovery made in the earlier decades of the sixteenth century. Such a discovery might have been made by the Portuguese—as it afterwards was by the Dutch—owing to storms driving ships out of their course while on the eastward passage to the Spice Islands. But it has left no trace in written records ; and to the generation which saw the opening of the seventeenth century Australia was still an unknown land.

The credit of its early exploration belongs almost entirely to the Dutch, but since it has long formed a field of British expansion some account of its discovery is necessary. The northern shore of New Guinea had been known to the sixteenth century navigators. In 1605 the Dutch authorities at Bantam despatched William Janszoon to make further investigations. Janszoon explored the south-western coast of New Guinea and the eastern side of the Gulf of Carpentaria, being thus the first recorded European to behold the shores of Australia. He thought that New Guinea and Australia were all one, not realizing that a passage existed between them.

That discovery was made very shortly after the Dutch expedition had left the coast. In 1605 two Spanish commanders sailed from Callao in South America with the object of exploring the South Pacific. They made various discoveries among the islands of Polynesia, and then separated, one only, Luis Vaez de Torres, persevering in the voyage. Torres sighted the eastern end of New Guinea and sailed along the whole of its south coast, thus proving it to be an island, and traversing the strait which now bears its discoverer's name. Torres returned in safety to America, but the Spaniards did not make public the information he had gathered, and the Dutch long afterwards believed New Guinea to be a part of Australia.

The next Dutch enterprise had no direct bearing upon Australian discovery, but proved, what had long been vaguely suspected, that Tierra del Fuego was not part of the great southern continent. Drake had made this discovery during his voyage of 1577-80, but for strategic reasons had not advertised it. English map-makers, however, had discarded the southern continent, at least in this region, soon after his return. There was now a commercial reason for attempting a voyage by the open sea. The Dutch East India Company's charter gave it a monopoly of the Indian trade, whether by the Cape of Good Hope or the Straits of Magellan. Isaac le Maire, an independent Dutch trader who seems to have intrigued with the French, determined to avail himself of the flaw in wording the charter. He despatched his son Jacob le Maire with William Schouten in 1615, to sail into the Pacific round Cape Horn. This they did successfully, the first time the feat had been accomplished, and arrived in the Eastern archipelago after making discoveries in Polynesia and on the northern coast of New Guinea. But at Batavia the authorities paid no heed to their ingenious evasion of the charter. Ship and goods were ruthlessly confiscated, and Jacob le Maire died of grief.

The exploration of Australia began again in 1616. Between that year and 1627 a series of Dutch voyages resulted in the charting of the western and half of the southern coasts. Most of these discoveries were made by merchantmen driven out of their course on the voyage from the Cape of Good Hope. Two voyages, in 1623 and 1636, revealed parts of the northern coasts to the west of the Gulf of Carpentaria.

The question whether Australia was an island or merely a projection of the supposed great continent was still an open one. In 1642 Abel Tasman sailed from Batavia to solve the problem. Going first to Mauritius, he then sailed far into the southern ocean, and turned eastwards until on November 4 he sighted a land which he named after Van Diemen, the governor-general of the Dutch Indies, but which is now called Tasmania. Leaving this coast he pressed on to the east until he discovered the South Island of New Zealand, which he supposed might be part of the southern continent. From New Zealand he sailed back to Batavia by the north of New Guinea. He had thus circumnavigated Australia and proved its insular character. But he had not sighted its eastern shore, which remained unexplored for another century, neither had he perceived the fact that Tasmania is a separate island.

Whilst Tasman was making his great voyage Martin de Vries had been charting the coasts of Japan, hitherto very vaguely represented on the maps. Previous Dutch voyagers had searched for other islands in the North Pacific, alleged to lie to the east of Japan and to be inhabited by civilized people. These rumours proved to be groundless.

With the voyages of Tasman and de Vries the exploration of Australia and the Pacific ceased until nearly the end of the century. The Dutch sought for rich trading lands rather than sites for settlement. The former they saw were not to be looked for in the south, and this accounts for the cessation of their interest in discovery. It was not until the nineteenth century that any European country had a sufficient surplus population to undertake the serious colonization of so distant a shore as Australia.[1]

(ii) *The Arctic*

In the Arctic the first three decades of the Stuart period witnessed a similar outbreak of energetic discovery, in which the English bore a preponderant part. Under Elizabeth Frobisher and Davis had searched for a north-west passage, and the Muscovy Company for one by the north-east. The last-named body had ceased from their efforts after the voyage of Pet and Jackman in 1580. The Dutch had then taken up the work, and their expeditions of 1594-7 had resulted in the discovery of Spitzbergen by Barents, with the prospect of commercial gain in the whale fishery. The Muscovy Company claimed the fishery as included in their monopoly. An offshoot from their corporation obtained a separate charter in 1613, but ultimately the Dutch beat them out of the field.

With the advent of the East India Company the North West Passage again assumed practical importance. In 1602 that body commissioned George Waymouth to search for it. He sailed up Davis Strait and returned by its western shore, the locality of Frobisher's discoveries. Finally, disaffection among his men forced him to give up the quest after he had penetrated some distance into Hudson's Strait. In 1605 Christian IV. of Denmark sent an expedition to Greenland to seek traces of the Norse colonies which had existed there in the Middle Ages. One of the ships was commanded by an Englishman, John Knight, who returned to his own country at the conclusion of the voyage. In the following year Knight sailed to the Labrador coast in a small vessel equipped by the East India and Muscovy merchants. He and four of his men landed to explore the country, and were seen no more. Immediately after his disappearance a swarm of Eskimos attacked the ship. The surviving members of the crew got her clear with difficulty, and sailed home by way of Newfoundland.

[1] Much of the foregoing is drawn from E. Heawood, *Geographical Discovery in the Seventeenth and Eighteenth Centuries*, Cambridge, 1912.

We come now to Henry Hudson, the greatest of the English explorers of this period. Exhaustive research has failed to reveal any certain information upon his early life and family. Several persons of his name were prominent in the Muscovy Company from its inception, either as investors or mariners, and it has been conjectured that Thomas Hudson, a London merchant associated with Walsingham and Doctor Dee in promoting Davis's voyages, was his uncle. Although his relationship to any of these persons has not been proved, it was in the Muscovy Company's service that he first became prominent. Whether by his own design or those of his successive employers, Hudson covered the whole area of the Arctic in his search for a northern passage to Asia, examining first the area due north of the British Isles, then the north-east, next the American coastline in the west, and finally the oft-traversed north-west where he met his fate after making his most important discovery. Such a comprehensive scheme, thoroughly carried out by one man, was precisely what had been lacking hitherto, and had it yielded purely negative results it would probably have put an end to the era of exploration for a century. Such, in fact, was its outcome in all directions except one—the north-west, where at the moment of the explorer's death he seemed to be on the verge of solving the great problem.

In 1607 Hudson sailed in a ship belonging to the Muscovy Company to accomplish the first part of his plan. He pushed northwards up the east coast of Greenland until stopped by ice, and then turned eastwards, following the edge of the ice barrier until he came to Spitzbergen. Everywhere in this stretch he failed to find any prospect of a passage through the ice. The voyage thus finally demonstrated the fallacy of the theory advanced by Robert Thorne eighty years before, that it was possible to sail right over the pole itself. In 1608 Hudson sailed again in the service of the Muscovy Company. His objective this time was the north-eastern sea between Spitzbergen and Novaia Zemlia. Here again the ice precluded all hope of a practicable channel. In this connection it must be borne in mind that the objects of Arctic exploration were not purely scientific, as in our own day. The merchants who financed the voyages looked for the discovery of a passage which could be regularly used for commercial purposes, and failing that, their servants were not justified in persisting in the search. The presence of a thick ice-barrier therefore satisfied Hudson that it was useless to continue in the north-east unless a route could be found along the coast of Siberia itself, a quarter in which the season of 1608 was now too far advanced for a proper exploration. He returned to London after examining the west coast of Novaia Zemlia.

Hudson now seems to have concluded that the west offered the best prospect of an Asiatic passage. He had been in communication with John Smith, the Virginia pioneer, who suggested that America might not after all be an unbroken continent, and that the region afterwards named New England might contain a channel to the Pacific. He

EARLY VOYAGES TO THE NORTH-WEST

had, however, to subordinate his views to those of his prospective employers. The Muscovy Company were unwilling to expend further sums on the project, and Hudson entered the service of the Dutch East India Company, whose predilections still favoured the north-east. In 1609 he sailed again in that direction in the Dutch ship *Half Moon*. He attempted to pass between Novaia Zemlia and the mainland, but ice and the insubordination of the Dutch crew put an end to his progress. Then, in order not to waste the remainder of the season, he steered boldly in the opposite direction, and coasted down the American shore until he reached the mouth of the river which has since borne his name. Thinking that this might be the desired passage through the American continent, he sailed the *Half Moon* inland until further progress was impossible and the truth was clearly established that he was in a river and not an arm of the sea. On the voyage home he touched at Dartmouth, where the authorities detained him and the English members of the crew. The Dutchmen went on to their own country, and their reports of the discovery led to the establishment of New Amsterdam at the mouth of the Hudson River.

The north-west was now the only quarter which Hudson had not attempted, and the north-west had always appealed most effectively to the imagination of English adventurers. A strong combination of the latter, including Sir Thomas Smith, Sir John Wolstenholme, Sir Dudley Digges and about twenty others, now prepared to finance the explorer in a voyage in this direction. In April, 1610, he set sail in a ship called the *Discovery*, a name which has become famous in the annals of exploration. His crew included Robert Juet, an old man who had been his mate in previous voyages, Robert Bylot, and Henry Greene, a man of bad character who owed much to Hudson's kindness. Passing in sight of Iceland and Greenland, the *Discovery* entered Hudson's Strait between Labrador and Meta Incognita (now Baffin Land). Many previous north-western explorers had gone so far, including perhaps Sebastian Cabot, the earliest of all. Hudson pushed on through the entire length of the strait. Having done so he turned southwards down the eastern side of Hudson Bay. He may now have supposed himself to be in the Pacific, or at least in a gulf having an opening to that ocean. Before he could proceed to the western shore of the bay, and so discover its true nature, the winter closed in and he hauled his ship ashore to preserve her from the ice. The long winter proved fatal to the discipline of the crew. Provisions ran short and sickness broke out. In June, 1611, Hudson was able to resume the voyage. In spite of starvation he seems to have determined to risk all in completing the discovery. His decision precipitated a mutiny. Headed by Greene and Juet the malcontents seized him and his son, placed them with the sick men in an open boat, and turned them adrift. None of the unfortunates were ever heard of again. Having committed this crime the mutineers elected Greene captain and sailed for England.

Greene and three others were killed in a fight with Eskimos. Juet died of hunger. The survivors reached home in September. Having but a lame account to give of themselves six of them were placed on their trial. Some documents relating to the case have been brought to light,[1] but the extent of their punishment nowhere appears. Robert Bylot, one of the accused men, took part in subsequent voyages.

Among the promoters of exploration the report of Hudson's discovery caused the greatest excitement, and many believed that the North West Passage was found. They hastened to subscribe funds for a new voyage to complete the work. In April, 1612, Captain (afterwards Sir) Thomas Button sailed with two ships. His orders were to traverse the passage, and after arriving in the Pacific to send back his smaller vessel with the news whilst proceeding to China and Japan with the other. Three months after his departure the adventurers, now nearly three hundred in number, secured a royal charter incorporating them as the Company of Merchants of London Discoverers of the North West Passage. Sir Thomas Smith became the governor of this body.

With these anticipations the return of Button was eagerly awaited. He made a good passage through Hudson's Strait, and sailed westwards across the bay until he came to its farther shore at a point which, for obvious reasons, he named Hopes Checked. He then coasted southwards and wintered at Port Nelson, suffering much hardship and losing one of his ships. In the other, Hudson's *Discovery*, he completed his examination of the western shore in the summer of 1613, and returned with news which, although of geographical value, fell far short of what his employers had expected. He did not admit, however, that hopes of the passage were at an end ; the set of the tides and other indications encouraged the belief that a channel might yet be found to lead westwards out of the bay. The members of the Company shared this belief for, besides setting forth other voyages, they took pains to keep secret the information obtained by Button, of whose discoveries only a meagre account has survived. Button's official relation was suppressed, and has never since been found.

Whilst Button was entering Hudson Bay in 1612 another explorer, James Hall, was examining the west coast of Greenland, apparently in the hope of finding gold. Hall had been a commander in a Danish expedition to the same region, in which some Eskimos had been kidnapped and carried off to Denmark. A relative of these unfortunates recognized Hall as one of the authors of the outrage, and murdered him in revenge. His crew then returned without making any discoveries of importance. In this voyage William Baffin took part as Hall's pilot, appearing for the first time in Arctic exploration. In 1614 Captain Gibbons, one of Button's companions, sailed in the service of the North West Passage Company to improve upon his former commander's discoveries. His voyage also proved unfortunate,

[1] See T. A Janvier, *Henry Hudson*, New York, 1909.

for he lost the season by becoming embayed on the Labrador coast in a place called Gibbons his Hole. When he freed his ship it was too late to proceed further.

The Company now took Baffin into its service and sent him out with Robert Bylot in 1615 to look for the passage through Hudson Bay. Baffin, like Davis in the previous century, was a well-educated seaman who made improvements of his own in the science of navigation; and, as in the case of Hudson, nothing has been discovered concerning his family antecedents, although there are indications that he was a London man.[1] In the voyage of 1615 he examined the northern parts of Hudson Bay and, finding that the ice increased and the water became shallow, came to the conclusion that no passage existed in that direction.

In the following year, 1616, Baffin and Bylot sailed once more under the same employers. Convinced that Hudson Bay was a *cul de sac*, they took up the line of discovery which John Davis had perforce abandoned in 1587. It will be remembered that Davis had desisted more on account of political and financial considerations than because he had lost hopes of success. Baffin therefore sailed up Davis Strait, and early in June passed his precursor's northernmost limit. He pressed on for three hundred miles into the stretch of water since called Baffin Bay. In the latitude 78° N. he found his further progress barred. He noticed passages leading out of his bay, but each was blocked by ice, and he returned to report that here again he saw no hope of a commercial route to the Pacific. His title to fame rests upon his chart of the discovery and his scientific observations. No other navigator covered the same ground until the opening of the nineteenth century. The remainder of his career was passed in the service of the East India Company. In 1622 he was killed at the siege of Ormuz. Whilst taking ranges for the artillery with his mathematical instruments, " he received a shot from the castle into his belly, wherewith he gave three leaps, and died immediately."

The North West Passage Company had now well-nigh exhausted its hopes and its capital. For two years it did nothing further. In 1619 it sent forth its last effort, in which William Hawkridge once more entered Hudson Bay, but failed to push the limits of discovery beyond those reached by his predecessors. Sir Thomas Smith was now growing old,[2] and withdrawing one by one from the enterprises he had so worthily invigorated. He retired from the management of the Virginia Company in 1619, and from the governorship of the East India Company in 1621. From this time onwards we hear no more of the North West Passage Company.

At the point where Baffin left it the discovery remained until 1631. In that year Luke Foxe of Hull obtained, after much petitioning, the

---

[1] *Voyages of William Baffin*, ed. Sir C. R. Markham, Hakluyt Society, 1881, pp. xxii xxiii.

[2] He died in 1625.

command of the ship *Charles* of the royal navy, and the equipment of his expedition by a body of private adventurers. Foxe was a middle-aged sea-captain who had studied the records of Arctic voyages and had long desired to lead an expedition of his own. Whilst Foxe's preparations were going forward the merchants of Bristol were stirred to undertake an independent enterprise with the same object—the discovery of an outlet from Hudson Bay. They committed their undertaking to the command of Captain Thomas James. We have thus the hitherto unprecedented coincidence of two English explorers sailing in the same year and with the same purpose, and yet without working in co-operation. Foxe expressed some contempt for James as a seaman, and there was considerable jealousy between the two expeditions from the outset. In the end neither accomplished anything remarkable. Foxe entered the bay and examined first its western and southern shores, where he encountered James. Then he tried its north-western exit, reaching a latitude of 67° N., " Foxe his Farthest." Sickness and ice then forced him to give up the search and return to England. James had a less fortunate voyage. His crew suffered many casualties from sickness and accident, and he decided to winter in the bay. Foxe was blamed for not doing the same, but, as he pointed out, it was possible to be in Hudson's Strait, by sailing from England in the spring, at a much earlier date than that of the break-up of the ice in the recesses of the Bay : wintering was therefore unnecessary. Each of the explorers wrote a book on his experiences, and each died within a few years of his return. With these voyages the quest for the North West Passage ceased for over a century.

CHAPTER VIII

THE PURITAN ASCENDANCY, 1649–1660

THE present-day view of the British dominions as transplanted portions of the nation, possessing the same rights to liberty as the parent stock and united to it in equality by ties of blood, is of comparatively recent development. In the seventeenth century the conception of empire was widely different. The men of that day regarded colonial expansion in terms of trade. To them overseas settlements were desirable only in so far as they afforded enhanced commercial facilities to the population at home. Parliament in 1649, appointing a commission to enquire into the affairs of the colonies, directed the members to consider " how they may be best managed and made useful for this Commonwealth ; how the commodities thereof may be so multiplied and improved, as those Plantations alone may supply the Commonwealth with what it necessarily wants." Here we have the essential character of the old empire clearly implied—a self-sufficient and exclusive trading corporation. It was natural for this system to be adopted, for it was the only one known to the time. Spain and Portugal, our precursors as colonial powers, had each taken it as the basis of their policy. In their case the royal authority had planted and developed the colonies ; in our own the same work had been done by private enterprise ; in both the capitalists at home had borne their part, and considered themselves as much entitled to share the fruits of success as were the pioneers who had now become colonists. In return for subjection to her economic system the mother-country afforded an undeniable benefit —defence by her armed forces against European enemies. The bargain was not altogether one-sided, and the statesmen of the seventeenth century therefore saw no valid reason why they should not mould the policy of the empire with a single eye to the prosperity of the British Isles.

This conception of a trading empire continued to flourish for nearly two hundred years. When, towards the end of the eighteenth century the older colonies would tolerate it no longer, and broke away ; and when at the same time the Industrial Revolution set in at home, and under these combined influences the mercantile system fell to pieces in the course of fifty years, the generation which witnessed the process had nothing to put in the place of the lost bond. It was commonly said that, the mercantile nexus being abolished, nothing remained to prevent the other outlying members of the British race from following the example of the United States. Only in the last seventy years has it become apparent that there exist means of cementing an empire other than a material system of profit-taking.

We see then that the men of the seventeenth century moulded the colonial policy of the following age, and that dominating their colonial policy was their commercial policy. Here again their outlook proceeded from a different angle to our own. To the modern economist trade is bound up with the maintenance of peace, and the well-being of one nation depends upon that of its neighbours ; wealth is increased by free intercourse, and no country becomes rich by making surrounding peoples poor. To the statesmen of 1649 this would have seemed an idle doctrine. Looking out upon their world they conceived its normal and natural state to be that of war—of universal competition for supremacy. This warfare was not always officially declared, but it was always implicit. Commerce to them was one of its processes— an attempt to seize the largest possible share from a body of world-wealth assumed to be a fixed quantity not capable of any great expansion. To extend their own country's industry and trade did not satisfy them ; they must also depress and uproot those of their rivals. They had therefore an elaborate strategy of trade comparable to the strategy of fleets and armies, and quite as assiduously studied. The modern critic often exclaims at the fatuity of navigation acts and monopolies and similar shackles upon enterprise, and marvels that intelligent men did not sooner realize their folly. The conception of commerce as an act of war and of merchants as organized and disciplined like soldiers, goes far to explain them. With such considerations in mind we are the better enabled to enter into the external policy of English governments under the Commonwealth and the Restoration.

The leaders of the Commonwealth had a stiff task before them in 1649. Scotland declared against them on the execution of the king. Ireland, long in a state of anarchy, was for the most part royalist in sentiment, and its leaders were busily raising forces for Charles II. A portion of the fleet had revolted in 1648, and was now under the command of Prince Rupert. The Isle of Man, Scilly, and Jersey were held by royalist garrisons and served as nests for privateers. Virginia, Maryland, Barbados and Antigua had all repudiated the authority of the parliamentary government. In Europe it could discern not a single friend ; in Spain, France, Portugal, even in barbarous Russia, it was looked upon as a gang of criminals, the enemies of mankind. With France there began a maritime war which, although unofficial, raged fiercely for several years. In the Channel and the Mediterranean French privateers preyed upon English commerce, capturing 5000 tons of shipping in the course of the first few months. As these privateers held letters of marque from Charles II. their activities were equivalent to the transference of the Civil War from the land to the sea.

The Puritan statesmen acted with resolution. Whilst Cromwell and the army struck down Ireland and Scotland, Sir Henry Vane and Robert Blake set about the strengthening of the navy and the re-establishment of English prestige throughout the world by its means. The first task was the hunting down of Prince Rupert. He had sailed from a Dutch port at the beginning of 1649 with eight ships. He failed to prevent Cromwell's transit to Ireland, being blockaded by Blake at Kinsale throughout the summer. In October he escaped and made for the coast of Spain. After capturing English merchantmen he entered the Tagus with his prizes, and received friendly recognition at Lisbon, where he was able to recruit his force to a considerable extent. For the Commonwealth government it was a crucial situation. Unless they could vindicate their claim to have Rupert treated as a pirate and not as the legitimate officer of the King of England the whole overseas interests of the country must go down before the hostile forces of Europe. Fortunately their contest cut across another, the war still going on between Spain on the one hand and Portugal and France on the other. In March, 1650, therefore, when Blake arrived off Lisbon in pursuit, he was able to obtain supplies from the Spanish coast and maintain a blockade throughout the summer. He soon received instructions to treat the Portuguese as enemies, and emphasized the position by detaining nine ships of the outward-bound Brazil fleet when they came down the Tagus to put to sea. In September he attacked the homeward-bound fleet from Brazil, and captured seven prizes. These measures caused a change in the Portuguese attitude, and Rupert ceased to be a welcome guest at Lisbon. In October, taking advantage of Blake's absence, the royalist leader set out once more. He entered the Mediterranean, lost the greater part of his squadron by wreck and in action, and took refuge with the remnant at Toulon.

One effect of Blake's proceedings was the recognition of the Commonwealth by Spain, which took place in December, 1650. In the following year Rupert evaded the English forces waiting for him in the Mediterranean, and once more gained the ocean. His intentions were now frankly piratical, and on that account he became politically less dangerous. For a year he cruised off the Azores and the African coast, capturing Spanish and English merchantmen. Only when the royalist cause had already perished in the West Indies did he sail thither in the summer of 1652. His force now dwindled away for lack of any support from a friendly shore. His brother Maurice perished in a hurricane near the Virgin Islands, and he himself, with only one of his fighting ships left, returned to Europe in the spring of 1653 to end his long adventure in a French port. In the meantime the Parliamentary forces had reduced the Scilly Islands and the other outlying royalist strongholds, and the victory of Worcester in 1651 had definitely put an end to civil war in the British Isles. A powerful supporter of the Stuart cause abroad had died in 1650 in the person of the Stadtholder William II., who left no successor of age to take his place. France was distracted by the troubles of the Fronde, and so, after two years of desperate uncertainty, the Commonwealth leaders might congratulate themselves on having weathered the storm.

The pursuit of Rupert, the war with the French, and the necessity for capturing the royalist strongholds round the English coast, had postponed the reduction of the rebellious colonies to the allegiance of the Commonwealth. In the autumn of 1651 this task was taken in hand. The colonies affected were Virginia, where Sir William Berkeley, appointed governor by Charles I. just before the outbreak of the Civil War, still ruled in the name of the dead king's son ; Maryland, where a faction had proclaimed Charles II. without authority from Lord Baltimore ; Barbados, controlled by Lord Willoughby and a body of active royalists ; and Bermuda and Antigua. The New Englanders had impassively accepted the triumph of Parliament, showing by their general attitude that they intended the rise and fall of English governments to remain a matter of indifference to them.[1]

The new Commission for Plantations appointed in 1649 was unable to take forcible steps at first for the reasons already considered. In October, 1650, it secured the passage of an ordinance forbidding all trade by foreign nations with the English settlements, but this remained a dead-letter until an English fleet could be spared to enforce it. A year later Sir George Ayscue arrived at Barbados with a strong squadron, and one of his first actions was to seize fourteen Dutch merchantmen which he found trading there in contravention of the ordinance. Ayscue found that a landing in Barbados would be a difficult matter, since there were 6000 royalists under arms, and they were encouraged by false rumours of a victory of Charles II. at Worcester in September. At length, on the receipt of the true tidings of Worcester, counsels of prudence prevailed. Colonel Modyford and the moderate party forced Willoughby to submit, and in January, 1652, Ayscue signed articles of capitulation with the Barbadians. They submitted to the Commonwealth and expelled Willoughby and the extremists on recognition of the island's financial and commercial independence, liberty of conscience, and the continuance of the General Assembly. Willoughby departed to watch over the interests of a colony he had planted two years before at Surinam in Guiana, of which we shall have more to say in the next chapter. Antigua, the Bermudas and the smaller island colonies gave little trouble after Barbados had been dealt with.

Early in March, 1652, three Parliamentary commissioners, headed by William Claybourne, appeared at Jamestown to exact the sub-

[1] G. L. Beer, *Origins, etc.*, pp. 369-70 ; Egerton, p. 57.

mission of Virginia. Berkeley and a royalist faction were ready to fight, but the assembly was lukewarm. After some discussion the Virginians surrendered, on the same general terms as the Barbadians. The assembly elected Richard Bennett, one of the commissioners, as governor in succession to Berkeley, who, however, remained in the colony, living in retirement until the Restoration, when he again assumed office. The Commissioners next proceeded up the Chesapeake to St. Mary's, where their presence with a single frigate secured the surrender of Maryland ere the month was out. Maryland, threatened by Claybourne and the Virginians with absorption into its southern neighbour, submitted on less favourable terms. William Stone remained governor, but Lord Baltimore's proprietary rights continued in abeyance until 1657, and the colony itself was the scene of disorders.

The general result of these transactions was that all the British dominions recognized the Commonwealth and its successor, the Protectorate. The trade of Massachusetts with England, by a grant made during the Civil War, had been free of all duties for some years. The remaining colonies, as they came in, obtained similar concessions of greater or less extent. In spite of centralizing theories of administration on the part of the Puritan government the colonial assemblies continued to follow their own devices, and the mercantile system with all that it entailed did not in practice obtain a firm grip upon colonial life until the Restoration.

The Parliamentary reorganization of the navy proved to be of paramount importance to the fortunes of England throughout the remainder of the seventeenth century. Already, before the king's execution, the Earl of Warwick, as Lord High Admiral, had clinched the loyalty of the seamen to Parliament by improving their food, pay and conditions of service. In 1649 the Commonwealth dismissed Warwick, and entrusted his office to a committee presided over by Sir Henry Vane. This committee realized that the vigorous foreign policy forced upon the republic as a condition of survival must be based upon a fleet of unprecedented strength. As dissensions began to appear between the Long Parliament and the army, jealousy of the latter force may also have been a motive; but Vane carried out his work with the assistance of a body of army officers, of whom Robert Blake and later George Monck were the most prominent. The successes of these middle-aged men, who had no previous experience of the sea service, form one of the most interesting chapters in naval history, especially as they were soon to be pitted against such accomplished seamen as Tromp and de Ruyter. Charles I. had made considerable improvements in the fleet with the proceeds of ship-money. Vane and his fellow-workers added forty-one new ships in 1649-51, practically doubling the existing force. In the eleven years ending in 1660, 207 new ships were built or acquired, of which 121 remained on the list in the latter year in addition to twenty-two inherited from

Charles I.[1] The work was necessary, but it was only achieved by an expenditure which plunged the country into debt and confiscation, and formed a considerable factor in the thankfulness with which responsible men welcomed the Restoration. At the height of the Dutch war the navy was costing nearly one-and-a-half millions a year—fifty per cent. more than the total revenue of Charles I.

Circumstances were soon to put the new navy to a severe test. The maritime war of reprisals with France which broke out in 1649 raised a crop of difficult questions upon the rights of neutrals, of whom the Dutch with their huge carrying trade were the most prominent. French merchants, in fear of English cruisers, shipped their wares in Dutch bottoms. The Dutch contended that a neutral flag protected the goods of belligerents, unless such goods were of military value. The English, on the other hand, claimed that all belligerent goods were fair prize wherever found. The Admiralty courts condemned such cargoes, although they released the ships which carried them. The question was of vital importance to Dutch interests. It was accentuated by the behaviour of individuals. Among the English people in general the echoes of the Amboyna tragedy had died away, and there was as yet no great national animosity ; but the seamen, whom Clarendon described as a separate nation in themselves, came into closer contact with their rivals, and had conceived a bitter hatred of them. When they overhauled a Dutch merchantman and could find no satisfactory evidence that the goods on board were French they tortured the crew until they obtained it. The practice was so common that the English Court of Admiralty had to threaten punishment if it were continued.[2] Dutch trade with English colonies persisted in spite of ordinances to the contrary, and led to such incidents as Ayscue's seizure at Barbados in 1651. England and the United Provinces were now in fact the two sea powers of the world. They had trampled down their older competitors and at last stood face to face. The situation was one which admitted of only two solutions —close alliance and a division of the spoil, or war to decide the supremacy.

The death in 1650 of the monarchical Stadtholder, the son-in-law of Charles I., seemed to offer a chance of the former. The States General decided to appoint no successor to the office. Both nations were Puritanical in religion, and both were now fully republican in government. In March, 1651, two English representatives, Strickland and St. John, travelled to the Hague to negotiate an alliance. The Dutch expressed willingness, but haggled over the terms, raising, in addition to the question of neutral rights, that of the English claim to sovereignty in the British seas, which involved a salute to the flag and a levy of tribute for the privilege of fishing in the North Sea. They

---

[1] Oppenheim, *op. cit.* pp. 307, 338.

[2] S. R. Gardiner, *Commonwealth and Protectorate*, vol. ii. London, 1897, pp. 108-9.

gravely produced the *Intercursus Magnus* of 1496, wherein some of
these matters were decided in their favour. They proposed further
a mutual opening of colonial trade in America and the West Indies
only, with joint squadrons to act against pirates. This was somewhat
reminiscent of the unhappy Spice Islands treaty of 1619. The English
negotiators, in fact, came to the conclusion that no alliance was possible
unless most of the concessions came from their own side, and at the
end of June they quitted the Hague in disgust.

The next move came from the English Parliament in the shape of a
new Navigation Act, to understand which it is necessary to consider
the legislation which preceded it. From the time of Richard II. to
the early years of Elizabeth there had been Navigation Acts for the
general purpose of securing for English shipping a fair share of the
trades between England and the continent of Europe. That purpose
had been achieved with the overthrow of the Hanse supremacy in
northern Europe and the establishment of English commerce in the
Mediterranean ; and Burghley had realized that the gain from the
maintenance of the old navigation laws was no longer commensurate
with its disadvantages. With the seventeenth century a new system
of oceanic trade had arisen. The early Stuart kings held that the
regulation of foreign trade pertained to the royal prerogative and not
to Parliament. They sought therefore to mould the new oceanic commerce not by Navigation Acts but by orders in council. The first
object was to ensure that English custom houses should collect duty
on all the produce of English colonies. In 1621 and 1625 the colonies
were ordered to ship their tobacco (then their sole considerable export)
exclusively to England, although there was as yet nothing to prevent
them from lading it in foreign ships. But in 1636 a royal instruction
enjoined the exclusive use of English shipping, and both aspects of the
full navigation policy were thus outlined. At the same time the
colonists were compensated for these restrictions by protection of their
goods in the English market, where much higher duties were levied on
foreign-produced tobacco than on the colonial product.[1]

The next development was the ordinance of 1650, already alluded to
in connection with the colonial rebellion against the Commonwealth.
It will be convenient to refer to this measure as the Navigation Act of
1650, for it was part of a new code of legislation that continued to live
and grow during the whole period of the Old Colonial Empire. The
Act of 1650 prohibited all trade with the rebellious colonies for the
duration of the rebellion, and was to that extent a temporary measure.
But it prohibited also trade by foreign vessels with all the colonies, and
this prohibition did not end with the rebellion, but remained permanently
in effect. After 1650 none but English ships might lawfully be found in
any colonial port. This was the first step in establishing a parliamentary
code in supersession of the royal prerogative and its regulations.

[1] For the early Stuart regulations see the author's *Caribbee Islands under the Proprietary Patents*, Oxford, 1926, pp. 95-102.

The second step was the more famous Navigation Act of 1651, which was intended not only to round off the process of excluding the Dutch from the trade of the new English Empire, but also to deprive them of the function of carrying goods from foreign countries to England. The measure forbade the import into England, Ireland and the colonies of goods from Asia, Africa and America unless in ships owned by Englishmen, Irishmen or colonists, and manned by crews of whom more than half were English, Irish or colonial. Imports into England from Europe might be brought only in English ships or in those of the nationality which originally produced the goods. Imports, in other words, might not be handled by " carriers ". Finally, aliens were forbidden to engage in the coasting trade or to bring salt fish into the country.

These two Acts concerned principally the interests of the Dutch. Their political effect must have been to render Anglo-Dutch relations more strained, and they contributed to the outbreak of war in the following year ; but they are no longer regarded as the major cause of the conflict. Their economic effects scarcely had a chance to show themselves until after the peace of 1654. From that date they remained in force until their supersession by a stronger measure in 1660. Their provisions were not fully insisted upon ; the American colonies seem to have evaded them, as the presence of Dutch factors at New Amsterdam enabled them to do with impunity. For this reason there is no clear evidence that the Acts of 1650 and 1651 increased English trade or damaged that of the Dutch. Yet the men of the time believed in their efficacy, for they were the only legislation of the Puritans to be singled out for perpetuation on the return of Charles II.

A Dutch embassy came to England in December, 1651, to renew the former negotiations and to ask for the reversal of the Navigation Acts. The latter was refused, and matters drifted steadily in the direction of war. As has often happened when two nations have been at variance on serious questions of policy, the final rupture turned upon a point of sentimental interest. The demand for a salute to the English flag caused intense irritation to the Dutch seamen. In the spring of 1652, while negotiations were still proceeding in London, both nations sent squadrons to sea in the interests of their commerce. Tromp, the Dutch admiral, determined to refuse the salute unless to a markedly superior force. On May 18 he encountered Blake off the Kentish coast. Both commanders were more ready to fight than to talk, and an indecisive cannonade ensued. Parliament sent commissioners to enquire into the circumstances. Cromwell was one of them, and although he disliked the idea of war with a Protestant nation and had striven for a settlement, he gave it as his opinion that Blake had been in the right. The Dutch envoys departed at the end of June, and the war began in earnest. One of the Dutchmen remarked with prophetic insight : " The English are about to attack a mountain of gold ; we, a mountain of iron."

The truth of the saying soon became evident. The Dutch had an immense sea-borne commerce, the English a relatively small one. The Dutch had to maintain their trade throughout the war, for its stoppage meant the starvation of a people too large to live upon the resources of its own territory. England could endure the partial or even the entire cessation of mercantile activity for a short period, for she was still in the main an agricultural nation, growing rich by trade and manufactures, but able to support life without them. In geographical position England held a permanent advantage, for the Dutch routes to western Europe, the Mediterranean and the oceans passed her southern and eastern shores; only the Baltic and the interior European routes remained unobstructed. In political organization England was united, her government controlling a single army and a single fleet and raising money by uniform taxation; Dutch authority, after the death of the Stadtholder, was split among seven autonomous provinces and five boards of admiralty, with illimitable suspicion and jealousy ready to break out at the first reverse. In fighting ships the two countries were almost equal in numbers, the English having the advantage in size and solidity, " we building our ships for seventy years, they theirs for seven," as an English captain described the difference. In the moral qualities of patriotism and religious fervour there was little disparity. The war was to be decided by material factors, amongst which two only told in favour of the Dutch—the numbers of their seamen and their understanding with Denmark, whereby they secured the closing of the Sound to the transit of English naval stores from the Baltic.

As might be expected, the fighting was close and deadly to a degree unknown in the Elizabethan wars. The English admirals were soldiers of the New Model Army, who atoned for their limitations in seamanship by a pugnacity which impelled them to continue every action to the bitter end. Ingenious manœuvres played therefore a subordinate part, and each battle developed into a ferocious melée from which neither side escaped undamaged. In the summer of 1652 Blake scattered the Dutch fishing fleets in the North Sea and then waited at Shetland for the Dutch East Indian trade known to be returning by the northern route. Sir George Ayscue at the same time cruised to destroy commerce in the Channel. Rightly or wrongly the English government thus made their enemy's commerce rather than his fighting fleet their chief point of attack. Tromp first sought to fall upon Ayscue, but was baffled by adverse winds and then sailed to seek Blake in the Shetlands. A great storm dispersed his fleet before he could engage, and his scattered vessels had to make for the Dutch ports to re-assemble. Public opinion blamed Tromp and insisted on replacing him by de Witt and de Ruyter. The latter in August convoyed a merchant fleet down the Channel and defeated Ayscue off Plymouth. In September Blake united the English fleet under his command and defeated de Witt at the Kentish Knock, near the

Thames estuary. Two months later the Dutch reinstated Tromp, who set out with some ninety warships to convoy 450 merchantmen through the Channel. Blake's force was much inferior, for some of his ships had been sent to the Mediterranean and many were under repair ; for the first time also the shortage of English seamen began to make itself felt. Nevertheless he decided to engage, and the battle began off Dungeness on November 30. Twenty of his captains held aloof, alleging that they had not sufficient men to ply their tackle. With the remainder Blake was heavily defeated, losing six ships. Under cover of darkness he retreated to the Downs, and the great convoy went on its way triumphant.[1]

England quickly recovered from the defeat. Ayscue retired and two more soldiers of distinction, Monck and Deane, joined Blake in the command, with a fleet made up to seventy sail. In February, 1653, they met Tromp at the mouth of the Channel returning with the Bordeaux trade, part of the convoy he had taken out in the previous year. In a straggling and indecisive battle, usually called that of Portland, Tromp saved his merchantmen at the cost of severe damage to his fighting ships. In May Tromp successfully guarded another convoy round the north of Scotland and conducted the inward trade by the same route to the Dutch ports. Next month occurred a decisive battle between the united fleets in the seas between Harwich and Dunkirk. Deane was killed, but the Dutch lost twenty ships and sought refuge in their own ports. A blockade of the Dutch coast followed ; trade came to a standstill, merchants were ruined by hundreds, and the population of Amsterdam were face to face with starvation. It was a condition which their past history had fitted them to endure. At the end of July Tromp and de Witt skilfully combined their scattered squadrons and faced Monck off the Texel in the greatest battle of the war. Tromp was killed and the Dutch lost twenty-six ships and 6000 men. But the English also suffered heavily and the blockade was broken whilst they repaired their losses. Peace negotiations followed, but the Dutch were not yet in extremity, and the hard terms which Cromwell offered goaded them to continue through the winter. At length the war came to an end by the treaty of April 5, 1654. The Dutch yielded in the matter of the salute, paid compensation for the Amboyna massacre, acquiesced in the Navigation Act, and entered into a defensive alliance. England agreed to freedom of the fishery in the North Sea.

The conclusion was not decisive, but the war itself had inflicted more damage upon the Dutch than upon the English. The latter took 1500 prizes during its course, a number estimated as double that of the existing English mercantile marine.[2] The load of public debt, however, counterbalanced the gain to individuals, and Dutch trade

---

[1] This was the occasion of the broom at the masthead story, for which modern research has discovered no foundation.

[2] Oppenheim, p. 307.

showed ere long an astonishing power of recovery. But England had at least proved her right to rank as a first-class power, a claim upon which the transactions of the Stuart reigns had cast some doubt.

During the struggle Cromwell had risen to supreme power in England, casting out his rivals of the Long Parliament in the spring of 1653. He had never wholly approved of the war, which ran counter to a great design of his own for a coalition of the Protestant nations to impose their will upon the world. In this matter he was somewhat after his time. The opportunity for such a scheme had passed with the death of Gustavus Adolphus twenty years before, and the Peace of Westphalia had closed the period of the religious wars. But Cromwell in his foreign policy regarded himself as the successor of Elizabeth, taking Spain at its face value, and not foreseeing that economic ambitions and the land-hunger of France were to be the disturbing influences of the future. It would have needed a prophet to forecast such changes in 1653, and Cromwell ever looked backward rather than forward. Had he lived longer there might have been no Age of Louis XIV. An indication of what was running in his mind appears in a document of September, 1653, embodying a scheme which the circumstances show to have met with his approval. This was for an ending of the Dutch war by an alliance between England and the United Provinces, which other powers might join, against all states maintaining the Inquisition. The Navigation Act was to be virtually rescinded by a mutual freedom of trade in all ports and plantations. English and Dutch were then to partition the colonies of the world, the latter taking Asia and buying out the interests of the East India Company ; all America, except Brazil, going to England ; and the African trade remaining divided. Then followed provisions for Christianizing the heathen and for an international commission to regulate disputes. Such a gigantic conception savours more of Napoleon than an English statesman, and Cromwell resembled Napoleon in this, that he was the only English soldier of modern times to wield absolute power in the state. The plan remained stillborn, but visions of it coloured the Protector's foreign policy until his death five years later.

For the present he had to make his profit from the contest between Spain and France. Of these, the latter had given more offence to the Commonwealth than the former. Many Puritans indeed favoured an alliance with Spain on the ground that she had now no Protestant subjects to oppress, and that the Holy Office had in practice long ceased to trouble Englishmen in Spanish ports. Cromwell hesitated between the two, contriving to keep each in doubt of his intentions. At the end of 1654 he sent Blake with twenty-four sail to the Mediterranean to indicate the potentialities of English intervention, and incidentally to chastise the Barbary pirates. At the same time he undertook single-handed a first instalment of the plan to drive Spain out of America.

The Western Design, as it is generally called, comprised a joint military and naval expedition to make conquests in the West Indies. The Protector did not intend it to lead to formal war in Europe. He regarded it as a reprisal for the Spanish attacks upon Providence and Association, and for the maltreatment which English crews received when driven by stress of weather into Spanish-American ports. The real point at issue was the Spaniards' claim, not to the monopoly of trade with their own possessions, but to the monopoly of all navigation in the Caribbean Sea. The claims of the Inquisition had become by this time merely a technical grievance, although Cromwell's mind, with its Elizabethan outlook, doubtless exaggerated their effect. A warfare of reprisal limited in scope was still generally distinguished from a regularly declared conflict, and Cromwell's instructions to General Venables, the military commander, show that this was his purpose : " Either there was peace with the Spaniards in the West Indies, or there was not. If peace, they had violated it, and to seek reparation was just." The locality of attack he left to the officers to decide when they should reach the spot. His general order was " to gain an interest in that part of the West Indies in possession of the Spaniards." The Isthmus of Panama he regarded as a favourable place ; the Spanish Main and Hispaniola also suggested themselves, and the commanders of the expedition chose the latter. Whichever they took first was to be viewed only as a beginning of the complete conquest of Spanish America.

General Venables and Admiral Penn collected their forces towards the end of 1654. The troops consisted of less than 3000 men made up of small drafts from the various regiments in the British Isles and a number of pressed civilians from the London streets. There were said not to have been a thousand trained soldiers among them, and they never even mustered as one body before embarking. At Barbados they were to be joined by as many West Indian colonists as the English islands could supply. Such a disorganized force was not in accordance with Cromwell's usual practice, but he considered that, however feeble, it would be sufficient for the purpose, and he did not expect to see any of the men come home again. His intention was that after making their conquest they should turn themselves into settlers and hold it permanently in that character. Venables evidently understood his mission in this light, for he took his wife with him. After picking up the colonial levies at Barbados, Venables landed in Hispaniola on April 14, 1655, and marched to attack San Domingo, the capital. Drake's landing place of 1585 was no longer available, and the commanders had to choose a point thirty miles from the city. The hunger, thirst and dysentery of this march demoralized the undisciplined troops. They made two attempts to approach the city, and each time broke in panic on being attacked by small bodies of Spanish horsemen. Venables, himself dangerously ill, saw that the idea of a siege was hopeless. He drew off, and sought for an easier prey as an alternative to returning empty-handed. In May the expedition appeared off Jamaica, an island almost unknown to the English, and inhabited by so few Spanish colonists that it could only raise five hundred fighting men to oppose the landing. Santiago de la Vega (Spanish Town) was easily taken, and the expedition then turned to the work of making a permanent plantation. Penn and Venables returned to England, and Cromwell in disgust sent them to the Tower, not, as is often said, for misconducting the enterprise, but for deserting their post and leaving their acquisition open to recapture.

The Spaniards, however, appear to have regarded Jamaica as lightly as did its captors, and made no immediate move to disturb the new colony.[1] At first it seemed that the forces of nature would alone exterminate the English settlers. Starvation and disease struck them down, and a terrible mortality ensued. It was not until the end of 1656 that things took a more hopeful turn. Then the discontented officers, who were doing more harm than good, were allowed to return home, and a capable governor took the problem in hand. The Protector advertised the advantages of Jamaica very widely in New England in the hope of attracting colonists, but the New Englanders would not stir. Finally he induced 1600 people to transfer themselves from Nevis. Even of this party, seasoned to the West Indian climate, two-thirds perished in the first three months. After these losses the colony very slowly attained to prosperity.

The poor outcome of the Western Design put an end to the Protector's colonial ambitions. It also involved him in war with Spain and ultimately in alliance with France. The Spanish war was less popular and less profitable than the Dutch. The Spanish fleets avoided action, and Spanish commerce was conducted principally in neutral vessels. The war had considerable political results, but its effects on English expansion were comparatively slight, and we need therefore enter into few details concerning it. At the beginning of 1656 Blake and Edward Montagu sailed too late to intercept a Plate fleet ; but in September of the same year Captain Stayner fell upon another near Cadiz, capturing half the treasure and sinking the remainder. Thirty-eight waggon-loads of silver rolled into the Tower, and the amount privately taken by the seamen was more than that received by the government. Through the winter of 1656-7 Blake maintained the blockade of Cadiz from the now friendly base of Lisbon. In the spring he heard that a Plate fleet had made for the Canaries to watch for an opportunity of reaching Spain. Sailing in pursuit he found the treasure landed and out of reach, and the ships anchored under the guns of Santa Cruz. He and Stayner entered the harbour, silenced the forts and destroyed the entire fleet, coming out safely on the turn of the tide with less than two hundred killed and wounded. In August Blake died as his ship sailed into Plymouth Sound. Meanwhile the

---

[1] Later, in 1658 and 1660, small Spanish forces demonstrated off the coast without effect.

declaration of war with Spain had given the royalists new hope. Charles II. moved into the Spanish Netherlands, where he organized Scottish and Irish regiments in the hope of using them to regain his throne. To Cromwell it was important to engage these royalist forces on foreign soil. Partly with this object, and partly in furtherance of the old scheme of a great northern coalition, he entered into an alliance with Cardinal Mazarin to finish the long war on the north-east frontier of France. Six thousand regular English troops crossed the Channel in 1657. In the following summer they assisted the great Turenne to defeat the royalist and Spanish army at the Battle of the Dunes beneath the walls of Dunkirk. The fall of that port followed and, in accordance with the agreement, it remained in English hands. Two months afterwards Cromwell died, and his great plan for using it as a base from which to dominate northern Europe perished with him. The Spanish war, with its two acquisitions of Dunkirk and Jamaica, gained at ruinous cost, has been reckoned the cardinal error of his foreign policy.

Although the statesmen of the Puritan ascendancy laid the foundations of a comprehensive and successful system of propagating British trade and shipping, it does not appear that any notable revival took place until after the Restoration. Commerce had suffered considerably from the effects of the Civil War, and the evil plight of the East India Company had been typical of the fortunes of the other chartered corporations. About 1650 there was a real general improvement, which the Dutch and Spanish wars were soon to neutralize. The ordinance of that year, prohibiting foreign trade with the English colonies, had a larger effect than the more famous measure of 1651.[1] The immense captures of the Dutch war paid some of its cost, but the Spanish war struck a deadly blow at English commerce. The privateers of Dunkirk and Ostend swept the Channel and the North Sea, and unparalleled expenditure on guards and convoys failed to cope with the evil. At Cromwell's death the state was practically insolvent, trade was dying and the people in great distress.[2] An argument based on the increased yield of the customs has pointed to a more favourable condition of affairs ; but it neglects to notice that the rates had been substantially raised and the methods of collection improved. One deduction from contemporary statistics is interesting ; they show that over seventy per cent. of the country's foreign commerce was conducted from London. This advance of the capital at the expense of the other seaports had been going on progressively from the beginning of the Tudor period.

The rule of Cromwell, and the short-lived experiments which followed it until 1660 showed that in public opinion at large the pendulum was swinging steadily backwards in the direction of monarchy and its accompanying institutions. In common with other democratic ideas, the agitation against the chartered companies, very evident during

[1] Beer, *Origins*, pp. 365-6.   [2] Scott, i. pp. 259-62.

the Civil War, gradually lost its force. When the Restoration took place there was a general acquiescence in the reconstitution of these monopolies, and a recognition of their usefulness to the interests of foreign trade. Cromwell, in fact, showed what monarchy might do for the nation, and outlined an imperial policy which bore its chief fruit under his successors.

CHAPTER IX

THE RESTORED STUARTS AND THE SHAPING OF THE MERCANTILE SYSTEM, 1660-1688

" The undoubted Interest of England is Trade, since it is that only which can
make us either Rich or Safe ; for without a powerful Navy we should be a Prey
to our Neighbours, and without Trade we could neither have Seamen nor Ships."
                                                    LETTER OF 1672.

" All Colonies and Plantations do endamage their Mother Kingdom, whereof
the Trades of such Plantations are not confined to their said Mother Kingdom
by good Laws and severe Execution of those Laws."
                                                    SIR JOSIAH CHILD, 1693.

WHEN Charles II. returned to England in 1660 he found the international position of his kingdom very different from that which it had
occupied under his father and his grandfather. It had been the work
of the Long Parliament and Cromwell to substitute considerations
bearing upon national power for the dynastic and personal motives
which had swayed the foreign policy of the early Stuarts. Puritan
external policy had been two-sided. Besides the conception of a
great Protestant coalition, which had been peculiar to Cromwell and
had perished with him, it had also promoted the secular aim of competing for the first place in the international race for wealth. To be
a great state, it had argued, England must be a rich state ; wealth
was best attainable by success in oceanic commerce, which entailed
the possession and exploitation of colonies ; for the colonial trade a
great mercantile marine was essential, and this in its turn would
demand the support of and at the same time would infuse life into,
a great fighting navy ; such a navy could only be maintained by the
wealthy state which its office was to defend. This has been described
as argument in a circle. But the simile creates a false impression.
The circle was not a closed one ; its diameter expanded with every
interaction of the forces revolving in its sweep, until at length it grew
into the wide base which supported the old empire through the French
wars of the eighteenth century and provided a foundation of sea-
power upon which to construct a new empire after the disasters of
1775-83.   This was the secular gospel which Charles II. and Restoration
England received from the Puritans. They cherished it and improved

upon it with as much zest as they displayed in casting away the religious gospel that accompanied it. In one aspect therefore we may regard the cynical and businesslike Charles II. as the dutiful heir of the pious yet also businesslike Oliver Cromwell.

Charles II.'s marriage followed shortly upon his accession. It was the first royal marriage deliberately planned to promote national rather than dynastic interests. Spain and France had concluded their long war by the Peace of the Pyrenees in 1659. In this peace Portugal was not included. Deserted by her late ally, she was left to face the probability of reconquest by Spain in spite of her gallant struggle for independence, maintained since 1640. England also had a question outstanding with Portugal's oppressor. The Spanish Netherlands had been Charles II.'s asylum during the later years of his exile, and the rulers at Madrid expected him on regaining his throne to restore to them Dunkirk and Jamaica. But without hesitation he identified himself with Cromwell's foreign policy, and refused to give up either of the Protector's conquests. His marriage with Catherine of Braganza quickly followed. Charles received in Tangier a coveted naval base in the Straits of Gibraltar, and in Bombay a new *point d'appui* from which to exploit the trade of the east. To quote his own words: "the principal advantages we propose to ourself by this entire conjunction with Portugal are the advancement of the trade of this nation and the enlargement of our own territories and dominions." England rendered service for the value received. Her auxiliaries helped to repel the Spanish invaders, and the independence of Portugal was formally acknowledged in 1668.

A strong element of mutual suspicion, neutralized only by the supple and feline personality of Mazarin, had coloured the military alliance between Cromwell and the French. With its object achieved in the fall of Dunkirk and the peace of 1659 that alliance would probably have given place to enmity had the Protector lived. Charles himself, although in his later years the dependent of Louis XIV., was by no means subservient at the outset. The Cromwellian Major Sedgwick had seized the French settlements in Nova Scotia in 1655, and Charles made no haste to return them upon his accession. His sale of Dunkirk to the French king has been much misrepresented. It was a justifiable act of policy, not a betrayal of the nation. Its garrison and defences cost £100,000 a year, and in itself it was not worth the price. Further, its retention would have entailed the abandonment of Tangier, for the English government could not afford to maintain two such fortresses. Charles saw good reason to prefer Tangier, and George Monck, whose honesty is unquestioned, concurred in the decision.[1] Already at the Restoration the instinct of the country saw in France a future enemy. Charles did not run counter to that instinct until some ten years had elapsed and financial entanglements, not all of his own making, drove

[1] Corbett, *England in the Mediterranean*, ii. pp. 12-16 ; *Polit. Hist. of Engl.* vol. viii. by R. Lodge, 1910, p. 23.

him into the secret anti-national intrigues which have brought disgrace upon his name.

Of more immediate consequence than the ambition of France was the attitude of the United Provinces. They had recovered with astonishing speed from the effects of the Puritan war. During the later years of the Protectorate they had been openly provocative, although Cromwell's Protestant bias had rendered him slow to take offence. The English alliance with Portugal now infuriated them, for they regarded themselves as the natural heirs of the dying Portuguese colonial empire. In fact, they had already seized the Portuguese stations on the Guinea Coast, from which they sought to monopolize the slave trade ; they had gained at one time an extensive grip upon Brazil, from which a Portuguese revival had, however, ejected them ; and they had almost completed the conquest of Ceylon. The English policy of the Restoration was therefore certain to bring about a renewed conflict with the Dutch, even had it not embarked upon the series of economic measures which we shall presently have to consider.

Such was the general position of England in the world when Charles II. took up the reigns of government. At his back he had a public opinion which showed that on the question of maritime expansion the nation was substantially united. The commercial interest had never enjoyed so much weight in politics before, and the landed interest as yet saw no reason to disapprove of the commercial policy. The amount of capital free for investment had steadily increased since the days of the Tudors, a stable government seemed now to have been attained, and a spontaneous outburst of national energy, comparable to that of the Elizabethans, sought its outlet, as theirs had done, in a new series of external adventures. In one direction it manifested itself in a revival and increase of the great trading organizations ; in another it took the form of the projection of new colonies by men of wealth and political influence. Of the leaders of the movement some had been royalist exiles, like James, Duke of York, Prince Rupert and the Earl of Clarendon ; others, like Monk, now Duke of Albemarle, Montagu, now Earl of Sandwich, Anthony Ashley Cooper, afterwards Earl of Shaftesbury, and Sir George Downing, were survivors of the Cromwellian regime. The success of these men in their new surroundings shows that nationalism had been the essential, Puritanism only an incidental, of those who carried out the external policy of the Puritan ascendancy.

It will be sufficient in this survey to summarize the history of the trading companies, its detailed treatment being reserved to a later chapter. The East India and Muscovy Companies, both moribund under the Puritans, received new charters and entered upon a fresh lease of life. The Duke of York founded the Royal Adventurers to Africa in 1662. Ten years afterwards this body gave place to the Royal African Company, which remained in existence until the abolition of the slave trade a century and a half later. In 1670 Prince Rupert and his associates received a charter as the Hudson's Bay Company, which continues its career to the present day. The Levant Company and the regulated corporations for the various European trades all shared to a greater or less extent in the revival of prosperity, although as conditions became more settled a growing tendency evinced itself to throw the shorter trade routes open to all comers as in modern times. The expansion of commerce continued progressively throughout the Restoration period, culminating in the decade beginning in 1682, a time, curiously enough, when internal political prospects were assuming a very gloomy aspect.

The Commonwealth, by the ordinances of 1650 and 1651, had sketched out a maritime policy which, as we have seen, was in itself a recapitulation of ideas previously existing in a vague and uncorrelated condition.[1] The foreign wars of 1652-9 have obscured the evidence bearing upon the actual utility of the Puritan legislation. All that we can say with certainty is that contemporary thought was unanimously in favour of its continuance. Accordingly the government brought forward a new Navigation Act in the Parliament of 1660, all the measures passed since the execution of Charles I. having automatically lapsed at the Restoration ; and the Act of 1660 combined the essential features of those of 1650 and 1651, and contained also a feature not found in those measures. The new Act declared[2] that certain European commodities, including all those of Russia and Turkey, must be imported only in English ships or those of the country of origin. The remaining European goods, if imported in foreign ships, were subject to additional duties. Foreign-caught fish was to pay heavy duties, and foreign ships were forbidden to trade between ports on the English and Irish coasts. So far as concerned trade with Europe the Act of 1660 was thus slightly less stringent than that of 1651. But its more important provisions concerned trade with other continents. From the non-English parts of America, Asia, and Africa no goods might be imported save in English shipping and direct from the place of origin or a port near to it. An important exception, however, provided that English ships might bring from Spain and Portugal the produce of those countries' colonies. Finally, the trade of English colonies, import and export, might be carried on only in English shipping, and certain enumerated colonial products (sugar, tobacco, cotton-wool, indigo, ginger and dye-woods) were to be shipped exclusively to England or other English colonies. Such colonial wares as were not in the enumerated list might still be sent direct to foreign countries. This enumeration policy, or restriction of important products to the English market, was a new and, to the colonists, an oppressive regulation. For the purposes of the Act English shipping included colonial and, at first,

[1] For an elaboration of this point see *Acts of the Privy Council*, Colonial Series, vol. i. ed. W. L. Grant and James Munro, 1908, pp. xxvii-xxix.

[2] For a fuller analysis see G. L. Beer, *The Old Colonial System*, New York, 1912, vol. i. pp. 61-74.

Irish [1] vessels, which had to be English, Irish or colonial built, and manned by crews at least three-fourths of English, Irish or colonial nationality. Scottish ships were not included in the scope of the privileges. The provisions relating to the manning of the ships, and the enumeration of all the more valuable colonial products, thus rendered the Act of 1660 much more restrictive upon colonial trade than that of 1651. The only colonial merchandise of first-class importance which escaped enumeration was the fish from the Newfoundland and New England fisheries. The restriction of Indian goods to the English market was provided for, apart from the Act, by the terms of the East India Company's Charter.

Under the Act of 1660 goods from the continent of Europe might still be sent direct to the colonies, in competition with English manufactures, provided they went in English bottoms. To put a stop to this the Staple Act of 1663 prohibited the introduction into English colonies of goods not of English origin, unless such goods were first brought to England and then re-shipped to the colonies. England thus became the "staple" for the supply of non-English wares to her possessions. A few exceptions were allowed to the operation of this law, the principal being that of salt from southern Europe for the Newfoundland and New England fisheries.

The free intercourse between the several colonies, and between New England (on the score of the fish trade) and the continent of Europe, led to evasion of the enumerating clauses of the 1660 Act. New Englanders bought tobacco and sugar in excess of their own colony's needs and shipped the surplus to foreign countries. To render this illicit trade unprofitable, the home government passed in 1673 the Plantation Duties Act, imposing at the place of lading additional duties on all shippers of enumerated goods who could not give security that they were taking the goods to England only.

The above Acts constituted the mercantile code of the Restoration. In themselves they appear unjustly restrictive of colonial trade and liberties, and have been severely criticized on that account. But it is untrue to regard the mother-country as taking all and giving nothing. She bore, almost alone, the burden of imperial defence, which included not only convoys and military expeditions in time of war, but continuous and expensive measures against the Barbary pirates in time of peace. In this way the tax-payer at home paid heavily for the mere existence of the colonies. The peopling of the plantations by emigrants from home was also, according to the ideas of the time, an economic loss to England, for which she could legitimately seek compensation. Colonial shipping shared the privileges accorded to English shipping. And, more important still, although colonial merchandise was debarred from free vent in the continental markets, it was heavily protected in the English market. The Book of Rates, drawn up contemporaneously with the Act of 1660, should be read in conjunction

[1] A later Act (1671) prohibited shipping of enumerated goods to Ireland.

with it. By assigning arbitrary values for the assessment of pound-
age on various classes of goods it gave the colonies an immense
advantage. Foreign sugar paid nearly three times as much duty as
colonial sugar ; foreign tobacco paid exactly three times as much ;
and foreign indigo more than three times as much. On minor products
the discrimination was still more marked.[1] The result was that the
enumerated goods had a practical monopoly of the English market.
Also, in case such goods were re-exported from England, the government remitted one-half, or on tobacco three-quarters, of the duties
paid at their entry into the country. Thus, by the incidence of these
duties the home consumer was heavily burdened in the cause of the
empire as a whole.

Armed with this code, the statesmen of the Restoration set out to
make their country rich as the centre of a trading empire. It has been
charged against them that their system was an unintelligent application
of crude and childish maxims by persons who enacted their laws
without thought, and turned at once to other matters in complete
heedlessness of the consequences. But this is to make the cavaliers
of the Restoration responsible for the follies of George III. and his
friends a century later. The original laws of trade and navigation
may have been voted by country squires ignorant of their true meaning ;
but they were certainly drafted and administered by men who were
deeply versed in the economic doctrine and practice of their time,
who had good reason drawn from experience for believing in their
efficacy for the purpose in view, who watched keenly for flaws in their
operation, and ever kept a sensitive finger upon the pulse of colonial
opinion. Officials overseas were encouraged to memorialize the
government, and a host of pamphleteers constantly discussed colonial
policy and ventilated grievances and new opinions. Some of these
writers were colonists themselves, and many were merchants of experience. Sir George Downing, who seems to have been the originator
of the enumeration policy and of the Staple Act of 1663, had resided
in Massachusetts, the West Indies and the United Provinces, was a
graduate of Harvard, and had gained experience in financial, administrative and diplomatic work under the Protectorate ere he came to
the task which enabled him to leave his mark upon the history of his
country. The Earl of Clarendon, again, the chief minister until 1667,
was at one with his sovereign in a sincere belief in the value of
colonization and the patriotic purpose of the legislation for its control.
It was after the passing of the Stuarts that the corrupt and tyrannous
aspects of the system became apparent, and it is one of the paradoxes
which arise from a comparison of our political with our external history
that the last two Stuart kings, whose arbitrary government at home
brought about the fall of their house, administered the colonies at
least as justly and as sympathetically as did the constitutional
monarchy which succeeded them.

[1] Beer, *op. cit.* i. 133-4.

In the latter half of the seventeenth century opinions concerning emigration underwent a complete change as compared with those held in the times of Elizabeth and James I. The transference of population across the Atlantic no longer appeared as a beneficial easement of congestion at home, a view which Hakluyt and his contemporaries had put forward as their principal incentive to colonization. Public opinion now held that England was under-populated, and that emigration was a distinct loss to the home country unless the emigrants supplied her with commodities which she could not produce on her own soil. Population was now appraised in terms of labour and, to a less extent, of military efficiency. An Englishman going to Massachusetts was a unit of wealth and a possible soldier lost to England without corresponding gain, since the products of Massachusetts competed with those of the English landowner. An Englishman going to Barbados, on the other hand, was held to compensate for this loss by the fact that he might there exploit the labour of a dozen negro slaves in producing the sugar which could not be grown upon English soil. The government therefore did not encourage wholesale and indiscriminate emigration from England, although it approved the introduction into the colonies of suitable foreigners from the Continent, such as the persecuted Huguenots of France. Scotsmen and Irishmen also, still regarded in some respects as aliens, were given facilities for settling in certain of the colonies. Emigration for religious reasons to a large extent fell off, the principal exception being that of the Quakers to the Jerseys and Pennsylvania; but the original settlers of those regions included a fair proportion of foreigners.

It followed from these considerations that the policy of the time concerned itself primarily with developing colonies of the slave-holding, plantation type, located in or near the tropics, and producing merchandise which would supplement rather than compete with that of the mother-country. Barbados satisfied these conditions brilliantly, and was thus accounted "the principal pearl in his Majesty's crown." Much was hoped for from the Leeward Islands, and Jamaica seemed to be a potential Barbados, more than twenty times the size of its prototype. The proprietors of the Carolinas expected to produce there the wines, oils, fruits and silks of Southern Europe, and so to render England independent of yet another foreign source of supply. Virginia and Maryland received but a qualified favour, for tobacco was falling rapidly in price and becoming a drug in the world's markets, and, moreover, the mercantilists at home could not forget that the western counties of England had proved themselves capable of tobacco-growing, and that the industry had been harshly suppressed in the interest of the colonists.[1] Farther north indeed, the reign of Charles II. witnessed the acquisition of New Jersey and New York, which

---

[1] Beer, *op. cit.* i. pp. 138-47. There were said at one time to have been 6,000 tobacco farms in Gloucestershire and the neighbouring counties. Troops were employed to destroy the plants, and much rioting took place.

certainly did not come up to the colonial ideals of the time. But England conquered these districts mainly for reasons of commercial strategy, and not because they were desirable in themselves. The presence of Dutch jurisdictions midway between New England and the southern plantations rendered impossible the strict enforcement of the Navigation Acts. New England itself remained the one unvalued dominion, a constant political anxiety and a source of weakness to the whole colonial system. It is within the truth to say that the Restoration statesmen were heartily sorry it had ever come into existence. With the exception of furs and a few ships' masts its exports had no value to their economic scheme. Even its fishery employed no English seamen, and contributed nothing to the available strength of the navy. It afforded a small market for English manufacturers, but it neutralized even that benefit by persistent infractions of the Staple Act in the ports of southern Europe. Newfoundland, on the other hand, remained highly prized. Care was taken to prevent the few settlers from doing much fishing, and the bulk of the catch was made by the English west-country mariners, who sold their fish in the Mediterranean, and returned to England with the proceeds, thus meriting the commendations of the mercantilists by improving the balance of English trade. The general approval of tropical colonies and the disfavour shown to those in temperate climates appears in strong contrast to the ideas of our own time. The conception of England as a mother of nations was non-existent; the English colonial planter was principally valued as a slave-driver, compelling negroes or white unfortunates to make wealth for the great maritime state of which the London counting-houses formed the core.

With the development of the plantation colonies the slave trade became a matter of vital importance to the empire. In the early years of the seventeenth century negroes had not played any large part, the manual labour of the plantations having been performed by the original settlers, by indentured servants, who were really slaves for a term of years, by transported criminals, and by prisoners of war taken principally in Ireland and Scotland in the civil troubles. Before 1660 Barbados seems to have been the only colony which used negroes extensively. After that date it became necessary to look to the supply. The Dutch had ousted the Portuguese from the Guinea Coast. English Guinea companies had hitherto been struggling and unsuccessful, although they maintained precariously a few African posts; and unattached traders, interlopers as they were commonly called, had carried on much of the trade. But slaving itself was a business which had changed since the days of Sir John Hawkins. Promiscuous kidnapping, such as he had indulged in, no longer yielded sufficient results. For a continuous supply it became necessary to buy from regular dealers who worked in the interior of Africa, and brought their captives down to the European stations on the coast. The prosperity of the plantations therefore demanded an organized trade, and the revived African companies, which we have already noticed, were the outcome. Their fortunes were closely bound up with those of the plantations, and they formed an essential part of the colonial system. The colonists, however, complained of the Companies' rapacity, Barbados alleging that the price had risen from £12-£16 a head under the open trade system to £25-£30 under the monopoly.[1] An English protest against the slave trade and its methods was published anonymously in London in 1684. It was possibly written by a Quaker. The Quakers of Pennsylvania certainly protested four years later ; but the world at large turned a deaf ear, and it was not until well on in the following century that any general sentiment of abhorrence became manifest.

Sea-power, as we have seen, was at once the object and the instrument of the colonial system ; and the growth of the mercantile marine was the critical test of that system's success in the eyes of those who devised it. On this head they were justified, for the mercantile marine unquestionably throve under the laws of trade and navigation. Between 1660 and 1688 its total tonnage was approximately doubled. Of this increase the West Indian trade accounted for the largest part, but that with the American colonies bore its share. In the decade 1660-1670 the value of the American traffic was one-tenth of the whole of our foreign commerce ; at the end of the century the proportion had risen to one-seventh ;[2] and since a ship commonly made but one double voyage a year across the Atlantic, whilst to the European ports it might make two or three, the above ratios under-represent the impetus given to English shipping. We may emphasize this point by a quotation from a recognized authority : " The Navigation Acts have been generally condemned by modern economists as having conduced neither to the naval nor commercial greatness of England, but this seems a difficult thesis to maintain in face of the well-attested fact that the carrying trade of England was, before their enactment, in the hands of the Dutch, and that afterwards, although not at once or at one bound, England became the great carrier of Europe." [3]

Side by side with the colonial and commercial system the Restoration rulers created an administrative machinery to operate it. The close of 1660 saw the supersession of Cromwell's Colonial Board of forty-three members by separate Councils for Trade (November 7) and for Foreign Plantations (December 1). These two bodies worked in co-operation, twenty-eight members being common to both. They consisted of privy councillors, ex-officials of the colonies, planters, and merchants. Their function was advisory : they heard evidence and made reports for the guidance of the Privy Council, which took action upon the information they supplied. In 1664-5 both these councils expired, their work being taken over by committees of the Privy Council. A few years later the earlier bodies were revived, the Council of Trade

[1] Beer, op. cit. i. p. 337.   [2] Beer, op. cit. i. pp. 13-15.
[3] H. E. Egerton, Short History of British Colonial Policy, p. 62.

in 1668, and that for Plantations in 1670; and in September, 1672, they were fused into one as the Council for Trade and Plantations. This body, whose members were paid for their services, did much good work during its short life, holding regular meetings twice a week, hearing petitions and complaints, and watching the actual working of legislation. But it was abolished in 1674, the Privy Council again assuming responsibility for its duties. The next year saw the evolution of a more enduring arrangement. The Privy Council Committee dealing with the colonies received a permanent secretary with a proper clerical staff and facilities for preserving archives; and, under the style of the Lords of Trade, did excellent work for twenty years to come.[1] It was during this period that the administration of the old empire reached its highest pitch of efficiency. The success of the Lords of Trade was largely due to the systematic labours of Sir Robert Southwell and William Blathwayt, the first permanent secretaries; and it is fair to say that from 1675 the government possessed for the first time something approaching to a colonial office in the modern sense of the term.

We may see from the foregoing that in the generation which followed the foundation of a colonial empire the English government was making a serious effort to cope with the administrative and economic problems to which it gave rise. The colonial system, firmly established for good or ill, represents the constructive achievement of later Jacobean statesmanship, which in internal politics has nothing comparable to it to show. For purposes of comparison the actual working of the system in the various colonies may here be briefly glanced at, although it will be more fully treated in subsequent chapters. The matter is one upon which varying opinions prevail, the principal question at issue being the extent to which the laws of trade and navigation were really enforced or evaded. Some investigators have held that in most of the colonies they were little better than a farce; others, including a recent and weighty authority [2] who has thoroughly sifted the statistical evidence, conclude that enforcement was the rule and evasion the exception. According to this latter view the administration of the Acts became more effective as the Restoration period progressed.

[1] Beer, i. p. 258; C. M. Andrews, *Colonial Self-Government*, New York, 1904, pp. 26-30.

[2] G. L. Beer, work cited. In a general summing-up of the navigation policy he says, "the actual end attained coincided with the aims of those enacting these measures." In dealing with each colony separately he comes on the whole to the same conclusion, although admitting exceptions. Prof. Egerton gives the general impression that the Acts were effective except in New England. Prof. E. Channing, *History of the United States*, vol. ii., takes the opposed view; but Prof. C. M. Andrews, in *Cambr. Hist. of the Br. Empire*, i. ch. ix, gives many instances of friction and discontent which could hardly have been so evident if the Acts had been a dead-letter. P. L. Kaye in *English Colonial Administration under Clarendon*, Baltimore, 1905, p. 149, gives the close of the Dutch wars (1674) as the opening date of practical enforcement.

Barbados continuously and bitterly complained of the working of the system. The year 1660 approximately marked the end of a period of almost incredible prosperity in the island. The numbers of the planters indeed decreased, but the fortunate individuals who engrossed the original small holdings into large estates revelled in an orgy of money-making which obviously could not last for ever. The Barbadians attributed the decline which then set in to the restriction of markets for their exports, but the increasing world-output of sugar, and the consequent fall in price, undoubtedly played a great part. There was some evasion of the enumeration regulations in the early years, but it ceased after 1681. The efficient administration of the Leeward Islands began in 1672. The trade laws were enforced and gave rise to fewer complaints. The prosperity of the islands steadily increased, but their combined wealth remained many times smaller than that of Barbados. Jamaica progressed slowly but steadily, and with an almost complete absence of grumbling against the colonial system. The operations of the buccaneers diverted its energies from industry, and its more rapid growth dates only from 1680, by which time buccaneering was on the decline.

On the mainland the Carolinas, first planted in 1663, grew very slowly during the seventeenth century. They failed to answer the expectations of their proprietors, and successfully resisted the efforts of the home government to enforce the laws of trade. But their relative weight in the empire during this period remained insignificant. Virginia and Maryland protested against the enumeration of tobacco. As with sugar, the fall in price was severe, but was admitted to be principally due to overproduction. Bacon's rebellion in 1676 is now recognized to have been due, not to the Navigation Acts, but to local political causes. In these two colonies there was no extensive violation of the Acts. The more northerly colonies were in a different position. They produced no enumerated goods of their own, but violated the Acts by purchase in the tobacco and sugar plantations and re-export to Europe. But the total of shipping thus employed, even when the illicit trade was most flourishing, bore a small proportion to that legitimately voyaging between England and the sugar and tobacco colonies. The middle states, New York and New Jersey, whilst in Dutch hands, undoubtedly rendered the navigation system abortive. After their conquest in 1664 the abuse diminished, but seems still to have remained considerable. The matter was not firmly taken in hand until after the close of the last Dutch war (1674). Even then evasion was never completely put down. Pennsylvania (founded 1680-1) did not develop sufficiently during the pre-revolution period for its relation to the colonial system to be defined. In New England the Navigation Acts long remained a dead-letter, even after the passing of the Plantation Duties Act of 1673. But here again the home government at length bestirred itself, and after a protracted dispute annulled the New England charters. Sir Edmund Andros took up the government of these colonies as a united dominion in 1686. In his short term of office he began to enforce the Acts, but the revolution at home in 1688 swept away the basis of his power, and left the constitutional monarchy to deal with the problem anew. On one point it is necessary to be clear. The restriction of enumerated products to the English market was the main cause of discontent and of such evasion as took place. But in New England and elsewhere there was no word of complaint against the exclusion of foreign shipping from the colonial trade. Here colonists and Englishmen were in agreement, for all shared in the protection accorded. When all has been said, however, we must admit that the colonial system in its actual working gave rise to a chronic friction between the colonists and the home population, which ultimately bore bitter fruit ; and its final justification must be that a colonial empire would not have been possible at all under any other arrangement.[1]

The Dutch recovery after the war of 1652-4, coupled with the vigorous colonial policy of the Restoration, caused the rivalry between the two nations once more to become acute. The Acts of 1660 and 1663 had the effect of prohibiting all Dutch trade, import or export, with the West Indian and American colonies. In the east the English acquisition of Bombay and the emergence of the East India Company from its long eclipse revived ancient controversies both in India and the islands, the Dutch being especially annoyed by the English alliance with Portugal. An English garrison at Tangier threatened their hold upon the Mediterranean trade, and the English African Company promised to cut short their projected monopoly of the slave supply. On the frontier between New Amsterdam and Connecticut the colonists of the two nations were face to face ; and in Guiana, where Lord Willoughby had for some years been developing his plantation of Surinam, there lay yet another cause of disagreement. Hostilities began in two separate regions in 1664, and war was formally declared in the following year—the first purely colonial war in English history. The French also had interests conflicting with those of England both in North America and the West Indies, and Louis XIV. joined in on the side of the Dutch in January, 1666. This French share in the conflict is very lightly touched upon by historians who concern themselves principally with home affairs, but it had a considerable effect on English colonial fortunes. Neither Charles II. nor John de Witt, the Grand Pensionary of Holland, had any keen personal desire for war, but the mercantile interests were too strong for them, and the nations as a whole were each equally ready to settle the question of maritime supremacy. " What matters this or that reason ? " said Monck. " What we want is more of the trade which the Dutch now have." And on the other side a corresponding sentiment prevailed.

The fighting in English waters resembled in its general character that of the earlier war—terrific combats fought to the bitter end with

[1] Cf. Channing, ii. p. 8.

alternating success, the stubbornness of the Dutch in battle not giving them a sufficient preponderance to neutralize the greater relative damage wrought upon them by the destruction of trade. The condition and the administration of the English navy had deteriorated since the days of Vane and Blake, but not, as the event showed, to such a marked extent as the disparagers of the Restoration would have us believe.[1] In 1665 the Duke of York went to sea as commander-in-chief of the English fleet, with Prince Rupert and the Earl of Sandwich as his subordinates. The Dutch under Opdam attacked him off Lowestoft on June 3, and were defeated with the loss of thirty-two ships and six thousand men, of whom two thousand were taken prisoners. The English loss was comparatively light. Sandwich then went in search of a great massed convoy of the Dutch East and West Indies and Levant trade, homeward bound by the north of Scotland route. He found the convoy refuging at Bergen, and attacked it in the port without first coming to an arrangement with the Danish government for sharing the spoil. The land defences therefore fired upon him and he was beaten off, but many of the merchantmen afterwards fell into English hands. In 1666 France declared war, and the report of a French fleet coming from the west caused the government to detach Prince Rupert, leaving Monck in inferior force in the Narrow Seas. De Ruyter, now in command of the Dutch, seized the opportunity. On June 1 he attacked Monck, beginning the celebrated Four Days Battle, one of the bloodiest ever fought upon the sea. For two days Monck, overmatched, continued the fight unassisted, the fleets gradually drifting westwards down the Channel. On the third Rupert rejoined, and the struggle ended on June 4 by both sides being too severely damaged to continue. The English lost twenty ships, five thousand men killed and two to three thousand prisoners. The Dutch lost six or seven ships and two thousand men.[2] Two months later the opponents met with equal forces off the North Foreland, and the English won a complete victory, inflicting a loss of twenty ships and seven thousand men with comparatively small casualties on their own side.

Whilst these events had been proceeding, the plague of 1665 and the burning of London in the following year had caused severe damage to English finances. Bishop Burnet says, " The plague broke the trade of the nation, and swept away about a hundred thousand souls." Charles II., destitute of funds, laid up the great ships of the fleet in 1667, and relied upon commerce destruction and negotiation to finish the war. In June de Ruyter raided the Thames estuary, entered the Medway, burned or captured many ships and bombarded Chatham. The material damage was considerable, and the loss of prestige by England still more important. This event marked the conclusion of hostilities in Europe.

[1] Cf. *Cambridge Modern History*, vol. v. ch. viii by J. R. Tanner and C. T. Atkinson.
[2] Accounts vary greatly as to the losses in this battle.

On the ocean and in the colonies the war had begun a year earlier than at home. In 1664 Admiral Robert Holmes, who played a notable part in commerce-destroying operations in this and the next war, sailed for the Guinea Coast with a force which included two king's ships. He inflicted some damage upon the Dutch trading posts, but after his withdrawal de Ruyter appeared with a stronger squadron to make reprisals. De Ruyter captured six stations belonging to the African Company, and caused enormous loss to its trade. In the same year Charles II. granted to his brother the Duke of York permission to capture New Amsterdam at the mouth of the Hudson, and the coast extending thence southward to Delaware Bay and eastward to Connecticut. The duke was to hold these territories as a proprietary colony. His representative, Colonel Richard Nicolls, carried out the conquest with a small force. New Amsterdam surrendered without fighting in August 1664, and Delaware in the following October. At the end of the year Charles gave orders for the expulsion of the Dutch from Tobago, and an expedition from Jamaica reduced the island early in 1665. All these hostilities took place before the declaration of war in Europe.

Francis, Lord Willoughby, had begun the plantation of Surinam in Guiana in 1650. Four years later he obtained a patent of proprietorship from the Protector, and Charles II. confirmed the grant in 1663. At the outbreak of war the colony had four thousand inhabitants and extended for forty leagues along the coast. It was beginning to yield crops of good sugar. Early in 1666 Willoughby captured the neighbouring stations of Paramaribo and Essequibo from the Dutch, and Cayenne from the French. He had then to return to resist the French in the Leeward Islands. As in Guinea, the Dutch delivered a heavy counterstroke. Later in 1666 seven Dutch warships with one thousand men retook their lost posts and appeared off Surinam. William Byam, the governor, showed fight, but had finally to surrender. In October, 1667, Sir John Harman once more captured Surinam for England, but the Treaty of Breda at home had already assigned it to the Dutch, and it had to be given up.[1] In the meantime the French had been actively attacking the English Leeward Islands. In April, 1666, they took the English portion of St. Kitts after heavy fighting accompanied by savage atrocities. In November they conquered Antigua and Montserrat, ruining the English plantations by carrying off the negroes to their own islands. Lord Willoughby was drowned in a hurricane at the end of the year whilst hurrying to the rescue. His brother William took up his command. In May, 1667, Nevis was also in danger, and a fleet action lasting four hours took place between English and French in the roadstead. The former, although in inferior force, were successful in saving the island. Later in the year William, Lord Willoughby, recaptured Antigua and Montserrat, and the war closed with the French in full possession of St. Kitts.

[1] *Calendar of Colonial State Papers, America and West Indies,* 1661-8, Introduction, pp. xli-xlii.

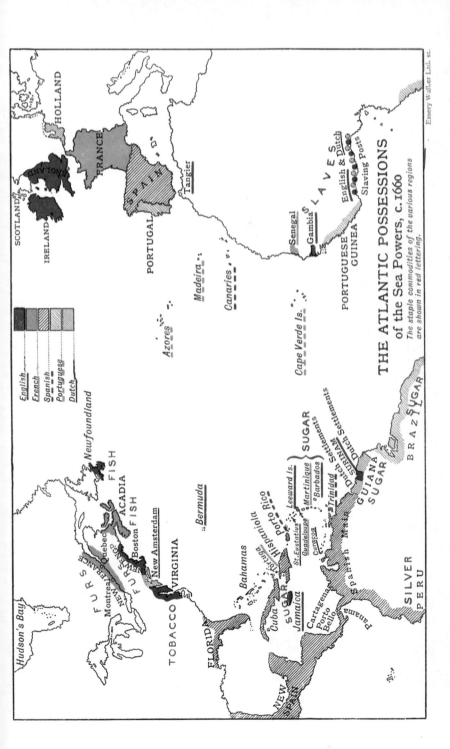

THE ATLANTIC POSSESSIONS
of the Sea Powers, c. 1660

The staple commodities of the various regions
are shown in red lettering.

Emery Walker Ltd. sc.

English
French
Spanish
Portuguese
Dutch

SCOTLAND
IRELAND
ENGLAND
HOLLAND
FRANCE
PORTUGAL
SPAIN
Tangier

Azores
Madeira
Canaries
Cape Verde Is.

SLAVES
Senegal
Gambia
PORTUGUESE GUINEA
English & Dutch
Slaving Posts

Hudson's Bay
Newfoundland
FISH
ACADIA
Quebec
Montreal
NEW FRANCE
FURS
FURS
NEW ENGLAND
Boston
New Amsterdam
VIRGINIA
TOBACCO
FLORIDA
Bermuda
Bahamas
Cuba
SUGAR
Jamaica
Hispaniola
porto Rico
Leeward Is.
St. Eustatius
Guadeloupe
Martinique
Curaçoa
Barbados
SUGAR
Trinidad
Tortuga
Cartagena
Porto Bello
Panama
Spanish Main
Dutch Settlements
SURINAM
Dutch Settlements
GUIANA
SUGAR
BRAZIL
SUGAR
NEW SPAIN
SILVER
PERU

By the Treaty of Breda, signed on July 21, 1667, England gave up to the Dutch Surinam and the claim to Pulo Run in the east; and to the French, Acadia, captured in 1655. The Dutch yielded New Amsterdam (New York), New Jersey and the Delaware estuary, thus retiring completely from the North American continent. France undertook to restore the English portion of St. Kitts, but the arrangement was only carried out after some delay.

One result of the second Dutch war was the beginning of a complete revulsion of public opinion in England. Hitherto English merchants, diplomatists and promoters of colonization had regarded the Dutch as their natural and principal enemies. This Dutch period had been a short one as compared with that of hostility to Spain, although the conflicts to which it had given rise had been far more intense. The growing military power of France under Louis XIV. now gave cause for a new alarm, and within a very short time the French took the place of the Dutch as the most dreaded competitors with England for colonial empire and European preponderance. The rapid French conquest of the Leeward Islands, and the possibility that Barbados might easily have shared their fate, revealed a hitherto unconsidered weakness in the English colonial system, to which these possessions were valuable out of all proportion to their size.[1] In the Spanish Netherlands also Louis began to make aggressions at the close of the war, with the ultimate aim of gaining control over that region of Europe which the sea powers regarded with the tenderest solicitude. The effect was a reconciliation of the former enemies in the Triple Alliance of 1668, a pact between England, the United Provinces and Sweden to resist the growing ambition of France.

Up to this point Charles II. had acted in substantial accordance with the interests of his people. From now onwards he adopted a secret foreign policy dictated entirely by considerations of internal politics. Briefly stated, his plan was to make himself absolute and to restore the Catholic religion in England with the financial and military aid of his cousin the French king. Louis' price was English co-operation in the conquest of the Netherlands. In 1669 the negotiations began, and in the following year they issued in the secret treaty of Dover embodying the above terms, of which the clauses relating to the Catholic religion remained undisclosed for a century. Charles had originally pressed for a share in the American colonies of Spain when Louis should have dominated that country, but this claim was not recognized in the treaty. The joint onslaught upon the Dutch by land and sea was timed for 1672. As a sequel to the real secret treaty Charles allowed his Protestant ministers to amuse themselves by making a sham treaty, by them believed to be genuine, in which no mention of the religious agreement occurred.

Under these auspices began the third Dutch war of 1672. In

[1] Even at the end of the century the imports from Barbados alone were ten times as great in money value as those from the whole of New England (Beer, i. pp. 41-2).

the previous December Charles suspended payment of interest on the government debts in order to raise money for a rapid equipment of the fleet. The Stop of the Exchequer, as it was called, was a short-sighted step, having disastrous effects on the credit and trade of the country.[1] It enabled Sir Robert Holmes to get to sea with a fleet intended to capture the Dutch Levant convoy homeward bound with cargoes valued at one and a half millions. The stroke, however, failed. Everything was done to arouse popular feeling against the Dutch, and two days before the declaration of war Charles issued a Declaration of Indulgence to Catholics under cover of the general excitement. In May, 1672, the Duke of York fought a terrific drawn battle with de Ruyter in Southwold Bay. The Earl of Sandwich was killed, and the French squadron, serving as auxiliaries in the English fleet, caused much dissatisfaction by holding out of the fight. On land the French armies overran the greater part of Holland, and Amsterdam was only saved by the flooding of the surrounding country. An angry mob at the Hague murdered John de Witt and his brother on account of their alleged neglect of the national defence. William III. of Orange, nephew of Charles II., became Stadtholder, and made some headway against the invasion. Protestant suspicions now gathered force against the English king. He had to withdraw the Declaration of Indulgence, and to consent to the anti-Catholic Test Act, which deprived the Duke of York of his command. In three naval battles of 1673 no decisive result could be obtained. The abstention of the French was again most marked, and Rupert declared that he would never serve side by side with them again. The impression was general that they were deliberately allowing the English navy to spend its strength whilst they themselves gathered experience as spectators. At length the popular outcry against the war became irresistible, and forced the king to end it by the Treaty of Westminster in February, 1674. The Dutch paid an indemnity and restored New York, which they had re-occupied in 1673. On the continent the war went on for four years more, until a general European coalition forced the Peace of Nymwegen on Louis XIV. In the later stages English opinion was in favour of joining the Dutch against the French, but Charles avoided compliance by not summoning parliament.

From this time until the Revolution of 1688, Charles II. and his brother remained largely subject to French influence. The growing absolutism of the crown and the consequent resort of its opponents to unconstitutional methods produced a reign of terror in England. In the colonies these political factors did not operate, and the period witnessed an expansion of trade and colonial enterprise, its principal achievement in the latter being the founding of Pennsylvania by William Penn in 1680-2. In New England, however, by reason of resistance to the Navigation Acts, there was a suspension of existing liberties similar to that in the mother-country. This was promoted

[1] Scott, *op. cit.* i. p. 287.

by the Duke of York and continued by him when he became king as James II. There is no evidence that he intended permanently to abolish representative government, and the New Englanders by their recalcitrant attitude had given cause sufficient to sting the mildest of home governments into asserting its authority.[1] Anglo-French relations in America followed the sentiments of the peoples rather than of their sovereigns. Bitter conflicts took place in Hudson Bay, and a situation verging upon war existed between the authorities at New York and at Quebec, each claiming the allegiance of the Iroquois Indians and sovereignty over the territory between the upper Hudson River and the St. Lawrence. The French menace provided an additional motive for consolidating the New England colonies into one dominion. During the last years of the Stuarts the navy extended its sphere of action and became increasingly an instrument of imperial administration. Warships were permanently stationed in colonial waters for the purpose of maintaining compliance with the laws of trade. Admiralty courts for the trial of delinquent shipping also came into existence in the West Indies, although not, prior to 1688, in the continental colonies. The possession of Tangier gave England a firmer hold upon the Barbary pirates, but Charles II. abandoned it in 1683 because the expense of its upkeep would have rendered necessary an appeal to parliament.

Although, as compared with other colonial administrations of the time, that of the later Stuarts had deserved well of its subjects, they had lost much of the personal loyalty which they had manifested during the misfortunes of Charles I. In New England, of course, no such sentiment was to be looked for, and the inhabitants eagerly imprisoned Andros and recognized the new government when news of William III.'s success came to hand in the spring of 1689. In the other colonies the course of events was similar. Carolina, Virginia, Maryland, Pennsylvania, New Jersey and New York made not the slightest effective resistance to the revolution which drove James II. from the English throne, and installed a constitutional monarchy in his place.

[1] The editor of the *Calendar of Colonial State Papers*, 1677-80 (Hon. J. W. Fortescue) expresses a strong opinion on the unfitness of seventeenth-century colonies for unlimited self-government. Colonial cliques, he says, were harsh, oppressive, dishonest and prevaricating, and needed a strong hand for their control. Maryland was the sole exception (Introduction, pp. liv-lvi).

CHAPTER X

THE EXTENSION OF ENGLISH COLONIZATION, 1660-1688

(i) *Carolina*

IN 1629 Charles I. had granted to Sir Robert Heath a patent for planting the region south of Virginia, and had bestowed upon it the name of Carolana. Heath had been unable to act upon his concession, which was considered to have lapsed by the time of the Restoration. A new combination of projectors, eight in number, now came forward, and in 1663 secured from Charles II. a patent constituting them the joint proprietors of the same coast under the slightly altered name of Carolina. These grantees were the Earl of Clarendon, now the chief minister of the crown; George Monck, Duke of Albemarle; Lords Ashley, Craven and Berkeley, Sir George Carteret, Sir William Berkeley, governor of Virginia, and Sir John Colleton, a planter of Barbados. They formed a combination of some wealth and unbounded political influence, and thus were able to enter upon their undertaking with fairer prospects than previous colonizing bodies had enjoyed. The patent granted them the usual proprietary rights, with additional provisos that they might allow liberty of conscience and must introduce a popular element into the legislature of their dominions. Later grants added the Bahama Islands to the Carolina proprietors, and defined their boundaries on the mainland as lat. 36° 30′ on the north and 29° on the south, with unlimited westward extension.

The object of the proprietors was no doubt partly to secure profit for themselves, but it is unfair to lay too much emphasis upon this as has often been done on the assumption that all the courtiers of Charles II. were unprincipled self-seekers. They must have known that plantations had seldom been lucrative to their first founders, and never immediately so. Bacon's dictum was already forty years old that "planting of countries is like planting of woods; for you must make account to lose almost twenty years' profit, and expect your recompense in the end." When he wrote it he had in mind Ireland and Virginia, but nothing had since occurred to modify his conclusion. In Carolina therefore the proprietors hoped to perform patriotic work by establishing a colony which should render the empire self-sufficient in certain articles of trade hitherto obtained from foreigners, and had they succeeded they would have been honourably entitled to some recompense for themselves. The products they had in view were silks, wines, fruits and oils ; they had no intention of planting tobacco or sugar and so competing with existing colonies.[1]

Public opinion in England was now unfavourable to any diminution of the home population by emigration, and the proprietors therefore decided to people their lands as far as possible with surplus inhabitants from the older colonies. Barbados at this time was undergoing the social change which accompanied the establishment of the sugar industry and resulted in the formation of large estates to the extinction of numerous smaller ones. Many Barbadians were therefore ready to try their fortunes in a new settlement. Virginia had a floating population of the poorer sort, ex-indentured servants, who could find no place between the aristocratic and servile strata of her society. New Englanders also were usually willing to emigrate afresh to lands which offered good prospects of success. It was principally from these elements that the Carolina settlements came to be formed. A minority of the original colonists came direct from Europe, and these included persecuted Huguenots and Scotch Presbyterians, leaving the English residue very small in proportion. The colonization of Carolina was therefore in accordance with the general Restoration policy which laid it down that the mother-country could ill spare desirable citizens of her own.

Although intended to form one homogeneous colony, the Carolina plantations fell from the outset into two distinct groups separated by many leagues of unoccupied territory. North Carolina, the first to be settled, sprang in its turn from two nuclei, one composed of a body of New Englanders occupying a post in the vicinity of Cape Fear, the other of Virginians who migrated in 1663 to the Albemarle or Chowan River. The Cape Fear settlement seems to have been independent of, and of prior date to, the Carolina grant. Its members finally dispersed and some were absorbed by the more permanent Albemarle River community, which thus became the colony of North Carolina.[2] The history of the latter ran quite apart from that of South Carolina, and it will therefore be convenient to follow it first through the period ending in 1688.

Seeing that the bulk of the inhabitants were Virginians, the proprietors requested Sir William Berkeley to send them a governor from that colony. In 1663 he appointed William Drummond to the office. Only a meagre record of the early transactions of the settlement has been preserved, from which it appears that in 1667 a constitutional government was established. Each of the eight proprietors appointed a deputy, and these sat in a single chamber with sixteen representatives elected by the colonists. Among the earliest enactments of this

[1] Beer, *op. cit.* ii. 178-9.
[2] Doyle, *Virginia, Carolina, etc.*, pp. 441-3 ; Channing, ii. pp. 13-14.

assembly were one exempting the settlers from all taxation for the first year, another debarring any proceedings against them for debts contracted out of the colony, and a third constituting a simple declaration of consent a valid marriage, if performed in presence of the governor. Such easy-going laws led the outside world to look unfavourably upon the North Carolinians, an impression which their subsequent record confirmed. Albemarle Sound in fact long remained a refuge for broken men and bad characters who had made the neighbouring colonies too hot to hold them.

None of the staple industries projected by the proprietors took root. The principal occupations were the raising of food-stuffs and the carrying on of an illicit trade in contravention of the Navigation Acts. For this the coast was peculiarly suitable. Its broken outlines and shallow waters, giving an advantage to those possessed of local knowledge, precluded effective supervision from without. Small craft brought cargoes from the sugar and tobacco colonies, and transhipped them to New England vessels which carried the goods to the continent of Europe. Privateers and even pirates found an undisturbed haven on the Carolina coast, and amid the general lawlessness the rights of the proprietors remained a dead-letter. In 1676 the scandal had grown to such dimensions that the proprietors determined to take it in hand. They sent out strict instructions for the enforcement of the laws, with the result that an insurrection broke out two years later. The rebels imprisoned the deputy-governor and his officials, and summoned an assembly which coolly passed an Act of Oblivion for the offences of its constituents. They then moderated their tone, and sent mildly worded messages to England. In the end they carried their point, mainly owing to the isolation of their position, and matters went on as before. Seth Sothel, a new governor, appointed by the proprietors in the hope of reducing the colony to order, fell into the hands of Barbary pirates on his outward voyage. When he recovered his liberty and took up his office he used it for his own ends during seven more years of virtual anarchy, and was finally banished by the colonists in 1688. The little band of advanced individualists who peopled North Carolina proved, in fact, uncontrollable from home throughout the Restoration period.

South Carolina, of somewhat later origin than its northern neighbour, was that part of their province upon which the proprietors lavished their greatest pains and expenditure. It received no permanent settlers until 1670, but from 1665 onwards exploring expeditions were active in reconnoitring its coast. Before we consider the actual plantation, however, the governmental plans of the proprietors demand some attention. The Commonwealth period in England had given rise to much abstract political speculation and drafting of paper constitutions. Some of the philosophers in this field had indeed found opportunity to put their schemes into practice, as in the Instrument of Government, and the impermanence of such institutions did not deter their successors of the Restoration from similar exercises when the country began to acquire new colonies. The two outstanding examples of this type are the Fundamental Constitutions of Carolina drawn up by John Locke and Lord Ashley (Shaftesbury) and the Frame of Government devised by William Penn for Pennsylvania. Although neither was ever put into practice they have an interest as indicating the current ideals of colonial management.

Locke, whose connection with Carolina arose from the fact that he was Ashley's secretary, devised his Fundamental Constitutions in 1667. They contemplated the settlement of the province by counties, each containing eight seignories, eight baronies and twenty-four colonies of 12,000 acres apiece. The seignories were to be reserved to the eight proprietors, the baronies to a colonial nobility bearing the titles of caciques and landgraves, and the colonies to the inferior settlers. Each of the proprietors was to fill some principal office of state such as chancellor, chief justice or admiral. The parliament was to consist of the proprietors, the nobility, and representatives of the freemen, sitting all in one chamber, although any order might meet separately and veto any proposed legislation. Slavery, both of negroes and white men, was recognized, the white servant or " leet-man " not obtaining his liberty after a term of years as in Virginia. Locke included other original and interesting ideas in his scheme.[1] When it first saw the light the colony was yet to be made, and the proprietors, as practical men, waited until it should attain a respectable population before introducing so complicated a system in its entirety. In the meanwhile the settlers evolved other and simpler institutions of their own, and resisted, persistently and successfully, all attempts to enforce the ready-made product of the philosopher's brain.[2] As will be shown, Penn's Frame of Government suffered a like fate for the same reason.

South Carolina began with the settlement of a group of Barbadians near Cape Fear. This failed to take permanent root, and the enterprise was apparently discontinued by the time the main expedition sailed from England in 1669. In that year the proprietors despatched three ships which went by way of the West Indies and picked up recruits at Barbados and Bermuda. Various misfortunes delayed the voyage, and the emigrants did not land in Carolina until April, 1670. They chose a site which they named Charlestown on the harbour of that name, although not on the spot occupied by the present Charleston. In 1671 a fresh contingent arrived from New York. Possibly owing to the diverse origins of the settlers there was much dissension in the early years, although the record of the community does not approach the disorderliness of North Carolina.

The policy of the proprietors was to concentrate the colonists as closely as possible in the neighbourhood of the chief town. They granted no lands more than sixty miles from it, and compelled every

[1] For a fuller analysis see Doyle, *op. cit.* pp. 446-50.
[2] Osgood, *op. cit.* ii. p. 211.

squatter to build a town house.   In 1672 Charlestown had 400 inhabitants.   Progress continued to be slow for some years, but in 1680 a renewed outburst of activity resulted in the removal of Charlestown to its present site.   At the same time Huguenots began to arrive, being especially favoured by the proprietors as likely to establish a silk industry.   The hope, however, proved illusory.   Scottish exiles followed the Huguenots, and formed a separate township of their own, for which they were regarded with some jealousy by their neighbours. Their undertaking failed to flourish, and after a few years the remnants of the Scots were massacred by the Spaniards of Florida.

As in North Carolina, the chief industries were the growth of foodstuffs for export to the West Indies, and the infringement of the Navigation Acts.   The colony was peculiar in its extensive enslavement of the Indians.   This took place contrary to the proprietors' orders, and produced a chronic state of warfare.   By the end of the century a quarter of the entire number of slaves were Indians.   On the whole the colony proved a disappointment to its founders.   They expended over £17,000 [1] upon it with practically no return, their only source of revenue being the quit-rents which were seldom paid.   Even from the larger point of view, of national rather than personal gain, they had apparently failed.   But in this the event justified them, for in the eighteenth century Carolina found its necessary staple industry, and took its place with a bound among the richest of the plantation colonies.   In 1700 the population was about 8000, of whom 5000 were in the southern settlement.

(ii) *New York and New Jersey*

The Dutch colony of New Netherland had been planted by the Dutch West India Company a few years after the discovery of the Hudson River.   In 1660 it consisted of settlements in the valley of that river extending as far inland as Rensselaerswyk (Albany) ; of others stretching along the coast eastwards until they came in contact with the ever expanding claims of Connecticut ; of a considerable occupation of Long Island, the eastern end of which had also been invaded by New Englanders since 1640 ; and finally, of a southwestward extension through what is now the state of New Jersey to the banks of the Delaware River, where the Dutch had in 1655 overrun and subdued a struggling Swedish colony planted some twenty years earlier.   The government of all these widespread territories centred in the fort of New Amsterdam at the mouth of the Hudson.   New Netherland differed from New England in that it was a collection of trading posts rather than a true colony.   Its inhabitants had little of that corporate consciousness and political independence which distinguished their neighbours ; their numbers were scanty in proportion to the extent of their territory, and they submitted apathetically to

[1] Beer, ii. p. 187 ; Channing, ii. p. 20, says £6000.

the somewhat unprogressive rule of the company which benefited by their industry.

England had for many years cast a jealous eye upon the Dutch coastline which interposed between her northern and southern groups of colonies. From the outset the English had viewed the Dutch as interlopers without any title to settle upon the American continent. The vaguely recorded voyages of the Cabots and the Virginia charters of James I. gave ground for denying the rights of all other nations. But claims based upon prior discovery were not honestly looked upon as conclusive, even in that age. All governments advanced and discarded them as occasion demanded, and the English themselves had expressly denounced them in their dealings with Spain and Portugal. The true title to possession was effective and unopposed occupation, and here the Dutch position would have been unassailable if only they had sent out sufficient emigrants to exploit their soil to its full advantage. This they never did, and the enterprising New Englanders by sheer force of economic pressure extended westwards into the region between the Connecticut and Hudson Rivers, and also became an increasing factor in the colonization of Long Island. In the latter, according to an English account, there were in 1663 some 1900 inhabitants, of whom about 600 were English. This penetration of the Dutch territories was in the main peaceful. Trading interests rendered Boston and New Amsterdam dependent upon one another, and Peter Stuyvesant, governor of the Dutch colony from 1647 onwards, maintained friendly relations with the rulers of Massachusetts. Englishmen even held official positions in the administration of New Netherland.[1]

This trade connection, so convenient to the New Englanders, was an offence in the eyes of the English government. In 1653, during the first Dutch war, Cromwell had despatched Major Robert Sedgwick to conquer the Dutch colony. Sedgwick intended to invade by land from New England, but the obstacles raised by the Boston authorities delayed his advance until with the peace of 1654 the opportunity passed away. The reconstructed colonial system of the Restoration again made the question an urgent one. Coasting vessels poured the enumerated commodities into New Amsterdam, and carried thence European goods which had not passed through English ports. English customs officers estimated the loss to the revenue at £10,000 a year, and the illicit trade was certain to increase if not checked. A Dutch entrepot, in fact, existing in the midst of the English colonies rendered the laws of trade unworkable. Massachusetts, whose port of Boston owned the greatest tonnage of colonial shipping, was the principal gainer. It was already showing dangerous symptoms of political independence. The home policy became accordingly that of raising Connecticut as a counterpoise,[2] fostering that colony's loyalty by a

---

[1] Doyle, *Middle Colonies*, London, 1907, p. 102.

[2] Doyle, *op. cit.* pp. 110-11.

new and favourable charter. Here was yet another incentive to a stroke at New Netherland, from whose conquest the Connecticut men would obtain territorial security, whilst their trading interests were small compared with those of Massachusetts. The larger significance of the Hudson River basin—its military value as affecting the French possessions in Canada—does not seem as yet to have dawned upon the English government.

The Duke of York, as brother of Charles II., was well fitted by his position to take the lead in all matters of trade and colonization which it was convenient for the crown to delegate to a powerful subject. He conducted such affairs with conspicuous energy throughout the reign, and were it not that his unhappy performance as king after Charles' death has overshadowed his colonial record, he would probably have lived in English history as a successful naval and imperial administrator.[1] Of him more than any of the Stuarts is it true that the external interests of the country brought out the best, as internal politics brought out the worst, in his character; and it is fair to remember that he was an admiral, colonial proprietor, and patron of commerce for twenty-five years, while his career as sovereign endured for but three years in the decline of his powers.

On March 12, 1664, Charles issued letters patent to the duke creating him proprietor of a stretch of territory north of New England reaching from the St. Croix River to the Kennebec, of all islands on the southern New England coast, and of the mainland from the Connecticut border to the Delaware estuary. The latter territory, of course, was coincident with the Dutch colonies, and the new grantee had immediately to put in hand preparations for converting his claim into a reality. He appointed Colonel Richard Nicolls as his deputy-governor, and equipped him for the enterprise with three warships, a transport, 450 soldiers, and £4000 in money. The close connection of the expedition with the whole system of colonial policy appears in the fact that Nicolls was simultaneously placed at the head of a royal commission to enquire into the affairs of New England. The undertaking was an act of military aggression, based upon expediency, and as such has been denounced by a foreign critic as " an unprincipled series of secret actions against a friendly nation." Had it occurred in the nineteenth century no such condemnation would have been too strong. But in the seventeenth the dividing line between mercantile and military warfare beyond the seas of Europe scarcely existed. The Dutch in 1664 were not a friendly nation as the words were understood at the time, and had given ground for reprisal by their encouragement upon the very scene of action of English subjects who were breaking their country's laws. Their unscrupulous doings in the East Indies and on the African coast were fresh in living memory.

[1] On this head the convergent testimony of independent investigators is striking; see particularly, Admiral Mahan, *Influence of Sea Power upon History*, pp. 174-5; and Hon. J. W. Fortescue, *Calendar of Col. State Papers*, 1685-8, p. xxxvi.

Colonel Nicolls with his armament sailed from Portsmouth in May, 1664, and arrived at Boston at the end of July. Remembering the delays which had frustrated Sedgwick's purpose, he relied principally upon his own force, and resumed his voyage to New Netherland after a very short stay in Massachusetts. That colony collected some troops which were too late to take part in the invasion ; Connecticut, more enthusiastic, furnished a contingent in time, under the leadership of the younger John Winthrop. Peter Stuyvesant had received notice of what was impending, and had exerted himself to make preparations for defence. But the West India Company had neglected the fortifications of New Amsterdam, the inhabitants were apathetic, and no serious resistance was possible. Nicolls appeared off Coney Island on August 18. He offered reasonable conditions—including one, continuance of trade with Holland, which it was not in his power to grant—and after protracting the negotiation in a desperate hope of relief Stuyvesant was forced by his own people to submit. On August 29 New Amsterdam surrendered without a shot having been fired. Nicolls detached Sir Robert Carr to take possession of the Delaware settlements, which was accomplished in October with some unnecessary plundering and bloodshed.

Thus at length the whole coast from Maine to Carolina was in English hands. To the captors the principal value of the conquest seemed to lie in its rounding-off of the fiscal system of their empire. On the continent of Europe little interest was expressed, even the Dutch making small effort to secure restitution. They had indeed lost little, for their feeble colony was indefensible at any time against its powerful neighbours in New England ; and at the Peace of Breda they obtained compensation elsewhere. The true losers were the French in Canada. They realized, as their superiors at home did not, that the Hudson basin was the key to North America. In a roadless country waterways were of priceless military and commercial worth. The navigable channel of the Hudson extended far inland from the Atlantic coast until it reached a point separated by a short march from the southern end of Lake Champlain, whilst its affluent the Mohawk stretched westwards towards the Great Lakes. Champlain in its turn issued northwards in the navigable River Richelieu, which entered the St. Lawrence between Quebec and Montreal. The Hudson therefore, in French hands, would have severed New England from the south and west and stifled its future development, at the same time giving Canada an ice-free access to the Atlantic. In English hands it threatened the existence of French power on the St. Lawrence. To adapt a well-known phrase, New Amsterdam under the English flag was a pistol pointed at the heart of Canada. The French Canadians were quick to perceive what damage had been wrought to their interests. "The King of England," said one when he heard the news, "doth grasp at all America." When the negotiations at Breda were in progress, Talon, the Intendant at Quebec, wrote home to urge that

France must before all things insist on the restitution of New Netherland to the Dutch, and that the French king must then purchase it
himself.[1] But his warning bore no fruit and the English retained their
prize, scarcely themselves aware of its full value.

In June, 1664, while Nicholls was still crossing the Atlantic, the
Duke of York had made over part of his prospective acquisition to
two of his friends, Lord Berkeley and Sir George Carteret. In commemoration of Carteret's heroic defence of Jersey in the Civil War
this territory received the name of New Jersey. It consisted of the
coastal strip between the Hudson and the Delaware, not including,
however, the ex-Swedish settlements to the southward of the latter
estuary. These, as a province, assumed the name of Delaware, and
remained attached to the duke's government. New Jersey was
sparsely inhabited by Dutch and Swedish settlers ; Nicolls considered
it the best component of the conquest and was proportionately annoyed
at his master's easiness in parting with it.

Nicolls himself ruled tactfully and well. He renamed the principal
places in the Hudson region, New Amsterdam becoming New York and
Rensselaerswyk, Albany. He preserved Dutch institutions for a
year, until English officials were equipped to take over the administration. The Dutch displayed no grief at their change of rulers, Stuyvesant himself setting the example by taking the oath of allegiance.
Nicolls was not empowered to set up representative government, a
thing much desired by the New England men in Long Island, but he
introduced there a code of laws with a New England flavour—subsequently known as the Duke's Laws—together with trial by jury and
freedom of conscience and worship. By 1673 this system extended
to the whole province of New York. Before that date Nicolls had
left America, to be killed on the deck of the duke's flagship in the
opening battle of the third Dutch war. That war entailed a temporary
loss of New York. In 1673 a Dutch fleet of twenty-three ships conveying 1200 soldiers raided the Chesapeake. Its commander, Cornelius
Evertsen, heard that New York was in no condition for defence, and
sailed northwards to capture it, although the undertaking had apparently not formed part of the original plan of his expedition. Colonel
Francis Lovelace, Nicolls's successor, was absent in Connecticut,
and New York surrendered after a feeble resistance. Its fall involved
that of New Jersey and Delaware, but all were restored to England
by the Treaty of Westminster early in 1674.

It is from this date that the real development of New York as a
member of the colonial empire begins. The duke sent out Sir Edmund
Andros (apparently pronounced Andrews) to take over the government.
He was a man of much force of character but somewhat lacking in
tact and imagination. He conceived his whole duty to be the maintenance of his master's interests, which he interpreted in a narrower spirit
than did the duke himself. His rule is therefore marked by disputes

[1] Doyle, *op. cit.* p. 151.

with the neighbouring colonies on questions of jurisdiction and boundaries. The Dutch reconquest had invalidated the former constitutional arrangements and rendered necessary fresh proprietary grants by the king and his brother. The English in Long Island had hopes of being taken within the government of Connecticut, but this was not allowed, neither was countenance given to their aspirations after self-government. Andros conducted the administration with the aid of a council of ten and the laws and revenue as arranged by Nicolls. Towards the end of his tenure of office the increasing stringency of the navigation system gave rise to some friction. In 1680 the duke recalled him, and two years later appointed Colonel Thomas Dongan to his place. Dongan was a man of large views, and an admirable governor. He came also armed with permission to establish representative government. The first assembly met in 1683 and passed a law known as the Charter of Liberties, settling the future details of the constitution. Dongan also realized the strategic value of the Hudson and the probability of a struggle with the French in Canada at some future date. He therefore entered into an alliance with the Iroquois tribes inhabiting the wooded country between the English and French colonies. He took these Indians under the duke's protection and interfered to save them from French aggression. The situation in North America, even before the fall of the Stuarts, was becoming a very sore point between England and France, in spite of the dependence of Charles II. and his brother upon Louis XIV. In 1686 the two governments signed a treaty intended to settle the difficulty, but it had little effect upon their respective colonists. Dongan was recalled in 1688, a few months before the overthrow of James II. Andros again took over the government of New York in conjunction with that of New England, but the story of his fall will be more conveniently considered in dealing with the latter region.

The history of New Jersey from its conquest to the Revolution is confused and fragmentary. Such as it is, it provides an illustration of the abuses of the proprietary system in cases where proprietary rights were easily alienable and could be sold like merchandise in the market. In 1664, as we have seen, the Duke of York granted the province to Lord Berkeley and Sir George Carteret, the former interesting himself mainly in the southern part towards the Delaware, commonly known as West Jersey, and the latter in East Jersey, the portion nearer to the Hudson. The two proprietors at first worked in concert and with some energy, advertising the advantages of the region, and attracting settlers from New and Old England by promises of constitutional government and religious liberty. The first New Jersey assembly met in 1668 and displayed an independence of temper which involved the colony in a contest with its proprietors.

Scarcely had this been settled when the Dutch reconquest of 1673 invalidated the patents and threw all into the melting-pot. The Quakers in England were at this time seeking for some place of refuge overseas, and before the Treaty of Westminster had determined the ultimate restitution of the middle colonies two of their leaders, John Fenwick and Edward Bylling, bought Lord Berkeley's rights as a speculation for £1000. After the peace of 1674 the Duke of York received a new patent for the entire territories of New York, New Jersey and Delaware, and Andros, as has been related, went out as his deputy. Andros refused to recognize the sale to the Quakers, and immediately asserted his jurisdiction over West Jersey, where Fenwick was trying to organize a Quaker state. Quaker settlers continued to arrive, but the conflict of authority necessarily retarded the development of the colony. In the meantime William Penn and others were negotiating with Sir George Carteret and his brother for the settlement of their co-religionists in East Jersey. The Quakers already had a footing there when Andros claimed and asserted jurisdiction in 1679. The aggrieved parties complained to the duke, who listened favourably and recognized their rights. In 1681-2, after the death of Carteret, William Penn and the Quaker syndicate bought out his heirs and united the Jersies under their rule. This arrangement also obtained the countenance of the duke, who seems to have been, at least in the colonies, a genuine supporter of religious toleration. He expressly instructed Dongan not to meddle with New Jersey. The life of the province continued peacefully until 1688, when its independence fell a victim to the large scheme of consolidation entered upon for the better enforcement of the laws of trade. New Jersey surrendered, along with New York, to the government of Andros, and so remained for the few months which elapsed before the overthrow of Stuart rule. The general result of the colony's vicissitudes had been to limit the powers of any corporate authority and to split up the population into small autonomous communities. Residents gave a very favourable account of the climate and the soil, but the colony remained unimportant in its relation to the general frame of the empire.

(iii) *Pennsylvania*

Of all the colonial proprietors of the seventeenth century William Penn has aroused the greatest interest, possibly because his true character remains something of a riddle to posterity. The son of Admiral Penn, who had shared the command of Cromwell's West Indian expedition, he had early in life adopted the religious tenets of the Quakers. To his principles he always remained faithful, although in his business career he sometimes allowed himself a latitude which is surprising in a member of a sect strict to the point of eccentricity. Examples of this apparent inconsistency are to be found in his close relations with the worldly court of Charles II. and his genuine friendship with the Catholic Duke of York. Some have ascribed it to mere time-serving and opportunism, but perhaps the most convincing explanation is that Penn was so broad in his tolerance as to be quite indifferent to dogma, and to condone in his friends conduct which he would not have permitted to himself.[1]

At the time of the admiral's death Charles II. owed him the sum of £16,000. William Penn, who had already interested himself in settling his persecuted sect in New Jersey, conceived the idea of commuting the royal debt for a grant of unoccupied land to the westward of that province. Charles acceded to his request, and in March, 1681, issued letters patent creating Penn proprietor of a new colony to be called Pennsylvania. Its boundaries marked a new phase in American settlement since they enclosed an inland area with no coastline, access to the Atlantic being gained by the Delaware River. That waterway was to form its eastern frontier, latitude 43° its northern, and a meridian 5° west of the Delaware its western limit, running through unexplored country. On the south the definition was less satisfactory, since a belt of land fifteen miles wide running westwards from Newcastle on the Delaware remained in dispute with Maryland for the greater part of a century.[2] The Duke of York, more complaisant than Lord Baltimore, resigned any claims he might possess to lands west of the Delaware. The charter expressly provided for the enforcement of the Navigation Acts, for representative government, and for religious toleration. Penn himself lost no time in circulating a prospectus of his colony not only in the British Isles but also on the continent of Europe. He declared his intention of treating the Indians as equal before the law with white men, of making provision for highways in the distribution of lands, of limiting the size of estates, preserving some part of the forests, and building a well-planned capital city. In his appeal to foreign emigrants we see the reflection of current views on conservation of the home population. Although he intended primarily to provide a refuge for oppressed Quakers he recognized that they alone would not be sufficiently numerous to fill his colony. This practical tolerance is in sharp contrast with the policy pursued by the founders of Massachusetts.

The west bank of the Delaware had already a few Swedish, Dutch and English inhabitants. The first contingent to go out from England sailed in October, 1681, under the command of William Markham, Penn's deputy-governor. The proprietor himself crossed with a larger body, including 400 Welsh families, in 1682. English, Irish, Welsh and Germans continued to emigrate to the colony in the succeeding years.

Before going to the scene of his venture Penn drew up his Frame of Government. According to this constitution the proprietor and a council of seventy-two members, elected by the freemen, were to draft the laws, which were then to be submitted to an assembly of 200. The latter body, however, had merely the right to confirm or reject the council's proposals, but not to discuss or amend them. One-third

---

[1] Doyle, *Middle Colonies*, pp. 480-4.

[2] The final boundary of Pennsylvania and Maryland was not laid down until 1767.

of the council were to retire annually. The freemen included all land-owners and taxpayers. Penn made not the least attempt to put his constitution into practice. Probably he saw that the new community was not ripe for it. In the meantime various legislative experiments were tried, that of 1683 consisting of a council of eighteen and an assembly of thirty-six members. The colonists showed no enthusiasm for the Frame of Government.

Penn remained in America for two years, supervising the early work of the settlement, and particularly that of founding Philadelphia The most memorable transaction of his personal government was his solemn compact with the Indian chiefs, wherein he guaranteed their rights and fixed the payments to be made for their lands. Although the intrusion of white men could not but be detrimental to the Indians' welfare, it was managed as humanely as possible. In 1688 the tact and firmness of the Pennsylvanian magistrates averted a threatened Indian rising. Four years before that date the state of affairs in England had compelled the proprietor to return. His dispute with Lord Baltimore was about to be heard before the Lords of Trade. The bitter persecution of the English Quakers in the last years of Charles II. also called for his personal intervention. When the Duke of York ascended the throne in 1685, Penn was instrumental in securing the release of 1200 of his imprisoned co-religionists. After Penn's departure his colony made rapid material progress, although politically its record was unhappy. There was little of that early period of suffering experienced by most of the older plantations. By 1685 Philadelphia had over 350 houses, and within ten years of the foundation Pennsylvania was exporting foodstuffs to the West Indies. But the success was clouded by perpetual discord in matters of government. Lofty ideals and material considerations proved to be incompatible. In vain Penn attempted to still the clamour. "For the love of God, me, and the poor country," he wrote, "be not so governmentish, so noisy, and open in your dissatisfactions." His colonists disregarded his precepts, and certainly forgot the considerable gratitude which they owed to him. Pennsylvania was the only one of the middle and northern colonies which preserved its charter in the general consolidation of 1686-8. Its escape was probably due to the personal friendship between its proprietor and James II. After the king's fall, Penn, finding that his friendship endangered his position at home and that the colonists repudiated his authority, appointed a non-Quaker, John Blackwell, as his deputy.

CHAPTER XI

THE OLDER COLONIES UNDER THE RESTORED STUARTS

(i) *The Island Colonies*

AFTER the recall of Sir David Kirke in 1651, the affairs of Newfoundland underwent a prolonged crisis for close on thirty years. During the whole of that period the future of English interests hung in the balance, and the uncertainty of the issue retarded the colony's development. The causes of this unhappy state of affairs lay in the conflicting claims of the settlers, the west-country fishermen, and the upholders of the colonial trading system in general, complicated, as time progressed, by the increasing grasp of the French upon the fishery, and their settlement upon the south-western coasts of the island.

At the Restoration the permanent English residents were few in numbers and scattered in tiny hamlets on the eastern and south-eastern shores. They were nevertheless true colonists, living by agriculture, fishing, and trade in local commodities, their future bound up with the life of their villages ; and they proved their title to recognition by the tenacity with which they resisted all the disheartening intrigues of the powerful interests seeking to dislodge them.[1] Their principal crime in the eyes of their enemies was that their settlements formed bases from which a local boat-fishing industry competed with the ship-fishermen who came out annually from England. The ship-fishery, as a training ground for seamen available for the national service, long remained of paramount importance in the eyes of the home government, and, had it not been for the rise of French power, would probably have succeeded in extinguishing the colony. In the opening years of Charles II., a partisan statement, which must be received with caution, shows the fishery to have declined considerably from the flourishing condition it had enjoyed in the decade 1630-40. The absolute falling-off may not have been serious—it had been largely reversed twenty years later—but there was undoubtedly a relative loss of ground to the French, whose fishermen became so active in the latter part of the century that the English lost their ancient market

---

[1] For a less favourable view of the colonists see *Acts of the Privy Council*, Col. Series. vol. i. (1908), p. xxxi.

in France, and had to confine their sales to the Mediterranean countries. Here the Newfoundland fish remained an important element in keeping up the favourable balance of trade desired by the mercantile economists. But they, although they looked kindly upon the fishery, grew perturbed at the use to which Newfoundland was put by the systematic violators of the laws of trade. Tobacco and sugar, brought by American coasters, found their way direct to the European continent, and in the reverse direction European manufactures reached America without complying with the Staple Act. The extent of the illicit trade is not precisely ascertainable; as elsewhere it has been exaggerated, and recent investigations tend to reduce it to unimportant dimensions.[1] Such as it was, it complicated the already tangled problem of Newfoundland. For yet another reason the directors of national policy were moved to keep a sharp eye on the fishery. At the time of the Restoration it was alleged that many of the hands failed to return with the ships in the autumn, going instead to settle in New England. Residing there, they still followed their trade, but were no longer available for the naval service. The government accordingly issued commands in 1670 that fishing skippers were to carry no passengers and to bring home every surviving member of their crews.

In 1661 French activities in Newfoundland took a new turn. Hitherto the Frenchmen had not wintered in the island, but in the year named Louis XIV. annexed the south-western coast of the Avalon peninsula, and put in hand the building of a fort at Placentia and its occupation by a permanent colony.[2] The threat to English interests was obvious; if the settlement should prove vigorous and expansive it might entail the exclusion of Englishmen from the fishery. It was thus the French menace which proved the determining factor in preserving the English settlers from the jealousies of their own fellow-countrymen. At first Placentia seemed formidable, its position being one of great natural strength. But the undertaking soon began to suffer from the besetting weakness of all the French colonizing projects —lack of a steady stream of emigrants. The colony therefore did not prosper, and ere long the authorities neglected their share of the work. In 1684 the fort of Placentia was described as "an old ruin," with only three guns out of twelve remaining mounted. The French fishery, on the other hand, increased enormously. At the end of the Stuart period it was reported to be employing 16,000 to 20,000 men annually and giving a corresponding accession to the power of the French navy. A contest for supremacy was obviously impending, and the matter became one of the most important due for settlement in the wars of William III. and Anne.

---

[1] Beer, *Old Colonial System*, ii. pp. 222-6.

[2] Prowse, *Hist. of Newfoundland*, pp. 177-80, says that as early as 1660-1 Charles II. made a secret agreement to hand over the island to Louis XIV.; but the evidence giving ground for the suspicion—it is nothing more—refers to a later date, that of the Treaty of Dover.

Meanwhile the agitation against the English colonists came to a climax. In 1670 the Privy Council rejected a proposal to transfer them all to other plantations. Five years later the newly appointed Lords of Trade reversed the decision and gave orders for the deportation of the luckless Newfoundlanders to St. Kitts and Jamaica or, in default, for the stringent enforcement of the old edict against residence within six miles of the coast. At last the dreaded blow seemed to have fallen, but at the eleventh hour the colony was saved by the public-spirited action of a naval officer. Sir John Berry, commander of the Newfoundland convoy, was certain that the Lords of Trade were acting under bad advice. He sent home a report which convinced them of their error, and caused them to admit that they had listened too readily to the short-sighted arguments of the fishermen. He added that if they persisted in their harsh policy, its effect would be to drive the settlers under the allegiance of the French.[1] The Lords of Trade, an enlightened and well-meaning body, accepted the reproof and extended their protection to the colony. In 1680 they rescinded the six-mile rule, decided on the appointment of a governor, and ordered the fortification of St. John's. Thenceforward there was no more talk of abandonment.

Berry's report and the subsequent enquiry gave rise to the collection of statistics which illustrate the condition of Newfoundland in 1677. There were at that date 523 permanent settlers, including women and children, living in twenty-eight different settlements, of which the largest was St. John's, with 87 inhabitants. In addition there were about 1300 boat-fishers, who came and went from place to place, but did not return to England with the fishing-fleet. The fleet consisted of 221 ships, averaging 74 tons apiece, armed with 688 guns, and manned by 5000 men.[2] For its protection the navy afforded convoy when necessary, as happened on fourteen different occasions between 1623 and 1675. In 1665 de Ruyter raided the fishery. Again in 1673 the captors of New York attempted to do so, but were beaten off from St. John's by Christopher Martin, a Devonshire skipper.

In our day it is somewhat difficult to realize that, judged by the standards of the old colonial empire, the West Indian islands were far more important than all the plantations on the mainland of America. Such nevertheless is the truth. A statesman of Charles II.'s reign, if asked to appraise the various colonies in the order of their value to the nation, would probably have placed Barbados first, followed by Newfoundland, Jamaica and the Leeward Islands ; after them Virginia and Maryland ; then the Middle Colonies and the Carolinas ; and last of all, New England.

A few figures will illustrate the pre-eminence of Barbados and also give some indication of the changes brought about by the growth of

[1] Beer, ii. pp. 214-6.

[2] *Hist. Geog. of Brit. Colonies*, vol. v. pt. iv. by J. D. Rogers, Oxford, 1911, pp. 82-4 ; the *Calendar of Col. State Papers*, 1675-6, pp. xxxv-xxxvi. gives slightly different figures.

the sugar industry.   The island itself was about the size of the Isle of
Wight, with a virgin soil whose richness began to deteriorate only
after thirty years of unsparing cultivation.   In 1643, when the sugar
industry took root, it had a population of 18,000 male whites, of whom
about one-half were proprietors ; at this time the negro element was
unimportant.   In 1666 the male white population was 8000, and two
years later the total white population was estimated at 20,000 ; but
of these less than 800 owned all the estates between them.   At the
same time the number of negro slaves had risen to about 40,000.   The
island, therefore, whilst growing in wealth, was losing the better elements of its population.   It is computed to have thrown off about
12,000 emigrants to other colonies in the twenty-five years prior to
1668.   On the riches of the aristocratic planters who remained, a
contemporary account is eloquent : " Their plate, jewels and household
stuff are estimated at £500,000, their buildings very fair and beautiful,
and their houses like castles ; their sugar houses and negroes' huts show
themselves from the sea like so many small towns, each defended by
its castle."   Under the navigation system some two hundred merchantmen, English built, owned and manned, laded the sugar annually
from the island quays ; the annual payment of customs on the out-
going sugar alone was about £20,000 ; and even at the end of the
century, when Barbados had reached its prime and the American
colonies were still rapidly expanding, the exports of the former were
worth £308,000, whilst those of all the latter together totalled £226,000.[1]
The period of most rapid expansion fell in the first twenty years
after the establishment of the sugar industry.   Thenceforward, as
mercantile relations adjusted themselves, and other plantations
began to grow sugar, the enormous profit-taking of the earlier period
ceased to be possible.   The island still went steadily forward, but its
planters prospered at a less feverish and perhaps more healthy rate.
They themselves refused to view the matter in this light.   They
regarded a natural reaction as due to the harsh measures of the home
government, and throughout the Restoration period they were loud
in their complaints.   Statistics show that they had little reason to
grumble ; too-dazzling success had, in fact, spoiled them.   The first
and greatest grievance was the enumeration of sugar under the Act of
1660.   It was the keystone of the colonial system, and unceasing
agitation failed to secure its reversal.   To a certain extent it delivered
the planters into the hands of the English merchants as a body.   But
the merchants competed amongst themselves, and we find no traces of a
ring or trust among them to regulate prices ; such a combination was
probably impracticable in the then state of society without the assistance of a government charter to ensure it a monopoly.   The Barbadians
also objected to the prohibition of direct trade with Scotland, but to
the clauses of the trade laws which protected the national shipping

---

[1] This refers only to exports direct to England, excluding intercolonial trade.   The
figures are from Beer's *Old Colonial System* and Lucas' *Hist. Geog. of Brit. Colonies.*

they seem to have given their approval, for they owned a certain number of small craft themselves. To represent their views, they maintained in London a Committee of Gentlemen Planters of Barbados, consisting of absentee owners and others with connections in the island. Another grievance lay in the method adopted to regularize the planters' titles to their land. The Caribbee Islands had originally been colonized under proprietary grants to English noblemen in the time of Charles I. The various claims became much complicated during the confusion of the civil wars, and when Francis, Lord Willoughby, returned to the governorship in 1663 he cut the knot by securing the passage through the assembly of an Act imposing an export duty of four and a half per cent. in return for the cancelling of all proprietary rights. The planters thus became freeholders, but they soon raised a never-ending clamour for the abolition of the duty. It remained in force, however, until 1838.

The neighbouring islands of the Windward group, which ultimately became important sugar colonies, received little development before the close of the seventeenth century. The French established themselves in Martinique, Grenada and St. Lucia prior to the Restoration. In 1664 Thomas Warner, the half-Carib son of the original planter of St. Kitts, led a thousand Barbadians against St. Lucia and drove them out ; France regained the island by the Treaty of Breda, but for many years did very little to colonize it. St. Vincent also, inhabited by an especially ferocious tribe, the offspring of Caribs and shipwrecked negroes, was left to itself during this period. Tobago changed owners several times, and finally became a no man's land until 1763 when the English entered into possession.

The Leeward Islands remained under the rule of Barbados until 1671, when they became a separate governorship. As we have seen, they suffered a great set-back when the French captured them all except Nevis in 1666. It was only after the restitutions effected by the Treaty of Breda that they began to develop into valuable colonies. By 1671 these readjustments were complete, and in the same year Colonel William Stapleton became governor of the group, retaining the office until 1686. The English part of St. Kitts began life anew with only one-third as many colonists as before the invasion. Antigua and Montserrat had both suffered a systematic plundering by their captors. Under Stapleton's efficient rule prosperity increased rapidly, each island having a deputy-governor and an assembly of its own. By 1678 the total population amounted to 10,500 whites and 8,500 negroes, of which Nevis had 3,500 and 3,800 respectively ; the Montserrat people were almost exclusively Irish. In addition to sugar the planters produced tobacco, indigo and ginger. They imported manufactures from England and foodstuffs from Massachusetts and her neighbours. Stapleton strictly enforced the laws of trade, against which his subjects raised fewer complaints than did the Barbadians.

Of Jamaica its original captors formed very high expectations ; it appeared to share all the advantages of Barbados in addition to being twenty-five times as large. Actually, for a variety of reasons, its progress was slow. The terrible mortality among the first colonists gave it an ill name, and the glamour of the buccaneers, who made it their principal base, tempted the more enterprising among the settlers from the paths of lawful industry. At the Restoration its people numbered about 4000 whites and 1000 negroes.[1] By 1673 the white population had doubled and the negroes had risen to nearly 10,000. From that time onwards growth proceeded at a more rapid rate, but it was only in the last decade of the century that the trade of Jamaica began to approach that of Barbados in value. In 1697-8 it amounted to about two-thirds of the latter's total. In the earlier years cocoa was the principal product of the plantations ; then a disease killed the trees, and sugar took its place. Indigo, tobacco, cotton and ginger were subordinate industries, and, unlike the other English islands, Jamaica was almost self-supporting in foodstuffs.

The refusal of Charles II. to restore Jamaica to Spain caused the continuance of a state of war in the West Indies until 1671. This was the period in which the buccaneers rose to their prime. They were recruited from seamen and colonists crowded out of the islands by the growth of large estates. They attacked primarily the commerce of Spain, but in practice there was often very little limit to their lawlessness. Their crowning exploit occurred in 1671 when, under the leadership of Henry Morgan, they landed on the Isthmus and sacked the town of Panama. Jamaica was for geographical reasons their headquarters, and its inhabitants grew rich by the sale of the spoils. In 1670 England and Spain signed the Treaty of Madrid. Its effects were not immediate, but ultimately it destroyed West Indian buccaneering by depriving it of its semi-legal status. Some of the buccaneers settled down into more sober means of livelihood ; Morgan himself became a knight and deputy-governor of Jamaica. Others frankly turned pirates, and roved far and wide in the Atlantic, the Indian Ocean and the Pacific. A bye-path of their activities, the cutting of log-wood in Campeche on the mainland of Central America, became a permanent trade, conducted from Jamaica and involving endless disputes with the Spanish government.

Jamaica received a constitution by royal proclamation in 1662, comprising the governor, a nominated council, and an elected assembly. The first assembly, of thirty members, met in 1664. Financial questions gave rise to disputes with the governor, and in 1678 the crown took an exceptional course by introducing the principle known in Ireland as Poynings' Law, to the effect that all legislation must originate with the English Privy Council, the assembly merely retaining the right of accepting or rejecting. The experiment was of short duration, and Jamaica soon regained its local autonomy. But bad relations between

[1] There are two conflicting estimates, one higher, the other lower, than the above.

governor and assembly long remained the normal state of affairs in the island. In these circumstances it is somewhat surprising that there was little outcry against the laws of trade and also, apparently, little evasion of their restrictions.

The Bahamas, granted to the Carolina proprietors in 1670, failed to derive much benefit from their new owners. They were backward and ill-governed, little better than nests of pirates, throughout the Restoration period. The Bermudas were a more reputable colony, since their population—stationary at about 9000—was engaged in productive industry. The Bermudians were however very independent, resenting outside control even after the islands became a crown colony in 1684. Long before this date they had fully attained their possible development, and the surplus population formed a useful element in planting newer settlements.

(ii) *Virginia and Maryland*

In the summer of 1660 rumours of the impending restoration of Charles II. began to circulate in Virginia, and the leaders of royalist opinion met with little opposition in assuming control. Sir William Berkeley, the last governor commissioned by Charles I., was still in the colony, although he had occupied no public office since his deposition by the Parliamentary commissioners. His friends still regarded him as *de jure* governor, and in July the assembly reinstated him. He was at this time personally popular and by long residence thoroughly identified with the views and interests of the Virginians. He was himself a tobacco planter on a large scale. In September came definite news of the king's return. The loyal Virginians hastened to appoint the anniversary as a public holiday and the thirtieth of January as a day of fast and mourning.

Their jubilation ere long received a check. The navigation ordinances of 1650 and the following year, in restricting the trade of the colony to English shipping, had restated a principle already familiar to them. The new Act of 1660 dealt them a severe blow by placing tobacco on the list of enumerated articles to be exported to the mother-country alone. At the same time the authorities in London began to entertain the idea of reconstituting the Virginia Company. To protest against these measures and to secure confirmation of his commission, Berkeley sailed for England in 1661.

That Virginia, considered as an isolated economic unit, suffered loss by the operation of the laws of trade is undoubted. But it was the price she had to pay for the privilege of belonging to a powerful maritime empire which gave her the protection of its armed force and an assured, if restricted, market for her tobacco. Suppose her to have attained economic liberty by withdrawing from that empire. How long would she, with her population of 40,000 souls, have continued to exist ere she became a prey to France or Spain ? For no great while ; neither would she have bettered her condition under an alien flag, for France and Spain adopted colonial systems as restrictive commercially, and politically far more repressive than did the much abused mother-country of England. Two things made a free-trade empire an idle dream in the seventeenth century—scarcity of population in the colonies themselves, rendering them unable to provide for their own defence ; and the exhausting drain imposed by naval armaments upon the revenue of states in which the wealth-producing methods of the industrial revolution were yet unborn. The Virginians therefore had to take the world as they found it ; and in fact, after the failure of Berkeley's protest, they ceased officially to remonstrate against the laws of trade. The Virginian assembly remains silent upon the point throughout the Stuart period.

The actual extent to which the colony suffered is a matter for divergent arguments, as is inevitable in a case where sentiment and impression, in default of exact statistics, form the basis of opinion. One writer says, "The Virginians were crushed with tremendous duties [1] on their tobacco and with ruinous restrictions upon their trade " ; another, "Virginia deserved well of the Stuarts ; but she offered a safe field for the spoiler and paid the penalty " ; a third, on the other hand, "In any reciprocal arrangement, mankind is prone to ignore the benefits conferred and to dwell solely on the restraints imposed. ... Would Virginia have welcomed complete free trade with the removal both of all restrictions and of all special privileges ? ... Unquestionably the gains and losses would have been so evenly balanced as to render a decision extremely difficult." [2] The question is obviously disputable. But one hard fact tells strongly against the "crushing and ruinous " interpretation : the population of the colony doubled itself during the reign of Charles II. It is generally admitted also that the colonial administration of the period was sympathetic and intelligent. It would not, for its own sake, have permitted vital damage to the interests of a colony which filled an important place in the empire it cultivated with so much care. Berkeley himself expressed the essence of the grievance with the pardonable emphasis of a partisan. It was that the English merchants absorbed an unfair share of the tobacco profits owing to the elimination of the foreign buyer. "The planters are the

[1] In sober truth the duties were not tremendous ; they amounted to 2d. per lb. on tobacco consumed in England, and only ½d. per lb. on that re-exported.

[2] The three authorities quoted are : (1) T. J. Wertenbaker, *Virginia under the Stuarts,* Princeton, 1914, p. 115 ; (2) Prof. E. Channing, *Hist. of U.S.,* ii. p. 63 ; (3) G. L. Beer, *Old Colonial System,* ii. p. 116. Channing mistook the valuation of tobacco for the actual duty imposed, and so overstated the latter. Wertenbaker apparently follows him. Beer corrects the error. Older authorities are not to be relied upon for the economic question. Winsor's *Narrative and Critical History,* for example, has contradictory statements on adjoining pages : "Under the monopoly of the Navigation Act ... the trade of the colony was almost extinguished " (vol. iii. ch. v., by Robert A. Brock, p. 150); "The resources of the colony continued [*c.* 1680] to be developed. The production and export of tobacco—the chief staple—steadily increased, and with it the prosperity of the colony." (*Ibid.* p. 152).

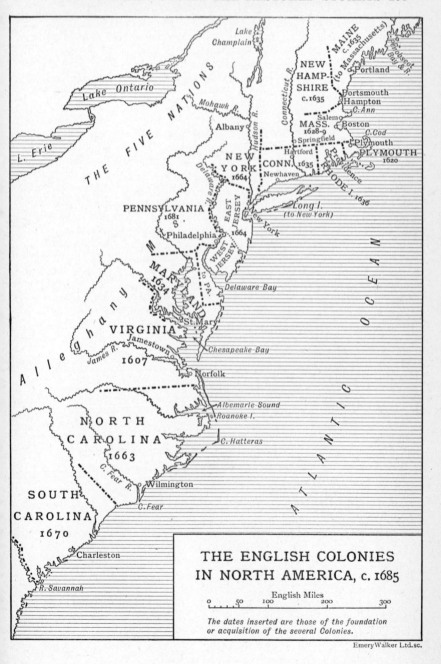

THE ENGLISH COLONIES
IN NORTH AMERICA, c. 1685

English Miles

0   50   100   200   300

*The dates inserted are those of the foundation
or acquisition of the several Colonies.*

Emery Walker Ltd. sc.

merchants' slaves " was the burden of his complaint. The planters nevertheless continued to increase and multiply and employ slaves themselves.

Although the enumeration of tobacco provided fair ground for remonstrance, the colonists were well aware that over-production was the principal cause of the fall in prices. The output of the English tobacco colonies more than sufficed to flood the home market. The surplus which was re-exported had to compete with the produce of Spanish America, and although smoking was on the increase throughout Europe, the supply exceeded the demand. The Virginians tried to cope with the evil by the old policy of the " stint," that is, limitation of the number of plants cultivated and destruction of the lower qualities of leaf. For this the co-operation of their neighbours in Maryland was essential. But Lord Baltimore, with an eye to his own immediate revenues, refused to sanction any mutual agreement. Maryland tobacco, of different flavour from that of Virginia, found its principal market in the Low Countries, and the divergence of interest was insuperable. An indirect means of effecting a stint, by the encouragement of other industries, also broke down. Berkeley returned in 1662 with instructions to favour the production of iron, flax, hemp and pitch. He expended much trouble on the attempt. But the industrial life of an aristocratic and servile community is not flexible like that of a modern democratic state. The social fabric of Virginia rested upon the tobacco plantations. It could not adapt itself to other means of livelihood.

From the foregoing it will be understood that there are two arguable views of the condition of Virginia under the Restoration, one holding that the colony was in chronic distress, the other that it prospered to a reasonable extent and that the dissatisfaction which undoubtedly existed sprang from other causes than the laws of trade. Those causes we shall consider below, merely remarking for the present that material prosperity is quite compatible with political unrest, as the example of England in the period 1678-88 amply illustrates. The testimony of population, as we have seen, favours the view that the colony was prosperous ; it increased steadily in the twenty years ending in 1670. In the latter year it amounted to about 40,000, including 6000 indentured servants and 2000 negroes.[1] In 1681-5 a conservative estimate placed it at 70,000 to 80,000, with white and black slaves numbering 15,000 and 3000 respectively. Another account of this time gives a still higher total.[2] The European war of 1672-8, in which England fought only during the first two years, produced a period of high prices whereof Virginia reaped the benefit.

The political history of the colony under the Restoration derives unity from the fact that long-continued abuses led to a dramatic climax in the revolt of 1676. The course of events was parallel to that in England. In 1660 the royalist Sir William Berkeley returned to

[1] Beer, ii. p. 129 ; Channing, ii. pp. 65 and 82.   [2] Beer, ii. p. 148.

power in an access of loyalty and popularity. The assembly elected in that year contained a large majority of his supporters, but, like the Cavalier parliament at home, it outstayed its welcome, for it sat undissolved for sixteen years. During that time the ruling party became a close oligarchy, managing all things for its own benefit amid a thickening atmosphere of corruption.[1] New men were crowding into the colony to find themselves deprived of political influence. Their new ideas and clear views, undimmed by long consuetude of existing abuses, found no legitimate outlet. They had no chance to exercise their votes. All appointments of officials and clergy, the whole patronage of the colony, rested with the governor's clique when they were not engrossed by strangers in England. Berkeley himself deteriorated. Originally a blustering, outspoken champion of his people's interests, he never consciously departed from that attitude ; but insensibly he became a morose, covetous old man, " broken in health, deaf and very irritable." His ideal of government was a paternal despotism, tempered by rough justice and common sense. Gradually the common sense departed. " I thank God," he wrote in his later days, " I thank God, there are no free schools, nor printing, and I hope we shall not have, these hundred years. . . . God keep us from both ! "

In 1673 Charles II., in a moment of generosity, dropped a bombshell into the stagnant pool of Virginian politics. He granted to Lords Arlington and Culpeper an interest in the colony which they had done nothing to merit. Their patent empowered them to make grants of land and to receive the quit-rents and escheats, to nominate sheriffs and surveyors, and to exercise all church patronage. It was a repetition on a huge scale of a similar grant made years before to certain courtiers, and covering only an outlying part of the province. The Virginian rulers received the news with " unspeakable grief and astonishment." They protested strongly, and sent agents to England to negotiate. Arlington and Culpeper, on their side, showed no keen desire to figure as political tyrants ; they preferred the safer rôle of blackmailers, and intimated that they would retire from their newly acquired rights for a consideration. To simplify the matter they resigned all but the quit-rents, from which Virginia prepared to buy them out. By the end of 1675 the terms of a charter had been framed whereby the Virginia colonists were to be incorporated for the purpose of jointly acquiring the quit-rents. The matter then hung in suspense, and the rebellion of the following year put an end to the scheme.[2]

---

[1] Cf. *Calendar of Col. State Papers*, 1677-80, p. iii : " The salaries of the members of the assembly were ridiculously high ; the cost of the liquor with which they enlivened their deliberations was charged against the public ; shameful jobs were perpetrated for the enrichment of their creatures . . . and, in fact, the whole settlement was plundered for their benefit."

[2] Channing, ii. p. 64, says the charter was issued ; but it never took effect and is not now extant.

In the colony the discontent with Berkeley's rule increased. Two incidents of the Dutch wars discredited the home and local administrations. In 1667 five Dutch warships raided the Chesapeake, caught the solitary guardship unprepared, burned seven merchantmen, and carried off thirteen. A long discussion on the question of building forts at the mouth of the James followed, but nothing was done. In 1673 the Dutch squadron which subsequently captured New York made a similar raid and destroyed eleven ships. Bad harvests and a devastating hurricane intensified local ill-feeling, and produced attempted risings in 1673 and 1674. Two years later the explosion occurred as the result of an Indian war.

The Indians had been quiescent for a generation, when reprisals for a petty theft gave the signal for an outbreak of massacre on the frontiers. The settlers concerned were much to blame. They murdered six Indian chiefs at a conference, beginning a medley of misunderstanding and treachery that issued in the killing of three hundred white men in the outlying plantations. Berkeley, old and set in his ways, would take no active steps to restore order. He had always regarded himself as the father of the Indians, and now his dimmed faculties refused to see the necessity of a campaign against them. In addition he was interested in the fur trade, and his opponents hinted that he was determined " that no bullets should pierce beaver skins." He sat still whilst the tale of slaughter mounted. Nathaniel Bacon, one of the new men lately arrived in the colony, had no such scruples. He raised a force on his own initiative, and led it against the savages. Berkeley, outraged at his independence, proclaimed him a traitor. The whole colony was now in a ferment. Berkeley dissolved the assembly and ordered an election, the first since the Restoration. The new house contained a majority against the governor, Bacon himself being elected to a seat. Amid the bewildering changes of front which followed the Indians were almost forgotten. Berkeley first pardoned Bacon, then denounced him again, quitted Jamestown, raised troops and returned, and was finally beaten out, whilst the place itself was burnt. A few facts stand out from the welter. Bacon's party in the assembly passed new laws intended to destroy the power of the oligarchy ; a bitter personal passion was aroused by the action of the Baconians in seizing Lady Berkeley and other womenfolk of their opponents, and exposing them to the fire of the besieged during the last attack on Jamestown ; and Bacon himself used language which showed him to be contemplating secession from the empire. The end came with Bacon's death from fever, upon which the revolt collapsed.

Berkeley was harsh in his vengeance. He confiscated estates, and executed the rebel leaders as they came in. An incident reveals him to us, remorseless and cynical. William Drummond, whom he had formerly made governor of Carolina, was one of the last to be captured. " Mr. Drummond," said the old man with a bow, " you are very welcome ; I am more glad to see you than any man in Virginia ; you shall be hanged in half an hour." " As your honour pleases," answered Drummond ; and hanged he was. Berkeley, however, confined his justice to the ringleaders. The total of executions fell short of forty, a moderate price for rebellion in the age of Jeffreys and Colonel Kirke. When all was over, three royal commissioners with a regiment of troops arrived from England. The commissioners, finding Berkeley still implacable, sent him home as the best means of restoring peace. He died in disgrace soon after landing, miserably ending a career which would have been reckoned honourable had it not lasted too long.

Virginia had two more governors of Stuart appointment. Lord Culpeper was chosen in 1679, but performed his duties by deputy until 1682, when he sailed to spend a few months in the colony. He was still in receipt of the quit-rents under the earlier patent, and he earned a name for rapacity among his subjects. Apart from this he acted with prudence and tact, promulgating a general pardon for the rebellion, and neglecting to put in force certain instructions from home tending to limit the power of the assembly. In 1684 Lord Howard of Effingham succeeded him. Howard was disliked by the colonists, but no important incidents marked his rule until the winter of 1688-9. Wild rumours then began to spread of events at home and of impending attacks by papists and Indians upon the colony. In April definite news arrived that James II. had fallen, and the revolution peacefully accomplished itself in Virginia.

In Maryland the period under review passed more tranquilly. Cecilius Calvert, the second Lord Baltimore, had great difficulty in maintaining his position under the Puritan régime. He was in fact between two fires ; the Puritans distrusted him for his religion, and the royalists for his time-serving. For several years his rights remained in practical abeyance, whilst factions disturbed the peace of the colony. In 1656-7 he made his peace with Cromwell and regained control which, by dexterous diplomacy, he retained at the Restoration. From then until his death in 1675 he continued " absolute Lord and Proprietor of the Province." His son, Charles Calvert, succeeded him. Unlike his father, he spent most of his time in Maryland, as governor from 1661 to 1675, and as proprietor from that date until 1684 when increasing perils to his patent recalled him to England. Although of ordinary ability, he was devoted to the interests of the colony.

Maryland itself was prosperous in a simple fashion, poorer than Virginia, but with its wealth more equally distributed. The strife of religions gradually decreased, the Catholic element tending to disappear. Tobacco remained the sole export, much of it in the early years being bought by New Englanders and illegally sent to Europe. After the passage of the Plantation Duties Act customs officials were sent out from England and the infraction of the trade laws diminished. Local feeling resented the increase of control. In 1684 George Talbot, the deputy-governor, murdered Christopher Rousby, the collector of customs, on board a ship of the royal navy. Talbot was condemned to death, but James II. commuted the punishment to five years' banishment. The proprietors, in fear for their patent, assisted the enforcement of the Navigation Acts. In spite of this, and also of the fact that they were Catholics, the third Lord Baltimore was not popular with James II, who favoured Penn in the matter of the boundary dispute. Amid the general confiscation of colonial charters which was in progress in 1688 Baltimore's rights stood in great danger, and would probably have been annulled had not the revolution intervened. In 1689 the news from home caused a Protestant rising against the proprietor and the election of a Maryland convention pending the decision of the colony's fate.

(iii) *New England*

In dealing with the history of New England under the restored Stuarts we are concerned more with measures than with men. The personalities of the period are not inspiring or even, for the most part, interesting. To the lofty clear-minded Winthrop and Bradford succeed a generation of leaders possessing indeed strength of will and subtlety of wit, but employing their talents by less noble means to less spiritual ends. All things move on lower planes, and of all the men with whom we came in touch on either side Clarendon alone fully merits the designation of a statesman.

Under the Puritan ascendancy New England was virtually independent, the outstanding feature of the period being the advance of Massachusetts, as compared with her neighbours. Massachusetts seized the administration of Maine and New Hampshire, the proprietary regions of Gorges and Mason upon her northern borders. She had visions also of annexing Rhode Island, to the southward, being anxious to make an end of that colony's religious toleration. Rhode Island, however, although barred from future territorial expansion, maintained its independence. Plymouth and New Haven, also, being closed in by their neighbours' occupation of the hinterlands, were unable to grow, and Connecticut was the only state which could make progress comparable to that of Massachusetts. The Navigation Act of 1651, by debarring the Dutch from the carrying trade, was beneficial to New England shipping. Boston ere long owned a promising fleet of coasters and merchantmen trading with the West Indies, the tobacco colonies, and Europe. Through its custom house passed most of the exports not only of Massachusetts but of all New England.

With the advent of the Quakers shortly before the Restoration there arose a new challenge to the Puritan hierocracy. The sect's offence was twofold. It frankly contemned the religious opinions of others, and it carried its ideas of human equality to such a pitch that it horrified all ordinary men with their rooted conceptions of a nicely graded social order. The Quaker of the seventeenth century refused to doff his hat in the presence of authority or to accord such titles as " Sir " and " Your worship " to those who considered themselves his superiors. Rhode Island, true to its principles, tolerated the new-comers, although it disliked them. Plymouth, mild in its intolerance, ordered them corporal punishment without danger to life or limb. Massachusetts imprisoned, scourged, and banished them, and on their reappearance pitilessly hanged four of the leaders, including a woman. This extreme act marks the climax of New England church governance. Thenceforward, as a natural reaction, a secular spirit began to make headway in the councils of the chief Puritan colony. The Boston rulers, called to account by the English government, wrote in extenu-ation : " The Quakers died not because of their other crimes how capital soever, but upon their superadded presumptuous and incorrigible contempt of authority."

Such a charge in the mouth of those who made it smacked of Satan rebuking sin ; for throughout the Restoration period the keynote of their own conduct towards the home government was this same contempt of authority, rendered the more galling by the smooth lip-service with which they accompanied it. The Council of Plantations appointed in 1660 was not long in framing a heavy indictment against the New Englanders, and against the Massachusetts men in particular : they had been tardy in proclaiming the king ; they habitually thought and spoke of themselves as a commonwealth, even in official documents ; they exceeded their chartered rights in imposing religious restrictions ; and they conducted their trade solely for their own benefit without regard to that of the mother-country. In short, they were bent upon practical independence whilst retaining all the advantages of member-ship in the empire. For technically complete separation they had no desire. They feared the French power on the St. Lawrence, and their trading interests throve under those clauses of the Navigation Acts which it suited them to recognize. Of sentimental attachment to England they showed little trace, which is not surprising in view of the circumstances which had driven their fathers to cross the Atlantic.

The Earl of Clarendon considered the report of his Committee of Plantations, and determined upon a moderate and far-seeing course of action. He rejected advice to annul the charters and consolidate New England as a crown colony, and sought instead to balance the dangerous influence of Massachusetts by according liberal treatment to Connecticut. In 1662 John Winthrop the younger, the leading man in the latter colony, travelled to England to negotiate for a new charter. Winthrop behaved with discretion, flattering the king and ingratiating himself with the men of science who were becoming a fashionable element in London life.[1] He therefore secured a grant whereby Connecticut received a favourable delimitation of its frontiers and permission to swallow up its smaller neighbour of New Haven. The

[1] He was afterwards made a Fellow of the Royal Society.

New Havenites, straitest of all the Puritans, protested in vain. They had to bow to superior force, and their colony disappeared as a separate political unit. Massachusetts received confirmation of its existing charter on condition of waiving the religious qualification for its franchise. This, in characteristic fashion, it made pretence of doing whilst maintaining in practice the prior state of affairs. Rhode Island also obtained a royal charter in 1663. Plymouth had never hitherto possessed such a document and declined it now, since the proposal was coupled with a condition that the crown should appoint the governor.

Having thus prepared the ground, Clarendon proceeded to the next step. Early in 1664 he appointed a royal commission of four members to go to New England and report upon the condition of affairs, with authority to take necessary steps for the enforcement of the laws of trade, the recovery of the king's interests in Maine and New Hampshire, and the removal of religious restraints. The chief commissioner was Colonel Nicolls, also charged with the conduct of the campaign against New Netherland. With him were Samuel Maverick, a pre-1629 settler and bitter enemy of the Puritans, and two others of less import- ance. Nicolls was undoubtedly the man to make the mission a success had he been able to devote his full attention to it, but unfortunately his military duties and subsequent governorship of New York absorbed his best energies. The commissioners therefore failed to reduce Massachusetts to obedience. At Boston they met with a polite reception coupled with a refusal to recognize their authority. " It is not so nominated in the bond " was the substance of the argument used against them. The Massachusetts charter indeed contained no explicit proviso that the colony must receive a royal commission, but the contention was a dangerous one to those who used it, for they had themselves overstepped their strict rights in more than one direction. However, a Dutch war was imminent, Massachusetts was protesting loyalty and ready with endless quibbles and evasions of the real issue, and Nicolls had to swallow the rebuff. He departed after setting up a royal administration in Maine, an arrangement which Massachusetts quietly reversed a few years later. In Rhode Island and Connecticut he had better fortune, for those colonies had given little offence to the government. Connecticut assisted in the conquest of New Netherland, and received a favourable frontier with the Duke of York's new province. In return she had to give up her claim on Long Island. Massachusetts, pleased at having foiled the king so easily, deprecated the royal rebuke by a present of masts for the navy, and the first diplomatic struggle with New England came to an end. The fall of Clarendon at the close of the Dutch war prevented its immediate renewal.

For some ten years New England maintained its isolation untroubled by the government at home. Its landsmen lived principally by agriculture and the production of foodstuffs for export, its maritime population by the coast fishery and by trade with the plantation colonies and with Europe.[1] To the latter it exported tobacco and sugar in contravention of the Navigation Acts. With the British Isles it had little direct intercourse. It received from them some manufactured goods and sent them a few furs, the whole on a scale petty as compared with the West Indian traffic.

In 1675 began a serious Indian rising known as Philip's War from the name of the leading chief of the redskins. The Indians of New England were debarred by the strong Iroquois tribes of the interior from retreating before the advance of white settlement. Economic pressure, the clearing of forests and extermination of game, drove them to despair. The revolt began near Providence, and flamed fitfully over all the New England colonies throughout the winter of 1675-6. Straggling and unprepared white men were massacred. Even larger bodies did not escape ; at Bloody Brook a force of ninety fell into an ambush and only ten survived. Philip was hunted down at the end of 1676, and many of his followers were sold as slaves to the West Indies. The war cost New England one-tenth of its men of military age, a dozen townships destroyed by fire, and £100,000 in money. Taxation rose to sixteen times its normal level ere the danger was overcome.

Massachusetts, as we have seen, resumed control over Maine after the fall of Clarendon. She did this at the request of the inhabitants. but without permission from home. About 1671 the heirs of Gorges and Mason, the original proprietors of Maine and New Hampshire, revived their claims to those territories, apparently with the object of creating a market for their disposal. The matter dragged on for some years, during which time Charles II. conceived the idea of acquiring Maine as an appanage for his illegitimate son, the Duke of Monmouth. Massachusetts, however, forestalled him, buying out the Gorges rights for £1250 in 1678. Charles was intensely annoyed, but the arrangement stood until the colonies passed from the British flag. New Hampshire received a separate government as a crown colony in 1679.

In the meantime the diplomatic attack upon Massachusetts independence had reopened. The passage of the Plantation Duties Act in 1672 presaged a new attempt to deal with the scandalous infringement of which the New Englanders were undoubtedly guilty. With the close of the last Dutch war and the appointment of the Lords of Trade the campaign for strict administration commenced. Its chief promoter was Edward Randolph, a civil service official, possessed of a resolute will and intense pugnacity tempered by very little tact or sense of proportion. His character had a great influence on the course of events, and he has been charged with " resolute malignity " towards the colonists,[2] although he seems in his crabbed fashion to have upheld what he regarded as their true interests.[3] In 1676 he went out to Boston to look into the commercial question. After a short stay he returned

---

[1] In 1665 Massachusetts owned 132 ships of which 52 were over 40 tons burden (Beer, ii. p. 246).

[2] Doyle, *Puritan Colonies*, ii. p. 253. [3] Channing, ii. p. 159.

to render a report charging the New England merchants with wholesale transgressions and a defiant attitude. He stated further that a majority of the people were hostile to the ruling oligarchy. In this he probably exaggerated.

From Randolph's report dates the movement to abrogate all chartered rights and combine the New England states into one large crown colony. The Lords of Trade supported the policy because they were convinced that self-government as understood at Boston was incompatible with the maintenance of the imperial fiscal system. Military strategists also backed it because division and autonomy rendered the colonies weak in presence of the growing power of France. Finally—and this undoubtedly was a weighty factor—the years 1678-88 were a period in which arbitrary government was for the last time raising its head in England ; French ideals and influences were predominant, and it was inevitable that a reflection of the general tendency should make itself apparent across the Atlantic. Thus all considerations, both of good government and of tyranny, pointed to a reduction of New England independence.

Randolph went back to Massachusetts as collector of customs in 1678. He pursued a headstrong course, bringing every trade offence, trivial or serious, before the courts. The latter generally refused to convict the defendants, and added to Randolph's fury by awarding damages against him for detention of shipping and cargoes. His personal unpopularity had much but not all to do with his failure. The trouble was really fundamental, going deeper even than the economic question. It was against the king's officer as such, rather than against the collector of taxes, that the New Englanders set their faces. At length, after years of ceaseless complaint by Randolph, browbeating of the colonial agents in London by the Lords of Trade, and alternate defiance and evasion by Massachusetts, the government took action. It issued a writ of *quo warranto* against the colony, and in 1684 declared forfeit the fifty-five years old charter of the Massachusetts Bay Company.

Consolidation was now the order of the day, and Charles II. designated Colonel Percy Kirke, lately returned from Tangier, as governor of New England. Randolph, much as he had suffered from the colonists, had no wish to see them handed over to the tender mercies of such a man, and he protested against the appointment. Charles died before signing the commission. The Monmouth rebellion followed, giving Kirke the opportunity of imprinting his name in the history of England ; and James II., more considerate to the colonists than to his subjects at home, decided not to confirm the late king's choice. As a temporary measure he appointed Joseph Dudley, a Massachusetts man, as governor. At the end of 1686 Sir Edmund Andros arrived at Boston to take over the duty from Dudley's hands. At first Andros ruled over Massachusetts, Maine, New Hampshire and Plymouth. But in the meantime proceedings had commenced against the remaining charters.

Rhode Island surrendered in 1686, and Connecticut was reduced by Andros in 1687 after a prolonged diplomatic contest. Nowhere, either in Massachusetts or elsewhere, was there any attempt at forcible resistance. Trade rather than religion was now the dominating motive ; and the New England traders knew that they were well off within the privileges of the empire, even with the Navigation Acts enforced.

The administration of Andros contained no popular element. He ruled with the aid of a nominated council consisting mainly of colonists, but the assemblies were entirely suspended. It was for this reason that men who had been accustomed to an active participation in their own governance could not reconcile themselves to the change. Andros was in a difficult position, but he acquitted himself well. He ruled justly and firmly, enforcing the Navigation Acts together with the new policy of religious toleration. For the first time since John Winthrop had founded the city, Boston witnessed the parades of redcoats and the celebration of an Anglican service by a surpliced clergyman. Still the new dominion grew. In 1688 Andros received orders to take over New York and the Jerseys. His authority now extended from the Delaware to the borders of Nova Scotia. Had its continuance not depended upon events at home a new and more beneficent era might have opened for America ; for there is nothing in James' previous record to indicate that he would have made permanent his suspension of the colonists' political rights. In a revolution such things must be, and the king fell before his colonial revolution was complete.

By the end of 1688 an intelligent anticipation of the conquest of England by William of Orange began to circulate in Boston. Definite news came by way of the West Indies in March of the following year, accompanied by William's declaration promising reinstatement to all dispossessed magistrates. Andros imprisoned its bearer for sedition, but he could not undo its effect in focussing all the latent disaffection among his subjects. A fortnight later Boston rose suddenly and unanimously. Andros with his handful of troops was powerless ; for throughout his authority had rested upon the far-distant resources of King James. He surrendered to the rebels, and the Dominion of New England was at an end. Here, as elsewhere throughout America, a pause followed, whilst all eyes turned towards London to see what edicts its new government would bring forth.

CHAPTER XII

THE GREAT TRADING COMPANIES UNDER THE RESTORATION

(i) *The East India Company*, 1657-1709

THE East India Company, set on its legs again by Cromwell's charter of 1657, participated to the full in the revival of trade inaugurated by the Restoration. The directors greeted Charles II. with an address of loyalty and a present of plate. He in his turn granted them a favourable charter and availed himself of their practical goodwill by accepting loans amounting to £170,000 in the space of sixteen years. His patronage thus had its price, but it was to be depended upon ; neither he nor his brother ever betrayed the Company's interests in the vacillating manner of the early Stuart kings. The charter of 1661 confirmed the privileges accorded by previous grants, and gave additional rights of jurisdiction over all Englishmen in the east and power to maintain fortifications and to raise troops for their defence. The paid-up capital with which the Company began the new era totalled £370,000. This became a permanent joint-stock upon which the directors could operate with greater confidence than in the old days of terminable adventures. They increased their resources by a judicious limitation of dividends in the first years and also by acting as bankers, accepting deposits repayable at short notice and on low rates of interest. The fact that the public were willing to trust them in this way illustrates the hitherto unwonted solidity of the Company's position.

A considerable item in Catharine of Braganza's dowry had been the promise to hand over the Portuguese possession of Bombay. Charles II. determined to hold the place as a crown colony, the first of its kind in Asia. In 1662 he sent the Earl of Marlborough with five ships and a military force to take it over. The exact extent of the territory concerned was in dispute, and Marlborough could not come to terms with the Portuguese governor. He came home in disgust, leaving his troops to perish for lack of supplies and a landing place. Surat could not receive them. for the Mogul would never have forgiven the presence of English soldiers in his dominions. At length the survivors, in number less than a quarter of the original strength of the force, gained admission to Bombay in 1665. In this inauspicious manner began the English tenure of the place which was to become their Indian headquarters at the close of the century. The ill fortune continued. Charles, weary of the profitless expense of his acquisition, made it over to the Company in 1668 for a rent of £10 a year. The Company's servants fared as badly in the early years as did the unseasoned troops from home. Cholera, a disease apparently new in their experience and thought to be of Chinese origin, swept them off by hundreds. Of the first five hundred English inhabitants of Bombay four hundred died there, and the average life of the English factor was reckoned at three years. Heroic determination triumphed over these odds. With unsparing labour the English erected fortifications, bettered the sanitary conditions by drainage works, and attracted trade and population. By 1677 the latter had risen from 10,000 to 60,000, and the commercial success of Bombay was assured.

The early history of the English in India consists, to a far greater extent than in other regions of the world, of the record of a few brilliant personalities overcoming seemingly hopeless conditions by sheer force of brain and character. For this the reason is not far to seek. In most other lands which have been the theatres of English expansion the principal foes to be overcome have been the forces of nature, and a struggle of this sort has demanded a high average standard of merit in the rank and file of the colonists. India, with its huge native populations, and the constant menace from European rivals, has exacted above all things excellence of individual leadership as the price of success, and at almost every period from the first settlement at Surat to the close of the Company's career one or more outstanding commanders are to be found upholding their employers' interests by the exercise of their talents. This biographical element in the record becomes especially prominent in the latter part of the seventeenth century.

A great change in the political condition of the country was about to set in. The Mogul Empire, which had hitherto preserved order in northern India and exercised a steadying influence beyond its immediate confines, had passed its zenith. Its outlying viceroys were seeking to assume the status of independent sovereigns, and the Marathas, a military nation scorning to be bound by territorial limits, were extending their plundering raids far and wide in central India and successfully challenging the power of the Mogul government. Aurangzeb, the last great emperor, reigned from 1658 to 1707, and spent the last five-and-twenty years of his life in a long campaign against the forces of anarchy. He displayed great energy and won many victories, but he could only delay and not avert the break-up of his empire. His career, of apparent splendour accompanied by the actual decay of his state, has been justly compared with that of Louis XIV. Surat, the English head factory, hitherto well within the zone of the imperial peace, witnessed a Maratha raid in 1664. The invaders plundered the town, but Sir George Oxenden, the English president, showed a bold front and beat them off from the walls of his unfortified factory with goods worth £80,000 in its cellars. The incident marks the beginning of the end of the old policy of unarmed trade laid down by Sir Thomas Roe. For the first time the Mogul had been unable to protect his clients ; henceforward they must prepare to defend themselves.

Realizing the necessity, Gerald Aungier, the president of Surat from 1669 to 1677, perceived also the importance of Bombay. Although pestilent, it was defensible ; it lay without the bounds of the emperor's jurisdiction, and the English could carry out their plans unhampered by the jealousy of his officers ; it lay also on the flank of the Maratha raids towards the north, in a position where English sea-power could command the respect of these formidable adventurers. Aungier it was, therefore, who developed Bombay, created a service of light craft to hold in check the coast pirates, made a treaty with Sivaji the Maratha chief, and diverted to his new place of arms half the shipping from England which had hitherto laded in Swally Road. In the year of his death he warned the Company that they must trade sword in hand or perish. His successors continued the policy he had inaugurated.

Madras, on the Coromandel Coast, saw itself threatened by the same forces of disorder. Francis Day's fortifications had fallen into decay, and the Company was as yet unconvinced that such expenditure was necessary. But here the need was even greater. The Dutch were strong in the Bay of Bengal ; the French appeared at St. Thomé, hard by, and established their first factory, which they removed later to Pondicherry ; the native powers were in a state of anarchy, the Marathas hovering watchful in the interior ; and, to cap all, the English were at war with one another. For three years, 1665-8, the Puritan George Foxcroft, the legitimate governor, was kept in durance by the royalist Sir Edward Winter, who only submitted to the Company's authority on the appearance of an armed fleet. In 1674 the Company determined to abandon the place as untenable. They changed their plan ere it was too late, and refortified it. Three years later Sivaji swept down upon the district, but the defences averted his attack. Aurangzeb, in the course of his campaigns, also threatened Madras, and for long it seemed the most precarious foothold of the English in India. In 1681 its president had to relinquish his control over the Bengal factories.

Amid the growing confusion these also experienced a time of trouble. The principal station was now the factory of Hughli which, like that of Kasimbazar, lay so far in the interior as to be beyond the reach of sea-going ships. The viceroy of Bengal, fast becoming an independent sovereign, was therefore able to oppress the Company's servants with impunity. After years of intolerable exactions a native attack upon Hughli in 1686 brought the grievance to a climax. In default of a remedy, the continuance of English trade in Bengal was impossible. As in Bombay, however, the time brought forth the man. Job Charnock, after thirty years' service in India, became head of the Bengal council in 1686. He had married a Hindu widow whom he was said to have rescued from her husband's funeral pyre. This fact, and his adoption of native ways of life, rendered him suspect to his fellow-countrymen, who falsely accused him of paganism. But, if there was something repulsive and uncongenial in his character, there was in it also a hard and unyielding trait which could dare all and suffer all, and which proved the salvation of his employers' interests in the Ganges delta. In 1686 he evacuated Hughli and moved thirty miles down the river to a spot where the rising bank overlooked an anchorage accessible to the Company's ships. On the land side jungle and swamps afforded defence against armies whilst they threatened death from disease. The place was uninhabited during the greater part of the year, and Charnock and his followers had to live in tents and boats under the burning sun. To the majority it seemed madness to settle there. Nevertheless on this site rose the city of Calcutta.

The viceroy of Bengal, now at open war with the English, followed with an army. Charnock had to leave his new post in 1687, only to stand stubbornly at two more points in succession and to return undaunted to Calcutta before the close of the year. Once more he abandoned the place, this time in compliance with orders from Madras. In 1690, peace being restored with the viceroy, he occupied Calcutta for the third time and finally. The mortality from disease was still terrible—" death overshadowed every living soul "—and the merchants would gladly have returned to the bondage and comparative ease of Hughli. But Charnock was resolute for a defensible factory at any cost. He died in January, 1693, but his work lived.[1] In 1697-8 his successors built Fort William on the scene of his labours, and by the end of the century the future capital had 1200 English inhabitants.

Charnock's war in Bengal had merged in a wider struggle which definitely marked the transition to the new policy of using armed force in India. In 1681 Sir Josiah Child and Sir John Child gained control of the Company's affairs, the former as governor in London, and the latter as president at Surat and Bombay. In spite of the common surname, they were not related to one another. Under their guidance the Company decided to make war upon the Mogul in order to extort fair play for its servants in Bengal and elsewhere. It underestimated the strength of the empire it was assailing, and failed to provide adequate forces for the grandiose campaign it had planned. To the two Childs it is but fair to say that others concurred in the decision and that they entered upon the adventure very unwillingly, conceiving it to be the only course open to them. The outcome in Bengal was happier than elsewhere. Aurangzeb turned fiercely upon the factories at Surat and Masulipatam, cutting

[1] For fuller details of Charnock's career see Hunter's *British India*, ii. pp. 249-71. For the foundation of Calcutta compare this with *Cambr. Hist. of Br. Empire*, iv. pp. 106-8.

off 'the trade and imprisoning the merchants. The English could retaliate only by stopping the pilgrims voyaging to Mecca by sea. In 1690 the Company was glad to patch up a peace on somewhat degrading terms, an arrangement facilitated by the death of Sir John Child, upon whom the emperor's resentment chiefly concentrated itself.

The two Dutch wars of Charles II.'s reign had little effect upon English fortunes in India. In the first a Dutch fleet cruised off Surat, but dread of the Mogul power forbade it to attack the factory. In the second the Company lost several ships, captured in the Bay of Bengal, and a Dutch force appeared off Bombay. Gerald Aungier had, however, made progress with his fortifications, and the enemy decided that the place was too strong to be attacked. Elsewhere the Company definitely abandoned its claim to Pulo Run, and in 1683 evacuated Bantam, intending thenceforward to concentrate its efforts upon India. St. Helena, occupied first under the Commonwealth, was lost and retaken in 1673. The crown granted it to the Company, which founded a small settlement on the island to serve as a resting place on the long voyage round the Cape of Good Hope.

The troubles experienced by the Company's servants in India were the inevitable accompaniments of Asiatic trade. They were seldom more than local in their effects, and whilst one factory was filling the record with its misfortunes the others were quietly making enormous gains for the shareholders. Figures best illustrate the Company's general prosperity under the Restoration. The sum of £370,000 paid up at the beginning of the period remained the nominal share capital until 1682. In that year the directors were able to double every holder's share out of the profits in hand, thus raising the total to £740,000.[1] In spite of this nominal doubling the market value of the entire stock ten years later stood at £1,069,000. In 1693 a new issue of stock brought the total to £1,488,000, valued in the following year at £1,213,000. The decline in the market price may thus be seen to have set in well after the fall of James II. It was in fact due to political changes arising from the events of 1688. During the whole period 1657-1691 the average annual dividend was about 25 per cent. In the decade 1672-82 the total division amounted to 380 per cent., of which 100 per cent. constituted the scrip dividend above mentioned, and the remainder was in cash. The stock reached its topmost price in 1683 when a £100 share fetched £500 in the market.

Such success was in itself dangerous. In the days of its adversity the Company had been accused of mismanaging a national asset; now the cry went up that a few selfish monopolists were engrossing the richest trade in the world. So long as Charles II. and his brother retained the throne the holders of their charters could afford to disregard the jealousy of outsiders. Both the royal brothers were

---

[1] The figures are taken principally from Scott's *Joint Stock Companies*, i. pp. 303, 308, 325, etc. As given above they are in round numbers, neglecting fractions of £1000

themselves stockholders, and both were anti-Dutch in their sympathies. But outside the court circle powerful influences were biding their time to pull down the favoured corporation. The feeling of the country became ever more inclined to the liberal institutions of Holland, and hostile to the tyrannous ideals of France upon which the Stuarts and their Company seemed together to rest their claims. Successful merchants and shipowners longed to take part in the eastern trade ; many of them could only do so under the stigma of interloping and by the use of false papers and clandestine clearances from Spanish ports. Textile manufacturers swelled the clamour, declaring that the import of muslins and calico took the bread from English craftsmen's mouths. The Levant Company complained bitterly of unfair competition, and pointed to its regulated constitution as the model of commercial liberty. All these rivals used every argument, sound and unsound, against the East India monopoly, and the old bullionist outcry of the country's peril from the export of silver once more exploited the credulity of the simple-minded.

The Company was not at first so selfish as its opponents declared. It allowed any English subject under the age of forty to dwell in India and engage in the port to port trade, reserving to itself only the monopoly of transport to Europe. Even for this it issued licences, as many as twelve " permission ships " putting to sea in the course of a single year. To its own servants it allowed generous opportunities for private ventures—at one time the employés' trade amounted to one-third of that done for the shareholders' account.[1] Perhaps by reason of this intentional laxity we find few complaints of interloping in the first half of Charles II.'s reign. But as the Stuart period drew to its close there was here as elsewhere throughout the empire a tightening of discipline by the authorities accompanied by a corresponding hardening of opposition to their control. At home and abroad Englishmen ranged themselves instinctively on the side of tyranny or of liberty, as some put it, of good government or disorder, as the alternatives appeared to others. The East India shareholders, as a body, were in no doubt as to their choice. Under the leadership of Sir Josiah Child they leaned to the court and their royal patrons, sharing with the French king the odium of financing the hated standing army, whilst Sir John Child revived their extreme claims in the east and marched interlopers in chains through the streets of Bombay.

Sir Josiah Child had, like many other leading men of the Restoration, served his apprenticeship as a Commonwealth official. His rise to Charles II.'s favour was slow, but he received a baronetcy in 1678 and became governor in 1681. His genius for finance, harshness of nature, and stubbornness of will moulded the Company's fortunes through its last years of prosperity, and strove desperately to avert the disaster for which they were in part responsible. At the time of his accession to power a minority of the shareholders were convinced

[1] Hunter, ii. p. 278.

that the monopoly could not for ever be made good against outside ambitions. Of this body Thomas Papillon became the leader. Politics embittered the dissension which thus broke out. Child was a monarchist, Papillon almost a republican. The former saw that the charter was as safe as the throne ; the latter envisaged the overthrow of both. When Child became governor Papillon was chosen deputy-governor. He and his party proposed to wind up the existing joint-stock and issue a new one, with the subscription-book open to all applicants. In this way the external advantages of the monopoly would have been preserved, and internally its basis would have been broadened so as to include the unprivileged outsiders. Sir Josiah stood firm for the maintenance of the vested interest, and he carried with him the majority of the five hundred shareholders. The reformers sold their stock and withdrew from the contest. Papillon was not allowed to retire unscathed. His enemies prosecuted him as an exclusionist. He was fined £10,000 for sedition, and fled overseas, to return a few years later in the train of William of Orange. At the same time Thomas Sandys, an interloper, challenged the general validity of royal charters for foreign trade. Jeffreys, the lord chief justice, presided at the trial of his case in Westminster Hall, taking care in his summing-up to bracket the presumptuous interloper with " the horrid conspirators against the King's life in this last hellish conspiracy " of the Rye House Plot. Judgment, as was inevitable, went in favour of the monopoly. It marked the culmination of Child's career and of the Old Company's prosperity.

The Revolution of 1688-9 was the precursor of misfortune. The Bill of Rights under which William and Mary undertook the government, although effecting little theoretical curtailment of the royal prerogative, practically made parliament the arbiter in all questions of national importance. Monopolies based solely on royal grants, whilst not absolutely more illegal than before, were thus rendered subject to reversal by legislation. The interlopers were quick to perceive that their time had come. With Thomas Papillon at their head they subscribed a fund, formed themselves into a society, and petitioned parliament in 1690 to throw open the Indian trade. A general election and the pressing business of the French war delayed their success. Child fought stiffly to the last, expending £80,000 in bribes in a single year. But the trend of events was against him. In July, 1698, his enemies obtained an Act of Parliament recognizing them as the New or English East India Company in contradistinction to the Old or London corporation. The grant was contingent upon the New Company lending £2,000,000 to the government at 8 per cent. All subscribers to the loan were to enjoy a proportionate share in the Indian trade, with liberty to organize themselves for that purpose in any way they thought fit. William confirmed the Act and gave three years' formal notice to the Old Company of the termination of its privileges.

But the Old Company did not accept defeat. If its rivals were strong at home, it was none the less firmly entrenched in the east, with factories, a loyal staff, and a century's hard-won experience. The subscription books for the two million loan were opened and in three days the great amount was underwritten. Among the entries appeared the name of John du Bois, for the sum of £315,000, nearly one-sixth of the whole. John du Bois was the secretary of the Old Company.

By this masterly stroke Child and the old hands stood to gain under the new Act almost as much as they were losing by the extinction of the royal charter. They might trade in what manner they pleased to the extent of their holding, and they determined to put to the proof their rivals' ability to establish factories, to attract trade, to negotiate with eastern courts, to accumulate prestige in a land which was conservative to the core. The New Company now realized that it yet had much to win. It proposed a fusion of interests, but received an evasive reply. It sent out presidents, factors and clerks to India with orders to open business at all places where the Old Company was already established. Its untrained servants had little success in face of their rivals' long-standing hold upon the country. In diplomacy the new corporation met with its heaviest defeat. Sir William Norris, whom it sent as ambassador to Aurangzeb, made himself ridiculous by his pretensions and his ignorance of the Mogul court, and narrowly escaped being murdered whilst making a retirement which resembled a flight.

On all hands the Old Company was foiling the New, but at ruinous cost to both. Amalgamation was the obvious remedy for a state of affairs rapidly becoming intolerable. The terms of the union now became the issue of the struggle. Both sides looked to parliamentary influence to carry the day, and in the general election of 1700-1 the din of the rival arguments eclipsed all questions of general politics. Bribes flowed like water, and the eighteenth-century system of borough-mongering was said to have taken shape from the electioneering methods of the East India Companies. At length, in 1702, the end was reached. By the Instrument of Union of that year the financial issues were adjusted, the Old Company received seven years' grace in which to wind up its affairs, and thereafter the two bodies were to merge into The United Company of Merchants of England trading to the East Indies. The amalgamation duly took place in 1708-9.

(ii) *The African Companies*

At the Restoration there was no organized trade with West Africa. Sir Nicholas Crisp's company,[1] long moribund, had transferred its assets on the slave coast to the East India Company in 1657. The latter body seems to have left the trade largely in the hands of private

---

[1] See *ante*, pt. iii. ch. i. p. 162.

adventurers, who are computed to have lost between them £300,000 in a few years. The Dutch West India Company was in fact rapidly monopolizing the slave trade. Its headquarters at Elmina, taken from the Portuguese in 1637, was the centre of a system which embraced some sixteen forts and trading stations,[1] some of which had in former years been in English possession whilst the remainder were inherited from the once magnificent African dominions of Portugal.

In 1660 Charles II. chartered a new company, the Royal Adventurers trading into Africa, with the Duke of York as its governor. At the out-set this body looked for its profit rather to the commodities of West Africa than to slaves. But the slave trade was the life of the West Indian plantations, and the statesmen who were consolidating the English colonial empire were obliged to challenge the Dutch monopoly. In 1662, therefore, the Royal Adventurers received a new charter which emphasized the slave trade as their principal business.[2] In 1664 Admiral Holmes went to the Guinea coast with a naval expedition, and added Elmina and other Dutch possessions to the posts which the Royal Adventurers had already received from the East India Company. Holmes also refounded James Fort (now Bathurst) on the Gambia River, whose banks have remained in English possession to the present day. Hard upon his track came De Ruyter with a more powerful squadron. De Ruyter successively took Goree, Satalone, Tacorady, Elmina and Anamabo. Repulsed from Cormantin, the English head-quarters, he returned to the attack after disposing of the minor garrisons. After hard fighting he prevailed, and Cormantin surrendered.

These reverses, occurring before the trade had been established, ruined the Royal Adventurers. By 1672 they were bankrupt, and a new chartered body, the Royal African Company, took over their stock and their remaining possessions of James Fort, Cape Coast Castle, and Sierra Leone. The Royal African Company, with the Duke of York as its governor, began business with a capital of £111,000.[3] At first it was prosperous, although never to the same extent as the other great trading companies of the Restoration. The war of 1672-8, in which the Dutch narrowly escaped annihilation as a free people, undoubtedly assisted the new venture to consolidate its position. For the six years 1676-81 its average annual dividend was 12½ per cent., and the stock rose to 245. In the period 1683-92 the annual average was nearly 5 per cent. ; thenceforward it dwindled to nothing. The Revolution of 1688-9 endangered the monopoly, which, like that of the East India Company, lacked parliamentary confirmation. The African Company was compelled to license private traders on payment of a royalty towards the upkeep of the forts. Its further history was

[1] Sir H. H. Johnston, *Hist. of the Colonization of Africa*, 2nd edit., Cambridge, 1913, pp. 123-4.

[2] *Cambr. Hist. of the Br. Empire*, i. pp. 440-1.

[3] For full financial details, see Scott, *Joint Stock Companies*, vols. i. and ii., numerous references.

one of continued disaster. In 1692 it quadrupled the nominal value of its stock, increasing the £111,000 to £444,000 without raising any further resources in actual cash. After this operation the market price stood at about 50 ; in 1697 it was 15 ; in 1708, 5 ; and in 1709-12, 2. By the latter date the Company was obviously in extremity, and a reconstruction inevitable. In 1713 this was carried out, the original shareholders losing four-fifths of their investment. The new Company at first enjoyed slightly better prospects, but was never a paying concern. In 1750 the joint-stock was wound up and the trade was continued under a regulated constitution and a new name—the African Company of Merchants. This arrangement existed until 1827, by which date the slave trade had ceased to be legal under the British flag. On the abolition of the regulated Company the trading stations fell to the crown.

The history of the English African companies is on the whole a melancholy one ; deservedly so, as some might be tempted to remark, by reason of the trade they carried on. Yet the fact remains that they did a useful and even an indispensable work in the economy of the old empire. Slaves were necessary to the development of the plantation colonies by which a maritime people could best thrive in the seventeenth and eighteenth centuries. It was only when Great Britain had gained, at the close of the latter, an industrial wealth greatly preponderating over that derived from the plantations, that she was strong enough to abolish the traffic which had made her rich.

The prime cause of the failure of the Companies was their inability to enforce their monopoly. The trade followed a triangular course— the outward passage to Africa, the middle passage across to the West Indies, and the homeward passage from thence to the British Isles. Of these the middle passage, economically the most important, was remote from government control. Interlopers and freelances of all sorts abounded. Even the Companies' servants had an eye principally to their private trade ; an observer remarked that the slaves who died on the voyage were always the Company's, whilst those belonging to the ship's captain arrived sound and well. The extent of the African coast, the difficulties of its navigation, and the sentiments of the western planters, all helped to render supervision difficult.

(iii) *The Hudson's Bay Company*

The exploration of Hudson's Bay by Hudson, Button, Foxe and James in the early part of the seventeenth century had created much excitement in English maritime circles at the time. When, however, it became apparent that these discoveries were not destined to open up a new passage to the Pacific Ocean the interest of contemporaries died away, and for nearly forty years the possibilities of commercial advantage in the north-west remained dormant.

In the meantime the French were extending their activities in the

M

St. Lawrence Basin.   Their pioneer in this region was Jacques Cartier of St. Malo, who had examined and charted the estuary of the great river in 1534 and the following years.   In 1605-8 Samuel de Champlain planted the first permanent post at Quebec and began to push westwards to the region of the Great Lakes.   A lucrative fur trade quickly sprang up and determined the future status of the Canadian settlements.   Instead of founding new homes—colonies in the true sense—as the New Englanders were doing, the French developed the fur trade to the exclusion of all else.   In the earlier decades they did not even produce enough foodstuffs in Canada for their own support, and the fall of Quebec in 1629 was due to the fact that English privateers captured the supply ships from France.   In 1627 Richelieu established the Company of New France to monopolize the trade.   This body developed its territories very slowly, and Louis XIV., under the advice of Colbert, replaced it by the Company of the West, with similar privileges, in 1664.   The general policy of the latter, as of its predecessor, was to employ the Indians as agents for the collection of furs.   Jesuit missionaries assisted the work by penetrating fearlessly into the wilds and striving to convert the savages, often at the cost of their own lives.   In one respect the French trading companies suffered from the same disadvantage as did their English contemporaries.   Their lucrative monopoly attracted interlopers who were often their own dismissed servants.   It was from the enterprise of two of these free lances that the English Hudson's Bay Company took its rise.

About the year 1659 Médard Chouart des Groseilliers and Pierre Radisson began a series of journeys in quest of furs in the unknown country around Lake Superior.   From the Indians they heard of a convenient overland route to the shores of Hudson's Bay, never hitherto visited by the French.   They returned to Quebec and attempted to convince the authorities that a rich producing area was but waiting to be tapped.   The time, however, was inopportune.   The new Company of the West was making an effort to crush individual enterprise, and discouraged the aspirations of the two pioneers.   Groseilliers then journeyed to Boston, arriving there in 1664 shortly after the appearance of Colonel Nicolls' commission from England.   At this point the scheme took the shape of a proposal to trade with Hudson's Bay by sea.   The Boston people thought well of it, but had no capital to spare, being fully occupied with the development of more certain enterprises nearer home.   Captain Zachary Gillam, however, a Massachusetts seaman, gave Groseilliers and Radisson a passage to Europe in his ship, and they crossed over to France in 1665 to lay their plans before Colbert and the government of Louis XIV.   Two years passed in discussion and ultimate discouragement, and Groseilliers at length travelled to London with letters of introduction to Prince Rupert from Lord Arlington, the English ambassador in Paris.   The Prince was in no great favour at court, and was also, for his position. a comparatively poor man.   Nevertheless he interested a few friends in the venture, and chartered two small ships to make a trading voyage into Hudson's Bay in 1668. One of these was the *Nonsuch* belonging to Zachary Gillam; the other need not concern us further, since her commander turned back before passing into the bay.[1]

Groseilliers accompanied Gillam, Radisson remaining in England. The *Nonsuch* penetrated into James Bay, the most southerly extension of the great inland sea, and on September 29, 1668, the adventurers landed at the mouth of Rupert's River and began the construction of Fort Charles, a wooden erection intended to serve as a stronghold and a trading depot. Before long the Indian tribes began to appear with supplies of beaver. By the following summer Gillam was able to sail for England with a good cargo, leaving Groseilliers to hold the fort.

Gillam's encouraging report paved the way for the next step. On May 2, 1670, Charles II. granted a charter of incorporation to the Governor and Company of Merchants Adventurers trading into Hudson's Bay. The governor was Prince Rupert, and the members, seventeen in number, included the Duke of Albemarle, Lords Craven, Arlington and Ashley, Sir Philip Carteret and Sir Peter Colleton, all of whom we have already noticed as interested in other trading or colonizing ventures of the time. The original capital was £10,500 of which Rupert was able to subscribe only £300. The charter conferred upon the Company the sole right to trade and establish settlements in Hudson's Bay, to maintain fortifications and armed ships, to make war and peace with non-Christian peoples, and to possess on a proprietary basis all the lands surrounding the Bay without inland limitation of frontiers. The vast and undefined territory thus assigned received the name of Rupert's Land.

As compared with other corporations of the period the Hudson's Bay Company began its career on a very modest scale as regards both numbers and wealth. One of its professed objects was the discovery of the North West Passage, but in practice it limited itself to the fur-trade. From the outset it displayed marked characteristics of its own. It maintained a policy of secrecy concerning its gains and the nature of its dominions, for long circulating the idea that the latter were unsuitable for colonization. It avoided also the public brawls and discussions which chequered the history of the East India Company, and, to a greater extent than did others, the unsound financial operations which involved nearly the whole of commercial England in the crash of the South Sea Bubble in 1720. It remains at the present day the only one of the Tudor and Stuart undertakings which survives as a working organization.

Twelve years of good fortune followed the Company's establishment. The European war of 1672-8 benefited it in common with the other branches of English expansion. An examination of economic details, in fact, leaves the conviction that this war, in which Louis XIV.'s ambitions seemed to reach their high-water mark of fulfilment, in

[1] G. Bryce, *Remarkable History of the Hudson's Bay Company*, London, 1900, p. 10.

reality completed the foundations of the English empire of the Restoration, and provided the basis of the maritime wealth which enabled England to overthrow France in America and India in the following century. In Hudson's Bay the English traded without effective disturbance until 1682, when the first French expedition made its appearance. By that date the Company had trading posts at Port Nelson, Charlton Island in James Bay, and Forts Churchill, Albany, York and Severn, in addition to the original establishment on Rupert's River. By this means they were able to exploit the trade of the whole southern and south-western shore of the Bay.

In 1682-3 the French began hostilities in earnest, claiming that the entire operations of the Company were an intrusion upon the territories of New France. Both sides alleged priority of discovery, the one by sea and the other by land, but such arguments were a waste of words amid the actual conditions of the period, when effective occupation overrode all considerations of international law. The French expedition of 1682, under the leadership of Radisson, who had deserted the English service, captured Port Nelson. The good understanding existing between the courts of Charles II. and Louis XIV. secured its restoration, and the Company at the same time strengthened Fort Churchill with walls seventeen feet thick and an armament of forty guns at a cost of £24,000. In 1686 a French force marching overland from Canada captured the whole of the Company's posts with one exception. But in that year England and France concluded a treaty of colonial neutrality, and Louis XIV. restored all the conquests except Fort Charles. Matters were in this condition when the English revolution involved the two nations in formal warfare at home and abroad. Their subsequent vicissitudes in Hudson's Bay will therefore be dealt with in a later chapter.

The financial history of the Company may, however, be conveniently treated to a somewhat later date.[1] Although it made large profits it seems to have refrained from paying dividends until 1683. The expedition of a single year during this period took out goods worth £650 and brought home furs to the value of £19,000. With its resources thus recruited it began the division of profits. In the ten years 1683-92 the annual cash dividend averaged $27\frac{1}{2}$ per cent. in addition to a scrip dividend in the latter year by which the nominal capital was trebled, becoming £31,500. An original investor who sold at market price at this time would have received nearly eight times his outlay. As with the other companies a period of depression followed when the full rigour of the French wars made itself felt, but the Hudson's Bay adventurers were fortunate in securing parliamentary confirmation of their charter and so escaping the additional perils which beset the old East India Company. From enemy action the Hudson's Bay Company suffered severely. The Treaty of Ryswick, owing to heedlessness on the part of the English negotiators, had the

[1] The figures are from Scott, vols. i. and ii.

effect of confirming its losses, and it was not until four years after the Treaty of Utrecht that it was able to resume the payment of dividends, intermitted since 1692. The subsequent French wars had a less adverse bearing upon its prosperity.

(iv) *The Regulated Companies*

The older regulated companies participated in the trade revival of the Restoration. We have already followed the history of the Merchants Adventurers and the Eastland Company to its conclusion.[1] The Levant Company suffered somewhat from the Dutch wars and from the competition of the East India Company in certain branches of its trade. But the English tenure of Tangier and the increasing amenability of the Ottoman empire to civilized diplomatic methods worked in its favour. In 1675 it concluded an advantageous treaty with the sultan. Under Colbert's régime the French began to supplant the Dutch as the Company's chief rivals in the Mediterranean. The Muscovy Company became a regulated body shortly after the Restoration, having been virtually in suspension under the Commonwealth. It had to struggle hard against Dutch competition, and never regained the exclusive position it had occupied at the outset of its career. Towards the end of the century its trade was again flourishing. In 1699 membership was thrown open to all on payment of a fee of £5 for admission.

AUTHORITIES. PART III
CHAPTER I. GENERAL SURVEY, JAMES I. AND CHARLES I.

For the general history of England during the period the chief authority is S. R. Gardiner, *History of England*, 1603-42, 10 vols., London, 1883-4, and *History of the Great Civil War*, 1642-9, 4 vols., London, 1893. In these works the internal history of the early Stuart period is exhaustively and accurately traced, and attention is given to some phases of external growth, particularly the Puritan emigration. *The Political History of England*, vol. vii., by F. C. Montague, London, 1907, is still a valuable authority. *The Oxford History of England*, the most recent treatment on a similar scale, includes *The Early Stuarts*, by Godfrey Davies. For diplomacy and international politics Sir J. R. Seeley's *Growth of British Policy*, 2 vols., Cambridge, 1895, is valuable.

For the commercial and economic aspects of expansion see W. Cunningham, *English Industry and Commerce in Modern Times*, vol. i. 5th edn., Cambridge, 1910; W. R. Scott, *Joint Stock Companies to 1720*, 3 vols., Cambridge, 1910; and chapters in *Cambr. Hist. of the Br. Empire*, vol. i. (1929). G. L. Beer's *Origins of the British Colonial System*, 1578-1660, New York, 1908, gives a clear explanation of the economic ideas underlying American colonization, and of the relation of the latter to the mercantile policy at home.

The administration of the colonies receives attention in *British Committees and Councils of Trade*, 1622-75, by Prof. C. M. Andrews, Baltimore, 1908.

For the navy the works of Laird Clowes, Hannay and Oppenheim, already

[1] *Ante*, pt. ii. ch. i.

cited, are still the leading authorities.   See also Sir J. S. Corbett, *England in the Mediterranean*, 2 vols., London, 1904, which throws original light on an otherwise neglected aspect of naval history in the Stuart period.

Throughout the period the *Dictionary of National Biography* is a most valuable authority, especially for the careers of individuals concerning whom no separate biographies have been published.

CHAPTERS II., III. AND IV.   VIRGINIA, MARYLAND AND NEW ENGLAND, 1603-49.

The history of the English colonies in America has given rise to the publication of a large number of works on both sides of the Atlantic, and from this multitude, of varying merit, it is not an easy matter to select a short list which will be of the maximum service to a student approaching the subject for the first time.

Taking first the histories which deal with all the colonies of the period, we find two great American works which lay the foundations of the modern treatment of the subject.   These are George Bancroft's *History of the United States*, New York, 1859 (5th edn., 1885) ;   and Justin Winsor's *Narrative and Critical History of America*, London, 1886-9.   Bancroft's work possesses great literary charm, but is somewhat sentimental and prejudiced by national controversies.   Winsor's is judicial and fair, and averse from exaggeration.   These two historians are of such standing that it is impossible to omit them from any list of authorities ;   most that is essential in them, will, however, be found embodied in later works.

Of these the first in importance is undoubtedly J. A. Doyle's *The English in America ;   Virginia, Maryland and the Carolinas*, London, 1882, and *The Puritan Colonies*, 2 vols., London, 1887.   These volumes have long formed the standard English authority on the subject.   They narrate the story of colonization in great detail, and are generally trustworthy, although corrected on a few minor points by more recent research.   They display a somewhat marked prejudice against James I., in whose favour there has of late been some revulsion of opinion. Doyle also contributed a summary of his work to the *Cambridge Modern History*, vol. vii. (1903), ch. i., *The First Century of English Colonization*.

Of the later American authors dealing generally with the subject we may select :   Prof. Edward Channing, *History of the United States*, 3 vols., New York, 1905-12, of which volume i. extends to the year 1660 ;   and L. G. Tyler, *England in America*, 1580-1652, New York, 1904.   Channing writes with the advantage of considerable research carried out after the publication of Doyle's works, and supersedes them in certain matters.   Tyler gives a detailed story of the English settlement, often novel in point of view.   He emphasizes the fact that at first the Colonies were simply outlying portions of the English nation, but that the Civil War gave them opportunity to develop on lines of their own.   H. L. Osgood's *American Colonies in the Seventeenth Century*, 3 vols., New York, 1904-7, is also an important authority in which the first two volumes tell the story from the colonial, and the third from the imperial, point of view.   The subject is treated mainly in its political and administrative aspect :   in the author's own words it is " an institutional history of the American colonies."   The most recent and weighty American general history is *The Colonial Period in American History*, 4 vols., 1934-8, by Prof. C. M. Andrews.   In this work the events, persons and institutions from the foundation of the colonies to the War of Independence are reconsidered and many earlier judgements are corrected.   The same author had previously published *Our Earliest Colonial Settlements*, New York, 1933, a series of lectures describing some salient features in the early records of the early Stuart colonies. G. L. Beer's work (see Auth. for ch. i.) ranges over the whole of the colonies from the economic side.   Of Prof. H. E. Egerton's *Short History of British Colonial*

Policy, London, 1897 (3rd edn., 1910), the first section covers the period ending in 1649.

Of works dealing with Virginia alone the following are important : P. A. Bruce, *Economic History of Virginia in the Seventeenth Century*, 2 vols., New York, 1896, which is exhaustive and accurate on the branch of the subject indicated by its title ; T. J. Wertenbaker, *Virginia under the Stuarts*, Princeton, 1914, a re-writing of the history of the state in the light of most recent research ; and Alexander Brown, *Genesis of the United States*, 2 vols., London, 1890, which, however, appeals principally to the student of original documents, of which it gives all available for the period 1605-16, reproducing them for the most part *in extenso*, together with many maps and illustrations. The best English life of Captain John Smith is that by A. G. Bradley (*Engl. Men of Action Series*), London, 1905. R. Johnson's *Captain John Smith*, New York, 1915, gives the outline of the career with faith in the explorer's own accounts, which some investigators have received with caution.

A number of writers have dealt especially with the history of Maryland. Among the more modern are : F. R. Jones, *Colonization of the Middle States and Maryland*, Philadelphia, 1904, one volume of a large and expensive series by various authors, containing many useful maps and illustrations ; C. C. Hall, *The Lords Baltimore and the Maryland Palatinate*, Baltimore, 1902, a reprinted course of lectures ; and W. J. Russell, *Maryland, the Land of Sanctuary*, Baltimore, 1907, written from the Catholic point of view. B. C. Steiner's *Maryland during the English Civil Wars*, 2 vols., Baltimore, 1906-7, enters more into detail.

On New England the special authorities are many and voluminous, owing to the political and theological interest which the subject has excited. A modern work covering the whole is that of B. B. James, *The Colonization of New England*, Philadelphia, 1904. Less detailed, but containing the essentials, is *The Beginnings of New England*, by J. Fiske, Boston, 1889, a reprint of a series of lectures. *The Pilgrim Republic*, Boston, 1888, by J. J. Goodwin, is a popular, but exhaustive, account of the Plymouth Colony, and should be read in conjunction with D. W. Howe's *Puritan Republic of Massachusetts Bay*, Indianapolis, 1899. Social and religious aspects are dealt with in *The Puritan in England and New England*, by E. H. Byington, Boston, 1896, and *Social Life in Old New England*, by M. C. Crawford, Boston, 1914. There are many other works on the same subject.

CHAPTER V.   NEWFOUNDLAND, GUIANA AND THE WEST INDIES.

The chief authority for the first of the three regions dealt with in this chapter is *The History of Newfoundland*, by D. W. Prowse, 2nd edn., London, 1896. It treats the subject in full detail, reprinting many original documents. A good deal of light on the early history of the island is also to be obtained from Sir C. P. Lucas' *Historical Geography of the British Colonies*, vol. v., part iv., by J. D. Rogers, Oxford, 1911. G. L. Beer (*op. cit.*) has some valuable remarks on the economic importance of the fishery. The subject is covered also in *The Cod Fisheries*, by H. A. Innis, Yale, 1940, a work of exhaustive research.

The materials for a history of the early Stuart ventures to Guiana are scanty, and to a less extent this is true of the first period in the West Indian islands. These topics are treated in the present writer's *The English in Guiana*, 1604-1668, Oxford, 1923, and *The Caribbee Islands under the Proprietary Patents*, Oxford, 1926 ; and in Prof. V. T. Harlow's *History of Barbados*, 1625-1685, Oxford, 1926. The story of the Providence Island Company is fully elucidated in A. P. Newton's *Colonizing Activities of the English Puritans*, Yale, 1914. Another of Newton's works, *The European Nations in the West Indies*, 1493-1688, London, 1933, is international in scope and a valuable commentary on the whole of the early colonial period. Ralegh's last expedition is treated by all his biographers and

---

also at some length in Gardiner's *History*, vol. iii. : the best exhaustive account and elucidation is in V. T. Harlow's *Ralegh's Last Voyage*, London, 1932. Relevant volumes issued by the Hakluyt Society are : *Colonising Expeditions to the West Indies and Guiana*, 1623-1667, ed. V. T. Harlow, 1924, and *Robert Harcourt's Voyage to Guiana*, 1613, ed. Sir C. A. Harris, 1926.

CHAPTER VI. THE EAST INDIA COMPANY, 1600-57.

In spite of its importance, there are comparatively few writers on this period of the Company's history. It is allotted only part of a chapter in *Cambr. Hist. of the Br. Empire*, vol. iv., a volume which, it should be noted, is identical with vol. v. of the *Cambridge History of India*. Sir W. W. Hunter's *History of British India*, 2 vols., London, 1899-1900, gives a comprehensive account of the Company's proceedings at home and abroad throughout the Stuart period ; it is a historical work of the first quality. Beckles Willson, *Ledger and Sword*, London, 1903, adds many additional details, as does Arnold Wright, *Early English Adventurers in the East*, London, 1917. W. R. Scott's *Joint Stock Companies* goes fully into the financial affairs of the Company. The prefaces to the *Calendars of Colonial State Papers* and Sir W. Foster, *English Factories in India*, 1618-21, are also valuable. *England's Quest of Eastern Trade*, by Sir W. Foster, London, 1933, covers this period in full detail.

CHAPTER VII. MARITIME DISCOVERY IN THE FIRST HALF OF THE SEVENTEENTH CENTURY.

A good general account of this subject is in E. Heawood's *Geographical Discovery in the Seventeenth and Eighteenth Centuries*, Cambridge, 1912. For further details on particular expeditions see T. A. Janvier, *Henry Hudson*, New York, 1909, and numerous publications of the Hakluyt Society, notably *Early Voyages towards the North West*, ed. J. Rundall, 1849 ; *Henry Hudson the Navigator*, ed. G. M. Asher, 1860 ; *Voyages of William Baffin*, ed. Sir C. R. Markham, 1881 ; *Voyages of Luke Foxe and Thomas James*, ed. M. Christy, 2 vols., 1894 ; and *Early Voyages to Spitzbergen*, ed. Sir M. Conway, 1904.

CHAPTER VIII. THE PURITAN ASCENDANCY.

The standard general history of the period covered by this chapter is S. R. Gardiner's *History of the Commonwealth and Protectorate*, 3 vols., London, 1894-1903, which devotes adequate attention to colonial and naval affairs. The author died before finishing his work, which was afterwards completed by Prof. C. H. Firth under the title of *The Last Years of the Protectorate*, 2 vols., London, 1909. Seeley's *Growth of British Policy*, previously mentioned, is particularly valuable as throwing light upon Cromwell's external ambitions.

On the commercial and economic side the chief authorities are the works of Cunningham, Scott and Beer described under the heading of Chapter I. of this part.

For the navy the leading authorities are also the same as there given. Full details of the Dutch war, with reprints of the original documents, appear in *Letters and Papers relating to the First Dutch War*, ed. S. R. Gardiner and C. T. Atkinson (vols. 13, 17 and 30 of the Navy Records Society's publications), London, 1894-9.

For the colonial policy of the Puritans see Beer's *Origins* and *Cambr. Hist. of the Br. Empire*, vol. i. ch. vii. ; also paper in the *American Historical Review*, vol. iv., *The Causes of Cromwell's West Indian Expedition*, by Frank Strong.

CHAPTER IX. THE RESTORED STUARTS AND THE SHAPING OF THE MERCANTILE SYSTEM.

The history of the reign of Charles II., on a scale comparable to that adopted by Froude or Gardiner, has yet to be written. Meanwhile the best modern accounts are those of Prof. R. Lodge in vol. viii. of the *Political History of England*, London, 1910 ; G. N. Clark, *The Later Stuarts*, Oxford, 1934 ; and David Ogg, *England in the Reign of Charles II.*, 2 vols., Oxford, 1934.

The colonial policy of the Restoration is exhaustively described in G. L. Beer's *The Old Colonial System*, part i. vols. i. and ii., New York, 1912. This author works mainly upon documentary evidence, much of it hitherto untouched, and contemporary pamphlet literature. His conclusions revolutionize previous conceptions of colonial administration, and the effect of the Navigation Acts. They should be read as a corrective to the remarks of earlier American authors who are somewhat prone to disparage both the motives and the results of English colonial policy. This branch of the subject also receives attention in Egerton's work already noticed (under pt. iii. chs. ii., iii. and iv.), and in authorities on the internal history of the colonies to be mentioned below. P. L. Kaye's *English Colonial Administration under Lord Clarendon*, Baltimore, 1905, is useful, although to some extent superseded by Beer's work. The Prefaces to the various volumes of the *Calendar of Colonial State Papers* and *Acts of the Privy Council*, Colonial Series, are also valuable. The Mercantile System is philosophically treated in G. Schmoller's *The Mercantile System and its Historic Significance*, English edn., London, 1896. For the purely economic aspect see Cunningham's *Modern Times* and Scott's invaluable *Joint Stock Companies*, already noted.

For the important naval history of the Restoration period the works of Laird Clowes, Hannay and Corbett (*England in the Mediterranean*) still hold good. Oppenheim's *Administration of the Royal Navy* is unfortunately no longer available, since it has never been continued beyond 1660. On the other hand, another classic authority, Admiral A. T. Mahan's *Influence of Sea Power upon History*, London, 1890, begins at that date. The *Cambridge Modern History*, vol. v. ch. viii., contains a good account of the organization of the fleet and of the Dutch wars of 1665 and 1672.

CHAPTERS X. AND XI. THE AMERICAN AND WEST INDIAN COLONIES UNDER THE RESTORATION.

For general remarks on the bibliography of this subject, as concerning the continental colonies, see the list of authorities for pt. iii., chs. ii., iii. and iv. Of the works of wide application there mentioned the following hold good for the Restoration period : those of Bancroft, Winsor, Doyle, Channing (vol. ii.), Osgood and Andrews. In addition Doyle's later volume on *The Middle Colonies*, London, 1907, takes up the story of New York, New Jersey and Pennsylvania, and treats it in the same ample fashion as adopted for the older settlements. Prof. C. M. Andrews' *Colonial Self-Government*, 1652-89, New York, 1904, forms a companion volume and continuation of Tyler's *England in America*, which ends at the former date. It provides a compact and accurate survey of the whole field of continental colonization for the period. Beer's *Old Colonial System*, described above, gives illuminating data on the trade of each colony separately. Here also may be mentioned two works of wider application : A. B. Keith, *Constitutional History of the First British Empire*, London, 1930 ; and J. B. Brebner, *The Explorers of North America*, London, 1933.

Useful leading authorities on the history of individual colonies are as follows :—
Carolina : C. L. Raper, *North Carolina, a Study in English Colonial Government*, New York, 1904, a work which goes thoroughly into institutional matters, but

is not concerned exclusively with the Stuart period ; E. M'Crady, *History of South Carolina*, 3 vols., New York, 1897-1901, and Hon. W. A. Courtenay, *Genesis of South Carolina*, Columbia, S.C., 1907, the latter being principally notable for a good reproduction of a contemporary map of the region.   Virginia : T. J. Wertenbaker, *Virginia under the Stuarts*, Princeton, 1914, useful for graphic details chosen from contemporary writings, but prone to exaggeration in economic matters upon which the author seems to ignore the authority of Beer ; P. A. Bruce, *Economic History of Virginia in the Seventeenth Century*, 2 vols., New York, 1896, and *Institutional History of Virginia in the Seventeenth Century*, 2 vols., New York, 1910, a very sound authority on the subjects treated.   Maryland : authorities as given for chs. ii., iii. and iv.   Pennsylvania : F. R. Jones, *Colonization of the Middle States and Maryland*, Philadelphia, 1904 ; see also art. on Penn in *Dictionary of National Biography*.   New York : numerous modern works, particularly Mrs. M. G. Van Rensselaer, *History of New York in the Seventeenth Century*, 2 vols., New York, 1909.   New England : authorities as given for chs. ii., iii. and iv. ; the subject is also thoroughly treated in the general works mentioned at the beginning of this section.

For Newfoundland Prowse and Rogers, as mentioned under authorities for ch. v. hold good.   Beer's *Old Colonial System* has a valuable chapter on the subject, and references occur in the Prefaces to the *Colonial Calendars* and *Acts of the Privy Council (Colonial)*.

For the West Indies the authorities are as given for ch. v. with the addition of Beer's *Old Colonial System* and the Prefaces to the *Calendars* ; also C. C. Higham, *The Leeward Islands under the Restoration*, Cambridge, 1920.   Two useful works applying mainly to this period are C. H. Haring's *Buccaneers of the West Indies*, London, 1910, and *Trade and Navigation between Spain and the Indies*, Camb., Mass., 1918.

CHAPTER XII.   THE GREAT TRADING COMPANIES UNDER THE RESTORATION.

For the financial history of the joint-stock companies Dr. W. R. Scott's work is the standard authority, and its detailed analysis is particularly valuable for the Restoration period.   All the companies, both joint-stock and regulated, receive attention in *Early Chartered Companies*, by G. Cawston and A. H. Keane, London, 1896, which is, however, planned on a smaller scale.   Passing references also occur in Cunningham's *Modern Times*.

The general history of the East India Company for the period is set forth in Hunter's and Beckles Willson's works mentioned under authorities for ch. vi. It is told more briefly in Sir A. Lyall's *Rise and Expansion of British Dominion in India*, 5th ed., London, 1910.

Sir H. H. Johnston's *History of the Colonization of Africa*, 2nd ed., Cambridge, 1913, is international in scope, but gives a few details on the doings of the Royal African Company and its predecessors.   Others are to be met with in the prefaces to the *Colonial Calendars*.

Two standard works on the Hudson's Bay Company are Beckles Willson's *The Great Company*, 2 vols., London, 1900, and G. Bryce's *Remarkable History of the Hudson's Bay Company*, London, 1900.   Agnes C. Laut's *Conquest of the Great North West*, 2 vols., New York, 1908, is written in a picturesque style and claims to revise the story on certain points.

PART IV

THE ZENITH AND FALL OF THE MERCANTILE
EMPIRE

CHAPTER I

FROM THE ENGLISH REVOLUTION TO THE TREATY OF UTRECHT

In the political history of England the Revolution of 1688 marks very definitely the end of one state of affairs and the beginning of another. A monarchy limited by vague checks from which it plotted always to free itself gave place to a monarchy bound by definite constitutional rules and reconciled to its position. The change was open, consciously made and realized by the nation. The Bill of Rights was its embodiment. Its implication, foreseen from the outset, was the responsibility of the executive ministers not primarily to the sovereign but to the representatives of public opinion.

Internationally also the Revolution involved a conscious change of front. The English and the Dutch, the peoples who had hitherto truly described themselves as the sea-powers, recognized that whilst they had been disputing the supremacy another had arisen which bade fair to overshadow both. Accordingly they combined their forces against France, and by so doing inaugurated a succession of colonial and maritime wars which constitute, for the western nations, the leading characteristic of the eighteenth century.

In the colonies beyond the Atlantic there was, on the other hand, no apparent indication that a turning-point in their history had been passed. In New England the half-completed schemes of James II. collapsed like a house of cards ; but since they had had little chance to show whither they would lead they left no permanent impression, and the arrangements which succeeded them savoured rather of restoration than of revolution. In the remaining colonies there was virtually no break at all in the visible current of development. Nevertheless, as history was in the fulness of time to unfold, the fall of the Stuart monarchy was silently responsible for shaping the future destiny of the American nation. It cut short the constructive plan of consolidation and firm control, and it gave free play to destructive tendencies at home and abroad which ultimately proved the ruin of the old empire.

The general attitude of the colonists was that of accepting the Revolution as an accomplished fact and awaiting a settlement of outstanding questions from home. A section of opinion in Massachusetts favoured a resumption of the government under the terms of the old charter, but the leaders hung back, conscious that the charter was by no means an ideal instrument for their purpose. Its drawback was that it did not legally cover all the proceedings which had been taken in its name. In other words, the rulers of the province had continually and extensively infringed it. Two years after his accession William III. found time to attend to the affairs of New England. He issued a new charter to Massachusetts, incorporating with it Plymouth and Maine and the regions claimed by England in Acadia and New Brunswick. Under the new order the governor, lieutenant-governor, and secretary were to be appointed by the crown. An assembly was to sit as before, but to be elected by voters qualified by ownership of property instead of by church-membership. A council was to be chosen in a general court consisting of the representatives and all the officials. The governor had a right of veto on legislation, and all Protestants were to enjoy religious liberty. As the first governor of the new series the crown tactfully appointed Sir William Phipps, a native of the colony and a self-made man who had risen from the position of a ship's carpenter.[1] At the same time New Hampshire was recognized as a separate colony, the condition which Charles II. had designed for it. As to Rhode Island and Connecticut, the crown lawyers decided that the confiscation of their old charters had been illegal, and they were therefore restored without modification. The northern colonies thus emerged from the Revolution as a block of four unfederated governments.

In New York matters took a somewhat different turn owing to the mixture of races in the population, the fear of French aggression on the northern frontier, and the presence of a large number of Catholic officials in the city. A suspicion gained ground that the Catholics intended to call in the French and hold the colony for King James. Jacob Leisler, a German of long residence, stood forward as the leader of the Protestant and revolutionary party. It was a position he was unable to maintain, since many of his opponents were as Protestant and revolutionary as himself. The contest was one in reality between two factions at issue on local questions. The deputy-governor of James II.'s appointment fled to England, and Leisler seized the supreme power which he exercised in arbitrary fashion in the name of William III. On the arrival of a new governor from England Leisler would not submit to his authority and was executed for treason. Although his actions had been by no means disinterested he seems to have been more harshly dealt with than he deserved. Ultimately his relatives obtained the reversal of the judgment and compensation for his death.

William Penn and Lord Baltimore both lost their proprietary rights in their respective provinces, the latter as a Catholic, and the former as a notorious friend of James II. Penn recovered his privileges after

[1] He had gained title and fortune by salving the cargo of a sunken treasure-ship in the West Indies.

the expiration of two years, but the Baltimores remained excluded from Maryland until 1715 when the head of the family became a Protestant. In general the crown tightened its hold upon the proprietary colonies by acquiring a right of veto upon the proprietors' appointments of deputy-governors. In 1702 Delaware obtained political separation from Pennsylvania, and the Jerseys were united as one crown colony, their proprietors surrendering their rights. Virginia and the Carolinas preserved unbroken the continuity of all their institutions.

On the whole the settlement effected by William III. perpetuated the arrangements made by Clarendon after the Restoration, with a slight addition to the power of the crown. The colonies were therefore in the condition of enjoying representative but not responsible government. Their elected assemblies could air their grievances and initiate legislation, but they had no direct means of enforcing their wishes or ridding themselves of executive officials who might be distasteful to them. The Commons of England had been similarly placed under James I. and Charles I., with civil war and revolution as the outcome. In New England the disadvantages of the system had shown themselves as soon as the later Stuarts set about the enforcement of the Navigation Acts, with the French menace hanging like a cloud upon the horizon to drive the lesson home. James II., with his Dominion of New England, had tackled the problem after one fashion. Had ten years been allowed him instead of three he might have made his experiment a success, in which case the empire would probably have become a military organization such as France contemplated in the eighteenth century, and world-democracy would have waited long ere coming into its own. William III. allowed the plan of consolidation to fall to the ground, never to be effectually resumed. He had still another alternative. He might have granted responsible government to the colonies with complete control of their own legislation and executive. The collapse of the laws of trade and the colonial system as then established would speedily have followed, a result which the ruling classes in England would have refused to tolerate for an instant. He chose therefore to leave the problem of colonial governance in an unsolved and unsatisfactory condition between two irreconcilable propositions : that the mercantile system demanded the economic subordination of the colonies to the mother-country ; and that a self-reliant population, steadily growing until it began to count itself in millions,[1] would not for ever remain subject to a government separated from it by a three months' voyage. The colonial system had been a good one in 1660—perhaps the only one possible. Thirty years later its very success demanded an overhaul of its machinery, and the opportunity was missed.

[1] In the eighteenth century the population of the American colonies roughly doubled itself every twenty years. That of England increased from about 5,500,000 in 1700 to about 6,500,000 in 1750

The question of the Navigation Acts soon came again into prominence. A short period of laxity in their administration followed the Revolution. Boston slipped back into its old ways. New York was an especial offender, one-third of its trade according to one estimate being contraband. Philadelphia also incurred suspicion, and Edward Randolph, returning to America in his old capacity, declared that even the Chesapeake colonies were shipping many illicit cargoes of tobacco to Europe. Extensive infringements penalized the merchant who complied with the law, and on the petition of the traders of London, Liverpool and Bristol the government took the matter up and passed in 1696 the last Navigation Act of general application. This measure, entitled An Act for preventing Frauds and regulating Abuses in the Plantation Trade, required that colonial governors should take oath to enforce the existing Acts under penalty of £1000 and dismissal, extended to colonial ports the entering and clearing formalities observed in England, invalidated all colonial laws contrary to the Acts, and decreed the setting up of admiralty courts in the American colonies. Subsidiary clauses also tended to the same end, the strengthening of the power of the crown officials to deal with evasions.[1] The Act seems to have had the desired effect, and a period of strict administration set in which lasted until the Duke of Newcastle took charge of colonial affairs under the premiership of Walpole.[2]

In 1696 also a new arrangement came into being for the conduct of colonial business in London. William III. at his accession had perpetuated the existing Lords of Trade, merely replacing individuals unfavourable to himself by others whom he could trust. Parliament, however, showed an increasing desire to take colonial affairs under its own supervision, and a strongly-backed bill was introduced into the Commons for that purpose. To prevent such an invasion of the royal prerogative William forestalled the initiative of Parliament by creating a new Board of Trade and Plantations consisting of eight salaried members chosen for their knowledge of colonial business, but not of necessity members of the Privy Council. Of the first Board the Earl of Bridgewater was president and John Locke and William Blathwayt were members. The chief ministers of state were also *ex officio* entitled to attend the meetings, but seldom did so. The Board of Trade, like the bodies which preceded it, had no executive power of its own. It was a consultative and advisory body looking to the king's ministers to carry out its recommendations. The minister specially charged with colonial matters was the secretary of state for the southern department, who issued instructions to the several governors, and exercised all colonial patronage. The Board of Trade during the first thirty years of its existence proved a vigorous and sensible body. It worked hard for the enforcement of the Navigation Acts, the sup-

[1] Channing, *History of U.S.*, ii. pp. 273-4.
[2] G. L. Beer, *Commercial Policy of England towards the American Colonies*, New York, 1893, p. 131.

pression of piracy, the increase of the power of the crown as exercised through colonial officials, and the consolidation of the colonies for military defence. In 1701, 1706, 1715 and 1722, it promoted parliamentary legislation for abolishing the colonial charters. It failed on each occasion, but it was mainly through its influence that the proprietors of New Jersey, and later those of Carolina, surrendered their rights to the crown. The earlier appointments to the board were nearly all of able men with a knowledge of their work. After the accession of the House of Hanover the large salary—£1000 per annum—proved a bait for needy place-hunters, and the increase of parliamentary corruption permitted a steady deterioration in the type of man appointed. The change was first noticeable about 1724, and by 1740 the board had become a farce.[1]

From the time of the Restoration, as we have seen, the dominant motive of the mercantilists who influenced English policy had been the maintenance of a favourable balance of trade, that is an excess of exports over imports, in their intercourse with foreign countries.[2] Their object, the amassing of national wealth, had been identical with that of the more ancient bullionists whom they supplanted and who had sought to achieve it by the simple process of prohibiting the export of the precious metals. The success of the East India Company, largely based upon the transference of silver to Asia, had cast doubts upon bullionist principles, and the ranks of the mercantilists had been largely recruited from the East India investors. Under the later Stuarts the colonists had been few in numbers and engaged for the most part in exploiting a virgin soil for the production of exotic wares such as tobacco and sugar, the bulk of which was re-exported from England to the European continent at a great profit. The mercantilists of that day therefore valued colonies principally as a source of supply. Towards the end of the seventeenth century a change of view gradually began to set in. New England, hitherto regarded as of little worth, increased mightily in population. The whole block of middle colonies, unproductive of tropical goods, sprang into existence and flourished rapidly. The southern colonists and the West Indian planters likewise multiplied, whilst confining their energies to producing a few staples to the exclusion of the general necessaries of life. A large and expanding colonial demand for European manufactures thus came into being, and the mercantilists at home awoke to the fact that the colonies as a market might be worth their attention to an even greater extent than as a source of stock-in-trade for exchange with European rivals.

[1] For the whole subject see O. M. Dickerson, *American Colonial Government*, 1696-1765, Cleveland, Ohio, 1912 ; and Channing, ii. pp. 230-1, 234-5.

[2] It is wrong to regard the mercantile theory as altogether fallacious in the time in which it was devised. Cf. W. A. S. Hewins, *English Trade and Finance in the Seventeenth Century*, London, 1892 : " The development of finance, the telegraph, and ocean-going steamers have destroyed the conditions which rendered possible the theory of the balance of trade. So far as it went, it was a sincere and more or less accurate attempt to solve an intricate problem " (p. 131).

Other factors contributed to the change. France, under the ministry of Colbert, had developed her West Indian, African and Asiatic interests until she had become a competitor with England in the sale of tropical produce. At home science was beginning to apply itself to industry, feebly, it is true, insignificantly as compared with later achievements, but to a sufficient extent to show an advance in industrial enterprise. In politics the employer of labour, in conjunction with the landed interest which supplied the raw material for the woollen manufacture, acquired an increasing weight by reason of the supremacy of parliament. The merchant pure and simple had no longer the preponderant voice in national concerns which he had enjoyed under the Restoration, when nearly every statesman, from the sovereign downwards, had taken part in oceanic trade.

All these considerations led, in the half-century following the Revolution, to a shifting of the centre of gravity of the mercantile system which entailed important consequences to British expansion overseas. The mercantilists still worshipped the balance of trade, but they sought more and more to attain it by fostering home industry by every means in their power, and by looking to the colonies first for an exclusive market and secondly for a supply of raw material whenever such could not be produced at home. An early landmark illustrating the process occurs in the reign of William III. About 1670 the East India Company had begun to import Indian textiles on a large scale. In 1688 an agitation against this business became pressing, and gathered force until it issued in an Act of 1699 (strengthened in 1721) prohibiting such imports in the avowed interest of the home woollen industry.[1] As we shall see, the same principles operated to the suppression, for the same reason, of infant American manufactures. All this did not, of course, imply that the colonial principles of the Restoration were lost sight of. They continued theoretically in full operation, although the extent of their practical application varied from time to time. What it did actually amount to was that henceforward two mercantile and colonial systems existed side by side— the old one, partly political in its intention, concerning itself with imperial self-sufficiency, the production of naval stores, the breeding of seamen and the increase of British shipping; and the new one, purely economic, solely and relentlessly bent upon fostering the industry and profits of the manufacturer at home.

Considering the mother-country and the colonies as a whole the Revolution made for no purifying of the administration or raising of social tone. There was at least as much suspicion of corrupt and

[1] Cunningham, *Modern Times* (part i.), pp. 463-5. On the whole question compare W. E. H. Lecky, *England in the Eighteenth Century*, London, 1892, ii. p. 240; N. A. Brisco, *Economic Policy of Robert Walpole*, New York, 1907, pp. 19-20, 126-31; G. L. Beer, *Commercial Policy towards Colonies*, pp. 77-90, and *British Colonial Policy 1754-65*, New York, 1907, pp. 135-40. The idea of colonies primarily as a market was an old one revived. It had been a prominent inducement to colonization in the mouths of the Elizabethan projectors.

unfair motives attaching to the parliamentary legislation after 1688 as to the royal control of trade and colonies in the preceding period. The very existence of a royal family in exile had its effect upon imperial policy. France supported the Stuarts. The future of the Whigs was bound up with their exclusion. France also had supplanted the Dutch as England's chief competitor. The Whigs were therefore warlike and protectionist, and thus determined the national prejudice and predilection until the old empire came to an end. Among the Tories on the other hand appeared the first germs of free-trade principles and a faint suspicion that national well-being might not after all depend wholly upon the depression of neighbouring peoples. Their tentative essays in this direction were merely instinctive, or perhaps even factious; but the commercial clauses proposed by Tory statesmen whilst negotiating the Treaty of Utrecht [1] were at least significant of a new trend of thought which had to wait until the end of the eighteenth century for its justification by rational argument.

In colonial enterprise during the period 1688-1713, apart from warlike acquisitions, the principal development occurred in South Carolina. Here, about the year 1688, began the planting of rice, a bag of seed having been given to a colonist by the captain of an East Indian ship. Rice-planting took root and flourished amazingly, becoming in a short time the staple industry which the colony had hitherto lacked. The commodity was not in great demand in England, but found a ready sale in Germany and also in the Mediterranean countries, where it ousted the rice formerly obtained from Egypt. In 1704, when the Carolina export had become considerable, it was placed on the enumerated list, so that it should be shipped solely by way of England. This had the effect of decreasing its sale in Portugal and the Mediterranean. But central Europe still took the bulk of the output,[2] and the prosperity of South Carolina continued to increase. The West Indian product of molasses, used in making rum, was enumerated at the same time. The outbreak of the Spanish Succession War gave occasion for another attempt to make the colonies a producing area for naval stores. The balance of trade with the Baltic countries was heavily against England, and Sweden in particular was adopting a hostile attitude which threatened to cut off the supply. An Act of 1704 accordingly provided for bounties to be paid on colonial hemp, timber, pitch and tar. On the supply of the two first-named articles the measure had little effect, but it stimulated a considerable industry in the last two in Carolina and the southern colonies.[3] The more rapid general progress of the American colonies as compared with the West Indian islands was a characteristic of the period. Barbados and the smaller islands had nearly reached the limit of their expansion, and were beginning to suffer from French competition and an extravagant standard of living among the planters. Exhaustion

[1] See below, pp. 336-7.   [2] Beer, *Commercial Policy, etc.,* p. 54
[3] *Ibid.* pp. 94-102.

of the soil was also becoming apparent ; in Barbados it was reckoned that 30 acres of sugar required 150 slaves, while in the French islands the same area was cultivated by 30 or 40 workers.[1] Jamaica gradually developed, and supplanted Barbados as the richest island. Its first capital, Port Royal, was destroyed by an earthquake in 1692, by a fire ten years later, and by a hurricane in 1722. Kingston, the present capital, became the seat of government in 1870.

Scotland had hitherto been shut out from all legitimate share in the English empire. The laws of navigation had, from their first enactment, sought to exclude Scottish ships and merchants from the colonial trade as rigidly as if they had been Dutch or French. In practice there had been some evasion, and in particular Scottish seamen had been tacitly accepted as forming part of the quota of national members necessary for the legal manning of ships. But the situation was such as a high-spirited nation could not endure for ever, and the years succeeding the Revolution seemed to provide a fit opportunity for Scotsmen to claim a share in oceanic enterprise. Of the scheme actually brought forward William Paterson was the originator. In 1695 an Act of the Scottish Parliament established a company to trade with Africa and the Indies, both East and West, with a licence to seize unoccupied lands and a monopoly for thirty-one years. Of the necessary capital £300,000 was to be raised in Scotland and a like sum in London, where Paterson hoped to obtain support from the rivals of the old East India Company. The latter body proved, however, sufficiently strong to secure the annulment of the English investment, and the royal veto on direct Scottish trade with India. Finally Scotland alone raised a subscription of £400,000, of which little more than half was actually paid up. At this point (1696) Paterson propounded the plan which was finally adopted. This was to form a trading colony upon the Isthmus of Darien or Panama, a point which Drake had long ago recognized as one of the great strategic centres of the world, and to make it an entrepot to replace the illusory North West Passage as a connecting link between the Atlantic and the Pacific. In the projector's own words, " this door of the seas and key to the universe will enable its proprietors to give law to both oceans, and to become arbitrators of the commercial world."

On paper the scheme was promising, but Paterson failed to allow for two factors which were to prove its undoing—the deadliness of the climate, and the power of Spain. He himself lost his controlling influence owing to financial irregularities which proved him to have been careless rather than dishonest, and when the first expedition sailed in 1698 he accompanied it in a subordinate capacity. Five ships and 1200 men quitted Leith amid scenes of tremendous enthusiasm. On their arrival at Darien towards the end of the year misfortunes

[1] F. W. Pitman, *Development of the British West Indies*, 1700-1763, New Haven, 1917, pp. 70-1.

at once began to fall upon the luckless colonists. After great sufferings the survivors abandoned the place in June, 1699. Five months later a relief force arrived in ignorance of the departure of the pioneers. Sickness smote the second body also, and the survivors capitulated to a Spanish force in April, 1700.[1]

The disaster paved the way for the union of Great Britain. The English government had been openly unsympathetic, and the West Indian colonies had afforded no relief to the hard-pressed settlers on Darien. Scotland, furious with the indignation, refused to be bound by the English arrangements for the succession after the death of Queen Anne, and there was a probability of a Jacobite restoration in Edinburgh when that event should take place. The only alternative was the union of the governments, which was finally carried in 1707 on terms which admitted Scotsmen in full equality to English commerce and colonies. An important factor in securing their acquiescence was the repayment by England of the money lost by the Darien investors.

In considering the colonial developments under William III. and Anne it is necessary to remember that they took place under the pressure of the most intensive foreign war which modern England had yet waged. The situation in 1689 was similar to that faced by the Commonwealth forty years before, with the added disadvantage that the greatest maritime power of the continent was openly supporting the cause of the exiled Stuart king. It was to the navy therefore that the Revolution government owed its survival and the preservation of its colonies. In a very real sense the American colonists, indirectly taxed as they were for the maintenance of imperial power, received a full return in security from French aggression during the Wars of the Grand Alliance and the Spanish Succession. It was a debt which they hardly admitted and very imperfectly realized, for the governments of that day condescended to no propaganda by which they might have explained the true position. Thus few Americans ever faced the fact that a squadron cruising in the English Channel might prevent the capture of New York.

After the close of the last Dutch war in 1674 Charles II. had allowed the fleet to fall rapidly into decay. Incompetence and dishonesty sapped its strength both moral and material; even newly-built ships were found unserviceable within a short time of their launch. The Duke of York regained control in 1684, and ascended the throne in the following year. In the short time allowed him he did much to restore efficiency,[2] but his general proceedings alienated the seamen in common with the rest of the people, and when the invasion came the navy was not enthusiastic in his defence. The Dutch fleet also deteriorated, more rapidly than the English, with the result that in 1688 the two combined were inferior to that of France, still benefiting by the maritime enthusiasm which Colbert had set on foot.

[1] See J. S. Barbour, *William Paterson and the Darien Company*, Edinburgh, 1907.
[2] *Cambridge Modern Hist.* v. pp. 170-1, 176 ; Mahan, *Sea Power, etc.*, p. 175.

William III. might never have landed on the English shore had it not been for the blunder of Louis XIV., who allowed his fine navy to stand idle whilst he concentrated all his force in an attack upon Germany in 1688. This permitted the invaders to sail unhindered down the Channel. The English fleet pursued, about a hundred miles behind, but were stopped by a change of wind which allowed William to land unmolested. By the end of the year James had fled and the Convention had been summoned to offer the crown to his nephew. James crossed to Ireland in 1689. The greater part of the country received him joyfully, and he might have secured it permanently if Louis XIV. had made full use of the French fleet.[1] But the latter did little to prevent the transit of William in pursuit in 1690, and the Battle of the Boyne drove James into exile for the second time. The remaining Jacobite forces capitulated at Limerick in the following year.

Too late to save Ireland, the French fleet sought the command of the sea in 1690. On the day of the Boyne victory the Comte de Tourville defeated a combined English and Dutch fleet at Beachy Head. The allies lost over a dozen ships, but their maritime resources soon enabled them to make good their deficiencies. Louis, on the other hand, did not follow up his success. He devoted less money to his fleet and more to his armies, with the result that the command of the sea fell to his enemies. In 1692 de Tourville opposed Admiral Russell with a very inferior force. He was defeated off Cherbourg and a part of his fleet was caught and destroyed at Cape La Hogue, whilst the remainder fled to St. Malo. Next year de Tourville appeared at sea for the last time with a fighting fleet. He captured part of a great convoy of merchantmen bound for the Levant. Thenceforward Louis ceased to employ his navy in great operations, but the seamen who were no longer wanted for the warships took service in privateers which inflicted immense damage on English commerce. This was the golden age of French privateering, but it had little effect on the issue of the war.

In America the war began with raids on the New York frontier towards Canada. The Iroquois or Five Nations with whom James II.'s governors had struck an alliance, held to their engagements, but frequently grumbled at the apathy of the English colonists who, they complained, left them to do all the fighting. In 1690 Massachusetts raised forces with which Sir William Phipps captured Port Royal in Nova Scotia. A more ambitious attempt on Quebec and Montreal later in the year failed utterly at a cost to the colony of £40,000. Frontenac, the governor of Canada, pointed out to his master the unfortified condition of New York, and urged him to capture it with a fleet from France.[2] But the transference of sea-power to the allies rendered the project impossible. In Hudson's Bay the adversaries were more equally matched. Port Nelson, regarded as the key-

[1] Mahan, p. 180.
[2] Hon. J. W. Fortescue, *Hist. of the British Army*, ii. p. 252.

position of the Bay, changed hands regularly nearly every season from 1691 to 1697. In the latter year the French captured it for the third time after a desperate naval action off the coast. Storm and battle annihilated the opposing squadrons and the French survivors, struggling to shore, nerved themselves to the capture of the fort as the alternative to starving in the wilderness. The Treaty of Ryswick, signed in 1697, had the effect of leaving Port Nelson in French hands, together with most of the remaining factories. Fort Albany, recaptured in 1693, was the sole remnant left to the Hudson's Bay Company of its once promising possessions in Rupert's Land. In other respects the treaty restored colonial matters to the state existing before the war.

The respite was of short duration, the struggle breaking out again as the War of the Spanish Succession barely four years later. Its object, so far as the English and Dutch were concerned, was to prevent the Spanish Netherlands and the sea power and colonies of Spain from falling into the hands of Louis XIV. The allies began with a great preponderance in naval force. They improved their position by the taking of Gibraltar, stormed by Sir George Rooke and Sir Cloudesley Shovell on August 4, 1704. The place had been weakly held by Spain, and its retention during the ensuing twelve months was a more arduous and heroic business than the original capture.[1] Three weeks after that event the French fleet from Toulon moved to retake it. The resulting Battle of Malaga, the only fleet action of the war, although inflicting no great damage, caused them to give up the project and retire to their ports. Thenceforward the English navy was supreme on every sea. France lost trust in her fleet, and allowed it to dwindle into feebleness. Even her privateering was far less successful than during the War of the Grand Alliance. Her commerce perished at the same time, whilst that of England, especially during the later years of the struggle, steadily increased. In 1710, 3550 ships, the vast majority English, cleared from English ports; in 1711, 3759; in 1712, 4267; and in the year of the peace, 5807.[2] In 1708 Great Britain further strengthened her hold upon the Mediterranean by the capture of Minorca, undertaken as an alternative to that of Toulon, for which the military aid of the allies was not forthcoming.

In America the Hudson's Bay Company, now financially exhausted, could do little towards the recapture of its lost factories, and the war in that region passed almost without incident. With the exception of Massachusetts, the colonies on the Atlantic seaboard remained apathetic, making no effort to rid themselves of the Canadian menace whose importance they fully realised. Massachusetts, however, contributed manfully to the attack upon the common enemy. In 1707 her levies failed to retake Port Royal, restored by the Treaty of Ryswick. Two years later a seriously planned invasion of Canada by colonial, regular and naval forces came to nothing owing to the non-

---

[1] Corbett, *England in the Mediterranean*, ii. p. 163.
[2] *Camb. Mod. Hist.* v. p. 439.

appearance of the fleet. In 1710, however, the Massachusetts men
with naval assistance finally took Port Royal, and with it the whole of
Nova Scotia. The town itself they renamed Annapolis. Next year
Quebec was once more attempted. Admiral Sir Hovenden Walker
and General Hill entered the St. Lawrence with twenty warships and
5000 troops. Ignorance of the local conditions ruined the expedition.
After 800 men had been lost by shipwrecks it withdrew without approaching Quebec. All these transactions tended to show the strength
of French Canada against an English attack, but the allied successes
in Europe secured greater gains at the peace than the fighting in America
had justified.

The treaties signed at Utrecht in 1713 assigned to England the
sovereignty of Nova Scotia, with an inland boundary which was never
properly defined, Newfoundland, with a reservation of French fishing
rights on its western shore, Hudson's Bay with the surrounding
territories, and complete possession of St. Kitts in the West Indies.
The cession of Nova Scotia did not include that of Cape Breton Island,
upon which the French shortly afterwards erected the fortress of
Louisbourg, " the Dunkirk of North America." The boundary of the
Hudson's Bay country was left to be decided by a commission, pending
which the French surrendered to the Company all the forts with their
guns and ammunition intact. Ultimately the parties agreed upon the
parallel of 49°—the present boundary of the United States—as the
dividing line between Rupert's Land and Canada in the trading country
north and west of the great lakes. In 1700 the Company had been
willing to accept 53°, which would have cut them off from the bottom
of the Bay.[1]

In Europe England retained Gibraltar and Minorca, thus confirming
the hold upon the Mediterranean which had been such a powerful if
silent factor in winning the war. Spain also conceded the Asiento or
exclusive monopoly of supplying slaves to the Spanish colonies, hitherto
enjoyed by the French Guinea Company. With this concession
went that of allowing one English ship yearly to trade at Porto Bello,
the entrepot between east and west on the Isthmus of Panama.
These two unlucky clauses proved, as we shall see, the cause of much
harm in later years.

The proposed commercial clauses of the treaty with France, which
failed to secure the assent of the British parliament, are of interest.
The French trade had, when freely carried on, shown a large adverse
balance against England. In consequence it had been forbidden in
1678 and only reopened later under duties so heavy as to be almost
prohibitive. The Tory statesmen now in power, Oxford and Bolingbroke, proposed a mutual reduction of tariffs so as to allow a comparatively free trade. England was already pledged by the Methuen
Treaty (1703) with Portugal, to admit Portuguese wines at a lower
rate than French. Apart from this a violent outcry arose from the

[1] Beckles Willson, *The Great Company*, i. pp. 237-8.

English woollen interest, which feared the competition of French textiles. All the prejudice of the nation lay in the same direction, and the combination of Whigs, manufacturers, port-drinkers and mercantile theorists carried the day. Duties on French goods remained so high that the major part of the cross-Channel trade was carried on by smugglers until the days of the younger Pitt.

The Treaty of Utrecht marked the beginning of a long period of peace during which Britain reaped the full reward of her maritime exertions in the war. Holland, although on the winning side, had lost rather than gained by the treaties. Of her ally and former rival, it has been well said : " Before that war England was one of the sea powers. After it, she was *the* sea power, without any second."

CHAPTER II

FROM THE TREATY OF UTRECHT TO THE FALL OF WALPOLE

A FEW years after the Treaty of Utrecht a speaker in parliament remarked : " The advantages from this peace appear in the addition made to our wealth ; in the great quantities of bullion lately coined in our mint ; by the vast increase in our shipping employed since the peace in the fisheries and in merchandise ; and by the remarkable growth of the customs upon imports, and of our manufactures, and the growth of our country upon export." And the settlement of 1713, inaugurating a long period of peaceful development and fixed, if unsatisfactory, political conditions, provides a fitting occasion for a general survey of the empire whose culmination and fall constitutes the history of British expansion in the eighteenth century.

In the far north the Hudson's Bay Company, restored once again to full possession of its posts in Rupert's Land, recovered gradually from its misfortunes and continued to develop the trade of the vast regions under its sway. It was careful to engage in trade alone, regarding any projects of settlement as inimical to its interests. After the Act of Union it took into its employment a large proportion of Scotsmen, who have left their mark upon the nomenclature of geographical features throughout the north-west. On the whole the Company was slow and conservative, and Bolingbroke's description of its directors as " these smug, ancient gentlemen " is a fair indication of their methods and their quiet success.

Newfoundland, in spite of the decision taken under Charles II., received no regular governor until 1728. There was little political development in the island. The fishery, still shared by the French, remained the dominant interest, with the result that the administration was conducted almost like that of a man-of-war.[1] Nova Scotia continued French in population for many years after its conquest. The inhabitants received fair treatment, including exemption from taxation, but their spiritual allegiance to the Bishop of Quebec was a source of trouble so long as the French ruled in Canada. The government invited New Englanders to settle in the province, but the pros-

[1] Egerton, *Colonial Policy*, p. 161.

pects, with the boundary undefined and the French ever plotting reconquest, were not sufficiently encouraging to secure any general acceptance of the offer.

Of the New England colonies Maine, under the dominion of Massachusetts, was scantily peopled, frequently ravaged by Indian warfare, and productive of little but lumber. Three only of its townships were sufficiently advanced to possess a church. New Hampshire was fertile, and produced corn and cattle in excess of its own wants. A ship-building industry flourished at Portsmouth, its only considerable town, from which also a roundabout trade in fish, timber, sugar and food-stuffs linked the colony with Newfoundland, the West Indies and Europe. Massachusetts was more closely settled, with a population of about 60,000. Boston had long been a thriving seaport with a vigorous intercolonial and European trade. Under pressure of this intercourse with the outer world much of the old Puritan idealism had disappeared, giving place to a sober pursuit of material prosperity. The abolition of the church qualification for citizenship contributed largely to the change. In political relations with the mother-country the old stubborn independence of spirit was still unbroken ; but it is fair to remember that, whilst the baiting and thwarting of the royal governor was an established pastime, the men of Massachusetts were distinguished from all the other colonists by their readiness to forget faction and fight for the empire in time of need. Agriculture and a few rudimentary manufactures occupied the inland population. On the coast the navigation laws fostered an extensive shipping and shipbuilding industry. In the reign of George I. the shipyards of Massachusetts turned out every year a hundred and fifty new vessels, many of which were sold in Europe at the conclusion of their first Atlantic passage. In Rhode Island, lacking the disciplined tradition of its greater neigh-bour, public standards were lower, and a good deal of smuggling and piracy was carried on. Newport had a fair share of the common New England trade with the West Indies and Europe. Connecticut preserved its Puritanism longer than did Massachusetts. Without good harbours, its shipping was unimportant. The excellence of its soil, however, enabled it to export large quantities of foodstuffs, most of which went through the port of Boston. The New Englanders in general were at this period almost exclusively of English descent. They had always given a cold welcome to settlers of other nationalities, including even those from Ireland and Scotland. The negroes among them were few, not much more than three per cent. of the whole.

In the middle colonies a more cosmopolitan population existed. New York in particular swarmed with a mixture of over half-a-dozen races—Dutch, English, German, Swedish, Irish, Walloon, French and Jewish—in which the Dutch were probably first in numbers, and the English second. The city itself was almost as large as Boston, and its trade perhaps half as great. Society was more prodigal but less cultured than in New England—New York boasted one printing-press whilst Boston had five—and the comparative absence of a civic sense led to connivance at many questionable undertakings and even to the patronage of known pirates. The Hudson, navigable far into the wilderness, connected the coast with a frontier population of hunters and traders of which Albany formed the centre. From this source came the furs which were exported in great quantities together with the foodstuffs and horses of the more settled region. When the French peril grew imminent New York and the Hudson waterway stood forth as the key of North America, affording an easier approach to Canada than that by the ice-strewn and dangerous St. Lawrence. New Jersey and Pennsylvania were also peopled from diverse sources, but here the British element predominated. The former province, although possessing a long coastline, had no seaports, and consequently remained an agricultural region with little direct foreign commerce. Pennsylvania, in which the Quaker element continued to be important throughout the eighteenth century, found its outlet to the sea by way of the Delaware River. This was the principal cause of the rise of Philadelphia to a position rivalling that of Boston, since all the trade of a large area passed solely through it. Negro slavery of the domestic type was fairly common in these colonies, the proportion of blacks to the whole population being about eight per cent.

The climate, industries and geographical conditions of the southern colonies rendered them very different in character from those of the north. The broken coastline of Virginia and Maryland, with its navigable estuaries, prevented the formation of any large seaport : almost every tobacco estate had its own landing-stage. The same peculiarity kept the population decentralized. The planter's mansion, with its surrounding group of huts for the slaves, formed the social nucleus, in place of the agricultural village of New England. Negro labour in the eighteenth century rapidly displaced the indented white servants with whom tobacco planting had originated. At this period the proportion of negroes was in Virginia about forty per cent. and in Maryland thirty. North Carolina, perpetuating its easy-going laws and commonly disregarding even their restraints, remained backward and unsatisfactory. It had no good harbour, no fixed seat of government and no slaves, its people sunk in sloth and barbarism and " living in a beastly sort of plenty," as one of its governors declared, upon the products of the soil. South Carolina, on the other hand, throve and expanded upon the cultivation of rice. Charlestown, its capital, was the entrepot of all its trade and the residence of its wealthy planters who left overseers to look after their estates. Its commerce more than doubled in the twenty years succeeding 1714. It was also notable as being the only continental colony in which slaves formed a clear majority of the population.[1]

----

[1] The above survey of the continental colonies is based principally upon Doyle's *Colonies under the House of Hanover*, London, 1907, pp. 1-61, which treats the subject in full detail.

As we have stated, the British West Indies after the Revolution made far less progress than did the American colonies. This relative ill-success was accentuated by the rapid advance of the French islands consequent upon reforms effected in 1717 in the French colonial administration, and by the superior business enterprise of the French planters. Before the date mentioned the English islands, in addition to supplying the wants of the mother-country, dominated the continental sugar markets both in America and Europe. After that date the re-exportation of sugar from Great Britain almost came to an end, and the American colonies developed a large trade with the French islands. Economically this was inevitable, for America needed a larger market for its ever-increasing output of fish, timber and agricultural produce, and the demand of the English sugar islands did not keep pace with the available supply. Europe, the northern colonies and the West Indies formed a triangular trade-route with the balance of produce flowing round it in the order named, and the balance of cash in the opposite direction. The growth of American population was the determining factor of the whole, and necessitated the inclusion of the French islands in the system. The West Indian planters maintained closer touch with the mother-country than did those of America. Many of them resided for the greater part of their time in England, and nearly all looked forward to retirement thither in their old age. Slavery in the West Indies was universal and exclusive of all other labour. By the middle of the century the negroes numbered over seventy per cent. of the whole population.

In the West African stations, whose ownership continued unchanged [1] throughout the wars of William III. and Anne, the slave trade increased with the western demand in spite of the financial troubles of the African Company. The latter body, by reason of Parliament's refusal to confirm its exclusive rights, developed more and more towards the status of a regulated concern open to any who could pay the requisite fees. The shipowners of Bristol and Liverpool availed themselves of the opening, and by the end of the eighteenth century the latter port held a predominant share of the trade. The United East India Company, finally consolidated in 1708, enjoyed peaceful and uneventful progress throughout the period now under review. But its French rival was equally fortunate, making after 1720 a wonderful recovery from a state of almost total suspension during the long war.

A few statistics will illustrate the condition and progress of the empire as a whole. The records are by no means complete, and some of the figures are conjectural. Those stated are based upon a comparison of information from various sources, some of which give mutually inconsistent results. The population of the American colonies in 1700 was about 200,000 ; in 1710, 280,000 ; and in 1720, somewhat over 400,000. This ratio of expansion was maintained as

[1] With the exception of the capture and loss of Goree from and to the French in 1692 and 1693 respectively.

the century advanced, so that by 1760 the continental colonies contained between one-and-a-half and two millions of people, or close upon one-third of the numbers in the mother-country. Of the 1720 total New England accounted for 114,000 ; the middle colonies, 98,000 ; and the southern colonies, 220,000, all inclusive of negroes, who numbered about a quarter of the whole. The British West Indies in the middle of the century had about 320,000 inhabitants, including 230,000 negroes. In 1713 the numbers were perhaps half as great.[1] In the African and East Indian trading factories the population of white men was of course insignificant. Throughout the colonies five towns only were sufficiently large to merit that designation in comparison with the European cities of the time— Boston, New York, Philadelphia, Charlestown, and Kingston in Jamaica. The total exports of Great Britain rose from £6,700,000 in 1700 to £7,700,000 in 1714, and £10,000,000 in 1737. Merchant shipping increased in a similar ratio ; in the latter year 503,568 tons of British shipping cleared from the home ports. In 1731 Boston owned 40,000 tons, and New York and Philadelphia 6000 tons each. In 1737 there were computed to be about 27,000 British (excluding colonial) merchant seamen. The navy kept on its books in time of peace about 10,000 officers and men, or enough to commission a dozen ships-of-the-line with a due proportion of auxiliary vessels and dockyard establishments. For the remainder it looked to the merchant service in time of need.[2] The tobacco export from Virginia and Maryland rose from 28 million lb. in 1700 to 85 millions in 1750. South Carolina exported an average of 26,500 barrels of rice a year in 1720-9, and 50,000 in 1730-9. The West Indies in 1730 sent 100,000 hogsheads of sugar to England alone, and in 1753, 110,000 ; their trade with the American colonies was certainly less stagnant. The East India Company, with its internal differences finally settled in 1708, traded prosperously for the next five-and-thirty years, making few acquisitions or changes of policy, but paying a steady dividend of eight, nine or ten per cent. By 1730 it was despatching about seventeen large ships annually to the east, and selling produce in England to the value of nearly £2,000,000 a year.

Although the prospect had in reality never before been so fair as in 1713-4, one circumstance overclouded it in the eyes of contemporaries, and gave rise to pessimistic forebodings of public bankruptcy and ruin. This was the existence of the national debt, which in 1701 had stood at £16,000,000, and by the accession of George I. had risen to £54,000,000. The amount was unprecedented, and the very idea of a standing debt had only been faced hitherto amid the excitement of a great war. Public opinion demanded its speedy reduction, and the

[1] See figures given in Pitman's *British West Indies*, pp. 372 *seqq.*

[2] The manning clauses of the Navigation Acts were usually suspended on the outbreak of war, so that foreigners might be available to replace the men taken out of the merchant service.

Whig ministers sought that end by the extension of a scheme bequeathed to them by their Tory predecessors.

In 1711 the floating debts had amounted to nine and a half millions. The Earl of Oxford (Harley) had incorporated the creditors as the South Sea Company, promising them six per cent. on the capital together with any profits they could make in excess from the monopoly of English trade with Spanish America. At the moment no such trade existed, but the government promised to obtain facilities in the forthcoming peace negotiations. The resulting concessions, the Asiento and the yearly general cargo at Porto Bello, fell somewhat short of expectations, and the Company never did a profitable trade. Its first ship did not even sail until 1717. Nevertheless the public hoped much from South America, then as now regarded highly as a potential field of business enterprise. In 1719-20 the improvement of credit and the embarrassment of the debt gave rise to a plan for a great extension of the South Sea Company, which was intended ultimately to take over all public obligations and pay the interest out of its trading profits. In the actual state of its affairs the project was insane, as those with inside knowledge must have been perfectly aware. But the people at large were ready to be gulled, and the promoters set on foot wild rumours of the golden nature of the adventure—such as that Spain was prepared to cede the mines of Peru in exchange for Gibraltar. A mania set in, no lie was too gross for belief, and the holders of the government debts fought with one another to exchange their scrip for South Sea Stock at ridiculous prices. In June, 1720, people paid £1000 and more for a £100 share in the enterprise. The inevitable crash followed, the cooler heads realizing their profits and the stock falling as rapidly as it had risen. To quote a recent authority : " By many writers the Bubble is still described as a national calamity. It really represented only a very rapid transference of riches from certain thousands of persons to certain other thousands—or hundreds," by the agency of " the new abstract commercialism, so different a thing from industry, a thing half conscious gambling and half conscious piracy." [1] Its interest to the present subject lies in the fact that the South Sea Company was the last chartered corporation of the early joint-stock series which had begun with the Muscovy Company in 1553, and also in that the implication of practically all the ministers in the fraud opened the way to power for Sir Robert Walpole, who directed the affairs of the empire from 1721 to 1742. The South Sea Company itself continued a precarious and losing trade until 1750, when a treaty with Spain abolished its special privileges.

The enthusiasm and the panic illustrate also a psychological matter which is the key to much of our history in the eighteenth century. The national character at that time was—on the surface at least— widely different from what it is now and from what it had been in

[1] Rt. Hon. J. M. Robertson, *Bolingbroke and Walpole*, London, 1919, pp. 101-5. See also Brisco, *op. cit.* pp. 42-9.

the seventeenth century. With no improvement in general education the people had lost the high ideals which had once possessed them. A covetous imperialism appealed strongly to them, they were extremely credulous, and at the same time pugnacious and irritable to an extent that passes belief—which some may attribute in part to the fact that the national consumption of gin, apart from other liquors, rose until it averaged nearly two gallons a year for every man, woman and child in the country.[1] This excitability brought in its train corresponding fits of depression : Walpole was using no figurative language when he said on the eve of war, " They are ringing their bells now ; they will soon be wringing their hands."

From the moment of taking office Walpole began a cautious policy of remedying abuses in the commercial and colonial system. He had to proceed slowly for fear of alarming those trading classes in England who were prone to conceive their interests imperilled by any reform ; and in one notable instance even he overstepped the limits of what was possible and experienced a sharp rebuff. The customs rates, moderate at the Restoration, had climbed higher and higher under the stress of wartime finance. The duty on colonial tobacco, 2d per pound under Charles II., had risen to 6⅓d. by 1714. That on beaver, 4d. per skin in 1660, had reached 16d. under William III. Sugar duties had also risen enormously. In addition there were export dues on many English manufactures. The first king's speech of Walpole's drafting (1721) laid down his policy : " to make the exportation of our own manufactures, and the importation of the commodities used in the manufacturing of them, as practicable and easy as may be." Accordingly he removed at a stroke the export duties on 106 articles of British manufacture and the import duties on 38 raw materials.[2] Thus far the new mercantilists were with him. There is little doubt that he would have gone farther had he dared ; but in the same year he was powerless to resist the demand for strengthened prohibitions on the import of East Indian fabrics.

The famous Excise Bill of 1733 illustrates his difficulties. Around the re-exportation of tobacco and the repayment of duties thereon a vast system of fraud had grown up. Traders and officials worked in collusion to alter the records and secure the repayment of more money than had been paid in ; tobacco was re-exported in ships, transferred to boats a few miles from the coast, and landed again immediately, the duty having in the meantime been remitted ; and many merchants imported tobacco, stripped the leaf from the stalks, and sent the latter on shipboard, the weight made up with dirt, to be thrown into the sea as soon as it had earned a repayment which was three times the value of the original goods.[3] Walpole himself said he was moved to

[1] Robertson, op. cit. pp. 150, 215.

[2] Lord Morley, Walpole, London, 1903 edit., pp. 166-7.

[3] Brisco, op. cit. pp. 108-9. An average price for tobacco in the plantations at this time was about 2d. per lb.

action as much by the complaints of the Virginian planters as by the loss to the revenue. He proposed accordingly to have all tobacco landed practically duty-free and placed in bonded warehouses from which it could be re-shipped without the passing of any cash between the merchant and the revenue officers. Only for home consumption was it to pay duty, on issue from the warehouse under control of excisemen with the usual safeguards, now of long standing in the case of other exciseable goods.

The scheme had already been applied to tea and coffee, and would have removed most of the possibilities of fraud. But Walpole failed to carry it in its larger application. Even before the details were known a factious opposition in parliament combined with the dishonest traders to mobilize all the forces of ignorance, cupidity and mob-violence. The storm shook the government, and even the constitution, to its base : " no assertion was too wild, no insinuation too incredible, no lie too glaring " ; Walpole narrowly escaped maltreatment in the streets ; officers solemnly reported that their troops, threatened with deprivation of their tobacco, could not be trusted to obey orders ; and the modest two hundred excisemen computed to be necessary under the scheme were magnified into an army of tyrants who would rival the enormities of the Inquisition. George II. stood by his minister, and the latter was ready to brave all things until he realized that the reform could only be effected by armed force. That, his Whig principles convinced him, was too great a price to pay, and he reluctantly abandoned the proposal. " There will be an end of the liberty of England," he said, " if supplies are to be raised by the sword."

In colonial administration he contended more successfully against the selfish interests, while ostensibly yielding to them. Here his instrument was the Duke of Newcastle, who took office in 1724 as Secretary of State for the southern department, which included control of the colonies. Newcastle shirked responsibility and made no attempt to grapple with the problems of his department. He filled the Board of Trade with men of like character to his own, and gradually destroyed its efficiency. The stories of his roomful of unopened despatches, his ignorance that Cape Breton was an island, his complaisant remark, " Yes, yes, Annapolis must certainly be fortified. Where is Annapolis ? "—are well-known. Such incompetence brought its Nemesis under the test of war. But for the peaceful progress which was Walpole's aim it had its advantages, for it enabled the great minister to nullify mischievous measures whose passage he could not avert.

As early as 1699 an Order in Council had prohibited the export of woollen manufactures from any of the colonies. In 1719 the Commons resolved " that the erecting of manufactures in the colonies tended to lessen their dependence upon Great Britain." An Act of that year imposed duties on American iron sent to England. Another of 1731 imposed heavy restrictions on the making of hats in the colonies,

and positively forbade their export, although this was a very suitable
industry for a country in which the beaver provided unlimited raw
material.   In 1733 the West Indian planters, strongly represented in
Parliament, secured the passage of the Molasses Act, which sought to
kill the New England trade with the French islands by prohibitive
duties on French-produced rum, molasses and sugar.   Walpole saw,
what few other men could see, that the prosperity of the colonies in
general outweighed that of special interests, and that the mother-
country would benefit rather than suffer by allowing colonial enterprise
free play.   For him the growth of American population, expanding
in geometrical progression, had its significance, whilst the more conservative economists viewed the plantations only through the glasses
of Clarendon and James II.   Accordingly he allowed full scope to his
maxim of *quieta non movere*.   There was no need of active intervention :
Newcastle's incompetence did what was necessary.   American manufactures developed in the modest manner which alone was natural
in a continent where land was cheap and urban population scanty.
The officials on the spot made no attempt to enforce the Molasses Act,
which remained a complete dead-letter until a much later time.   The
administration of certain sections of the older laws of trade seems also
to have been fairly lax.

Of constructive reform he was able to effect something.   He
agreed to the enumeration of beaver in 1722 whilst lowering the
duties by over sixty per cent.   On the other hand he partially
freed rice and sugar from the same restriction.   In 1729 he allowed
Carolina to export rice to all destinations south of Cape Finisterre without transhipment in England, and in 1734 the infant
colony of Georgia received the same privilege.   This had the effect
of recapturing the lost Portuguese market.   In 1739 the West Indies
were also allowed to send sugar direct to southern Europe, but in
their case the concession availed little in recovering what had been
lost to French competition.[1]

In political administration his mild methods are open to greater
criticism.   Colonial defence remained unorganized, the perennial
squabbles between governors and assemblies were never cleared up,
and the position of crown officials was often so undignified that self-
respecting men hesitated to accept such posts.   In general all the old
sores rankled still.   These matters Walpole did not touch.   But,
while he reigned long, his position was never secure.   He was plagued
always by the most dishonest and ungenerous opposition which English
politics have ever produced ; and, as he told an adviser who wished
him to impose a direct tax on the colonies, he could not afford to raise
up gratuitous enemies on the other side of the Atlantic.   Since even
his detractors could not accuse him of lacking courage, his judgment

[1] On these matters see particularly Beer, *Commercial Policy*, and Brisco, *Walpole's
Economic Policy* ; also *American Historical Review*, vol. xx., *Anglo-French Commercial
Rivalry*, 1700-50, by Prof. C. M. Andrews.

was probably correct. American politics at this period belong more particularly to the internal history of the colonies, and will conveniently be treated at greater length in a subsequent chapter.

The colonization of Georgia, the last of the thirteen states founded under British rule, was taken in hand in 1732. It originated in philanthropic motives, somewhat suggestive of the doctrines of Hakluyt a hundred and fifty years before. General James Oglethorpe was concerned at the unhappy fate of men committed to debtors' prisons, and came to the conclusion that a specially organized colony was needed to give such characters a fresh start in life. The government was favourable to his scheme because it desired to set up a buffer to protect the plantations of South Carolina from Spanish incursions. Oglethorpe and his associates therefore obtained a charter making them proprietors of the coast between the Savannah and Altamaha rivers, that is, between Carolina and Florida. In January, 1733, he crossed the Atlantic with his first party of emigrants, and founded the town of Savannah in a good military position upon the river of that name. Oglethorpe lived for some years in his colony, directing its early efforts and striving to render it a means of the moral reformation of its inhabitants. Some of his ideas were unsuitable to the local conditions. He allotted the land in very small parcels, which could not be worked as economically as the great estates in South Carolina. He also attempted to prohibit slavery, but the settlers ere long found means of evading this rule. The Spaniards in Florida were of course hostile, and there was much desultory fighting with them in the early years. This led to no decisive results except the general retardation of the colony's progress. The proprietary grant had been made terminable after twenty-one years, that is, in 1753. Before that date, however, the promoters saw the control of the undertaking slipping from their grasp, and were glad to resign their rights. In 1751 Georgia became a crown colony. By 1760 its white population was about 6000 in numbers, principally engaged in rice cultivation.

Shortly after the peace of 1713-4 the East India Company had to face new competition from an unexpected quarter. As part of the settlement the Spanish Netherlands were assigned to the Emperor Charles VI., and figure as the Austrian Netherlands in the later history of the eighteenth century. Charles was sore at what he considered his desertion by England in the last stages of the war. He permitted accordingly a Belgian revival in oceanic trade, which took the form of voyages from Ostend to India and China. British Jacobites assisted the enterprise. Factories were established at three points in India— Covelong, Bankipur and Kasimbazar, and from 1718 to 1721 at least fifteen large ships sailed out of Ostend for the east. In 1722 Charles formally chartered the Imperial and Royal Company of the Austrian Low Countries, granting it a thirty years' monopoly of trade with Africa and the East and West Indies. Three years later he effected a treaty with Spain by which the South American ports were thrown

open to his Company's ships.   English trading interests took alarm ;
in their usual exaggerated language they declared that " the liberties
of England will be no more, and the Protestant religion destroyed."
In fact, the shares of the East India Company fell 15 per cent.   Walpole
yielded to popular pressure and mobilized the fleet, sending one
squadron to the Baltic, another to the Spanish coast, and a third to
Porto Bello.   Spain accepted the challenge and laid siege to Gibraltar.
British sea power was, however, too strong, and the emperor gave way
before the war became general.   In May, 1727, he agreed to suspend
the Ostend Company for seven years.   Before their expiration he
abolished it altogether.   The whole incident affords proof of the
maritime supremacy to which Great Britain had risen and of the
methods by which the high-handed imperialism of the time was prepared to deal with its rivals.[1]

The same forces brought about the fall of Walpole and of the
precariously maintained peace upon which they had been nourished.
English industry and trade had advanced at a much greater rate than
had the population, until the influential classes were drunk with
prosperity and convinced that no obstacle could withstand their
aggression.   The state of politics afforded an outlet to predatory
ambitions.   The great minister's overbearing personality would permit
no man of parts to share his power, and drove all that was active and
vigorous in the younger generation into the ranks of the opposition.

A West Indian dispute with Spain afforded Walpole's enemies their
opportunity.   The Treaty of Utrecht had conceded to England the
Asiento and with it a very limited general trade in Spanish America.
It had left unregularized the illicit traffic with the same region always
carried on to a greater or less extent since the days of Queen Elizabeth.
In the long peace this contraband trade had grown in volume in unison
with the remainder of our commercial undertakings.   At the same time
the Spanish government had shown signs of recovering from the
lethargy into which it had fallen in the seventeenth century.   The
situation therefore was that English merchants had come, by long
prescription, to imagine that they had almost a right to defy the
Spanish navigation laws, whilst a Spanish force of *guarda costas* came
into being with the object of enforcing those laws by stopping and
searching for contraband any English ship they found sailing in the
Caribbean Sea.   It is clear that legitimate English traders were hardly
treated. | The word *guarda costa* suggests a government force under
regular pay and discipline.   In fact the *guarda costas* were not of that
status.   They were privateers who fitted out armed vessels as a speculation.   They searched British merchantmen, sometimes far from territorial waters, and arrested them if they found any goods that might
be of Spanish origin. | Once condemned, the prize went mainly to the

---

[1] See G. B. Hertz, " England and the Ostend Company," *Engl. Hist. Review*, xxii.
pp. 255-79.   Carlyle described the undertaking as " a mere paper company " ; but it
paid an aggregate dividend of 125 per cent. in seven consecutive years.

captors, and in practice it was impossible to obtain restitution even if the judgement were set aside by higher authority in Spain.[1] This was the right of the British case, but linked to it was another motive, that of the conquest of rich colonial possessions. The merchants' grievance could have been settled by negotiation. The ulterior object demanded war. Public opinion, seeking as a warcry some concrete embodiment of the abstract principles involved, pitched upon the case of Jenkins' Ear. Captain Jenkins, skipper of a West Indian trader, testified that he had been arrested by *guarda costas* on the high seas, hanged to his own yard-arm, let down half-dead, and deprived of an ear, which his persecutors had mockingly told him to take as a present to King George. The story secured enthusiastic credence, and the opposition made it their text upon which to preach a war with Spain.

Walpole was averse from the adventure. As a statesman he recoiled from fighting over a question which could have been settled by negotiation. Perhaps also at the back of his mind lay an uneasy suspicion that the mighty naval machine upon which the war party relied for an easy victory had grown somewhat rusty by long disuse. He resisted the war fever as long as he could, and even succeeded in patching up an unsatisfactory agreement with Spain, which the opposition rejected with contempt. Their object, in the political world, was simply to pull down the minister, and they cared nothing for consistency in their methods of achieving it. They shouted for war and at the same time moved a reduction of the army ; and when they had forced Walpole to set the world ablaze, they coolly accused him of doing so on his own motion, in order to cover the traces of his own malpractices. Prominent among the younger members of this party was William Pitt, and seldom has a really unselfish and patriotic statesmen been involved with such unsavoury associates. The true explanation is probably that of a contemporary foreign observer, that he was conscious of great talents but as yet knew little of the world. The political opposition could not have forced the minister's hand if the country had not been on their side. Here, as the weight of evidence lies, the motive was not so much the wrongs of British seamen as sheer lust of plunder. In spite of all the disillusionments of the past, South and Central America were still Eldorado in the public mind. Spain was rich and weak, and promised to be an easy prey. The war party never ceased their clamour ; and in November, 1739, Walpole gave way, sorely against his will. With that decision, although he retained office for three more years, his work as a statesman virtually ends.

[1] R. Pares, *War and Trade in the West Indies*, Oxford, 1936, chs. i. and ii.

CHAPTER III

THE OLD FRENCH COLONIAL EMPIRE

THE fall of Walpole marks the opening of a generation of warfare between Great Britain and the French and Spanish branches of the House of Bourbon. In this struggle the old British Empire reached its climax by the acquisition of Canada and the hegemony of India, and was shattered by the loss of the original American colonies in 1782-3. The old French Empire also attained the height of its power and glory, and swiftly went down under a series of crushing defeats some twenty years prior to the disruption of its victorious British rival. Before entering upon an account of this dramatic period it is necessary therefore to glance briefly at the colonial edifice of France and the methods by which it had been built.

In the successive stages of its development French oceanic enterprise runs on parallel lines to that of England. First there was a period of desultory voyages of discovery, inspired by the hope of a short passage to the east, and coupled with fishing on the Newfoundland banks. This period stretches from the discovery of America to the death of Francis I. in 1546. In the middle of the sixteenth century there followed, as in England, a vigorous attempt to open a trade with the regions claimed by Portugal in Guinea and Brazil. In these matters the French record is obscure, but their success seems to have been at least as great as that of the London merchants under Edward VI. and Mary. Next, in the later decades of the same century, the religious wars drove the Huguenots to the sea, and inspired a plundering campaign against the Spanish colonies in the west, which somewhat antedated that of Drake and his followers. Here again the full details have perished, for Huguenot France produced no Hakluyt to preserve its record of adventures on the ocean. Arising out of the same movement were small, ill-supported, under-capitalized efforts to plant colonies—by Villegagnon in Brazil and by Ribault and Laudonnière in Florida. These, like the undertakings of Gilbert and Ralegh, failed and left no trace. Then, in the first half of the seventeenth century, the reunion of France under the House of Bourbon and the strong rule of Cardinal Richelieu afforded a basis upon which to commence the building of a real colonial empire. Permanent colonies established

350

themselves in Canada and Acadia, the former but a short twelve months after the landing of John Smith and his comrades upon Virginian soil. French settlers appeared also in the West Indies—at St. Kitts in the same year as Thomas Warner and his English pioneers, at other islands a little later.   To the east also the French merchants began to feel their way by a series of experimental voyages in the wake of the English and the Dutch.   This was in France the age of the chartered companies, far more numerous than in England, and on the whole far less successful. It was a method of expansion which appealed strongly to the bureau-cratic French mind.   The companies were more tightly bound than ours by government control, and they made the mistake of under-taking colonization as well as trade, two functions which English experience soon showed to be incompatible.   In the latter half of the seventeenth century the broad parallel still holds good.   Corresponding to the constructive colonial policy of the English Restoration statesmen we find in France the administration of Colbert (1664-83), whose watch-words were territorial expansion with a view to trade, naval power for its protection, and the fostering of national wealth, the whole under a system of unified control, minutely vigilant in method, delicate in touch.   Colbert's work was mighty ; its defect was that it depended too much upon the guidance of a master hand.   After his death it fell into the power of lesser men, and the wars of 1688-1713 brought a decline amounting almost to an eclipse of the French colonial empire, whilst the more hardy and self-reliant system of England survived and even flourished under the shock.   A revival followed the Treaty of Utrecht.   John Law, the Scottish adventurer, although he failed in his vast financial schemes, gave an impetus to French commerce and expansion, and the monarchy continued his work on sound and sensible lines.   By 1740 the French empire had grown rich and strong, and fit in outward appearance to challenge the supremacy of its British rival.   In the west as in the east it was the French who showed the greater military power and who willingly took the offensive against their more sluggish and reluctant neighbours.

Upon the earlier stages of French expansion we cannot dwell in detail.   French fishermen flocked to Newfoundland in the opening years of the sixteenth century, and the Normans, Bretons and Basques long outnumbered the mariners of western England in that region. In 1522 Giovanni da Verrazzano, an Italian seaman in the service of Francis I., captured some homeward-bound Spanish ships conveying rich cargoes from the West Indies.   The incident excited the desire of the French king to acquire similar possessions across the Atlantic. He despatched Verrazzano to make a coasting voyage from Florida northwards to the Gulf of St. Lawrence.   Neglecting the prior claims of English discovery, he proclaimed the annexation of the continent under the name of New France (1524).   The Spaniards afterwards captured Verrazzano and hanged him as a pirate.   The St. Lawrence estuary seemed to offer a prospect of penetrating by a westward passage to the Pacific. In 1534 Jacques Cartier of St. Malo sailed to investigate the region, and his work in that and the following year resulted in a fairly correct delineation of the surrounding coasts upon the charts. Other seamen of northern France followed his example, and at Dieppe there sprang up a school of cartographers who made a notable contribution to the advance of geographical science. Cartier returned to the St. Lawrence in 1540, and two years later François de Roque, Sieur de Roberval, attempted to plant a colony on its banks. But France, like England, had yet a long apprenticeship to serve in the art of colonization, and this early effort was soon abandoned.

In the meanwhile French traders were reaching the coast of Brazil in defiance of Portuguese prohibitions. The country appeared suitable for a Huguenot colony of refuge, and in 1555, under the patronage of Coligny, Nicholas Durand (otherwise known as Villegagnon) led a fairly large body of pioneers to make the experiment. He settled on an island near Rio de Janeiro and, with the arrival of reinforcements, the colony seemed to promise well. Theological controversies, however, proved its ruin. The settlers quarrelled with their leader and deserted the island, the survivors making their way northwards along the coast until they were picked up by European merchantmen. Another Huguenot enterprise had a longer life and a more tragic ending. Early in 1562 Captain Jean Ribault, also one of Coligny's men, examined the coasts of Florida and Carolina, and chose a site on the latter for a colony which he left under the charge of Albert de la Pierria. Ribault returned to France and wrote an account of his voyage, which has survived, curiously enough, only in an English translation. Left to themselves, the colonists murdered Pierria and sailed for home, most of them dying of starvation on the way. In 1564 René Laudonnière planted the colony anew, and Sir John Hawkins was able to afford it some assistance on his homeward voyage from the West Indies in the following year. Ribault also came out again with reinforcements, but soon after his arrival a Spanish expedition fell upon the settlement, determined to root out heresy in America ere it could fully establish itself. The Huguenots were taken by surprise. Laudonnière and a few others escaped by sea. Ribault and every other Frenchman whom the Spaniards could catch were ruthlessly massacred. The Spaniards then took possession of the fort and settled down in their victims' places. In 1567 Dominique de Gourges with another French expedition recaptured the place and hanged every Spaniard in it by way of revenge. But the Huguenot colony was not replanted.

Farther north there was no renewal of the projects of Cartier and Roberval until the close of the century. Then, in 1598, the Marquis de la Roche planted a small settlement in Acadia. This failed to prosper, and was abandoned in 1603, at which time only twelve persons were left. In 1605 the Huguenots founded Port Royal (afterwards Annapolis) in the same region, abandoning it two years later. The next attempt proved a permanent success. In 1608 Samuel de Champlain sailed up the St. Lawrence and established a trading post at Quebec, and at about the same time Port Royal was also re-occupied. The two provinces of Canada and Acadia thus began their careers side by side. In the former the purpose was rather trade with the Indians than agricultural settlement, but the latter, after long years of precarious hardship, became a true colony, self-supporting and to a large extent cut off from the outside world. Canada was governed by officials appointed by the crown, whilst a company provided the funds and drew profit from the fur trade. The result was that Quebec depended upon food supplies from home, and the scanty French population ranged over a far greater stretch of territory than they were able effectively to occupy.

The next step belongs to the year 1627, shortly after the accession of Cardinal Richelieu to power in France. Richelieu took a wider view of colonization than any of his predecessors had done, forecasting the all-embracing mercantile policy characteristic of both England and France in the latter half of the seventeenth century. The machinery he favoured was that of the chartered company with monopoly rights. In the year mentioned he formed the Company of the Hundred Associates (or of New France) and the Company of the Isles of America, the former to exploit the continent, and the latter the West Indies. African undertakings also sprang up during his ministry, and in the year of his death he chartered the Company of the Indies to resume the eastern trade which had failed to prosper under its smaller predecessors. A French authority counts it as a fundamental error that he failed to perceive the unsuitability of companies for the work of colonization.[1]

The Company of the Hundred Associates secured widespread privileges, including sovereignty and the monopoly of trade from Florida to the Arctic. Virginia and the Pilgrims' colony of Plymouth were already in existence at the time of the grant, but Richelieu, at war with Charles I. and Buckingham, ignored the English achievements. English and Scotch pioneers nevertheless administered a rude shock to his pretensions. Sir William Alexander occupied Acadia in 1627 and two years later Sir David Kirke captured the French foodships and starved Champlain into surrender at Quebec. For the moment the French flag disappeared from North America. But in 1632 Charles I., compelled by his political ambitions to gain peace at any price, restored both Canada and Acadia, and Richelieu's company was able to resume its operations. During the next thirty years, however successful it may have proved as a trading concern, it did little for the cause of colonization. By 1663 the French population of Canada amounted only to 2500 persons. The Jesuits, who sent out their first mission in 1625, were active in exploration and conversion of the Indians. The latter fell into two great groups, the Hurons and Algonquins who inhabited Canada and the shores of the great lakes,

---

[1] Paul Leroy-Beaulieu, *De la colonisation chez les peuples modernes*, 4th edit., Paris, 1891, p. 146.

and the Iroquois confederacy who held the watershed between the St. Lawrence and the Hudson River. The former group fell under French influence ; the latter preserved their independence but leaned usually towards alliance with the English colonies. The French pioneers of the seventeenth century were commonly more successful than the English in their dealings with coloured races, whether with the red men of America, the Caribs of the West Indies, or the more civilized peoples of the east. Their natural courtesy was an asset in comparison with the rougher manners of their rivals, the Jesuit teaching had the merit of uniformity and simplicity as against the discordant systems of the various Protestant sects, and the French as a rule adapted themselves without scruple to native ways of life. A governor of Canada attended a meeting of Indian chiefs painted and befeathered like his hosts ; in the West Indies Frenchmen discarded European clothes and lived naked among the Carib cannibals ; and in general they displayed little antipathy to the mixed marriages which were anathema in New England.[1]

In the West Indies the Company of the Isles of America developed the French portion of St. Kitts and inaugurated settlements in Martinique and Guadeloupe and the western end of Hispaniola, named St. Domingo by the French. None of these islands rivalled the early prosperity of Barbados, but all made steady progress in preparation for the flood-tide of success which came to them in the eighteenth century. In one respect the Caribbean colonies were more promising than New France : they were the only region to which Frenchmen would emigrate at all freely. In the period 1670-80 their population was between four and five times that of Canada. The question of emigration was in reality the rock upon which the old French empire split. It produced daring soldiers, seamen and explorers in profusion ; but never a sufficiency of sober, hard-working cultivators of the New England and Maryland type. The comparative success of the West Indian plantations indicates what might have been done elsewhere, for it took place in spite of and not as a result of the efforts of the Company of the Isles of America. The latter body sought to grind the faces of the planters by buying their produce cheap and selling them French goods dear. The colonists therefore disregarded its monopoly and invited Dutch traders to deal with them. Dutch sea-power reaped the benefit, and the French Company fell into a state of bankruptcy.

French merchants directed their thoughts to the east almost as early as did the English and the Dutch. Henry IV. chartered an East India Company in 1604, and Louis XIII. another in 1611, but neither

---

[1] Leroy-Beaulieu, *op. cit.* p. 140, says of the French as colonists : " Il n'est pas de peuple qui sache mieux se plier à tous les climats et à toutes les conditions d'existence, qui soit plus sympathique aux races étrangères et primitives, qui sache mieux se fondre avec les aborigènes et s'approprier aux différents milieux." On the other hand he finds coupled with these very qualities two causes of French failure, " le gout outré des aventures et la facilité à prendre les mœurs et les idées des populations primitives.'

of these projects came to the stage of action. In 1615, however, the persons concerned obtained a new grant, and despatched two expeditions to the Eastern Archipelago with very moderate success. Little further was done until 1642, when Richelieu, as we have seen, founded the Company of the Indies. This body determined, as its first step, to plant a settlement in Madagascar to serve as a base from which to develop the Indian trade. The effort absorbed all its capital, and after precariously maintaining its hold for some years against the native tribes of the island, it too sank into impotence.[1]

Such was the generally disappointing condition of the French empire when the Age of Louis XIV. began with the death of Cardinal Mazarin in 1661. Louis determined to be his own chief minister and to reduce the officers of state to a position strictly subordinate to himself; but to Jean Baptiste Colbert, who took charge of finance, the navy, commerce and the colonies, he allowed a free hand in his own department. Colbert took office with his policy already framed. Some years earlier he had written to Mazarin : " We must re-establish or create all industries, even those of luxury ; establish a protective system in the customs ; organize the producers and the traders in corporations ; ease the fiscal bonds which are harmful to the people ; restore to France the marine transport of her productions ; develop the colonies and attach them commercially to France ; suppress all the intermediaries between France and India ; develop the navy to protect the mercantile marine." [2] This was the system which was becoming, and was to remain for over a century, the gospel of all the sea-powers. In France for some twenty years it found its most brilliant exemplification and produced its most striking results. It is therefore justly known by the name of Colbertism, although no single man can claim to have been its inventor.

In pursuit of his first object of universal and detailed control Colbert determined to sweep up all external enterprises into two great company organizations, one for the East Indies and the other for the West. In 1664 he obtained his edicts. The Company of the West was given the control of all American, West Indian and African possessions, the latter—the slaving stations—being rightly regarded as belonging to the western colonial system. At the same time the new East India Company obtained a fifty years' monopoly of trade in the Indian Ocean and the Pacific, and a government guarantee against financial loss for the first ten years.

The Company of the West thus took over the purely colonial business of France in addition to vast trading interests. But, taught by experience, Colbert laid down stringent conditions to prevent the former from being sacrificed to the latter, and the crown kept in its hands the appointment of all the principal colonial officials. In

[1] For details of the Madagascar colony see H. Castonnet des Fosses, *L'Inde française avant Dupleix*, Paris, 1887, pp. 40-5.

[2] Henry Weber, *La Compagnie française des Indes*, Paris, 1904, p. 100.

Canada three men shared the administration : the governor, the titular chief, who concerned himself principally with military matters ; the intendant, who managed civil and fiscal affairs and was often able to overrule the governor ; and the Bishop of Quebec, who controlled the important missionary department and thus incidentally dealt with much of the business of exploration. In Talon the minister found an intendant after his own heart, and the two worked hard for the advancement of the colony. Talon was the first official, either English or French, to see the importance of the Hudson River to the future of North America, and he vainly urged the acquisition of New York by diplomatic or warlike means. Louis XIV. was not sufficiently impressed to make a bid for the place, and the Treaty of Breda confirmed it to England. In Canada itself the care of the administration produced a revival of energy and for the first time a perceptible growth of population. The numbers trebled in the years 1664-74, and reached nearly 10,000 by 1679. Canada differed absolutely from the English colonies in that there was no representative government. All control was bureaucratic, the land was held on feudal tenures, and the French division of classes into *seigneurs* and peasants reproduced itself. This retarded agriculture by keeping the more independent spirits in the ranks of the hunters and pioneers who could push into the wilderness beyond the reach of social restraints. The careers of Radisson and Groseilliers, who did such good service to the English Hudson's Bay Company, furnish an illustration of this tendency, and the loss which it caused to French interests.

In the Caribbean the Company of the West was financially more successful than its predecessor, but by enforcing the trade restrictions which the latter body had only asserted it seems to have retarded the development of the islands as colonies. One result of Colbert's work was that the royal navy of France made its first appearance in the West Indies in 1666, assisting in the reduction of the English islands which the Treaty of Breda restored in the following year. In spite of its success in this region the Company of the West as a whole fell into difficulties, and ten years' experience convinced Colbert that the control of the crown was the proper means of developing the colonial empire. In 1674, accordingly, he abolished the Company and continued the administration directly in the king's name.

During this period Canadian energy in certain directions was very evident. In 1669-73 the Jesuits had completed the exploration of the great lakes. They now struck southwards to the headwaters of the Mississippi and its affluents. In 1682 La Salle traversed the great river to its mouth in the Gulf of Mexico. At once the project arose of colonizing the Mississippi delta and ultimately its whole basin. The new region received the name of Louisiana, and La Salle lost his life in a vain attempt to plant it in 1687. The first permanent settlement did not take place until the close of the century, and New Orleans, its later capital, only dates from 1717. In the meantime the trend of events was launching Canada upon a course of military adventures very congenial to its restless inhabitants. Colbert died in 1683 at a juncture when colonial and European rivalries were once more growing acute. Louis XIV. bent all his energies to the aggrandisement of France along her eastern frontiers. A reaction set in against the high consideration hitherto given to the colonies, and thenceforward until the Revolution the ruling circles at the French court, although patronizing overseas interests in time of peace, sacrificed them to the lure of military conquest on the Rhine in time of war. The French nobles who governed Canada were thus left very largely to frame their own policy and carry it on with their own resources ; and considering the scantiness of the means, their work was undeniably brilliant. The Comte de Frontenac served his first term as governor from 1672 to 1682. He established forts Frontenac and Niagara at the eastern and western ends of Lake Ontario, and made some progress towards winning the Iroquois from the English alliance. He could not, however, agree with the intendant, and was recalled. In his absence hostilities broke out with the English in Hudson's Bay, and the Iroquois made war upon his successor, who lost the Ontario forts. At the outbreak of the general war in 1688 Frontenac was reinstated. He kept the frontiers of New York and New England in constant alarm, discouraged the Iroquois, and recaptured Acadia, overrun by the New Englanders in 1691. But for the lack of naval support he would certainly have done more. D'Iberville, his most brilliant subordinate, all but destroyed the English hold on Hudson's Bay, and ravaged the little English settlements in Newfoundland. The favourable colonial terms obtained by France at the Treaty of Ryswick were largely due to Frontenac's work. He died in 1698. In the renewed war of 1701-13 Canada was less enterprising and the home government even less able to afford assistance. The Treaty of Utrecht therefore accorded the fringes of New France—Newfoundland, Acadia and Hudson's Bay —definitely to Great Britain. The loss was partly attributable to neglect of the fine navy which Colbert had built up.

The revived East India Company of 1664 enjoyed a longer lease of life than did that of the west. It attempted at first to resume the project of a Madagascar colony, but found the opposition of the natives too strong. As an alternative it occupied the smaller islands of Bourbon and the Isle of France, now known as Réunion and Mauritius. Here after many years it was successful in founding the desired naval base in the Indian Ocean. In India itself François Caron established the first French factory at Surat in 1668. The grant of another post at Masulipatam on the Bay of Bengal followed in 1669. The Company now acted with great vigour, and sought to gain a footing at Trincomalee in Ceylon. A Dutch force, however, evicted the French, who proceeded next to St. Thomé on the Coromandel Coast. Dutch hostility pursued them thither, and in 1674 the garrison of St. Thomé had to capitulate. The French commander, François Martin, had made a gallant defence, and secured permission to withdraw with the honours of war. He had anticipated the situation, and had already surveyed another position on the same coast. To this place, afterwards known as Pondicherry, he led the sixty followers who were left to him. He remained there for some years, working hard to establish his countrymen in the goodwill of the native powers.

In spite of Martin's success the French company was not at this period financially prosperous. When the next Dutch war broke out in 1688-9 it was able to send little help to its servants in India. In 1693 therefore Pondicherry surrendered to a great Dutch armament, to be restored by the Treaty of Ryswick in 1697. In the meanwhile the Surat factory had decayed and had been abandoned, but in compensation the French had obtained a footing at Chandernagore in Bengal, receiving a formal grant for a factory in 1688. On recovering Pondicherry the Company made it their head factory and the seat of their director-general in the east. François Martin was the first holder of the post, dying in harness in 1706.[1] At this juncture the history of the Company resembled that of its English rival half a century before. Its servants were making headway in India, but at home its affairs were in the utmost disorder. The disastrous wars and the general ruin of the French finances reacted upon a business which had never been sound to such an extent that it was reduced to licensing private merchants to carry on the trade. From 1712 onwards it despatched no ships of its own for nearly eight years, and Colbert's once promising bid for eastern commerce seemed destined to collapse. One point is noticeable in the wars of 1688-1713 : there is little record of hostilities in India between the English and the French. Neither side was sufficiently established to risk a struggle in presence of strong native powers, and both accordingly entered into local agreements for neutrality. In 1707, however, occurred the death of Aurangzeb, the last Mogul emperor to exercise real authority beyond the environs of Delhi. This event, presaging a period of revolution and insecurity, was destined ultimately to modify the position and policy of all Europeans in the country.

In the years succeeding the Treaty of Utrecht the main interest of French colonial history centres in the mother-country. Louis XIV. died in 1715, leaving his kingdom in a condition of bankruptcy and distress which contrasted strongly with the prosperous state of England. The Duke of Orleans assumed the government as regent for Louis XV., and gave his countenance to the proposals of John Law, a Scottish financier who came to France at this time. Law's plan for the repayment of the debt and the re-establishment of prosperity bore some resemblance to the South Sea Scheme in England. He developed it by

---

[1] In Martin's time : " Pondichéry offrait une physionomie toute particulière et différait des autres villes que les Européens possédaient en Asie. Les habitants vivaient entre eux avec cordialité. Les antipathies de race et de couleur y étaient inconnues." Castonnet des Fosses, *op. cit.* p. 129.

degrees, its ultimate form being the establishment of a huge and universal trading company to take over all the overseas interests of the country, absorb the national debt into its own stock, and command the necessary confidence by means of a close alliance with the government. He began with a renewed Company of the West in 1717, which, like the older body of the same name, controlled the trade and the public lands of Canada and Louisiana. In Canada its actual influence was small, but on the Mississippi it began vigorous measures, sending out 5000 colonists and founding New Orleans. In 1719-20 it absorbed the East India Company, the Barbary, St. Domingo, and Guinea Companies, and a China Company established some years previously. The two last-mentioned bodies were in a moribund condition similar to that of the East India Company. In addition to these undertakings, Law's great corporation, now styled the Perpetual Company of the Indies, had a tobacco monopoly and a banking business. The end resembled that of the South Sea Bubble. The stock was inflated out of all proportion to the profits actually made, and the crash came in 1720 when a panic succeeded the mania for speculation. Nevertheless some permanent good remained. The East India Company emerged from the chaos with its trade set in motion once more, and enjoying not only its former traffic with India but that with China, St. Domingo and Louisiana in addition. The latter colony suffered a relapse from the activity of 1717, but never fell quite to its former insignificance.

After the fall of Law the French empire enjoyed over twenty years of peace. During this time, both at home and abroad there was a general revival of prosperity and rebirth of sea-power. Canada, although still far behind the English colonies, participated in the movement. In 1713 its population was about 20,000; in 1721, 25,000; in 1744, 54,000. It was therefore tending towards the same ratio of increase as in the remainder of North America—a doubling of numbers every twenty years. The military efficiency of this population was high in proportion to its political and economic primitiveness. It was homogeneous and at the sole disposal of its governor. All men between the ages of fourteen and seventy were liable to service in the militia, and were regularly exercised and officered by *seigneurs* to whom they paid instinctive obedience. This contrasted strongly with the condition of the English colonial militias, divided among a dozen uncoordinated governments, seldom called out except in time of emergency, accustomed to cavil at the orders, or rather the entreaties, of the king's representatives, and to treat their own officers with democratic familiarity. Nevertheless New England alone possessed five times the population of New France, and this superiority of weight must have proved decisive had the colonists been left to decide their quarrels without interference from home.

The rulers of Canada by no means admitted as final the territorial losses sustained at Utrecht. The disastrous failure of the English expedition which attempted to ascend the St. Lawrence in 1711 led them to believe that the heart of their colony was unassailable. As a further safeguard they planted the banks of the Richelieu River, flowing between Lake Champlain and the St. Lawrence, with disbanded soldiers and their officers. In 1720 they began the construction of the great fortress of Louisbourg on Cape Breton Island. This was intended as a refuge for a French fleet and a base from which to reconquer Newfoundland and Nova Scotia. The latter province they kept in a constant state of insecurity by boundary disputes and religious propaganda among the French inhabitants. In the Mississippi valley they were also active, building a series of fortified posts along the course of that river and never losing sight of the project of linking-up Canada and Louisiana as one continuous dominion.

The French West Indies also date a forward movement from the days of Law. Although his method of expansion had been that of the chartered company, his organization had been so closely bound to the state that it escaped many of the vices to which commercial control of colonies was prone. From 1717 the West Indian trade enjoyed freedom from the too excessive restrictions imposed by Colbert. By reason partly of this freedom and partly of the fact that their soil had not yet been exhausted, the French islands shot ahead of the English. By 1738 St. Domingo was exporting twice as much sugar as Jamaica, and Martinique and Guadeloupe were more prosperous than Barbados. The English planters lost the bulk of their European market to this competition. The French monarchical administration showed greater enlightenment than English parliamentary mercantilism by permitting the refining of sugar in the colonies in despite of the theoretical loss to home industry. The revival of the French Newfoundland fishery, and the progress of Canada and above all of the West Indies, did much to rescue French sea-power from the extinction into which Louis XIV. had allowed it to fall.

The East India Company resumed its independent life in 1723, having already recommenced its trade under Law. Pondicherry became a large and well-governed town, with growing fortifications and a trade which in 1730 enabled it to send five and a half million francs worth of goods to France. The Company's port of Lorient in Brittany was busy with the despatch of cargoes and the building of large merchantmen. At the Isle of France Bertrand de la Bourdonnais, a seaman of established reputation appointed governor in 1735, created a thriving colony and a dockyard capable of repairing warships and serving as a refuge for a fleet. In India itself the Company acquired the additional factories of Mahé on the Malabar Coast and Karikal in Tanjore. Chandernagore in Bengal, hitherto a minor station, received as its governor in 1730 Joseph François Dupleix, who in eleven years made it the richest European settlement in the province. According to accounts formerly received, Dupleix during this period meditated and worked out his daring and original plans for a French subjugation of India, gaining experience and building up a system of native connections by means of which he intended to expel the English from the country.[1] This project he continued after his promotion to the governor-generalship at Pondicherry in 1741, and the outbreak of hostilities soon afterwards gave him a chance of putting it to the test.

Great as was the advance of the British empire in the generation of peace after Utrecht, that of the French was more striking and seemed to promise unbounded future success. In 1715 the French mercantile marine comprised but 300 vessels ; in 1735 it numbered 1800, of which sixty ranging from 400 to 800 tons each belonged to the East India Company.[2] It was progress of this sort which excited the forebodings of William Pitt, the most disinterested of Walpole's opponents, and caused him to welcome the opportunity of trying a fall with the Bourbon monarchies. The Anglo-Spanish war of 1739 and the Austrian Succession war of 1740, in which England and France fought first as auxiliaries and later as principals, thus afforded an outlet to restless ambitions long pent up on either side of the Channel.

[1] His career, from this point of view, is narrated by Tibulle Hamont, *Dupleix d'après sa correspondance inédite*, Paris, 1881. A later historian, however, Prosper Cultru, *Dupleix*, Paris, 1901, claims to have examined Dupleix's papers with equal care and to have discovered in them no trace of any great pre-arranged plan. In his preface he says : " Je crois avoir demontré : 1° que la Compagnie n'avait pas les moyens de suivre une politique, et n'en a jamais eu aucune ; 2° que Dupleix, avant 1749, n'en eut pas plus qu'elle ; 3° que l'entreprise qu'il a tentée alors, née des circonstances, ne devait pas avoir de lendemain et n'a été poussée qu'au hasard ; qu'il a agi au jour le jour et n'a pas eu de plan arrêté avant 1753 ; 4° que, par suite, il a manqué des ressources nécessaires ; et quant à ses chefs, ils n'ont pu apprécier à temps le valeur de projets tout à fait contraires à leurs traditions." Farther on he deprecates the popular conception of " ce Dupleix légendaire, sans vice et sans faiblesse, presque divin," and asserts that the Governor of Chandernagore is revealed by his own letters as " un commerçant actif mais malheureux, un homme ambitieux, non de conquérir un empire, mais d'aller vivre bourgeoisement en France." H. H. Dodwell, in *Dupleix and Clive*, London, 1920, and in *Cambr. Hist. of the Br. Empire*, iv. ch. v. (1929), agrees with the rejection of the legendary Dupleix and represents the French leader as an able but self-seeking man of the type common among Europeans in India during the period.

[2] Castonnet des Fosses, *op. cit.* p. 224.

CHAPTER IV

THE ANGLO-FRENCH STRUGGLE IN INDIA

(i) *Dupleix and the Carnatic Wars*

THE chequered history of English trade with the east gave place after the union of the companies to a long period of tranquil and uneventful progress, unbroken by wars abroad and scarcely disturbed by faction at home. The United East India Company possessed the staff, the factories and the prestige of the old corporation, together with the parliamentary charter of the new. It expressed the solidity of its position by its choice of a motto : Auspicio Regis et Senatus Angliae. An additional factor promoting that solidity lay in its large loans to the state. By 1737 its subscribed capital amounted to £4,200,000, the whole of which was in government hands. It carried on its trade upon the interest received for this sum, the rate standing originally at 8 per cent., but falling by successive stages to 3 per cent. as the eighteenth century advanced. Its own business was generally lucrative, unlike that of its French rival, so that it was enabled to pay the shareholders an average dividend of about 9 per cent. In 1720 its stock reached its highest quotation of 455, and even at the end of a disastrous decade of war, thirty-five years later, it fell no lower than 148. In 1715, after preliminary experiments, it opened a regular trade with China, and tea became an important—ultimately the most important—article which it brought into England. Its exports still consisted of bullion and manufactured goods, the value of the former being originally three times that of the latter, although towards the end of the century the disproportion lessened until merchandise predominated. It exported woollen goods at a loss, but found it expedient to continue, in order to conciliate the manufacturing interest and the general mercantile opinion of the time. Walpole remained always the Company's good friend. In 1720 it displayed readiness to sacrifice its own advantage to assist him in straightening out the South Sea tangle. Ten years afterwards he showed his gratitude by adroitly quashing a new agitation for an open trade to the east.[1]

---

[1] On these matters see F. P. Robinson, *The Trade of the East India Company*, 1709-1813, Cambridge, 1912 ; and *Cambridge Modern History*, vol. vi. pp. 529-30.

In India, as in Europe, the tranquillity of the time was deceptive and destined not to last. The successors of Aurangzeb became progressively more feeble, whilst the *subadars* or rulers of the six

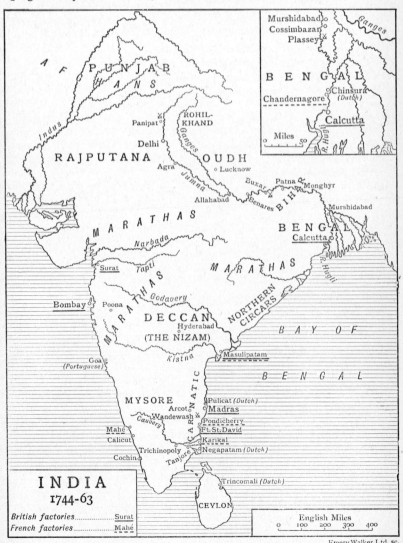

INDIA
1744-63

British factories...............Surat
French factories...............Mahé

English Miles

Emery Walker Ltd. sc.

great provinces into which he had divided his empire sought more and more the status of independent sovereigns. The process of disruption spread further, the nawabs and rajahs of the smaller states disregarding also the authority of their superiors. Persian and Afghan adventurers poured over the north-west frontier. Some departed with their plunder, others remained to found dynasties by the sword. In the centre and the south the Maratha confederacy, against which the great Moguls had struggled with little success, extended the area of their plundering raids and increased their redoubtable military power. In the space of two years, 1740-2, they killed the Nawab of the Carnatic, raided Bengal, and alarmed Madras and Bombay. It was their destiny, in fact, to prepare the whole country for European domination by destroying in detail the Mohammedan governments which emerged from the wreck of the Mogul empire.[1] By 1740, " the Indian people were becoming a masterless multitude swaying to and fro in the political storm and clinging to any power, natural or supernatural, that seemed likely to protect them. They were prepared to acquiesce in the assumption of authority by any one who could show himself able to discharge the most elementary functions of government in the preservation of life and property. In short, the people were scattered without a leader or protector ; while the political system under which they had long lived was disappearing in complete disorganization." [2]

With India in such a state of anarchy the rival European trading bodies could not for ever stand aloof from its politics. They must secure their hold by military and political action, or perish. The Dutch loosened their grip. They withdrew more and more from their Indian interests and concentrated their energies upon the archipelago where their supremacy was unchallenged. The English and the French held on, and the war which broke out between their governments at home in 1744 merely hastened a struggle which must have begun independently in the east at a slightly later date. In the geographical distribution of its settlements the English Company had an advantage. At Bombay, Madras and Calcutta it possessed three establishments of the first rank in widely separated regions. It was unlikely that all three would be menaced at the same moment, and one or two were therefore able to continue trading whilst misfortune overwhelmed their fellows. Bombay, in fact, never fell to any conqueror, European or Indian, and its harbour served as a refuge to British fleets when the monsoon season forbade them to remain upon the Coromandel Coast. The French, on the other hand, possessed only one headquarters, Pondicherry, which became the centre of strife. Chandernagore, their river factory in Bengal, was easily blockaded and inaccessible to their sea-going fleets. The latter also could find no retreat from the monsoon nearer than the Isle of France, far away in the western Indian Ocean. Karikal and Mahé, their southern factories, had little trade and were useless for naval and military purposes. For these reasons the French entered the contest with a severe handicap.

---

[1] Sir A. C. Lyall, *Rise and Expansion of British Dominion in India*, 5th edit., London, 1910, p. 85.

[2] *Ibid.* pp. 64-5.

Their best asset was the good repute with the native princes, which successive governors of Pondicherry had laboured to acquire.

La Bourdonnais, as we have seen, had displayed great energy during his governorship of the Isles of France and Bourbon. Among his notable achievements had been the creation in the former island of a fortified dockyard and harbour, Port Louis, capable of sheltering the largest fleet likely to be used in eastern waters. Returning to France in 1739 he learned that war with England was probable. He proposed therefore to Cardinal Fleury that he should take out an armed squadron to Port Louis and there await the opening of hostilities in readiness to strike the first blow on the Coromandel Coast. After delays and modifications the plan was adopted. He sailed in 1741 with five ships and 1700 soldiers and seamen. But the directors of the French Company had no wish to fight their English competitors ; they preferred instead to seek an agreement for neutrality as in the previous war. Accordingly they prevailed with the aged cardinal to send La Bourdonnais an imperative instruction to return the ships immediately to Europe. The admiral, revisiting the Isle of France after a preliminary cruise on the Indian coast, found this unwelcome order awaiting him. He obeyed it. Scarcely had he done so than a counter-order arrived permitting him to keep the ships ; but they were already out of his reach. The whole transaction was characteristic of the French administration at this period.

In the meantime Dupleix had left Chandernagore to take over the governor-generalship at Pondicherry. He arrived towards the end of 1741, and found that the events of that year had raised French prestige to a high level in the eyes of the native powers. A large Maratha army had ravaged the Carnatic and demanded from Pondicherry a tribute and the handing over of certain refugees who had placed themselves under French protection. M. Dumas, the out-going governor-general, had refused with so bold a front that the raiders had drawn off without venturing to attack. Dupleix communicated with La Bourdonnais early in 1742 and approved his plans against the English, undertaking on his part to collect all materials for a siege of Madras. La Bourdonnais then retired to the islands to await the signal from France, only, as we have seen, to find himself deprived of his armed squadron and left apparently destitute of resources.

When war broke out the British government sent four warships to the east. They arrived at Madras in 1745, and their commander made preparations to attack Pondicherry. The French Company had forbidden Dupleix to spend anything on the defences, and the town seemed likely to fall an easy prey. But Dupleix turned his native connections to good account. He induced the Nawab of the Carnatic to forbid hostilities upon his territory. The Madras authorities gave way, on condition that a like prohibition should protect them from the French if ever the balance of power should incline in favour of the

latter. The English had yet to learn that neutrality guaranteed by a
native prince was a broken reed upon which to lean.

La Bourdonnais heard of the outbreak of war in the autumn of 1744.
His action upon receipt of the news proved him to be a great leader and
organizer. He detained every French merchantman which touched at
Port Louis, silenced the objections of their commanders, armed them
with the few light guns he could collect, trained their crews as soldiers
and gunners, and formed negro companies to increase his numbers.
" La Bourdonnais determined to make what he had not. He himself,
carpenter, engineer, tailor and smith, constructed with his own hands
the model of all the articles that were required. . . . Working in this
way, he soon found himself at the head of a body of men well taught
and well disciplined, and ready to undertake any enterprise he might
assign to them." [1]   In January, 1746, a seventy-gun ship of the line
arrived from France, in company with four more Indiamen. This
raised his force to ten armed or partially armed vessels.

La Bourdonnais had still to contend with fortune. After leaving
the Isle of France to join the ships which he had sent to await him on
the coast of Madagascar he was overtaken by a hurricane. One
vessel foundered, the only battleship lost all her masts, and the
remainder sustained injuries more or less severe. Six more weeks of
terrific labour were necessary before he could resume the voyage to
the Coromandel Coast. He reached that locality towards the end
of June, and immediately fought an action with the British squadron.
The result was not decisive, but his opponents withdrew to the southwards, leaving the way clear for him to sail to Pondicherry. At this
point began the differences between La Bourdonnais and Dupleix
which ended in a complete rupture. The governor was anxious for an
immediate attempt upon Madras, but the admiral hesitated. At
length, after a long delay the French force sailed. It found its task
unexpectedly easy. The English governor, Nicholas Morse, was not
a strong man, neither were his defences prepared for a siege. He
appealed to the Nawab to enforce neutrality according to his promise,
but did not hold out long enough to co-operate with the force which
would have come to his aid. After a week's siege, in which the English
had five casualties and the French none, Madras capitulated in the
middle of September.

By the terms of the surrender La Bourdonnais undertook to restore
the place on payment of a ransom. He was afterwards accused of
receiving a bribe from the English on account of this complaisance.
At his trial in France he was acquitted, but recent investigation allows
little room for doubt that he was guilty.[2] The eighteenth century
scarcely regarded such a transaction as a breach of honour, and for La

[1] Col. G. B. Malleson, *Hist. of the French in India*, 2nd edit., re-issued, Edinburgh,
1909, p. 122.

[2] Sir G. Forrest, *Life of Clive*, 2 vols. London, 1918, i. pp. 45-6 and 461-3. The
subject is discussed at length in Malleson's *French in India*.

Bourdonnais fair excuses may be urged. His instructions had forbidden him to make permanent conquests, he had no sympathy with
Dupleix's projects, and he had a shrewd suspicion that the close of the
war would, as so often before, see all colonial gains restored. He therefore took what seemed to him the commonsense course of paroling the
English officers and accepting their bills for the ransom together with
others for his private purse. Dupleix was furious. In the midst of
their recriminations the monsoon burst, and its first gale well-nigh
destroyed the French squadron lying off Madras. With the shattered
remnant La Bourdonnais quitted the coast, arriving at the Isle of
France in December. Thence he sailed for Europe, but was taken on
the way by an English cruiser. The courtesy with which his captors
behaved increased the suspicions of his countrymen and helped to earn
him the three years' confinement in the Bastille which awaited him ere
his innocence was declared.

Up to this point the main interest of the story has lain on the French
side, for the initiative had been theirs, and the English had done little
but submit passively to fate. But when, on the departure of La
Bourdonnais, Dupleix refused to honour the latter's engagements [1]
and declared his intention of keeping Madras, the more energetic
Englishmen were stung to action. Considering that Dupleix's breach
of faith absolved them from their parole they made their escape to
Fort St. David, a minor English settlement lying on the coast a few
miles south of Pondicherry. One of these Englishmen was Robert
Clive, hitherto a civilian servant of the Company, and now at the
threshold of his military career.

Dupleix was not able immediately to proceed against Fort St.
David. He had first to secure Madras against another party who
complained of his tricky diplomacy. When despatching La Bourdonnais to the attack, he had quieted the protest of the Nawab of the
Carnatic by a promise to hand over the prospective conquest to his
keeping. The Nawab now claimed fulfilment, and Dupleix refused.
An assault upon Madras by native forces followed, but M. Paradis, a
Swiss officer in command of a small French force, inflicted a decisive
defeat on the Nawab's troops, and the danger passed.

At Fort St. David, a small but strong place, with the native town of
Cuddalore adjoining it, the English made preparations for a stout
resistance. The governor, Hinde, possessed greater energy than
Morse, and English ships soon brought reinforcements from other

---

[1] Hamont and Malleson, as whole-hearted admirers of Dupleix, declare that as the
latter never signified his consent to La Bourdonnais' treaty with Morse, he was justified
in infringing its terms. La Bourdonnais, however, expressly told Morse that the
Pondicherry government had consented to the ransom. Sir G. Forrest (i. p. 49)
concludes that it had in fact done so. Whatever may have been Dupleix's personal
responsibility, the English of Madras, having received a promise of ransom from the
officer to whom they capitulated, were undoubtedly the victims of a breach of faith.
Professor Dodwell, in *Cambr. Hist. of the Br. Empire*, iv. p. 121, is less inclined than
any of his predecessors to allow Dupleix credit for patriotic plans. He says : " the
question was really, Who was to make money out of Madras? "

parts of India. Clive received a military commission and took an active share in organizing the garrison. At the opening of 1747 the French began their attack. Paradis, their ablest officer, was no longer in chief command, and the attempt miscarried. Two other movements against the fort had no better success, and with the passage of time the English grew stronger and the French weaker. On the first day of 1748 Major Stringer Lawrence arrived from England as commander-in-chief of the Company's forces. In the subsequent years he rendered invaluable services and imparted his professional training to the natural genius of Clive. News also came to hand that Admiral Boscawen was leading to the Indian Ocean the strongest European squadron which had yet appeared there. At the end of July he dropped anchor off Fort St. David, and, joining to his force the vessels already on the coast, he had under his command thirteen ships of the line and about twenty smaller craft.

Boscawen, aware that the war was drawing to its close, lost no time in laying siege to Pondicherry. Although he had a great force misfortune dogged the enterprise from the outset. His engineers proved incompetent, and Major Lawrence, his best military officer, was captured in a preliminary fight. Dupleix, within the town, although not by taste or training a soldier, conducted a brilliant defence.[1] At length, after a two months' siege, Pondicherry baffled its assailants. Boscawen drew off, not so much because he had lost hope of taking the place as on account of the approach of the monsoon, which imposed a time limit upon his operations.

In December arrived the news that France and Great Britain had ceased hostilities in the previous April. The terms of the Treaty of Aix-la-Chapelle became known in the following year, among them an article to the effect that Madras had been exchanged against the British conquest of Louisbourg in America ; and in August, 1749, Boscawen formally received the restitution of the town before sailing for Europe. In this manner La Bourdonnais was justified and the first bout in the struggle for India came to an end. Clive resigned his commission, and the English on the Coromandel Coast betook themselves once more to their merchandise " in the prospect of a firm and lasting peace."

Their satisfaction did not long endure. Even before the restoration of Madras a series of events had begun which was destined once more to plunge the Carnatic and its rival trading companies into war. Dupleix had long been upon uncomfortable terms with the Nawab, Anwar-u Deen. He seized in 1749 the opportunity of promoting the interests of a rival claimant to the throne. This was a prince named Chanda Sahib, a firm friend of the French and a man of military talent and European as well as Eastern culture. Chanda Sahib invaded the Carnatic in company with Muzaffar Jang, son of a *subadar* of the

---

[1] Forrest (i. pp. 77-8) refutes the aspersions of Macaulay and Mill on Dupleix's courage.

Mogul Empire. In the event of success it was agreed that Chanda
Sahib was to be Nawab of the Carnatic, while Muzaffar Jang was to
seek, with French help, the superior office of Nizam of the Deccan.
In July, 1749, the two adventurers met Anwar-u Deen at the battle
of Ambur. Four hundred Frenchmen, sent by Dupleix, decided the
fortune of the day. Anwar-u Deen was killed, and his conquerors
proceeded first to Arcot, where they proclaimed themselves in their
respective dignities, and then to Pondicherry, where Dupleix received
them with open arms. Mohammed Ali, the son of the slain Nawab,
fled to Trichinopoly in the southern end of the province, and there shut
himself up and implored the help of the English. A pause now ensued.
The English still clung to the idea of peace, and were unwilling to give
Dupleix a pretext for withholding the restoration of Madras. The
French on their side were desirous that Boscawen with his great fleet
should leave Indian waters in accordance with the orders he had
received ; and Boscawen was known to be debating the propriety of
remaining on account of the uncertain condition of affairs. Finally
the French gave up Madras, and Boscawen set sail. Immediately
Dupleix despatched his allies to conquer Trichinopoly and so to complete their triumph. Contrary to his wishes they turned aside to levy
blackmail on the Rajah of Tanjore. The business detained them
longer than they expected. In the interim Nasir Jang, a new claimant
to the Deccan, entered the field with a great army. He invaded the
Carnatic, and was joined by an English contingent.

English and French were now for practical purposes again at war,
although they maintained the fiction of peace for some time by pro-
fessing to serve their respective allies as auxiliaries. Dupleix has been
credited with beginning this policy of native alliances with the definite
purpose of creating an empire. In reality it would seem that his
actions were the result of opportunism, were suggested to him rather
than initiated by him, and that his object at this time was the narrower
and more obvious one of depressing the English power.[1] Both companies now had more troops in India than they cared to maintain in
idleness, but neither dared disarm in face of the other. They had
therefore a strong incentive to intervene in the disputed successions as
a means of recouping their expenditure. The supposed original plans of
Dupleix thus arose naturally from the circumstances, and were pursued
contemporaneously by his opponents.[2] But he may fairly be credited
with superior ability and grasp of essentials in their execution.

The year 1750 witnessed a medley of fighting, treachery and intrigue
in which Dupleix found full scope for his talents. On the French side
the struggle disclosed the presence of a general comparable to Clive in
genius. This was the Marquis de Bussy, an impoverished nobleman
who had come to India with the intention of seeking, in a very literal

[1] Cultru, *Dupleix*, pp. 226-7, 236-7.
[2] Cf. Lyall, *op. cit.* pp. 91-2 ; this is also the conclusion of *Cambr. Hist. of the Br. Empire*, iv. pp. 125-6.

sense, fortune and fame. He succeeded so well that in twenty years he was able to retire to his native land with the reputation of being one of the ablest leaders and richest men living. Nasir Jang, the English candidate for the Deccan, alternately buffeted and cajoled by Dupleix, was at length murdered by his own people ; Mohammed Ali once more took refuge in Trichinopoly ; Muzaffar Jang bestowed a huge reward and the title of nawab upon Dupleix ; and at the close of the year French affairs were at the high tide of prosperity.

Their successes continued for some months longer. Early in 1751 Dupleix despatched Bussy to conduct Muzaffar Jang to the Deccan and install him as Nizam. On the march the prince was shot in a wayside scuffle with some malcontents who resisted his passage. Nothing daunted, Bussy selected another puppet, Salabat Jang, as Nizam in his place, and established him at Haidarabad, the capital of the province. In the Carnatic a new personality came upon the scene—Thomas Saunders, who moved from a minor factory to take up the governorship of Madras, and determined at once that the English should intervene actively on behalf of Mohammed Ali. The latter was still at Trichinopoly, and at the outset English aid brought him little comfort. He was defeated by some local adversaries whom he attempted to punish, and a large body of his troops went over to Chanda Sahib. Thereafter, with a small English detachment sent to relieve him, he was closely besieged by the French and their allies, stripped of every inch of his territory outside the walls, and apparently destined to succumb to the star of Dupleix.

Robert Clive had been a civilian since the Peace of 1748. He had, however, been employed on commissary duties with the armies in the field, and had seen for himself the desperate position of Mohammed Ali, with whose fortunes those of the English were bound up. At this juncture, in July, 1751, he desired to be a soldier once more, and Saunders granted him a captain's commission. Since Lawrence had temporarily quitted India, Clive became by common consent the leading British officer in the Carnatic. He immediately set out for Trichinopoly, fought his way through the besiegers, and returned with a discouraging report and his mind made up that only the boldest of measures could retrieve the situation. The measure he proposed was a surprise blow at Arcot, the capital, which Chanda Sahib had denuded of troops for the siege of Trichinopoly. Saunders approved, and forwarded the preparations with all the means in his power. His utmost efforts could only provide Clive with a force of 200 Europeans and 600 sepoys, and this left less than 150 men in the garrisons of Madras and Fort St. David. Saunders, however, was a man who could risk all in the hands of a soldier he trusted. Clive entered Arcot on the first day of September, and took possession of the fort without difficulty. As he had calculated, Chanda Sahib, was severely hit by the loss of his capital, and detached a large proportion of his army from Trichinopoly to retake it. For fifty days Clive and his handful held the fort against from fifteen to twenty times their own numbers. The watchful Marathas were struck with admiration, and Morari Rao, one of their chiefs, undertook to come to the relief of the English. As a last resort the besiegers attempted to storm the fort, and after a night of furious fighting they were beaten off. Then they broke off the siege, and retreated in disorder, leaving Clive triumphant with less than half his original force surviving. Throughout the siege he had had but three British officers to help him.

The defence of Arcot changed the aspect of the war. By reviving English prestige it placed the contending nations on a greater equality than before. Dupleix, with Bussy far away in the Deccan, looked in vain for a general to command his forces. He had capable officers, but none with the fearless genius of Clive. The latter took the field immediately, and improved his success. In December, 1751, he defeated Chanda Sahib's army and its French auxiliaries at Arni, and took Conjevaram, a strong position commanding the road from Madras to Arcot. The English, hitherto confined to the walls of their factories, were now beginning to overrun the province in the interest of their claimant, Mohammed Ali.

All now depended upon the fate of Trichinopoly, which would long since have fallen but for Clive's enterprise elsewhere. The French officer in command of the besiegers was Jacques François Law, nephew of the financier. He was sluggish and obstinate in his methods, and nothing that Dupleix could urge sufficed to goad him to action while there was yet time to achieve success. Early in 1752 Lawrence arrived again in India and assumed the chief command. In company with Clive he set out to relieve Mohammed Ali. They defeated Law under the walls of Trichinopoly, and the French leader then took refuge in an island hard by, formed by two channels of the River Cavery. Dupleix appointed D'Auteuil, an aged officer, to march to the rescue. In several weeks of confused fighting Clive foiled and ultimately captured D'Auteuil. Chanda Sahib also fell into the hands of his enemies, and finally Law and his troops surrendered. Trichinopoly had become the pivot of Dupleix's schemes, had drawn like a magnet all the fighting forces in the country, and was now the scene of a disaster which proved the ruin of the French statesman.

Chanda Sahib did not long survive the failure. The chief who was guarding him took an early opportunity to strike off his head and send it to Mohammed Ali. The latter assumed the full state of Nawab of the Carnatic, and Clive and Lawrence, with other British officers, spent the remainder of 1752 in making his power a reality by capturing the French garrisons spread over the country. In the following year Clive returned to England for the sake of his health. Dupleix showed a wonderful talent for retrieving misfortune. Recruits reached him from France, and he undertook once more to recover Trichinopoly in the interest of Chanda Sahib's son. Bussy, secure in the Deccan, reached out northwards to Masulipatam, and conquered the Northern

Circars, the coast province to the north of the Carnatic. Bussy indeed looked somewhat patronizingly upon Dupleix's struggles, and recommended him to make peace with the English and concentrate upon the central Indian prospects. Dupleix, however, held on. In his long duel with Lawrence he gained some military successes, but his treasury was now empty, and nothing but strong support from home could ultimately save him. Such was his position when a sudden blow ended his Indian career in the summer of 1754.

News took long to reach Europe in the eighteenth century, and that of the Trichinopoly disaster of 1752 only came to hand in the following year. The directors of the French Company had long been dissatisfied with their governor-general, whose political projects they did not understand,[1] and whose indifference to trading interests enraged them. They now entered into negotiations with the English Company and determined to recall Dupleix. Godeheu, his successor, reached Pondicherry in August, 1754. According to his instructions he sent Dupleix home in the next ship to sail, and made with the Madras government a treaty by which Mohammed Ali was recognized as Nawab, and both sides undertook to interfere no more in native politics. The French retained their own factories, and Bussy was left undisturbed in virtual control of the Deccan.

Admirers of Dupleix have described this treaty as a base betrayal. Opinion on the spot regarded it as favourable to the French, in view of the actual position of affairs. Dupleix himself claimed that he was on the point of victory. He lived nine years longer, suffering persecution and poverty, and composing the memoirs in which he built up that theory of his career which has, until recent times, been accepted at its face value. Modern writers have tended to react strongly against him. One emphasizes the fact that Bussy's expedition to the Deccan was a mistake, since it removed from the coast the one general who could have stood up to Clive and Lawrence : " The advantages derived from Bussy's exploits were showy rather than substantial . . . The Deccan was not worth conquering." [2] Another coldly describes his magnificence and his use of intrigue as " a commonplace mistake," holding that " a European should meet Orientals not with their weapons but with his own." [3] This at least is probably true, that he never realized the nature of the defence with which a continued success would have brought him face to face—the sea-power of the British nation.

(ii) *Clive in Bengal*

Throughout the bitter struggle in the Carnatic the English and French in Bengal had traded side by side exactly as though a profound

---

[1] Dupleix fully explained his plans to his Directors for the first time in a memorandum of 1753 (Cultru, pp. 279-84).

[2] H. Dodwell, *Dupleix and Clive*, London, 1920, pp. xvi, 101-2.

[3] Lyall, *op. cit.* pp. 101-5.

peace had prevailed.   The contrast between the course of events in
Bengal and in Southern India was largely due to the fact that in the
former province the Europeans were in presence of a real native power,
which would have enforced the neutrality of its territories.   This
power was wielded from 1742 by Alivardi Khan, one of those adventurers
who had crossed the north-western mountains to carve for himself
a kingdom in the Indian plains.   As long as he lived affairs went well,
although he was growing somewhat alarmed at the manner in which
the foreign traders were taking root in his province.   He died in 1756,
leaving his throne to his nephew, a violent youth named Surajah
Dowlah.[1] Immediately grievances old and new came to a head.
The Company's servants had a long-standing privilege of trading free
of the internal tolls levied within the country.   They had abused it
by allowing natives to traffic under their passes, and so to defraud the
revenue.   The authorities at Calcutta gave offence by sheltering a
wealthy refugee from the Nawab's displeasure and refusing to give him
up.   The news from the Carnatic, to the effect that native sovereigns
were rapidly sinking to the status of vassals to the foreigners, was
alarming to the Bengal ruler.   His suspicions that a like fate was in
preparation for himself gained ground from reports that new fortifications were in progress at Calcutta.   Alivardi Khan, old and desirous
of peace, had left these problems to his successor.   Surajah Dowlah
determined to strike before the odds against him grew heavier.

In actual fact the fortifications and garrison of Calcutta were in-
commensurate with the size of the town and the wealth they had to
defend.   Prolonged immunity from the misfortunes which had assailed
Madras had rendered the English authorities neglectful and incompetent
in all save commercial affairs.   The measures which alarmed Surajah
Dowlah were a belated effort to prepare the place for defence, not
against himself, but against the French, in view of the approaching
declaration of a new European war.   Hostilities between Britain and
France had been going on in America and at sea since the spring of
1755, and it seemed inevitable that they must shortly extend to India.[2]
The Calcutta merchants sent the Nawab information to this effect
when he questioned them about their new works.   He saw his suspicions
confirmed : the Europeans were bent upon making his province a
second Carnatic.   " I swear by the Great God and the prophets," he
wrote, " that unless the English consent to fill up their ditch and raze
their fortifications . . . I will not hear anything on their behalf, and
will expel them totally out of my country."   His displeasure fell
likewise upon the French at Chandernagore, but they were discreet
enough to turn away wrath by a suave answer.

Finding the English unimpressed by his menaces, to whose serious

[1] There are many variations of the name.   The above spelling is, if not the most
accurate, the most familiar to the general reader.

[2] The formal declaration of the Seven Years' War took place in May, 1756, and the
news reached India at the close of the year.

import they apparently gave little attention, Surajah Dowlah gathered a large army, seized the minor factory at Kasimbazar, and marched upon Calcutta. The objects of his wrath had spoken the truth when they had declared that their preparations were against a French attack, for the new batteries were all on the river front, whilst on the land side the walls were ruinous and the field of fire obstructed by buildings. What followed constitutes the most terrible story of British India prior to the Mutiny, a story of desperate heroism rendered fruitless by years of incompetence, of storm and panic followed by black tragedy. Macaulay's version of it is still the most widely read by the general student, and it does a great injustice to many of his fellow countrymen, for the writer, here as elsewhere, did not hesitate to sacrifice accuracy to sweeping literary effect. He says : " The servants of the Company at Madras had been forced by Dupleix to become statesmen and soldiers. Those in Bengal were still mere traders, and were terrified and bewildered by the approaching danger. The governor, who had heard much of Surajah Dowlah's cruelty, was frightened out of his wits, jumped into a boat, and took refuge in the nearest ship. The military commandant thought he could not do better than follow so good an example. The fort was taken after a feeble resistance ; and great numbers of the English fell into the hands of the conquerors." [1] This suppresses much of the truth and suggests a very false impression of what took place. Sir George Forrest, on the other hand, shows that there was lack of direction and lack of all necessary materials, but that the majority of the Calcutta inhabitants, civilian as well as military, behaved with devoted courage, and that the resistance, although hopeless, was by no means feeble. Want of understanding caused the orderly evacuation to develop into a scramble for the ships, and the governor yielded to a momentary panic after freely exposing himself to the enemy's fire. Those who remained fought until the Nawab's troops had penetrated the defences under a flag of truce : " For three days a few soldiers and a motley gathering of civilians held a range of fragile buildings, encircled by a mouldering wall, against an army furnished with guns and Europeans trained to use them, and a vast host of armed men inspired by hatred and fanaticism. It ended in disaster, but the men who did the fighting showed at the siege of Calcutta English courage at its very best." [2]

One hundred and forty-six Europeans surrendered when further resistance was useless. Their leader, John Zephaniah Holwell, was led before Surajah Dowlah and obtained a promise of good treatment. But the same night all the prisoners were thrust into the Black Hole, a narrow guard-room cell intended for two or three occupants. The stifling heat and lack of air killed the majority of them ere morning brought release : Holwell and twenty-two others alone came out alive. The atrocity was the work of a subordinate, but the Nawab made no

---

[1] *Essay on Clive*, collected edit., 1889, p. 513.

[2] Forrest, *op. cit.* i. pp. 311-12.

move to punish him, and expressed no regret for what had happened. He thus identified himself, in the minds of the English, with the author of the crime, although his attitude at the interview with Holwell had suggested a certain amount of goodwill.   A few days after the tragedy of Calcutta he returned to his capital of Murshidabad in the belief, apparently, that his dealings with the English were finished.   That they would send an army to bring him to account seems not to have entered his head.

Towards the close of 1755 Clive had returned to India.   He was now lieutenant-colonel of the Company's forces and a member of the Council of Madras.   He landed, however, at Bombay with a view to operations for the expulsion of Bussy from the Deccan.   The Bombay authorities did not think fit to proceed with this plan, but they found work for Clive and his troops in a campaign against the pirates who for a century past had infested the coast to the south of Bombay.   Clive, in concert with Admiral Watson, destroyed the pirate strongholds and put an end to a nuisance which was beginning to have serious effects upon trade.   He then sailed for Madras and took his seat on the Council. Shortly afterwards he became deputy-governor of Fort St. David.

At this juncture came news of impending war with France, and the formation at Brest of a great naval and military expedition destined for the Carnatic.   The Madras government expected the blow to fall within a few months, and considered themselves none too well prepared to meet it.   Their consternation and perplexity were therefore considerable when they heard in August of the fall of Calcutta and the necessity of a punitive expedition for its recovery.   After some discussion they decided to take the risk of sending to Bengal most of their available troops under Clive and the whole of the naval squadron under Admiral Watson.   Clive received orders not only to recover Calcutta, but also to obtain confirmation of all former privileges and reparation for the losses sustained.   Nevertheless, if definite news arrived of the expected European war, he was to be ready to return immediately with the greater part of his force for the defence of Madras.

The expedition sailed in the middle of October, 1756, and took six weeks to reach the mouth of the Hugli.   In January the ships and the army advanced up the river, expelling the Nawab's troops from the forts on its banks and retaking Calcutta with small difficulty.   Soon afterwards the long expected declaration of war arrived from home, and the three hundred French troops at Chandernagore became potential allies of Surajah Dowlah.   They, however, showed no eagerness to assist the tyrant, and there was some talk, ultimately abandoned, of an Anglo-French neutrality in Bengal as in former wars.   The Nawab now approached Calcutta with a great army.   Clive fought an indecisive action against great odds, and the Nawab, disconcerted at the rough handling he received in place of an anticipated triumph, proposed to negotiate for peace.   Clive, anxious to deal separately with Chandernagore, and alarmed for the safety of Madras, thought

it best to comply. In February he agreed to a treaty by which he
obtained all he had been sent to demand, except compensation for the
losses of private individuals at the sack of Calcutta.

The treaty did not terminate Clive's difficulties. He could not return
to Madras without disposing of the French peril. Bussy was expected
to march into Bengal from the Deccan, and his junction with the
garrison of Chandernagore would afford the Nawab a prospective
means of revenge upon Calcutta. For the moment, however, Chandernagore was at Clive's mercy. The Frenchmen there desired to
treat for neutrality, but they confessed they had no power to bind
their superiors at Pondicherry to honour the agreement. Clive therefore reluctantly decided that he must take the French settlement.
Much intricate negotiation ensued with the Nawab, who would not
consent to the step. A rich native named Omichund acted as inter-
mediary, and appears to have fomented strife by misrepresenting and
betraying both parties. At length Clive and Watson cajoled the
Nawab into sending an equivocal letter which they interpreted as a
consent. In March they attacked Chandernagore, which capitulated
after a desperate resistance. Surajah Dowlah was furious, but an
Afghan invasion of northern India was causing him anxiety, and he
did not yet dare to break openly with the English. They could see,
nevertheless, that he intended mischief, and it seemed as if the departure
for Madras must be indefinitely postponed.

A solution of the problem now presented itself, which led to the
establishment of British sovereignty in Bengal. The wealthy and
powerful men at the Nawab's court were weary of a master who
rivalled Nero in cruelty, violence and fickleness. No subject who
was worth plundering felt safe. Some of these malcontents therefore
conspired to seek English aid in dethroning the tyrant and setting up
another ruler in his place. They chose Mir Jafar, one of their own
number, to be the new Nawab of Bengal. Through the agency of the
shifty Omichund they communicated the design to Clive. He had
no scruple in acceding to it. Bussy was still thought to be marching
from the Deccan ; Surajah Dowlah delayed the expulsion of the remaining Frenchmen from Bengal, and was reported to have enlisted
them secretly in his own service ; and the importunities of the defenceless Madras government became ever more urgent. Clive therefore
wrote soothing letters to Surajah Dowlah, and issued orders to his
own troops which seemed to indicate that he had given up all ideas
of a continued campaign. The plot appeared to be going well when
Omichund revealed his true nature. He demanded a share of the
plunder of the Bengal treasury which would have amounted to a
million sterling. In default he threatened to betray all to the Nawab
and compass the murder of the English envoys at his court. But in
blackmailing Clive he mistook his man. Clive laid the matter before
the Council at Calcutta, and proposed to hoodwink the too confident
traitor. Two versions of the agreement with Mir Jafar were drawn

up, the one on white paper, the other on red. The former, to be treated as genuine, contained no mention of Omichund's reward ; the latter, to be disavowed at the final settlement, conceded his demands in an explicit clause. Omichund was shown only the sham treaty. It bore the names of Clive and all the leading Englishmen in Bengal. One signature was a forgery. Admiral Watson had refused to put his name to the document, and the others had written it for him.[1]

In the middle of June Clive began his march from Calcutta with 3000 men to the battle which was to decide the fate of Bengal. He knew Surajah Dowlah's army many times outnumbered his own, but he counted upon Mir Jafar's promise to desert with a large part of it when the moment came. On approaching Plassey, where the enemy was encamped, he began to experience misgivings, for it became probable that Mir Jafar was either false or so unnerved that nothing could be expected from him. A council of war advised delay, and Clive himself agreed with its opinion. A fresh assurance from Mir Jafar, however, caused him to reverse the decision, and he ordered his army forward.[2] During the night of June 22 the British force arrived at Plassey Grove, an orchard of mango trees with a brick house adjoining. Surajah Dowlah with 50,000 men lay encamped a mile to the northward. In the morning Clive drew out his troops on the edge of the grove, whilst the enemy extended in a semicircle over the wide plain in front, preparing to attack. A four hours' cannonade followed, and Surajah Dowlah, a prey to indecision, listened to the advice of those who were plotting his ruin and ordered his army to draw back to its camp. Clive intended to let them go, thinking that he could best decide the campaign by a night attack on the undisciplined host. But a subordinate officer forced his hand by advancing without orders. Clive therefore continued the movement ; the Nawab's army broke up in panic and streamed away towards Murshidabad, Surajah Dowlah

---

[1] The exact truth regarding this transaction has never been fully cleared up. Col. G. B. Malleson in his *Life of Clive*, London, 1882, pp. 229-33, throws doubt upon Omichund's treachery. But Sir G. Forrest (*Clive*, i. pp. 419-20) shows that that at least rests upon substantial evidence. Neither is it doubtful that Watson declined to sign the red treaty. But certain witnesses, examined fifteen years later, and retailing in part hearsay evidence, declared that although he would not actually sign, he made no objection to his name being forged, and that it was done with his full cognizance. Such a jesuitical quibble is certainly strange in a British admiral, and especially in one so candid, stubborn and fearless as Watson showed himself to be. A witness hostile to Clive stated that the admiral was not privy at the time to the imposture. He died two months after the framing of the treaty, leaving no record of his own side of the matter save that embodied in conversations with the above-mentioned witnesses. The latter seem to have committed nothing to writing at the time, and their recollections in 1772 were naturally vague and discrepant. The extent of Clive's responsibility for the forgery thus remains undecided. His treatment of Omichund will ever be variously judged so long as men take their stand upon absolute or relative canons of conduct. Macaulay decides against him, arguing that the whole position of the British in the east depends upon the inviolability of their pledged word. But society, in our day at least, has no mercy for the blackmailer, and its guardians show no scruple in outwitting him by such means as Clive adopted.

[2] Forrest, i. pp. 446-8.

himself setting the example ; and Mir Jafar, who had hovered all day on the edge of the fight without committing himself, rode in to congratulate the victors.

Clive concealed the contempt which he must have felt for the timeserver, and accompanied him to Murshidabad. Surajah Dowlah fled as they entered the city. Within a few days he was betrayed, brought back, and murdered by Mir Jafar's son, who made haste to accomplish the deed before the English could intervene. With the traitor Omichund the conquerors dealt next. He was told the story of the sham treaty and inexorably denied a penny of his demand. The treasury indeed contained not a twentieth part of its expected riches, and the Company had to be content with payment by instalments of its inflated claims. With the establishment of Mir Jafar upon the throne the difficulties of the English did not cease, for it speedily became apparent that English force alone could keep him there. The Nawab's dominions comprised the three provinces of Bengal, Behar and Orissa, with a vast population, industrious and unwarlike, ruled by an official class mainly recruited from the Mohammedan adventurers of the north-west. Permeating the whole mass were thousands of professional soldiers belonging to the fighting races of India, living by civil war, and ready to sell their swords to any who would lead them to plunder. The English had effectively destroyed the prestige of the Nawab's government. If they had attempted to subside into their former status of mere traders universal anarchy would have followed ; they had therefore to stand by the throne of their puppet and endeavour to rule the country through him. Clive perceived that the scheme was faulty and that its logical outcome was full British sovereignty,[1] but for the present he had to do his best to make it a success. The year 1758 was passed in asserting the Nawab's authority over the outlying chiefs. Early in 1759 Clive defeated an invasion by an outside coalition led by the Nawab of Oudh and a son of the Mogul emperor. In reward Mir Jafar granted him a *jagir* or estate worth £30,000 a year, an acquisition which afterwards cost him dear. In the same year a Dutch armament appeared in the Hugli with the thinly-veiled intention of disputing the British supremacy. Although the two nations were at peace in Europe Clive did not hesitate to attack and destroy the Dutch ships and capture the Dutch factory of Chinsura, holding that a reference of the matter to the distant home authorities would entail irreparable damage in Bengal. In February, 1760, he quitted India for the second time, leaving to his successors in Bengal a gigantic problem of administration which his energy had temporarily soothed but had not solved.

Clive bears the immediate responsibility for the whole British policy towards Surajah Dowlah and for the conquest of his country. It is a transaction which brings us face to face with the ethics of the eighteenth century. By the standards of a later age, based upon the

---

[1] He wrote to Pitt to that effect in 1759 (Lyall, *op. cit.* p. 144).

moral obligation of the strong European to the dependent native, it is hardly defensible. But to Clive and his fellows the future was a sealed book. In their own eyes they were the weaker side, and the native powers of incalculable strength and wealth ; and to the weak all weapons were permissible. In the use to which they put their incredible victory later generations have found much that is sordid and shameful. They enriched themselves, they exploited their conquest for the benefit of their Company, they showed little concern for the feeble population which produced the wealth they seized. In this again they were but men of their age, the product of the mercantile imperialism which judged all issues by the interest of the parent state, basing its power as much upon kidnapping and massacre in unknown African villages, and upon slave-gangs labouring in the western plantations, as upon the stored-up plunder of the east. The man of action has little time in which to consider the ethics of his deeds. He takes them ready-made from his priests and philosophers. And so far these latter classes in England, and indeed in all Europe, had made little protest against the empire-building methods of their day. But the time was now at hand when a new humanitarian school was to arise to insist upon fair treatment for the coloured races under the white man's rule.

(iii) *Lally and the fall of French India*

Whilst Clive was establishing British and destroying French influence in Bengal a complementary destruction of French power had been accomplished in southern India. Its story is no less important than the one we have just related, but it has a simplicity of plot and a concentration of interest which enable its salient facts to be told in a shorter space. It is in effect the single-handed struggle of a violent and masterful personality, unbalanced though tinged with genius, unaided and even thwarted by subordinates, against a combination of sane and level-headed mediocrities, true to their salt and standing loyally by one another. The latter party triumphed, less perhaps by reason of their own merits than by the preponderance of material resources upon their side.

The Comte de Lally, son of an exiled Irish Jacobite, was a man upon whose character historians are in substantial agreement. He was utterly without fear, headstrong and passionate, personally honest and contemptuous of dishonesty in others, prejudiced in opinions which he formed on slender information, and suspicious of the motives of all who held views contrary to his own. At the opening of the Seven Years' War he was fifty-four years of age and the holder of a brilliant military record gained in the European campaigns of the French army. His timely action at the critical moment was said to have snatched victory from defeat at Fontenoy ten years before.

The French government contemplated a strong expedition to India from the time when a new war with England became imminent in 1755. They continued to toy with the subject throughout the next two years, in spite of Lally's derisive recommendation, when asked for his advice, that " whatever course you adopt, it is primarily necessary that you should think and act at the same time." It happened therefore that, whilst Clive and Watson were actually upon the Coromandel Coast in May, 1756, Lally did not even sail from France until May, 1757. About six months of this delay was due to the admiral of the expedition, Comte d'Aché, who returned to port for trivial reasons after first sailing, and afforded the government an opportunity of reducing the strength of the force by one-third. As finally constituted Lally's army numbered about 2000 regular troops, and the fleet nine ships, of which one belonged to the French navy and the remainder to the East India Company. The passage to India occupied nearly twelve months more, for which again Lally blamed d'Aché, and the ships did not drop anchor at Pondicherry until the end of April, 1758. We have already seen the disturbance to English plans which the mere menace of the expedition had caused. Had it arrived a year earlier it might have prevented the conquest of Bengal.

Lally reached Pondicherry in no amiable frame of mind. His instructions were to attack the English strongholds on the coast, to ignore the interior and the system of native alliances dear to Bussy and Dupleix, and to recall the former from the Deccan if he thought fit. He had been warned also that corruption was rampant at Pondicherry, and enjoined to effect reforms with a strong hand.[1] What he found on his arrival confirmed the prejudices with which he had set out. M. de Leyrit, the governor, had made no preparations for a campaign, could give him no information about the topography of the country or the defences of the English settlements, and protested that his treasury was empty. Lally did not conceal the fact that he thought the Pondicherry officials were rogues and traitors, and they on their side placed their hatred of the general before their duty to their country. Ere long he was describing the place as " this Sodom, which it is impossible but the fire of the English must destroy sooner or later, even though that of heaven should not."

In spite of his exasperation with de Leyrit he acted without a moment's loss of time. On the day of his landing he collected the troops in Pondicherry and marched them to Cuddalore, which he took without difficulty. Meanwhile d'Aché, with the soldiers from Europe still on board his fleet, fought an action with Admiral Pocock, Watson's successor, whom Clive had despatched from Bengal a month before. D'Aché, although he lost none of his ships, had the worst

---

[1] Lally's instructions are given fully in Tibulle Hamont's *Lally-Tollendal*, Paris, 1887, pp. 66-71. The corruption at Pondicherry was of long standing : Dupleix had held that the amassing of private fortunes by the Company's servants was perfectly defensible (Dodwell, *op. cit.* p. 110).

of the encounter and suffered severely in casualties to his crews, already enfeebled by the long voyage. Lally demanded from Pondicherry the provision of transport and the enlistment of coolies for the service of his army. The officials folded their hands and gave him no help. Then, according to an English account, he pressed indiscriminately every brown-skinned man whom he could catch, irrespective of caste or status, and set them to drag his guns to Fort St. David. By this action he forfeited the respect and affection for France which Dupleix had so laboriously built up. For the moment, however, his tempestuous energy carried him to success. A month after his first landing Fort St. David, reckoned the strongest fortress in India, hauled down its flag. Clive, who knew the place, expressed bitter contempt for the defenders; but they complained that they were short of powder and that the bombardment had destroyed their water-supply.

Lally's next object was the capture of Madras, to be followed by an expedition to Bengal. But Madras was far away, and the undertaking demanded an expenditure of treasure which Pondicherry could not or would not supply. D'Aché also had left him, and had gone to cruise for British merchantmen in the neighbourhood of Ceylon. De Leyrit and Lavaur, a Jesuit priest who had been a confidant of Dupleix, now suggested a quarter in which they were certain the money could be raised. The kingdom of Tanjore lay to the southwards, close to the French settlement of Karikal. One of the Fort St. David prisoners was a native prince with pretensions to the throne. Why not use him as an instrument for blackmailing the existing rajah into the payment of fifty-six lacs of rupees said to be due under an old bond of 1750 ? Lally, averse to native entanglements, demurred, but at length, seeing no alternative, consented. It is open to doubt whether his advisers were disinterested.[1] Lally marched his hungry soldiers down the coast to Karikal, where he counted on finding victuals. He found on arrival that d'Aché's fleet had carried off the bulk of the supply. From the countryside also he got no help, for the natives fled in terror at his approach. Nevertheless, plundering and threatening, he entered Tanjore and began the siege of the capital. The rajah had been willing to compromise until an English reinforcement and a brutal threat from Lally to send him as a slave to the Isle of France determined him to resist to the last. The English fleet again defeated d'Aché, who then quitted the coast in despair. Lally found himself without supplies to finish the campaign, and retreated to Pondicherry at the end of August.

In the meanwhile the French at Pondicherry had seized a rich Dutch vessel under pretext of reprisal, and the money found in her gave Lally new hopes of besieging Madras. Before doing so he insisted upon a step which completed the ruin of Dupleix's work. Whilst marching

---

[1] Hamont (pp. 103-4) describes Lavaur as " le tentateur " and " le plus dangereux des intrigants," and plainly states at a later stage that he was bent upon Lally's ruin. Dodwell (p. 155) holds that Lavaur was at this time sincere.

on Tanjore he had sent orders to Bussy to abandon the Deccan and join him with all his troops except a detachment under the Marquis de Conflans for the retention of the Northern Circars. Bussy was cut to the heart, but he obeyed. On meeting Lally he pleaded to be sent back. Lally listened coldly and declined to alter his decision. In his own mind he was convinced that Bussy, like all other Franco-Indians, was a dishonest schemer thinking first of his own interests. Bussy on his side, considering his superior's proceedings, set him down as a madman marked for destruction. To increase Lally's disgust the French colonels, although of higher military rank than Bussy, requested that the latter should be second-in-command in supersession of their own claims.

Thus reinforced, Lally, in the last days of 1758, set out to besiege Madras. The governor was now George Pigot, a worthy successor of Saunders, and the veteran Colonel Lawrence commanded the troops. Having long notice of what was intended, they had made full preparations for defence, calling in the outlying garrisons to their assistance. On the French side few had hopes of success, and the general attitude was well expressed by an officer who said that it was better to die by a bullet on the glacis of Madras than of hunger in Pondicherry. Clive also, looking on from Bengal, was in nowise perturbed. " I am confident," he wrote to Pitt, " before the end of this year, they will be near their last gasp in the Carnatic, unless some very unforeseen event interpose in their favour." He based his confidence on superior sea-power and the wealth and supplies of Bengal. Lally fixed his headquarters outside the walls in Pigot's country house, which the governor had considerately left furnished for his use. The French occupied the Black Town, but could make little progress with their works against Fort St. George. They missed their one great opportunity when a large proportion of the garrison, retiring from an unsuccessful sortie, might have been cut off and captured. The unlucky Bussy, it was said, interfered for some unexplained reason to forbid the movement which would have compassed their destruction. The siege dragged on with Lally personally commanding in the trenches whilst many of his officers and men were busy conveying their plunder to Pondicherry. The besieged had more to eat than the besiegers, for bands of native horsemen scoured the country in the English interest cutting off the supplies of the French. Lally himself declared that he had not eaten bread nor tasted wine for eleven days. At length he could hold on no longer. Although the breach was imperfectly opened he gave orders for the assault. But a few hours before the time appointed sails appeared on the horizon. It was Admiral Pocock's fleet with substantial reinforcements. The siege at once broke up, and Lally returned to Pondicherry amid the jeers of its inhabitants.

On the same day (March 7, 1759) another siege was beginning in the Northern Circars. The native chiefs of that region, finding Bussy's strong hand withdrawn and the feeble Conflans left in his place, revolted and applied to Calcutta for assistance. Clive saw the prospect of a great advantage and despatched Colonel Francis Forde with a force equal to that of the French. Forde defeated Conflans at the Battle of Condore in December, 1758, and after an interval followed him to Masulipatam, the strongly fortified capital of the region. Forde's prospects before Masulipatam seemed almost as hopeless as those of Lally at Madras. Finally, when a native force sent by Salabat Jang was approaching in relief, he stormed the place by night and compelled Conflans to lay down his arms. The Nizam of the Deccan then abandoned the French alliance and ceded the whole of the Northern Circars to the English Company.[1]

After the failure at Madras the war in the Carnatic languished for a time. Lally was at the end of his resources, and the English were not yet strong enough for active measures against him. Towards the end of 1759 Colonel Eyre Coote, an officer who had served at Plassey, arrived at Madras to take over the command from the aged Lawrence. At the same time Lally took the field, with discontented officers and mutinous troops, to endeavour some stroke for the restoration of his position. Lally laid siege to the fortress of Wandewash in the country south-east of Arcot. Coote came up to its relief, and a battle followed which was decisive principally by reason of the engagement in it of nearly all the European troops on either side. For a time the fortune of the day was doubtful. Then the disaffection which had long been the bane of the French once more displayed itself. Lally called upon his cavalry to charge, and they refused to follow him. At the same moment a panic broke out in another part of his line owing to an accidental explosion. Bussy, attempting to retrieve the misfortune, was taken prisoner. Lally himself was wounded, and his army fled from the field. This battle (January 22, 1760) was the prelude to the siege of Pondicherry.

The siege did not begin for some months. Coote occupied that time in capturing all the French strongholds in the Carnatic so that there should be no hope of relief when at last he invested his enemy's capital. Arcot, Karikal, Fort St. David and Cuddalore fell in quick succession. Lally heard from D'Aché that the French government had forbidden the fleet to return to the Coromandel Coast, and at the same time men

---

[1] Hamont regards Forde's expedition as the culminating stroke of Clive's career. " C'en était fait ! Clive avait le droit d'être fier ; à force de jugement, de clairvoyance, de volonté, d'énergie, d'habileté à profiter des circonstances, d'esprit de suite, de génie, pour tout dire en un mot, il triomphait. Et quel triomphe que le sien, le fruit de la politique et de l'épée ! Depuis le début de sa carrière, ce héros avait fait bien du mal à notre pays. C'était lui qui avait inventé tout un système de lutte contre Dupleix. Sur les champs de bataille où il avait paru, la France l'avait vu ébranler sa fortune. . . . La conquête de Mazulipatam couronnait tous ces exploits ; elle les dépassait même, car elle était d'une portée politique immense. C'était le coup mortel donné à l'influence française. Notre pays ne perdait pas seulement une armée et une forteresse, il perdait l'Inde. Le Dékan aux mains de l'Angleterre, c'était le donjon de la citadelle aux mains de l'ennemi " (Lally-Tollendal, pp. 190-1).

and munitions were pouring into Madras. In September the close siege of Pondicherry began, although the town had for some time been virtually cut off from the outside world. Coote showed no eagerness to anticipate by an assault the result which he knew to be inevitable. Lally, thwarted and baited unceasingly by the civilian officials, held out to the last. On January 16, 1761, when his victuals were finished to the last grain of rice, he surrendered. The victors demolished the fortifications and the houses, and removed the population to their own settlements.

The Treaty of Paris in 1763 restored to France the skeleton of her Indian possessions—Chandernagore, Pondicherry and the rest, unfortified, denuded of their supporting districts, and denuded by consequence of most of their trade. In every subsequent war they fell into British hands, and at each subsequent peace they have been restored on the like terms. But the events of 1757-61 were nevertheless decisive, for never since that time has there been the least prospect of a French empire being founded in India. Two other events round off the long drama. On May 9, 1766, Lally, after long confinement in the Bastille, was led out to the Place de Grève and beheaded. He had, declared his enemies, betrayed Pondicherry to the English, the nation which he hated in every fibre of his being. The sentence was a judicial murder, and has long been recognized as such. Three years afterwards a royal decree abolished the French Company of the Indies and threw open the remnants of the trade. The Company had never paid its way, and since 1725 had lost capital to the amount of 169 millions of francs.

CHAPTER V

THE CLASH OF EMPIRES, 1739-1763

In 1739 the competition between the colonial empires of Britain and France transferred itself from the commercial to the military stage. The declaration of that year was indeed launched against Spain. But in the minds of those who used Jenkins' Ear and the political unpopularity of Walpole as a means of subverting the peace there lurked a suspicion that behind Spain stood France. A Bourbon world-power, they declared, united in defiance of the Treaty of Utrecht, was preparing to challenge the world-power of Great Britain. The suspicion was in part justified. Six years previously the two Bourbon monarchs had signed the Family Compact, a secret treaty designed, amongst other objects, for the recovery of Gibraltar and the curtailment of England's commercial privileges. But in France two parties and two policies co-existed. The court and the inner circle of statesmen thought first of European aggression, the conquest of the Netherlands, the advance to the Rhine. Outside this circle was what passed, in the then state of French society, for a popular movement, the work of the adventurers and the poorer noblesse, to whom active military service offered the only means of livelihood. These men wearied of the tedious subtleties of the higher statesmanship, and they directed themselves to maritime and colonial aggression. It was their ambition which commercial England feared. In India it produced its Bussy and its Dupleix; in America a series of combative governors, the stronghold of Louisbourg, and the fortified link of the Ohio between New France and the Mississippi. But all the while the inner circle of government at home was betraying it. The French army grew, whilst the French navy stagnated. When war came the fleet was only half as strong as England's; neither had France urged upon her Spanish partner the importance of due naval preparation.

France, then, cumbered herself with two simultaneous ambitions, mutually destructive because she was unable to support simultaneously the cost of both. England also, of necessity and not of choice, was hampered by a European care. The King of England was also the Elector of Hanover, wedged defenceless between the predatory armies of Prussia and France. Honour and policy alike forbade the sacrifice of the Electorate in an English quarrel, and the obligation went far to neutralize the preponderance of England upon the sea. Unless our armies and our gold could defend Hanover our fleets must make conquests in vain, for what they gained in war would have to be surrendered as ransom at the peace. The great conflict had therefore its continental as well as its oceanic side. The former is, in its details, beyond the scope of this book, but we must never forget its existence while considering the fortunes of the latter.

For convenience we have treated separately the Indian aspect of the struggle. That remained always in the minds of the combatants accessory to the play of events in the main theatre, the Atlantic Ocean and its islands and continental coasts. Here lay the great quadrilateral of trade and sea-power, with its controlling points in Europe, Africa, the Antilles and America. Here passed and repassed the ships of the three nations, bearing their slaves and sugar and skins and foodstuffs, their rum and muskets and scalping-knives wherewith to set red men killing white. For the monopoly of this arena the old empires staked their wealth and their future with the true gambling frenzy of the eighteenth century, and for it all three perished, the French at once, the British and the Spanish in the second and third generations ; and out of their ruins grew the modern world in which we live to-day.

Before Walpole declared war upon Spain he had already sent a fleet under Admiral Vernon to the Caribbean Sea. In November, 1739, this armament captured Porto Bello, the successor of Drake's Nombre de Dios. Vernon destroyed and abandoned his prize, but the ease with which he had taken it convinced Walpole's opponents of the rightness of their policy, and set them planning a more systematic campaign against the wealth of South America. With this object in view two expeditions were prepared in 1740, the one consisting of a fleet and army to reinforce Vernon and enable him to subjugate the Spanish Main and Indies as Cromwell had planned to do a century before, the other a squadron under Admiral George Anson, to round Cape Horn, raid the Pacific coasts of Chili, Peru and Mexico, and prey upon the rich traffic plying between China, the Philippines and Panama. Anson's expedition, consisting of five ships of war and three auxiliaries, was the first to sail, in September, 1740. Its composition shows that Walpole had been wise in his forebodings, for the warlike resources of the country were in a state of incredible confusion. The troops ordered on board were five hundred out-pensioners of Chelsea Hospital : " Mr. Anson was greatly chagrined at having such a decrepit detachment allotted to him . . . and solicited strenuously to have them exchanged ; but he was told that persons who were supposed to be better judges of soldiers than he thought them the properest men that could be employed on this occasion. And upon this determination they were ordered on board the squadron on the 5th of August ; but instead of five hundred, there came on board no more than two hundred and fifty-nine, for all those who had limbs and strength to walk out of Portsmouth deserted,

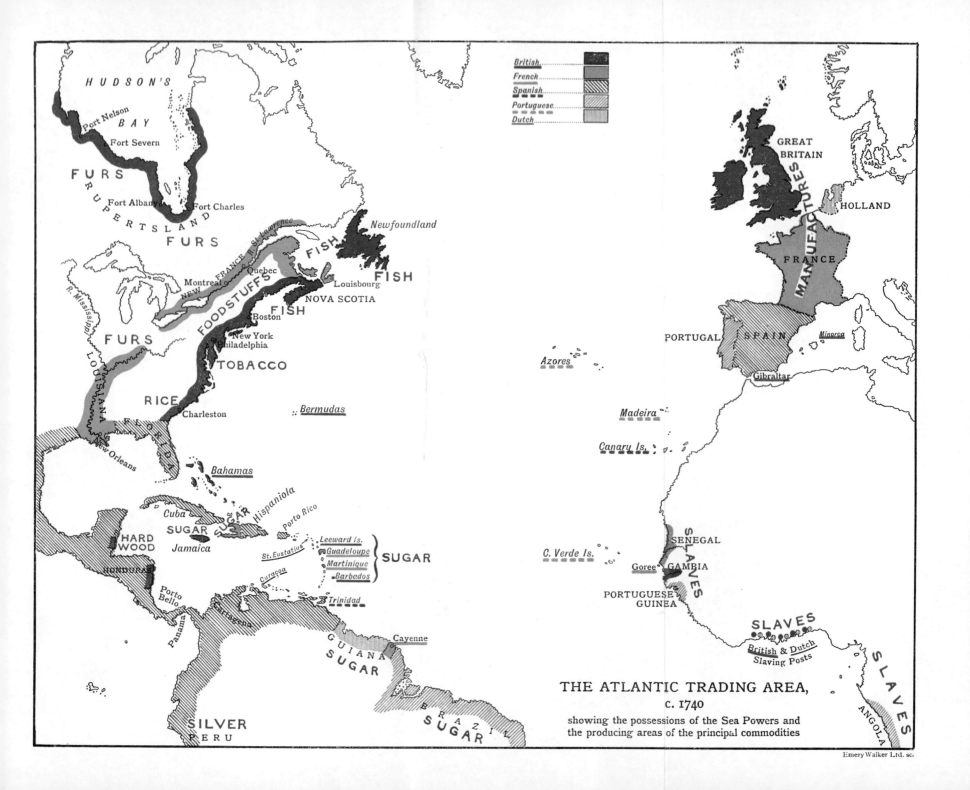

HUDSON'S
BAY

Port Nelson

Fort Severn

FURS

RUPERTSLAND

Fort Albany · Fort Charles

FURS

FURS

Newfoundland

FISH

FISH

NEW FRANCE R. St. Lawrence

Montreal
Quebec
Louisbourg

FOODSTUFFS

NOVA SCOTIA

FISH

Boston

New York
Philadelphia

TOBACCO

R. Mississippi

LOUISIANA

RICE

Charleston

FLORIDA

New Orleans

Bermudas

Bahamas

Cuba
SUGAR
SUGAR
Hispaniola
Porto Rico

HARD
WOOD

Jamaica

St. Eustatius

Leeward Is.
Guadeloupe
Martinique
Barbados

SUGAR

HONDURAS

Porto
Bello
Panama
Cartagena

Curaçoa

Trinidad

GUIANA
SUGAR

Cayenne

B R A Z I L
SUGAR

SILVER
PERU

British ....
French ....
Spanish ....
Portuguese ....
Dutch ....

GREAT
BRITAIN

HOLLAND

FRANCE

MANUFACTURES

PORTUGAL
SPAIN
Minorca

Gibraltar

Azores

Madeira

Canary Is.

C. Verde Is.

SENEGAL

Goree
GAMBIA

SLAVES

PORTUGUESE
GUINEA

SLAVES

British & Dutch
Slaving Posts

SLAVES

ANGOLA

THE ATLANTIC TRADING AREA,
c. 1740

showing the possessions of the Sea Powers and
the producing areas of the principal commodities

Emery Walker Ltd. sc.

leaving behind them only such as were literally invalids, most of them
being sixty years of age, and some of them upwards of seventy." [1]

Many of the seamen were in no better state than the soldiers : the
grim sufferings which inevitably followed may be read at length in
the account from which the above extract is taken. Perhaps the
most extraordinary fact of all is that Anson fulfilled his mission. He
entered the Pacific, took some of the smaller places on the coast, and
captured a rich galleon with a lading worth £500,000. He then
traversed the Indian Ocean and rounded the Cape of Good Hope,
reaching home in 1744 with one ship and one-fifth of his men surviving.
Had he been better equipped, his historian contends, he might have
made Chili an independent state under British protection, opened
communication with Europe across the Isthmus, and permanently
severed the neck of Spanish America as other strategists had sought
to do in former days. Perhaps it was fortunate for his country that
such dreams were not fulfilled.

In the meanwhile Vernon collected at Jamaica a great fleet with
15,000 seamen and a landing force of 10,000 troops, some of the latter
being American colonists. With these he laid siege to Cartagena,
the principal city of the Spanish Main. The Spanish government was
nerveless and indolent, and its colonies ill provided with tangible means
of defence. But, just as a Russian Tsar boasted of his General January
and General February, so Spanish America might claim to be under
the protection of General Pestilence. A terrible outbreak of fever
smote Vernon's command and forced it to quit the attempt on Cartagena after it had failed to succeed by assault. A descent upon the
coast of Cuba had the like result, and the wrecks of the greatest armament which England had yet sent to the Caribbean drew off without
accomplishing any of the conquests expected at the opening of the
struggle. This was practically the end of the Jenkins' Ear War.

In 1740 the question of the Austrian Succession had called Europe
to arms. England and France took opposite sides, at first in the
character of auxiliaries. In 1743 the Bourbon kings renewed the
Family Compact, and early in the following year war was formally
declared between George II. and Louis XV. French aggression in
the Netherlands had brought the Dutch also into the field, and George
II., crossing to the continent in person, had won the battle of Dettingen
with the assistance of his allies. Early in 1744 the French government
planned an invasion in the Jacobite interest, collecting over 10,000
troops at Dunkirk and a large fleet at Brest. There were at the
moment not 7000 regular soldiers in England, and the old county
militia had been suffered to decay out of existence. The Brest fleet
came into the narrow seas and the invading army began to embark.
A British squadron under Sir John Norris sighted the enemy off

[1] *Anson's Voyage*, by Richard Walter, chaplain of the flagship. *The Dictionary
of National Biography* states that Walter wrote his account practically from Anson's
dictation.

Dungeness, but ere the opponents could engage a great storm scattered them. The French lost twelve transports with their troops and gave up the project. The Anglo-French war began at the same time in the Mediterranean. A fleet commanded by Admiral Mathews pursued twelve Spanish warships into Toulon and blockaded them there. In February, 1744, they came out in company with the French Mediterranean squadron. Mathews engaged them and suffered something like a defeat, chiefly owing to dissensions among his officers. By the sentence of the subsequent courts-martial he and some of his captains were cashiered, but Captain Edward Hawke emerged from the affair with credit, having captured the only prize taken in the action.

In America fighting began in the same year, the French from Louisbourg descending upon Nova Scotia and taking its capital, Annapolis. Since this was the only town, and the agricultural population were exclusively French, the event amounted to a virtual conquest of the province. New England took alarm, and Massachusetts under its energetic governor William Shirley was foremost in preparing for a counterstroke in 1745. Shirley adopted the bold plan of attacking Louisbourg itself, although it was strongly situated and its defences were reckoned to have cost £1,000,000. He organised some 4000 New England volunteers and entrusted their command to William Pepperell, a Boston merchant. A British naval squadron under Commodore Warren co-operated. In six weeks " with the help of gunners from the fleet and extraordinary good fortune " Pepperell took Louisbourg and its garrison of 2500 professional troops. The news aroused intense enthusiasm in London. It was the first real success of the war, whilst in other directions the outlook was gloomy in the extreme, for the Duke of Cumberland had just been beaten on the continent at Fontenoy and the Young Pretender had landed in Scotland and routed the English at Prestonpans. Shirley and Pepperell received baronetcies, and the American colonist stood forth for the first time as a fighting man in the eyes of the home population. Shirley, his appetite whetted by success, urged the complete conquest of Canada, and prepared to raise 10,000 Americans for the work in 1746. The British government agreed, and promised five regular regiments and a fleet. But the Duke of Newcastle changed his plan and diverted the English forces to an attempt upon Lorient, and Shirley alone could effect nothing of importance.

During the war the French navy grew steadily weaker as the result partly of the capture of merchant seamen and partly of the financial demands made by the army. Two battles in 1747 completed its ruin. In May Anson destroyed off Cape Finisterre a joint squadron, part of which was destined for the reconquest of Louisbourg and part for the support of Dupleix in India. Of nine French battleships and eight armed Indiamen, the English captured six and four respectively, and by so doing rendered impossible any further French offensives in America and India. In October Hawke, now an admiral, with a

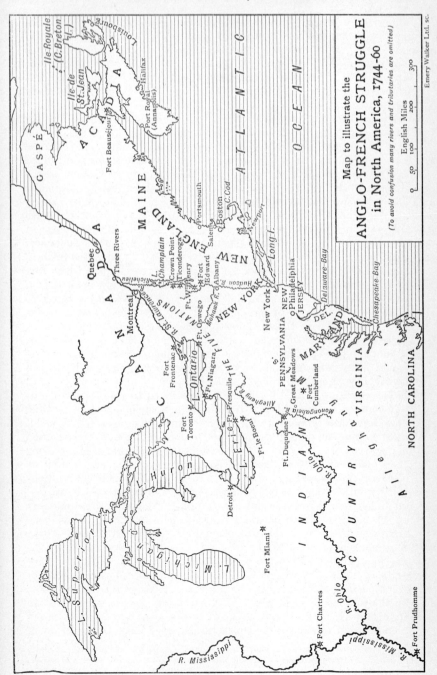

Map to illustrate the
ANGLO-FRENCH STRUGGLE
in North America, 1744-60
(To avoid confusion many rivers and tributaries are omitted)

English Miles
0   50   100   200   300

Emery Walker Ltd. sc.

superior force destroyed six ships-of-the-line at Belleisle, the French fighting a hopeless battle in order to save a rich West India convoy which they were guarding. On land, however, the French army, to which Louis XV. had sacrificed his fleet, carried all before it. By the end of 1747 it had a firm grip upon the Austrian Netherlands. But eight years' warfare had exhausted the combatants and all were ready for a truce.

The Peace of Aix-la-Chapelle (April, 1748) was little more than that. It left unsettled all the questions upon which Great Britain had fought the Bourbons. France evacuated Flanders and Madras to secure the return of Louisbourg. Gibraltar and Minorca remained in English hands, together with the little colony of Georgia, which the Spaniards claimed to be an infringement of their territorial rights. The frontiers of Nova Scotia and New York remained as vague as ever, although the negotiators, in shirking the matter, salved their consciences by providing for a commission to settle it at some future date. In the West Indies again, four disputed islands—St. Lucia, Dominica, St. Vincent, and Tobago—were declared neutral. And in the Spanish treaty not a word appeared about the right of search upon which Pitt and his friends had thundered so eloquently ten years before.[1] On this point Burke wrote : " Some years after, it was my fortune to converse with many of the principal actors against that minister [Walpole] and with those who had principally excited that clamour. None of them—no, not one—did in the least defend the measure or attempt to justify their conduct. They condemned it as freely as they would have done in commenting upon any proceeding in history in which they were totally unconcerned."

The cessation of hostilities in Europe seemed to give fresh impetus to colonial animosities in North America, and the question of the Ohio now came into prominence for the first time. The reason for its not having done so during the war is intelligible : whilst it had been necessary for the colonists of both nations to stand on their guard along their old frontiers they had had no men to spare for encroachments in new regions, and in addition, the kind of expansion which ambitious men on either side had in mind was most conveniently to be carried on under the guise of peaceful penetration. From their first discovery of the Mississippi and occupation of its delta, the French had been familiar with the idea of linking Canada with the Gulf of Mexico by a continuous route of which the greater part could be traversed by water. The line of the Ohio, whose affluent the Allegheny flowed within fifty miles of Lake Erie, seemed to offer the most promising means of accomplishing this plan. Accordingly the French governors followed up the establishment of Fort Frontenac at the northern end of Lake Ontario with that of Fort Niagara at its southern extremity, and thence began to survey the southern shores of Lake Erie. In doing

---

[1] A commercial treaty with Spain was signed in 1750, putting an end to the Asiento. In general its terms were less favourable than those of 1739, but Pitt approved of it.

so they were something more than the exponents of a Canadian ambition. France itself was awake to the importance of the colonial question. A home official wrote at this time : " The English will rule the seas through their fleets and the land through their wealth, and America will furnish them with the means of dictating to Europe . . . France alone is in a position to prevent this catastrophe, and France must do so for her own sake and that of all Europe." [1]

The English were by no means content to admit a French monopoly even of the Great Lakes, and in 1727 Governor Burnet of New York had built at his own expense Fort Oswego on Lake Ontario midway between Niagara and Frontenac. At the same time the people of Virginia and Pennsylvania awoke to the possibilities of the Ohio region, and British traders were active there as early as 1740. Shortly after the close of the war in 1748 some leading men in England and Virginia formed a partnership known as the Ohio Company and secured a royal grant of 500,000 acres in the Ohio valley. They began immediately to push their scheme, undertaking to settle two-fifths of their territory within a few years and to use the remainder as an area for Indian trade. In 1749 another group calling itself the Loyal Company received 800,000 acres somewhat further to the southwards in the country lying west of Virginia and North Carolina ; and two years later yet another Virginia concern, the Greenbriar Company, obtained a title to 100,000 acres on the Greenbriar River, a tributary of the Kanawha, in which region they immediately began surveying operations.[2] It is thus evident that the English colonists were preparing to cross the mountains in force.

As the English moved westwards the French simultaneously pressed southwards from the lakes ; it is indeed difficult as well as profitless to decide which party was technically in the right. In 1749 small bodies of French troops descended the Allegheny and the Ohio, and began to trade with the Indians and set up inscriptions claiming the country for France. La Galissonière, governor of Canada, was active in pursuing this policy, recognizing that in effective occupation by non-military colonists the English were certain to outstrip the Canadians. Sir William Johnson, who had interests in the western Indian trade, sent warnings to New York and Pennsylvania, and Robert Dinwiddie, the governor of Virginia, also realised that a crisis was at hand. In 1751 the French arrested English traders on the Ohio and warned them not to persist in their business. At the same time Dinwiddie was considering a plan to build a fort at the point where the Allegheny

---

[1] *Cambridge Modern History*, vi. pp. 411-12.

[2] Detailed information concerning these companies appears to be scanty. References to their doings occur in R. G. Thwaites, *France in America*, 1497-1763, New York, 1905, pp. 152-3 ; B. Fernow, *The Ohio Valley in Colonial Days*, Albany, 1890, pp 88-90 ; and J. S. Johnson, *First Explorations of Kentucky*, Louisville, 1898, introd. pp. xv-xvi. The latter gives 1748 as the date of foundation of the Ohio Company, although indications exist that the scheme was mooted prior to the outbreak of war in 1744.

and the Monongahela unite to form the Ohio. Ultimately the Virginians did plant a small and shortlived post in this neighbourhood. In 1753 operations on both sides became more intensive. The French built a fort at Presqu'ile on Lake Erie, another named Fort le Boeuf on the road to the headwaters of the river, and a third, Fort Duquesne, which supplanted the Virginian post at the important fork above referred to. In 1754 Dinwiddie despatched George Washington, a young officer who had visited the Ohio in the previous year, to evict the French in their turn. Washington defeated the French garrison and killed its commander, but a stronger French force compelled him to capitulate at Great Meadows on terms which allowed him to retreat to Virginia. With this action the dispute definitely assumed the status of a war—and of a war which, although few concerned then guessed it, was to decide the ownership of North America.

Having regard to the small numbers of white troops available on either side, it is evident that the attitude of the Indians was an important factor in the situation. The English traders were able to undersell the French in trade goods. The French, on their side, in addition to their unfailing tact in dealing with savages, were able to point to the purity of their motives. They were careful to proclaim that they wished only to hunt and trade, employing the red men as allies and agents on terms favourable to both parties. The English, they declared, were enemies of the Indian, destroying his hunting grounds and driving away the game in order to plant crops and farmsteads.[1] On the whole, the Ohio Indians saw the matter in this light, and those who did not remain neutral consistently supported the French.

Whilst the great colonial war was beginning on the banks of the Ohio the contributory trouble of the Nova Scotia boundary was entering an acute stage. Although various treaties in the seventeenth and eighteenth centuries had dealt with the ownership of the province none had attempted to define its true limits. The French claimed that the cession of 1713 had included something less than the whole peninsula which the Bay of Fundy almost separates from the mainland. The British claimed not only the entire peninsula, but also the still larger area to which it is attached, stretching northwards to the St. Lawrence and southwards to the confines of Maine. The divergence of view was too wide for peaceful bargaining to bridge, and the boundary commission provided by the Treaty of Aix-la-Chapelle never achieved any useful result. Until 1749 the population was entirely French. The British government ruled it tenderly, respecting its religion and refraining from taxation, and it multiplied threefold at least during the forty years following the annexation. The restoration of Louisbourg to France, however, renewed an obvious danger, to counter which it was determined to introduce British settlers. The Peace of 1748 had involved in England the disbandment of numerous soldiers and

---

[1] R. Waddington, *Louis XV. et le renversement des Alliances*, Paris, 1896, pp. 7-8.

seamen, who commonly took to crime as a means of livelihood and perished on the gallows without profit to themselves or their country. Captain Thomas Coram, the philanthropic founder of the Foundling Hospital, suggested the equipment of these men as colonists in Nova Scotia. George Dunk, Earl of Halifax, recently made President of the Board of Trade, approved the plan ; and in 1749 he despatched 3000 ex-soldiers and their families to the eastern coast, where they settled round a harbour since known by the name of Halifax. The enterprise precipitated trouble with the French. The rulers of Canada saw the value of Louisbourg diminished by the establishment of a rival stronghold. They retaliated by sending religious and political agents to stir up discontent among the French Acadians, already offended by the intrusion of the new settlers. Predatory Indians in the Canadian service added to the woes of the province, murdering the English colonists and such Frenchmen as refused to take part against the government. By 1755 the once peaceful existence of Nova Scotia was at an end, and raids and massacres were of daily occurrence. The British officials then took a step they had long meditated. They collected all the French inhabitants they could lay hands on and shipped them to various centres in New England and the Middle Colonies. They carried out this stern measure only after repeated warning, and they could fairly urge that the Canadian government itself had rendered it inevitable by waging scarcely-veiled hostilities in time of peace and by tampering with the allegiance of British subjects.

The Seven Years' War, as between Great Britain and France really opened in 1755, although the formal declaration was withheld until the following year, when also the complementary struggle upon the continent of Europe broke out with Frederick the Great's invasion of Saxony. In England the Duke of Newcastle had been prime minister since the death of his brother, Henry Pelham. Anson was at the head of the Admiralty and the Lord Chancellor Hardwicke, a lawyer of great wisdom and breadth of view, was an influential member of the cabinet. Pitt had for some time been Paymaster of the Forces, but the office was not of cabinet rank, and he had no hesitation in opposing the government's policy. Owing to the terms of existing treaties Newcastle had a difficult game to play. If he attacked France, Spain might declare against him. The defensive alliance also between England and the Dutch required either party to come to the other's assistance with a specified force, but only in case of attack by a third power. It was important therefore for England to avoid being the technical aggressor in the conflict which was now inevitable. Newcastle, of course, held that the French were the aggressors on the Ohio, but it was a recognized convention of the time that hostilities confined to the colonies did not constitute an irrevocable declaration of war in Europe. It remained to be seen how far this principle would apply to fighting at sea on either side of the Atlantic Ocean. This diplomatic preoccupation goes far to excuse the want of decision with which Newcastle conducted the opening moves of the war.[1] The French, on their side, were equally handicapped. Their true policy, with their strong army and relatively weak navy, was to invade Hanover in order to secure a guarantee against colonial losses. But Frederick the Great, their nominal ally, was not to be trusted, and they had not yet accomplished that union with Austria, their former enemy, which a year later was to clear their path of obstacles. Both England and France therefore contented themselves with sending naval and military forces to America, and left it to chance to dictate the future extension of the war.

The British expedition sailed first. Newcastle's government, moved by Washington's defeat and Dinwiddie's strong representations, ordered two regular regiments to Virginia under the command of General Edward Braddock. The latter was instructed to raise colonial forces and to expel the French first from Fort Duquesne on the Ohio, then from Lakes Erie and Ontario. At the same time the active Shirley in New England was to obtain a British footing upon Lake Champlain, from which the River Richelieu flows into the St. Lawrence below Montreal. All these were to be represented in Paris as defensive measures such " as may make the French ministers ashamed to complain of them." Braddock failed to achieve even the first part of his mission. Some of the colonies were apathetic, particularly New Jersey and Pennsylvania, where the Quaker scruples against warfare were strong. New York and Maryland also gave little help, but in Virginia he obtained a few hundreds of militiamen. He had left England early in 1755, and in June he began his march through the forests and over the mountains to Fort Duquesne. When within nine miles of his destination he fell into an ambush laid by a French and Indian force. He and his disciplined troops, trained for the wars of Europe, were outmatched by an enemy without formation or cohesion, invisible in a densely wooded country, and taking little harm from the mechanical volley-firing of the regulars. Braddock, three-fourths of his officers, and more than half his men fell on the field.[2] The survivors retreated, leaving the Ohio still in French occupation. Washington was one of the few officers who escaped. During the succeeding months he strove with little success to defend the frontiers of Virginia and Pennsylvania against an avenging swarm of red men who poured over the Alleghanies under French leaders, and carried fire and slaughter through all the outlying settlements. In the north the New Englanders had little better success. Six thousand of them, raised by Shirley and commanded by Sir William Johnson, were repulsed in like manner near Lake Champlain. Shirley himself failed in an expedition against the

---

[1] A full explanation of these matters occurs in Sir J. S. Corbett's *England in the Seven Years' War*, London, 1907, vol. i. chap. iii.

[2] An interesting description of the battle from the French side appears in Waddington, *op cit.* pp. 420-5. The French had only 43 casualties : the English, about 900.

French on Lake Ontario ; but a detachment of Massachusetts militia captured Fort Beauséjour on the border of Nova Scotia.

Shortly after Braddock's departure the French government despatched 3000 soldiers and a fleet to Canada. Newcastle, for the reasons already stated, found it inadvisable to intercept this expedition near the shores of France. Trusting, however, that an action off the American coast might have less serious diplomatic results, he despatched Admiral Boscawen in pursuit. Boscawen attacked his quarry near the Gulf of St. Lawrence. He captured only two ships with troops on board. The others eluded him. Some stayed to reinforce the garrison of Louisbourg ; the remainder reached Quebec, where they placed New France above the risk of serious attack by the forces which the English had in America. By this unlucky action Newcastle and Boscawen had given a diplomatic advantage to France whilst inflicting little material damage in return.

Newcastle, nevertheless, scored an important success. He kept Spain neutral and won over Frederick of Prussia to the British side.[1] Only with the Dutch was he unsuccessful. France now determined to begin the war in earnest, and from that moment Newcastle lost his grip of the situation. The English arrangement with Frederick precluded for the moment an attack upon Hanover, and the French planned instead the invasion of England and the capture of Minorca. The first of these undertakings never took effect, although the threat of it caused a panic to break out in London, for it was computed that 35,000 men at home and in America was the utmost strength to which the British army could be raised ; and the French had 50,000 concentrated in the Channel ports alone. British sea-power, however, prevented them from embarking. The expedition against Minorca sailed from Toulon, landed in the island in April, 1756, and laid siege to Port Mahon, the capital. The British government had some little warning by means of intercepted despatches, and sent Admiral John Byng with an inadequate fleet in relief. Byng fought an action off the island with the French squadron under La Galissonière. He inflicted and received no decisive damage, but despaired of saving the place and concluded that his duty was to sail westwards to protect Gibraltar. The French were delighted by his departure, for his mere presence would have placed their besieging army in a serious plight by interrupting its supplies. Newcastle replaced Byng by another admiral, but it was too late. Port Mahon capitulated on June 28. A violent outcry arose in England, and Newcastle saved the government by sacrificing Byng. The unhappy admiral was tried by court-martial and his personal courage vindicated. But he was convicted of failing to do his utmost against the enemy and shot on the deck of the flagship in Portsmouth Harbour. Pitt braved unpopularity in seeking to save him, and the Duc de Richelieu, commander of the

---

[1] By the Convention of Westminster, January, 1756, Frederick guaranteed the neutrality of Hanover.

captors of Port Mahon, wrote chivalrously from France in his behalf. Voltaire did the same and ironically remarked, after the tragedy, that it was a British custom to shoot some of their commanders " pour encourager les autres."

In America the year 1756 brought renewed disasters. Along all the western frontier the Indians raided and massacred to their hearts' content. The only remedy was to strike at Fort Duquesne; but Virginia conceived that she had done enough, and Pennsylvania still refused to vote a man for the public cause. The New Englanders alone showed any spirit, and they naturally thought first of their own defence. From Europe new commanders-in-chief arrived for both sides, the Marquis de Montcalm for France and the Earl of Loudon for England. Loudon, like Byng, was apt to see the gloomy aspect of his task. He collected boats, stores, and the New England militia throughout the summer on Lake George, an offshoot of Lake Champlain, but hesitated to take definite action. Montcalm, on the other hand, struck a useful blow by capturing Fort Oswego, the English post on Lake Ontario, which menaced the water-borne communication between Canada and the Ohio.

These events, in their details, must be read elsewhere. The crucial point amid all the confusion of 1756 lay at home, in the play of individual forces and the effects of disaster upon the emotions and opinions of the British nation. As the bad news came in by every post— Braddock's defeat, Shirley's failure, Boscawen's failure, the threatened invasion, the loss of Minorca, the loss of Oswego—the nation's confidence in its destiny fell to the lowest point it had touched since England became an oceanic power. In the spring and summer panic was the order of the day. Hardly the coolest and most level-headed of men had any faith that the country could emerge with credit from a war so unhappily begun; and the general tone of English society was by no means cool and level-headed. The Duke of Newcastle, vacillating, timid, unfit for any strong decision, blown this way and that by every clamour and rumour, typified the government. The merchants, fearing for their sea-borne wealth, besieged him with claims upon the navy, and seriously hampered the work of Anson, a really capable administrator. Up and down the country men looked hourly for a landing of the French. Disaffection was rife, and it was said that all had felt more secure even when, ten years before, the Pretender had marched on London. George II., old and harassed, washed his hands of England and devoted himself to saving his beloved Hanover. The army was insignificant in size, and it seemed impossible to augment it by the methods then in vogue. The navy indeed had more ships than that of France, but no admiral had yet been found with the luck or skill to lead it to success. Seventy years of political corruption were bearing their inevitable fruit : " to contend with the power of France seemed to many a hopeless task : to hold up against it in their own lifetime the most they could hope with such a ministry." [1]   In part

[1] B. Williams, *Life of Pitt*, London, 1913, i. p. 252.

no doubt the fault lay with the nation as a whole. Financial gain
from trade supremacy was a poor moral basis upon which to stand in
such a crisis, and that to most was the true object of the war. It gave
no such uplift as the Puritan faith of 1649 or the call of freedom in
1588. Hardwicke, himself as despondent as any, put his finger on the
sore when he stigmatized the national policy as " vexing your neighbours for a little muck."

But, through it all, one man kept his faith, seeing clearly the path
to victory, never doubting his own power to tread that path if the
nation would trust him as its guide. Pitt had no misgiving on the
score of right. He accepted, as a thing ordained, the materialist
canons which governed the relations of state to state. France was the
challenger of his country's supremacy in the Atlantic : France was
therefore the foe of mankind, and her flag must be blotted from the
seas. He had no personal ends to serve, no finger in colonial trading
ventures, no dishonest share of the public funds to claim. All his
thoughts were for the aggrandizement of his country along established
lines, and the very simplicity of his creed gave him the moral stamina
which others lacked. Already in 1755 his speeches had embarrassed
the government and enraged the king, earning thereby his dismissal
from the paymaster's office. All through the ensuing year he followed
relentlessly the same course, arousing his countrymen from their
despair and bringing them to see that in his leadership and in their
own efforts lay salvation. The war, he said, was for sea-power and
America. Let the country spend its money upon the fleet and the
army in that theatre, and let Hanover be left to sink temporarily
beneath the flood. Victory such as he envisaged over the ocean
would restore that and all other things at the peace. Most violently
he denounced the payment of subsidies to the German princes-of-
fortune, the favourite panacea of George II. The unlucky singling-out
for fame of one phrase of his, of " conquering America on the plains of
Germany," has done more than all else to obscure the true story of
his work. He spoke the words long afterwards, in different circumstances, and in a context which modifies their apparent sense. In
1756 they represent the exact opposite of the policy he preached, and
for that reason his name was anathema to the German king. Nevertheless Pitt and the nation would not be denied. Newcastle would
have clung to office, trusting that some lucky chance would save him.
But his supporters shrank from the storm. Henry Fox, who studied
nothing but his own fortune, resigned. William Murray, cowed by
Pitt's invective, did the same, becoming Lord Chief Justice and
Baron Mansfield. Newcastle bowed to the inevitable and himself
recommended his rival to the king. On November 15, 1756, Pitt
became Secretary of State and virtual premier, although the Duke
of Devonshire, as First Lord of the Treasury, nominally held that
rank.

Whilst Pitt had been forcing his way to power the confused situation on the continent had taken definite shape. In May, 1756, France and Austria signed an alliance. In September Frederick of Prussia made war upon Austria and suddenly invaded Saxony. The vexed question whether Frederick or Maria Theresa was the real aggressor need not detain us here. The result of the year's intrigues was that Austria, France and Russia coalesced for the dismemberment of Prussia, and that the latter country became from force of circumstance our firm ally, for the fate of Hanover was bound up with that of Frederick's dominions. Pitt realised this fact and began to modify his attitude towards German subsidies.

He was not yet, however, prepared to send any large proportion of the British army to the German campaign, and consequently did not obtain the real confidence of George II. In other respects his position was insecure. He had come to power as the great commoner, the chosen leader of the middle classes who voiced the opinion of the nation at large. As such he was regarded with distrust by the great families who monopolized parliamentary power and looked to the Duke of Newcastle as their head. His ministry lasted therefore only five months. It was not that Newcastle's men conspired actively against him in Parliament. They passively refrained from supporting him, and the blow came from the court. In the spring the Duke of Cumberland, before setting out to command the Hanoverian army against the French, persuaded his father that Pitt was not sound on the question they both had nearest to heart ; [1] and George II. dismissed his minister on April 6, 1757.

To expel Pitt was easier than to replace him. Newcastle was obviously unfit to conduct the war, and his previous proceedings were at that moment the subject of an inquiry which might easily lead to his impeachment. The king turned to Lord Waldegrave, who tried to form a ministry and failed. Fox was capable of undertaking this or any other task, but his greed and selfishness had made him hopelessly unpopular. Meanwhile the country was roaring for Pitt, and the empire, during the critical months of the campaigning season, was without a government. So it went on until June, when the king, with certain ruin as the alternative, submitted once more. The parliamentary inquiry had whitewashed Newcastle, and Pitt had forborne to press the case against him. Hardwicke now acted as a soother of differences, and the coalition ensued which was to change the fate of the war. Newcastle became nominal head of the government with undisputed control of the jobbery and patronage which constituted internal politics. Pitt returned as Secretary of State for the southern department with virtual command of the forces, the colonies, and foreign affairs. The holder of the northern secretaryship, through whose office passed the correspondence with the German powers, was a nonentity who took his orders from Pitt. Anson took the admiralty again, and Hardwicke filled the post of general adviser and composer

[1] Corbett, op. cit. i. p. 158 ; Cambridge Modern History, vi. p. 405.

of disputes. Fox, excluded from the cabinet, consoled himself with the rich prize of Paymaster of the Forces.

So Pitt at length came to grips with his task. It was high time, for the year had brought a repetition of the woes of 1756. The Earl of Loudon had planned the first step towards the conquest of Canada— the capture of Louisbourg at the gate of the St. Lawrence. To this end he denuded the New York and New England frontiers of most of the regular troops, and sailed from New York to Halifax with a large force. At Halifax he learned that, owing to naval miscalculations, the French fleet in Louisbourg was stronger than his own, and that his army would be in danger of a great disaster if he attempted to go on. He therefore abandoned the project and returned to the English colonies without coming in sight of Louisbourg. During his absence Montcalm had been alert. Collecting all the available Frenchmen, Canadians, and Indians, he descended Lake Champlain and appeared on Lake George. There he laid siege to Fort William Henry. After a week's fighting the garrison capitulated on the understanding that they were to withdraw freely to Fort Edward on the Hudson River. As the unhappy party marched out after surrendering their arms Montcalm's Indians fell upon them and massacred a large number. Montcalm, who was blamed for his negligence in taking no steps to prevent such a crime, exerted himself to save the survivors ; but the affair embittered the feelings of the British against Canada and hardened them, when the tide of fortune turned, to demand inexorably the expulsion of the French from the American continent.[1] Montcalm might now have proceeded to the invasion of the Hudson valley. But it was imperative for him to allow his militia to return home for the harvest ; for Canada, even after this lapse of time, produced barely sufficient food for its own inhabitants, and to feed the regular troops in addition it was necessary to depend on precarious supplies from France. With these events then the campaign of 1757 came to an end in America. In Europe things had gone equally ill. The Duke of Cumberland was completely beaten by the Duc de Richelieu, lost nearly the whole of Hanover, and agreed to the Convention of Klosterzeven by which he was to disperse his army and leave the French in possession of their gains. Pitt, taking office too late to influence the main course of events, attempted to draw away some of the French armies by a naval and military raid upon Rochefort in the Bay of Biscay. But this also failed to produce much effect.

During the winter Pitt worked hard at his plans for 1758. His purpose was to tie the French down in Europe by supporting Frederick and the Hanoverians, by more attacks upon the French coast, and by a strong naval blockade, and in the meantime to promote vigorously

---

[1] The standard French authority, Richard Waddington, *La Guerre de Sept Ans,* 5 vols., Paris, 1899, etc. gives a full account of the massacre, and is in substantial agreement with the English historians (i. pp. 263-8). At Oswego in the previous year Montcalm's Indians had murdered some of the prisoners (*Ibid.* p. 233).

the conquest of Canada.   To accomplish the first of these objects he
agreed to the policy he had formerly denounced, the payment of
subsidies and the employment of British troops in Hanover under a
Prussian general, Ferdinand of Brunswick.[1]   A useful outcome was the
closing of the breach between Pitt and the king : George II. overlooked
the past, and put full trust in his minister until his own life ended two
years later.

The influence of the master mind, working unhampered for the
first time, at once displayed itself.   In Hanover Ferdinand regained
most of what Cumberland had lost.   On the French coast there was
perpetual alarm and waste of French resources.   In June the British
landed near St. Malo and destroyed twelve armed ships and over seventy
merchantmen.   In August the same force captured and destroyed the
port of Cherbourg with all it contained, twenty ships and a quantity
of warlike stores.   Landing again near St. Malo, however, the British
were repulsed with heavy loss at St. Cast.   Pitt claimed nevertheless
that this expeditionary force had kept employed throughout the
summer three times its own number of Frenchmen.   In the Mediterranean a French squadron seeking to make for America was defeated
off Carthagena and turned back to Toulon ; whilst in the Bay of
Biscay Hawke defeated and drove back yet another fleet intended for
the reinforcement of Louisbourg.   The effects soon showed themselves
across the ocean.   There the British generals, now in overwhelming
strength, undertook nothing less than the conquest of New France.
At the end of July, Amherst and Wolfe took Louisbourg and destroyed
a French squadron in its harbour.   The great fortress upon which
France had spent so much was dismantled and deserted for ever, and
its inhabitants deported to Europe.   In the end its terrors had proved
to be more of a pretence than a reality, for the works were incomplete
and in bad repair.   In the west a similar bold effort brought an even
tamer ending.   General John Forbes set out from Pennsylvania to do
that which Braddock and Washington had attempted in vain.   He
marched resolutely upon Fort Duquesne, refusing to listen to counsels
of retreat.   When he reached the fortress it was burnt and empty.
Its garrison had retired to Canada, and not a Frenchman remained upon
the Ohio, the tragic river where the world-conflict had begun.   Only
on Lake Champlain had the defenders of New France succeeded.   There,
at Ticonderoga, General Abercrombie, the commander of the largest
British army, attacked Montcalm and was terribly repulsed.   Hundreds
of his men fell in assaulting an impregnable position, and the fate of
Canada was deferred for a year.   Nevertheless, a detachment of his
force took Fort Frontenac and cut off the Canadians from any hope
of regaining the Lakes and the Ohio.

[1] Sir J. S. Corbett points out that there was no real inconsistency.   What Pitt
denounced was making the continent the main theatre of British effort ; what he did
was to make it a useful accessory to the conquest of America (i. pp. 155-6, 190-1).
Cf. Williams, op. cit. i. pp. 356, 364.

Pitt had hitherto made North America the object of his chief efforts. The circumstances which led up to the war had left him no other choice. But now that its conquest was reasonably provided for he showed himself fully conscious that the prize of the struggle was supremacy in the whole Atlantic trading area. During his first ministry Thomas Cumming, a merchant known as the Fighting Quaker, approached him with a scheme for the reduction of the French African settlements of Goree and Senegal. Cumming had entered into relations with the native chiefs and was confident of success ; but the critical condition of affairs at that time would not admit of the project being taken up. In 1758 Pitt was able to spare a small expedition for the purpose, and on May 1st Cumming and Captain Marsh made a bloodless conquest of Fort Louis in the Senegal River. They found themselves too weak to take the island of Goree, the other French slaving centre to the southward. In November, however, Pitt had greater forces at his disposal, and despatched Admiral Keppel with five ships-of-the-line. In the first days of 1759 Keppel captured Goree. With it fell the whole French slave trade, the vital support of their sugar plantations. Economically the result of the expedition was out of all proportion to the military outlay.

Rumours that France was about to sue for peace made it advisable to extend the area of conquest to the West Indies without further delay. To mercantilists of the old school this appeared as obvious as it was desirable, for the sake of the sugar islands themselves and the merchant shipping to which they gave employment.[1] Pitt was an adherent of the newer school which preferred continental colonies capable of supporting a large population to " take off " the manu- factures of the mother country. He was looking also to the recovery of Minorca, which he reckoned essential to British security. At the close of 1758 he was living in fear of a peace which would leave his work half done, and he therefore planned a West Indian campaign primarily with an eye to seizing something which he could exchange for the Mediterranean stronghold.[2] Later, when victory exceeded even his anticipations, he was as loud as any for the retention of the West Indian gains. The French possessed in the Caribbean Grenada, Guadeloupe, Martinique and the western and richer portion of His- paniola. They had also, in spite of the treaty of 1748, begun to plant the so-called neutral islands of Dominica, St. Lucia and St. Vincent, of which the first two were larger and more promising than Barbados. Hitherto neither side had done more than protect its own and prey upon its enemy's commerce. It is significant that for this purpose each had employed naval forces three times as great as those allotted to Watson and d'Aché in the Indian Ocean.[3]

---

[1] William Beckford, a city merchant and ex-planter of Jamaica, was active in urging the West Indian campaign (A. von Ruville, *William Pitt*, English translation, London, 1907, ii. pp. 222-3).

[2] Corbett, *op. cit.* i. pp. 371-6.   [3] *Ibid.* p. 369.

The West Indian expedition sailed in November, 1758, simultaneously with that for Goree. It consisted of 6000 troops, escorted by ten battleships and some frigates. It arrived first at Martinique, but found Fort Royal, the principal harbour, too strong to attack. It sailed next to Guadeloupe, and after persistent and heroic efforts captured the island. On the day after the capitulation a French fleet arrived in relief, but was then too late to change the issue. In England there was at first some dissatisfaction with the achievement, for the value of Guadeloupe was not recognized owing to the fact that it shipped all its produce through the custom-house of Martinique. In reality it was the richest French island after Hispaniola.

With the conquest of Canada unfinished, Pitt was not yet prepared to do more in the Caribbean. Having obtained his insurance against a premature peace he devoted all the country's energy once more to the north. To subdue the heart of New France in 1759 he provided two main armies, one under Amherst on Lake Champlain, to strike north- wards at the St. Lawrence, the other under Wolfe to sail up that river to Quebec. With Wolfe went a strong fleet under Sir Charles Saunders. Wolfe's part achieved the most striking success and is perhaps the best-known exploit in our history. It has been the inspiration of many volumes, and its bare outline alone can be related here. Early in June the fleet and the army entered the estuary, on a mission rendered doubly perilous by the unknown dangers of the navigation and the unknown strength of the capital they were to attack. The last attempt of the kind, in 1711, had failed disastrously by shipwreck at the outset. Saunders and the seamen did wonders, taking the great ships-of-the-line through channels which the French pilots with a century's experience had only traversed with small merchantmen. Montcalm had received warning in the spring. He had no direct aid to hope from France. His rôle was to waste the short summer months in a stalemate, trusting that events in Europe might yet turn the scale and save the colony. He almost succeeded. Wolfe found his opponent in a position which forbade direct access to Quebec and defied all efforts at dislodgment. In mid-September, when the ships must soon leave and hope was nearly dead, Wolfe's genius triumphed. He deceived Montcalm as to his intentions, found an unguarded path up the cliffs, and climbed by night to the Plains of Abraham, where no natural obstacle stood between him and the ramparts of Quebec. Montcalm hurried to interpose, and in the short struggle on the heights both leaders fell. Part of the French army retired to Montreal. The remainder surrendered a fortnight later with the capital.

Still Canada was not conquered. Amherst had failed to reach the St. Lawrence, and round Montreal were gathered all the broken forces which still served under the flag of France. Before the winter was out it became doubtful whether the British would hold their hard-won conquest of Quebec. When the ice gripped the river and the ships sailed for England General Murray remained with 7000 men. By

April, 1760, scurvy and starvation had reduced them to 3000. De Lévis, Montcalm's successor, knew of their straits and advanced upon them from Montreal. In the desperate battle which ensued Murray lost one-third of his remnant and retired within the broken walls. Both sides expected supplies from home when the navigation reopened ; and the first ships to arrive would thus decide the fate of Quebec. On May 9 a frigate came in sight of the beleaguered town. It showed the British flag, and a British fleet followed in its wake. De Lévis left his siege-guns and retired to Montreal. There the curtain fell upon the long drama. From all sides Amherst and Murray and the subordinate leaders closed in upon those who had fought so pluckily for France. On September 8, 1760, the last French governor of Canada surrendered, and the wide continent with all its splendid possibilities passed to the British crown.

At home a statesman had arisen who might hope to vie with Pitt. Towards the close of 1758 the Duc de Choiseul became a leading spirit in the French government and, like his great antagonist, absorbed ere long the direction of the war. He realized that France, now definitely inferior at sea, could not hope to save Canada by defeating Amherst and Wolfe. He decided instead to retrieve all things by a blow at the heart, by the invasion of the British Isles whilst the British fleets and armies were extended over the broad Atlantic. In spite of Pitt's far-flung enterprise the ships under Hawke in the Channel were stronger than those under Conflans at Brest. But, as invariably happens in a maritime war, the neutral nations were seriously aggrieved at belligerent interference with their commerce. Sweden, Denmark and Holland all complained of the blockade and the high-handed action of English privateers. If Choiseul could win them over he might yet launch his troops across the Channel, for together they possessed sufficient naval strength to turn the balance. The Dutch in particular had been skilfully embroiled, for France had relaxed her laws of trade and thrown open her sugar islands to their merchantmen. Britain had replied by proclaiming that neutrals had no right to engage in time of war in a trade closed to them in time of peace. The contention had rough justice on its side, but that made naturally little appeal to such tenacious dealers as the Dutch.

As the summer of 1759 advanced the invasion project was seen to be no idle boast. Newcastle was frightened, and did his best to breed a panic. Pitt refused to call home a man or a ship from the west. He pacified the neutrals, however, by bringing the most lawless priva-teers to heel, taking them into naval pay and employing them to watch the Narrow Seas. Choiseul was thus left to invade with his own resources, and step by step his project fell to pieces. In August the French squadron from Toulon escaped, passed Gibraltar and sought to make for Brest. Boscawen fell upon it and destroyed it in Lagos Bay on the coast of Portugal. A force of smaller vessels got out of Dunkirk, but was driven far eastwards to Sweden, and played

no part in the main effort. At Brest the greatest fleet was blockaded
all the summer. In November the Comte de Conflans brought it out,
determined to risk all ere the year closed. With Hawke in pursuit
he sought refuge in Quiberon Bay, and there on a stormy afternoon
Hawke followed him regardless of the reefs and shoals and the gathering
darkness. The Englishman lost two ships, but he took and destroyed
six of the French, and four others escaped so damaged that they
never went to sea again. The invasion was finished, although hardly
one French soldier had embarked. On the continent Ferdinand of
Brunswick had completed the year of victory by defeating the French
at Minden.

The following year witnessed, as we have seen, the end of the war in
Canada. Until that was decided Pitt undertook nothing great elsewhere, and the small strokes in Africa and the West Indies had already
been accomplished. At home an event occurred which paved the way
for his downfall. In October, 1760, George II. died with unexpected
suddenness. He had long been reconciled to his minister and had
given his genius full rein. The new king, young and ambitious, at
first seemed disposed to do the like, but ere long a coldness arose, and
lesser men conspired to break the authority of the real master of
England.

In 1761, with Canada fallen, Pitt turned to securing the conquest
in Germany, by reinforcing the armies wherewith Ferdinand was
making head against the French. He found strength to assist also by
his favourite method of raids against the coast of France. In this
kind of enterprise the year witnessed his greatest success in the capture
of the island of Belleisle near the mouth of the Loire. Choiseul had
still one card to play. The old and inactive King of Spain had died
a year before George II. His successor Charles III. was a bitter enemy
of England, anxious to revive old disputes which had slept since
Aix-la-Chapelle. Choiseul therefore opened peace negotiations in
1761, demanding more than Pitt was willing to concede, skilfully
making Spain a party to the discussion, and exciting his neighbour to a
renewal of the Family Compact by pointing to the unreasoning arro-
gance of the British attitude. On August 15 the third Family
Compact was signed at San Ildefonso, Spain undertaking to pool
commercial privileges with France, to put her forces in order and to
declare war upon England by May, 1762, unless a general peace had
been concluded by that date. With the compact in his pocket
Choiseul took so high a tone that the English broke off the negotiations
in September.

The abortive and insincere haggling of 1761 was of more avail to
France than the gain of many battles, for it thrust Pitt into the gulf
which had been silently opening since George II.'s death. The great
minister was for rendering permanent the destruction of French
sea-power. But at the moment when at length this was possible some
of his colleagues drew back. England must beware, they said, of

aiming too high. If she seized the universal control of the seas she would set all the world against her ; and they pointed to the ambition of Louis XIV. and its results. The whole question centred ultimately round the Newfoundland fishery : should or should not France be allowed to regain a share in that training ground of seamen ? Choiseul, with an air of moderation, played this card with consummate skill. *" Donnez-nous de la pêche,"* he said, *" et sauvez-nous le point d'honneur pour Dunkerque, car ce n'est que cela, et la paix est faite."* [1] At length Pitt, by producing proof of Choiseul's duplicity, and by sheer violence of speech at the council table, carried the others unwillingly with him. But dissension broke out again on the point which followed. Spain was obviously preparing for war, waiting only for her treasure fleet to come in from the Indies. For Pitt there was now only one Bourbon power. Spain was France, and France was Spain ; and he was for instant attack. The others refused. All appealed to the king, and George III. decided for the majority. They would have preferred for Pitt to retain office until the end of the war, but with the parting words, " I will be responsible for nothing that I do not direct," he resigned on October 5, 1761.

During these events the activity of the British fleets had never slackened. In June an expedition from America took Dominica. The force was immediately augmented, and its commanders proceeded next to the coveted and wealthy Martinique. The island surrendered in February, 1762, and its fall was followed by that of St. Lucia, Grenada and St. Vincent. The remnant of the French possessions in the Caribbean and the Gulf of Mexico would probably have been taken also but for the intervention of Spain and for a somewhat ominous symptom in America. The colonists, since the fall of Canada, had displayed a lessening interest in the struggle, and now they practically refused to co-operate further.[2] At the opening of 1762 Spain duly declared war, and at once the miscalculation underlying Choiseul's clever diplomacy made itself apparent. His ally was so feeble that, far from saving France, she began to lose her own possessions. On August 14 Havana, the capital of Cuba, surrendered after a two months' siege, with a fifth of the Spanish navy in its harbour. In October an expedition from Madras took Manila, the head city of the Philippines.[3] There remained scarcely a ship or an island of the Bourbon powers which was not either taken or imminently threatened.

The Earl of Bute, the king's favourite minister, had taken Pitt's place as head of the government. His first action was to renew the negotiation which had fallen to the ground in 1761. In the following

---

[1] Waddington, *op. cit.* iv. pp. 541-2, 543. The " point of honour " about Dunkirk arose out of the English claim that that port must not be fortified.

[2] *American Historical Review,* vol. v. "Chatham's Colonial Policy," by H. Hall, p. 672 ; Beer, *British Colonial Policy,* 1754-65, New York, 1907, pp. 67-8.

[3] See Von Ruville, *op. cit.* iii. pp. 61-8. The capture of the two capitals did not by any means involve that of the whole of the respective colonies.

year, whilst the Bourbon colonies fell in quick succession and Choiseul
was meditating one last desperate plan for the invasion of England,
the preliminaries of peace were framed.   Convergent motives dictated
a haste which entailed large concessions : George III. hated the
German aspect of the war, and was determined to be done with it ;
Bute was conscious of incapacity and dreaded the commission of some
huge mistake ; and the Duke of Bedford voiced the opinion of many
who stood aghast at the measureless ascendancy their country had
attained, and looked with prophetic insight to some fearful Nemesis
in the years to come.   On Pitt the same foreboding acted in a different
manner.   He would have deprived France of every colony and put
it for ever out of her power to seek revenge upon the sea.   But the
moderate view prevailed and restitution was the order of the day.   It
involved a choice between restoring Canada or the West Indies.
Already, since 1760, the subject had been actively discussed and many
pamphlets had appeared on either side.   The trade of Guadeloupe
and Martinique was many times more valuable than that of Canada.
It was frankly recognized also that the removal of the French menace
might bring in its train a revolt of the American colonists.   Nevertheless
the newer mercantilists, who placed the colony as a market before the
colony as a source of supply, gained the day.[1]   The growing population
of America kept English manufacturers busy.   It was hoped that
Canada would contribute to the same end.   Pitt backed this view.
Mere size of territory appealed to him, and he scouted the idea of
colonial disloyalty.   If concessions there must be, he preferred to
give back the sugar islands ; but he denounced the whole business, and
particularly the readmission of France to the Newfoundland fishery.
Nevertheless the peace went forward.   Bute and Choiseul agreed to
the preliminaries in the autumn, and the definitive Treaty of Paris
was signed on February 10, 1763.

    Great Britain received from France the whole of Canada, Nova
Scotia and Cape Breton Island, Minorca, Senegal, Grenada, St. Vincent,
Dominica and Tobago ;[2] and restored to France the fishing rights
on the banks of Newfoundland and in the Gulf of St. Lawrence, with
the little islands of St. Pierre and Miquelon as fishing stations ; Belleisle,
on the Biscay coast ; Guadeloupe, Martinique and St. Lucia ; and
Goree as a necessary slaving station.   Great Britain received from
Spain Florida, the logwood concession in Honduras, and a resignation
of Spanish fishing rights in Newfoundland ; and restored to Spain
the island of Cuba.   The wording of the treaty also entailed the restoration of Manila, the news of whose capture did not come to hand before
the signature.   France completed her withdrawal from America by
ceding Louisiana to Spain as some compensation for losses incurred
on her behalf.

    [1] For a compendium of the arguments used see *American Historical Review*, vol.
xvii., "Canada versus Guadeloupe," by W. L. Grant.
    [2] Tobago had previously been neutral and unoccupied.

The Treaty of Paris marks the culminating point of the old mercantile British Empire, and of that fierce competition for sea power and colonial wealth which took its origin in the Portuguese discoveries of the fifteenth century. Five nations had, during three hundred years, engaged in the contest for supremacy, and now, after one last terrific struggle Great Britain had emerged the undisputed mistress of the seas. Her commerce grew during the war, and at its close she had 8000 sail at sea and her navy alone employed 70,000 veteran mariners. It is strange that only in the moment of the victory did doubts arise concerning its outcome. Had the views prevailed in 1739 which now dictated a partial readmission of the Bourbon powers to the spoils of the Atlantic, a torrent of blood might have been spared, and the old merciless system of colonial exploitation might have evolved peacefully to better things. For already the men were living who were to discredit mercantilism, abolish the slave trade, and raise the standards of British conduct in the east. Pitt's sure and fearless vision told him that the victorious Treaty of Paris was but the prelude to new dangers. He had led the country so far on the path of ascendancy that compunction at the final step was fatal. The Bourbons, in fact, began immediately to plot revenge. France reconstituted her navy whilst George III., the would-be patriot king, neglected his imperial duty to enter upon insane political adventures. In twenty years Bedford's prophecy was fulfilled to the letter, and a great maritime coalition had laid the old empire in the dust. So, in appearance, was Pitt justified. But it is doubtful if even he could have followed his course to the end, and certain that no other man could. The judgment of history upon all ascendancies has been the same, whether of the priest, the merchant or the soldier. All have flourished until they have become intolerable, and all have perished at the hands of enemies they have despised.

CHAPTER VI

THE PROBLEM OF INDIAN GOVERNMENT, 1760-1784

WHEN Clive left Calcutta in 1760 the Company's servants were the virtual although not the legal rulers of Bengal and its dependent provinces. They wielded the effective military power of the region, and the Nawab, of their own creation, was a puppet in their hands. Nevertheless the political institutions were still those of the native régime, and they were operated by native officials acting in the name of the titular Nawab. There were thus two jurisdictions in the country overlapping and depending upon one another. The Nawab's duty was to collect the revenue and to hand over a large part of it to the English conquerors who had enthroned him. They on their side concerned themselves more with the results than the methods of his procedure. The arrangement, as Clive had partly foreseen, was certain to be full of difficulties. It was rendered intolerable by the fact that the Company was in the first place a trading concern whose proprietors at home looked first to financial profit, and hardly realized that they were responsible for the good government of millions of subjects; by the exaggerated notion, everywhere current, of the wealth of Bengal, an error of long persistence; and by the attitude of the Company's servants on the spot, long accustomed to supplement their pay by private speculations, and recognizing that the new conquest presented a golden opportunity for the making of their own personal fortunes. Out of this jumble of misunderstanding and sordid motive British statesmanship had to evolve some sound and honest system of government. It took a quarter of a century to do so, and deplorable transactions took place before it had solved the problem.

For the first five years the principal feature is the conduct of the Company's servants in the province. On the whole it may justly be described as infamous, although some part of the responsibility rests with the proprietors at home who should have foreseen and controlled the wrong-doing. On Clive's departure the governorship was temporarily filled by Holwell, who possessed little natural integrity, and in whom the sufferings of the Black Hole had killed all sympathy with the people of Bengal. Holwell gave place after a few months to Henry Vansittart of Madras, who never displayed the firmness necessary to control his unruly subordinates. Holwell and Vansittart became dissatisfied with Mir Jafar, who was now old and infirm. In 1761 the Calcutta council determined to depose him in favour of his son-in-law Mir Cassim. Their precedent was obviously the dethronement of Surajah Dowlah by Clive. That event had taken place under pressure of extreme peril from the French. They imitated it for less urgent reasons after the French flag had disappeared from India. Mir Cassim, an ambitious man, undertook to make large payments to the English councillors,[1] and the revolution was bloodlessly effected in the presence of the English military force. Mir Cassim soon showed that he had no mind to be a puppet-ruler. He would have worked in harmony with the English had he been able to preserve his own dignity by so doing, but he looked back regretfully to the days when the foreigners had been mere traders under the jurisdiction of the native prince. He saw that the possession of an army had rendered them supreme, and he therefore took in hand the creation of an army of his own. He removed his residence from Murshidabad to Monghyr, farther from Calcutta, and began to train a force on European methods.

Whilst the senior officials were enriching themselves directly from the Bengal treasury their subordinates were exploiting the internal trade of the province. The English claim to trade free of tolls and dues along the roads and waterways of Bengal was of ancient standing. So long as the Nawab had been the effective ruler the privilege had been kept within bounds ; at times it had been totally disallowed. Now, under a weak and corrupt governor, the Company's servants pushed the advantage to its extreme limits in reckless disregard of the ruin they were bringing on the country. They had little need for personal enterprise. The easy method was to sell their passes to native financiers and to a crowd of nondescript adventurers whom the spoil attracted from all quarters. These persons hoisted the British flag over their goods, forced the populace to buy dear and sell cheap, and even dressed their retainers in the uniforms of British sepoys.[2] The genuine native trader had to pay heavy tolls and was consequently forced out of business, and the finances fell into disorder. Mir Cassim complained bitterly of these abuses, and Warren Hastings, then a subordinate officer, openly denounced the whole system. Vansittart felt some compunction. In 1762 he and Hastings made an agreement with the Nawab for trade under the Company's passes to pay a duty of 9 per cent., a much lower rate than that exacted from natives. The Council refused to ratify the arrangement, and in retaliation Mir Cassim abolished the dues on all alike. From this point the Nawab and the council drifted into war.

[1] Col. Malleson in his *Life of Clive*, Oxford, 1893, pp. 152-3, says that Mir Cassim bought his throne from the council, and this seems to be the plain truth of the matter.

[2] For details see Forrest's *Clive*, ii. pp. 224-9 ; also Dodwell, *Dupleix and Clive*, chaps. iv. and v.

In June, 1763, Ellis, the agent of the factory at Patna, made an attempt to seize the city. He failed and was made prisoner with all his men. The Company's forces then advanced against Mir Cassim's new army, and defeated it after some hard fighting. Mir Cassim fled into Oudh, after massacring Ellis and the Patna captives to the number of 150 persons. The council then brought out Mir Jafar from his retirement and reinstated him as Nawab. In Oudh Mir Cassim obtained the support of the Nawab Vizir, Shuja-ud-daula, and of Shah Alam, the titular Mogul emperor, then an exile from his own capital of Delhi. These allies invaded Bengal in 1764 and were defeated with great slaughter by Sir Hector Munro at the Battle of Buxar. The Mogul and the Nawab of Oudh submitted to the English, and Mir Cassim ultimately escaped out of their ken. Early in 1765 Mir Jafar died, and the Calcutta councillors made the occasion the source of another rich haul for themselves. They enthroned his natural son in preference to his legitimate grandson, and extorted large presents in defiance of instructions recently received from home forbidding the practice.

In the meantime the directors and proprietors in London were becoming aware that all was not well in Bengal. Their servants were transmitting huge private fortunes to England, but the Company's trade was falling off. Remedial action was delayed by dissensions in the Company. The proprietors, that is, the shareholders, believed in Clive and were anxious to see him again in control in Bengal. Among the directors there was a strong feeling against him. They had not forgiven him for his suggestion to Pitt that the crown should take over their conquests, and they were offended at the high tone he had often taken in his correspondence with them. Of this party Lawrence Sulivan was the head. Soon he and Clive were declared enemies, and when, in 1764, Clive consented to sail for Bengal he stipulated for Sulivan's removal from control.[1]

Clive had been unwilling to quit once more the life of ease to which his achievements and his ill-health entitled him. Only a sense of duty impelled him to take up a task which he foresaw would be difficult and thankless ; but he knew that he was probably the only man who could restore order and decency in the province he had won. In May, 1765, he reached Calcutta, with a commission as governor and commander-in-chief and a free hand to do as he thought fit. His first action was to suspend the council and substitute for it a select committee of his own choice. The councillors had no defence ; they had carried out their last job with flagrant haste in order to anticipate his expected arrival. Clive then made provision for future good conduct. He enforced the signing of covenants against taking presents from natives. He took up also the question of private trade, and his handling of it showed that he was prepared to be just as well as stern to his old

[1] For these matters see Beckles Willson, *Ledger and Sword*, ii. pp. 137-9, 149-50, 155-6, 171-2, which presents the case against Clive more fully than do his biographers.

comrades in the service. He admitted that the Company's salaries
were inadequate and that a man who risked his health in their employment had a right to a competence on retirement. He was also
determined to stop privileged youngsters from piling up fortunes in a
few years and returning to enjoy them without having rendered any
good service to their country's cause in the east. He therefore formed
the internal trade in salt into a regulated monopoly of which the
Company received a part of the profits and its senior servants the
remainder, the juniors having to await their turn for admission to
the benefits. At the same time he forbade individual trading. The
directors ultimately disapproved of the scheme and cancelled it after
it had been two years in operation. They distributed instead a bonus
of 2½ per cent. on the net revenues as a supplement to the salaries.
These reforms put an end to the worst abuses of the preceding period,
although after Clive's departure private trading and the taking of
presents continued to a modified extent. His unswerving justice
raised against him a host of enemies who pursued him vindictively
to the end of his life.

The relations of Bengal to the exterior native powers also claimed
his attention, and the fruits of the victory at Buxar remained to be
gathered in. Shah Alam, the Mogul, would have had him march to
Delhi, expel the Afghans,[1] and extend the British protectorate over the
whole of northern India. Clive, in common with other British statesmen, was not favourable to such an expansion of sovereignty. He
decided instead to make Oudh a buffer state against the independent
powers. The Nawab of Oudh consented to the arrangement and
agreed to pay for the Company's troops to come to his assistance when
necessary. He also ceded certain of his territories to Shah Alam,
whose imperial pretensions were to be further supported by a subsidy
from the revenues of Bengal. In return the Mogul granted to the
Company legitimate possession of the Northern Circars and the *diwani*
or right of administering the revenue of Bengal, Behar and Orissa.
By this step the power of the purse was added to that of the sword,
and the Company's hold upon Bengal and its dependencies became
complete. Henceforward the Nawab was a mere shadow in the background of affairs.

Clive left India for the last time in January, 1767, after putting
down with characteristic firmness a mutiny of the military officers who
were enraged at a reduction of their pay. The rulers of the Company
at home were still under a delusion with regard to the wealth of their
possessions. They adopted a faulty system of investment, and entered
into engagements with the British government which they were unable
to maintain. From 1765 onwards it is computed that they paid,
directly and indirectly, some two millions a year into the exchequer.

---

[1] In 1761 the Afghan king, Ahmed Shah, had routed the Marathas at the great battle
of Panipat. In the succeeding years the Afghans gradually loosened their hold, and
the Marathas returned to the control of the Delhi region (Lyall, *op. cit.* pp. 152-3).

By 1770 they were at the end of their tether and had practically to confess insolvency. At the same time wealthy Anglo-Indians were streaming home and buying estates in the country and seats in parliament. The old suspicions against the Company broke forth and the old cry that it was mismanaging a national asset was revived. A parliamentary enquiry began in 1772, and Clive's enemies seized the opportunity to drag into the light his dealings with Surajah Dowlah in 1757, his deception of Omichund, and his rich reward from Mir Jafar. Some of his accusers were men whose own villainy he had put down, and their action was dictated by personal spite cloaking itself in the guise of public service. To a superficial view he had done successfully what he had punished them for doing. But they could plead neither his great necessity nor his great deserts. Nevertheless the stigma remained. Parliament, judging him by new standards which it made retrospective, censured him not in plain words but by implication for his acquisitions, and praised him for his great services. His pride could not endure the very partial triumph of his ignoble accusers ; his physical ailments also became a torment, and he committed suicide in 1774.

Whilst dissension and misfortune were paving the way for a reorganisation of the Company at home the affairs of Bengal improved only in comparison with the scandals of 1760-5. In the earlier period, to quote an investigator, "the troubles of Bengal had been due to trade abuses ; from 1765 to 1772 they were due to the inherent defects in the new government machinery." [1] Under the *diwani* concession the English received and expended the revenue, but it was still collected by native officials to an accompaniment of plunder and oppression. Much of the taxation accrued from land held on complicated tenures with whose details British administrators were yet unacquainted. In 1769-70 a terrible famine broke out, and about one-third of the population perished. Nevertheless, the revenue remained as high after the calamity as before. In the former year the Company appointed commissioners to effect a new reform, but the ship which carried them foundered with all hands, and a year was lost ere they could be replaced. The scramble for wealth recommenced, and the problem of good administration seemed as unsolved as ever.

In 1772 Warren Hastings became governor. Acting on instructions from home, he carried out a change in the *diwani*, removing the treasury from Murshidabad to Calcutta and appointing English collectors under the control of a Revenue Board at the capital. Part of this arrangement was subsequently reversed. He established also two courts of appeal, civil and criminal, the latter presided over by a native judge. The wider politics of India once more claimed attention. The Marathas constituted a fighting power which considered itself, with fair justice, the equal of the East India Company. In the south the Hindu kingdom of Mysore had fallen to Hyder Ali, a Mohammedan adventurer, who

[1] M. E. M. Jones, *Warren Hastings in Bengal*, 1772-4, Oxford, 1918, p. 63.

seemed likely to prove an unquiet neighbour to the British in the Carnatic. The Madras government became entangled in 1767 with disputes in the interior from which it emerged with little credit. The Marathas, recovering from their defeat at Panipat, once more became masters of Delhi, and made incursions into Rohilkand, the district lying on the north-west frontier of Oudh. Finally Shah Alam, the Mogul emperor, unwisely returning to Delhi in 1771, became a semi-prisoner of the rovers who were disturbing the whole of India. These events presaged another period of warfare at a time when the Company's finances were at a low ebb. Hastings on taking control at Calcutta discontinued the subsidy due to Shah Alam under the treaty of 1765, since its payment now constituted a tribute to the Marathas. He also lent part of the Bengal army for the conquest of Rohilkand. The suggestion came from the Nawab of Oudh, who took possession of the province, and made a substantial payment to the Company's treasury. This transaction at a later date gave ground for Hastings to be accused of tyranny and oppression. It should be noted that the dispossessed chiefs were themselves alien usurpers of a generation's standing and that Hastings personally reaped no benefit from their overthrow.[1]

Meanwhile it was evident at home that some attempt must be made to separate the Company's functions of government and trade, and that the king's ministers must have some voice in the former. Lord North therefore passed his Regulating Act in 1773, the measure coming into force in India in the following year. It effected a unification of policy in the country by making the governments of Madras and Bombay subordinate to that of Bengal, the head of the latter becoming governor-general. The governor-general, however, was to enjoy a very limited power. He had attached to him a council of four members appointed by parliament. If they were equally divided he had the casting vote, but if three of them disagreed with him they were to override his wishes and reduce his power to a nullity. In addition the Company was bound to submit all its correspondence on civil and military affairs to the king's ministers, who could disallow its decisions. The Act further set up at Calcutta a Supreme Court of Judicature consisting of a chief justice and three assistants. The court's jurisdiction was undefined and might easily collide with that of the council. Warren Hastings was nominated first governor-general, with Richard Barwell, Philip Francis, Sir John Clavering and Colonel Monson as his councillors, and Sir Elijah Impey as chief justice. The scheme was obviously ill-considered in detail and full of perils, and any chance it might have had of working satisfactorily was destroyed by the fact that all the councillors except Barwell were known opponents of Hastings. This

---

[1] The general tendency is now to acquit Hastings of substantial oppression. Dr. Berriedale Keith is an exception. In his *Constitutional History of India*, London, 1936, he takes an unfavourable view of Hastings. Mr. P. E. Roberts in his chapters in *Cambr. Hist. of the Br. Empire*, iv., gives a generally favourable impression, with reservations.

may have been their recommendation in the eyes of a generation which had a taste for checks and balances in theoretical politics.

Hastings and Barwell received the other three councillors from England at Calcutta in October, 1774, and hostilities between the two parties immediately commenced. For the next two years the governor-general was in the position of a man on his trial before a tribunal already convinced that he was guilty of fraud on a vast scale, and seeking only to collate the evidence before proceeding to judgment. The majority demanded to see his correspondence for the period 1772-4, interfered with his diplomacy with the native powers, reversed his decisions, and went far to destroy British prestige at a time when the clouds of a coming storm were gathering against the empire in all parts of the world. They had not been six months in the country when Raja Nuncomar, a wealthy Brahmin who had an ancient grudge against Hastings, came forward with a document purporting to prove that the governor-general had received a bribe from a native heiress. The evidence was afterwards shown to be a forgery, but Francis and his collaborators received it with credulous delight. At this moment, however, Nuncomar was struck down from an independent quarter. A native against whom he had a lawsuit accused him of another forgery having no connection with politics. He was brought before the Supreme Court, and Impey, after an impartial trial, sentenced him to death. The council majority, seeing their tool discredited, turned their backs upon him and disregarded even his petition for a respite. He was accordingly hanged without delay. The verdict was just, but the sentence was reckoned too severe ; for although forgery was a capital offence by English law, it was more cheaply rated in native eyes. Nevertheless Nuncomar, although he was condemned for a common felony, was at the same time guilty of a conspiracy against the governor-general which really amounted to treason. Francis in later years made persistent attempts to prove Hastings guilty of instigating and influencing the prosecution of Nuncomar, but not a scrap of evidence was ever brought to light to show his connection with it. The affair remained a coincidence which men might interpret according to their own estimate of Hastings' character.

The governor-general had escaped from a dire peril, but the negation of all government continued until Monson and Clavering died in 1776 and 1777 respectively.[1] At that juncture not even the cutting-off of Washington and Franklin could have been more opportune for the empire than the deaths of these two mediocrities. Delivered from them, Hastings just contrived, and no more, to preserve British power in India during the general calamities of 1778-83. Had they been still at his elbow all would have been lost. In their places he received two more manageable assistants, one of whom was Sir Eyre Coote, the victor of Wandewash and Pondicherry. Francis, now in the

[1] The details of these disputes are mainly of biographical interest. See Malleson's and other *Lives of Hastings*.

minority, patched up the quarrel for a brief period, but ere long it broke forth again.   In 1780 Hastings formally charged him before the council with lying and dishonesty.   A duel followed, and Francis went down with a bullet in his side.   On his recovery he quitted India to carry on the war at home.

Amid such preoccupations Hastings faced a combination of the Marathas and Hyder Ali, the able soldier who had seized the province of Mysore.   Since 1775 the Bombay Presidency had involved itself in a contest with the Marathas of Poona.   Bombay had backed a pretender to the Maratha throne on the understanding that when successful he should cede the port of Bassein and the island of Salsette. Hastings had not approved the adventure, but when it began to turn out badly he felt obliged to support Bombay, for the sake of his country-men's prestige.   His intervention in 1780 saved the Bombay forces from disaster and secured an eventual compromise at the Treaty of Salbai in 1782, by which the British obtained Salsette.   The Madras officials had managed their affairs even worse than had those of Bombay. The Nawab of the Carnatic had raised loans on extortionate terms from English adventurers, who exploited his country to obtain satisfaction of their claims.   While Hastings had been at a deadlock with his own council, the party of corruption at Madras had gone so far as to im-prison their governor, Lord Pigot, for attempting to curb them.   They had also offended Hyder Ali by neglecting to carry out a treaty they had imprudently made with him.   In 1778 came news of war with France.   Hastings seized Chandernagore without difficulty.   The Madras forces took Pondicherry after a seventy days' siege, and moved next to the capture of Mahé on the Malabar coast.   Hyder Ali immedi-ately objected, saying that Mahé was under his protection.   French agents were already busy with him and with the Marathas, promising munitions and the advent of an expedition to drive the English from India.   Mahé was nevertheless taken, and in 1780 Hyder Ali declared war, invaded the Carnatic, and ravaged the country to the very walls of Madras, whose feeble government made no effective resistance.

On receiving the news Hastings sent Sir Eyre Coote with men and money to the scene of his former triumphs.   A squadron of French warships appeared on the coast, and found at the moment no English fleet to oppose them.   The Carnatic wars of the previous generation had shown the advantage to be drawn from such a situation, but the French did nothing for their allies and retired to the Isle of France. Coote was now old and on the brink of the grave, but he defeated Hyder Ali at Porto Novo in 1781, and his son Tipu Sultan at Arni in 1782. Gradually and at enormous cost to Hastings' crippled finances the Carnatic was cleared of invaders.

Meanwhile the Comte de Suffren, the ablest French admiral of the century, was approaching with twelve ships-of-the-line, and behind him the Marquis de Bussy with more ships and troops.   Through no fault of their own Suffren and Bussy were each a little too late.   News of war with Holland preceded the former in time to allow the English to occupy Negapatam and Trincomalee before his arrival, and Sir Edward Hughes with an inferior British fleet was ready to dispute his operations on the Coromandel Coast. In 1782-3 Hughes and Suffren fought no less than five desperate actions, in which neither obtained a decisive victory over the other. Bussy appeared early in 1783, to find that Hyder Ali had died two months previously and that his son had withdrawn from the Carnatic. The French general landed on the Madras coast, and was making some headway against the English when the Peace of Versailles put an end to the fighting in the middle of the year. By this treaty the French recovered their trading stations as they had done after the Seven Years' War. Tipu Sultan made a separate peace with the English in 1784 on a basis of mutual restoration of conquests.

Hastings had saved the British hold on India and had prevented the exploitation of the country from falling to the revived maritime power of France. He had done so at a time when he could receive no help in men and money from home, for the mother-country was struggling against the American colonists, the fleets and armies of France, Spain and Holland, and the political enmity of all the rest of Europe. The war in India had taken place in the Bombay and Madras presidencies. It had touched only remotely Bengal and its dependent states. From these latter therefore Hastings had felt obliged to raise the money necessary to carry on the struggle. Two of the measures he adopted had an important bearing on the general principles of British government. The Raja of Benares was the holder of lands upon which he paid a fixed revenue to the Bengal treasury. In 1778 Hastings demanded from him an additional war contribution. He paid it in that and the following year, and then resisted further demands. Hastings somewhat rashly arrested him in the midst of his people with the result that a general rising brought the governor-general's own life into peril. Hastings controlled the situation by his courage and presence of mind, and finally deposed the Raja for contumacy. The other case concerned the tributary state of Oudh. The Nawab was in debt to the Company and at the end of his resources. But his mother and grandmother, the Begums of Oudh, had possessed themselves of rich state lands and treasure to which they could show no legal title. Hastings, at the request of the Nawab, required them to disgorge, and sent a military force which compelled them to do so. The coercion of women, however legitimate, is a task from which no government can derive credit. Hastings was aware of the fact, and consciously sacrificed his reputation to his duty. These transactions furnished the principal material for his impeachment in later years.

The Regulating Act of 1773 had now revealed its folly and weakness. During its operation the governor-general, responsible for all things, had seen his council reverse his orders, cancel his appointments, and reject his considered policy, not once only, but as a matter of routine.

No man could say definitely whether the crown or the Company was sovereign of the Indian provinces.   Parliament appointed the governor-general, but he was the servant of the Company.   The king's ministers could veto the directors' orders, but they had apparently no responsibility for the results of the policy with which they could interfere. Hastings and Impey were personal friends ; yet a bitter dispute had raged between them on the extent of their jurisdictions as governor-general and chief justice.   The theorists who drafted the Act had calculated that balanced powers would carry the course of administration along a moderate middle line without excess in any direction. In actual working they had produced an anarchy tempered only by the patience and breadth of view of a chief magistrate whose qualities were not likely to be repeated in subsequent appointments to the office.   Lord North's Regulating Act was a disastrous failure.

In 1783 North had fallen and had returned precariously to power in coalition with his former opponent Charles James Fox.   The latter introduced a new India Bill to transfer Indian sovereignty to parliament and the crown.   Since the measure never became law its details need not detain us here.   The principal objection to it was made on the score of English and not Indian interests, for it was argued that by granting all Indian patronage to the crown it would give the king's ministers a dangerous means of corrupting members of parliament.   Its failure to pass entailed the overthrow of the cabinet.

The younger William Pitt succeeded as prime minister.   In 1784 he brought forward his India Bill and duly passed it into law.   By this Act a Board of Control was to take charge of all civil, military and revenue affairs, the board consisting of a Secretary of State with a seat in the cabinet, the Chancellor of the Exchequer, and four privy councillors.   The king's ministers were to appoint the governor-general, who was to be primarily their servant, receiving his orders from the Board transmitted through a secret committee of three directors of the Company.   In India the governor-general was to be assisted but not controlled by a council of three members.   The Company remained in control of its trading interests and of the mass of Indian patronage. The introduction of a Secretary of State [1] and his close relations with the governor-general substantially transferred the sovereign power to the home government.   The arrangement proved workable, and under it India continued to be ruled for over seventy years.   Warren Hastings was disappointed, for personal reasons, with Pitt's attitude.   Still in the prime of life, he would have liked to show what he could do under a constitution which gave him a reasonable chance to govern well. But he was made to realize that his day was over, and he quitted India in February, 1785, before the arrival of his successor.

---

[1] He was not formally Secretary of State for India, an office which dates from 1858, but one of the pre-existing Secretaries of State.   Since the powers of the Board of Control soon fell almost entirely into the hands of its President, that minister became " virtually a secretary of state for India."—Keith, *op. cit.* p. 99.

CHAPTER VII

AMERICAN POLITICS, 1689-1763

Our view of American history in the eighteenth century is inevitably coloured by its known outcome—the severance of the colonies from British rule ; and for the purpose of this book it is most useful to regard the matter frankly from that standpoint, and to concentrate attention chiefly upon those issues which prepared the way for independence.

Before turning to the working of political institutions it is important to know clearly the people with whom we have to do. Before the revolution of 1688-9 the only colony which contained a large non-British element in its white population was New York. There the Dutch predominated, and there was also a considerable proportion of Frenchmen. The other colonies were mainly peopled from the British Isles. New England was almost exclusively English. Pennsylvania contained a large Welsh element, and Catholic Irish were numerous there and in Maryland. Irishmen and Scotsmen were also to be found throughout the southern colonies. After the revocation of the Edict of Nantes in 1685, many Huguenots went from France to America, settling principally in New York, Virginia and South Carolina. Exact or even approximate figures are not obtainable, but it seems clear that until the second decade of the eighteenth century the sum of all these emigrations was not sufficient to modify the predominantly British colouring of the American population. After 1709, however, a great German wave began to pour across the Atlantic. In that year no less than 13,000 persons from the Rhine country appeared in England seeking passage to the colonies. A few were diverted to Ireland, but the government, with a mercantile motive for expanding colonial population, favoured the wishes of the remainder. Some Germans and Swiss went to North Carolina, many to the frontier regions of New York, and a still greater number to Pennsylvania, where they were sufficiently numerous to retain their own speech and customs. The German emigration to this colony long continued in large volume. Twenty years after its commencement thousands were still arriving annually : in 1739 and 1743 two German newspapers were founded in Pennsylvania.[1] Successive arrivals took service as "redemptioners" or indentured servants with established colonists of their own nationality. Negroes were also sold into America at a much greater rate than during the seventeenth century. Upon those colonists of British descent changed environment and climate were beginning to work a subtle alteration of outlook and to weaken the ties of instinctive allegiance. In addition, the duration, hardship and expense of the Atlantic passage, coupled with the absence of all but the most primitive postal arrangements, formed a barrier to sunder those family ties which nowadays preserve the affection of the wandering Englishman for the land of his birth. The result was that insensibly the Americans became a distinct race. "In 1660 the people of England and of the English colonies . . . formed parts of one nation ; in 1760, this was no longer true. . . . In all that constitutes nationality, two nations now owed allegiance to the British crown."[2]

Constitutional machinery was of one general type throughout the colonies : each had a governor representing the crown ; a council which advised the governor, assisted in legislation, and acted also as a supreme court of law ; and a lower chamber or assembly composed of elected representatives. The methods of appointment to these offices were various. Connecticut and Rhode Island, having recovered their old seventeenth-century charters, appointed their own governors and councils. In Pennsylvania, Maryland and the Carolinas the proprietors selected the governors subject to the royal veto. The Penn and Baltimore families had each lost their rights in 1689. The former recovered theirs two years afterwards, and the latter in 1715. Thereafter proprietary government continued, in name at least, in their respective colonies until British rule came to an end. In the Carolinas, on the other hand, the proprietors surrendered their rights to the crown, for the southern province in 1719, and for the northern in 1728. In the remaining colonies the governors were of royal appointment throughout the period under review. In the choice of the councillors also there was no strict uniformity. Massachusetts, Connecticut and Rhode Island had locally elected councils. In the other colonies the crown or the proprietors had the principal share in the selection. The assemblies were all popularly elected, although the franchise qualification varied. Generally it may be said that most freeholders possessed the vote. To maintain touch with the home government each colony sent one or more agents to reside in London, their duties being very similar to those of the consuls of foreign powers. In the negotiations and disputes which preceded the War of Independence some of these agents, notably Benjamin Franklin of Pennsylvania, played a prominent part.

Colonial administration at home was in the hands primarily of the secretary of state for the southern department. He was supposed

---

[1] E. B. Greene, *Provincial America*, 1690-1740, New York, 1905, p. 232.

[2] Channing, *History of United States*, ii. pp. 598-9. The subject is fully treated in chap. xiv. of the same volume : "The Coming of the Foreigners."

to act upon the expert advice of the Board of Trade. That body, as we have seen, was active and efficient until about 1724. Thenceforward it declined in quality and prestige until by 1748 it had become completely insignificant. In that year the Earl of Halifax became its president and set himself to revive its influence. Halifax, by the force of his personality, restored to the Board the deliberative functions which the Duke of Newcastle, as colonial secretary, had usurped. In 1757 the president was, in virtue of his office, admitted to a seat in the cabinet. Before this he had succeeded in acquiring for the Board the power of recommending to the higher colonial appointments and the general exercise of colonial patronage. The Board of Trade, during the periods in which it was in active working order, tried to follow a consistent policy of subordinating colonial governments to that of the mother-country. It strove honestly, in so far as it had the power, to treat imperial problems in a broad and generous spirit. " The Board did not advocate a selfishly narrow trade policy, but believed that the colonies and the home country should form one commercial unit, as nearly independent of all others as possible." [1] Up to 1689 the English parliament had shown little desire to meddle in colonial administration. After that date parliamentary interference increased, and the Commons frequently took the initiative in such matters as amendments to the laws of trade and the devising of shackles upon American manufactures. This influence was not generally for good, and the supremacy of the House of Commons, regarded at home as a guarantee of liberty, came to be looked upon in America as the source of irritating restrictions.

Colonial administration on either side of the Atlantic had grown up piecemeal and uncoordinated. No single element—assembly, governor, Board of Trade, or secretary of state—could claim to be in the last resort a supreme authority with final power to resolve a disputed question. Such questions therefore dragged on for years until sheer weariness rather than established principles laid them to rest. At the opposite extremes were commonly to be found the home authorities and the colonial assembly. The governor usually occupied a middle position, his duty urging him to support the former and his immediate interests the latter. " Every proprietary Governor," remarked a contemporary observer, " has two masters ; one who gives him his Commission, and one who gives him his Pay." [2] Much therefore depended upon his personal character ; and although the governors of the eighteenth century were not as a rule such needy and unprincipled place-hunters as some have depicted them, they were equally seldom men of outstanding power and determination. On the whole they reflect pretty faithfully the qualities of the politicians who appointed

---

[1] O. M. Dickerson, *American Colonial Government*, 1696-1765, p. 312. The book consists principally of a detailed analysis of the functions and influence of the Board of Trade.

[2] Greene, *op. cit.* p. 198

them—limited in outlook, honest in intention, anxious to avoid disputes with their difficult subjects, disinclined to push theoretical rights to their logical conclusion in action. Each looked only to a short term of office, and of each the besetting temptation was to tide over difficulties in a makeshift fashion leaving his successor to face the consequence. It is not of such stuff that tyrants are made.

Three subjects of dispute were of continual recurrence—the salaries of the governor and royal officials, the right of colonies to issue paper money, and the right of the crown to veto colonial legislation. It was a settled principle of the home administration that once a colony was fairly established it should defray the salaries of the officials appointed to govern it. In the West Indies this principle had been enforced, not without loud complaint on the part of the planters. In the American colonies a long struggle on the point ended with the defeat of the central government. The salary dispute raged most fiercely in Massachusetts. It began under Sir William Phipps, the first governor appointed under the new charter of 1691. He and his successors were instructed from home to demand a fixed and permanent stipend of at least £1000 a year. The colonial leaders steadily refused compliance. They were careful to lift the struggle to the plane of principle by making voluntary and temporary grants often exceeding the amount demanded. But on the principle they were adamant, and however generously they provided for their governor they would do so only for a year at a time, reserving the right to cut off supplies should they see fit. In the power of the purse lay the real freedom of an elective assembly ; lacking that it might sink to the status of a debating society. The Commons of England had fought the battle and won it in the seventeenth century, and they were now disinclined to share the victory with the American colonists. But they won it also by their steady persistence. Successive governors, receiving no money from home, accepted temporary grants in default of a permanent salary, and under Jonathan Belcher, who took office in 1729, the central government at length gave way and assented to the colonial view.[1] In New York and other colonies the same principle prevailed, although the salary question was interwoven with other issues and not clearly isolated as in Massachusetts. Political opinion in England never truly faced the deeper implication of the dispute—that colonial freedom was incompatible with subordination to the will of the mother-country. From the standpoint of the present day we who take pride in the firmness of Elyot and Hampden cannot logically condemn the colonial leaders who strove for similar objects.

On the question of paper currency the British government occupied a sounder position. Owing to the balance of trade being continually adverse to the colonies they suffered always from a deficiency of the precious metals. In consequence they were tempted to issue paper

[1] Belcher and other governors were themselves colonists, but this did not modify the attitude of their subjects.—*Camb. Hist. of the Br. Empire*, i. pp. 388-9.

money at times when extraordinary expenditure was necessary.
Some colonies, notably Rhode Island, did this to excess, and their
currency became heavily depreciated. This in its turn had unfavourable effects upon commerce, and led the mercantile interest at home to
complain. The home authorities passed Acts of Parliament and
issued instructions to the governors to curb what was undoubtedly an
abuse. But here again the colonial assemblies had usually the last
word and the views of British statesmen were only partially enforced.

The vetoing of colonial legislation was a source of perpetual ill-
feeling. Throughout the period the crown sought to exercise overseas
the right which it had allowed to fall into abeyance in England. Sometimes governors received instructions in advance to disallow certain
classes of legislation. More usually the veto was imposed at home when
the acts of the colonial assemblies came up for review. The legislation
which was vetoed was in most cases of a type which sought, directly
or indirectly, to subvert the operation of the imperial laws of trade ;
and again the principle at stake was that of colonial liberty as opposed
to mercantile subordination. The colonists did not deny the crown's
right to veto. They found means of circumventing it by passing
temporary Acts and renewing them as often as they fell to the ground,
relying upon the fact that an interval of two or three years commonly
elapsed before the decision of the home government was promulgated.[1]
The outcome of all these trials of strength emphasized the unsatisfactory nature of representative government unaccompanied by full
responsibility of the executive officers to the assembly.[2] It illustrated
also the chronic weakness, rather than the tyranny, of the British
administration, which was continually asserting powers theoretically
justifiable but incapable of enforcement.

The project of federating the colonial governments had first appeared
when the New Englanders banded themselves together for common
defence in the time of Charles I. James II. had pursued it from a very
different point of view when he consolidated the northern and middle
colonies under Sir Edmund Andros. The high-handed proceedings of
Andros and his master rendered the Americans averse from any future
plans of federation imposed from without, and the social and religious
differences between the various regions long prevented the rise of any
motion to union from within. All had their disagreements with the
home government, but none had sufficient sympathy with their neighbours to fight their battles in common. Nevertheless, the French
peril from 1689 onwards rendered co-ordination at least of military
effort desirable, and plans were discussed from time to time which,
whilst themselves abortive, kept alive the idea of union which bore
fruit at length in the Philadelphia Congress of 1774. In all these plans
the initiative came from the British government or its representatives ;
the royal officials in fact were almost the only men in America who

---

[1] *Channing* ii. pp. 240-4.
[2] Egerton, *British Colonial Policy,* p. 133.

showed any interest in the matter.[1] In the time of William III.
Penn suggested a colonial congress, and the Board of Trade, on the
representation of the colonial governors, proposed to appoint a captain-
general of the combined military forces of the northern colonies. The
chartered colonies, however, declined to agree to what they considered
an infringement of their liberties. Again in 1721 the Board in a
report to the crown recommended the creation of a governor-general
of America, with trading concessions as a bait to secure the colonists'
compliance. But Walpole's reign of *quieta non movere* was setting in
and nothing came of the proposal. A like fate befell another memorandum from the Board five years later, suggesting a consolidation on
autocratic lines accompanied by a stamp tax to pay the expenses of
the new government. The most promising attempt at federation
came in 1754 when the French menace was again becoming acute.
In that year representatives from all but two of the colonies met at
Albany to treat with the chiefs of the Five Nations. Benjamin
Franklin proposed to the meeting a plan of union whereby a president-
general was to be appointed by the crown and a grand council of forty-
eight was to be elected by the colonies. This body was to take charge
of Indian affairs and military defence, with power to raise money for
those purposes. The representatives approved of the scheme, but the
colonial assemblies, jealous of their own authority, all refused to
ratify it.[2]

The colonists indeed, except during the short period of Pitt's ministry,
were extremely backward in defending their own territory against
the French. To this Massachusetts and Connecticut were honourable
exceptions. The others, as a rule, expected the imperial government
to take all necessary measures by land as well as by sea. In time of
peace tiny detachments of the British army were stationed in Newfoundland, Nova Scotia, New York and South Carolina. On the
outbreak of war the government began by requesting the colonies to
call out their militias in addition. New York, although comparatively
wealthy and exposed to attack, usually haggled and procrastinated
until the time for action had passed. The Quaker colonies had religious
motives for standing aloof, although after the outbreak of the Seven
Years' War the Quaker politicians of Pennsylvania withdrew from
public affairs in order to allow their fellows a free hand in carrying out
measures they could not themselves approve. Virginia found a few
men for the operations against Fort Duquesne, but was parsimonious
in paying and supplying them. The more southerly colonies, with
their preponderance of slave labour, were never in a position to turn
out large forces. In general the colonies were slow to move, and when
they did so, were often unwilling to trust their men out of their own
jurisdiction. Under Pitt's sympathetic leadership they did better.
He gave colonial officers an equal status with regulars of the same

[1] Doyle, *Colonies under the House of Hanover*, p. 63.
[2] Beer, *Policy*, 1754-65, pp. 20-22.

rank, and he explained fully his policy and his needs. In 1760, the year of the final assault upon Canada, the colonies contributed 16,000 men, of whom Massachusetts provided 5,000, Connecticut 4,000, Virginia 1000, and Maryland and the Carolinas nil.[1] After the fall of Canada the colonists' enthusiasm died away. They failed to provide the expected numbers for the West Indian campaign of 1762, and although they shared in the capture of Havana, the movement against Louisiana had to be given up. One authority holds that the colonial attitude was largely responsible for the retrocessions of territory at the Treaty of Paris. It was plain that the Americans would take little share in garrisoning the new acquisitions, and the magnitude of the national debt rendered it imperative to cut down military outlay at home.[2]

In another matter connected with the war the outlook of the colonists was curiously narrow. Although they desired the conquest of Canada, and knew that the chief disability of the French was lack of victuals, they persistently sold food-stuffs to the enemy during the struggle. With the French West Indies this unpatriotic commerce went on with scarcely any disguise. Numbers of vessels from the middle and northern colonies went down to Martinique under pretext of exchanging prisoners, and passes for the purpose were openly sold in Boston. Responsible statesmen indeed made a move to stop the traffic, and in 1755-6 the legislatures of Virginia, Pennsylvania, Massachusetts, New York and Maryland all passed laws to that end. Nevertheless it continued. Louisbourg and Quebec were largely victualled from New England, and when the navy interfered to stop the West Indian business a depot was formed on the neutral Spanish coast of St. Domingo where a great interchange of produce went on. Finally General Amherst intervened by ordering an embargo in the American ports, and the customs officers began for the first time to enforce the Molasses Act of 1733.[3]

The old colonial system, as we have seen, was based upon the ideal of self-sufficiency, of a self-contained empire in which the mother-country produced all the manufactured goods required, and the colonies all the raw material and the tropical luxuries which were fast becoming necessities of civilized life. At home this ideal was fanatically and almost universally held ; it was the common factor of all shades of mercantile opinion. The colonists, on the other hand, regarded it coldly. Whilst quite content to benefit by those sections of the Navigation Acts which protected their shipping against foreign competition, they grumbled always against the restriction of market for enumerated wares and the prohibition against the import of manufactures direct from the continent of Europe. They commonly

---

[1] Beer, *op. cit.* p. 65.   [2] H. Hall in *American Historical Review*, v. p. 672.

[3] Details in Beer and Hall, works cited, pp. 72-127 and 666-7 respectively. The latter holds that it was an intolerable grievance for the colonists to be stopped from supplying warlike stores to the common enemy : " the sacrifice seemed too great even for their simple loyalty." Of these two authors the American is more generous to British policy than the Englishman.

ignored the advantage they derived from sacrifices in the imperial interest imposed upon the home population. Of these sacrifices the ruthless suppression of the west of England tobacco culture was only one. English shipbuilders asked for protection against their New England competitors, but never obtained it. The English consumer paid monopoly prices for empire-grown sugar ; his tea and his silks and other articles of non-British manufacture cost him more than the colonist paid for the same goods, owing to the system of remissions of duty upon re-exported merchandise ; and as a taxpayer he found the money for the bounties upon naval stores and other productions which the imperial administration sought artificially to foster in America. The whole policy involved sacrifices upon both sides for corresponding benefits. It has already been considered at length, but it has been necessary to summarize it again in this chapter because it was undoubtedly the chief factor in producing that colonial discontent which a few tactless measures kindled rapidly into the flame of insurrection. Rightly or wrongly the suspicion prevailed in America that the mother-country was getting the better of the bargain ; and such an impression was inevitable so long as the whole imperial administration was centred at Westminster in the hands of British statesmen with the merchants and manufacturers of London close by to whisper in their ears. On the issue of imperial self-sufficiency the practical question is not only whether such a policy can be fairly conducted, but further, whether it can be made to appear fair and just to all who live under its operation ; in the eighteenth century it certainly could not.

The study of British history primarily from the standpoint of our internal politics has led to the general suppression of a truth which was always patent in America. The question of colonial independence leapt suddenly into prominence at home in the early years of George the Third. Opposition speakers were prone to emphasize the iniquities of the government by contrasting the then unsatisfactory state of affairs with a condition of ideal contentment and unquestioning loyalty which they alleged to have prevailed until the advent of George Grenville and Lord North. Burke's phrase about the bonds, " light as air yet strong as iron," which had bound the colonies to the mother-country, has passed into a commonplace of our school books. But in actual fact the hankering after independence had coexisted with the whole development of the American provinces. The Puritan emigrants of Charles I.'s day had regarded their movement as a definite breaking-away from the English state. They had contented themselves with the substance of independence whilst yielding the shadow of allegiance for two material reasons, fear of the French and the profits of inter-imperial commerce. The growth of the French peril and the revolutionary settlement under William III. had strengthened the imperial tie ; yet always we find observers who realized that it depended largely upon expediency. In Oliver Cromwell's time James Harrington wrote in his *Oceana* : " the Colonys in the Indies, they

are yet Babes that cannot live without sucking the breasts of their
Mother Citys, but such as I mistake if when they com of age they do
not wean themselves." Harrington spoke of colonies in general.
More particular is the statement of Lord Cornbury, governor of New
York in the reign of Anne : " If once they can see they can cloath
themselves . . . without the help of England, they who are already
not very fond of submitting to Government would soon think of putting
in Execution designs they have long harbourd in their breasts." In
1711 fears were expressed that the projected conquest of Quebec
would dissolve the bond of colonial loyalty.[1] In 1748 again, the
Swedish traveller Peter Kalm asserted that it was common talk in
America that within thirty or fifty years the colonies would be an
independent state. And at the close of the Seven Years' War it
was certainly common talk in France, to which British statesmen
paid some attention, that we were doing a foolish thing in driving
the French from Canada, since the inevitable result would be
a revolt of the Americans, relieved of their principal motive for
submission.

Such evidence proves that the idea of independence existed long
before the quarrel became acute. It does not prove that it was widely
or seriously entertained, and there is on the other side a considerable
body of testimony to the goodwill of the colonists. The attitude of
the majority seems to have been that they were determined to maintain
the measure of independence they already enjoyed, and to encroach
whenever possible upon the powers which the British government still
exercised. So long as they were permitted to do this, and to infringe
the more objectionable portions of the laws of trade, they were quite
willing to continue under the vague suzerainty of the British crown.
What they hated in England was the control of her politicians and the
mercenary measures of her parliament. For the sovereign, even for
George III. personally, they professed a loyalty which is somewhat
surprising.[2] This then was the actual position in 1763 : thirteen
separate states existed on the American seaboard, each with rights of
self-government in internal affairs limited in theory but scarcely in
practice by the wishes of the home administration, and all moulding
their external business more or less upon the code of laws composing
the colonial system. Between these semi-independent states were
diversities of racial origin, religion, social ideals and material interest,
so great that they had never yet seemed capable of acting together for a
common object ; and of their uniting to make themselves by force of
arms a nation there appeared still less likelihood, for their mutual
animosities were in some cases more bitter than their grievances
against the mother-country. Nevertheless affairs were in an unstable
condition ; development on either side of the ocean was following
divergent lines ; in numbers the Americans were no longer hopelessly
inferior ; and if they did not yet constitute a nationality of their own

---

[1] Egerton, *op. cit.* pp. 143-4.   [2] Egerton, pp. 181-2.

it was equally evident that they had ceased to be Englishmen of the type which now inhabited the land of their birth.

Pitt, with his practical experience of colonial government, was conscious that things could not long remain as they were. There are indications that he had some great scheme of imperial development in his mind, although, since he had no opportunity of putting it to the test, we do not know the precise form it would have taken. Among his papers two plans have been found which were apparently submitted to him by others, although they may well have been consonant with his own ideas. One, dated 1770, suggests an imperial Parliament to comprise, in addition to the representatives of Great Britain, ten peers and fifty members of the commons for America and the West Indies as well as ten peers and thirty commoners for Ireland. The other contains a detailed allocation of the fifty representatives among the several colonies, each having from one to four members according to size of population. An appended note remarks : " It's not unlikely that the Americans may wish for some restrictions on their maritime and internal trade to be taken off in case of an union, and that may be considered afterwards. The Act of Navigation [*i.e.* that of 1660] at all events should be preserved inviolate." [1] An investigator of this phase of Pitt's policy [2] in summing up says : " That he would have triumphed over all difficulties with the colonies we may well believe, though this might have involved a scheme of imperial federation, a scheme which might have altered the whole course of our history, which might in fact have detached England from continental politics, which might have led to the consolidation of an unbroken sphere of Anglo-Saxon influence in the North Atlantic and Pacific Oceans." All this, however, was destined to remain in the realms of hypothesis whilst the actual conduct of affairs fell into the hands of men devoid of sympathy with the Great Commoner and his works.

[1] B. Williams, " Chatham and the Representation of the Colonies in the Imperial Parliament," *English Historical Review,* xxii. pp. 756-8.

[2] H. Hall, *op. cit.* p. 672.

CHAPTER VIII

THE AMERICAN REVOLT, 1763–1778

THE American revolt in effect began soon after the peace of 1763, in reaction to British measures for the strengthening of imperial trade and defence. George Grenville, younger brother of Earl Temple, and brother-in-law of William Pitt, was a subordinate member of the Bute administration which concluded the Peace of Paris. Public resentment at the terms of the peace forced Bute to resign shortly after its ratification, and Grenville then took office as the leading spirit in a ministry distasteful to the king and destined to enjoy but a short career. Grenville's task was to restore the national finances and to provide for the military defence of the empire against that Bourbon revival which even then appeared certain sooner or later to take effect. He proposed to accomplish it by distributing a strong garrison throughout the colonies and paying for it by colonial taxation, by overhauling and readjusting the laws of trade, by diminishing colonial dealings with the French West Indies, and by substituting strictness for the laxity hitherto characteristic of the royal officials in America. His watchword, in short, was efficiency; he was determined to put the colonial theory into practice to the uttermost letter; and never had the advent of a like character to power appeared more timely than after the victorious extravagance with which Pitt had made England the mistress of the sea.

Grenville began by looking into the state of the American customs service. He found that many officials lived quietly in England, performing their duties by deputy. He ordered them at once to their posts, and at the same time instructed governors and naval officers to be active in enforcing the laws of trade. In the following year, 1764, he amended those laws in several particulars. The enumerated list was now made to include coffee, pimento, cocoanuts, hides, whale-fins, raw silk, potashes, colonial iron and lumber, in addition to the staples formerly embraced by it.[1] Many European manufactures had hitherto been cheaper in America than in England by reason of the remissions of duty on re-exportation. Grenville abolished the greater part of this arrangement, and so indirectly increased the colonial share

[1] Beer, *Colonial Policy*, 1754-65, p. 221.

of taxation.[1] The Molasses Act of 1733, with its prohibitive duties on French produce, had been ignored until the late war and then enforced avowedly with the intention of stopping intercourse with the enemy islands. It was now remodelled as the Sugar Act, the duties being lowered until they were no longer prohibitive, but became instead a source of revenue if strictly collected.

These reforms barely sufficed to make the colonial customs pay for the cost of collection, an amplitude they had never before attained. But the policing and defence of the empire were reckoned to need a force of 10,000 regular troops, of whom three-fourths would be stationed in America and the remainder in the West Indies. With the object of defraying somewhat less than half the cost Grenville passed the Stamp Act of 1765. The measure extended to the colonies, on a mitigated scale, duties which had long been levied in England. The minister no doubt considered that he had paid full deference to colonial feelings by warning the governors in advance that he meant to impose a tax and asking them to suggest an alternative if their subjects found the stamp duty distasteful. It was to allow time for discussion that the Stamp Act had not been included with the measures of 1764. When it came before parliament in the following year it excited little notice and passed by a large majority. Immediately afterwards George III. dismissed the Grenville ministry for reasons unconnected with their colonial policy.

Meanwhile two events of 1763 had already shown that the conquests from France had created serious problems. The Indians of the vast region between the settled colonial areas and the Mississippi were aggrieved at the transfer of these territories to the British, who would be more likely than the French to expand their population and evict the natives. The tribes rose under a chief named Pontiac and were put down only after severe fighting. Before this news reached England the government had determined to safeguard Indian interests. The region was proclaimed an Indian reserve, in which white men might trade but not settle, and in which future land-purchases should be by the king's officers and not by private speculators. But the decision gave deep offence to colonial pioneers who had dreamed of obtaining rich lands cheaply at the Indian's expense.

In England Grenville's tightening-up of the colonial system had gone smoothly enough. In America it was the signal for an outburst of violent agitation which astonished many of the colonists themselves, and showed the depth of the fissure which had silently opened between the two chief constituents of the empire. It must be remembered that the Walpole and Newcastle régime had been one of lax enforcement of commercial restrictions. During the war Pitt had insisted upon collecting the molasses duties for an object which was more military than economic, and on the restoration of peace the Americans looked to a resumption of the French Indies trade which was so essential to

[1] Channing, iii. p. 40.

their prosperity. They now found that this was to take place under heavy restrictions which were to be not only theoretical but real. In their own view also they needed financial relief rather than additional burdens. Some of the colonies had incurred war debts of their own, and were imposing local taxation to pay them off. Yet, although they grumbled at the legislation of 1764, it is probable that they would have submitted ; for the laws of trade were a recognized institution against which practical men thought it useless to repine. The Stamp Act, however, was a very different matter. It was an internal tax for the sole purpose of raising a revenue, with none of those commercial compensations which were supposed to flow from the manipulation of tariffs ; and it was " granted " to the crown by a House of Commons which contained not a single member for the areas it affected. Trivial therefore as the stamp duties were, they had an enormous result. They gave every colony an identical grievance, thus facilitating combined resistance ; and they provided a simple war-cry, " No taxation without representation," with an appeal to the meanest and laziest intelligence. It is worth noting that this particular outcome was unlooked-for, even by those who were hostile to imperial control. Some of the colonial leaders had themselves at the outset accepted posts as stamp-distributors under the Act.

The inhabitants of Massachusetts and Virginia took the lead in disaffection. The former were already ruffled by the Sugar Act and the stricter administration of 1764. At the end of that year the Boston merchants had formed a non-importation society, pledged to dispense with English manufactures until the grievance should be redressed. The Stamp Act intensified the movement. James Otis and John and Samuel Adams wrote vigorous protests and sought to bring the other colonies into line. By December, 1765, 250 Boston merchants had joined the combination, and those of New York and Philadelphia were following suit.[1] The Virginia resistance proceeded largely from the fiery personality of one man, Patrick Henry, a lawyer of pronounced political opinions. Henry took the position that free men have certain fundamental rights, definable apparently at the pleasure of their owners, and that no authority, constitutional or otherwise, can enact any binding law contrary to those rights. Although a daring reference to King George in one of his early speeches in the assembly evoked cries of " Treason! " his eloquence fell ere long upon sympathetic ears. Virginian industry was depressed, and many of the leading citizens were discontented. Some, like Washington, were bitterly incensed at the conduct of the king's troops in the late war ; and all were annoyed by the condescending treatment accorded to " colonials " when they visited England or sent their sons there to be educated. Franklin himself, at that date an Anglophile, noticed this attitude : " Every man in England," he wrote, " seems to consider himself as a piece of a

[1] A. M. Schlesinger, *The Colonial Merchants and the American Revolution*, 1763-76, New York, 1917, pp. 59-80.

sovereign over America ; seems to jostle himself into the throne with
the King, and talks of *our subjects in the colonies.*" The ancient
cavalier loyalty of Virginia had long come to an end, and she now
furnished more leaders to the American revolution than did any other
state.   The question of parliament's right to tax the colonies was one
upon which no agreement was possible.   It was fatally easy for either
side to justify itself by arguments which were perfectly logical and
advanced in good faith.   In general we may say that the English
government proved its point by appeal to strict legal technicality,
and that its opponents took their stand upon those moral rights which
every man acknowledged in his heart.

In the sphere of action the Stamp Act was a hopeless failure from
the outset.   In every colony the people refused to do business on
stamped documents ; in some the officials were intimidated by physical
force from attempting to perform their duties.   At Boston a mob broke
into the houses of the chief justice and others, and burned all the
moveables in the street.   In North Carolina the inhabitants of Wilmington seized the stamp distributor and compelled him to resign his
office on the spot.[1]   In most places the revolt was comparatively good-
humoured, and the burning in effigy of the collector was reckoned a
suitable emphasis of refusal to buy his wares.   Nevertheless on refusal
all classes were determined.   Whilst the mob broke windows and
danced round bonfires the men of substance acted with more dignity.
At the invitation of Massachusetts a congress assembled at New
York.   Nine colonies sent representatives, who drafted resolutions
asserting the popular view.   For the first time a majority of the
thirteen had taken common action upon their own initiative.   Other
symptoms of a new spirit followed.   In New York and New England
the radicals organized themselves as Sons of Liberty.   The impossi-
bility of using stamps and the illegality of dispensing with them
paralysed such commerce as escaped the non-importation movement.
Exports to America fell off, and distress in the manufacturing towns
at home became clamorous.   Early in 1766 the Marquis of Rockingham,
Grenville's successor, repealed the hated Act.   At once there was a
revulsion of feeling in America.   General joy was expressed, and the
New Yorkers went so far as to raise a statue to George III.   The
figure was of lead, and a few years later its owners were making it into
bullets wherewith to shoot the king's troops.   At the time the satisfaction bade fair to be permanent.   Six months after the first news
John Adams, the radical leader of Massachusetts, declared, " The
repeal of the Stamp Act has composed every wave of popular disorder
into a smooth and peaceful calm." [2]

Grenville protested bitterly against the repeal, and George III.,
at odds with his late minister on most other matters, shared his

---

[1] G. E. Howard, *Preliminaries of the Revolution*, 1763-75, New York, 1905, p. 153,
gives details of similar compulsion in nine colonies.

[2] Sir G. O. Trevelyan, *The American Revolution*, London, 1905, etc., i. p. 2.

resentment in this. Rockingham's own position was insecure, and
expediency rather than principle seems to have dictated his action.
As a sop to his opponents he therefore accompanied the repeal by a
Declaratory Act asserting the abstract right of parliament to levy
taxes on the colonies. At the same time he amended the Sugar Act
by reducing from threepence to one penny the duty on every gallon
of molasses taken from the French islands to America, and extended
the lowered impost to the produce of the British West Indies as well.
Amid the general satisfaction in the colonies this extension passed
almost unnoticed. But it contained an important principle : the
duty, being levied on British and alien goods alike, was no longer
colourable as a measure of trade protection, and became one of revenue
production pure and simple. Thus was laid the foundation of another
quarrel two years later. The significance of the withdrawal of the
Stamp Act has been variously estimated. One view is that if the
ruling circles in England had honestly accepted the rebuff, there
would have been, there and then, an end of trouble with the colonies ;
another is that repeal was tantamount to the admission of independence,
since the American radicals were so elated with their victory that they
proceeded at once to proclaim the laws of trade a nullity. The truth
probably lies between the two, for in matters of this sort a clear-cut and
unqualified statement can hardly ever be made to cover all the facts.[1]

The cry against the Stamp Act had been " No taxation without
representation," but it is fairly certain that the majority of Americans
had no desire for representation in an imperial parliament. They
regarded it as impracticable and dangerous to their interests, and they
were probably right. To George III. and the Whig statesmen the
scheme was equally distasteful, and it had therefore little chance of
reaching the stage of experiment. Nevertheless certain proposals of
imperial federation saw the light at this time and deserve a brief
notice. Pitt's dalliance with the idea we have already referred to.
Thomas Pownall, a former governor of Massachusetts, produced in
1764 a scheme for a combined parliament to sit in London, and appealed
to the Anglo-Scottish union of 1707 as a general precedent. His work
was widely read, but gained him few adherents. Somewhat later
Joseph Galloway, a Pennsylvanian politician, proposed a colonial
parliament to sit in America under a president-general appointed by
the crown. All its Acts relating to common taxation and imperial
interests were to be ratified by the parliament at Westminster, and
conversely those of the latter were to be passed by the American body
before attaining the force of law. In internal matters the two branches
of the empire were to remain completely self-governing. The arrangement obviously presupposed a British readiness to forego the laws of

[1] Trevelyan, op. cit. i. pp. 2-7, holds the former view ; and S. G. Fisher, The Struggle
for American Independence, 2 vols., London, 1908, repeatedly asserts the latter (particularly in vol. i. pp. 62-3, 106-7, and 110). Prof. Egerton, pp. 192-3, emphasizes
the truth that the Stamp Act and its failure were mainly important because they
revealed a pre-existent but unsuspected condition of discontent.

trade : in the absence of that an immediate deadlock would have resulted. Galloway, although too advanced a liberal for British tastes, was a genuine loyalist, and backed his opinions by abandoning his property and going into exile after the Declaration of Independence.[1] In reality the conceptions of politics in Britain and America were too widely sundered to allow a chance of success to combined institutions. In America the representatives sought to control the executive ; in England they had sunk to the status of its pensioned dependents. The entire deeply rooted system of rotten boroughs and organized corruption stood in the way of federation. Franklin's account of a general election spoke volumes in a sentence : " The whole venal nation is now at market, and will be sold for about two millions, and might be bought . . . by the very devil himself." [2]

Rockingham went the way of Grenville in 1766, and colonial policy was thrown once more into the melting-pot. Pitt, although still disliked by the king, accepted the Earldom of Chatham and the leadership of the new administration. His health broke down soon after he had taken the seals, and whilst he lived in seclusion and on the verge of insanity others conducted the business of the empire in his name. Thus it came about that the Chatham ministry revived the animosities which the repeal of the Stamp Act had temporarily stilled, and embarked upon an American policy to which Chatham himself was opposed. The principal culprit was Charles Townshend, the chancellor of the exchequer. In 1767 he undertook to increase the revenue by new duties upon tea and manufactured goods—paper, glass, lead and colours—entering the American ports. The necessary Act was accordingly passed through parliament in that year. To a certain extent Townshend's hand was forced, for Grenville and others of the opposition were loudly demanding American taxation and holding out a reduction of the English land tax as an attractive possibility which would then ensue.[3] Townshend, however, chose an absurd method of effecting his purpose. The new taxes were to be collected in American custom-houses. Had they been levied in the English ports of departure they might have caused little resistance. Their total estimated yield also was only £40,000 a year, a sum trivial in comparison with the serious issues involved. In view of such circumstances it is difficult to resist the impression that some sinister influence behind the scenes was bent definitely upon reviving the controversy which had begun with the Stamp Act.[4] Townshend died in September, 1767, after making provision for another innovation which was duly carried into effect. This was the creation of an American Board of Customs Commissioners to reside across the Atlantic and enforce the laws of trade, which were again relapsing into ineffectiveness since Grenville's hand had been removed.

---

[1] On these matters see G. B. Hertz, *The Old Colonial System*, Manchester, 1905, pp. 118-130.

[2] Egerton, pp. 189-90.   [3] Channing, iii. p. 83.   [4] Trevelyan, i. pp. 6-7.

Chatham recovered his health and resigned his office in 1768. The Duke of Grafton, his principal colleague, carried on for two years more, with the addition to the ministry of Lord North, the king's personal nominee. In 1770 North became the prime minister and so remained for twelve years. His long tenure marks the triumph of the king's efforts to gain the ascendancy over the great Whig families, and his administration was in reality the personal government of George III. In 1768, also, a belated change was made in the machinery of administration. A new office, that of secretary for American affairs was created, with a seat in the cabinet for its holder. The step was a sound one, but the government made an unfortunate choice in appointing Lord Hillsborough as the first secretary. He combined the incompetence of Newcastle with an affectation of solemn profundity which irritated the practical and plain-spoken men with whom he had to deal.

Townshend's new customs commissioners seem to have been at least partially successful in enforcing the observance of the laws of trade. The revenue from this source, inclusive of the new duties, rose from £2000 per annum in 1763 to £30,000 in 1768-74.[1] In the latter period it substantially exceeded, for the first time, the cost of collection. Resistance, however, broke out once more on the former lines. The radical politicians revived their Sons of Liberty organizations, and goaded the American merchants to renew their pledges of non-importation. The latter policy, as regarded the dutiable articles, was pursued in every colony save Georgia from 1767 to 1770. It failed to achieve its object of bringing the pressure of the manufacturing interest to bear upon the British government, because the period was one of extraordinary briskness in European trade and home industry was therefore in a flourishing condition.[2] It emphasized, nevertheless, the ugly spirit which spread everywhere in the colonies during these years. George III. met the rising tide of resistance by ordering troops to Boston in support of the commissioners, and by increasing the naval patrols upon the coast. Boston was to him always the fountain of disloyalty. " The capital of Massachusetts, in the eyes of its Sovereign, was nothing better than a centre of vulgar sedition, bristling with Trees of Liberty, and strewn with brickbats and broken glass ; where his enemies went about clothed in homespun, and his friends in tar and feathers." [3] By 1769 there were nearly 4000 soldiers quartered among the 17,000 inhabitants of the town. At first the redcoats were well received, but later collisions occurred. An incident of 1770 has found its way into history as the Boston Massacre. Some loafers pelted a sentry, and taunted him and his comrades with cries of " Lobsters ! "

---

[1] Channing, iii. pp. 90-1. The figures there given throw doubt on the view that the laws of trade were never effective after the repeal of the Stamp Act.

[2] Schlesinger, *op. cit.* pp. 237-8. The whole non-importation movement is fully analysed for the first time by this author. See especially chaps. iii-v.

[3] Trevelyan, i. p. 10.

and " Bloodybacks ! " the latter in reference to the floggings which
were common in the regular army.   After one of their number had been
felled to the ground the soldiers fired and killed four persons.   Some
have magnified the affair as the first outpouring of patriot blood in
the cause of liberty, but the civilian magistrates of Boston showed what
they thought of it by inflicting a minor punishment on two of the
soldiers and acquitting the remainder.

Both enforcement of and resistance to the new duties had now
become a matter of principle rather than of practical utility.   All
except the tea duty were doing more good than harm to the colonies,
for by raising the price they stimulated colonial manufacture of the
articles concerned.   The British government, in fact, was setting up
a protective tariff against the products of home industry.   Lord
North realized this, and on assuming control of the government in
1770 decided to remove all the Townshend duties except that on tea.
The Duke of Grafton wished to abolish that also, but by a majority
of one the cabinet voted for its retention, in order to keep alive the
principle of parliamentary taxation.   The concession actually made
was sufficient to restore partial tranquillity in America.   The colonial
merchants were tired of non-importation, and gladly seized the excuse
for abandoning it.   Tea, even when legally imported, was undeniably
cheap, and a great deal, especially at New York and Philadelphia,
paid no duty at all.   Discontent therefore subsided, and for three
years the American question ceased to trouble the serenity of British
politics.   But a deceptive appearance of calm was the effect of distance.
Viewed closely, the colonies were not tranquil but seditious, as was
shown when the smuggling interest surprised and burnt the king's ship
Gaspée which had run ashore on the Rhode Island coast in 1772.

We have seen the contest between parliament and the colonies twice
blaze forth and twice subside ; and on each occasion taxation had been
the issue.   In 1773 the British government renewed the attack upon
a different line, and this time the quarrel grew without intermission
until it ended in complete revolution.   The East India Company had
reached a stage of development as a sovereign power which rendered
necessary a closer supervision by the king's ministers, and legislation
to accomplish that end was now inevitable.   The Company was in
financial distress, and therefore asked for a trading concession in
return for the political power it was surrendering.   It had hitherto
been compelled to sell its wares, of which tea had become the largest
item, by public auction in London.   British and American merchants
had thus handled the business of re-export and distribution in the
colonies.   Lord North now passed a Tea Act granting the Company a
complete refund of British duties, together with the right to export the
tea in its own ships to America and sell it through its own agents in
American ports.   The object in view was twofold, to enable the Company
to dispose of some seventeen million pounds of surplus tea in its warehouses, and to put an end to the tea-smuggling which still continued

in the colonies.   Smuggling would cease to be a paying business when the Company was selling tea free of English duty whilst the smugglers could only obtain supplies which had paid that duty.[1]

In theory, and had there been no smuggling, the cost of tea to the American consumer would have been halved by this arrangement. But the interests, both of the smugglers and of the legitimate American merchants, were attacked.   In England itself there had been much resentment against the great Company's monopoly ; and to extend it to mutinous colonies was soon shown to be a blunder against which the financial concession was but a straw in the balance.   The first fleet of tea-ships reached America towards the end of 1773.   At Philadelphia the inhabitants firmly demonstrated to the Company's officer that they would not allow his cargo to be discharged.   He therefore withdrew without landing a single chest.   At New York the same course was taken, and there also violence was avoided.   At Charleston the tea was landed, but remained unsold in the warehouse. At Boston three ships entered the harbour, and in face of a violent agitation the governor insisted that their ladings should be discharged. On December 16, the day before that appointed for the work to begin, a party of disguised men boarded the ships and threw the tea into the water whilst the townspeople lined the shore in enjoyment of the spectacle.

The defiance was too open and too well organized to be overlooked. But before considering the counter-measures which led rapidly to war, it will be as well to glance briefly at the attitude of prominent statesmen towards the question.   Benjamin Franklin had resided almost continuously in England since the end of the Seven Years' War.   He was the colonial agent for Pennsylvania and later for Massachusetts and other colonies in addition.   Whilst maintaining generally the colonial view he had worked honestly for conciliation, being a lover of England and a personal admirer of George III., of whom he said, " I can scarcely conceive a king more truly desirous of promoting the welfare of all his subjects."   Franklin's high reputation and his influence with British statesmen afforded the best hope of a settlement until 1773.   In that year an incident arose which converted him into an enemy.   He had obtained possession of certain private letters which reflected unfavourably upon the conduct of royal officials in Massachusetts. He sent them to his friends in Boston, with a request that they should not be made public.   The Bostonians, however, printed them. Franklin was called before the Privy Council in England and subjected to an hour's abuse by the solicitor-general, who plainly called him a thief.   He listened without moving a muscle, but he never forgave the ministers who were present at the scene.   The Earl of Chatham, after his resignation in 1768, lived ten years longer in broken health and without assuming any public office.   He spoke frequently in the House of Lords, and was the one figure in the ranks of British statesmen

[1] Schlesinger, pp. 262-70, gives the best account of the whole transaction.

whom the colonists regarded with affection and respect. It is doubtful, however, whether he could have done more than postpone an outbreak had he been in power. He declaimed against direct taxation of the colonies, but he was a passionate believer in the mercantile system and the ideal of self-sufficiency which was the real root of the trouble ; and whilst denouncing the Stamp Act he had asserted the right of parliament to legislate for the empire in all other matters. His faith in imperial federation might have led him to a constructive policy, but he never put his proposals into definite shape until the time for them was past. George III. was hostile to colonial claims from the outset, although the Americans long considered him as their friend, possibly because he hated Grenville. The colonial question really filled a secondary place in his mind until his victory over the Whigs in 1770. Then his irritation grew until it culminated with the news from Boston in 1774. After that date he was on the side of uncompromising repression. Among the men of minor weight Edmund Burke agreed with Chatham on the theoretical supremacy of parliament, but he was no lover of the mercantile system and disliked any measures which savoured of tyranny. " Great empire and little minds," he said, " go ill together." " Freedom . . . is the true Act of Navigation which binds you to the commerce of the colonies, and through them secures to you the wealth of the world." His political influence at the time was small in comparison to the opinion his speeches and writings have gained him with posterity. Lord Shelburne, a member of the ministry until 1768, resigned in that year as a protest against the Townshend measures. He represented a rising school which saw little utility in the possession of colonies of any kind.

On the subject of American opinion it is also necessary to be clear. Right up to the opening of hostilities, and even for some time afterwards, it would seem that the majority of the radicals had no desire for complete separation. What they worked for was emancipation from the control of parliament and from the shackles of the mercantile system. Having obtained that, they would have been content with the status of a self-governing dominion under the British crown. One authority holds that this solution would have been acceptable until the very moment of alliance with France in 1778.[1] The language of Washington and others supports such a view, and the exiled Galloway testified that in 1775 not one-fifth of the colonists sought independence. And always, it must be remembered, there was a considerable body of positive loyalists, by some estimated at half the total population, who had no sympathy with insurrection even for a limited object. The American revolution, like most others, began in fact with a negative rather than a positive purpose, and it was from its own fires that there emerged a new patriotism to be satisfied only by the working out of its destiny in the guise of complete national independence.

The royal answer to the Boston outrage was not long delayed. In

[1] Egerton, pp. 221-2.

March, 1774, Lord North introduced in parliament the retaliatory measures by which George III. hoped to make a signal example of those who had despoiled the East India Company. The Boston Port Act decreed the closing of Boston and the removal of its custom-house to Salem, until such time as the inhabitants should offer repara-tion for the wasted tea. The Massachusetts Government Act, which followed, abolished the local election of the councillors and jurymen, and the holding of town meetings, thus practically annulling the charter. The Transportation Act allowed the trial in England instead of in the colony of officers accused of murder committed in the course of their duties, that is, in aiding the governor to repress the inhabitants. The fourth of the series, the Quebec Act, appears to have been independent of the retaliation policy, and to have been passed in the ordinary development of Canadian business.[1] Its terms, however, proved as offensive to the Americans as those of the other measures, and its effects thus belong to this part of the subject. It granted to the French Canadians the free practice of the Catholic religion, still rigorously banned in New England, and extended the area of Canada to include the whole region north of the Ohio and east of the Mississippi, the country already marked down for the future expansion of the older colonies. Whilst passing these Acts Lord North strengthened the troops in Boston and transferred the governorship to General Gage, the commander-in-chief on the spot.

The other colonies at once took up the cause of Massachusetts, and gifts of food and resolutions of sympathy poured into Boston from all parts of America. To concert common measures delegates from every colony but Georgia met at Philadelphia in September. This meeting is known as the First Continental Congress. Here Joseph Galloway brought forward his plan of imperial federation already referred to. Many members of the Congress approved of it, but, considering that America was the aggrieved party in the present dispute, they preferred to proceed instead to a Declaration of Rights. This document, whilst expressly allowing the authority of parliament to control imperial trade, declared that the Americans could not submit to the laws of 1774 and other objectionable measures which preceded them. The delegates next bound themselves and their constituents to an association for a general stoppage of commercial intercourse with England until grievances should be redressed. The tone of the Congress was dignified and restrained, but throughout the colonies a violent persecution of loyalists and officials broke out, and at Boston Gage found himself virtually beleaguered through the autumn, in a condition bordering upon warfare with the revolutionary countryside.

On the nineteenth of April, 1775, the first blood was shed. Gage had despatched a column from Boston to destroy some warlike stores collected at Concord. On its way the force encountered the colonial

¹ Egerton, pp. 243-6.

militia at Lexington, passed through it after a skirmish, and fulfilled its mission. Then, retiring to Boston, the soldiers were harassed all along the route by ever growing bands of marksmen, who picked them off from behind cover until they reached their shipping on the northern shore of Boston Bay. In all the British force of 1000 men lost about a quarter of its numbers, whilst the American casualties amounted to less than a hundred. The news set the continent ablaze. Everywhere the militias were called out and the enlistment of a regular army began. Two months after Lexington a large New England force was blockading Boston, where Gage had received reinforcements bringing his strength up to 7000 men. In June the Americans occupied the Charlestown peninsula on the northern side of Boston harbour, and erected batteries from which it was possible to bombard the shipping and the town. Gage found it necessary to dislodge them, and the Battle of Bunker Hill ensued. Two assaults failed with terrible loss ; the third succeeded largely because the defenders had run short of ammunition. There had been much loose talk about the cowardice and indiscipline of the Americans, to which the event of the battle came as a harsh corrective ; for although the British troops were left in possession of the ground they had paid a heavier toll for it than in any victory of the Seven Years' War. The colonial leader who said, " I wish we could sell them another hill at the same price," had good reason for his exultation.

In the interval between these two military actions a second Congress had met at Philadelphia. It forwarded the organization of the army and appointed Washington to the chief command. But it considered itself as acting against the illegal measures of the ministers, and not against the royal supremacy of George III. The latter was still recognized as king even in Massachusetts after the fight at Lexington.[1] The constitutional fiction was similar to that under which Pym and Hampden had taken up arms in 1642. It was vitally important to maintain it, for it alone left the way open for a peaceful settlement. The Congress therefore proclaimed that it was resisting arbitrary and novel aggressions upon the recognized liberties of the people, and that it would lay down its arms when the danger of such aggressions came to an end. It embodied these pronouncements in a memorial to the king commonly known as the Olive Branch Petition, and offering in effect to return to the position of 1763. To do so would have been to abandon parliamentary supremacy over the colonies, and to that scarcely a man in England was ready to consent. Even Chatham and Burke demanded its recognition as a preliminary to the concessions they were now urging upon the government. George himself was in no mood for compromise, and from him came the decision that arms alone must decide the question. Lord North, with many forebodings, obeyed his master, and it was British policy which deliberately converted rebellion for a limited object into a war to the death for complete independence or complete submission.

To later generations the fate of Canada appears as one of the most important decisions of this critical year. Since the conquest the province had been under semi-military government, and the French population had settled down with less friction than might, on the whole, have been expected. The British officials had been competent and fair-minded men, a description which was eminently true of Sir Guy Carleton, who now filled the post of governor. Generations of warfare with New England had left a hatred which a few years' peace could not efface, and the Quebec Act, by legalizing the Catholic religion, had convinced the Canadians that they had more to gain from the British connection than from throwing in their lot with their Puritan neighbours. Constitutional theories, also, made little appeal to the French *seigneurs* and the illiterate peasants who had always rendered obedience to absolute power. Canada had submitted without question to the Stamp Act. When, therefore, in the summer of 1775, the Americans seized the frontier posts on Lake Champlain and proceeded later to march into the province, they found little support from the inhabitants. Carleton concentrated his defence at Quebec. In attacking the town the American leader Montgomery was killed, and his colleague Benedict Arnold found his troops melting away by desertion and disease. He persisted in the attempt until the summer of 1776, and then withdrew. The expedition, although ostensibly a failure, had the effect of diverting large British reinforcements from the American coast to the St. Lawrence, where they were almost useless for the main purpose of the war.[1]

The prospect of a long war opened up by George III.'s determined attitude paved the way for an extension of American claims. In the winter of 1775-6 Washington's army adopted a new national flag, a visible symbol to every beholder of a definite breach with the past. George III. returned no answer to the Olive Branch Petition, but Lord North passed an Act through parliament prohibiting all trade with the rebellious colonies. Thomas Paine, an English radical, published a widely read pamphlet assuring the Americans that independence was their only road to freedom and that by proclaiming it they would secure foreign aid. Men of property dreaded the mob-rule and disorder which threatened to raise their heads in the absence of any legitimate government. American debtors owed British creditors between three and six million pounds, all of which might conveniently be wiped from the slate by some irrevocable act.[2] All these were contributory circumstances, but the rapid movement which changed the professed loyalty of 1775 into the enthusiastic casting-off of allegiance in 1776 proceeded chiefly from the mere act of rebellion itself. America had combined to set on foot an army. An army to be effective presupposed a nation behind it, with its corporate spirit and its patriotism resting upon

---

[1] Channing, iii. p. 243   For fuller details on the invasion of Canada see below, part v. chap. ii.

[2] Hertz, *op. cit.* p. 129.

some definite foundation. That foundation Congress supplied in the Declaration of Independence, agreed to without a dissentient [1] at Philadelphia on July 4, 1776. Its drafting was the work of Thomas Jefferson of Virginia ; its substance embodied the political theories of Locke and the claims of natural liberty which the colonists had urged during the past twelve years. By it the colonies constituted themselves the United States and a sovereign power, capable of negotiating alliances as an equal with other prospective enemies of Great Britain. The concurrent intention of framing a common government proceeded more languidly, and was not practically achieved until after the close of the war.

George III. was determined upon a military conquest, although from the outset he did not lack advisers who told him that in face of united resistance it was impossible. American resistance in fact was not united. The Declaration was the work of an energetic minority. Every state had its loyalists, and the doubters and waverers were still more numerous. Washington even in the early years had hard work to keep his soldiers together, and the difficulty increased as time went on. They deserted to the English in hundreds and to their own homes in thousands. The active loyalists fought on the British side : one authority mentions fourteen regiments principally recruited from among them.[2] It may well be that the king was right, and that if Britain and America had stood alone in the world he would have worn down his rebels in the end. How he could then have rebuilt his ravaged empire save by the very concessions which would have obviated fighting at the outset is not evident. Probably the subject never entered his mind. But he was not left to work his will without interference. His generals failed in 1775-7 to make much impression upon the Americans. After the latter date the war merged into a world-wide struggle in which the Bourbon monarchies and the minor sea-powers of Europe combined to reverse the decision of 1763, and to pull down the supremacy which Pitt had established. For the present we have to consider briefly the events of the first, uncomplicated period, when there was still a chance of victory or compromise.

Whilst Arnold was failing to conquer Canada in 1775-6, a British expedition under Sir Henry Clinton made an equally unsuccessful attempt to reduce the Carolinas. Clinton relied upon the loyalists of the south, but they were already dispersed before his arrival. He was defeated in an attack upon Charleston and retired to join the main army, where Sir William Howe had succeeded Gage in the chief command. In March, 1776, Howe evacuated Boston, being convinced that no useful result could be obtained by lingering in the New England capital. He sailed away by sea to Halifax, and thence in July proceeded to open a new campaign in the middle states. These latter, he was assured, were, unlike New England, luke-warm in the rebellion, and offered the best opening for the work of reconquest. In July

---

[1] The New York delegates abstained from voting.   [2] Hertz, *op. cit.* p. 96.

and August Howe occupied Staten Island and Long Island, defeated Washington's men at Brooklyn, and entered New York. Washington, with less than 5000 men remaining, retreated across the Delaware to Philadelphia, and the American cause seemed lost. Washington himself confessed that " the game was pretty well played out." At this point Howe, who was a skilful commander in action, was smitten with an unaccountable fit of dilatoriness. At the end of the year Washington reorganized his forces, recrossed to New Jersey, annihilated a Hessian detachment at Trenton, and remained in occupation of the interior parts of the province, whilst the British still held the environs of New York.

The year 1777, had the British plans been fulfilled, should have seen the back of the rebellion broken. That it did not do so was due partly to the incompetence of the home government, which failed to co-ordinate the actions of its generals, and still more to the peculiar nature of the American resistance, whereby armies broken in the field were able to subsist on the countryside and reunite after their enemies had passed, and large bodies of ostensible civilians turned themselves temporarily into soldiers and gathered in superior numbers round any threatened point. This was especially true in New England, where the male population formed an armed militia able to carry on its civilian labour until the moment for action arrived. The object of the British plans was to bring the army under General Burgoyne, which had gone to Canada in the previous year, down the Hudson valley into the main theatre of the war. Howe at New York seems to have considered that Burgoyne could accomplish this task without assistance, and he therefore continued his campaign against Philadelphia in the opposite direction, trusting that Burgoyne's move would prevent the New Englanders from reinforcing Washington. According to one account the carelessness of the secretary-at-war, in neglecting to send off a despatch, prevented Howe from learning until too late what was required of him. The miscalculation entailed the disaster which ended the first phase of the war.

Howe remained at New York until the end of July. Then he embarked his army and sailed to Chesapeake Bay, at whose northernmost limit he landed a month later. From this point to Philadelphia was no great distance. He defeated Washington at the Brandywine River, and entered the city on September 26. There he commenced another long period of inaction, which lasted until his supersession in the following year.

In the meantime Burgoyne quitted Canada in July with an army of 7000 men, of whom nearly half were German mercenaries. By the end of the month he had traversed Lake Champlain and reached Fort Edward on the Hudson River. At this point his difficulties began. His force diminished by the lengthening of his communications, and by fighting with the New Englanders who gathered in ever increasing numbers about his line of march. On August 16 he lost 800 men at the

Battle of Bennington. By the end of September he had only 5000 left, and was being encircled by 20,000 Americans in a hilly, wooded and roadless country with whose intricacies the enemy were familiar. A swift retreat, regardless of the loss of his immense train of guns and baggage, might have saved him, but he still trusted to be succoured by a force moving up the river from New York. Sir Henry Clinton, left by Howe at that city, did indeed attempt a diversion, but his numbers were too small and his move too late to save Burgoyne. The latter, after losing more men at the two battles of Freeman's Farm (September 19 and October 7), surrendered the remains of his army to General Gates at Saratoga on October 17.[1] The loss of 7000 men was not, in the then condition of the empire, an irretrievable military disaster. But in its effect upon European politics Saratoga was decisive, for it brought into the field those enemies of Great Britain who had hitherto hesitated to take up the cause of the United States. During three years the British armies had failed to subdue the rebellion. They never again had the chance to do so unhampered by the spectators of the contest.

---

[1] By the terms of the capitulation the troops were to be disarmed and transported to England ; but Congress violated the agreement and detained them as prisoners. For these campaigns in detail see Fortescue's *British Army*, vol. iii. An excellent short account is in *Political History of England*, vol. x., by W. Hunt (1905).

CHAPTER IX

THE FALL OF THE MERCANTILE EMPIRE, 1778-1783

WILLIAM PITT, in criticizing the treaty of 1763, had said : " You
leave to France the possibility of reviving her navy." He had predicted
a disastrous outcome from such lenity, and the Duc de Choiseul
immediately set to work to prove him right. Even before the peace
Choiseul had set on foot measures for reconstructing the French marine,
and after it he never slackened the energy with which new ships were
built, new models elaborated, artillery improved, the maritime con-
scription overhauled, and officers, seamen and gunners trained
unceasingly for the sole object of revenge—revenge upon the power
which had seized the supremacy of the seas and heedlessly, out of
the plenitude of its conquests, returned to the Bourbon sovereigns
some crumbs of their lost colonial possessions. By 1770 he had
doubled the paper strength and probably trebled the value of the fleet
as compared with that of 1763. There were at the end of these seven
years of effort sixty-four ships-of-the-line actually afloat, and the
dockyards and arsenals had been brought to a high state of efficiency.
Nor did the work stop there, although Choiseul himself disappeared
from public life. In 1778 the number of capital ships had risen to
eighty, there were 67,000 seamen on the books, and 10,000 gunners
drilled regularly every week. In the two decades which followed the
Seven Years' War the spirit of Colbert returned for the first and last
time to the old navy of France.

Concurrently with the naval renascence Choiseul elaborated a
great diplomatic plan of campaign. In his mind the events of the
future hinged upon the coming revolt of the American colonies, which
he regarded as certain from the day when Canada changed hands,
and as imminent from 1766 when agitation enforced the repeal of the
Stamp Act.[1] To utilize the expected opportunity he sought a close
alliance with Spain and a concentration of naval and mercantile effort
in the Mediterranean and Caribbean Seas. By control of the former,
he held, France would be rendered secure against European attack ;
by that of the latter she would be able to dictate the course of events

[1] Henri Doniol, *La Participation de la France à l'Établissement des États-Unis*, 5 vols.,
Paris, 1886-98, i. pp. 4-5.

in America, and to build up a tropical empire to compensate the loss
of Canada. For that loss he seems tacitly to have felt relief rather
than regret, in common with other French thinkers of the time. It
was recognized that, as a colony, Canada had always been a failure,
and its recovery after 1763 never formed part of the national plans.
In realizing his programme Choiseul made some progress until his
public career was abruptly cut short by a miscalculation in 1770.
In the Mediterranean he carried out the conquest of Corsica (1768-9),
securing a naval station to neutralize the British possession of Minorca.
He had also in view designs upon Egypt, from which, like Napoleon,
he had visions of a new line of advance towards India. With the
Spanish alliance he succeeded so far that in 1765 Charles III. made
tariff concessions having the effect of favouring the export of French
goods to the Spanish colonies. The French West Indies recovered
their prosperity, but an attempt to plant new French colonies in
Guiana ended in failure. In the meantime Choiseul watched keenly
the progress of disaffection in British America and of party discord in
England. In 1770 he judged, somewhat prematurely, that the time
had come. A Spanish force from Buenos Ayres sailed to the Falkland
Islands and expelled with a high hand a few British settlers who were
established there. The Spanish government appeared ready to justify
its action by declaring war, and Choiseul was anxious to support his
ally. Louis XV., however, old and disillusioned, refused his consent.
He dismissed Choiseul and backed out of the dispute, and Spain
surrendered to the British contentions. The events of the next ten
years proved Louis to have been right and Choiseul wrong, for war in
1770 would probably have resulted in another Bourbon humiliation
and the strengthening of the British supremacy. For this reason Choiseul has been denounced as a visionary and a fanatic. Nevertheless
he was a true prophet and his work contributed vastly to the shaping
of the world's history.

The mantle of Choiseul fell upon the Comte de Vergennes, a cooler
and more patient man, not less inspired with the thirst for revenge,
but able to wait until the times were really propitious to the project.
In 1774 Louis XVI. succeeded to his grandfather's throne, and Vergennes took direction of foreign affairs in a ministry wherein the great
Turgot had charge of the finances. Turgot, like certain new thinkers
in England, conceived that the whole system of colonial monopolies
was fallacious and valueless, and he had therefore no sympathy with
wars for the transference of colonial power. He warned the king that
the finances of France in particular could not sustain another conflict.
Vergennes also had his reasons for delay, and France remained a
spectator of the opening campaigns in America. To Vergennes the
deterrent was an abiding fear of the Earl of Chatham. The French
state papers of 1775 depict this terror as carried to an almost ludicrous
pitch. If England crushed her colonies would she not, flushed with
triumph, employ her resuscitated armies and fleets in conquering

the Bourbon West Indies ? If the colonists foiled her, would she
not seek indemnification in the same quarter ? Had Chatham
deliberately stirred up the revolt in order to return to power as a
mediator ? Was he, with perfidious subtlety, seeking that position
in order that he might rally under his command all the forces of British
and American patriotism and lead yet another crusade against the foes
whom he had spent his life in despoiling ? [1] Such were the pictures
which the French statesmen conjured up in the opening year of the
rebellion, and so wildly were they out of touch with the reality, of an
England torn by faction and governed by such Machiavellis as Lord
North and George III., and of Chatham as he was, a wreck in body
and mind, his counsels shunned by sensible men, and his eloquence
reduced to mere raving and denunciation.

When the fighting of 1775 failed to subdue the colonists Vergennes
recovered his confidence and began to think that the occasion might
be at hand for the Bourbons to intervene. In the following year he
at one time advised immediate war if Spain would consent to take the
lead. But Spain, although hostile to England, loathed the Americans
as heretics and supplanters of her own ancient claims to all the west.
French naval preparations also were not complete, and the British
success at New York decided Vergennes to wait once more. He
himself had no love for colonial aspirations. " France," he wrote,
" may be content to remain a spectator whilst Englishmen rend their
own empire to pieces. Our concern in the matter is that this war
should last." He therefore granted a loan to the States, threw open
the French ports to American privateers, and connived at the supply
of munitions by French capitalists. In July, 1776, Silas Deane arrived
in Paris to conduct this business on behalf of Congress. He distributed
commissions broadcast to privateers and military adventurers. and did
his best to spread the belief that if France intervened she should
obtain, for sentimental reasons, the European monopoly of American
trade. In the following year Benjamin Franklin appeared as the
senior American envoy. He was received with enthusiasm by society,
as a sage of antiquity returned to earth. A gust of sentiment over-
spread the country for the virtuous republicans of the west, and
volunteers flocked across the Atlantic to place their swords at
Washington's disposal. Many returned disillusioned by practical
contact with democracy, and one wrote at the close of 1777, " there is
a hundred times more enthusiasm for the revolution in any Paris café
than in the whole of the United States." [2]

---

[1] Doniol, op. cit. i. pp. 42, 81, 117.

[2] Fortescue, British Army, iii. 297. The popular sentiment for democratic ideals
was undoubtedly a factor in the French decision. But it was a subordinate factor,
serving to bring the French people into line with the policy their government had long
determined on. M. Jusserand, in his introduction to J. B. Perkins' France in the
American Revolution, Boston, 1911, holds that love of liberty was the principal motive
of France, and that the people forced the hands of the court, which contained many
Anglophiles who had renounced designs of revenge for the Treaty of Paris. But the

Whilst these transactions were going forward Vergennes negotiated
with Spain.   That country had a long list of ancient and recent grudges
against England—the successive losses of Jamaica, Gibraltar, Minorca
and Florida, and the age-long infringement of the Spanish laws of trade.
But the countenance of rebellious colonists seemed too high a price to
pay for the satisfaction of these grievances, for the loyalty of Spain's
own South American possessions was by no means above suspicion,
and the example of the north might prove contagious.   She therefore
hung back and left France to take the initiative.   Throughout 1777
Franklin worked in Paris with unexampled tact and assiduity.   The
great figure of Chatham still haunted the imagination of Vergennes,
and the capture of Philadelphia, coupled with rumours of smashing
victories by Burgoyne on the Hudson, counselled delay to the wary
court of France.   At length on December 2 came news of the actual
truth, the surrender at Saratoga six weeks before.   Within a fortnight
France recognized the United States as an independent power, and the
framing of an alliance was taken in hand.   On February 6, 1778,
Vergennes and Franklin signed treaties of commerce and military
co-operation.   True to Choiseul's policy, France placed first the
disruption of the British empire.   Neither she nor America were to
make peace until England had acknowledged the independence of
the United States.   France then renounced all claim to Canada or any
territory upon the mainland of the continent east of the Mississippi,
but she reserved a free hand to make conquests in the West Indies
and elsewhere.

For England the alliance altered the whole aspect of the struggle.
Lord North announced the news to parliament in March, and all
realized that the civil war in the colonies was merging into a conflict
with the maritime powers of the world.   For a moment it seemed as
though the British government might do as Vergennes had feared—
call off its forces from America and fall, with a united nation behind it,
upon the Bourbon powers.   In February North had abolished the tea
duty, renounced the right to tax the colonies, and repealed the Boston
Port and Massachusetts Government Acts.   Amherst, the veteran of
the Canadian conquest, recommended a naval blockade only against
America, and a military withdrawal would have been popular with
the Opposition, which had received the news of Saratoga " with a howl
of insulting triumph." [1]   In spite of this display Fox and his followers
were keen to beat the French : Chatham himself, who had forbidden
his son to serve against America, despatched him with his blessing to
take his place in the garrison of Gibraltar.   But George III. refused to
face the facts.   The Americans were his prime enemies, and he declined

balance of evidence is against this view.   French statesmen were not controlled by
public opinion, and Vergennes and his coadjutors, although they may have admired
English institutions hated the British world-power, and were determined to bring it
low.   Compare Perkins, *op. cit.* 210 ; Sir G. O. Trevelyan, *George III. and Charles Fox,*
i. 205-8 ; Doniol, i. 566-78.

[1] Fortescue, iii. p. 244.

to relax his grip upon them.   The colonial war therefore continued,
and the flower of the army and navy remained upon the American
seaboard instead of blockading the Bourbon coasts and sweeping up
their possessions as they had done in the Seven Years' War.   In this
decision the king's evil genius was Lord George Germaine, the secretary
for America, and, to a less extent, Lord Sandwich, who took control
of the navy.   Both these ministers are unanimously accused of adopting
and adhering to false strategic views ; and still worse, of acting consistently as the enemies of the unhappy commanders afloat and in the
field.   Under their administration every general and admiral knew
that for the least mishap his reputation would be blackened by the
government which employed him.[1]   Not so had Pitt drawn victory
from disaster.

The interest of 1778, the first year of the new war, centres around the
proceedings of the fleets.   On April 15, the Comte d'Estaing sailed
from Toulon with a strong squadron, passed the Straits of Gibraltar,
and made for America.   His passage was very slow, and news of his
coming preceded him.   Sir Henry Clinton, knowing that New York
was open to capture, hastily quitted Philadelphia in order to march
to its defence ; and Lord Howe, the British admiral, escaped with his
warships and transports from the Chesapeake ten days before d'Estaing
sailed in.   Had the latter, who took twelve weeks to cross the Atlantic,
arrived sooner he might have captured both fleet and army and ended
the war at a stroke.[2]   At New York a little later the same chance
presented itself.   Howe, whose ships were far inferior in force, showed
a bold front, and d'Estaing avoided the encounter and passed on to
Rhode Island.   This had been occupied by the British in 1776, and
served as a naval base after the evacuation of Boston.   Howe followed
d'Estaing and again by superior leadership foiled him without fighting
a battle, and saved both the port and its garrison.   After these failures
d'Estaing sailed for the West Indies at the beginning of November.
His conduct led to much dissension between the French and the
Americans, and to a suspicion that France was not eager to see the
colonies independent before she had made her own profit out of
the war.   In home waters Admiral Keppel went to sea at the head of
the Channel fleet.   He met the Comte d'Orvilliers off Cape Ushant and
fought an indecisive action, principally memorable for its demon-
stration of the effect of politics upon naval efficiency.   Keppel, a
Whig, was balked of a victory by the refusal of a Tory subordinate
to obey his orders.   The Tory ministers then had the admiral tried
for his life on charges brought against him by the man who had been
in fault.   The court-martial vindicated Keppel, but such was the
disgust aroused by the whole incident that some of the ablest officers in

---

[1] Pamphleteers and journalists, well known to be in government pay, were employed
to poison the public mind against Burgoyne, the Howes, Clinton and Keppel.   See
Trevelyan, *George III. and Fox, passim.*

[2] Admiral Mahan, *Navies in the War of Independence,* London, 1913, pp. 62-3.

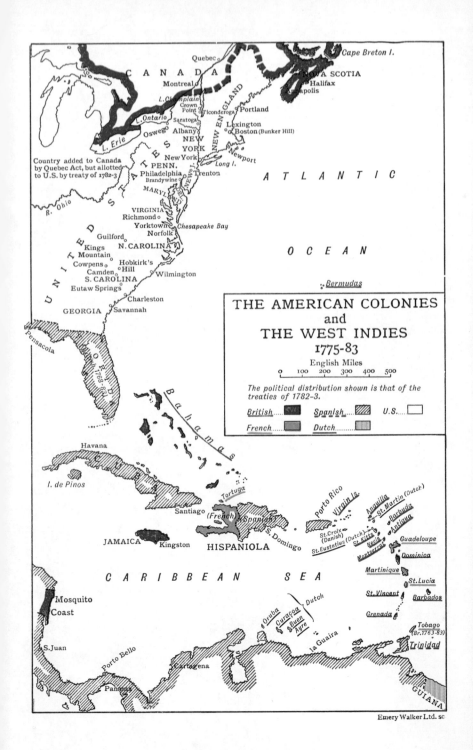

CANADA

Quebec
Montreal
L. Champlain
Crown
Point Ticonderoga Portland

NOVA SCOTIA
Cape Breton I.
Halifax
Annapolis

L. Ontario
Oswego
Saratoga
L. Erie
Albany
NEW
YORK
Lexington
Boston (Bunker Hill)

Country added to Canada
by Quebec Act, but allotted
to U.S. by treaty of 1782-3

New York
PENN.
Philadelphia
Brandywine
Long I.
Newport
Trenton

R. Ohio

MARYLAND

ATLANTIC

VIRGINIA
Richmond
Yorktown Chesapeake Bay
Norfolk
Guilford
Kings
Mountain
Cowpens
Camden
Hobkirk's
Hill
S. CAROLINA
Eutaw Springs
Charleston
GEORGIA Savannah
N. CAROLINA
Wilmington

OCEAN

.: *Bermudas*

U N I T E D   S T A T E S

Pensacola
FLORIDA
Br. 1763-83

Bahamas

THE AMERICAN COLONIES
and
THE WEST INDIES
1775-83
English Miles
0   100   200   300   400   500

*The political distribution shown is that of the
treaties of 1782-3.*

British   Spanish   U.S.
French   Dutch

Havana
C U B A
I. de Pinos
Santiago
Tortuga
(French)(Spanish)
Porto Rico
Virgin Is.
Anguilla
St. Martin (Dutch)
Barbuda
Antigua
St. Croix
(Danish)
St. Kitts
Nevis
St. Eustatius (Dutch)
Montserrat
Guadeloupe
Dominica

JAMAICA
Kingston
HISPANIOLA
S. Domingo

Martinique
St. Lucia

C A R I B B E A N   S E A

St. Vincent
Barbados

Mosquito
Coast

Grenada

Aruba
Curaçoa
Buen
Ayre
Dutch

Tobago
(Br. 1763-83)

S. Juan
Porto Bello
Cartagena
Panama
la Guaira

Trinidad

G U I A N A

Emery Walker Ltd. sc

the service refused to accept commands while Lord Sandwich remained in power.[1]

D'Estaing's departure from America to the West Indies was dictated by a geographical factor which had a regularly recurring effect throughout the war. From the beginning of August to the beginning of November the islands were subject to violent hurricanes and unsafe for the operations of large warships. At the end of the hurricane season winter conditions were setting in on the American coast. The great fleets on either side are therefore usually found in the West Indies in the spring and early summer, on the continental seaboard in the late summer and autumn, and returning to Europe or the West Indies in the winter. In 1778 a British force left New York for Barbados on the same day as d'Estaing sailed from Boston for Martinique. The governor of the latter island had already taken Dominica. The British now retaliated by capturing St. Lucia, although d'Estaing as before was in superior force. In the summer of 1779 the French took St. Vincent and Grenada. There was at this time considerable disaffection among the planters in the British West Indies, many of them sympathizing more or less openly with the enemy. The Bermudians even went so far as to send delegates to Congress.[2]

In the winter of 1778-9, the British government came to the decision to employ the bulk of its forces in a reconquest of the southern states, Georgia, the Carolinas, and Virginia. This region was accordingly the scene of the later campaigns of the American war. New England after Saratoga was not again assailed. New York remained the British headquarters, linked with the armies in the south by sea communications depending for their maintenance upon the superiority of the British fleets to those of France. That superiority, as we shall see, was overthrown at a critical moment, and the whole plan ended in disaster. Its inception was largely due to Lord George Germaine, who was persuaded that the loyalists were in the majority in the southern states and would make their conquest an easy matter. As a beginning a British force sailed down to Georgia at the end of 1778 and took Savannah on December 29. In the succeeding two months the whole of Georgia was overrun and apparently subdued. D'Estaing, returning from the West Indies in the hurricane season of 1779, made an attempt to recapture Savannah but was beaten off.

The most important event of 1779 was the entry of Spain into the war. On April 12 she signed a treaty of alliance with France, and the Bourbon powers undertook the invasion of England and the siege of Gibraltar. Spain, however, never expressly allied herself with the Americans, and displayed no interest in securing their independence.

---

[1] A full account of the court-martial appears in Trevelyan's *George III. and Fox*, chap. v. It throws a clear light upon the almost incredible vileness of political life at the time.

[2] Fortescue, iii. pp. 259-60.

Her motives were simply the recovery of possessions lost to England in previous wars.

At this point it is opportune to survey the opposing forces. At sea the Bourbon powers had some 140 ships-of-the-line, those of France being extremely efficient, those of Spain excellently built but poorly handled. England had nominally 150, but many existed on paper only, having been allowed to fall into such decay that they were never able to go to sea. In the strength of fleets actually afloat the British were usually much inferior to the allies. In frigates and privateers the latter, aided by the Americans, were also stronger. It was computed that 3000 British ships, about one-third of the mercantile marine, were captured during the war. France possessed, for those days, an enormous regular army, unhampered by the continental campaigns which had drained its strength in the Seven Years' War. This army was always available for the invasion of England, and its presence on the Channel coast forbade the sending of proper reinforcements to the British in America. The Spanish troops were also sufficiently numerous to besiege Gibraltar and Minorca simultaneously and to appear in superior force in the Gulf of Mexico. The British army, as always in the warlike eighteenth century, was inadequate in numbers. It consisted for the most part of the highest and the lowest orders in society, supplemented by mercenaries hired in Germany. The professional classes, the tradesmen, and the working men above the line of pauperism were scarcely represented in it, and it never occurred to anyone that they should be. The people who amongst them furnished the bulk of public opinion were thus hardly touched in person by these long wars, which perhaps accounts for the persistent jingoism of the times. The militia, as distinct from the regular army, was a force for home service only. It had been reconstituted by Pitt in the Seven Years' War. In 1778, on the threat of invasion, it was called out and trained to the number of 39,000 men. Thus poorly equipped the old mercantile empire faced the world-wide coalition of the enemies its successes had raised up. A contemporary writer, summing up the history of 1779, declared : " Whether it proceeded from our fault, or whether it was merely our misfortune, mankind seemed to wait, with an aspect which at best bespoke indifference, for the event of that ruin which was expected to burst upon us." [1] And the worst was yet to come.

Spain formally declared war in June, 1779, having already concerted plans of invasion with the French. In July the united Bourbon armada entered the Channel and hovered off Plymouth. To its sixty-six battleships the British could not oppose half the number. But divided counsels caused delay, and a terrible epidemic broke out, particularly in the Spanish ships. A gale drove the great fleet from the English coast, and it was too disordered to return. The greatest menace of the century passed away with scarcely a shot fired. The Comte d'Orvilliers, the allied commander-in-chief, was so heartbroken that he entered a monastery and died shortly afterwards.

On the American side d'Estaing left for Europe after his failure at Savannah. In his absence the British undertook the second instalment of their southern reconquest. Sir Henry Clinton withdrew the British troops from Rhode Island and led an expedition to the siege of Charleston, the capital of South Carolina. In May, 1780, the city surrendered with nearly 7000 American soldiers. Clinton returned to New York, leaving Lord Cornwallis in command in the south. Cornwallis overran the Carolinas but had never sufficient men to secure his gains. The republican forces continually reformed behind him, and the presence of numerous loyalists in his ranks rendered the fighting the most bitter and barbarous in the war. In the victories of Camden, Guildford and Hobkirk's Hill, and the defeats of King's Mountain and Cowpens, his forces melted away. By the spring of 1781 the British held little more than the three coast capitals of Savannah, Charleston and Wilmington ; and Clinton at New York, watched by the French and American armies, could send but scanty aid.

During this period the Bourbon fleets concerned themselves little with the fortunes of the colonists In 1780 de Guichen, the French commander, operated in the West Indies, and when the season became unsuitable he returned to France. Sir George Rodney, the British admiral, fought an indecisive action with him near Martinique, and the balance of power in the islands remained unchanged. A British attempt to revive the ancient project of seizing central America succeeded so far that San Juan in Nicaragua was taken. Then sickness annihilated the expedition and the remnant withdrew. Nelson, as a young officer, was present, and barely escaped with his life.

At home the situation grew steadily worse. The minor sea-powers of Europe complained bitterly of the British contention that all enemy goods in neutral ships were contraband of war. Vergennes on the other hand had proclaimed that France repudiated this doctrine and would maintain the right of neutrals to convey all but actual munitions of war. Frederick of Prussia, although not appearing as a principal, instigated the neutrals to take action,[1] and Catherine II. of Russia stood forward as the champion of the weaker powers. Russia, Sweden and Denmark together formed the Armed Neutrality, pledged to fight for the principle that " free ships make free goods," that contraband of war did not include naval stores, victuals or general merchandise, and that a blockade to be legal must be really effective with the blockading ships lying close to the ports concerned. Prussia and the German Empire joined the league in 1781, Portugal and even Turkey in 1782. The isolation of Britain was complete.

Holland went to greater extremities. Her concern in the contraband trade was larger even than that of the Baltic countries. Her West Indian island of St. Eustatius, which she threw open to the shipping

[1] Trevelyan, *op. cit.* ii. p. 77.

of the world, became a huge depot for the supply of munitions to America. In 1780 John Adams, the New England politician, travelled to the Hague and, with an ability comparable to that of Franklin, won over the Dutch statesmen to a recognition of American independence. The British government, apprised by captured despatches of what was going on, seized the excuse for declaring war in December, 1780. It was perhaps the only firm and well-judged stroke to the credit of Lord North's cabinet, for Holland, with her colonies defenceless in the East and West Indies alike, was less dangerous as an open than as a secret enemy. In the following year Rodney captured St. Eustatius and the neighbouring island of St. Martins, with £4,000,000 worth of booty and nearly 200 sail of contraband traders. In the east the fall of the Dutch factories of Trincomalee and Negapatam followed shortly on the news of the war.

The war in America now drew towards a decisive result. In the spring of 1781 Cornwallis saw much of his work in Carolina already undone and considered that the conquest of Virginia was indispensable to the establishment of the British position in the south. Germaine in England persuaded himself that the Carolinas were firmly subdued, and also held the invasion of Virginia to be the next step. He therefore authorized Cornwallis to march northwards. Clinton at New York disliked the idea but was obliged to acquiesce. He sent such forces as he could spare to the Chesapeake to assist Cornwallis. Washington was also prepared to stake all upon a great stroke. In his case it was a counsel of despair. His troops were mutinous, diminishing in numbers and worse provided than ever before, and he saw in Congress and the people at large an increasing selfishness and indifference to the outcome of the war. His only hope lay in utilizing the services of a fine French force which had crossed the Atlantic under the Comte de Rochambeau in the previous year. France at last realized that she must render efficient aid or witness the collapse of the American cause. The Comte de Grasse sailed for the West Indies with a great fleet in the early summer. He found awaiting him an appeal from Washington and Rochambeau to co-operate on the American coast. He collected troops and money in the French islands and arrived in Chesapeake Bay at the end of August. Cornwallis was already in Virginia, having entrenched himself at Yorktown in anticipation of aid from New York. Washington and his French allies now marched southwards to crush Cornwallis whilst de Grasse held the approach by sea. Rodney, sixty-seven years old and a martyr to gout, had gone to England to recover his health, leaving Admiral Graves on the American coast. Graves, with nineteen ships against twenty-four, attacked de Grasse in the Chesapeake. He was beaten off and retired to New York to refit. During his absence the siege of Yorktown moved to its conclusion. Cornwallis found himself penned in by land and sea, the greater part of his men sick, and his camp swept by the French and American guns. He surrendered his whole force on October 19, 1781.

This was virtually the end of the American war.   George III. was for carrying it on, but he found himself alone in that opinion.   Parliament decided to take no more offensive action by land against the colonists, and early in the following year Lord North resigned, together with his tragic ministers for war and marine.   By neglecting every maxim which Pitt had exemplified they had ruined the empire.   In the words of Admiral Mahan, " No hostile strategist could have severed the British army more hopelessly than did the British government."

Whilst the British forces evacuated successively Savannah, Wilmington, Charleston and New York (1782-3), the Bourbons still remained to be dealt with.   In 1781 Suffren led a fleet to the Indian Ocean with results which we have detailed in a previous chapter.   In the west Rodney's forces followed the capture of St. Eustatius with that of Demarara and Essequibo on the mainland of Dutch Guiana. But whilst this was going on the Spaniards from New Orleans took Pensacola and by so doing reconquered the whole of Florida, which they had ceded to Britain in 1763.   De Grasse, before leaving for Yorktown, had taken the small island of Tobago.   On his return in November, 1781, the French rapidly recaptured the lost Dutch colonies, St. Eustatius, St. Martins, Demarara and Essequibo, and proceeded to the conquest of the British Leeward Islands, St. Kitts, Nevis and Montserrat.   At the same moment a Spanish expedition overran the Bahamas.   The Bourbon leaders now concerted a design upon Jamaica, and it seemed as though the British flag was fated to disappear from the West Indies as well as from the continental colonies.

At this critical juncture Rodney arrived once more from England. The ships which he brought with him rendered his united fleet about equal to that of de Grasse.   He brought the latter to action on April 12, 1782, near the Saints, some small islets between Dominica and Guadeloupe.   The result of the battle was a British victory, the only decisive one gained against the French in this war.   Rodney broke the French line, captured de Grasse himself and five battleships, took two more a few days later, and ruined the whole French fleet.   At once the position of affairs was completely altered.   Nothing more was heard of the conquest of Jamaica, and the smaller islands were again at the mercy of Great Britain.

In European waters in 1781-2 the war was waged more fiercely than ever.   In both years Bourbon fleets cruised in the Channel and threatened, without accomplishing, a landing on the English coast. Sir Hyde Parker encountered a Dutch squadron in the North Sea and barely defeated it after a stubborn battle.   Gibraltar had been since 1779 a focus of interest.   In that year the Spaniards blockaded it, and later they developed their operations into an active siege.   During a defence lasting for three years and seven months the garrison under General Eliott were three times relieved and revictualled.   On the first occasion Rodney, sailing for the West Indies at the close of 1779, destroyed a Spanish squadron off Cape St. Vincent and conducted his supply ships to the rock. Again in April, 1781, nearly a hundred sail with food and troops broke the cordon. In the following year the allies, seeing peace imminent, made a supreme effort to take the fortress. For a week, in September, 1782, an unprecedented bombardment and the use of novel engineering devices were tried in vain. Shortly afterwards Lord Howe carried out the third relief, and the long siege ended with the war in February, 1783. Minorca was less fortunate. A Spanish army began the siege of Port Mahon in July, 1781, and in the following February the citadel was surrendered after a heroic defence.

Apart from this loss and that of Florida the British Empire had made good its possessions against the Bourbon powers, although the American colonies were irretrievably gone. Financial exhaustion was now everywhere apparent. Lord North had raised his last loan at ruinous interest, France was far gone in the bankruptcy which Turgot had predicted, and the American Congress had subsisted from the outset on paper money which was now hardly worth the cost of printing. The destruction of the commercial and maritime wealth of all the combatants had been enormous. These considerations rather than any decisive victory of the fighting forces led to the opening of peace negotiations in 1782.

Lord Shelburne was now the British prime minister. Although he still boggled at independence, and was willing to make large concessions in return for a purely nominal allegiance, he was obliged to concede a full recognition of the sovereignty of the United States. On important details the British negotiators gave way in two notable instances : they failed to secure protection for the loyalists from the vengeance of their fellow-countrymen, and they agreed to the nullification of the Quebec Act in so far as it concerned the lands between the Ohio and the Mississippi. The Act (of 1774) had annexed this territory to Canada ; it was now confirmed to the United States, having been in effect conquered during the war by an American partisan leader. Other boundary questions were left to be settled at a later date. As to the loyalists, their lot was a hard one. Vindictive persecution, of which Washington approved, drove them from the land of their birth. Many settled in Nova Scotia and Canada, and the British government compensated them for their losses to the extent of £4,000,000. Their claims amounted to more than double that sum. On these terms Great Britain provisionally acknowledged the independence of the United States in November, 1782, pending the conclusion of peace with her other enemies.

With France and Spain preliminaries were agreed to early in 1783, and the definitive treaty was signed at Versailles in September. Between Britain and France there was in the West and East Indies a mutual restoration of conquests, except that France retained Tobago. In Newfoundland the French fishing rights were strengthened and the British gave an undertaking not to settle the western shores of the

island. In Africa, France kept Senegal, taken in 1779, and Britain
returned Goree, taken in the same year. Spain retained her reconquered
possessions of Minorca and Florida. A separate treaty restored to
Holland her lost posts in India and the Caribbean with the exception
of Negapatam, which was kept by the East India Company.

The Treaties of Versailles mark the end of much that has hitherto
bulked largely in this history—of the three centuries of competition
between the western nations for sea-power and colonial wealth, of the
mercantile empire which Great Britain had built upon the ruins of her
rivals' undertakings, even of the economic beliefs which had underlain
the whole conduct of the civilized world. Democracy had won its
first victory, and social questions were soon to supplant the old struggle
for national wealth as the mainspring of men's actions : it was but
a short six years from the peace of 1783 to the fall of the Bastille. The
old British empire was torn into two portions, and the larger was lost
to it—the thirteen states had contained five-sixths of the white men
who dwelt overseas under the British flag. At home industrial changes
and the birth of new ideas in economics and ethics were teaching a new
generation to doubt that political and racial ascendancy were the true
goals of national life. Adam Smith published his *Wealth of Nations*
and Lord Mansfield pronounced the first judgment against slavery
whilst the American conflict was in progress. And after the independence of the United States the mother-country's trade with them,
contrary to prediction, increased more rapidly than ever before.

The causes of the great American revolt have appeared from time
to time in our narrative from the day when Endicott and Winthrop
arrived in Massachusetts Bay. They group themselves broadly
under two heads, political and economic. In politics, comparing
colonial administration before and after 1688, we see that the victory
of Parliament in that year, the establishment of responsible government in England, was not conducive to better administration of the
colonies. Insular interests acquired a too crushing weight in the
national counsels : an irresponsible king, even of the Stuart type, had
always realized that he was the ruler not of England only, but of Ireland
and the colonies as well ; the members of the Commons who influenced,
and in the last resort controlled, the ministers of the eighteenth century
were prone to take a narrower view and to regard the colonists, not as
fellow Englishmen, but as potential rivals and competitors who could
not be safely allowed the same political rights as Englishmen at home.
Hence the political victory of the " glorious revolution " of 1688 was
not extended to America. The electors of England, few and corrupt
as they were, at least could remove the executive if it became intolerable
to them. Those of America could denounce their governors and
bring about a deadlock which prejudiced the welfare of the state, but
their governors still held office until an outside authority chose to
remove them. American constitutional rights remained in the Stuart

stage throughout the eighteenth century. But when all is said, it was the working of the mercantile colonial system which exemplified the political grievance and prepared the way for the explosion. In importance the economic was to the political as the concrete to the abstract. The system was devised with an eye to the plantation colonies of the Restoration, weakly populated by white men and incapable of self-defence against naval attack. In nurturing those colonies in their sickly stage it cannot be denied that the system worked to admiration. Without the protection of its sea-power they would have perished as New Netherland and New France perished in the fierce colonial wars. But in the hands of a Parliament wherein vested interests had too great a weight the system was inelastic. When the New England and middle colonies throve and supported a large population mercantilism could see in them an exclusive market for home manufactures, and nothing more ; it could not endure that these rising peoples should take a share in the rich plantation trades. The idea permeated and vitiated all intercourse : colonials were not equals but subjects of the citizen at home. Amid these wide considerations particular measures sink a little from the prominence which their labels have acquired for them : " It was not the Stamp Act nor the repeal of the Stamp Act, it was neither Lord Rockingham nor Lord North, but it was that baleful spirit of commerce that wished to govern great nations on the maxims of the counter." [1] After all analysis of details these words of a contemporary seem best to sum up the truth of the matter.

Of the separation it is customary for English writers to speak with regret, and to expatiate upon the means by which it might have been avoided or at least postponed. But, from the perspective of the present day, is it not a matter for congratulation that it happened when it did ? Had the colonies remained part of the empire the great cosmopolitan emigration of the nineteenth century would still, so far as we can see, have taken place. Germans, Slavs, Latins, Scandinavians and disaffected Irish have combined to produce in America a nationality, English-speaking indeed, but out of sympathy with England on many important issues. The facts of population are inexorable. The effective government of such an empire would have moved ere long from the banks of the Thames to those of the Hudson. The great British dominions of the nineteenth century would have been exploited as much by Americans as by ourselves. And the people of the British Isles might now or in the future—if the suggestion is not too fantastic —be contemplating their own forlorn war of independence against the great non-British combination which had engulfed them.

---

[1] Arthur Young, quoted by Lecky, ii. p. 241. Cf. Adam Smith, 1776 : " The sneaking arts of underling tradesmen are thus erected into political maxims for the conduct of a great empire. "

AUTHORITIES. PART IV.

General : For the detailed English history of the period covered by this part the classic authorities are Lord Macaulay's *History of England* and W. E. H. Lecky's *History of England during the Eighteenth Century.* More modern works dealing with the same period are *The Political History of England,* vols. viii., ix. and x., by R. Lodge, I. S. Leadam and W. Hunt respectively ; and two volumes of the *Oxford History of England,* namely *The Establishment of the Hanoverians,* by Basil Williams, and *The Reign of George III.,* by G. S. Veitch. For naval history the leading authorities are the same as those mentioned for part iii., ch. ix. The Hon. J. W. Fortescue's *History of the British Army,* vols. ii. and iii., London, 1899, etc., becomes increasingly valuable for colonial as well as military history as the eighteenth century progresses. Other works useful throughout the period are Prof. H. E. Egerton, *British Colonial Policy,* already mentioned, and Sir J. R. Seeley's *Expansion of England,* London, 1883. The *Cambridge History of the British Empire,* vols. i. and iv. (India), and A. B. Keith, *Constitutional History of the First British Empire* (1930), authoritatively cover this period.

CHAPTERS I. AND II. FROM 1688 TO 1739.

The history of the American colonies during this period is told in J. A. Doyle's works mentioned among the authorities for part iii., up to 1714. From that date onwards the same author unites the whole subject in one volume, *The Colonies under the House of Hanover,* London, 1907. A good American work on the same period is E. B. Greene's *Provincial America,* 1690-1740, New York, 1905. The second volume of Prof. Channing's *History of the United States* (New York, 1908) is valuable also. *The Colonial Policy of William III,* by G. H. Guttridge, Cambridge, 1922, is a detailed study and record. O. M. Dickerson in *American Colonial Government,* 1696-1765, Cleveland, Ohio, 1912, gives a full explanation of the Board of Trade and its influence. The late Mr. G. L. Beer did not live to continue his *Old Colonial System* for the period subsequent to 1689. He had treated it summarily, however, in his first work, *The Commercial Policy of England towards the American Colonies,* New York, 1893. The West Indies in their economic aspect receive detailed treatment in F. W. Pitman's *Development of the British West Indies,* 1700-63, Yale, 1917, which is a mine of statistical information. A useful view of colonial matters in general is contained in the introduction to *Acts of the Privy Council, Colonial Series,* vol. ii. (1680-1720), 1910, ed. by W. L. Grant and James Munro. The sentiments of the English people towards colonial subjects, especially in relation to economic doctrines, are fully explained with a wealth of illustration from contemporary sources by G. B. Hertz in *The Old Colonial System,* Manchester, 1905, and *British Imperialism in the Eighteenth Century,* London, 1908. For Walpole's colonial and commercial policy see Lord Morley's *Walpole,* London, 1889 (re-issued, 1903) ; N. A. Brisco, *The Economic Policy of Robert Walpole,* New York, 1907 ; and Rt. Hon. J. M. Robertson, *Bolingbroke and Walpole,* London, 1919. Two useful monographs are those of G. B. Hertz, " England and the Ostend Company," *Eng. Hist. Review,* xxii. 255-79 ; and J. S. Barbour, *William Paterson and the Darien Company,* Edinburgh, 1907.

CHAPTER III. THE OLD FRENCH COLONIAL EMPIRE.

The Cambridge Modern History, vol. vii. ch. iii. (by Miss Mary Bateson), gives an excellent short account of the planting and development of French colonies in America and the West Indies. Longer works are Francis Parkman's *Pioneers of France in the New World* and other books by the same author ; and R. G.

Thwaites, *France in America*, 1497-1763, New York, 1905. On the economic side, see S. L. Mims, *Colbert's West Indian Policy*, Yale, 1912, and Pierre Bonnassieux, *Les Grandes Compagnies de Commerce*, Paris, 1892. The period 1880-1900 saw the issue of a number of French works on colonial history, contemporary with a renewed French interest in colonization. Some of these should be read with caution, since they were not purely historical in their inspiration : they partook to some extent of the nature of propaganda, the argument being that the French colonial empire in the eighteenth century would have been a magnificent success but was thrown away by the ineptitude of the Bourbon government. To this period belong H. Castonnet des Fosses, *L'Inde Française avant Dupleix*, Paris, 1887 ; and Tibulle Hamont's *Dupleix*, Paris, 1881, and *Lally-Tollendal*, Paris, 1887. Col. G. B. Malleson's *History of the French in India*, 2nd ed. (re-issued), Edinburgh, 1909, an earlier work, gave the lead in glorification of Dupleix. Prosper Cultru's *Dupleix*, Paris, 1901, is more critical in method and goes far to shatter the legend. A good general history is Henri Weber's *La Compagne Française des Indes*, Paris, 1904, written in a lively and emphatic style, and dealing with much besides purely Indian affairs. Henri Grolous in *La Compagnie Française des Indes Orientales de 1664*, Paris, 1911, treats the subject in its administrative and financial aspects. *De la Colonization chez les Peuples Modernes*, by Paul Leroy-Beaulieu, 6th edn., Paris, 1908, is international in scope, as its title indicates.

CHAPTERS IV. AND VI. INDIA, 1709-1785.

The most authoritative general history covering the period is vol. iv. of *Cambridge History of the British Empire* (1929), whose text is identical with that of vol. v., *Cambridge History of India*. *The Constitutional History of India*, by A. Berriedale Keith, London, 1936, deals with a subject that becomes important towards the end of this period. The commercial interests of the Company are treated in F. P. Robinson's *Trade of the East India Company*, 1709-1813, Cambridge, 1912. A more recent book dealing with the subsequent period may be read as a commentary on this topic, namely C. N. Parkinson's *Trade in the Eastern Seas*, 1793-1813, Cambridge, 1937. Other useful general histories are B. Willson's *Ledger and Sword*, vol. ii., London, 1903, and Sir A. C. Lyall's *Rise and Expansion of British Dominion in India*, 5th edn., London, 1910. J. R. B. Muir's *Making of British India*, 1756-1858, Manchester, 1915, reprints important documents. Lives of Dupleix and Lally have been noticed under the heading of Chapter III. Lives of Clive are numerous, among the more useful being Sir G. W. Forrest's *Life of Clive*, 2 vols., London, 1919, and H. Dodwell's *Dupleix and Clive*, London, 1920. The career of Warren Hastings has inspired more controversy than that of any other Indian statesman. Burke was closely connected with it, and a recent biography, *Edmund Burke*, by Sir Philip Magnus, London, 1939, not only describes Burke's crusade for purer government, but also shows that he was involved in Indian financial transactions which would now be considered discreditable. Sir A. C. Lyall's *Warren Hastings (English Men of Action)*, London, 1889, is concise and impartial. Sir G. W. Forrest's *Administration of Warren Hastings*, Calcutta, 1892, uses newer documentary evidence ; and *Warren Hastings in Bengal*, 1772-4, by M. E. M. Jones, Oxford, 1918, is an economic study of a short period. Macaulay's *Essays* on Clive and Hastings are still read for their literary vigour, but they are prejudiced and inaccurate.

CHAPTER V. THE CLASH OF EMPIRES, 1739-1763.

Cambr. Hist. of the Br. Empire, vols. i. and iv., have chapters covering this subject, which may be read in its wider bearings in the general English histories dealing with the period. A valuable detailed study is *War and Trade in the West*

Indies, 1739-63, by R. Pares, Oxford, 1936. For naval history, Admiral H. W. Richmond's *The Navy in the War of* 1739-48, 3 vols., Cambridge, 1920, should also be consulted. For the Seven Years' War there are in addition some excellent guides. For English readers the most illuminating is Sir J. S. Corbett's *England in the Seven Years' War*, 2 vols., London, 1908, which is especially valuable for Pitt's principles and methods and his justification against criticisms which have been levelled at him. The works of M. Richard Waddington, *Louis XV. et le Renversement des Alliances*, Paris, 1896, and *La Guerre de Sept Ans*, 5 vols., Paris, 1899, etc., enter into full detail from the French point of view whilst maintaining strict impartiality in matters of controversy. They show the colonial struggle in its true relation to European affairs. The campaigns in Canada are well described in A. G. Bradley's *Fight with France for North America*, London, 1900, and, more technically, in A. Doughty's *Siege of Quebec*, 6 vols., Quebec, 1901, etc. Colonial policy in relation to the struggle receives attention in G. L. Beer, *British Colonial Policy*, 1754-65, New York, 1907 ; Miss Kate Hotblack, *Chatham's Colonial Policy*, London, 1917 ; and Miss G. S. Kimball, *Correspondence of William Pitt with Colonial Governors*, 2 vols., New York, 1906, the latter giving the text of the despatches. Beer's work should be compared with an article by H. Hall on the same subject in *American Historical Review*, vol. v. p. 672. Two *Lives of Pitt* should also be studied—those of A. von Ruville, 3 vols., English translation, London, 1907, and B. Williams, 2 vols., London, 1913. The former gives a German view which somewhat disparages certain aspects of Pitt's career. The latter is a whole-hearted eulogy. Certain authorities bearing upon the Ohio question have been referred to in the footnotes.

CHAPTER VII. AMERICAN POLITICS, 1689–1763.

For this chapter the chief authorities are those given for colonial affairs under the heading of chaps. i. and ii., and more particularly the works of Doyle, Egerton, Greene and Channing. For the latter part of the period see also L. H. Gipson, *The British Empire before the American Revolution*, 3 vols., Idaho, 1936 ; Beer's *Colonial Policy*, 1754-65 ; and H. Hall's paper in the *American Historical Review*. An article by B. Williams, " Chatham and the Representation of the Colonies in the Imperial Parliament," *English Hist. Review*, xxii. p. 756, also has some bearing on the subject.

CHAPTERS VIII. AND IX. THE AMERICAN REVOLT AND THE FALL OF THE MERCANTILE EMPIRE, 1763–1783.

Of the immense literature, general and special, dealing with this subject it is necessary to make a somewhat narrow selection of works pre-eminently useful for the various points of view. In addition to the longer histories already mentioned which take the American Revolution as a whole in their course, the following works should be noted : G. E. Howard, *Preliminaries of the Revolution*, 1763-75, New York, 1905, and C. H. van Tyne, *The American Revolution*, New York, 1905. These are complementary to one another, being consecutive volumes in a large series on American history. They present a clear, fair and straightforward account of the period. A standard English work is that of Sir G. O. Trevelyan, *The American Revolution*, 4 vols., London, 1899, etc. It begins with the Stamp Act and goes on to 1778. The same author continues the subject in *George the Third and Charles Fox*, 2 vols., London, 1912-14. He is sympathetic towards American contentions and especially valuable for his account of contemporary English politics and their relation to the great affairs. S. G. Fisher, in *The Struggle for American Independence*, 2 vols., London, 1908, advances novel views on some points, but should be read with caution and in comparison with other authors. A. M. Schlesinger's *Colonial Merchants and the American Revolution*, 1763-76, New York, 1917, is a valuable elucidation of a matter hitherto obscure, the origin and effects of the non-importation policy. G. B. Hertz's *Old Colonial System* is very illuminating on the social, economic and sentimental aspects of the struggle. Beer's *Colonial Policy*, 1754-65, gives in its later chapters the best account available of Grenville's fiscal measures. For the participation of the Bourbons in the war J. F. Ramsey, *Anglo-French Relations*, 1763-70, Berkeley, Cal., 1939, a study of Choiseul's foreign policy, is a good preliminary to Henri Doniol's *Histoire de la Participation de la France à l'Établissement des États-Unis*, 5 vols., Paris, 1886-99, a great work which must be regarded as the final authority on the subject. Those who desire a more condensed account will find much of Doniol's substance embodied in J. B. Perkins, *France in the American Revolution*, Boston, 1911. For the military campaigns there are many authorities. Fortescue's *British Army*, vol. iii., is the most recent and comprehensive, dealing with all the world-wide aspects of the contest. The author is emphatic upon the half-hearted nature of the revolt and the fact that it was more than once upon the verge of collapse. This is somewhat damaging to the revolutionary epic as formerly conceived in America, and has drawn some adverse criticism in reply. Admiral Mahan's *Influence of Sea Power upon History* is especially full on the naval campaigns ; the same author has also reprinted his contribution to Laird Clowes' *Royal Navy* under the title of *Navies in the War of Independence*, London, 1913. Another work dealing with the same subject is G. W. Allen's *Naval History of the American Revolution*, 2 vols., Boston, 1913, especially interesting for personal and biographical details, and the privateering warfare upon which Mahan touches only lightly. On the British side the best naval account is *The British Navy in Adversity*, by Capt. W. M. James, London, 1926, in which the mistakes in naval and general policy are examined.

INDEX

[In order to facilitate the rapid following-up of the history of an institution or policy through a long period, entries relating to such matters have been made as exhaustive as possible and grouped under comprehensive headings. Examples are: Colonial policy and administration, Navigation Acts, Slave trade and slavery. All organizations for foreign trade and colonization are grouped under Companies.]

Abercrombie, General, 400
Acadia, *see* Nova Scotia.
Aché, Comte d', 380, 381, 383.
Achin, English at, 216.
Adams, John and Samuel, 430 ; John, 431, 452.
Adams, William, in Japan, 222.
Admiralty Courts in colonies, 271, 328.
Afghans, Afghanistan, eighteenth century, 363-4, 411 *n*.
Aquila, Juan de, 147.
Aix-la-Chapelle, Treaty of, 368, 390.
Albany (New York), 276, 280, 340.
Albemarle River, settlement at, 273, 274.
Albuquerque, Affonso de, 65.
Aldworth, Thomas, 223, 225.
Aleppo, 12, 43, 53.
Alexander VI., bulls of, 62-4.
Alexander, Sir William, 206, 207, 353.
Alexandria, 12, 43.
Amadas, Philip, 130.
Amazon, English colony on, 156, 209.
Amboyna, 217, 219, 220 ; massacre, 221-2, 249.
Ambur, Battle of, 369.
America, Norse discovery of, 54-5 ; Columbus' discovery, 60-2.
American Import Duties Act, 433, 435.
American Loyalists, 437, 441, 454.
American revolt, forecasts of, 406, 425-6, 444 ; causes of, 455-6.
Amherst, General, 400, 402-3, 424, 447.
Andros, Sir Edmund, 265-6, 280-1, 282, 302-3.
Annapolis, 207, 334, 335, 336, 345, 352-3, 388.
Anson, Admiral George, 386-7, 388, 393, 398.
Antigua, *see* Leeward Islands.
Antonio, Don, 142.

Antwerp, English traders at, 24, 25, 41.
Anwar-u Deen, 368-9.
Arab traders, 12, 64, 67.
Arcot, Clive at, 370-1.
Argall, Samuel, 175, 177, 207.
Arlington, Lord, 295, 314.
Armada, the Great, 137, 138-42.
Armed Neutrality, 451.
Arnold, Benedict, 440.
Ashehurst, Thomas, 72-3.
Ashley, Lord, *see* Shaftesbury.
Asiento, the, 336, 343.
Association Island, *see* Tortuga.
Atlantic, importance of, in eighteenth century, 386, 401.
Aungier, Gerald, 306, 308.
Aurangzeb, Emperor, 305-6, 307-8, 311.
Australia, discovery of, 231-2.
Austrian Succession War, 387.
Ayscue, Sir George, 243, 248-9.
Azores, discovery of, 57 ; fighting at, 122, 138, 143, 146.

Babington conspiracy, 137.
Bacon, Francis, 205, 272.
Bacon, Nathaniel, 296.
Baffin, William, 237-8.
Bahamas, 213, 272, 291, 453.
Balasor, English at, 225.
Baltic, trade with, 16, 19, 22-3, 24, 26, 31, 42-3, 50, 248, 331.
Baltimore, Lord ; first, 154, 155-6, 183-4, 206 ; second, 156, 184-7, 243, 244, 294, 297 ; third, 284, 297-8, 326.
Bannister, Thomas, 116.
Bantam, English at, 216, 217, 218, 220, 308.
Barbados, 156, 211-2, 241, 243, 251, 261, 265, 287-9, 331-2.
Barbary pirates, 166, 250, 259
Barker, Andrew, 93, 109,

INDEX

Charles I., policy of, 159, 167-8, 182, 195, 206, 207, 211, 222, 228-9.

Charles II., policy of, 256-7, 266, 269-71, 295, 304-5.

Charles V., Emperor, 45, 50.

Charles VI., Emperor, 347-8.

Charleston (Charlestown), 275-6, 340, 342, 436, 441, 451, 453.

Charnock, Job, 307.

Cherbourg, raid on, 400.

Chidley, John, 112.

Child, Sir John, 307-8, 309 ; Sir Josiah, 255, 307, 309-11.

China, trade with, 362 ; Portuguese in, 65.

Chinsura, 378.

Chios, 43, 44, 49.

Choiseul, Duc de, 403-5, 406, 444-5.

Clarendon, Earl of, 257, 260, 272, 299-300.

Clavering, Sir John, 413-14.

Claybourne, William, 183, 185-7, 243-4.

Clinton, Sir Henry, 441, 443, 448, 451, 452.

Clive, Robert, Lord, 367-8, 370-1, 375-9, 381, 382, 383 n., 408, 410-11, 412.

Cloth manufacture and export, 5-6, 15-16, 24.

Coddington, William, 199-200.

Coen, Jan, 220-1.

Colbert, Jean Baptiste, 314, 317, 330, 351, 355-7.

Colleton, Sir John, 272 ; Sir Peter, 315.

Colonial defence, 423-4, 429.

Colonial policy and administration, British, to 1660, 113, 125-6, 127, 128, 155, 156-8, 160-1, 164, 166-8, 198-9, 204, 240-1, 244, 263 ; 1660-88, 258-62, 263-6, 272-3, 286, 287, 291-4, 295, 297, 299-300, 302-3 ; 1689-1783, 325-7, 328-31, 332-3, 344-7, 419-23, 424-5, 428-9, 432, 433, 434-8, 455-6 ; Dutch, 154-5, 219-22 ; French, 314, 330, 341, 353-61 ; Portuguese, 222-4, 240 ; Spanish, 100, 210, 240.

Colonial Secretary, Colonial Office, 345, 398, 434.

Columbus, Christopher, 60-2, 65.

Commerce, British (including colonial), 5, 6-8, 10, 13-18, 21, 28, 30, 50, 81-2, 113, 125, 161-4, 193, 198, 218, 226-8, 244, 253, 257-8, 288, 335, 338-42, 348. See also Companies.

Commercial policy, British, to 1485, 10-11, 15, 17-18, 18-20, 22-3, 24-5, 25-6, 30-2 ; 1485-1558, 40-4, 44-6, 46-7, 85-6 ; 1558-1603, 50-1, 98, 215 ; 1603-49, 156-7, 163-4, 167-8, 226-30 ; 1649-60, 229-30, 241, 246-7 ; 1660-88, 255-6, 259-60 ; 1689-1783, 329-31, 336-7, 343, 344-7, 401, 406, 424-5, 456. See also Navigation Acts.

Commercial policy, Dutch, 154-5, 219-22 ; French, 353, 355, 358-9.

Commercial policy, theories of, 28-9, 40, 51, 164, 226-7, 241, 255-6, 329, 330, 355, 401, 424.

Commissions for Trade and Plantations, 1625-75, 161, 167, 199, 200, 204, 206, 243, 263-4, 299, 300 ; from 1675, see Lords of Trade and Board of Trade.

Commonwealth, policy of, 240-7.

Companies, Austrian, Imperial and Royal (Ostend), 347-8.

Companies, British :
Adventurers to the New Found Land, 73.
African Company of Merchants, 313.
Amazon, 208-9.
Cathay, 119-20.   Darien, 332-3.
East India, to 1709, 95, 123-4, 162, 163-4, 214-30, 233, 257, 304-11, 330 ; 1709-84, 341, 347-8, 362-84, 408-17, 435-6 ; financial details, 216, 217, 218, 227-8, 229, 304, 308, 310, 311, 342, 362, 411-12.
Eastland, 22-3, 25-6, 52-3.
Greenbriar, 391.
Guiana, 156, 209.
Guinea, Tudor, 83-6, 98-100, 103 ; 1618, 162 ; 1630, 162-3, 311.
Hudson's Bay, 257-8, 313-17, 334-5, 336, 338.
Levant, 53, 123, 161-2, 258, 317.
Loyal, 391.
Massachusetts Bay, 159, 194-7, 302.
Merchants Adventurers, 7, 23-4, 25, 27, 30-1, 41-2, 45-6, 52.
Merchants in Spain, 48-9.
Merchants of the Staple, 7, 14-15, 47.
Muscovy, 86-91, 94, 114-16, 117, 126, 162, 163, 233, 234, 257, 317.
New England Council, 170, 188, 190, 192, 194, 198, 201.
Newfoundland (Guy's), 205-6.
North-West Passage, 237-8.
Plymouth (for Virginia), 170, 188.
Providence Island, 159, 212-13.
Ohio, 391.
Royal Adventurers, 257, 268, 312.
Royal African, 257, 312-13, 341.
Sir H. Gilbert's, 128.
Sir Nicholas Crisp's, see Guinea, 1630.
Sir William Courteen's, 163, 228-9.
Somers Islands, 210.
South Sea, 343.
Turkey, 53, 116-17.
Venice, 53.
Virginia, 160-1, 169-80, 189, 210, 291.

Companies, Dutch, East India, 123, 154, 162, 219-22, 236 ; West India, 276-7, 279, 312.

Companies, French, Barbary, 359 ; China, 359 ; East India, 306, 341, 353, 354-5, 357-8, 359, 360-1, 372, 384 ; Guinea, 336, 359 ; of the Hundred Associates, see of New France ; of the Isles of America, 353, 354 ; of New

BY JAMES A. WILLIAMSON

A SHORT HISTORY OF
BRITISH EXPANSION

Vol. I. THE OLD COLONIAL EMPIRE. *Third Edition.*
Vol. II. THE MODERN EMPIRE AND COMMON-
WEALTH. *Fourth Edition.*

THE
FOUNDATION AND GROWTH
OF THE BRITISH EMPIRE
Fifth Edition

THE BRITISH EMPIRE AND
COMMONWEALTH

A NOTEBOOK OF
COMMONWEALTH HISTORY

MACMILLAN AND CO., LTD., LONDON

PRINTED IN GREAT BRITAIN
BY ROBERT MACLEHOSE AND CO. LTD.
THE UNIVERSITY PRESS. GLASGOW